GUIDE TO RURAL ENGLAND

THE SOUTH OF ENGLAND

By Peter Long

Published by:
Travel Publishing Ltd
7a Apollo House, Calleva Park
Aldermaston, Berks, RG7 8TN

ISBN 1-902-00772-7

First Published: *2002*

Country Living Guides to Rural England:

East Anglia
The South East of England
The South of England
The West Country

Please Note:

All advertisements in this publication have been accepted in good faith by Travel Publishing and they have not necessarily been endorsed by *Country Living* Magazine.

All information is included by the publishers in good faith and is believed to be correct at the time of going to press. No responsibility can be accepted for errors.

Editor:	Peter Long
Printing by:	Scotprint, Haddington
Location Maps:	© Maps in Minutes ™ (2000) © Crown Copyright, Ordnance Survey 2001
Walk Maps:	Reproduced from the 2001 Pathfinder 1:25,000 Ordnance Survey Maps by permission of Ordnance Survey on behalf of the Controller of Her Majesty's Stationery Office, © Crown Copyright MC 100035812
Cover Design:	Lines & Words, Aldermaston
Cover Photo:	A view of "White Horse Country" near Wantage: © photo by Anthea Kemp
Text Photos:	Text photos have been kindly supplied by the Britain on View photo library and the Southern Regional Tourist Board © www.britainonview.com © Southern Regional Tourist Board

Photograph by Hugo Burnand

Foreword

From a bracing walk across the hills and tarns of The Lake District to a relaxing weekend spent discovering the unspoilt hamlets of East Anglia, nothing quite matches getting off the beaten track and exploring Britain's areas of outstanding beauty.

Each month, *Country Living Magazine* celebrates the richness and diversity of our countryside with features on rural Britain and the traditions that have their roots there. So it is with great pleasure that I introduce you to the *Country Living Magazine Guide to Rural England* series. Packed with information about unusual and unique aspects of our countryside, the guides will point both fair-weather and intrepid travellers in the right direction.

Each chapter provides a fascinating tour of the South of England, with insights into local heritage and history and easy-to-read facts on a wealth of places to visit, stay, eat, drink and shop.

I hope that this guide will help make your visit a rewarding and stimulating experience and that you will return inspired, refreshed and ready to head off on your next countryside adventure.

Susy Smith, Editor of **Country Living** ***Magazine***

P.S. To subscribe to **Country Living** ***Magazine every month, call 01858 438844.***

Introduction

This is the second *Country Living Magazine* rural guide edited by Peter Long, an experienced travel writer who spent many years with Egon Ronay's Hotel and Restaurant Guides before joining the Travel Publishing team. As with the East Anglian edition Peter has ensured that *The Country Living Magazine Guide to Rural England* covering the southern counties is packed with vivid descriptions, historical stories, amusing anecdotes and interesting facts on hundreds of places in Bedfordshire, Berkshire, Buckinghamshire, Gloucestershire, Hampshire (including the Isle of Wight), Hertfordshire, Oxfordshire and Wiltshire.

The coloured advertising panels within each chapter provide further information on places to see, stay, eat, drink, shop and even exercise! We have also selected a number of walks from Jarrold's Pathfinder Guides which we highly recommend if you wish to appreciate fully the beauty and charm of the varied rural landscapes of the South of England.

The guide however is not simply an "armchair tour". Its prime aim is to encourage the reader to visit the places described and discover much more about the wonderful towns, villages and countryside of these counties. Whether you decide to explore this region by wheeled transport or by foot we are sure you will find it a very uplifting experience.

We are always interested in receiving comments on places covered (or not covered) in our guides so please do not hesitate to use the reader reaction form provided at the rear of this guide to give us your considered comments. This will help us refine and improve the content of the next edition. We also welcome any general comments which will help improve the overall presentation of the guides themselves.

Finally, for more information on the full range of travel guides published by Travel Publishing please refer to the details and order form at the rear of this guide or log on to our website at www.travelpublishing.co.uk

Travel Publishing

Locator Map

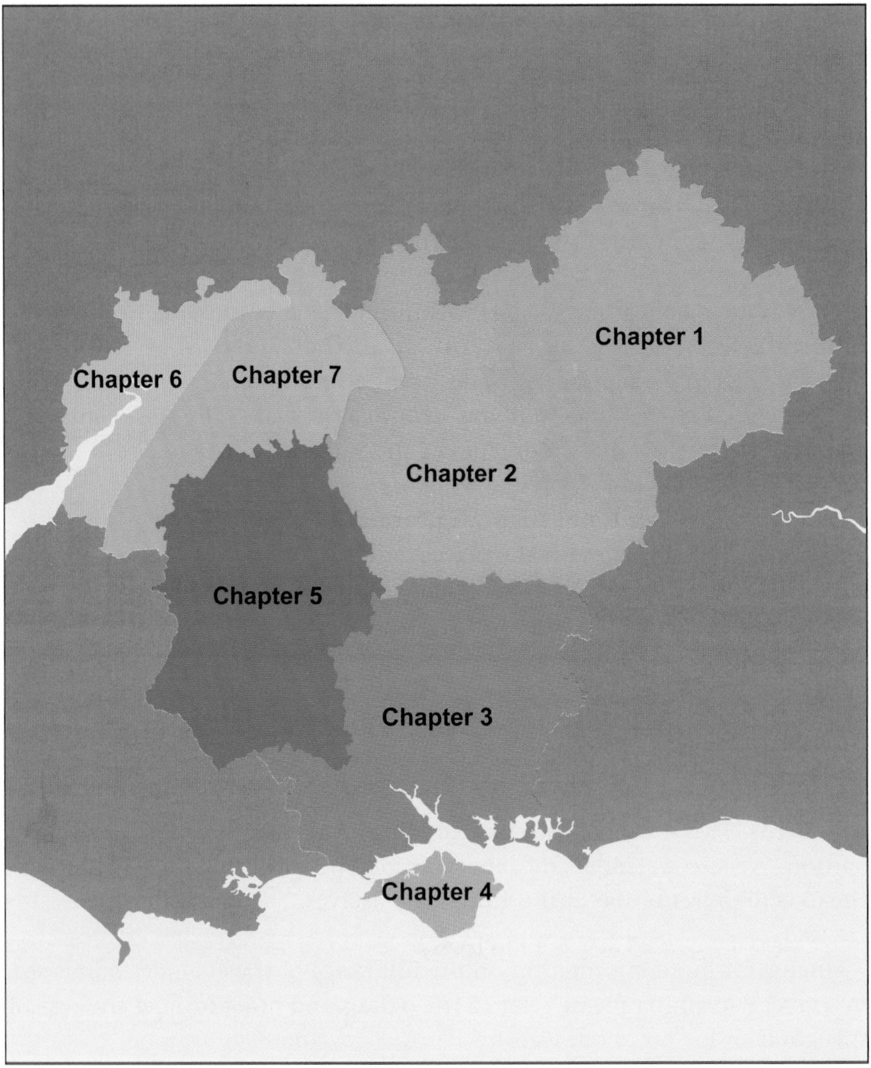
Chapter 1
Chapter 2
Chapter 3
Chapter 4
Chapter 5
Chapter 6
Chapter 7

Contents

1 THE CHILTERNS

The Chilterns run in an arc from Goring-on-Thames, where they meet the Berkshire Downs, to a point near Hitchin, and are set mainly in the counties of Hertfordshire, Bedfordshire and Buckinghamshire. In an area that is part of the commuter belt around London, the Chilterns nonetheless offer the visitor plenty of unspoilt countryside and much of the range is in an Area of Outstanding Natural Beauty.

Westmill, Hertfordshire

In Buckinghamshire the Ashridge Estate includes the main ridge of the Chilterns, from Ivinghoe Beacon to Berkhamsted on the border with Hertfordshire. Ashridge Commons and Woods and Ivinghoe Hills are Sites of Special Scientific Interest, and the estate is rich in archaeological remains. The Bradenham Estate, four miles from High Wycombe, includes Bradenham Woods, an area of ancient beech that is among the best in the Chilterns. Beech predominates throughout, but under the management of the National Trust oak, whitebeam, ash and wild cherry are also being encouraged here.

Sutton, Bedfordshire

The highest points in the Chilterns are at Wendover Woods and Coombe Hill, both over 800 feet above sea level and both offering superb views. The woodland in the Chilterns is less extensive than formerly but is still noted chiefly for beech trees that were instrumental in the growth in the 18th century of chairmaking, one of the most important of the Chilterns crafts. The centre of the industry was High Wycombe, where the Windsor chair was the most famous product. Several skills and several woods were involved in the making of this classic chair: bodgers used the ubiquitous beech for the legs; benders shaped ash for the bowed backs; and bottomers made use of the sturdy elm for the seats. The history of the chair-making industry is told in High Wycombe Museum.

Many have found peace and inspiration in the Chilterns. Chalfont St Giles was the temporary home of John Milton when he fled the plague in London; at Stoke Poges Thomas Gray wrote his *Elegy in a Country Churchyard*. Other notable residents include the statesman and writer Benjamin Disraeli and Sir Francis Dashwood, founder of the notorious Hell-Fire Club.

Pitstone Wharf, Buckinghamshire

LOCATOR MAP

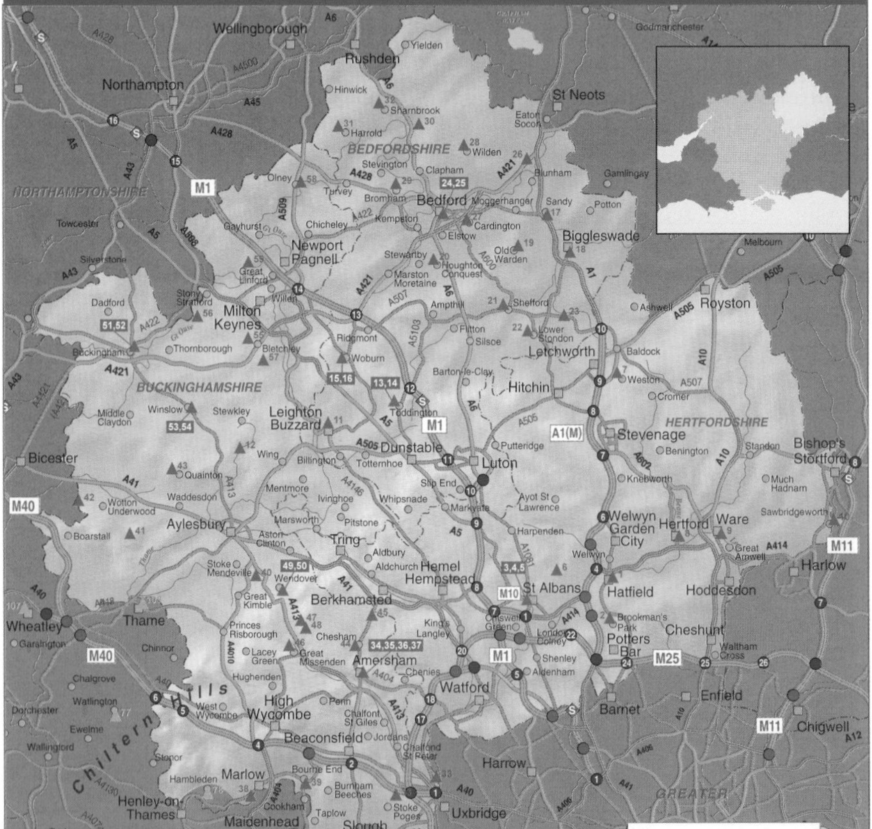

ADVERTISERS AND PLACES OF INTEREST

HERTFORDSHIRE

Benington, Hertfordshire

Like its neighbours, urban and suburban development in Hertfordshire has taken away large chunks of what was open countryside, but there is still some excellent walking and splendid scenery. Most notable is the National Trust's Ashridge Estate, where the woodlands and downlands are home to a wide variety of wildlife, and the views from the highest points are magnificent. The southern part of the county, closest to the capital, was essentially a rural area until the building of the Grand Union Canal and the development of the railways brought industry and expansion. The more southerly towns also grew as residential areas for commuters, and after World War II, with an acute housing shortage in the blitzed capital, the New Towns were created to cater for the thousands of Londoners who had lost their homes. The strongest historical ties in the county are to be found in the ancient city of St Albans, while Hatfield combines old and new elements: it was designated a New Town after World War II, but the old town survives, along with the magnificent Hatfield House and part of the Royal Palace, once the home of the future Elizabeth I. Close to Hatfield lies Welwyn Garden City, conceived by Ebenezer Howard and built in the 1920s with the aim of providing working people with a pleasant and attractive place to live, with easy access to the countryside. One of the best known monuments in Hertfordshire is the Eleanor Cross at Waltham Cross, one of 13 such crosses erected by Edward I to commemorate the resting places of the funeral cortege of his Queen, Eleanor of Castile.

HEMEL HEMPSTEAD

This is a place with two distinct identities: the charming old town centred around the ancient Church of St Mary and tranquil Gadebridge Park; and the new town, one of the first to be built following World War II, planned as an integrated series of communities, each with its own individual centre.

Gadebridge Park is an extensive expanse of open parkland through which runs the River Gade. The park's attractive walled garden adjoins the High Street of the old town alongside the grounds of the church, which has a 200 foot timber spire that was added in the 14th century, two centuries after the main building. Evidence of a settlement here long before the Norman Conquest can be found surprisingly close to the town's industrial area. Protected by a fenced enclosure and visible from the road lies the mound of a

Bronze Age barrow. By the time of the compilation of the Domesday Book, Hemel Hempstead was an attractive market town with several mills along the banks of the River Gade. The **Charter Tower**, just inside one of Gadebridge Park's entrances, is reputed to be the tower from whose upper window Henry VIII handed down Hemel Hempstead's royal charter, but the tower was in fact built long after the charter was given. On the road close to the railway station is a curious stone tablet known as **Snook's Grave**, marking the spot where James Snook, a notorious highwayman, was hanged and buried. Thought to be the last person in England to be taken back to the scene of his crime for the ultimate punishment, Snook was found guilty in 1802 of robbing a postboy and killing him in the process.

The village of **Bedmond**, three miles southeast of Hemel Hempstead, was the birthplace of Nicholas Breakspear, the only British Pope, who was crowned in office as Adrian IV in 1154.

AROUND HEMEL HEMPSTEAD

Watford

5 miles S of Hemel Hempstead on the A411

Originally a country market town, Watford was transformed in the 19th century by the arrival of the railway, which brought new industry and new building. Among the few earlier buildings to survive the rapid development are the five-gabled **Bedford Almshouses**, which date back to 1580, and the early 18th century Fuller and Chilcott school. On the high street stands the splendid Mansion House, once the offices of the Benskin Brewery and now home to **Watford Museum**, where visitors can learn about the industrial and social history of the town; the local brewing and printing industries feature prominently, along with a tribute to Watford Football Club.

In the north of the town, off the A411 Hemel Hempstead road, Watford Council manage the gardens at **Cheslyn House**; the 3½-acre garden has woodland, lawns, a bog garden, rock garden, splendid herbaceous borders and an aviary and is open from dawn to dusk every day except Christmas

King's Langley

2 miles S of Hemel Hempstead on the A4251

The home of Ovaltine. A Swiss doctor called George Wander invented the drink in 1865 and his son Albert later took over the business. The King's Langley factory was built in 1912 and greatly expanded subsequently. Local farms produced eggs, barley, milk and malt for the popular drink, and the factory even had its own narrow boats on the Grand Union Canal. One of these boats has been renovated and bears the name *Albert*.

TRING

Situated on the edge of the Chiltern Hills and on the banks of the Grand Union Canal, Tring is a bustling little market town whose character has been greatly influenced by the Rothschild family. However, the members of this rich and famous family are not the only people of note to be associated with the town and in **St Mary's Church** can be found the grave of the grandfather of the first US president, George Washington, while the 17th century **Mansion House**, designed by Sir Christopher Wren, was reputedly used by Nell Gwynne.

The town's narrow winding High Street, off which lead little alleyways and courtyards, contains many late Victorian buildings, all designed by local architect William Huckvale. Of particular note is the **Market House**, built by public subscription in 1900 to commemorate, albeit a little late, Queen Victoria's Diamond Jubilee. A fine example of the Arts and Crafts style, so popular at the turn of the century, the building was later converted into a fire station and today it is home to the town council chamber. The old **Silk Mill**, first opened in 1824, once employed over 600 people, but towards the end of the 19th century the silk trade fell into decline and Lord Rothschild ran the mill at a loss to protect his employees rather than see them destitute. Unable to carry on in this fashion, the mill closed to the silk trade and, after losing some its height, the building was converted into a generating station. From 1872 to the 1940s, the Rothschild family lived at Tring Park and from here they exercised their influence over the town. Perhaps their greatest lasting feature is the **Walter Rothschild Zoological Museum**, which first opened in 1892 and, on Walter's death in 1937, became part of the British Museum (Natural History). An eccentric man with a great interest in natural history, Walter collected over 4,000 rare and extinct species of animals, birds and reptiles. Tring's focal point is **The Square**, remodelled in 1991 and featuring an ingenious **Pavement Maze** in the form of a zebra's head - a tribute to Walter's work. The town's war memorial, unveiled in 1919, stands in The Square, as does the flint and Totternhoe stone Church of St Peter and St Paul. Dating chiefly from the 15th century, this parish church contains some fine medieval carvings as well as 18th century memorials.

AROUND TRING

Marsworth

2 miles N of Tring off B489

Mentioned in the Domesday Book and situated on the banks of the Grand Union Canal, Marsworth was known as Mavvers to the canal people. The village is also home to the **Tring Reservoirs National Nature Reserve**. The four reservoirs were built between 1802 and 1839 to store water for the then Grand Junction (now Grand Union) Canal, which reached its summit close by. Declared a nature reserve in 1955, this is a popular place for birdwatchers, and there is also a nature trail and a variety of trees and marshland flora.

Aldbury

2 miles E of Tring off A4251

This picturesque village, with its green, pond, stocks, village shop, timber framed houses and parish church, dates back to Saxon times and is often used as a film location. There was once a castle in the village that is said to have disappeared in a flash of light sometime during the 14th century. The story goes that the castle's owner Sir Guy de Gravade, in league with the Devil, raised the dead from their

Aldbury Manor, Hertfordshire

graves and from them learned the secret of turning base metals into pure gold. One night a servant, having seen his master at work, decided to experiment on his own; the results were disastrous, for the castle and all the residents within were engulfed in a flash of lightning. On dark moonless nights, the castle is said to reappear and through the windows the ghosts of Sir Guy and his servant can be seen working in their everlasting quest for gold. The village lies on the western boundary of the **Ashridge Estate**, formerly part of the estate of Lord Brownlow and now owned by the National Trust. With grounds and woodland extending to some 4,000 acres on the Hertfordshire-Buckinghamshire border, this is a lovely place for walking and spotting the wealth of local flora and fauna. The focal point of the area is the **Bridgewater Monument**, an impressive tower that was erected in memory of the Duke of Bridgewater, who was famous for his pioneering work in the development of canals. Open on afternoons between April and October, the tower offers magnificent views across the countryside.

To the east of Aldbury, a mile south of Little Gaddesdon off the A4146, lie the 150 acres of **Ashridge Management College**, 90 acres of gardens and the rest woodland. Designed by Humphry Repton (he presented his Red Book to the 7th Earl of Bridgewater in 1813), the gardens were actually laid out by Sir Jeffrey Wyatville. Among the highlights are an Italian garden and fountain, a circular rosarie, a large oak planted by Princess (later Queen) Victoria, an avenue of Wellingtonias, a Bible garden, a sunken garden once used as a skating pond and a grotto constructed from Hertfordshire pudding-stone.

Northchurch

3 miles SE of Tring on A4251

On the south wall of the Church of St Mary is a memorial plaque to Peter the Wild Boy, who is buried close to the porch. Found living wild in a wood near Hanover, Germany, in 1725, he was brought to this country by the royal family and entrusted to the care of a farmer in this parish. He died in 1785 at an estimated age of 75. Though the full length of the **Grand Union Canal** towpath, in Hertfordshire, can be walked, the section of canal from Northchurch to Tring has been developed with recreational use particularly in mind. As well as the attractive canalside walk there are numerous maintenance and conservation projects to preserve this magnificent waterway and the wealth of wildlife and plant life found along its banks.

Berkhamsted

4 miles SE of Tring on the A4251

It was in this historic town - one of Hertfordshire's five boroughs at the time

Motte and Bailey Castle, Berkhamsted

of the Domesday Survey - that William of Normandy, William the Conqueror, two months after the Battle of Hastings, accepted the British throne from the defeated Saxons. Shortly afterwards, William's half-brother Robert, Count of Mortain, commenced work on **Berkhamsted Castle**, which as a precaution against the low lie of the land was surrounded by a double moat. The castle entertained many distinguished visitors down the years: the Black Prince on honeymoon with his bride Joan, the Fair Maid of Kent; King John's wife Isabel, besieged in 1216 by the Barons; Thomas à Becket when he was Lord Chancellor; Geoffrey Chaucer as Clerk of the Works. The castle was a place of considerable importance until at least the 15th century, but is now all but ruined. One of the most interesting of the town's surviving ancient buildings is **Dean John Incent's House**, an impressive black-and-

white timbered and jettied building in the main street opposite the 13th century Church of St Peter. A notable feature of this church is a window dedicated to the poet William Cowper, who was born at the local rectory in 1731. The town's cultural connections reach modern times through Graham Greene, son of Berkhamsted School's headmaster, and frequent visitor JM Barrie, creator of Peter Pan.

HATFIELD

This historic town grew up around the gateway to the palace of the abbots and Bishop of Ely. Beside the palace gatehouse is the parish church which is dedicated to St Etheldreda, the East Anglian princess and first abbess of Ely in the 7th century. The novelist Lady Caroline Lamb and her husband Henry William Lamb, 2nd Viscount Melbourne,

HATFIELD HOUSE

Hatfield, Hertfordshire AL9 5NQ
Tel: 01707 287010 Fax: 01707 287033
website: www.hatfield-house.co.uk

Hatfield House, where Elizabethan history began, is a superb redbrick Jacobean mansion built by Robert Cecil, 1st Earl of Shaftesbury and Chief Minister to King James I, in 1611. The house has been in the Cecil family ever since, and is the home of the Marquess of Salisbury. Superb examples of Jacobean craftsmanship can be seen throughout the house, notably in the Grand Staircase with its elaborately carved wood and in the stained-glass window in the private chapel. The state rooms are treasure houses of the finest furniture, world-renowned paintings, exquisite tapestries and historic armour; they include the fabulous Marble Hall, the Long Gallery and King James' Drawing Room.

The gardens at Hatfield House are a great attraction in their own right, laid out by John Tradescant the Elder and planted by him with many species never previously grown in England. The gardens, where restoration started in Victorian times and still continues, include herb, knot and wilderness areas which can be visited when the house is open to the public (Easter Saturday to September 30 in 2002); the East Gardens, which include the Kitchen Garden and the formal parterres, are open on Fridays (Connoisseurs' Days). With over 100,000 visitors in 2001, Hatfield House was the winner of that year's Visitor Attraction of the Year and Regional Excellence Awards. Special events for 2002 include Living Crafts (9-12 May), Festival of Gardening (7-9 June), Art in Clay (2-4 August) and the Flower Show (6-8 September).

Hatfield House

Salisbury. The pub also features in Dickens' *Oliver Twist*, as following the murder of Nancy, Bill Sikes 'shaped his course' for Hatfield and, in the tap room of the Eight Bells, a fellow drinker saw the blood on Sikes' hat. The fire which Sikes helped to extinguish was perhaps inspired by the fire that had recently ravaged Hatfield House. The idea of Hatfield New Town was nothing new in post World War II Britain as in 1848 proposals for a new town were advertised to coincide with the completion of the railway line in 1850. Though some development did take place, it was not until the 1950s that the rapid expansion began. However, the two areas remain separate, on either side of the railway line and, fortunately, much of the older part of the town has survived.

are buried in a vault here. The Viscount, who was Prime Minister in 1834 and from 1835 to 1841, has a memorial in the church, but there is no mention of Lady Caroline, whose public infatuation with Lord Byron had brought about their separation in 1825. Elizabeth I spent her early life in the Royal Palace of Hatfield, of which only a single wing remains. This can be seen in the delightful gardens of the impressive Jacobean mansion, **Hatfield House** (see panel opposite), which now stands on the site.

Back in the centre of town lies the Eight Bells pub, which was frequented by Charles Dickens when, as a newspaper reporter for the *Morning Chronicle*, he visited Hatfield to report on the fire, which not only destroyed a substantial part of Hatfield House but also resulted in the death of the Dowager Lady

AROUND HATFIELD

BROOKMANS PARK
3 miles S of Hatfield on the A1000

A quiet residential area with a large commuting population. To the east lies **Northaw Great Wood**, the remains of the forest that once covered a large part of Hertfordshire. It is now preserved with conservation in mind, and visitors can

wander through the woodland and perhaps spot muntjac deer, badgers, foxes and some of the 60 or so species of birds that have been sighted here.

Welwyn Garden City

2 miles N of Hatfield on the A1000

As the name of this town would suggest, Welwyn is indeed a Garden City, one of two in Hertfordshire that followed the ideas and plans of Ebenezer Howard. After seeing the squalor in which people lived in the cities, particularly London, Howard conceived the idea of providing working people with an opportunity to live in well spaced out housing with access to the clean air of the countryside and the industrial areas close by. The land for Welwyn Garden City was first acquired in 1919 and the building began a year later, with the present station completed in 1926. Howard's ideas are still perhaps best seen here, as the railway line also acts as the demarcation line for the two areas of the town: industry to the east; the shopping and commercial areas to the west; and the residential areas, with extensive planting and many open spaces beyond.

Just to the south of the town lies **Mill Green Museum**, in the tiny hamlet of Mill Green. Housed in the workers' cottages for the adjoining watermill, this was, between 1911 and 1973, a private residence. There are two permanent galleries here where local items from Roman times to the present day are on display, including pottery, craft tools, underwear and school certificates. A further gallery is used for temporary exhibitions. The adjoining **Mill Green Mill** is a wonderful watermill restored to full working order. Standing on the site of one of the four such mills in Hertfordshire that featured in the Domesday Book, Mill Green Mill was originally owned by the Bishops of Ely. Reconstructed and altered many times, the mill finally ceased to grind corn at the beginning of the 20th century when the incumbent miller emigrated to Australia. Milling recommenced in 1986, after much careful restoration work by the Mill Green Water Mill Restoration Trust, and not only can it be seen working but freshly ground flour is on sale.

Welwyn

1 mile N of Hatfield on the A1(M)

This historic town has grown up along the route of the Great North Road, which became the High Street, but, since the construction of the A1(M) took the route away from the town centre, Welwyn is now relatively traffic-free. During the excavations for the new motorway, the famous **Welwyn Roman Baths** were uncovered. Part of a 3rd century villa or farm, the bath house is preserved in a steel vault within the motorway embankment.

Ayot St Lawrence

3 miles NW of Hatfield off the B653

The most famous resident of the village was the playwright George Bernard Shaw, who lived here from 1906 until his death in 1950. It seems that while on a visit to the area looking for a country home he saw a headstone in the churchyard with the inscription 'Her time was short'. The lady in question has in fact died at the age of 70, and Shaw thought that if 70 was considered a short span of years, this was the place for him. The house in which he lived, Shaw's Corner, has been preserved by the National Trust as it was in his lifetime and contains many literary and personal mementos of the great Irish writer. In the lovely garden is the revolving writing hut where he did much of his writing and which could turn to catch the sunlight. His ashes and those of

Ayot Green

ST ALBANS

This historic cathedral city, whose skyline is dominated by the magnificent Norman abbey, is a wonderful blend of the old and new. One of the major Roman cities in Britain, the remains of **Verulamium** were excavated only quite recently, but there was already a settlement here before Julius Caesar's invasion in 54 BC. Attacked and ruined by Boadicea in the 1st century, the city was rebuilt and today the remains of the walls, Britain's only Roman theatre (as opposed to an amphitheatre) and a hyopcaust can still be seen in **Verulamium Park**. Also in the park is the **Verulamium Museum**, where the story of everyday life in a Roman city is told; among the displays are ceramics, mosaic

his wife Charlotte Payne-Townshend were scattered in the garden. Close by, just south of Ayot St Peter, runs **Ayot Greenway**, an attractive footpath, rich in flora, that follows part of the route of the old Luton, Dunstable and Welwyn Junction Railway, which hit the buffers under the Beeching axe in 1966.

St Albans Cathedral

who lived in St Albans for the last five years of his life. In the town's central market place stands the **Clock Tower**, the only medieval town belfry in England, built between 1403 and 1412. Originally constructed as a political statement by the town, it asserted the citizens' freedom and wealth in the face of the powerful abbey as the town was allowed to sound its own hours and ring the curfew bell. The original 15th century bell, Gabriel, is still in place. Close to the peaceful and tranquil Verulamium Park, on the banks of the River Ver, is **Kingsbury Watermill**, a wonderful 16th century mill that is built on the site of an earlier mill that was mentioned in the Domesday Book. Beautifully restored, the waterwheel is still turned by the river and visitors can not only enjoy this idyllic setting but also see the working milling machinery and a collection of agricultural implements. Two other museums in the town are very well worth

floors, personal possessions and room re-creations. Designated as a Cathedral in 1887, **St Albans Abbey** was built on the site where Alban, the first British martyr, was beheaded in 303 for sheltering a Christian priest. Dating from the 11th century and built from flint and bricks taken from the Roman remains, the Cathedral has been added to and altered in every century since. Among the many notable features, the medieval paintings, said to be unique in Britain, are the most interesting. In the nearby Church of St Michael are the tomb and life-size monument of the Lord Chancellor Francis Bacon (1561-1626), 1st Baron Verulam and Viscount St Albans,

ST ALBANS MUSEUMS

Hatfield Road, St Albans,
Hertfordshire AL1 3RR
Tel: 01727 819340 Fax: 01727 837472
e-mail: museum@stalbans.gov.uk
website: www.stalbansmuseums.org.uk

The fascinating story of historic St Albans, from the departure of the Romans to the present day, is told at the **Museum of St Albans**. The range of lively displays covers the rise of the market town that grew up around its abbey through to its development as a modern commuter city. The museum is also home to the famous Salaman Collection of trade and craft tools that was put together by Raphael Salaman, author of the *Dictionary of Woodworking Tools*.

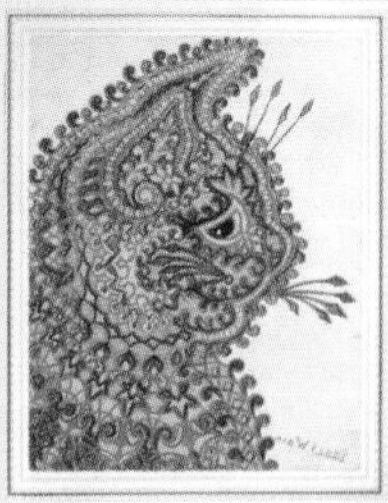

Just outside St Albans, at Verulamium, is the Museum of everyday life in Roman Britain, set in attractive parkland. Home to some of the best Roman mosaics and wall plasters outside the Mediterranean, the museum houses recreated Roman rooms and there is also an Iron Age gallery.

Finally there is the town's ancient Clock Tower that was erected in the early 15th century by the townsfolk of St Albans so they could sound their own hours and so assert their freedoms from the town's abbey.

a visit. The **Museum of St Albans** (see panel opposite) relates the fascinating history of the town from Roman times through to the present day and among the exhibits on show is the famous Salaman collection of trade and craft tools that is considered to be the finest in the country. In **St Albans Organ Museum** (open on Sundays) visitors can enjoy the stirring sounds of an amazing collection of working mechanical musical instruments, which include two theatre organs, musical boxes, and reproducing pianos, all of which have been lovingly restored. All the most famous manufacturers are represented, including Mortier, Decap, Bursens, Wurlitzer and Steinway. In the 15th century St Albans was the home of Hertfordshire's most famous witch, Mother Haggy. Said to have changed, late in life, from a white witch to a black witch, she rode around the town at noon on a broomstick and crossed the River Ver in a kettle.

Just to the north, in the tiny hamlet of **Redbournbury**, lies **Redbournbury Mill**, an 18th century watermill that stands on the site of a mill that was mentioned in the Domesday Book. Once belonging to the abbey at St Albans, the mill was seized by the crown following the Dissolution of the Monasteries. First coming into private hands in 1652 when it was sold to an ancestor of the present Earl of Verulam, it stayed in the family until 1931 when it once again became Crown property. Now back in private hands, this splendid mill, on the banks of the River Ver, has been restored to its former glory and is now in full working order, powered by a large 1935 Crossley oil engine. Open to the public on Sundays from March to October, and on other days for special events, the mill also sells its own stoneground flour and bread.

AROUND ST ALBANS

Chiswell Green

3 miles SW of St Albans on A414

This village is home to probably one of the biggest attractions in Hertfordshire, the **Gardens of the Rose**, a site, currently being greatly expanded, that contains one of the most important rose collections in the world. The Royal National Rose Gardens can boast some 30,000 rose trees and upwards of 1,700 varieties. It is not necessary to be a horticultural enthusiast to appreciate the sheer natural beauty of gorgeous displays such as The President's Walk or The Queen Mother Rose Garden, named after the Garden's patron, which contains some of the oldest varieties of rose, including Damask, Gallicas, Albas and Portland. With the model gardens, the

Coleman Croft Saddlery

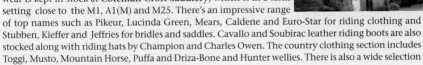

Coopers Green, Nr St Albans, Hertfordshire AL4 9HJ
Tel: 01707 274239 Fax: 01707 271256
e-mail: mail@colemancroft.com website: www.colemancroft.com

An amazing range of high-quality saddlery, riding clothing and country wear is kept in stock at **Coleman Croft Saddlery**, which is in a farm setting close to the M1, A1(M) and M25. There's an impressive range of top names such as Pikeur, Lucinda Green, Mears, Caldene and Euro-Star for riding clothing and Stubben, Kieffer and Jeffries for bridles and saddles. Cavallo and Soubirac leather riding boots are also stocked along with riding hats by Champion and Charles Owen. The country clothing section includes Toggi, Musto, Mountain Horse, Puffa and Driza-Bone and Hunter wellies. There is also a wide selection of horse rugs and equestrian books to choose from.

miniature roses, and the breathtaking pergola, it would be difficult to exaggerate the beauty of this place, which really has to be visited to be appreciated.

London Colney

3 miles S of St Albans off the A414

Among the interesting old buildings in this pleasant village on the River Colne is the late-Victorian All Saints Convent, which stands within the former Colney Park. Begun in 1899 as an Anglican establishment, with a church added in the 1920s, it was bought by the Roman Catholic Church in 1973 as a pastoral centre. A mile south of London Colney, aircraft enthusiasts will be in their element at the **Mosquito Aircraft Museum**, which is run by the de Havilland Aircraft Museum Trust. It was here in 1940 that the first Mosquito aircraft was built and taken by road to the de Havilland airfield at Hatfield. In addition to the prototype Mosquito there is a collection of other de Havilland planes, plus various engines and displays of all kinds of aeronautical memorabilia. To the east lies Colney Heath, where highwaymen would prey on the stagecoach passengers journeying to and from London on the Great North Road.

Shenley

4 miles S of St Albans on B5378

A traditional country village with, at its centre, two inns, a pond, the site of a former pound for stray animals, and the village lock-up. One of several in Hertfordshire, this **Lock-up** is a brick beehive-shaped construction where the village's drunks and petty criminals were locked up overnight before being put before the magistrate the next day. On either side of the door is the warning sign: 'Be sober, do well, fear not, be vigilant'.

Just north of the village lies the impressive moated **Salisbury Hall**, built by the Treasurer of Henry VIII and modernised in the 17th century. The architect Nicholas Hawksmoor lived near Shenley and is buried in the churchyard of the neighbouring village of Shenleybury. Here, too, is the grave of the dashing racing driver Graham Hill, who was killed in a flying accident at Arkley, 3 miles from Shenley.

Aldenham

6 miles SW of St Albans on the B462

The greatest feature of **Aldenham Country Park**, established in 1971 on what was formerly Aldenham Common, is a large reservoir that was dug by hand by French prisoners of war in the 1790s. Designed to maintain the levels of local rivers following the building of the Grand Union Canal, it is now used for recreational purposes and also supports a wealth of wildfowl and plant life. Coarse fishing is available by permit. The park has a lakeside nature trail and woodland walks and is home to several rare breeds of domestic animals, including Longhorn cattle. Families can have fun in Winnie the Pooh's '100 Aker Wood', where the homes of Pooh Bear, Christopher Robin, Piglet, Eyeore and Owl have been recreated in association with the Disney Corporation.

Markyate

7 miles NW of St Albans off the A5

Markyate's narrow main street is part of the great Roman road, Watling Street, the route between London and Holyhead. A mansion in the village, built on the site of a medieval nunnery known as Markyate Cell, became famous as the home of Lady Katherine Ferrers, the notorious highwaywoman of Nomansland Common near Sandridge, just north of St Albans. Married as a teenager to a man she did not like, Katherine found escape and adventure by disguising herself as a highwayman and holding up the coaches that plied the busy Watling Street. She kept both her disguise and her booty in a secret room above the kitchen in the house. Famed and feared for her audacity, the Wicked Lady, who always rode a jet black horse, eventually died at the door of her room after struggling home wounded during a hold-up. She was buried quietly by her husband, who had her room sealed in the hope that her secret would die with her. It did not.

Harpenden

4 miles N of St Albans on A1081

The whole of the town centre is now a conservation area and, in particular, the High Street is lined with many listed 17th and 18th century buildings. The **Harpenden Local History Centre** is an ideal place to find out more about this charming old agricultural community and, as well as the small permanent collection there are regularly changing themed exhibitions. The **Harpenden Railway Museum**, a small private collection that was begun in 1963, contains several thousand items of railway memorabilia, many of which originate from the county. The ashes of the comedian Eric Morecambe were scattered in the garden of remembrance next to the Church of St Nicholas.

STEVENAGE

Designated the first of Britain's New Towns in 1946, the town grew up along the Great North Road, and as traffic increased from the 13th century it developed round its parish church, the main road becoming its High Street. The idea of New Towns grew from the severe shortage of housing following the World War II air raids on London, and the first new houses in Stevenage were occupied in 1951; the new town centre was completed in 1958. Within the new town area, by a roundabout near the railway station, lie **Six Hills**, reputed to be Roman burial mounds. The history of the town, from the earliest days to the development of the new town and the present day, is told in **Stevenage Museum** in the undercroft of St George's Church.

AROUND STEVENAGE

Knebworth

2 miles S of Stevenage off A602

The town is best known today for the open-air rock concerts held in the grounds of **Knebworth House**. The home of the Lytton family since 1490, the present magnificent Gothic mansion

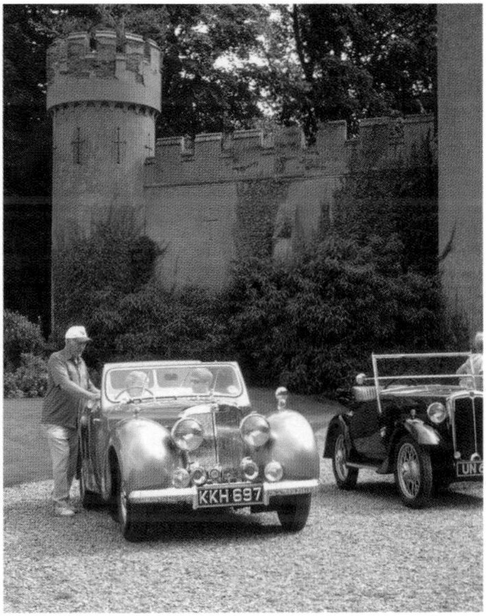

Classic Car Show, Knebworth

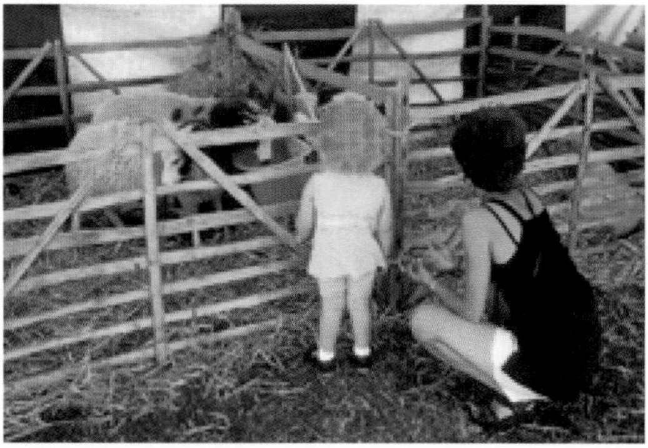

Craft Fair, Knebworth

house was built during the 19th century to the design of the Victorian statesman and novelist, Edward Bulwer-Lytton, who wrote *The Last Days of Pompeii*. However, fragments of the original Tudor house remain, including parts of the Great Hall, and there is also some superb 17th century panelling. Other members of the Lytton family of note include Constance, a leading figure in the suffragette movement, and Robert, Viceroy of India. An exhibition at the house brings to life the story of Lord Lytton's viceroyship and the Great Delhi Durbar of 1877. The house has also played host to such notable visitors as Elizabeth I, Benjamin Disraeli, Sir Winston Churchill and Charles Dickens, who is said to have taken part in amateur theatrical performances here. Dickens was a close friend of Sir Edward and the success of the performances prompted the two gentlemen to embark on the financing of a charity to establish a Guild of Literature and Arts with the aim of providing housing for poor and aged actors and artists. Dickens christened his tenth child Edward Bulwer Lytton Dickens in honour of their great friendship. The grounds of Knebworth House are also well worth visiting and as well as the beautiful formal gardens laid out by Lutyens there is a wonderful herb garden established by Gertrude Jekyll, a lovely Victorian wilderness area, a maze that was replanted in 1995 and acres of grassland that are home to herds of red and sika deer. Children will enjoy the adventure playground, where they will find Fort Knebworth, a monorail suspension slide and a bouncy castle among the amusements.

Benington

3 miles E of Stevenage off the B1037

One of the county's most attractive villages, Benington has a lovely green fringed by 16th century timber-and-plaster cottages. The village church dates from the 13th century, and next to it, on the site of a largely disappeared castle, is a large Georgian house known as **Benington Lordship**. The house is set in superb grounds that include lakes, a Norman keep and moat (the remains of the castle), kitchen, rose and water gardens, a charming rockery, magnificent herbaceous borders and a splendid folly dating from 1832.

Cromer

4 miles NE of Stevenage on the B1037

Half a mile east of the village, on the B1037 towards Hare Street, stands Hertfordshire's sole surviving post mill. **Cromer Windmill** was built on an artificial mound where windmills have stood for over 600 years. The present mill dates back at least to 1720, possibly as early as 1681. Blown over in a storm around 1860 and subsequently rebuilt, it was in use until the 1920s, by which time milling by wind had become uneconomic. The mill was basically left to deteriorate until an appeal by local people in 1967 saved its life. On completion of the first phase of restoration work the mill was presented to the current owners the Hertfordshire Building Preservation Trust. The first open days were held in 1991 and the mill was restored to full working order in 1998 with the help of grants from the Heritage Lottery Fund and English Heritage. The mill can be visited on Sundays, Bank Holiday Mondays and the second and fourth Saturdays from the second Sunday in May until the end of August.

Royston

12 miles NE of Stevenage on A10

This light industrial town grew up at the intersection of the Icknield Way and Ermine Street and is named after a wayside cross erected by Lady Roysia. A favourite hunting base for royalty, **James I's Hunting Lodge** can still be seen, though the only original features which remain are the two large chimneys.

Discovered in 1742 below the junction of the two ancient thoroughfares is the man-made **Royston Cave**. Bottle-shaped and cut out of the chalk, the cave is 28 feet deep and 17 feet across. Inside the chamber is a series of crude carvings on the walls, including St Christopher and the Crucifixion; the purpose of the cave and the date of the carvings have never been determined.

Therfield, nr Royston

The **Royston Museum**, in the former Congregational Schoolroom building, houses the Royston and District Local History Society collections, which relate to the history of this late medieval town and the surrounding area. Also here is a substantial collection of late-19th century ceramics and glass.

Weston

4 miles N of Stevenage off the A6141

A scattered village atop the Weston Hills. Two stones mark the grave of Jack o'Legs, a friendly giant who occasionally turned highwayman, robbing the Baldock bakers of their batches of bread. Caught, bound and about to be killed, he asked to be buried where his arrow landed.

Baldock

5 miles N of Stevenage on the A6141

A settlement of some size during the Iron Age and Roman times, the Baldock of today dates from the 13th century; it was founded by the Knights Templar and takes its name from the Old French for Baghdad. The Church of St Mary has an impressive 14th century tower and spike steeple, and the town boasts many handsome Georgian houses, both in the tree-lined main street and in the side streets.

Ashwell

9 miles N of Stevenage off the A505

One of the five boroughs of Hertfordshire in medieval times, Ashwell, which took its name from the ash trees around the source of the River Rhee, later prospered through a malting industry that only ceased in the 1950s. The 14th century **Church of St Mary** has the highest tower in the county, at 176 feet, and several inscriptions referring to the Black Death of 1349 and the plague and great storm of 1361. **Ashwell Museum**, in the restored Town House, affords a fascinating insight into the natural history, social history and archaeology of the town.

Letchworth

6 miles N of Stevenage on A505

This attractive country town is proud to be the first Garden City, where the ideals of Ebenezer Howard were put into practice (see under Welwyn Garden City). The site for Letchworth was purchased in 1903 and Barry Parker and Raymond Unwin were appointed architects. The residential cottages were designed and built by different architects for the 1905 Cheap Cottages Exhibition and, with none costing more than £150, they each demonstrated new techniques and styles of building and living accommodation. The Parker and Unwin office is now home to the **First Garden City Heritage Museum**, a unique place which traces the history and development of this special town; among the many displays are the original plans and drawings of Letchworth. **Letchworth Museum and Art Gallery** is home to displays of local natural history and archaeology including finds of late Iron Age and Roman origin that were unearthed at Baldock.

Hitchin

4 miles NE of Stevenage on A600

Situated on the banks of the River Hiz, this old town was, during medieval times, a vast market area where straw was purchased for the local cottage industry of straw plaiting and where the completed plaits were sold. As the trade in straw declined so the market at Hitchin reduced in size but there is still a small market place today, west of the parish church. Many of the town's older buildings have survived, if now surrounded by newer developments. The oldest parts of **St Mary's Church** date from the 12th century, though there was a minster church here at the time of the Domesday Survey. The low tower is the only part of the original building which survived an earthquake of 1298. Rebuilt in the 14th century, the grandeur of the church reflects the prosperity which Hitchin once enjoyed. Standing on the site of a Gilbertine Priory is **The Biggin**, constructed in the early 17th century. For a while it was a private residence, then a school, before becoming, in 1723, an almshouse for 'poore auncient or middle aged women', a function which it still performs today. Another building worthy of a mention is **The Priory**, which takes in fragments of a Carmelite Priory founded in the 14th century. Built in 1770 by Robert Adams as the private residence of the Radcliffe family, it was extensively renovated in the 1980s after being disused for many years.

Finally, **Hitchin Museum**, home to the county's largest collection of period costumes, is an excellent place to visit. It shares a building with the **Museum of the Hertfordshire Imperial Yeomanry** - a band of men mustered to repel Napoleon's threatened invasion. As well as the numerous displays of local social history, part of the museum includes the **Victorian Chemist Shop** and **Physic Garden**. This re-creation of a chemist's shop uses many of the stock and fittings from Perks and Llewellyn, who ceased trading as a pharmacy in 1961; the original cabinets still contain the lavender toiletries for which the firm was world famous. To carry the connection further between the town and pharmacy, the medical pioneer Lord Lister had family ties with Hitchin and began his education here. The Physic Garden reflects the historical and modern importance of plants as a source of medicine.

HERTFORD

Dating back to Saxon times, the town was founded at a ford across the River Lea, at that time the boundary between Saxon and Viking England. A once important waterway linking Hertford with London, the River Lea, which became the Lea (Lee) Navigation at

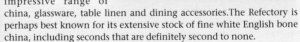

Hertford, was used to transport flour and grain but today its traffic is leisure cruises. The **Hertford Nature Walk** is situated in the meadows between the Rivers Lea and Beane, and takes in the canal basin, known as **The Folly**.

Hertford is very much a mix of the old and new, and among the interesting buildings are the particularly beautiful Norman **Church of St Leonard, Bengeo** and the **Quaker Meeting House**. Said to be the oldest purpose-built meeting house in the world that has been in constant use as a place of worship, the meeting house dates from 1669 and stands behind a walled courtyard; it has a unique four-tiered platform for the ministers that is screened from the entrance. The collections at **Hertford Museum** were started in the 1890s and cover a wide variety of subjects relating to the town and the surrounding area. The Museum is located in a 17th century town house that is complemented by a reconstructed Jacobean garden.

Little remains of the original **Hertford Castle**, which was built by King Alfred's son Prince Edward to protect London from the Danes. However, the 15th century gatehouse is still standing and, now modernised, is used as administrative offices for the borough council. The site of the castle is now a public park and evidence of the castle's original motte and bailey can still be seen in the lie of the land. A short length of the massive Norman flint wall, complete with a 14th century postern gate, is also preserved in the park.

To the south of the town lies **Cole Green Way**, a delightful nature trail that follows the route of the now disused Hertford and Welwyn Junction Railway. Passing through attractive meadowland, the trail runs from Hertford to Cole Green, where the former station provides a pleasant picnic spot.

AROUND HERTFORD

Hoddesdon

2 miles S of Hertford on the A1010

The town grew up around the road along the Lea Valley that replaced the Roman Ermine Street in Saxon times. In Lea Valley Park stands the 15th century **Rye House Gatehouse**, a fascinating historic attraction which includes an exhibition where visitors can eavesdrop on the conspirators in the Rye House Plot. In 1683, Rye House was the scene of a plot to assassinate Charles II as he passed through the town on his way back from Newmarket to London. The plot failed and the conspirators, including Richard Rumbold, the then tenant of Rye House, were executed.

Cheshunt

8 miles S of Hertford off the A10

In 1564 Lord Burghley, Chief Minister to Elizabeth I, built his great house Theobalds here. Later, James I was so taken with the house that he persuaded Burghley's son Robert to exchange the house for his palace at Hatfield. The house was all but destroyed in the aftermath of the Civil War, and what remains of the building stands in the public **Cedars Park**. Also in the park is **Temple Bar**, designed by Wren and originally erected at the Fleet Street entrance to the City of London after the Great Fire of 1666. By the 1870s London's traffic had increased to the extent that the gateway was causing an obstruction, so it was removed and rebuilt in the park.

Waltham Cross

9 miles S of Hertford on the A1010

The town takes its name from the cross built in the centre in 1291. It is an Eleanor Cross, one of three survivors of the 12 which Edward I erected to commemorate the resting places of the funeral cortege of his Queen, Eleanor of Castile. Eleanor died in Lincolnshire and the cortege took 13 days to travel to Westminster Abbey, where she is buried. The building materials in the cross include Caen stone, Sussex and Purbeck marble and precious stones, and it is recorded that the total cost was £95. The other surviving crosses are at Northampton and Geddington, and a Victorian replica stands in the forecourt of Charing Cross Station. In 1859 Anthony Trollope came to live in Waltham Cross. He kept pigs, tended his garden and wrote some of his best work while living here.

Ware

3 miles E of Hertford on the A1170

Situated at the point where Ermine Street crosses the River Lea, Ware was the scene of a famous encounter between King Alfred and the Danes in 895 and, during the Middle Ages, it became a trading rival to Hertford. The construction of a viaduct in the 1970s to carry the A10 across the valley has removed much of the traffic from the town and, despite development over the years, Ware still retains many of its original buildings. Behind the east end of the High Street, there is access to Blue Coat Yard where, on the right, stands **Place House**, possibly one of Ware's two Domesday manor houses, which was rebuilt during the 13th century as a splendid aisled hall and in the 1680s was purchased by the governors of Christ's Hospital for use as a school for boys being fostered in Ware. Most of this building still remains and on the opposite side of the yard stand the cottages which were built in 1698 and provided accommodation for a foster mother and up to 14 boys.

The Fashion Doll Specialist

36 High Street, Ware, Hertfordshire SG12 9BY
Tel: 01920 467874
e-mail: barbiegirl9595@aol.com
website: www.fashiondollspecialist.co.uk

The Fashion Doll Specialist on Ware's busy main street is the country's leading stockist and source of information on the worldwide phenomenon that is the Barbie Doll. If there is anything to be known about Barbie Dolls, this is where they know it, and what started as a collecting hobby for Susannah Williams has turned into a business whose name and repute have spread to all parts of the globe. The first-floor shop is crammed with Barbie products and, once inside, the true Barbie aficionado will be very difficult to budge! Besides the dolls themselves, the shelves and racks have all the Barbie paraphernalia, from clothes for all occasions to furniture sets, location sets and a vast range of accessories without which no Barbie and no Ken would feel complete.

The prices start at less than £10 for a beach doll to vintage reproductions and - from a recent catalogue - a very rare Qi-Pao Barbie from Hong Kong for a cool £500. The complete range runs into thousands, with many being added all the time, and the fashion dolls include dozens of characters besides Barbie and Ken. Shop hours are 9.30 to 4 Monday to Friday and 9 to 5 on Saturday, and there's also a flourishing mail order business. The name on the shop front is Marjorie Williams, Susannah's mother, who with her husband runs the florist shop on the ground floor. Their stock fills the interior and spills out into colourful pots and vases on the pavement.

The High Street crosses the River Lea at Bridgefoot, and here can still be seen some unique 18th century gazebos, many of which has been restored to their former glory. The riverside path leads on into an attractive public garden behind what was once a Franciscan Priory, of which only a few traces remain. Founded in 1338 as a friary, the priory became a private house in 1568 and remained so for several centuries. In 1920, the owner, Mrs Page-Croft, gave the house and gardens to the town and, fully restored in 1994, the building stands pristine surrounded by seven acres of parkland.

No trip to Ware would be complete without a visit to **Scott's Grotto**, built by the poet John Scott in the late 18th century and located off the A119 Hertford Road. The son of a wealthy Quaker family, Scott devised this elaborate series of six chambers linked by passageways and air tunnels during the 1760s; they are lined with flints, fossils, minerals and thousands of shells. On a hill above the Grotto is an octagonal summerhouse approached by horseshoe-shaped steps. The Grotto was described by Scott's friend Dr Johnson as 'a fairy hall', adding that 'none but a poet could have made such a garden'. The Grotto was extensively restored in 1990, and the replacement shells came from local donors and from as far afield as Japan. It is open every Saturday and Bank Holiday Monday from April to the end of September.

The history of Ware and its major role in the malting industry is explained in **Ware Museum** at Priory Lodge.

Great Amwell

3 miles E of Hertford off the A10

Between 1609 and 1613 the **New River** was created to carry fresh water from local springs by way of Hoddesdon and Cheshunt to the New River Head reservoir at Clerkenwell in London. Wooden pipes then carried the water to the houses and businesses of North London. This enterprise was the brainchild of Sir Hugh Myddelton, whose achievement is commemorated at Great Amwell by an island laid out by the architect of the New River Company in 1800. Just south of the village church lie the imposing buildings of Haileybury College, which was established in 1809 as a training school for the East India Company. The architect was William Wilkins, whose best-known work is the National Gallery in Trafalgar Square.

BISHOP'S STORTFORD

The name of this delightful rural town derives from two sources: the River Stort on which it stands and the fact that the Bishop of London was, at the time of the Domesday Book, also Lord of the Manor here. Malting and brewing were the major industries in the 19th century, and Bishop's Stortford was an important stop on the coaching route from London to Norwich. But the town's chief claim to fame is as the birthplace of Cecil Rhodes, and his exploits are documented in his former home, Nettlewell House, now the **Rhodes Museum and Commonwealth Centre**.

AROUND BISHOP'S STORTFORD

Much Hadham

3 miles W of Bishop's Stortford on B1004

A large and largely unspoilt village, which still retains many old timber-framed houses and cottages, the oldest of which dates back to the 15th century. The **Forge Museum and Victorian Cottage Garden** not only tells the story of the work of the blacksmith over the years but is also home to a delightful cottage

Much Hadnam

garden. As well as displaying and growing plants that would have been familiar to a 19th century country gardener, the garden houses an unusual 19th century bee shelter.

Nearby **Perry Green** became the home of Henry Moore: following bomb damage to his Hampstead studio in 1941, the famous sculptor moved with his wife Irina to the peace and tranquillity of the village and he remained there for the rest of his life. The Henry Moore Foundation, which operates from Dane Tree House, Perry Green, and from the Henry Moore Institute in Leeds, was established in 1977 'to advance the education of the public by the promotion of their appreciation of the fine arts and in particular the works of Henry Moore'. The Perry Green site comprises several studios and two converted barns containing the Foundation's collection of Moore's work, as well as tapestries based on his drawings which were woven at West Dean College in Sussex. On the far side of the village green is a visitor centre selling books, posters, postcards and

other Moore-themed merchandise along with a limited number of original prints. The estate contains many fine trees and hedgerows, much loved by Moore and to be seen in many of his works, and it was Irina who over the years created the garden areas in which the studios and sculptures are sited. The Foundation is open to the public from April to September by appointment (call: 01279 843333). Moore, who died in 1986, is buried in the village churchyard.

Standon

5 miles W of Bishop's Stortford on A120

This old village, which once had a weekly market and two annual fairs, derived its importance from the families who held the manor and also from the Order of St John of Jerusalem. Though there is little evidence today, the order established a commandery, a hospice and a school, which is believed to be the building now known as Knights' Court.

In a field to the west of the village lies the **Balloon Stone**, a giant sandstone boulder which marks the spot where, in 1784, Vincenzo Lunardi completed the first balloon flight in England. He began his flight in Finsbury, north London, and landed here some two hours later having first touched down briefly in a field at North Mimms.

BEDFORDSHIRE

Bedfordshire is a county of multifarious delights, all within easy reach of London and major road and rail networks. In the Bedfordshire Heartlands are to be found two of England's leading animal attractions, Woburn Safari Park and Whipsnade Wildlife Park. There are picturesque villages and historic houses, transport and heritage museums, mills and farms, woodland and nature reserves, great views from the Chilterns escarpment and well-established walking and cycle routes. The Great Ouse and the Grand Union Canal, once commercial arteries, are finding a new role as leisure attractions, with miles of scenic walks or leisurely cruises to be enjoyed. The south of the county is dominated by the towns of Luton and Dunstable, while the central region of Bedfordshire is an area of ancient settlements and a rich diversity of places to see. Here is perhaps the most impressive dovecote in the country, with nests for 1,500 birds, while just outside Sandy are the headquarters of the Royal Society for the Protection of Birds. At nearby Cardington the skyline is dominated by the huge hangars where the R100 and R101 airships were built. Houghton House at Houghton Conquest is widely believed to have been the inspiration for the House Beautiful in John Bunyan's *Pilgrim's Progress*. Bunyan was born in the village of Elstow, a little way south of Bedford, and many of the places most closely associated with the writer can be visited, in both the town and the village. Bedford, the county

Grand Union Canal, Linslade

capital, offers a blend of history and modern amenity, all set against the backdrop of the River Great Ouse, which passes through the town and many pleasant villages on its journey across the county.

LUTON

The largest town in Bedfordshire and perhaps best known for Luton Airport and Vauxhall cars, Luton first began to prosper in the 17th century on the strength of its straw plaiting and straw hat making industries. At the centre of this essentially modern town is **Wardown Park**, a traditional town park with tennis, bowls and boating, and, housed within a delightful Victorian mansion, **Luton Museum and Art Gallery**. The park was opened to the public in the early years of the reign of Edward VII, but not the house, which was first a restaurant and then, during World War I, a military hospital. It was not until 1931 that the town's museum and art gallery, originally housed in the library, moved here. As well as featuring a re-creation of a Victorian shop and pub, the museum is also home to a range of collections covering the hat trade, costume, local history, archaeology and childhood. As lace making was one of the two main cottages industries in Bedfordshire, visitors will not be surprised to learn that the museum also has the largest collection of lace anywhere in the country outside London. Although Luton has expanded rapidly from a market town in the early 19th century to a major industrial centre by the mid-20th century, visitors can also take a step back in time by seeking out **Stockwood Craft Museum and Gardens**. Housed in a Georgian stable block, the museum has a collection of Bedfordshire craft and rural items

Luton Town Centre

enhanced by frequent craft demonstrations. The walled garden is equally impressive and the Period Garden includes knot, medieval, Victorian, cottage, Dutch and Italian sections. The Hamilton Finlay Sculpture Garden showcases six pieces of sculpture by the internationally renowned artist Ian Hamilton Finlay in a lovely natural setting. Also here can be found the **Mossman Collection** of over 60 horse drawn vehicles, the largest of its kind on public display in Britain. The story of transport comes into the 20th century in the Transport Gallery, whose exhibits include bicycles, vintage cars and a model of the Luton tram system. Replicas of some of the vehicles on display here have found their way into such films as *Ben Hur* and *Out of Africa*.

Just to the south of the town is the magnificent house **Luton Hoo**, originally designed by Robert Adams and set in 1500 acres of parkland landscaped by Capability Brown. Construction of the house began in 1767, though it was extensively remodelled in 1827 and again in 1903, when the interior was given a French style for Sir Julius Wernher, who installed his fabulous art collection in the house. Luton Hoo is no longer open to the public.

Luton Hoo

Just southeast of Luton is **Someries Castle**, the remains of a fortified medieval manor house dating from the middle to late 15th century. The earliest surviving brick building in the county both the gatehouse and chapel have survived and are still a very impressive sight. The original castle on this site belonged first to the de Someries family and then to the Wenlocks, and the house, of which only a romantic ruin remains, may have been built for the Lord Wenlock who died at the Battle of Tewkesbury in 1471, when the Yorkist victory ended the Wars of the Roses.

AROUND LUTON

Slip End

1 mile S of Luton on the B4540

Woodside Animal Farm is home to hundreds of animals and birds to see and feed; its many attractions include a walk-through monkey house, red squirrel enclosure, alpaca family and hand-reared racoons. There are indoor and outdoor picnic and play areas, pony and tractor rides, a bouncy castle, farm shop, craft shop and coffee shop.

Whipsnade

5 miles SW of Luton off B489

This small village with a charming, simple church is surrounded by common land on which stands **Whipsnade Tree Cathedral**. After World War I, a local landowner, Edmund Kell Blyth, planted a variety of trees which have grown into the shape of a cathedral, with a nave, transepts, a chancel and cloisters. A curiously moving place, particularly as the trees have matured, the Tree Cathedral, where services are held during the summer, is in the care of the National Trust. To the south of the village can be seen the white silhouette of a lion cut into the green hillside, which is reminiscent of the much older White Horse at Uffington. A magnificent landmark, the lion also advertises the whereabouts of **Whipsnade Wild Animal Park**, the country home of the Zoological Society of London. Whipsnade first opened its doors in 1931, attracting over 26,000 visitors on the first Monday, and in the 70 years since it has grown and developed and continues to provide fun and education for thousands of visitors each year. There are 2,500 animals on show in the park's 600 acres, and behind the scenes

Whipsnade is at the forefront of wild animal welfare and conservation, specialising in the breeding of endangered species such as cheetahs, rhinos and the scimitar-horned oryx. There are daily demonstrations - penguin feeding, sealions, free-flying birds - and other attractions include a railway safari, Discovery Centre, Children's Farm and Adventure Playground. Feeding time for the animals is always a popular occasion, while humans who feel peckish can make tracks for the Café on the Lake or (in summer) the Lookout Café, or graze on ice cream and snacks from the many refreshment kiosks in the park.

Totternhoe

6 miles W of Luton off the A505

This attractive village is situated below **Totternhoe Knolls**, a steeply sloped spur of chalk that is now a nature reserve known nationally for its orchids and its butterflies. On the top of the spur are the remains of a motte and bailey castle dating from Norman times.

Putteridge

2 miles NE of Luton on the A505

The University of Luton and the Hertfordshire Garden Trust have restored the gardens at **Putteridge Bury** to the original designs of Sir Edwin Lutyens and Gertrude Jekyll; one of the highlights is a superb rose garden.

Dunstable

2 miles NW of Luton on the A505

Dunstable is a bustling town that grew up at the junction of two ancient roads, Icknield Way and Watling Street, and was an important centre in Roman Britain, when it was known as Durocobrivae. The town's finest building is undoubtedly the **Priory Church of St Peter**, all that remains of a Priory founded by Henry I in 1131; only the nave actually dates from that time. It was at the Priory that Archbishop Cranmer's court sat in 1533 to annul the marriage of Henry VIII and Catherine of Aragon. On the B4541 Dunstable-Whipsnade road, **Dunstable Downs** commands some of the finest views over the Vale of Aylesbury. Designated a Site of Special Scientific Interest and a Scheduled Ancient Monument, it has much to attract the visitor, including a Countryside Centre with interpretive displays and gifts, circular walks and a picnic area; it's a popular spot with hang gliders and kite flyers, and a refreshment kiosk is open all year round. South of Dunstable Downs at the junction of the B4541 and B4540, Whipsnade Heath is a small area of woodland containing some unusual plants and fungi.

Billington

8 miles W of Luton on the A4146

Mead Open Farm is home to a variety of established farm animals and offers a particularly wide range of attractions for children, including an indoor play barn,

(Continued page 30)

Priory Church of St Peter, Dunstable

WALK 1

Dunstable Downs

Start	Robertson Corner, Dunstable Downs visitor centre
Distance	4½ miles (7.2km)
Approximate time	2½ hours
Parking	Dunstable Downs visitor centre
Refreshments	Kiosk at visitor centre, pubs at Whipsnade
Ordnance Survey maps	Landranger 166 (Luton & Hertford), Explorers 181 (Chiltern Hills North) and 182 (St Albans & Hatfield)

The Dunstable Downs form part of the steep western escarpment of the Chiltern range, and from their open, grassy slopes there are extensive views over the Vale of Aylesbury and further afield towards the flat country bordering the East Midlands and East Anglia. From the visitor centre on top of the downs the route heads across pleasant, undulating country to Whipsnade Heath, passing by the 'Tree Cathedral' at Whipsnade before returning to the edge of the escarpment. The finale is a splendid 1 mile (1.6km) ramble along the crest of the downs with grand views all the while. This is a well-waymarked walk as it follows one of Bedfordshire County Council's 'Circular Routes'.

From the visitor centre turn right along the road to the point where it forks at Robertson Corner. A monument here reveals how this road junction got its name: two brothers called Robertson were killed in World War I and a third brother gave the surrounding land to the National Trust as a memorial. At the fork take the left-hand road, pass the entrance to Kensworth Quarry, and after ½ mile (800m) – just after passing a house and before reaching a radio mast – turn left through a waymarked gap in a hedge (A).

Walk along the left-hand edge of a field, by a hedge on the left, and in the field corner keep ahead through trees and then continue along the right-hand edge of the next field, by a hedge on the right, heading downhill. Just before reaching the bottom corner of the field, turn right and then immediately left to walk along a track, keeping right at a fork and continuing, by a hedge and line of trees on the left, towards Kensworth Quarry. Look out for a yellow waymark which directs you to the right to continue along a pleasant path through a belt of trees. Climb a stile on the edge of the trees, keep ahead across a sloping field, just below the steepest part of the slope on the left, climb another stile and bear slightly right to head downhill across the next field to climb a stile in the bottom corner.

Turn right to walk along the right-hand edge of a field, by a hedge on the right. Climb a stile, pass to the left of a barn, turn right over another stile in front of a gate and then turn left to continue in the same direction as before, along a track that heads uphill to a cattle-grid. Keep along a hedge-

WALK 1

lined track and, just before reaching a barn and metal gate, turn left over a stile in the hedge and continue along a narrow path, climbing a stile on to a road. Turn right, and at a public footpath sign turn left **B** over a stile and walk across the middle of a field, passing a solitary tree, to a stile. Climb the stile and walk along a narrow path, between a hedge on the left and wire fence on the right. Pass between a wooden barrier on the edge of trees and continue through woodland to go through another barrier on the far side. Keep ahead across Whipsnade Heath car park to a road **C**.

Turn right, keep ahead at a crossroads and continue along the road into Whipsnade village – the road is busy but there is a verge for most of the way. Continue along the right-hand edge of the spacious green, opposite Whipsnade's brick church, and at a sign for 'Tree Cathedral' turn right **D** along a potholed, tarred lane. Turn right at the sign for the Tree Cathedral and go through the gate at the far end of the car park into the grounds of Whipsnade Tree Cathedral, a variety of trees planted in the shape of a cathedral. This was created in 1931 by Edmund Blyth and was inspired by the building of Liverpool Cathedral, his experiences in World War I and the loss of friends killed in that war. He bequeathed it to the National Trust.

The route continues along the left edge of the 'cathedral grounds' to a kissing gate, after which hug the left-edge of the meadow to use another kissing gate and continue to a T-junction of paths. Turn right, following both Circular Route and Icknield Way signs, along a pleasantly tree- and hedge-lined path to reach the edge of the escarpment. Ahead is a magnificent view over the Vale of Aylesbury, with the line of the Chilterns stretching away to the left. The path bears right, but almost immediately turn left along a narrow path to a finger-post and turn right, in the Dunstable Downs direction, to a gate.

Go through the gate on to open downland for the superb finale. As you continue gently uphill across the slopes of the downs, there are extensive views over flat country to the left and ahead of the curving escarpment. The path leads back to the car park and visitor centre. ●

0 200 400 600 800metres 1 KILOMETRES
0 200 400 600yards ½ MILES

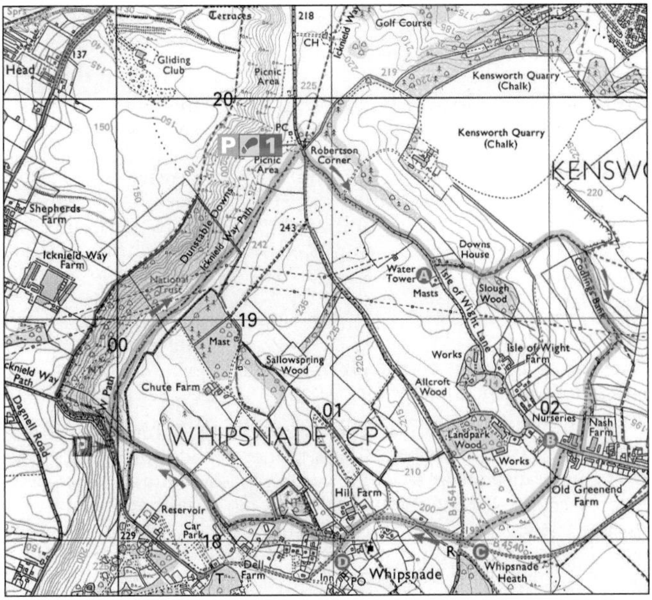

Leighton Buzzard Railway

Page's Park Station, Billington Road, Leighton Buzzard, Bedfordshire LU7 4TN
Tel: 01525 373888 Fax: 01525 377814
website: www.buzzrail.co.uk

One of England's premier narrow gauge heritage railways, **Leighton Buzzard Railway** was established in 1919 to carry sand from the quarries, which had opened up to supply the demand for sand during World War I, in the north of the town through to the town's railway sidings and canal wharf. Built using war surplus materials and equip-ment, the line, since 1968, has carried a passenger service, mostly steam hauled, from Page's Park to Stonehenge Works in the countryside near the village of Heath and Reach. Operated by volunteers of the Leighton Buzzard Narrow Gauge Railway Society, the trains pass through a modern housing estate before emerging into rolling countryside with views of the Chiltern Hills in the distance. The railway is now the home of the largest collection of narrow gauge locomotives in Britain and, of the 50 here, some 12 are steam driven. The oldest engine dates from 1877 whilst the newest is a diesel locomotive built especially for the line in 1999. The return journey takes just over an hour and the railway operates on Sundays and Bank Holiday weekends between March and October.

activity house, sandpit, indoor pets corner and ride-on toys. There's also a tea room and shop and a number of daily activities and weekly events.

Leighton Buzzard

9 miles W of Luton on A505

The town's interesting name tells a lot about its history: Leighton is Old English and refers to a centre for market gardening whilst the Buzzard is a reference not to the bird of prey but to a local clergyman, Theobald de Busar, the town's first Prebendary. The town's past prosperity as a market centre is reflected in the grandeur of its fine Market Cross, a 15th century pentagonal structure with an open base and statues under vaulted openings all topped off by pinnacles. The market is still held here every Tuesday and Saturday. The spire of **All Saints' Church** is over 190 feet high and is a local landmark. This big ironstone church dates from 1277 and inside there are a number of endearing features in the form of graffiti left by the medieval stonemasons: one shows a man and woman quarrelling over whether to boil or bake a simnel cake. Seriously damaged by fire in 1985, the church has been carefully restored to its medieval glory;

Leighton Buzzard Canal

Lakeside Trout & Coarse Fishery

Wing Road, Cublington, Leighton Buzzard, Bedfordshire LU7 0LF
Tel: 01296 682201 Fax: 01296 682215

Sarah Ellis and her family provide a warm, friendly welcome and year-round fishing at **Lakeside Trout & Coarse Fishery** in a delightful rural setting below the Chilterns. Two well stocked lakes offer excellent sport, and Sarah, an experienced competitor, can provide free tuition in the art of fly fishing. Rods can be hired, and there's a useful half-day beginners' course. Fishermen like their peace and quiet, so this is not a place to bring noisy children! The Fishery is open seven days a week, and a fine lunch is served in a nearby Cublington pub.

the painstaking work included regilding the roof, which is particularly fine, with carved figures of angels. Leighton Buzzard and its neighbour Linslade are on the Grand Union Canal and visitors can now take leisurely boat trips along this once busy commercial waterway on the *Leighton Lady*. Historic forms of transport seem to be the thing in the town as visitors can also take a steam train journey on the **Leighton Buzzard Railway** (see panel opposite). For life at a more leisurely pace than steam trains, the town lies at one end of the **Greensand Ridge Walk** which extends across Bedfordshire to finish some 40 miles away at Gamlingay, Cambridgeshire. The name Greensand comes from the geology of the area, a belt of greensand which stretches from Leighton Buzzard up to Sandy and beyond.

AMPTHILL

This historic town, situated on a rise and with fine views over the surrounding countryside, was a great favourite with Henry VIII; it was here that Catherine of Aragon stayed during the divorce proceedings conducted by Henry's court at Dunstable. At that time there was also a castle here, built by Sir John Cornwall for his bride, the sister of Henry IV. On the site now stands Catherine's Cross, erected in 1773, which bears the arms of Castile and Aragon. On land given to his family by Charles II, the 1st Lord Ashburnham built the castle's replacement, **Ampthill Park**, in 1694. The house was enlarged a century later and the 300-acre park was landscaped by the ubiquitous Capability Brown. Ampthill Park is famous for its old oak trees and visitors can also enjoy the views from the Greensand Ridge Walk, which runs through the grounds. The most interesting building in the town is the large Church of St Andrew, which has a fine west tower. Inside can be found some 15th century brasses and a 17th century monument to Richard Nicholls that includes the cannon ball that killed him during the Battle of Sole Bay in 1672. This man Nicholls, who was born and lived most of his life in Ampthill, served the Stuart kings and named New York after the Duke of York, later James II.

AROUND AMPTHILL

Flitton

2 miles SE of Ampthill off the A507

Next to the 15th century church is the **de Grey Mausoleum**, a series of rooms containing a remarkable collection of sculpted tombs and monuments to the de Grey family of Wrest Park (see section below).

Silsoe

3 miles SE of Ampthill off A6

Although the manor of Wrest has been held by the de Grey family since the late 13th century, the house standing today dates from the 1830s. Built for the 1st Earl de Grey from the designs of a French architect, it follows faithfully the style of a French chateau of the previous century. Parts of the house at **Wrest Park** are open to the public but the real glory is the gardens. They are a living history of English gardening from 1700 to 1850 and are the work of Charles Bridgeman, with later adaptations by Capability Brown. The layout remains basically formal, with a full range of garden appointments in the grand manner - there is a Chinese bridge, an artificial lake, a classical temple, and a rustic ruin. Two buildings of particular interest are

Poplars Nursery & Garden Centre

Harlington Road, Toddington, Bedfordshire LU5 6HE
Tel: 01525 870201 Fax: 01525 873905
e-mail: david@poplars.co.uk
website: www.poplars.co.uk

Follow the brown signs from Junction 12 of the M1 on to the A5120 to find **Poplars Nursery & Garden Centre**; it is owned and run by the Little family, outstanding in the field of horticulture for over 100 years. The first garden centre opened here in the early 1970s and has grown steadily year after year. Quality and service have always been watchwords, and the staff are all willing and able to give good sound advice on all aspects of growing plants. The buying team source the best plants from specialist growers across Europe, but local and British-grown plants predominate in the vast range that runs from seedlings to mature trees.

There's an equally impressive selection of bulbs and seeds, and Poplars specialises in offering the highest quality seed potatoes and onion sets. Besides the plants, the centre is well stocked with everything for the garden, from pots and baskets to fencing, paving, turf, sand, barbecues, lighting, heating and stylish garden furniture. In the gift shop a constantly changing choice of original gifts is on display, and in Poplars Pantry Coffee Shop visitors can enjoy delicious home cooking and freshly prepared teas and coffees throughout the day. Other services available at this outstanding place include a carry-to-car service, local home delivery, garden design, gift wrapping, free leaflets and sharing with customers an unrivalled knowledge of local growing conditions.

Toddington Manor Gardens

Park Road, Toddington, Bedfordshire LU5 6HJ
Tel: 01525 872576 Fax: 01525 874555 website: toddingtonmanor.co.uk

Toddington Manor Gardens have been developed by the owners Sir Neville and Lady Bowman-Shaw into one of the most attractive in the county. Amid the six acres of gardens and 20 acres of woods are a lovely lime avenue leading into a cherry walk, a walled garden with beds of delphiniums and peonies, a fine herb garden, old-fashioned roses and a very impressive double herbaceous border. There's also a wild garden and three small ponds with nets and buckets available for children to go dipping. Other attractions include rare breeds of livestock, plants for sale, picnic area and a magnificent collection of over 100 vintage tractors. Open noon to 5pm 1 May to 31 August; closed Sunday.

Wrest Park Gardens

the Baroque Banqueting House, designed by Thomas Archer, which forms a focus of the view from the house across the lake, and the Bowling Green House, dating from about 1740 and said to have been designed by Batty Langley, who was best known as a writer of architectural books for country builders and built little himself. Immediately beside the house is an intricate French-style garden, with an orangery by the French architect Cléphane, flower beds, statues, and fountains. The village of Silsoe contains over 130 listed buildings.

Toddington

5 miles S of Ampthill on A5120

Situated on a hill above the River Flitt, this village is often overlooked, particularly by those travelling the nearby M1 who think only of the service station of the same name. However, the village is an attractive place, with cottages and elegant houses grouped around the village green. Unfortunately all that remains of **Toddington Manor** house is a small oblong building with a hipped roof which is believed to be the Elizabethan kitchen of the large quadrangular house that was built here in around 1570. Toddington is a place which makes much of its folklore and is host to Morris dancers in the summer and mummers who tour the village providing traditional entertainment at Christmas. Local legend also has it that a witch lives under Conger Hill - which is actually a motte that would, at one time, have had a castle on top - and, on Shrove Tuesday, the children put their ears to the ground to listen to her frying pancakes.

Ridgmont

4 miles W of Ampthill on the A507

Part of the Woburn Estate, this is a typical estate village where the owners of the land (in this case the Bedford family) provided the houses and other buildings. Here the workers lived in gabled, redbrick houses. The church, designed by George Gilbert Scott, was also built at the expense of the estate. Ridgmont is the birthplace of the Countess of Strathmore, the mother of Queen Elizabeth the Queen Mother.

Woburn

6 miles W of Ampthill on the A4012

First recorded as a Saxon hamlet in the 10th century, and again mentioned in the Domesday Book, Woburn grew into a small market town after the founding of the Cistercian Abbey here in 1145. All but destroyed by fire in 1720, this pretty village has retained many of the pleasant Georgian houses that were built subsequently and the attractive shopfronts give the place a cheerful air. Situated at a major crossroads, between London and the north and Cambridge and Oxford, Woburn also saw prosperity during the stagecoach era and by 1851

Woburn Abbey

Woburn, Bedfordshire MK17 9WA
Tel: 01525 290666 Fax: 01525 290271
e-mail: enquiries@woburnabbey.co.uk
website: www.woburnabbey.co.uk

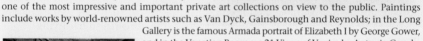

Built on the site of a Cistercian monastery founded in 1145 by Hugh de Bolebec, **Woburn Abbey** was given to the 1st Earl of Bedford in the will of Henry VIII and has been the home of the Dukes of Bedford for over 400 years. The original building was partially destroyed by fire and the present stately home dates mainly from the 18th century. Woburn Abbey houses one of the most impressive and important private art collections on view to the public. Paintings include works by world-renowned artists such as Van Dyck, Gainsborough and Reynolds; in the Long Gallery is the famous Armada portrait of Elizabeth I by George Gower, and in the Venetian Room are 21 Views of Venice by Antonio Canale, better known as Canaletto.

The collection also includes 18th century English and French furniture and some wonderful porcelain, notably the fabulous Sèvres dinner service given to the 4th Duchess by Louis XV. The Sculpture Gallery was originally built as an Orangery in 1789 by Henry Holland. The Temple of Liberty, housing busts of leading political figures, was added in 1802 and in 1818 the Orangery was enlarged by Jeffery Wyatville to house the 6th Duke's collection of marble statuary and reliefs. The Gallery, whose centre is supported by eight marble columns dating from the 2nd century AD, is full of treasures, from Greek and Roman sarcophagi to superb vases and paintings and reliefs from many periods. The Gallery is a wonderful venue for anything from conferences and product launches to fashion shows, wedding receptions and dinner dances. In the same part of the Abbey complex is Woburn Abbey Antiques Centre, opened in 1967 and now one of the largest centres of its kind outside London.

Over 50 dealers are housed under one roof in a reconstruction of city streets in bygone days, with genuine 18th century shop facades that were rescued from demolition many years ago. The centre's stock encompasses period English and Continental furniture, oil and watercolour paintings, porcelain, glass, brass and copperware, treen, silver, clocks and watches, textiles, antiquities and jewellery - and not a modern reproduction or 'collectable' in sight! Another attraction within the estate boundaries is the deer park, which, like the private gardens, was landscaped by Humphry Repton for the 6th Duke. There are ten species of deer in the park, including the Père David, which originated in China and was saved from extinction by the 11th Duke. Visitors to this marvellous place will also find gift shops, a pottery and a coffee shop. The Abbey will be closed from 28 October 2002 to the end of the year.

A mile from the Abbey is one of the country's leading animal attractions, Woburn Safari Park, among whose residents are lions, tigers, elephants, hippos, rhinos, eland, zebra and sea lions. Also close by is the Woburn Golf & Country Club with its three championship golf courses and newly opened " Inn at Woburn " with 53 rooms plus 7 luxurious cottages.

THE COUNTRY CROSS-STITCHER

19 Bedford Street, Woburn, Bedfordshire MK17 9QB
Tel: 01525 290070 Fax: 01525 290072
e-mail: mail@countrycrossstitcher.co.uk
website: www.countrycrossstitcher.co.uk

A love of needlework prompted Rosemary Sharman to open the **Country Cross-Stitcher**, which is located in a row of Georgian cottages in the town of Woburn on the Bedfordshire/Buckinghamshire borders. Retailer of the Year for the South East in 2000 and 2001, the thriving shop is packed with items connected with needlework, with a huge range of fabrics, threads, kits and accessories, which Rosemary seeks out from all parts of the world. She also runs the Woburn School of Needlework in a building opposite the shop.

there were 32 inns here. **Woburn Abbey** (see panel opposite), ancestral home of the Dukes of Bedford, is renowned for its art treasures, its deer park and its antiques centre. A short distance north of the Abbey is the **Wild Animal Kingdom and Leisure Park**, home to a vast range of animals including eland, zebra, hippos, rhinos, lions, tigers, elephants and sealions.

There are fine views of Woburn Abbey and of Milton Keynes from **Aspley Woods**, one of the largest areas of woodland in Bedfordshire, set between Woburn and Woburn Sands. The woods offer peace, tranquillity and miles of tracks for walking.

Woburn Abbey Wild Animal Kingdom

MARSTON MORETAINE

3 miles NW of Ampthill off the A421.

Marston Vale Millennium Country Park is a new amenity that offers a splendid day out in the countryside for all the family. The wetland habitat is home to a wide variety of wildlife, and the park provides excellent walking and cycling; bikes can be hired from the Forest Centre, which also has an interactive 'Discover the Forest' exhibition, café bar, art gallery, gift shop, free parking and children's play area.

BIGGLESWADE

On the banks of the River Ivel, which was once navigable through to the sea, Biggleswade was an important stop on the Great North Road stage coach routes. It also has another link with transport as the home of Dan Albone, the inventor of the modern bicycle. He produced a number of variants, including a tandem and a ladies cycle with a low crossbar and a skirt guard, but is best known for his racing cycle, which in 1888 set speed and endurance records with the doughty CP Mills in the saddle. Dan Albone's inventiveness was not confined to bicycles, as he also developed the Ivel Agricultural Tractor, the forerunner of the modern tractor.

SANDY

3 miles N of Biggleswade on A1

The sandy soil that gave the town its name helped it rise to fame as a market gardening centre in the 16th century. The 14th century Church of St Swithun contains some interesting statues, including one of Captain Sir William Peel, who was awarded one of the first Victoria crosses for heroic action in the Crimean War.

RSPB Nature Reserve, Sandy

Close to the town run the paths of two long distance walks: the **Ridgeway Long Distance Path**, which is England's oldest such route and runs from Avebury to Ivinghoe Beacon, and the **Greensands**

Ridge Walk, which covers some 40 miles across the county. A little way southeast of the town, at **The Lodge**, are the headquarters of the Royal Society for the Protection of Birds and the nature reserve set in over 100 acres of open heath and woodland. As well as offering a great deal to those interested in birds, the Lodge

HIGHFIELD FARM

Great North Road, Sandy, Bedfordshire SG19 2AQ
Tel: 01767 682332 Fax: 01767 692503
e-mail: margaret@highfield-farm.co.uk

In the secluded **Highfield Farm** just seconds off the southbound A1, Margaret Codd, with her husband, son and daughter in law, offers outstanding hospitality and comfort in Bed & Breakfast accommodation. With a rating of 5 Diamonds by the English Tourism Council, the standards are the highest and guests can choose from a total of ten rooms, all beautifully appointed and kept in immaculate order. Three rooms are in the farmhouse, two in adjacent stables and five in a recently converted barn with lovely old beams and wooden floors. All the rooms have tv and hospitality trays, and guests have the use of a delightful sitting room and beautiful gardens. In the charming dining room the day starts with a superb breakfast, Crumps of Ashwell, a local award winning butcher, provides the top-quality bacon and sausages; the kippers are the finest, plumpest Scottish specimens; eggs come coddled, fried, scrambled, poached, or even in an omelette.

Gunns of Sandy provide the excellent bread, honey is produced on local farms, and the marmalade is made by Mrs Codd herself. The delights of the farm and the proximity of the A1 giving easy access to many of the county's leading places of interest mean that Highfield Farm is a very popular base for touring the area. Booking well ahead is recommended. It's a very short drive to Sandy where the 14th century Church of St Swithin is well worth a visit. Close by is the Lodge, the national headquarters of the Royal Society for the Protection of Birds.

Gardens, formal gardens first created in the 1870s, were restored in the 1930s by Sir Malcolm Stewart and are well worth visiting in their own right. Also on the site is a newly developed wildlife garden.

MOGGERHANGER

5 miles N of Biggleswade off the A1

Grade I-listed Moggerhanger Park was built by Soane and is set among gardens and parkland designed by Humphry Repton. The estate is currently undergoing major restoration.

BLUNHAM

5 miles N of Biggleswade off the A1

This quiet rural village was the home of the poet John Donne while he was rector from 1622 to 1631, a post he held while also Dean of St Paul's in London. Donne began his working life as a secretary to the Lord Keeper of the Great Seal, Sir Thomas Egerton. Donne angered his employer by secretly marrying his niece and was forced to leave that position. Ordained in 1615, Donne postponed his clerical career to sail with the Earl of Essex on two of his expeditions. Donne divided his time between London and Blunham, where he stayed in the house opposite the parish church; in the church can be seen a chalice which he presented in 1626 as well as some fine Norman work and interesting bosses.

OLD WARDEN

3 miles W of Biggleswade off B658

This charming village of thatched cottages along a single street has developed its unique character as a result of the influence of two local families. In the early 18th century, Sir Samuel Ongley, a London merchant, shipowner, and former director of the South Sea Company, bought this country seat for himself and his family, who stayed here for over 200 years. In 1776 Robert Henley Ongley was awarded an Irish peerage for his services to Parliament, and it was his grandson, also called Robert, who created Old Warden as it is seen today. Taking the original estate cottages, and also building new ones, Sir Robert developed this rustic village and also embellished

THE SWISS GARDEN

Old Warden Park, Biggleswade, Bedfordshire SG18 9ER
Tel: 01767 627666

The **Swiss Garden** is set in 10 acres where visitors can wander among splendid shrubs and rare trees, at the centre of which is the Swiss Cottage. It brings together tiny follies, ornate bridges and winding ponds. Visitors can discover the breathtaking fernery and grotto, or lose themselves on the serpentine walks. In season the early bulbs and

primroses, the rhododendrons and the old-fashioned roses make wonderful displays. Old Warden is a place of many other attractions, notably the Shuttleworth Collection. The Swiss Garden is licensed to hold civil wedding ceremonies. The Garden is open from 10am to 6pm on Sundays and from 1pm to 6pm every other day from March to September. Also open Sundays (and New Years Day) in January, February and October from 10am to 4pm. No dogs.

the 12th century church with some interesting Belgian woodwork. However, Sir Robert's most famous piece of work is the **Swiss Garden**, laid out in the early 19th century (see panel on page 37)

In 1872, his fortune depleted by the extensive building and remodelling programme, Sir Robert sold the estate to Joseph Shuttleworth. A partner in a firm of iron founders, it was Joseph who led the way to the development of the steam traction engine and also built the Jacobean-style mansion house that can still be seen today. A recently added attraction on the estate is the **English School of Falconry** at the **Bird of Prey & Conservation Centre**. 300 birds of various species are on public display and in addition to training and flying birds of prey from around the world, the centre is firmly committed to conservation and education, working with schools to create displays and informative workshops. Regular flying demonstration times are 10.30am for free-flying indigenous species, 12.30pm for the falconry pageant, 2.30pm for 'Out of Africa' featuring vultures, secretary birds, eagles, owls and falcons, and at 4pm, in summer only, the Falconers Fun Demonstration. Here, too, is the famous **Shuttleworth Collection** of historic aircraft (see panel below).

A short drive north of Old Warden are two delightful villages, **Ickwell** and **Northill**. The former, which has a

The Shuttleworth Collection

Old Warden Park, Biggleswade, Bedfordshire SG18 9EA
Tel: 01767 627288 e-mail: collection@shuttleworth.org
Fax: 01767 626229 website: www.shuttleworth.org

The origin of the magnificent **Shuttleworth Collection** is born in tragedy. Already a keen motor racing driver and collector of motorcars, in 1932, the 23-year-old Richard Ormande Shuttleworth, who had inherited the estate, bought his first aircraft and so laid down the foundations for this world famous collection. At the outbreak of World War II, Richard, naturally, joined the RAF and he was killed in a flying accident in 1940s. After the war, Richard's mother founded a trust that resulted in the Shuttleworth College for Agriculture and for the promotion of education and training in the science, practice and history of aviation and automotive transport.

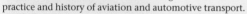

However, Richard's mother also saw that the collection that her beloved son had started was allowed to grow and, from his first aeroplane, a de Havilland Moth, the collection has expanded to contain nearly 40 airworthy historic aircraft most of which are unique.

Now housed within eight hangars, the aircraft, which date from 1909 to 1955, are complemented by a number of vehicles, motorcycles and bicycles. Along with viewing the craft, throughout the year there are a number of flying days, some of which are themed, where visitors have the added excitement of seeing many of the collection's planes take to the skies. The collection, too, has a long list of film credits and these include such memorable pictures as *Reach for the Skies*, *The Battle of Britain* and, more recently, *Pearl Harbour*.

Northill Village

Maypole standing permanently on the green, is the birthplace of the great clockmaker Thomas Tompion. The 14th century Church of St Mary, which dominates the village of Northill, is noted for some fine 17th century glass and a one-handed clock built by Tompion, who developed new techniques in the making of clocks and watches. Some of his clocks could run for a year without rewinding and he also made barometers and sundials, including pieces for King William III.

STEWARTBY

10 miles W of Biggleswade off the A421

Stewartby was built in 1926 for the employees of the local brickworks, which were thought to be the largest in the world and at their peak turned out 650 million bricks a year. The kiln took over a year to reheat after World War II.

HOUGHTON CONQUEST

9 miles W of Biggleswade off the B530

That this village is home to Bedfordshire's largest parish church seems fitting, as Houghton Conquest also has links with the county's most famous son, John Bunyan. On a hilltop a little way south of the village stands **Houghton House**, reputedly the inspiration for the House Beautiful in *The Pilgrim's Progress*. Built in 1615 for Mary, Countess of Pembroke, the house was visited by Bunyan in his days as an itinerant tinker. The property later came into the hands of the Dukes of Bedford, one of whom had it partially demolished, and the ruins are now in the care of English Heritage.

SHEFFORD

5 miles SW of Biggleswade on the A507

The small town of Shefford grew up, as the name suggests, around a sheep ford across the Rivers Hitt and Flitt and enjoyed a brief status as an inland port

THE KNIFE & CLEAVER

The Grove, Houghton Conquest, Bedfordshire MK45 3LA
Tel: 01234 740387 Fax: 01234 740900
e-mail: info@knifeandcleaver.com website: www.knifeandcleaver.com

The Knife & Cleaver is a friendly, atmospheric old country inn and owners Pauline and David Loom have made this one of the top eating places in the county, serving delights such as shellfish bouillabaisse, grilled Dover sole, rack of Welsh lamb or chargrilled ribeye steak. A bar food menu is available for lighter or quicker meals, and the fine food is complemented by a carefully selected list of wines. Real ale is on pump in the oak-panelled bar, with a large range of malt whiskies and French fruit brandies. The Knife & Cleaver is also a superb place to stay with nine en suite rooms available including three de luxe rooms in the converted stable block.

S & S Timms Antiques

2-4 High Street, Shefford, Bedfordshire SG17 5DG
Tel: 01462 851051 Fax: 01462 817047
e-mail: info@timmsantiques.com
website: www.timmsantiques.com

Sue and Steve Timms, with their son Robbie, own and run **S & S Timms Antiques**, a business started in Chelsea in 1930 by Steve's father. Their shop, which they opened three years ago after relocating from Ampthill, occupies a prominent corner site on the main street of Shefford. Dating from the 17th century and at one time a bank, it comprises nine showrooms on two floors, filled with antique furniture made mainly in the 18th and 19th centuries, with some early 20th century pieces.

Their stock always includes numerous occasional tables, dining room tables, dressers, chaises longues and sets of chairs. The Timms family are among the most prominent buyers and sellers in their field and also exhibit at major fairs such as Chelsea and the Commonwealth Institute. The shop is open 7 days a week. Attractions in and around the town of Shefford include a hedge maze in an orchard, a specialist in dried flowers and Chicksands Priory, where swans swim serenely on the River Ivel.

Stondon Transport Museum

Station Road, Lower Stondon, Henlow, Bedfordshire SG16 6JN
Tel: 01462 850339 Fax: 01462 850824
e-mail: info@transportmuseum.co.uk
website: www.transportmuseum.co.uk

Stondon Transport Museum invites visitors to take a trip down memory with its marvellous collection of over 400 exhibits. A hobby that got out of hand is how curator and director Maureen Hird describes the enterprise started by John Saunders and now one of the leading attractions in Bedfordshire. John is a former design engineer whose design work has included a one-man submarine and an amphibious caravan. Most of the exhibits are displayed under cover in a small area, thus keeping walking to a minimum and ensuring that the museum is accessible to all ages.

The exhibits cover all forms of transport, from motorcycles to helicopters, and spans the period from the beginning of the 20th century to the recent past. One of the greatest appeals of the collection is that it includes vehicles that are not usually museum pieces, among them a Bedford Dormobile open truck, a Jowett Javelin and a London bus. The centrepiece of the collection is a life-size replica of Captain Cook's bark *Endeavour*, in which he undertook one of his most important voyages of discovery, in 1768. The ship was constructed using the original plans. Regular guided tours of the ship take place each day, and the whole fascinating museum is open from 10 to 5 seven days a week. A café on site sells refreshments and snacks throughout the day. The museum is located on the A600 next to Mount Pleasant golf course.

on the Ivel Navigation. This waterway was built primarily to bring coal from Kings Lynn by way of the River Ouse. In North Bridge Street a wall plaque marks the house of the pastoral poet Robert Bloomfield, a poor farm labourer and shoemaker who found fame when he published *The Farmer's Boy* in 1800. The poet, who died, as he had lived, in extreme poverty, is buried in the churchyard at nearby Campton, the village of Shefford's mother church. In Hitchin Road is a hedge maze in an orchard, with a picnic site and plenty of space for children to romp.

LOWER STONDON

6 miles S of Biggleswade off the A600

Lower Stondon attracts visitors from near and far to its renowned **Transport Museum** and garden centre (see panel opposite).

BEDFORD

This bustling town on the Great Ouse was already a thriving market place before the Norman Conquest and the Church of St Peter de Merton, built in the 10th century, has some substantial Norman additions. The fine Norman south doorway, though, was not actually intended for this building but was brought here from the Church of St Peter in Dunstable. St Peter's is not Bedford's main church: this is St Paul's Church in the centre of the market place, a mainly 14th and 15th century building, with some interesting monuments and brasses and a stone pulpit where Wesley preached in 1758. Outside the church is a statue of one of the best-known sons of Bedford, John Howard, an 18th century nonconformist landowner who denounced the appalling conditions in

HOLLAND RESTORATION

The Hollies, 23 Stotfold Road, Arlesey, Bedfordshire SG15 6XL
Tel/Fax: 01462 733874 e-mail: info@hollandrestoration.co.uk
website: www.hollandrestoration.co.uk

Quality re-upholstery of modern, traditional and contract furniture is the main facet of **Holland Restoration**. The owners Tina and Peter Holland offer their customers a complete furniture service including cane work, polishing, restoration and repairs. Customers visiting the workshop, have a huge range of fabric books to choose from and can enjoy viewing work in progress. The workshop is one of the few that still specialise in traditional cane, sheet cane and rush weaving and customers will travel from afar to have their furniture restored to its former glory. Over the years, the owners have been privileged to work on many pieces of furniture for personalities, stores and country homes.

MADE IN BEDFORDSHIRE - THE DIRECTORY OF LOCAL FOODS & CRAFTS

Made in Bedfordshire offers the consumer a rich diversity of products and produce that are made or grown locally. The Directory aims to raise people's awareness of the many benefits of shopping locally, such as reducing food miles, helping to support local growers, producers and the local economy, and the health benefits of buying fresh local produce. The easy to read Directory has 66 entries which Bedfordshire County Council hopes will tempt readers to enjoy exploring and discovering the wealth of local products that are 'Made in Bedfordshire'. Made in Bedfordshire is updated regularly. A FREE copy can be obtained by contacting Jo Faul, Bedfordshire County Council, on 01234 228739, or can be viewed on the County Council website: www.bedfordshire.gov.uk. Click on 'About Bedfordshire', then 'local events and information'. Alternatively, contact the Bedfordshire Tourist Information Centres or visit Bedfordshire local libraries. Enjoy!

jails and prison ships. His name lives on in the Howard League for Penal Reform.

Beside the river and running through the heart of the town are the **Bedford Embankment Gardens**, which provide a year-round display of plants. Close by is also the **Priory Country Park**, an area of 206 acres with a diverse habitat, which represents the flood meadows, reed beds and woodland that once surrounded the town. With such a variety of plant life, the park is able to support a wide diversity of animals, insects and birds as well as providing recreational opportunities for local residents and visitors with angling and lake and river walks. In Park Road North, Hill Rise Wildlife Area is a site for nature conservation specialising in butterflies, amphibians and small mammals.

For an insight into the history of the town and surrounding area the **Bedford Museum** is well worth a visit. Among the many interesting displays is a piece of wall which shows the construction of the wattle walls that were an essential building technique in the 14th century. Housed within the unlikely combination of a Victorian mansion and an adjoining modern gallery, the **Cecil Higgins Art Gallery** was started in 1949 by a wealthy Bedford brewery family. Visitors can not only see the internationally renowned collection of watercolours, prints, and drawings but also some fine glass,

Cecil Higgins Art Gallery

ceramics, and furniture. The Gallery hosts several important exhibitions each year: among those planned for 2002 are a Celebration of Bedfordshire Lace (23 July-22 September) and Tissot and his London Circle (1 October-5 January 2003) featuring works by the painter on loan from the V&A and British Museum). On permanent display is a needle panel entitled 'Bunyan's Dream'. It was designed by Edward Bawden in 1977 to

Sue's Little Bits

4 Mill Yard, Mill Street, Bedford, Bedfordshire MK40 3HD
Tel: 01234 360284 website: www.sueslittlebits.co.uk

Sue is Sue Fermor and her **Little Bits** are an amazing range of dolls houses and miniature collectables. In her bright, cheerful little shop in a modern precinct, everything the dolls house-proud owner could want is in stock, including DIY lighting and a full range of furniture, and among the high-class accessories are the Warwick range, including hand-painted items and silver tableware, copper and brass items, and Peter Clark's bird and animal collection. Also a range of collectable bears. The shop is open from 9.30-5.00 Monday to Saturday.

commemorate the tercentenary of the publication of *Pilgrim's Progress*, the 350th anniversary of John Bunyan's birth and the Queen's Silver Jubilee. Bedford's most famous son, Bunyan was born just south of the town, in Elstow, and lived and was imprisoned in Bedford in the 1660s and 1670s. The son of a tinsmith, Bunyan followed the same trade as his father and so was able to travel the countryside more than most people of that time. In the 1650s, Bunyan met John Gifford, the then pastor of the Independent Congregation which held its meetings at St John's Church. It was their lengthy discussions that led to Bunyan's conversion and he was baptised shortly afterwards by Gifford in a backwater that leads off the Great Ouse. St John's Rectory, 300 yards south of the river, is now occupied by St John Ambulance but one room has been set aside for Bunyan memorabilia and is open to the public by arrangement. It was while preaching in the villages of Bedfordshire that Bunyan came into conflict with the authorities. He was arrested in 1660, near Ampthill, and put in prison for the first of two such confinements. It was during his first imprisonment, between 1660 and 1672, that he wrote many of his works, including his most famous, *Pilgrim's Progress*. Following his release from prison in 1672, Bunyan was elected pastor of the Independent Congregation.

River Ouse, Bedford

One of his first tasks was to find a permanent meeting place and he promptly bought a barn to act as a temporary measure which was used until 1707 when the meeting house was finally built. The church seen today was constructed in 1849 and the magnificent bronze doors, with illustrations from *Pilgrim's Progress*, were given to the church by the Duke of Bedford in 1676. Within the church is also the **Bunyan**

Woodworx Of Cardington

Cardington Courtyard, Harrowden Lane,
Cardington, Bedfordshire MK44 3ST
Tel/Fax: 01234 743939
e-mail: woodworx@ic24.net

Easy to find on the A600 just a minute's drive off the Bedford by-pass, **Woodworx of Cardington** leads the field in hand-crafted, made to measure furniture that is guaranteed to enhance any room in any home. The showrooms and workshops occupy former dairy buildings set in a rectangle round a courtyard, and the skill with which the site was cleared and the conversion made is a tribute to the expertise and experience of the partners in the business, Barry Gyford and Jason Whybrow.

Hand-crafted kitchens are the speciality of Woodworx, from concept and design to the manufacture and assembly on site and the detailed finishing work such as the hand-painting of cornices. Pride in their work is paramount, whether the commission is a complete kitchen or a single small item; no corner or angle is too awkward, and furniture can be made with special height adjustments to provide for the personalised needs of disabled users.

The range of furniture is impressive, embracing Woodworx' own distinctive designs and customers' individual requirements, and in the showrooms and workshops the visitor might see anything from a gazebo for the garden or a barbecue with a tiled roof to dressing tables, wardrobes, cabinets, dining room suites and four-poster beds. Woodworx of Cardington is open from 8 to 5 Monday to Saturday and from 12 to 4 on Sunday; there is ample parking space in the courtyard.

Woodworx is unique in its own sphere and has a unique neighbour in the imposing shape of the giant hangars that were built to construct and house the great airships of the 1930s and were later the workshops for the barrage balloons built to defend London in World War 2. The village of Cardington itself is an attractive place, with many houses built by the Whitbread family, and the Church of St Mary is well worth a visit.

Museum, which tells graphically the story of the man as well as the times through which he lived. Among the many displays are the jug in which his daughter Mary brought him soup whilst in prison, his chair, his tinker's anvil, and the violin and flute which he made in prison. Another tribute to Bunyan in the town is **Bunyan's Statue**, which was presented to the town in 1874 by the Duke of Bedford. Made of bronze, the statue is the work of Sir JE Boehm; around the pedestal of the 9ft figure, which weighs more than three tons, are three bronze panels depicting scenes from *Pilgrim's Progress*.

Elstow Moot Hall

A building with more modern connections is the Corn Exchange in St Paul's Square, from where Colonel Glenn Miller frequently broadcast during World War II. A bust of the bandleader who gave the world *In the Mood* and *Moonlight Serenade* stands outside the Exchange, and in 1994 a plaque was unveiled on the 50th anniversary of his mysterious disappearance over the English Channel. Another regular at the Exchange was also a bandleader, Billy ('Wakey! Wakey!') Cotton, whose parents lived in retirement in nearby Flitwick.

AROUND BEDFORD

Elstow

1 mile S of Bedford off the A6

John Bunyan connections are everywhere in Elstow. The cottage where he was born in 1628 no longer stands, but its site is marked by a stone erected in Festival of Britain Year, 1951. The **Abbey Church of St Helena and St Mary** has two renowned stained glass windows, one depicting scenes from *Pilgrim's Progress*, the other scenes from the Holy War. Here, too, are the font where Bunyan was christened and the Communion Table used when he worshipped and rang the bells. Bunyan's mother, father and sister are buried in the churchyard. The Church also tells the story of the ill-fated R101 airship (see under Cardington), and there's a handsome memorial in the churchyard. Elstow **Moot Hall** was built in the 15th century and served as a place for hearing disputes and as a store for equipment for the village fair. Restored by Bedfordshire County Council, it is now a museum depicting life in 17th century England with particular reference to Bunyan. The Council also restored Elstow Cottages, a row of Tudor cottages looking once again as they did in Bunyan's time.

Cardington

1 mile E of Bedford off the A603

The Whitbread family of brewers are closely connected with Cardington. The first Samuel Whitbread was born in the village in 1720, and it was another Whitbread, also Samuel, who restored the church, whose font was designed in black basalt by Josiah Wedgwood. But Cardington is best known for the two giant hangars that dominate the skyline. Built in 1917 and 1927 to construct and house the airships that were once thought to be the future of flying, they are best known as the birthplace of the R100 and the R101. The R101 first took off from Cardington in October 1929 with 52 people on board for a five-hour flight over the Southeast. The passengers enjoyed a four-course lunch in the luxurious dining saloon and were amazed at the airship's quietness - they could hear the sounds of traffic and trains below. In July 1930 the R101 started her maiden flight across the Atlantic and tied up in Montreal after an uneventful flight of 77 hours. In October of that year the world's biggest airship left the hangars at Cardington for her first trip to India. Disaster struck not long into the journey when the R101 crashed into a hillside near Beauvais in France. 44 people, including the Air Secretary Lord Thomson of Cardington, died in the crash, which was believed to have been caused at least in part by lashing rain that caused the ship to dip suddenly. The Church of St Mary contains memorials to both Samuel Whitbreads, and in the churchyard extension is the tomb of those who perished in the R101 disaster.

Wilden

4 miles NE of Bedford off the A421

Thousands of visitors come here each year to discover the delights of **Bedford Butterfly Park**, which has quickly become one of the county's leading family attractions (see panel below).

Stevington

4 miles NW of Bedford off A428

This is a typical English village with a church that was certainly here at the time

Stevington Post Mill

Bedford Butterfly Park

Renhold Road, Wilden, Nr Bedford, Bedfordshire MK44 2PX
Tel: 01234 772770 Fax: 01234 772773
e-mail: enquiries@bedford-butterflies.co.uk
website: www.bedford-butterflies.co.uk

Bedford Butterfly Park is located in ten acres of land untouched by modern faming practices and was specially chosen by its founder Andrew Green. The site revealed no fewer than 60 varieties of wild flowers and is home to over 60 species of butterfly, some in the Millennium Garden, others in the colourful tropical house. The Wondrous World exhibit shows the variety of life found in rain forests and features leaf-cutting ants, giant snails and tarantulas among others. Attractions include exhibitions, adventure playground, tea room and gift shop.

River Great Ouse, Bromham

of the Domesday survey, a village cross decorated with capitals and a large finial, and a holy well that attracted visitors in the Middle Ages. However, the most important building in the village is the **Post Mill**, the only one of the county's 12 remaining windmills that still retains its sails. Dating from the 1770s, the mill continued to operate commercially until 1936, having been rebuilt in 1921. Extensively restored in the 1950s, it is in full working order today. Though milling was an important part of village life here for many years, lace making too was a thriving industry and mat makers also settled here, taking advantage of the rushes growing on the banks of the nearby River Ouse. Stevington also has connections with the supporters of John Bunyan and a Baptist meeting place was established here in the mid 17th century, some 70 years before the present church was built in 1720. Stevington Country Walk follows two miles of the former Bedford-Northampton railway line.

Turvey

6 miles W of Bedford on the A428

Turvey lies close to the county border and Buckinghamshire can be reached by crossing the Great Ouse by the long bridge, some of whose 16 arches are thought to date from the 13th century.

Bromham

2 miles W of Bedford off A428

This quiet residential village also has a splendid ancient bridge, this one with no fewer than 26 arches. Close to the river is a watermill that dates back to the 17th century. Now fully restored and in working order, **Bromham Mill** is also home to displays of natural history, crafts and other special exhibitions (see panel below). Charles I is known to have stayed at Bromham Hall, the home of Royalist Sir Lewis Dyve, who made his

Bromham Mill And Gallery

Bridge End, Bromham, Bedfordshire MK42 8LP Tel: 01234 824330

Bromham Watermill sits on the River Great Ouse, not far from Bedford, where it is crossed by a historic 26-arched bridge. A huge iron waterwheel is the source of power. Flour has been milled here for hundreds of years and is still produced today. The Mill houses an art gallery, where contemporary craftwork and fine art exhibitions change regularly and much is offered for sale by interest free credit. Textiles are usually represented, with a range of jewellery and small gifts. Afternoon tea can be taken outdoors or in the mill overlooking the river and visitors can enjoy the tranquillity, watching kingfishers dive from the banks. Bromham Mill is open 1pm to 5pm Wednesday to Saturday and 10.30am to 5pm on Sundays and Bank Holidays. The Mill is closed November to February.

North End Barns

Bletsoe, Nr Bedford, Bedfordshire MK44 1QT
Tel/Fax: 01234 781320

On a working arable farm six miles north of Bedford, an outstanding barn conversion has created highly recommended Bed & Breakfast accommodation in a lovely country setting. Welcoming hosts and owner-farmers Paul and Chris Forster have been farming here for 30 years and began the B&B side in 1997. The long redbrick barn has eight spacious en suite bedrooms with tv and tea/coffee makers; one room on the ground floor is suitable for disabled guests. An excellent breakfast is served between 7.00 and 8.45 in the handsome 16th century farmhouse, and there are numerous eating places for lunch and dinner in the local villages and in Bedford.

The rural setting is both peaceful and attractive and guests can enjoy a gentle stroll around the farm. There's a tennis court on site, and the owners have long-term plans to provide golf and fishing facilities. Fishing and sailing are available at Grafham Water, riding at Thurleigh and Keysoe and some of the best clay pigeon shooting in the country at nearby Riseley village. The rooms at North End Barns are all non-smoking, and pets are not accepted.

Harrold-Odell Country Park

Carlton Road, Harrold, Bedfordshire MK43 7DS
Tel: 01234 720016 (Park) 01234 720002 (Café)

Set in the beautiful countryside of north Bedfordshire beside the River Great Ouse, **Harrold-Odell Country Park** is an ideal place to spend the day. Two lakes cover half the park's 144 acres and water meadows, riverside and woodland make up the rest. The variety of scenery and habitat provide a peaceful location for walking, picnicking, watching wildlife or just relaxing. A surfaced path around the main lake is suitable for all visitors and there are informal paths through the water meadows and nature sanctuary. The park is also the starting point for many walking and cycling routes, providing easy access to the countryside further afield.

The park is a haven for wildlife, the lakes attracting both winter wildfowl and migrating summer birds. Wildflowers flourish in the water meadows and nature sanctuary through the spring and summer.

The Visitor Centre is home to the Café in the Park, where visitors can enjoy delicious home-made treats including summer salads, winter soups and irresistible cakes, all made with as many organic and locally grown ingredients as possible. The Centre has an information room with displays about the park and the local area. The Centre has wheelchair access and baby changing facilities, and parking is free. The park is open every day and dogs are welcome in most areas, provided they are with a responsible owner! The park is signposted from Harrold and Carlton villages.

Ivy Lodge Nurseries

Bedford Road, Sharnbrook, Bedfordshire MK44 1ND
Tel/Fax: 01234 782108

In the same family for four generations, **Ivy Lodge Nurseries** is a small rural concern specialising in traditional country plants. Rebecca Jacques and her father Peter grow a wide selection of herbs, perennials, shrubs and bedding plants, and can 'plant up' anything from a hanging basket and old sinks to a pair of wellies. They sell a lot of reclaimed buckets, watering cans, old clay pots and organic peat-free compost, and at Christmas they do a roaring trade in trees, door rings, holly wreaths, mistletoe and swagging for fireplaces.

escape from the house during the Civil War by swimming the river.

Sharnbrook

7 miles N of Bedford off the A6

Situated in the heart of beautiful countryside, this pleasant village boasts many fine old buildings, including, at Stoke Mills, an old flour mill that has been converted into a popular theatre.

Harrold

7 miles NW of Bedford off the A428

A typical country village with an old bridge and causeway, an octagonal market house and an old circular lock-up that was last used in the 19th century. Close by is the **Harrold-Odell Country Park**, which covers 144 acres of landscaped lakes, river banks and water meadows that are home to a wealth of plant, animal and bird life (see panel opposite).

Hinwick

10 miles NW of Bedford off the A6

Built between 1709 and 1714, **Hinwick House** is a charming Queen Anne building that is still home to the descendants of the Orlebar family for whom it was constructed. Occasionally open to visitors, this delightful brownstone house with details picked out in lighter coloured stone has a particularly pleasing entrance hall and an interesting collection of furniture and paintings. This tiny village is home to another attractive house, **Hinwick Hall**. Although the oldest parts of the hall date back to about 1540, the house was given a new front in the early 18th century, with motifs that are very similar to those of Hinwick House.

Yielden

10 miles N of Bedford off the A6

A village on the River Til, guarded by the earthworks of a long ruined castle. Mentioned in the Domesday Book, Yielden Castle, of which only an oblong motte, two large baileys and stone foundations can be seen, is reputed to have been built on the site of the battle between the Romans and the Iceni in which the warrior queen Boadicea (Boudicca) was killed. On one Christmas Day John Bunyan came to the village to preach in the church, as a result of which the incumbent vicar, William Bell, was removed from his post for allowing Bunyan this freedom.

BUCKINGHAMSHIRE

The south of the county, with the River Thames as its southern boundary, lies almost entirely within the chalk range of the Chiltern Hills, most of which is classed as an Area of Outstanding Natural

Milton's Cottage, Chalfont St Giles

Beauty. The county town since the 18th century has been Aylesbury, the market centre for the attractive Vale of Aylesbury, which runs from the Chilterns in the south to Buckingham in the north. Here, the visitor will discover a rural patchwork of secluded countryside, woodland and valleys, waterways, charming villages and busy market towns. A thousand miles of footpaths include the ancient Ridgeway, and the quiet country lanes and gentle undulations make cycling a real pleasure; the Vale is at the heart of the new National Cycle Network. The area around the former county of Buckingham is perhaps the least discovered part of the county, still chiefly rural, with a wealth of attractive villages and a number of fine houses, including Ascott House, a former Rothschild residence; Claydon House, where Florence Nightingale was a frequent visitor; Winslow Hall, designed by Wren; and Stowe, where the deer park is being restored to its former glory. In this area are also two outstanding churches, the Saxon Church of All Saints at Wing and St Michael's Church at Stewkley, one of the finest Norman churches in the whole country. The northern region of the county is dominated by the new town of Milton Keynes, developed in the 1960s but incorporating many much older villages.

CHALFONT ST GILES

Among the various ancient buildings of interest in this archetypal English village there is an Elizabethan mansion, The Vache, that was the home of friends of Captain Cook and, in the grounds is a monument to the famous seafarer. However, by far the most famous building in Chalfont St Giles, with an equally famous resident, is **Milton's Cottage**. John Milton moved to this 16th century cottage, found for him by fellow Quaker and former pupil Thomas Ellwood, in 1665 to escape the plague in London. Though Milton moved back to London in 1666, he wrote *Paradise Lost* and began work on its sequel, *Paradise Regained,* while taking refuge in the village. The only house lived in by the poet to have survived, the cottage and its garden have been preserved as they were at the time Milton was resident. The building is now home to a museum which includes collections of important first editions of Milton's works and a portrait of the poet by Sir Godfrey Kneller.

Another fascinating and unusual place to visit in the village is the **Chiltern Open Air Museum**, which rescues buildings of historic or architectural importance due to be demolished from across the Chilterns region and re-erects them on its 45 acre site. The buildings rescued by the museum are used to house and display artefacts and implements that are appropriate to the building's original use and history. Also on the museum site is a series of fields farmed using medieval methods where, among the historic crops, organic woad is grown, from which indigo dye is extracted for use in dyeing demonstrations. Madame Tussaud, famous for her exhibitions in London, started her waxworks here in the village, and another well-known resident was Bertram Mills of circus fame. His tomb stands beside the war memorial in the churchyard of St Giles.

AROUND CHALFONT ST GILES

Jordans

1 mile S of Chalfont St Giles off the A40

This secluded village reached down a quiet country lane is famous as the burial place of William Penn, Quaker and founder of Pennsylvania. He and members of his family are buried in the graveyard outside the Quaker meeting house that is among the earliest to be found in the country. In the grounds of nearby Old Jordans Farm is the Mayflower Barn, said to have been constructed from the timbers of the ship that took the Pilgrim Fathers to America.

Chalfont St Peter

2 miles S of Chalfont St Giles on the A413

Now a commuter town, Chalfont St Peter dates back to the 7th century and, as its name means 'the spring where the calves come to drink', there is a long history here of raising cattle in the surrounding lush meadows. First mentioned in 1133, the parish Church of St Peter was all but destroyed when its steeple collapsed in 1708. The building seen today dates from that time as it was rebuilt immediately

Bucks Country Parks

Countryside Centre, Black Park Country Park,
Black Park Road, Wexham, Buckinghamshire SL3 6DR
Tel: 01753 511060 Fax: 01753 550280
e-mail: countryparks@buckscc.gov.uk
website: www.buckscc.gov.uk/countryside/countryparks

Buckinghamshire County Council administers three outstanding country parks within easy driving distance of London. Neighbours **Black Park** and **Langley Park** and nearby **Denham Country Park** comprise hundreds of acres of woodland, heathland and parkland, lakes and rivers, open every day of the year to provide the ideal surroundings in which to relax and play. All three offer a wide variety of walks, and the differing scenery gives the visitor ample opportunity to discover the abundant wildlife.

Black Park's extensive coniferous and mixed woodland has enabled the Park to double for Turkey, Germany, Scandinavia and Scotland in films (Pinewood Studios are next door). Pedaloes can be hired on the lake , which balances the conservation of designated Sites of Special Scientific Interest alongside income-generating activities such as the filming and commercial forestry. It also has a café by the lake. Langley Park started life as a deer park stocked with animals from Windsor and evolved first into a Tudor hunting ground and then into a beautiful estate landscaped by Capability Brown. It is also known for its formal arboretum, its magnificent rhododendrons and azaleas. and its superb half-mile avenue flanked by handsome mature oaks. Five miles away, Denham Country Park borders the Rivers Colne and Misbourne and the Grand Union Canal and offers excellent opportunities to study the wildlife of both wetland and woodland. A fourth park is **Thorney Park** and the focal point here is a 25-acre lake that is a haven for migrating and over-wintering water birds.

after the disaster.

Housed in a barn at Skippings Farm is the **Hawk and Owl Trust's National Education and Exhibition Centre**. Dedicated to conserving wild birds of prey in their natural habitats, the Trust concerns itself with practical research, creative conservation and imaginative educational programmes.

Cliveden House

Stoke Poges

6 miles S of Chalfont St Giles off the A355

It was by in the churchyard in this surprisingly still rural village that Thomas Gray was inspired to pen his *Elegy Written in a Country Churchyard*. Often visiting Stoke Poges to see his mother, who was staying with her sister in a large late Georgian house built for the grandson of the famous Quaker, William Penn, Gray was obviously taken with the village and its surroundings. He lies buried with his mother in the church, and, to the east, is the imposing **Gray Monument**, designed by James Wyatt and erected in 1799. The Church of St Giles itself is very handsome and dates from the 13th century but perhaps its most interesting feature is the unusual medieval bicycle depicted in one of the stained glass windows. Behind the church is an Elizabethan manor house where Elizabeth I was entertained and Charles I imprisoned.

Taplow

8 miles SW of Chalfont St Giles off the A4

The name is of Taplow is derived from Taeppa, a Saxon warrior whose grand burial site high above the Thames was excavated in 1883. Nothing is known of Taeppa himself, but the items discovered at the site are on display in the British Museum. To the north of the village lies the country house of **Cliveden**, once the home of Lady Nancy Astor, the first woman to take her seat as a Member of Parliament. The first house on the site was built in 1666 for the Duke of Buckingham, but the present magnificent mansion, most of which is now a hotel, dates from the 19th century. The splendid grounds include a great formal parterre with fountains, temples and statuary, a water garden and a wonderful rose garden. Some of the great names in architecture and garden design had a hand in the Cliveden of today: the house and terrace are the work of Sir Charles Barry, the rose garden was designed by Sir Geoffrey Jellicoe, and the renowned Italian country house architect Giacomo Leoni was responsible for the **Octagonal Temple**, now a chapel, where the American-born millionaire William Waldorf Astor, his son Waldorf and the ashes of Waldorf's wife Nancy are buried.

Burnham Beeches

5 miles SW of Chalfont St Giles off the A355

A stretch of land bought in 1880 by the Corporation of the City of London for

Burnham Beeches

use in perpetuity by the public, and since then a favourite place for Londoners to relax. Burnham Beeches was designated a National Nature Reserve in 1993 and this extensive area of ancient woodland and heathland includes an important collection of old beeches and pollarded oaks.

Beaconsfield

3 miles SW of Chalfont St Giles on the A40

This is very much a town in two parts: the old town, dating back to medieval times and, to the north, the new town which grew up following the construction of the Metropolitan line into central London and consisting chiefly of between the wars housing. The old town is best known for its literary connections. The poet and orator Edmund Waller was born in the nearby village of Coleshill in 1606 and had his family home just outside Beaconsfield. After getting involved in a plot to seize London for Charles I in 1644, he was banished from Parliament and spent some time in exile before returning to Beaconsfield after a pardon to concentrate on writing. Somewhat wiser than in his youth, Waller took care to write poems in favour of Cromwell and, after his restoration to the throne, the King. Waller's tomb in the churchyard of St Mary and All Saints is marked by a very tall, sharply pointed obelisk with a tribute from fellow poet John Dryden. The church itself is one of the finest in the county. Waller's first family home was Gregories, which was bought in 1768 by the statesman and political theorist Edmund Burke, whose grave is inside the church. Beaconsfield was also the home of the writer of the *Father Brown* books GK Chesterton (his grave is in the nearby Catholic church), the poet Robert Frost and the much loved children's author Enid Blyton.

For a unique step back in time to the 1930s, or for anyone wanting to feel like Gulliver in Lilliput, a trip to the model village of **Bekonscot** is a must. The oldest model village in the world, Bekonscot was begun in the 1920s by Roland Callingham, a London accountant, who started by building models in his garden. As the number of

Bekonscot Model Village

Enlightenment By Design Ltd

Forge End, The Broadway, Old Amersham,
Buckinghamshire HP7 0JP
Tel/Fax: 01494 432020
e-mail: info@enlightenmentbydesign.co.uk
website: www.enlightenmentbydesign.co.uk

Enlightenment By Design Ltd is a Specialist Lighting Retailer with a wide range of contemporary and traditional lighting. Owned and run by Adrian Forrest, the premises are filled with many beautiful and different ideas for the lighting of your home be it fittings, lamps or shades – for inside or outside. Enlightenment also stock a range of accessories and giftware. The friendly owner and staff are happy to give impartial advice and help with ideas or, if you don't see what you want, they will try to source it for you. They stock ranges from leading manufacturers in Britain and abroad and customers can browse through the many brochures looking for enlightenment. A very popular service they offer is the shade-making or re-covering service – beautiful shades, handmade in this country.

One of the main attractions is the stunning contemporary lighting by Fabbian of Italy – so different and so beautiful. Enlightenment also import Italian Ceramics and among their other suppliers are Prices candles, Poole Pottery, Fantasia Fans and Waterford Crystal.

Opening times are 11.30 – 5.30 on Monday, 9.30 – 5.30 Tuesday to Friday and 9.30 – 6.00 on Saturday. There is free parking on the Broadway for 1 hour and a public car park is just round the corner by the Toyota Garage.

Carringtons

6 Market Square, Old Amersham,
Buckinghamshire HP7 0DQ
Tel: 01494 432045
e-mail: s.ribeck@btinternet.com

In a 17th century building on Old Amersham's market square, with car parking adjacent, **Carringtons** fulfils the dual role of delicatessen and café. The front part is the well-stocked delicatessen, with a separate counter, and the café offers the choice of stools at a little bar or chairs and tables at the back. Owner Susan Ribeck believes in offering her customers the very best in quality and care, and everything on the menu is freshly prepared by the chefs on the premises.

Sandwiches in baguettes, ciabatta or cornbread are made to order with a choice of some two dozen fillings, from egg mayonnaise or ham & salad to turkey & avocado, smoked salmon with cream cheese or goat's cheese with tapenade and sun-dried tomato. Main dishes also provide a plentiful choice, both hot and cold, including poached eggs and smoked ham, seafood salad and pasta with pesto, and for the sweeter tooth there are Danish pastries, fruit tarts, slices, flapjacks and cheesecake. The café and deli are open from 8am to 7pm every day, and across the road, in the same ownership, is Carringtons Restaurant serving an excellent selection of evening meals.

buildings and models grew, Callingham purchased more land and, with the aid of a friend from Ascot who added a model railway, created the village seen today. When the model village first opened, people started throwing coins into buckets for charity and, even today, all surplus profits go to charity. Enid Blyton's house Green Hedges is depicted in Bekonscot, and she wrote a story about two children who visit the model village.

South of Beaconsfield, on the other side of the M40 at **Wooburn Common**, an entertaining day out is guaranteed at **Odds Farm Park**, home to many rare and interesting animals. The park was created particularly with children in mind and the regular events include pigs' tea time, pat-a-pet, bottle feeding lambs and goat milking. As one of 20 approved rare breed centres in the country, the farm combines the family attractions with the breeding and conservation of many of Britain's rarest farm animals.

PENN

3 miles N of Beaconsfield on the B474

A centre of the tiling industry after the Norman Conquest, Penn provided the flooring for Windsor Castle, the Palace of Westminster and many churches. But the village is best known as the ancestral home of William Penn, the Quaker and American pioneer, and in the village church are several memorials to the family. In the churchyard of Holy Trinity is the grave of the diplomat spy Donald Maclean, who died in Moscow in 1983. His ashes were brought back to England by his brother and buried in the family grave.

AMERSHAM

3 miles N of Chalfont St Giles on the A413

The Romans were farming around Amersham in the 3rd and 4th centuries, the Saxons called it Agmodesham and to the Normans it was Elmondesham. So

POP ANTIQUES

12 The Broadway, Old Amersham, Buckinghamshire HP7 0HP
Tel: 01494 434443
e-mail: gretta@popantiques.com
website: www.popantiques.com

The residents of Old Amersham gained a splendid new opportunity for antique hunting and finding a really special gift when Gretta Colligan opened **Pop Antiques** in the summer of 2001. Young, enthusiastic and knowledgeable in all matters artistic, Gretta has stocked her shop with

all manner of antiques, high-quality reproduction pieces and matching items, from cushions to dining suites.

Pop Antiques source the world to gather the finest furniture, mirrors and decor with the aim of bringing beautiful and original items to Amersham, supplying customers throughout the UK and beyond. In the shop, which occupies part of a Grade II-listed building in the centre of the village, the space is filled with highly desirable pieces, including antique and high-class reproduction furniture, soft furnishings, lamps and mirrors, crystal and porcelain. Painted designer furniture is something of a speciality, and nay of the items are French inspired. The business has proved an instant success, with a rapid turnaround of items large and small, and warehousing facilities in West London allow a much larger stock to be held.

The Kings Arms

Old Amersham, Buckinghamshire HP7 0DJ
Tel: 01494 726333 Fax: 01494 433480
website: www.kingsarmsamersham.co.uk

The Kings Arms, one of the country's oldest public houses, consisted originally of two separate timber-framed buildings dating from about 1450. Modernised in the 16th century and later an important coaching stop, the two buildings were amalgamated into what is now a marvellous traditional inn and separate restaurant, with the additional amenities of meeting rooms and a banqueting hall. Many original features survive, including open hearths, timbers and ceiling trusses, and the walls of the dining area are filled with a collection of interesting old cartoon prints and pictures.

Diners can choose between fixed-price and à la carte menus that combine both classic and contemporary elements, and taking their inspiration from the global cuisine. Flying the traditional flag could be Parma ham with melon and figs, navarin of lamb and pear Belle Hélène, while dishes with a more modern ring might include sun-dried tomato and goat's cheese baked in filo pastry with a basil dressing, or brochette of monkfish flavoured with Chinese spices with black linguini and a soya butter sauce. At regular times during the year patrons can push the boat out with the spectacular plateau de fruits de mer comprising oysters, crab, langoustines, mussels, clams, whelks, winkles, prawns and shrimps, with lobster added for a real indulgence. The present landlord John Jennison took over the lease in 1977, acquired the freehold in 1993 and with his wife is still busy restoring this marvellous old inn, which is closed Sunday evening and Monday.

the town has plenty of history, much of which is told in the Museum. Amersham was an important staging post in coaching days, and the Crown Hotel, one of the town's many coaching inns, was featured in the film *Four Weddings and a Funeral*. Old Amersham, by the River Misbourne, boasts many fine old buildings, including Sir William Drake's Market Hall of 1682 and the Church of St Mary with some fine stained glass and monuments to the Drake family. Close to the town is Gore Hill, the site of a battle between the Danes and the Saxons in 921. It is recorded that in 1666 the Great Fire of London could be seen raging from the hill.

Chenies Manor

Chenies

3 miles E of Amersham off the A404

This picturesque village, with a pretty green surrounded by an old school, a chapel and a 15th century parish church, is also home to **Chenies Manor**, a fascinating 15th century manor house. Originally the home of the Earls (later Dukes) of Bedford, before they moved to Woburn, this attractive building has stepped gables and elaborately patterned high brick chimneys. Built by the architect who enlarged Hampton Court for Henry VIII, the house has played host not only to the king but also his daughter Elizabeth I, whose favourite oak tree still stands in the garden. Naturally, there is a ghost here, that of none other than Henry, whose footsteps can be heard as he drags his ulcerated leg around the manor house in an attempt to catch Catherine Howard in the act of adultery with one of his entourage, Tom Culpeper. The house has much to offer, not just from the exterior but also inside where there are tapestries, furniture and a collection of antique dolls, but the elaborate gardens should not be overlooked. Among the delights are a Tudor style sunken garden, some fine topiary, a turf maze, a kitchen garden and a physic garden with a variety of herbs that were used for both medicinal and culinary purposes.

HIGH WYCOMBE

The largest town in Buckinghamshire, High Wycombe is traditionally known for the manufacture of chairs and, in particular, the famous Windsor design. It is still a centre of furniture manufacture today as well as being a pleasant town in which to live for those commuting to London. Originally an old Chilterns gap market town, High Wycombe still has several old buildings of note. The **Little Market House** was designed by Robert Adams in 1761 and is of a rather curious octagonal shape, while the 18th century Guildhall is the annual venue for a traditional ceremony showing a healthy scepticism for politicians when the mayor and councillors are publicly weighed - to see if they have become fat at the expense of the citizens. Located in an 18th century house with a flint facade, the **Wycombe Museum** has displays which give the visitor an excellent idea of the work and crafts of the local people over the years. There is, of course, a superb collection of chairs and other furniture, and children are well catered for with special activities and trails and a 'Discovery' centre. In the landscaped grounds of the museum is a medieval motte which would normally indicate that a castle once stood here but, in this case, the structure was probably little more than a wooden tower. The oldest standing building in the town is All Saints Church, a large, fine building dating from the 11th century.

AROUND HIGH WYCOMBE

MARLOW

4 miles S of High Wycombe on the A4155

An attractive commuter town on the banks of the Thames, Marlow is famous for its suspension bridge built in 1832 to

River Thames, Marlow

Marlow Suspension Bridge

the design of Tierney Clarke, who built a similar bridge linking Buda and Pest across the Danube. The High Street is lined with elegant houses, and Marlow has a good supply of riverside pubs; in one of them, the Two Brewers, Jerome K Jerome wrote his masterpiece *Three Men in a Boat*. Other literary connections abound: Mary Shelley completed *Frankenstein* while living here after her marriage to the poet Percy Bysshe Shelley and TS Eliot lived for a while in West Street, as did the author Thomas Love Peacock while writing *Nightmare Abbey*. Marlow hosts an annual regatta and is one of the places the Swan Uppers visit each year counting and marking the swans belonging to the Queen and to two London Livery Companies.

BOURNE END
4 miles SE of High Wycombe on the A4155

A prosperous commuter town on the banks of the Thames; it began to expand in the late 19th century as the Victorians developed a passion for boating on the river. It was once the home of the writer Edgar Wallace, who died in Hollywood during work on the screenplay for *King Kong*. He is buried in the village cemetery at nearby Little Marlow.

TOWN FARM

Bisham, Marlow, Buckinghamshire SL7 1RR
Tel: 01628 473781 Fax: 01628 472257

Home-produced meat and poultry is the speciality of **Town Farm**, a long-established business run by farmer's wife Sally Philp. In the shop, which is situated next to the farmhouse on the farm where many of the animals are raised, customers can be absolutely sure of the freshness and quality of what they are buying, be it beef, lamb, pork, game, poultry or sausages,

and freezer packs and free-range organic eggs are also available. The shop, which is open every Friday and Saturday, lies off the A404 very close to Bisham Abbey.

PICTURES PLUS

The Garden Centre, Hedsor Road, Bourne End,
Buckinghamshire SL8 5EE
Tel: 01628 528222

Paul Matthews trained as a photographer before establishing his picture-framing business, located inside the covered garden centre on the Cookham side of Bourne End. **Pictures Plus**, one of the largest commercial galleries in the land, is filled with the work of numerous contemporary artists, including original oils, watercolours and pastels, posters, etchings, silk screens, and limited edition prints. Customers can consult with Paul and choose from the numerous examples displayed in the workshop. Paul also frames customers' own pictures, along with badges, bats, trophies and many other items. Pictures Plus is open from 9 to 6 Monday to Saturday and from 10.30 to 4.30 on Sunday.

Hambleden

6 miles SW of High Wycombe off the A4155

This much filmed village was given to the National Trust by the family of the bookseller WH Smith - who later became Viscount Hambleden. He lived close by at Greenlands, on the banks of the River Thames and is buried in the village churchyard. The unusually large **Church of St Mary**, known as the cathedral of the Chilterns, dates from the 14th century and, though it has been altered over the years, it still dominates the area with its size and beauty. Inside the building's 18th century tower is a fascinating 16th century panel which is believed to have been the bedhead of Cardinal Wolsey - it certainly bears the cardinal's hat and the Wolsey arms.

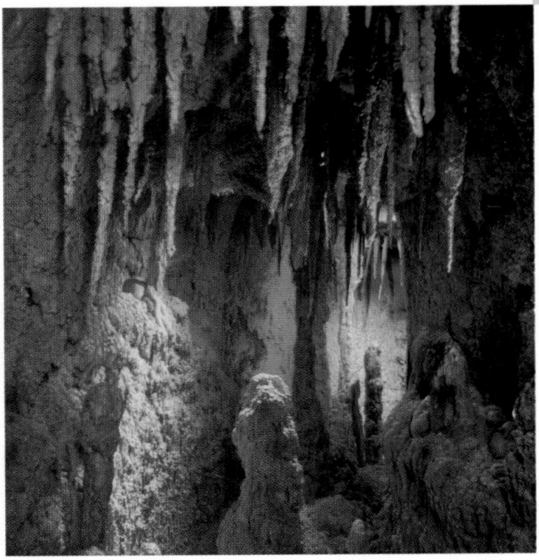

West Wycombe Caves

The village's other building of interest, Hambledon Mill, can be found by the River Thames and is reached by a road that was first used by the Romans.

West Wycombe

2 miles NW of High Wycombe on the A40

This charming estate village, where many of the houses are owned by the National Trust, has a main street displaying architecture from the 15th through to the 19th century. Close by is **West Wycombe Park**, the home of local landowners the Dashwood family until the 1930s and now a National Trust property. Of the various members of the family, it was Sir Francis Dashwood who had most influence on both the house and the village. West Wycombe house was originally built in the early 18th century but Sir Francis boldly remodelled it several years later as well as having the grounds and park landscaped by Thomas Cook, a pupil of Capability Brown. Very much a classical landscape, the grounds contain temples and an artificial lake shaped like a swan, and the house has a good collection of tapestries, furniture and paintings. Hewn out of a nearby hillside are **West Wycombe Caves**, which were created, possibly from some existing caverns, by Sir Francis as part of a programme of public works. After a series of failed harvests, which created great poverty and distress amongst the estate workers and tenant farmers, Sir Francis employed the men to extract chalk from the hillside to be used in the construction of the new road between the village and High Wycombe.

The village **Church of St Lawrence** is yet another example of Sir Francis' enthusiasm for remodelling old buildings. Situated within the remnants of an Iron Age fort, the church was originally constructed in the 13th century. Its isolated position, however, was not intentional as the church was originally the church of the village of Haveringdon, which has long since disappeared. Dashwood remodelled the interior in the 18th century in the style of an Egyptian hall and also heightened the tower, adding on the top a great golden ball where six people could meet in comfort and seclusion. The **Dashwood Mausoleum** near the church was built in 1765; a vast hexagonal building without a roof, it is the resting place of Sir Francis and other members of the Dashwood family. Sir Francis had a racier side to his character and, as well as being remembered as a great traveller and a successful politician, he was the founder of the Hell-Fire Club. This groups of rakes, who were also known as the Brotherhood of Sir Francis or Dashwood's Apostles, met a couple of times a years to engage in highly colourful activities. Though their exploits were legendary and probably loosely based on fact, they no doubt consumed large quantities of alcohol and enjoyed the company of women. Traditionally, the group meetings were held in the caves, or possibly the church tower, though between 1750 and 1774, their meeting place was nearby Medmenham Abbey.

Hughenden

2 miles N of High Wycombe off the A4128

This village is famous for being the home of the Queen Victoria's favourite Prime Minister Benjamin Disraeli; he lived here from 1848 until his death in 1881. He bought **Hughenden Manor** shortly after the publication of his novel *Tancred*. Though not a wealthy man, Disraeli felt that a leading Conservative politician should have a stately home of his own and, in order to finance the purchase, his supporters lent him the money so that he could have this essential characteristic of an English gentleman. The house, now in

Hughenden Manor

the hands of the National Trust and open to the public from March to early November, is a remodelled 18th century house refaced with various coloured bricks; the interior is an excellent example of the Victorian Gothic style. Here can be found an interesting collection of memorabilia of Disraeli's life as well as his library and pictures and much of his furniture. The garden is based on the designs of Disraeli's wife Mary Anne, and the surrounding park and woodland offer some beautiful walks. Disraeli, who was MP for Buckinghamshire from 1847 to 1876 and Prime Minister in 1868 and from 1874 to 1880, is buried in the churchyard of St Michael. In the chancel of the church is a marble memorial erected in his memory by Queen Victoria. Disraeli was the son of a writer and literary critic, Isaac d'Israeli, who lived for a time in the village of **Bradenham** on the other side of High Wycombe. The Bradenham Estate, also owned by the National Trust, includes Bradenham Woods, an area of ancient beech that is among the finest in the whole Chilterns region. Although beech predominates, other trees, including oak, whitebeam, ash and wild cherry are being encouraged.

AYLESBURY

The county town of Buckinghamshire since the 18th century, Aylesbury lies in rich pastureland in the shelter of the Chilterns. Postwar development took away much of the town's character, but some parts, particularly around the market square, are protected by a conservation order. At various times in the Civil War, Aylesbury was a base for both Cromwell and the King, and this period of history is covered in the **County Museum**. The museum, housed in a splendid Georgian building, also has sections on Louis XVIII of France, who lived in exile at nearby Hartwell House, and on Roald Dahl, who lived near Great Missenden.

AROUND AYLESBURY

MENTMORE
6 miles NE of Aylesbury off the B488

The village is home to the first of the Rothschild mansions, **Mentmore Towers**, which was built for Baron Meyer Amschel de Rothschild between 1852 and 1855. A splendid building in the Elizabethan style it was designed by Sir Joseph Paxton, the designer of Crystal Palace, and is a superb example of grandiose Victorian extravagance. However, the lavish decoration hides several technologically advanced details for those times, such as central heating, and, as might be expected from Paxton, there are large sheets of glass and a glass roof in the design. In the late 19th century the house became the home of Lord Rosebery and the magnificent turreted building was the scene of many glittering parties and gatherings of the

THE CHILTERN BREWERY

Nash Lee Road, Terrick, Aylesbury, Buckinghamshire HP17 0TQ
Tel: 01296 613647 Fax: 01296 612419
website: www.chilternbrewery.co.uk

The ancient and revered art of the English brewer is alive and flourishing at the **Chiltern Brewery**, which was established by Richard and Lesley Jenkinson in 1980. Richard had been a founder member of the Campaign for Real Ale in the early 1970s, and they were founder members of SIBA, the trade association for small brewers. Their brewery specialises in the production of hand-crafted draught and bottled beers, the latest being Battle of Britain Ale launched in December 2001 in association with RAF Halton.

They also produce a unique range of goods made with beer, hops or malt, including prize-winning beer cheeses, beer bread, beer chocolate, hop pickled onions and hop cologne. Own label bottled beers and supplies to farmers markets are recent successful developments, in the care respectively of Richard and Lesley's sons Tom and George. A wide range of specially arranged tours is offered, with all the brewing processes explained and a tutored beer sampling. Optional extras include food, either a help-yourself cold buffet or a princely feast of bangers & mash and spiced onion gravy followed by barley wine fruitcake. The Chiltern Brewery, which lies on the B4009 off the Wendover bypass (A413), is also home to the fascinating little Buckinghamshire Breweries Museum, the first micro-brewery museum in the country.

most wealthy and influential people in the country. However, in the 1970s the house was put up for auction and, while the furniture and works of art were sold to the four corners of the world, the building was bought by the Maharishi Mahesh Yogi and it is now the headquarters of his University of Natural Law. Mentmore Towers is occasionally open to the public.

Ivinghoe

7 miles E of Aylesbury on the B488

As the large village church would suggest, Ivinghoe was once a market town of some importance in the surrounding area. In this now quiet village can be found **Ford End Watermill**, a listed building that, though probably much older, was first recorded in 1767. The only working watermill, with its original machinery, left in Buckinghamshire, the farm in which it is set has also managed to retain the atmosphere of an 18th century farm.

To the east lies the National Trust's **Ivinghoe Beacon**, a wonderful viewpoint on the edge of the Chiltern Hills. The site of an Iron Age hill fort, the beacon was also the inspiration for Sir Walter Scott's *Ivanhoe*. The Beacon is at one end of Britain's oldest road, the **Ridgeway National Trail**. The other end is the World Heritage Site of Avebury in Wiltshire, and the 85-mile length of the Ridgeway still follows the same route over the high ground used since prehistoric times. Walkers can use the whole length of the trail (April to November is the best time) and horseriders and cyclists can ride on much of the western part.

Pitstone

7 miles E of Aylesbury off the B489

Though the exact age of **Pitstone Windmill**, owned by the National Trust, is not known, it is certainly one of the oldest post mills in Britain. The earliest documentary reference to its existence was made in 1624. It is open to the public on a limited basis. Also in the village is a **Farm Museum**, where all manner of farm and barn machinery, along with domestic bygones, are on display. A delightful hour or two can be spent cruising from Pitstone Wharf along a lovely stretch of the Grand Union Canal.

Pitstone Windmill

Stoke Mandeville

2 miles S of Aylesbury on the A4010

The village is best known for its hospital, which specialises in the treatment of spinal injuries and burns. Just south of Stoke, on Old Risborough Road, **Bucks Goat Centre** has the most comprehensive collection of goat breeds in the country. Visitors can groom, cuddle and feed them with vegetables from the Farm Shop. Also here are the famous Aylesbury ducks and other poultry, pigs, small pet animals and donkeys, facilities for children, shops and a café.

GREAT KIMBLE

5 miles S of Aylesbury on the A4010

Though the village is home to a church with an interesting series of 14th century wall paintings, its real claim to fame is the nearby 16th-century mansion, **Chequers**, the country residence of the British Prime Minister. Originally built by William Hawtrey in 1565, but much altered and enlarged in the 18th and 19th centuries, the house was restored to its original form by Arthur Lee in 1912. Later, in 1920, as Lord Lee of Fareham, he gave the house and estate to the nation to be used as the prime minister's country home. The first Prime Minister to make use of Chequers was Lloyd George, and many who have known the house have since moved, or stayed, in the area: Ramsay MacDonald's daughter lived at nearby Speen; Harold Wilson bought a house in Great Missenden; and Nye Bevan owned a farm in the Chilterns.

BOARSTALL

12 miles W of Aylesbury off the B4011

A curious feature here is the 17th century **Duck Decoy** set on the edge of a lake to catch birds for the table. The site, run by the National Trust, contains a nature trail and exhibition hall. The National Trust is

also responsible for **Boarstall Tower**, the 14th century stone gatehouse of a long demolished fortified house.

WOTTON UNDERWOOD

8 miles W of Aylesbury off the A41

In this secluded village stands the privately owned **Wotton House**, a charming early-18th century building said to be practically identical to the original Buckingham Palace. The gardens, which feature more than a dozen follies, were laid out between 1757 and 1760 by Capability Brown.

WADDESDON

4 miles NW of Aylesbury on the A41

The village is home to another of the county's magnificent country houses, in this case **Waddesdon Manor**. Built between 1874 and 1889 for Baron Ferdinand de Rothschild, in the style of a French Renaissance château, the house is

Waddesdon Manor

GATEHANGERS INN

Lower End, Ashendon, Nr Aylesbury, Buckinghamshire HP18 0HE
Tel: 01296 651296
e-mail: crisprichpat@aol.com

Patricia and Richard Crisp's **Gatehangers Inn** is a 400-year-old building with a striking redbrick facade topped by an equally eyecatching red-slate roof. The two bars have the cosy, inviting look and feel of a typical village inn, complete with real ales on tap, and there is a separate restaurant where excellent lunches (not Monday or Tuesday) and evening meals are served. The inn, which has a rear garden and off-road car parking space, is located about 5 miles west of Aylesbury off the A41 or A418. This is a popular walking area, and there are many places of interest nearby.

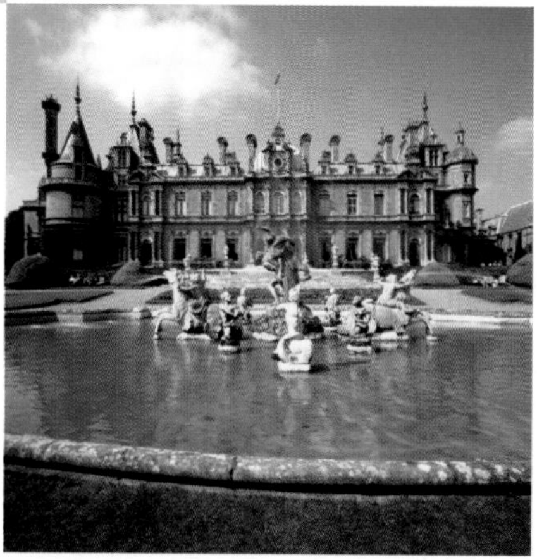

Waddesdon Manor

of the best collections of 18th century French decorative arts in the world, including Sèvres porcelain, Beauvais tapestries and fine furniture. There are also paintings by Gainsborough, Reynolds and 17th century Dutch and Flemish masters on display.

QUAINTON
5 miles NW of Aylesbury off the A41

A pleasant village with the remains of an ancient cross on the green, a number of fine Georgian houses and a row of almshouses built in 1687. Here, too, is another of the county's windmills, **Quainton Tower Mill**, built in the 1830s and 100ft high. Quite early in its life it was fitted with a steam engine, but despite this innovation the mill's working life extended barely 50 years. Just south of the village, at Quainton Railway Station, is the **Buckinghamshire Railway Centre**, a working steam museum where visitors can relive the golden age of steam (see panel opposite).

set in rolling English countryside and borrows elements from several different French châteaux, surrounded by formal gardens and landscaped grounds. These contain, among many treasures, a French-style aviary in a part of the gardens designed by the popular 20th century American landscape artist Lanning Roper, hundreds of trees both native and foreign, a fabulous parterre, Italian, French and Dutch statuary, and a huge pheasant named Ferdinand made from 15,000 bedding plants on a steel frame. The French influence even extended to the carthorses used on the site - powerful Percheron mares that were imported from Normandy. Now in the hands of the National Trust, the house is home to one

CHESHAM

A successful combination of a commuter town, industrial centre and country community, Chesham's growth from a sleepy market town was due mainly to its Metropolitan underground railway link with central London. Chesham was the

BERNWODE PLANTS

Kingswood Lane, Ludgershall, Buckinghamshire HP18 9RB
Tel: 01844 237415 Fax: 01844 238920
website: www.bernwodeplants.co.uk

Derek and Judy Tolman started **Bernwode Plants** in the mid-1980's when they acquired fields a mile outside of Ludgershall. The nursery is set among 30 acres of hay meadows, and grows and sells a huge range of old-fashioned herbaceous perennials, herbs, shrubs and fruit trees. With over 2,500 varieties, all grown on the premises,the choice is among the widest anywhere in the land. Staff are on hand to give expert advice on growing needs and plant habits. The nursery is open six days a week in season and plants can be sent by courier to customers anywhere on the UK mainland.

birthplace of Arthur Liberty, the son of a haberdasher and draper, who went on to found the world famous Liberty's department store in London's Regent Street in 1875. Another resident of note was Roger Crabbe who, having suffered head injuries during the Civil War, was sentenced to death by Cromwell. After receiving a pardon, Crabbe opened a hat shop in the town where he is reputed to have worn sackcloth, eaten turnip tops and given his income to the poor. Perhaps not surprisingly, Crabbe was used by Lewis Carroll as the model for the Mad Hatter in *Alice in Wonderland*.

Buckinghamshire Railway Centre

Quainton Road Station,
Quainton, Aylesbury,
Buckinghamshire HP22 4BY
Tel: 01296 655720

A working steam museum set in a 25-acre site, the **Buckinghamshire Railway Centre** was established in 1968 and boasts one of the largest collections of preserved steam and diesel locomotives in the country, including items from South Africa, the USA and Egypt as well as from Britain. Visitors can ride behind full-sized stream locomotives and on the extensive miniature railway. The Railway Centre is also home to the beautifully restored Rewley Road Station, which dates from 1851 and was moved here from Oxford, and is now the main visitor centre. Open Wednesdays to Sundays from March to the end of October, the steam trains operated on Sundays and on Wednesdays in the school holidays.

Chessmount Nurseries

41b Chessmount Rise, Waterside, Chesham,
Buckinghamshire HB5 1RB
Tel/Fax: 01494 772051
e-mail: john@chessmount.freeserve.co.uk

The oldest family business in Chesham, **Chessmount Nurseries** was established in 1946 by the father of Verity May, who now runs it with her husband John. Father also still helps out at this splendid traditional plant nursery, which offers an impressively wide selection of perennials, alpines, shrubs, bedding plants and trees. Quality is second to none, prices are competitive, and the range includes many rare and unusual varieties.

Helpful, knowledgeable staff are on hand to help with the selection of the right plant for the right position, and landscaping services are also available. The nurseries are located about half a mile from the centre of Chesham, a little way off the A416. Visitors should allow plenty of time to explore all the nooks and crannies of the nurseries, the paths and the open beds, the glasshouses and the tunnels, and to admire the glorious countryside views which alone would make a visit worthwhile. Opening hours are 9 to 5 Monday to Saturday, 9 to 4 Sunday, and there's plenty of free parking. Chesham itself, a pleasant town situated among wooded hills, is easily reached from London by either road or rail.

The Old Farm

Hog Lane, Ashley Green, Chesham,
Buckinghamshire HP5 3PY
Tel/Fax: 01442 866430
e-mail: gillian.theoldfarm@virgin.net

Gillian and Terry Potter offer quiet, comfortable self-catering accommodation in tranquil, scenic surroundings close to the A416 between Chesham and Berkhamsted. The Barn comprises a double-bedded room with en suite bathroom, and a living/dining room with armchair, sofa, dining table, tv and video recorder, cooking unit, microwave, toaster, fridge, sink unit, washing machine, iron and ironing board. French doors open out on to a small terrace with garden chairs. The Annexe, attached to the owners' 16th century farmhouse, has similar facilities, but with accommodation for four and a separate kitchen. The double bedroom has an adjacent bathroom and WC, and a sofa in the large sitting/dining room transforms into a capacious double bed. Bed linen and towels are supplied in both The Barn and The Annexe, and a cot and high chair are available on request. The accommodation is strictly non-smoking, and pets are not allowed. The Old Farm is an excellent place for a quiet break and, with ready access to the main road network, a good base for touring the sights of the area or for enjoying the local leisure facilities, including several golf courses.

Peterley Manor Farm

Prestwood, Great Missenden,
Buckinghamshire HP16 0HH
Tel: 01494 863566 Fax: 01494 862959

Peterley Manor Farm is a family-run business which has been steadily expanding since the Brills bought the property in 1982. Roger Brill is the fourth generation of the farming family of Brills in the business, and he now runs the show with his wife Jane and other members of the family spanning three generations. It's a great place to come to take the country air, to Pick Your Own fruit and vegetables, to visit the nursery and farm shop and to say hello to the friendly resident alpacas. The Pick Your Own season runs from mid-June to October, with berries of all kinds, plums, apples, beans, peas, beetroots, carrots, spinach and potatoes all available at their appointed times in the season. This produce is also for sale in the farm shop (open Tuesday to Sunday), along with home-produces apple juice, cut flowers, free-range eggs, local honey, traditional preserves and chutneys, ice creams, cakes and self-service frozen fruit and vegetables. Herbaceous plants, fuchsias, geraniums, lobelias and petunias are among the extensive stock at the nursery, along with a huge selection of ready-planted hanging baskets and patio planters. Other offerings at this excellent establishment include home-grown pumpkins for Halloween and Christmas trees and festive gifts and produce.

Great Missenden

3 miles W of Chesham off the A413

Home to the only other court house in the Chiltern Hundreds (the other is at Long Crendon), Great Missenden's **Old Court House** dates from the early 1400s. Also in this village is an attractive flint and stone church and Missenden Abbey, which was founded in 1133 by the Augustinian order. A daughter community of St Nicholas's Abbey in Normandy, the abbey has long since gone and in its place stands a fashionable Gothic mansion dating from 1810. The village has had its fair share of famous visitors and among them is Robert Louis Stevenson, the author of *Treasure Island*, and the anti-slavery campaigner, William Wilberforce. However, Great Missenden is probably best known as being the home of Roald Dahl, the internationally recognised author particularly loved for his children's books. He lived here for 30 years and is buried on the hillside opposite his home, Gipsy House, in the churchyard of St Peter and St Paul. His daughter Olivia, who died at the age of 7, is buried at Little Missenden in a plot that was intended for Dahl himself and his first wife, the actress Patricia Neal. But this plan was changed when Dahl and Neal were divorced in 1983, seven years before his death. The gardens of his home are open the public once a year.

Lacey Green

8 miles W of Chesham off the A4010

Lacey Green is home to another of the county's preserved windmills, this one a **Smock Mill**, in which only the cap carrying the sails rotates to meet the wind. As a result, the body of the mill where the machinery is housed can be

(Continued page 70)

WALK 2

Great Hampden and Little Hampden

Start	Cockshoots Wood car park and picnic area. Turn off A413 about 1¾ miles (2.8km) south of Wendover along lane signed to Cobblers Hill, car park is ½ mile (800m) along this lane
Distance	6½ miles (10.5km)
Approximate time	3 hours
Parking	Cockshoots Wood
Refreshments	Pub at Little Hampden
Ordnance Survey maps	Landranger 165 (Aylesbury & Leighton Buzzard), Explorer 181 (Chiltern Hills North)

Apart from one fairly steep climb near the end, this is a gently undulating walk through a peaceful, rolling and well-wooded landscape in the heart of the Chilterns. The route passes two remote and interesting churches at Great Hampden and Little Hampden.

Cockshoots Wood is crisscrossed by a multiplicity of paths and tracks, but following the directions and bridleway waymark arrows as outlined here should keep you firmly on track. Put your back to the lane at the car park entrance and look right to find and take the waymarked bridleway that starts at a gap in the fence. This well used and potentially muddy track snakes gently up through scrubby undergrowth to enter woodland. Bear right at the waymarked post and continue up the bridleway to emerge into an extensive clearing near the crest of the hill. Trace the wide path straight across this open area to re-enter woodland, bearing slightly right once within the trees and then keep left at a fork. In a further 100 yds (91m) or so is a complicated, waymarked junction of routes. Go left, then immediately right, a blue bridleway arrow painted on a tree confirming the way. The wide path winds through the woods to emerge at a junction of lanes and paths (A). The way is ahead along the tarred lane, passing the corner-stile on your left. Ignore the next lane to the left, then at the sharp right bend keep ahead along the rougher track to reach another tarred lane, along which turn left.

At a public footpath sign turn left through a metal gate. Walk along a grassy, hedge-lined path and, emerging into a field, turn right to continue along the right-hand edge of the field, by a hedge on the right. The path later keeps along the right inside-edge of woodland. On leaving the wood bear right along a track, then bear left, at a white arrow, going downhill along the right-hand edge of a field, by a hedge and trees on the right. Go through a hedge gap in the field corner and continue down-hill across the middle of a field to a road.

Cross the road, take the lane ahead and at a public footpath sign turn right (B) up steps and walk along a narrow path between a wire fence on the left and a hedge on the right. Where the fence on the left ends, continue along the right-hand edge of a field. At the field corner the path continues ahead through woodland; it is narrow, overgrown and indistinct in places but there are white arrow-markers. Keep more or less in a straight line, later the path becomes more obvious. At a T-junction indicated by arrows on a tree trunk, turn sharp left, head gently uphill and, where arrows indicate the next path junction, turn right and continue uphill; the path curves left to reach a crossroads of paths. Turn sharp right, between a white-arrowed tree and a white-arrowed telegraph pole, to climb a stile and continue across a field to another one. Climb this and keep ahead over a third stile on to a lane.

Turn left along the lane for 200 yds (183m), and at a public footpath and bridleway sign turn right C through a metal gate to walk along the right-hand edge of a field, by trees and then by a wire fence on the right. Keep in a straight line along the right-hand edge of a series of fields, going through a succession of metal gates and finally continuing along the left-hand edge of woodland to a road. Bear left, keep ahead at a crossroads – in the direction of Great Hampden, Speen and Princes Risborough – and where the road bends sharply left, continue along a tarmac drive to pass between Hampden House on the right and Great Hampden church on the left. The most famous member of the Hampden family – lords of the manor – was John Hampden, a Parliamentary opponent of Charles I, whose refusal to pay ship money in 1641 helped to trigger the Civil War. He was killed in 1643 while fighting for the Parliamentary army. Hampden House was almost totally rebuilt in the 18th century.

Where the tarmac drive turns right into the grounds of the house, keep ahead through a gate and immediately turn right over a stile D. Walk across a field, passing the front of Hampden House, climb a stile and head gently downhill through mixed woodland to climb another stile at the far end. Continue straight across a field to climb a stile on to a road E. Cross the road and climb a stile opposite, at a public footpath sign. Take the path ahead through more woodland. At a crossroads of paths a white arrow directs you to the right to emerge into a field. Continue straight across the field heading towards a gap in the hedge at the far end.

Go through this gap, head uphill through a conifer wood, and on leaving the trees bear slightly left and walk across a field making for the trees on the far side. Here, at a white arrow on a tree, continue along a path, by a wire fence on the left – later the path becomes a drive – to a lane in the hamlet of Little Hampden. Turn right, heading downhill along the lane to the tiny Little Hampden church, noted for its 15th century timber-framed porch.

Opposite the church turn left F, at a public bridleway sign, along a track that heads downhill, meandering along the left-hand edge of a field, and then climbs up to the edge of woodland. Pass through a gap in the trees to head uphill through the wood, keeping on the main path all the while; at the top emerge from the trees and continue between wire fences to a metal gate. Go through the gate and keep ahead along a concrete path, by a hedge on the left, to a farm. Pass to the left of the farm buildings to reach a lane G.

Cross straight over the lane and go along the rough driveway opposite, signed as The Chiltern Way and The South Bucks Way. Just before the edge of the woods turn left along the waymarked footpath, almost immediately fork left alongside a fence and follow the wide path for 300 yds (274m) to a junction and waymark post. Turn left here and retrace your initial route back to the car park.

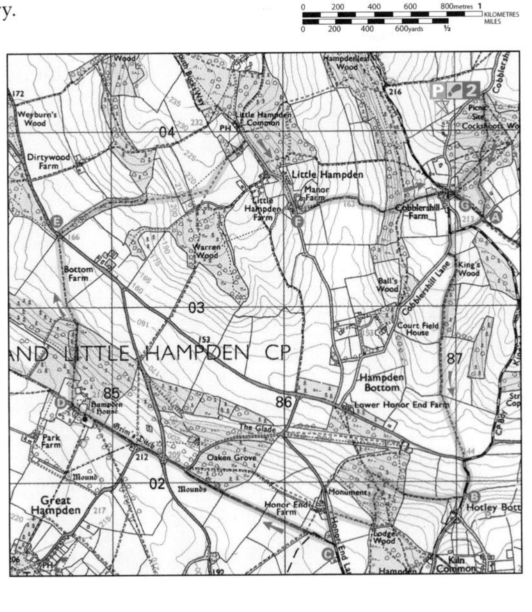

Wimpennys At The Pheasant

Ballinger Common, Nr Great Missenden,
Buckinghamshire HP16 9LF
Tel: 01494 837236 Fax: 01494 837120
website: www.wimpennys.com

An exciting modern European style of cooking brings a discerning clientele to **Wimpennys at the Pheasant**, a bright conservatory restaurant that was formerly the Pheasant Inn. Pastel shades and lush plants create an attractive, relaxed ambience in which to enjoy a meal prepared by two talented and enthusiastic young chefs, Stuart Ginger and Paul Scott. Their menus reflect the very best in taste, making fine use of locally supplied meat and dairy produce, garden herbs and vegetables hand-picked at the market, and fish and shellfish fresh from the sea.

The choice runs from appetising light lunches to a full à la carte menu on which every dish is a triumph of well-balanced textures and flavours. Starters such as squid ink tagliatelle with roasted langoustines and shellfish cream, or rabbit and black pudding terrine pave the way for superb main courses like turbot with boulangère potato, parsley butter crust and baby leek velouté or pot-roast partridge with bean cassoulet, sautéed lamb sweetbreads and ventrèche bacon. Desserts like tarte tatin with cider brandy ice cream and caramel sauce keep the enjoyment level sky high right to the end, and the fine food is complemented by an excellent wine list. The restaurant, which is owned by Patricia and Nigel Wimpenny-Smith, overlooks the common in a quiet village off the A413, a short drive from Amersham.

bigger, heavier and stronger. This example was built in the mid 17th century and was moved from Chesham to this site in 1821. Lacey Green is the village where the young poet Rupert Brooke used to spend his weekends in the company of friends at a local pub. The son of a master at Rugby School and a student at Cambridge University, Brooke began writing poetry as a boy and travelled widely in the years leading up to World War I. Early on in the war, in which he fought, his poetry showed a boyish patriotism, but his later works were full of bitter disillusion. He died in 1915 while on his way to the attempted landings at the Dardanelles in Turkey. Close to the village lies Speen Farm and the **Home of Rest for Horses**, whose most famous patient was Sefton, the cavalry horse injured in the Hyde Park bomb blast of the early 1980s.

Princes Risborough

9 miles W of Chesham on the A4010

The Prince in the name of this Chilterns Gap market town is the Black Prince, the eldest son of Edward III, who held land and had a palace here. The town has many 17th and 18th century houses, but the most interesting building is the Market House dating from 1824. The ground floor is an empty space providing shelter for market stalls, while in the room above the Town Council meets. Off the market square, opposite the church, the National Trust's **Princes Risborough Manor House** is a 17th century redbrick house with a handsome Jacobean staircase.

Wendover

6 miles NW of Chesham on the A413

This delightful old market town, situated in a gap in the Chiltern Hills, has an attractive main street of half timbered, thatched houses and cottages of which the best examples are **Anne Boleyn's Cottages**. A picturesque place, often seen as the gateway to the Chilterns, Wendover also has a fine selection of antique shops, tea rooms and bookshops.

The town also offers visitors an opportunity of seeing the glorious countryside through the medium of **Wendover Woods**. Created for recreational pursuits - there's a mountain bike course at Aston Hill - as well as for conservation and timber production, these Forestry Commission woods offer visitors numerous trails through the coniferous and broadleaved woodland. It is one of the best sites in the country to spot the tiny firecrest, a bird that is becoming increasingly rare.

Wendover Cottages

Off the B4010 a short drive west of Wendover, **Coombe Hill** is the highest point in the Chilterns and affords superb views across the Vale of Aylesbury, the Berkshire Downs and the Cotswolds. On the summit is a monument dedicated to the men who died in the Boer War. The National Trust have introduced a flock

WENDOVER OUTDOORS & COUNTRY WEAR

3 Icknield Court, Back Street, Wendover, Buckinghamshire HP22 6EB
Tel/Fax: 01296 624988 e-mail: charleschaney@dial.pipex.com

Part of a modern redbrick block in a street running parallel to the High Street, **Wendover Outdoors & Country Wear** explains itself in its title. It is owned and run by Charles Chaney, a keen outdoors man who numbers walking and coarse fishing among his favourite pursuits. He has a very thorough knowledge of his stock, which encompasses country and outdoor wear for all the family, and is happy to recommend and advise on what to wear for any outdoor activity. The range covers boots, trousers, waterproofs, moleskins, shooting and fishing jackets, gilets, fleeces, hats, socks, gloves and accessories for every outdoor occasion by all the leading manufacturers.

NUMBER ONE

1 High Street, Wendover, Buckinghamshire HP22 6DU
Tel: 01296 623150 Fax: 01296 625138

Sisters Kim White and Karen Sheehey own and run **Number One**, which stands at one end of the High Street in the ancient Chilterns town of Wendover. One of numerous quaint old buildings, Number One dates from the middle of the 16th century, and its spick and span triple-windowed frontage tempts passers-by with an eyecatching display of high-quality gifts for all occasions. Inside, the whole range is on show, including plants, flowers, accessories for home and garden, and gifts of all kinds. The shop is open from 9 to 5.30 Monday to Friday and from 9 to 5 on Saturday.

Buckingham Nurseries & Garden Centre

Tingewick Road, Buckingham, Buckinghamshire MK18 4AE
Tel: 01280 813556 Fax: 01280 815491
e-mail: enquiries@hedging.co.uk website: www.hedging.co.uk

Buckingham Nurseries & Garden Centre is very much a family affair, with Richard and Pauline Brown running the Garden Centre and Nursery, son Peter the Aquatics Centre and other son David the IT side, including the excellent website. The nursery was established in 1945 by Richard's father and has occupied its present site since 1970. The bright, spacious Garden Centre produces on site a wide range of perennials, alpines and unusual bedding plants, and also available are pot-grown shrubs and trees, and in season an extensive selection of hedging plants and fruit, forest and ornamental trees. The stock includes house plants, fertilisers, tools and accessories and an enormous range of seeds and bulbs.

In the busy season over 70 people are employed in the various areas of the business - Garden Centre, Mail-order department,heated glasshouses, unheated propagation areas, the aquatics centre (stocked with cold water, tropical and marine fish) and the restaurant the 'Gardeners' Retreat', where visitors can relax inside or outside over a cup of tea or coffee or enjoy a meal chosen from the menu of home-baked dishes. Knowledgeable staff are always on hand to answer questions and to give advice at the Centre, which has won several prestigious awards and is highly recommended by the Royal Horticultural Society and many leading gardening correspondents. The Centre, which is fully accessible to wheelchair users and has a large car park, lies about four miles from the magnificent Stowe Landscape Gardens and close to the National Trust's Claydon House and Waddesdon Manor.

Homeflair

8 Meadow Row, Buckingham, Buckinghamshire MK18 1PU
Tel/Fax: 01280 812399

Owner Wendy Harris runs a very successful and long-established business in a small shopping complex. **Homeflair** is an attractively renovated stone cottage in a row of cottages, each with its own distinctive character and charm. A small bay window filled with goods tempts passers-by inside, where smart, well-lit pine units display a wide-ranging collection of gifts and cards for all ages and occasions. Fashion jewellery is one of the specialities, and many of the other items stocked include china, glassware, frames, fragrant gifts and a wide range of toys including Galt and Orchard, plus many more.

The stock at Homeflair changes constantly, so Wendy's loyal band of regular customers will always have plenty of new things to look at. Buckingham is a fine old market town, largely rebuilt after a ruinous fire in 1725. Many of the best buildings are therefore Georgian, and even the old jail (now a museum) opposite Homeflair has an unexpectedly elegant air.

of sheep on to the hill to control the invasion of scrub and to encourage the grass.

BUCKINGHAM

This pleasant town, the centre of which is contained in a loop of the River Ouse, dates back to Saxon times and was once granted a charter by Alfred the Great. Although it became the county town in AD 888, when King Alfred divided the shires, from an early date many of the functions of a county town were performed by the more centrally located Aylesbury. According to the Saxon Chronicle, it was Edward the Elder who fortified the town in AD 918 when he brought his army here during his advance on the Danish invaders. The stronghold he built, on which later stood a Norman castle, is now the site of the parish Church of St Peter and St Paul. In 1725 a disastrous fire destroyed much of the town. Many buildings were replaced and the town now boasts some fine Georgian houses of which Castle House in West Street is the best example. In the centre of Buckingham, the early-18th century gaol, one of the first purpose-built county gaols in England, today houses the **Old Gaol Museum**, which not only reflects the building's history but also has displays on the town's past and the county's military exploits. A high-tech glass roof was added in 2000, spanning the original prisoners' exercise yard to create a new light-filled area for special exhibits and an educational resource centre. One building that did survive the devastating fire in the 18th century is the **Buckingham Chantry Chapel**. Now owned by the National Trust, the chapel was constructed in 1475 on the site of a Norman building whose doorway has been retained. Well worth a visit, the chapel was restored by George Gilbert Scott in 1875. A much more recent addition to this delightful country market town is the **University of Buckingham**, which was granted its charter in 1983.

Buckingham Town

AROUND BUCKINGHAM

Stewkley

10 miles SE of Buckingham on the B4032

Stewkley, renowned as being the longest village in England, is even better known for its wonderful church, one of the finest Norman churches in the land, with spectacular zigzag patterns and a massive tower.

Winslow

5 miles SE of Buckingham on the A413

A small country town of ancient origin, where Offa, the King of Mercia, stayed in AD752. The village's most prominent

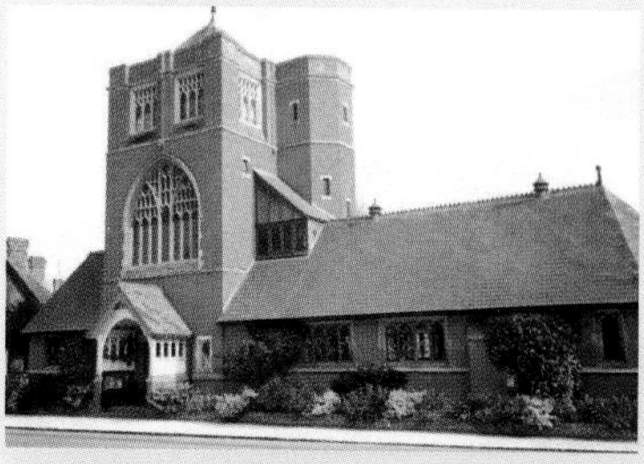

The Congregational Church

15 Horn Street, Winslow, Buckinghamshire MK18 3AP
Tel/Fax: 01296 715717

A handsome red brick **Congregational Church** built in 1889 fulfilled its original role for 100 years before becoming a private residence. Owner Sarah Hood has created an unusual home and offers Bed & Breakfast accommodation of unique appeal; three letting bedrooms are on one side of the aisle, each with its own distinctive character, and a bathroom and shower room are on the other side. Guests have their own sitting room with television, and an excellent breakfast is taken in the old school room, now the kitchen.

CB Winslow Pizzeria

40 High Street, Winslow, Buckinghamshire MK18 3HB
Tel: 01296 712222 Fax: 01296 715932
e-mail: cb@winslow90.freeserve.co.uk
website: www.cbwinslow.ltd.uk

Carmela Pisapia, born in Rome but resident in England since the age of 11, runs **CB Pizzeria** with her husband Dominic. In the cheerful 40-cover restaurant in a row of shops on Winslow's main street, they serve a range of pizza and pasta; and at the front of the pizzeria is a small bakery and delicatessen selling excellent Italian bread and prepared goods making extensive use of fresh local produce, much of it organic. Winslow lies on the A413 four miles southeast of Buckingham.

building is **Winslow Hall**, a delightful Wren house set in beautiful gardens. House and gardens are open for visits by appointment only.

Wing

12 miles SE of Buckingham on the A418

Another village famous for its church. All Saints Church, standing on a rise above the Vale of Aylesbury, retains most of its original Saxon features, including the nave, aisles, west wall, crypt and apse. The roof is covered in medieval figures, many of them playing musical instruments. This remarkable church also contains numerous brasses and monuments, notably to the Dormer family who came to Ascott Hall in the 1520s. Just east of the village, **Ascott** was bought in 1874 by Leopold Rothschild, who virtually rebuilt the original farmhouse round its timber-framed core. Now in the care of the National Trust, the house contains a superb collection of fine paintings, Oriental porcelain and English and French furniture. The grounds are magnificent, too, with specimen trees and shrubs, a herbaceous walk, lily pond, Dutch garden, an evergreen topiary sundial and two fountains, one in bronze, the other in marble, sculpted by the American artist Thomas Waldo Story.

Middle Claydon

5 miles S of Buckingham off the A413

The village is home to **Claydon House**, a Jacobean manor house that was remodelled in the 1750s at a time of great enthusiasm for all things Oriental. The home of the Verney family for over 350 years and now owned by the National Trust, the house contains a number of state rooms with magnificent carved wood and plaster decorations on an Oriental theme. What makes the house particularly interesting is its associations with Florence Nightingale.

Florence's sister married into the Verney family and the pioneer of modern hospital care spent long periods at the house, especially during her old age. Her bedroom in the house and a museum of her life and experiences during the Crimean War can be seen here. Florence died in 1910 after a long career which embraced concerns of public health as well as the training of nurses; she was the first woman to be awarded the Order of Merit.

Chinese Room, Claydon House

Dadford

3 miles N of Buckingham off the A422

Just to the south of the village lies **Stowe School**, a leading public school which occupies an 18th century mansion that was once the home of the Dukes of Buckingham. Worked upon by two wealthy owners who both had a great sense of vision, the magnificent mansion house, which was finally completed in 1774, is open to the public during school holidays. Between 1715 and 1749, the owner, Viscount Cobham, hired various well known landscape designers to lay out the fantastic gardens that can still be seen around the house. Taking over the house in 1750, Earl Temple, along with his nephew, expanded the grounds and today they remain one of the most original and finest landscape gardens in Europe. Worked on by the best designers of the day, the gardens at Stowe contain temples, alcoves and rotundas scattered around the landscape that were placed to evoke in the onlooker a romantic and poetic frame of mind. It is one of the more intriguing quirks of fate that Lancelot Brown, always known as Capability Brown because he told his clients that their parks had capabilities, was head gardener at Stowe for 10 years. He arrived here in 1741 and began to work out his own style, a more natural style of landscape gardening which was to take over where gardens like the ones at Stowe left off. Brown's concept was to ensure that the landscape element of the garden, the tree

Stowe School

planting, lakes and lawns, should look as natural as possible. **Stowe Landscape Gardens** are now in the hands of the National Trust and are open to the public.

Silverstone

5 miles N of Buckingham off the A43

The home of British motor racing, Silverstone is best known as the venue for the British Formula I Grand Prix. But it hosts many varied motorsport events throughout the year, including the Silverstone Historic Festival, British F3, GT, Touring Car and Superbike championships. It is also the place of dreams for boy racers, who can try their hand at driving a wide range of cars round the circuit, including single-seaters, rally cars, 4X4s, E-type Jaguars, Lotus Elises and Porsche 911 Carrera Supercars.

Thornborough

3 miles E of Buckingham off the A422

This lively and attractive village is home to Buckinghamshire's only surviving medieval bridge. Built in the 14th century, the six-arched structure spans Claydon Brook. Close by are two large mounds which were opened in 1839 and revealed a wealth of Roman objects. Though it was known that there was a Roman temple here its location has not been found.

MILTON KEYNES

Most people's perception of this modern town is of a concrete jungle but the reality of Milton Keynes could not be more different. The development corporation that was charged, in 1967, with organising the new town has provided a place of tree-lined boulevards, uncongested roads, spacious surroundings, and acres of parkland. It is too, of course, a modern town, with new housing, high-tech industries, modern leisure facilities, and a large covered shopping centre. One of the town's most notable buildings is **Christ Church**, built in the style of Christopher Wren; the first purpose-built ecumenical city church in Britain, it was opened in March 1992 by Her Majesty the Queen. While Milton

Bletchley Park

The Mansion, Bletchley Park, Milton Keynes, Buckinghamshire MK3 6EB
Tel: 01908 640404 Fax: 01908 274381
website: www.bletchleypark.org.uk

Bletchley Park, also known as 'Station X', was home to the famous code breakers of World War II and was the birthplace of modern computing communications. It is now a heritage site run by a charitable trust, with historic Victorian and wartime buildings, exhibitions and tours for visitors, community activities and non-residential conference facilities. Along with military vehicles and a mass of World War II memorabilia, there is the Cryptology Trail that allows visitors to follow the path of a coded message from its interception through decoding to interpretation. Though it is interesting and amusing today during World War II over 12,000 people worked here in secret doing just that and, in particular, some of the finest brains in the country were assembled here to break the unbreakable code of the German Enigma machine. A truly fascinating place, Bletchley Park uncovers a side to wartime Britain that few people were aware of at the time. The park is open every weekend from early March to the mid December. There is an admission charge.

Milton Keynes Museum

Keynes is certainly a place of the late 20th century, it has not altogether forgotten the rural past of the villages, which are now incorporated into the suburbs of the town. **Milton Keynes Museum**, run by a large and active group of volunteers, has a large collection of industrial, domestic and agricultural bygones that illustrates the lives of the people who lived in the area in the 200 years leading up to the creation of the new town. A Victorian house features a working kitchen and laundry, and among other eye-catching exhibits are a local tramcar and an impressive collection of working telephones.

AROUND MILTON KEYNES

Bletchley

2 miles S of Milton Keynes on the A421

Now more a suburb of Milton Keynes, Bletchley is famous for **Bletchley Park**, the Victorian mansion which housed the wartime codebreakers who beat odds of 150 million million million to 1 and cracked the Nazi Enigma cypher, the backbone of German military and intelligence communications (see panel opposite).

Though Bletchley is now all but merged with its larger neighbour, it still retains a distinctive air. The original

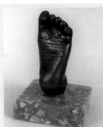

village here dates back to Roman times and was first recorded as a town in 1108.

STONY STRATFORD

3 miles NW of Milton Keynes off the A5

Often considered to be the jewel in the crown of the villages around Milton Keynes, Stony Stratford was a popular staging post on the old Roman road, Watling Street. Richard III, as the Duke of Gloucester, came in 1483 to detain the uncrowned Prince Edward before committing him to the Tower of London, and other notable visitors include Charles Dickens, Samuel Johnson and John Wesley, who preached under the tree that still stands in the market place.

GAYHURST

4 miles N of Milton Keynes off the B526

Built during the reign of Elizabeth I, **Gayhurst House** was given to Sir Francis Drake in recognition of his circumnavigation of the world, though the building seen today was not the one that Drake have lived in. It was later occupied by Sir Everard Digby, one of the conspirators behind the Gunpowder Plot of 1605.

OLNEY

8 miles N of Milton Keynes on the A509

This pretty town on the banks of the River Ouse is famous for its association with William Cowper, who came to the town to be under the ministry of the Reverend John Newton. Newton was a reformed slave-trader as well as a fiery preacher; he is buried in the churchyard of St Peter and St Paul, where he was the curate. This church is a spacious building dating from the mid 14th century and its spire rises some 185 feet to dominate the skyline of Olney. For over 300 years, Olney was a centre of lace-making by hand, using wooden or bone bobbins. When lace was at its most expensive, in the 1700s, only the well-to-do could afford to buy it, but the rise in machine-made lace from Nottingham saw a fall in prices and a sharp decline in Olney lace. A revival of the trade was tried by Harry Armstrong when he opened the Lace Factory in 1928 but, although handmade lace is still produced locally, the factory only lasted until Armstrong's death in 1943. The house in which Cowper lived from 1768 to 1786 is now the **Cowper and Newton Museum**, an interesting place that not only concentrates on Cowper's life and work but also has some exhibits and collections concerned with times in which he lived and the life of Olney. Each of the rooms of the large early 18th century town house has been specially themed and there are numerous displays of Cowper's work, including the 'Olney Hymns'. Cowper wrote 67 of these and the remaining 281 were written by Newton, most famously *Amazing Grace* and *Glorious Things of Thee are Spoken*. William Cowper was also a keen gardener

THE NEW STUDIO/STUDIO 2

Rose Court, Olney, Buckinghamshire MK46 4BY
Tel: 01234 711815/711994 Fax: 01234 241405
e-mail: keren@thenewstudio

The New Studio/Studio 2, opened in 1997 by Keren Monnickendam, is located in a 17th century building in a courtyard just off the main square in Olney. 1,600 square feet of space on two floors are given over to showcasing the work of talented British artists and crafts people, and the range includes paintings, ceramics, woodwork, metalwork, glassware, textiles and jewellery. Studio 2 contains designer furniture and sculpture.

Church of St Peter and St Paul, Olney

and the summer house, where he wrote many of his poems, can still be seen out in the rear garden where he also chose to experiment with plants that were new to 18th century England. Also at the Museum is the nationally important Lace Collection and items particular to the shoemaking industry which was another busy local trade in the 19th and early 20th century.

The town's present day claim to fame is its annual Pancake Race held every Shrove Tuesday. Legend has it that the first 'race' was run in the 15th century when a local housewife heard the Shriving Service bell ringing and ran to church complete with her frying pan and pancake. Today's re-enactment is open to any lady of Olney over 18 years of age; the rules state that she must wear a skirt, an apron and a scarf as well as carry a frying pan and pancake.

Nearby **Emberton Country Park,** located on the site of former gravel pits, is an ideal place to relax. Not only are there four lakes and a stretch of the River Ouse within the park's boundaries but facilities here include fishing, sailing, and nature trails.

Chicheley

5 miles NE of Milton Keynes on the A422

This attractive village is home of **Chicheley Hall**, a beautiful baroque house that was built in the early 18th century for Sir John Chester and which remains today one of the finest such houses in the country. Down the years it was used by the military and as a school, but in 1952 it was bought by the 2nd Earl Beatty and restored to its former glory. The Earl's father, the 1st Earl, was a particularly courageous naval commander and, as well as receiving the DSO at the age of just 25, he was also a commander in the decisive battle of Jutland in 1916.

Newport Pagnell

3 miles NE of Milton Keynes on the A422

Modern development hides a long history at Newport Pagnell, which local archaeological finds indicate was settled in the Iron Age and during the Roman occupation. It was an important administrative centre, and in the 10th century the Royal Mint was established here. Lacemaking was once an important industry, and the town is also associated with the car-maker Aston Martin, which started life in the 1820s as a maker of coaches for the nobility. In the distinctive red, white and black Victorian police station visitors are invited every Tuesday to look round the Police Museum, where the exhibits include over 600 models of police cars, truncheons, handcuffs and a 1903 hand-drawn ambulance. *The Blue Lamp* and *Dixon of Dock Green* are remembered in the nostalgic Jack Warner Corner.

Great Linford

2 miles N of Milton Keynes on the A422

Situated on the banks of the Grand Union Canal, this village, which is now more or less a suburb of Milton Keynes, has a 13th century church, a 17th century manor house, and a **Stone Circle**, one of only a few such prehistoric monuments in the county. Despite the encroachment of its much larger neighbour, the village has retained a distinctive air that is all its own.

The central block of the present manor house was built in 1678 by Sir William Pritchard, Lord Mayor of London. As well as making Great Linford his country seat, Pritchard also provided a boys' school and almshouses for six unmarried poor of the parish. The manor house was extended in the 18th century by the Uthwatt family, relatives of the Lord Mayor, and they used various tricks to give an impressive and elegant appearance to the building. The Grand Union Canal cuts through the estate, whose grounds are now a public park. Brick kilns survive at Great Linford from

the days when bricks were in great demand for the new railway towns of Wolverton and New Bradwell.

WILLEN

1 mile N of Milton Keynes on the A509

The village Church of St Mary Magdalene, built in the late 17th century, is an elegant building in the style of Sir Christopher Wren, but Willen is also home to another house of prayer, the **Peace Pagoda and Buddhist Temple**, opened in 1980. It was built by the monks and nuns of the Nipponsan Myohoji, and it was the first peace pagoda in the western hemisphere. In this place of great tranquillity and beauty, a thousand cherry trees and cedars, donated by the ancient Japanese town of Yoshino, have been planted on the hill surrounding the pagoda, in memory of the victims of all wars.

GREAT LINFORD LAKES

Parc Farm, Little Linford Lane, Little Linford, Buckinghamshire MK19 7EB
Tel: 01908 612052 Fax: 01908 615776

Trout fishing and shooting are among the facilities offered by owner David Marle at **Great Linford Lakes**. Three hundred and fifty well-kept acres on the northern outskirts of Milton Keynes were originally gravel beds, where extraction started in the 1940s and included the supply of building material for the construction of the town from 1967 to 1969.

It then returned to nature and became a wildlife reserve, and bird watching and the study of the indigenous flora and fauna remain popular activities. The site contains extensive woodland, 12 lakes and 2½ miles of river frontage, and is open for both individual visits and corporate events that could include guided walks as well as excellent lake and river fishing and clay pigeon shooting. The nearby village of Great Linford, on the banks of the Grand Union Canal, has several attractions, including a 13th century church, a fine 17th century manor house and a Stone Circle, one of very few in the county.

2 THE THAMES VALLEY

The Thames has played a major role in the history of England down the centuries; it rises in the Cotswolds and wends its way through the varied landscapes of several counties and on through London before entering the North Sea at Tilbury; the total length is some 210 miles and its tributaries include the Churn, Coln, Windrush, Evenlode, Cherwell, Kennet, Loddon, Wey and Mole. Most of its length was eventually made navigable by barges, with the help of locks, and nowadays long stretches are used for leisure and sport. The Victorians and the Edwardians, with their passion for boating, were responsible for the development of many fashionable towns and villages along the Thames. One of the best known places on its banks is Henley-on-Thames, famous for the annual regatta that has attracted visitors and competitors for over 150 years. Villages and ancient crossing points are scattered along the river, and the banks and towpaths afford pleasant walks and delightful scenery. At various points along the river, visitors can watch the annual tradition of swan upping, an event that dates back to the 12th century. Every year, in mid-July, the swan marking begins at Sunbury and finishes at Abingdon Bridge. The birds are examined for beak marks which distinguish the royal swans (unmarked beaks) from those with nicked beaks; the latter belong to the ancient livery companies of Vintners and Dyers. The cygnets, which are about two months old at the time of the upping, have their beaks nicked or not nicked according to the stretch of the Thames in which they are examined. Much of the ceremonial survives, with different colours for the uniforms of the various participants in their wooden skiffs, but the occasion is also an opportunity to monitor the welfare of the birds, which increasingly risk damage from the growing numbers of anglers and river traffic. In the west of the county the Berkshire Downs spread across the border, and among the ancient towns and villages and landmarks are Wantage, the birthplace of Alfred the Great, and the region's most famous sight, the Uffington White Horse cut in chalk on a hillside. Oxford, the city of dreaming spires, began to develop from a small walled Saxon town with the influx of students and scholars in the 12th century. With over 40 colleges making up the University, this seat of learning has

Kennet Horse Boat

Henley-on-Thames

influenced thinking throughout the world for centuries, and the thousands of visitors who flock here each year can see some of the finest buildings in the whole country. The region has revealed many traces of prehistoric settlement, but it was with the Norman Conquest of 1066 that the strategic importance of the Thames Valley was recognised and the first Windsor Castle built.

The Ridgeway, Oxfordshire

LOCATOR MAP

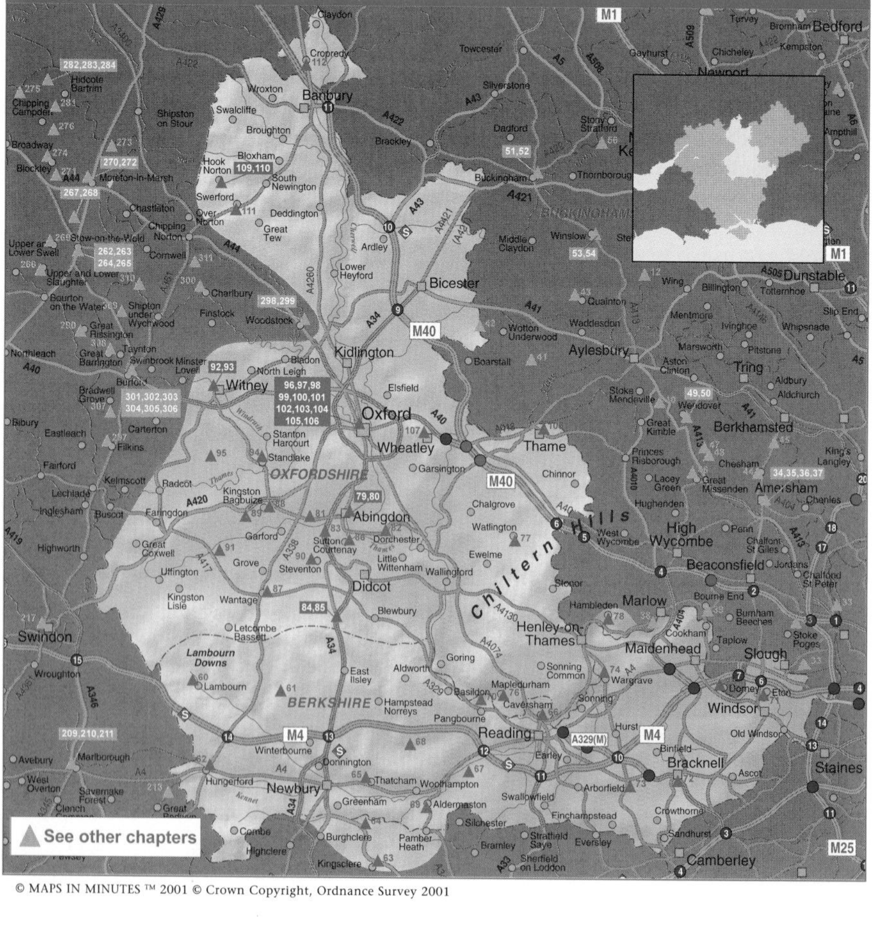

ADVERTISERS AND PLACES OF INTEREST

BERKSHIRE

The county of Berkshire extends over some 485 square miles in the valley of the middle Thames and is divided into six main districts. The western area of the county is important for racing and the training of racehorses, with a top-class course at Newbury and the training centres of Lambourn and East Ilsley. Another feature of West Berkshire is the number of communication routes that flow across the region linking London with the West Country, dominated today by the M4 motorway. The ancient Ridgeway Path, England's oldest road, follows the county border with Oxfordshire, and the Kennet and Avon Canal, completed in 1810, crosses southern England from Bristol to join the River Thames at Reading. Entering the county at Hungerford, this major waterway passes through a charming rural landscape as it winds through villages and market towns. The canal prospered until the arrival of the Great Western Railway in 1841, after which it inevitably declined; by the 1950s it was largely unnavigable. After a full clearing and restoration programme the canal can now once again be travelled its full length, providing a wide variety of leisure activities for thousands of visitors each year. The central region of Berkshire is dominated by Reading, a thriving commuter town with excellent links to both London and the West Country. Though seeming to be very much a product of the last two centuries, it has a long and interesting history. The Thames, forming the northern county border with Oxfordshire, has, especially along its southern banks, many delightful villages which became fashionable thanks to the Victorian and Edwardian passion for boating and remain fashionable to this day. The most important landmark in the east of the county is the 900-year-old Windsor Castle, one of three official residences of the Queen and a major tourist attraction. Across Windsor Great Park, the remains of a royal hunting forest, lies Ascot racecourse, founded in 1711 by Queen Anne. Five days in June see the world's of fashion and horseracing meet at the highest level at the Royal Ascot meeting, but the course stages many meetings throughout the year.

LAMBOURN

Lying up on the Berkshire Downs, in the extreme west of the county, this village, which has the feel of a small town, is best known as a major centre for the training of racehorses. Over 1,200 horses are trained here, there are more than 100 miles of gallops, and the **Lambourn**

Lambourn

Trainers' Association organise guided tours of the stables and trips to the gallops to view the horses going through their paces. Lambourn has been home to some of the greatest trainers in the history of the racing game, including Fred Winter and Fulke Walwyn over the jumps and Barry Hills and Peter Walwyn on the flat. Apart from the horses, Lambourn has plenty to amuse and occupy the visitor. Its medieval **Church of St Michael** is one of the finest parish churches in Berkshire. Originally Norman and constructed on the cruciform plan, it has been greatly altered and extended, though the west end still has its Norman doorway, complete with zigzag ornamentation. The lychgate was dedicated to the memory of William Jousiffe, who brought horses from Newmarket to Lambourn in the 1870s and thus established a still-flourishing industry.

To the north of the village are **Lambourn Seven Barrows**, one of the most impressive Bronze Age burial sites in the country and actually comprising no fewer than 32 barrows.

AROUND LAMBOURN

EAST ILSLEY
10 miles E of Lambourn off the A34

This attractive downland village has managed to retain several interesting features and in particular the winding mechanism of the now long disused village well by the pond. It was on sheep that the village chiefly prospered and from the beginning of the 17th century East Ilsley held fortnightly sheep fairs that were second only in size to Smithfield, London. At their peak in the 19th century, permanent pens were erected in the main street to contain the animals and, on one day, it was recorded

THE HARE & HOUNDS

Lambourn Woodlands, Lambourn,
Berkshire RG7 7JD
Tel: 01488 71386 Fax: 01488 72329

Fine food, a good choice of wines, well-kept ales and a friendly, relaxed ambience keep the customers coming back to the **Hare & Hounds**, which stands on the B4000 at Lambourn Woodlands (Junction 14 or 15 from the M4). The enormous pub sign depicts a hare and two hounds sitting at a table enjoying a drink together, while inside, the bars boast many attractive features, including flagstones, wooden pillars and beams, country furniture, pictures, prints and a handsome gilt-framed mirror.

The bar and restaurant manager, Anita Andrews, has the services of an outstanding team of chefs. They produce a variety of dishes, some familiar pub favourites, others less often seen on pub menus. Among the former could be bangers and mash or Aberdeen Angus steaks, direct from their suppliers in Aberdeen, while the mouthwatering printed menu, which is changed regularly, might include such tempting choices as seared scallops and seafood risotto flavoured with crab bisque, confit of duck leg or slow-roasted chump of lamb served with gratin dauphinois, boudin blanc and a thyme and garlic jus. And few diners can resist desserts like honey-roasted figs with blueberry ice cream.

that 80,000 sheep were penned. During the 19ᵗʰ century the station in the nearby village of **Compton** became an important centre for the passage of sheep to and from the great East Ilsley sheep, but with the decline in the sheep trade resulted in the closure of the station. About a mile south of Compton lie the remains of an Iron Age fort, Perborough Castle, while to the northeast, just above the Ridgeway, is Lowbury Hill, where traces of a Roman temple and a Roman military outpost can be seen. Today, along with its neighbour, West Ilsley, the village is associated with racehorses, which use the gallops on the downs as their training grounds.

Hampstead Norreys
12 miles E of Lambourn on the B4009

Just to the north of the village lies **Wyld Court Rainforest**, an education and conservation charity devoted to the raising of awareness about the world's rain forests. Here, at the indoor rainforest, where the temperature never falls below 70°C, visitors have the opportunity to walk through the humid and shadowy jungles of the Lowland Tropical Forests, the cool, orchid-festooned and ferny Cloudforests, and the Amazon with its amazing flowers and wonderful bromeliads. There is also a unique collection of spectacular and rare plants, tranquil pools, the sounds of the

topics, and rainforest animals including a pair of time marmosets, tree frogs, iguanas, and Courtney the dwarf crocodile. Also on site are a shop selling plants and gifts, and a tea shop.

NEWBURY

This crossroads town has, for many years, dominated the rural area of West Berkshire. Prospering during the Middle Ages, and afterwards, on the importance of the woollen industry, the town became famous as **The Cloth Town**. Among the various characters who made their money out of the weaving of the wool the best known is Jack of Newbury, who died in 1519. Asked to raise two horsemen and two footmen for Henry VIII's campaign against the Scots, Jack raised 50 of each and led them himself. However, they only got as far as Stony Stratford in Buckinghamshire before news of the victory of Flodden reached them and they turned for home. In fact, Jack of Newbury, christened John Smallwood and also known as John of Winchcombe, was rather more than just a local merchant and his life story has become a local legend. The son of a draper, he was apprenticed to a rich Newbury clothmaker, and when his master died, Jack married the widow and upon her death inherited the prosperous business. Over the years he became one

The Ibex

Main Street, Chaddleworth, Newbury, Berkshire RG20 7ER
Tel: 01488 638311

This is good walking country, and ramblers are among the many visitors who enjoy the friendly service and happy atmosphere of the **Ibex**. Karen Munday took over the lease after working at this splendid pub for ten years, and the sturdy redbrick building remains firmly at the social hub of village life. The inside of the Ibex is agreeably traditional, with old beams and open fires. Ruddles Best is one of the many ales in the bar, and Karen offers a full menu of home-cooked dishes such as potato skins with chilli or beef and mushrooms in red wine. At the back of the pub is a delightful beer garden and patio.

The Kennet, Newbury

of the town's leading merchants, employing as many as a thousand people. After displaying his loyalty to the king, Jack was offered a knighthood which he turned down on the grounds that he wanted to remain equal with his workers. Evidence of the town's wealth can be seen in the splendid 'Wool' **Church of St Nicholas**, which was constructed between 1500 and 1532. Built on the site of a Norman church, no expense was spared and Jack of Newbury gave the money for the magnificent five-bayed nave. The church has seen much restoration work, particularly during the Victorian age, but the fine pupil and elaborately decorated nave roof have survived.

During the Civil War two battles were fought nearby, in 1643 and 1644, and following the war, the town's clothing industry declined. However, the 18th century saw the construction of turnpike roads and Newbury became a busy coaching stop on the road from London to Bath. The town further opened up to travellers and the needs of carriers with the completion of the **Kennet and Avon Canal** in 1810. **Newbury Lock**, built in 1796, was the first lock to be built along the canal and it is also the only one to have lever-operated ground paddles (the sluices that let in the water) which are known as 'Jack Cloughs'. Back in the centre of the town, in the Market Square is the **Newbury Museum**, housed in the 17th-century cloth hall and the adjacent 18th century granary, a store used by traders travelling the canal. As well as the archaeological section, the history of the town is fully explained, including the two battles of Newbury during the Civil War.

Just to the north of the town lies **Shaw House**, a splendid example of Elizabethan architecture and the finest in Berkshire. It was built around 1581 by a wealthy clothing merchant, Thomas Dolman, who chose to put his money into this elaborate house rather than his business, much to the displeasure of his workers. The house is not open to the public but can be glimpsed from the road.

Those arriving in Newbury from the south will pass the **Falkland Memorial**, which has nothing to do with the 1980s conflict in the South Atlantic. It is in fact a memorial to Lord Falkland, who was killed at the first battle of Newbury in 1643. Battles of a less lethal kind are fought just five minutes from the town centre at Hot Shots, one of the country's most popular paint ball sites, attracting up to 200 shooters each day. To the east of the town lies **Newbury Racecourse**, which stages top-quality flat and National Hunt racing throughout the year.

AROUND NEWBURY

DONNINGTON

1 mile N of Newbury on the B4494

Despite being so close to the town of Newbury, Donnington has managed to retain its village identity and atmosphere. To the west of the village,

Donnington Castle

and visible from the road, is Donnington Grove House. Built in 1759 and designed by the architect John Chute, this was the home, in the late 18th century, of the Brummell family; Beau Brummell, the instigator of the Bath Society, lived here as a child. However, most visitors to the village come to see **Donnington Castle**, a late-14th century defence that was built by Sir Richard Abberbury. Once a magnificent structure, only the twin towered gatehouse survives amidst the impressive earthworks. Owned by English Heritage, the castle had its most eventful period during the Civil War when it was the scene of one of the longest sieges of the conflict. Charles I's troops were held here for 20 months and this was the time when most of the castle was destroyed. During the second of the two battles of Newbury, Charles I stayed at nearby Shaw House, while Sir John Boys defended the castle.

WINTERBOURNE

3 miles N of Newbury off the B4494

Just south of the village lies **Snelsmore Common Country Park**, one of the county's most important natural history sites. The common comprises several different habitats, including woodland, heathland and bog, and it supports a correspondingly wide variety of plant and animal life.

HUNGERFORD

8 miles W of Hungerford on the A4

Although not mentioned in the Domesday Book, by the Middle Ages this old market town was well established, and the manor of Hungerford had some distinguished lords including Simon de Montford and John of Gaunt. Hungerford's heyday came in the 18th century when the turnpike road from London to Bath was built, passing through the town. By 1840, the town had eight coaching inns serving the needs of travellers and the prosperity continued with the opening of the Kennet and Avon Canal, but the building of the railway took much of the trade away and the town reverted to its early, gentle lifestyle. However, several of the old coaching inns have survived and, in particular, The Bear Hotel. Although it has an impressive Georgian frontage, the building actually dates back to 1494, making it one of the oldest in the town.

Kennet and Avon Canal, Hungerford

HIGHCLOSE FARM SHOP & PICK YOUR OWN

Bath Road (A4), Hungerford, Berkshire RG7 0SP
Tel: 01488 686770 Fax: 01488 681380
e-mail: sophie@thefarmshop.co.uk
website: www.thefarmshop.co.uk

Top-quality farm produce is the mainstay of **Highclose Farm Shop & Pick Your Own**, which operates from a large modern barn-style building set back from the main A4. Alan and Christine Holland started the PYO facility back in the 1960s as an adjunct to their farming enterprise. Alan and son Jonathan now concentrate on the 14,000 acre farm ('everything except sheep and chickens'), while Jonathan's wife Sophie runs the farm shop.

Completing the team at the top is Steve Gallimore, who manages the PYO side and the increasingly

important involvement in farmers markets. The 40 acres of PYO land provide a splendid choice of fruit and vegetables, which can also be bought in the shop. Other goods for sale in the spacious barn include organic and free-range meats, an extensive range of farmhouse cheeses, jams and preserves, chutneys, relishes and sauces, dairy produce, smoked salmon, quails' eggs, ice creams, meringues, hot and cold pastries, fresh bread, delicatessen items and frozen fruit and vegetables. In one corner is Brambles Coffee Shop, where morning coffee, lunches and afternoon teas are served.

It was here, in 1688, that a meeting took place between William of Orange and representatives of James II, which culminated in the end of the House of Stuart and the flight of James II to France. As well as still holding a weekly market, the town also continues the ancient tradition known as the Hocktide Festival or Tutti Day (tutti meaning a bunch of flowers). Held every year on the second Tuesday after Easter, the festival was originally used as a means of collecting an early form of council tax. During the colourful event, two men carrying a six-foot pole decorated with ribbons and flowers go around each household collecting the tax. To ease the burden of their visit, the men share a drink with the man of the house, give him an orange, and kiss his wife before collecting their penny payment. Today, however, though the visits are still made, no money is collected.

COMBE
7 miles SW of Newbury off the A338

The isolated hamlet of Combe is overlooked by **Walbury Hill**, which at 974 feet is the highest point in Berkshire and the highest chalk hill in England. A popular place for walking and hang-gliding, the hill offers terrific views and the bonus of an Iron Age fort on its summit. Close to the hill stands **Combe**

Combe Gibbet

Gibbet, one of the last public hanging places in the country. This gibbet was first used in 1676 to hang a pair of adulterous murderers, George Broomham and Dorothy Newman, and has a crossbar with a 'his' side and a 'hers' side.

BURGHCLERE

4 miles S of Newbury off A34

The village is home to the **Sandham Memorial Chapel**, which was built in the 1920s to remember the dead of World War I. What makes this chapel so interesting are the internal murals, which entirely cover the walls and are considered by many to be Stanley Spencer's greatest achievement. An extraordinary project, the murals illustrate the artist's experiences as a medical orderly during the war and the everyday routine of a soldier's life. The pictures reach a climax with the huge *Resurrection of the Soldiers* which

completely fills the east wall. This modern chapel is found amid beautiful and tranquil scenery with views across **Watership Down**.

GREENHAM

1½ miles SE of Newbury off the A34

Greenham Common and the adjacent **Crookham Common** make up the largest area of lowland heathland in Berkshire. In 1941 the common land was taken over by the Air Ministry and became an important military base, first for British squadrons and then for the American Air Force. In 1981 nuclear-armed Cruise missiles arrived at Greenham and the site became notorious for the anti-nuclear demonstrations. The airbase is gradually being returned to nature and the site is once again open to the public; designated a Site of Special Scientific Interest (SSSI), it is home to many rare and endangered plants and animals.

BY APPOINTMENT

The Old Miller's House, 18 Swan Street, Kingsclere, Berkshire RG20 5PJ
Tel: 01635 297113 (workshop 01635 299066)
e-mail: batlegg@bun.com

The local miller has long gone, and his house is now the home of **By Appointment** and its owners Barbara Legg and Mark Townsin. An interior designer by discipline, with many years' experience in the retail business, Barbara has stocked her splendid little shop with high-quality items large and small, including 18th and 19th century furniture, treen, accessories and gifts to suit any purse and any occasion.

Porcelain trinket boxes, lamps and lampshades, cachepots and jardinières, walking sticks, cushions, candles, glasses and quilted notice boards are just a few of the stock on display in the window and on floors and shelves throughout the shop. Four miles away from the shop is the workshop of Barbara's partner Mark Townsin, a skilled antique restorer and cabinet maker who will undertake commissions large or small. The workshop also offers the services of antique furniture restoration, French polishing, upholstery, gilding, china repairs, carving and caning. Open only two days a week, the shop hours are 9.30 to 5.00 Friday and Saturday - and by appointment outside of these times. Kingsclere is an attractive village with a pleasing mix of architectural styles, a mix seen at its most appealing in Swan Street, where By Appointment is located.

Darling Buds Of May Plants Nursery

Newbury Road, Headley, Thatcham,
Berkshire RG19 9LA
Tel: 01635 269308 Fax: 01635 269828

Since they took over **Darling Buds of May** in 1996 partners Sheila and Kevin have added the wealth of experience that has made the plant nursery what it is today. Darling Buds is a business born out of passion: Sheila's love of growing plants from seeds and cuttings means that each and every plant from the wide range of perennial (shrubs and herbaceous borders) and annual (bedding and basket) plants is lovingly home-grown on site for quality and value for money. Pottering round the nursery is an experience that is both relaxing and enjoyable, and the River Enborne running through the property is an added delight.

Darling Buds stocks only the best, and professional advice on gardening and garden design is always close by from Sheila and her many reference guides. As a local grower the nursery can offer not only competitive rates but the friendly, personal service that brings people back again and again. Hanging baskets are a speciality, and in 2000 they supplied the winner of the 'most floriferous pub in North Hampshire' award. Customers can bring their own tubs or baskets to fill, choose their favourites and have them expertly arranged or take their pick from the selection of ready-filled baskets and tubs.

Thatcham

2 miles E of Newbury on the A4

Believed to be the oldest village in Britain, it is hard to imagine that this now large suburb of Newbury was once a small place. **Thatcham Moor** is one of the largest areas of inland freshwater reed beds in the country and, as well as the reeds which can grow up to six feet in height, the area supports numerous species of marshland and aquatic plants. Birds also abound here and it is an important breeding ground for reed and sedge warblers.

Thatcham Nature Discovery Centre, a multi-activity based centre, situated close to the Thatcham Moors Local Nature Reserve (see panel on page 92).

READING

This thriving commuter town, which took its name from the Saxon chief Reada, is a delightful combination of over a thousand years of history and a vibrant and modern city. There are Victorian brick buildings nestling beside beautiful medieval churches, famous coaching inns opposite high tech offices and some of the best shopping in the area. However, Reading began as a Saxon settlement between the Rivers Thames and Kennet and as a defensible site was used by the Danes as a base for their attack on Wessex in the 9th century. The town grew up around its **Abbey**, which was founded in 1121 by Henry I, the youngest son of William the Conqueror, and it was consecrated by Thomas à Becket in 1164. The abbey went on to become one of the most important religious houses - its relics include a piece of Jesus' shoe, the tooth of St Luke, and a slice of Moses' rod - and Henry, its great benefactor, was buried in front of the High Altar in 1136. Today, the

Thatcham Nature Discovery Centre

Muddy Lane, Lower Way, Thatcham, Berkshire RG7 3FU
Tel: 01635 874381 Fax: 01635 866991

Thatcham Nature Discovery Centre is situated off Lower Way on the northern side of Thatcham Lake close to the Thatcham Moors Local Nature Reserve. The centre is a multi-activity base where visitors are encouraged to look, listen, touch and learn through an exciting range of interactive exhibits. In Discovery Hall they can find out what lives below the lake, get a bird's eye view of the world or relax and watch the wildlife from the comfort of the lakeside observation area. Upstairs is the Green Gallery, which invites visitors to consider the benefits of sustainable lifestyle choices.

The reserve is one of outstanding importance for nature conservation, as the reed beds represent one of the largest stretches of inland reeds remaining in the country. The area is home to a variety of birdlife, including large breeding populations of reed and sedge warblers; many rare insects are also to be found, among them the spectacular Scarlet Tiger Moth.

Outside, visitors can watch birds from the hide, and enjoy a walk round the nature trails and lakeside footpaths. There are picnic tables, and two exciting adventure playgounds. The site is enhanced by the local council's innovative approach to works of art in public places: artists and craftspeople have been allowed to bring their imagination, vision and talents to the reserve, seen notably in some beautiful and unusual pieces in local wood by sculptors Alison Crowther and Claire Wilks. The Discovery Centre runs a full and varied programme of events including a rural craft day, summer holiday activities and in the Café gallery, exhibitions of art, sculpture and photography for visitors to enjoy over a cup of cappuccino and slice of homemade cake. The RSPB education service run from the centre is a high quality field work programme where all courses have been designed to meet the requirements of the National Curriculum. Specially trained field teachers involve and instruct the children providing a day which is fun, educational and thought provoking.

atmospheric abbey ruins stand in **Forbury Gardens** on the banks of the River Kennet; these gardens are also home to the **Maiwand Lion**, which commemorates the men of the Berkshire Regiment who died in the Afghan War of 1879. Reading boasts several other pieces of distinguished public art, including the Robed Figure by Dame Elizabeth Frink and the Soane Obelisk designed by Sir John Soane, architect of the Bank of England. Adjacent to the abbey ruins is another of Reading's famous buildings - **Reading Gaol**. Hardly a tourist attraction, it was here that Oscar Wilde was imprisoned and where he wrote *De Profundis*. His confinement here also inspired the writer to compose the epic *Ballad of Reading Gaol* whilst staying in Paris in 1898. Though the town developed during the Middle Ages as a result of a flourishing woollen industry, it was during the 18th century with the coming of both the turnpike roads and the opening of the **Kennet and Avon Canal** which saw the town boom. By the 19th century, Reading was known for its three Bs: beer, bulbs, and biscuits. As the trade of the canal and River Thames increased, the movement of corn and malt explains the growth of the brewing trade, and the leaders in the bulb trade were Sutton Seeds, founded here in 1806 but now just a memory. The world renowned biscuit-making firm of Huntley & Palmer began life here in 1826, when Joseph Huntley founded the firm, to be joined, in 1841, by George Palmer, inventor of the stamping machine.

The Story of Reading, a permanent exhibition at the **Museum of Reading**, is the ideal place to gain a full understanding of the history of the town, from the earliest times to the present day. Here, too, can be seen the world's only full size replica of the Bayeux Tapestry, made in the 19th century and featuring Edward the Confessor, once Lord of the Royal Manor in Reading, as a central figure. As a contrast to the museum's displays depicting the life of the town in the 20th century, The Silchester Gallery is devoted to the describing day to day life at Calleva Atrebatum, the Roman town of Silchester, using Roman artefacts unearthed there during early excavations. This museum, one of the most go-ahead in the country, has special events and changing exhibitions throughout the year, so every visit will reveal something new and exciting to see.

Situated on the banks of the River Kennet and housed in a range of canal buildings, **Blake's Lock Museum** describes the life of the town in the 19th and early 20th centuries. Originally part of a pumping station built at Blake's Weir in the 1870s, the buildings themselves are also of interest and are superb examples of Victorian industrial architecture combined with decorative Reading brickwork. In 1925 Reading

Blake's Lock Museum

Extension College became a university in its own right. Lying to the south of the town centre at Whiteknights, the university campus is home to the **Rural History Centre**, the national centre for the history of food, farming and the countryside. The centre has one of the country's finest collections of artefacts relating to daily life and work in the countryside, an extensive library and archives and over 750,000 photographic images of rural life. Also in the university building are the Ure Museum of Greek Archaeology and the Cole Museum of Zoology.

River Thames, Sonning

AROUND READING

Caversham

1 mile N of Reading on the A4155

An old settlement that was once an important place of pilgrimage. Visitors travelled great distances to St Anne's Well, where they believed that their ailments could be cured.

Sonning

3 miles NE of Reading off the A4

This pretty little village leading down to the Thames is a popular spot to visit, especially on summer weekends. In 1399, after he had been deposed, Richard II brought his young bride Isabella here to be looked after in the palace of the Bishops of Salisbury. Her ghost is said to appear on the paths beside the river. On Grove Street stands **Turpin's**, a house which belonged to the aunt of Dick Turpin and provided occasional refuge for the notorious highwayman. Behind the wall of the old bishop's palace is Deanery Gardens, a house built in 1901 to the design of Sir Edwin Lutyens.

Hurst

4½ miles E of Reading off the A321

This attractive, scattered village is home to a Norman church, well endowed with monuments, and a row of fine 17th century almshouses. The village bowling

The Clock Workshop

17 Prospect Street, Caversham, Reading, Berkshire RG4 8JB
Tel: 0118 947 0741 Fax: 0118 947 4194
e-mail: theclockworkshop@supanet.com

John Michael Yealland, FBHI, offers a high-quality restoration service for clocks, barometers and scientific instruments at the **Clock Workshop**, which stands in a row shops near the Thames at Caversham. All types of mechanical and dial restoration, gilding, case repairs and lacquer work are undertaken, and the shop also stocks a wide range of fully restored antique clocks and barometers for sale. John, who trained in London and spent five years with the renowned Strike One, set up in Caversham in 1981 and runs the shop with a staff of four.

green is said to have been made for Charles II.

Just to the south lies **Dinton Pastures Country Park**, a large area of lakes, rivers, hedgerows and meadows rich in wildlife. Until the 1970s, this area was excavated for sand and gravel, but the former pits are now attractive lakes and ponds; one of them has been stocked for coarse fishing and the largest is set aside for canoeing and windsurfing.

FINCHAMPSTEAD
8 miles S of Reading off the A327

To the east of the village lie **Finchampstead Ridges**, a popular spot for walkers that offers wonderful views across the Blackwater Valley. Simon's Wood has a varied mixture of conifers and broad-leaved trees, and in the wood and on the heath are siskin and flycatchers, dragonflies, damselflies and a wide range of invertebrates and lichens.

ARBORFIELD
4 miles S of Reading on the A327

Arborfield Garrison is the home base of REME, the Royal Electrical and Mechanical Engineers, and the site of their museum. To the south is **California Country Park**, a wooded beauty spot where the woods support 34 different species of tree and the bogland provides a range of habitats for the many animals, birds and plants that are found here.

SWALLOWFIELD
5 miles S of Reading off the A33

This ancient settlement has been inhabited since prehistoric times and in 1071 the manor was held by Roger de Breteuil, the originator of the Domesday Survey. Since then, the manor house, **Swallowfield Park**, has been associated with both royalty and other notables. The present house (unfortunately now but a shell) was built in 1678 by Wren's assistant William Talman for the 2nd Earl of Clarendon, who acquired the estate upon marrying the heiress. In 1719, the park was purchased by Thomas Pitt, a former Governor of Madras, who used the proceeds of the sale of a large diamond he bought while out in India. The diamond can now be seen in the Louvre Museum, Paris, and Pitt's story was the basis of the novel, *The Moonstone*, by Wilkie Collins, who visited the house in 1860. The Italian Doorway, by Talman, is probably the house's most outstanding remaining feature and it marks the entrance to the walled garden. Here can be found a dog's graveyard where lies one of Charles Dickens' dogs, which the novelist bequeathed to his friend and owner of the house, Sir Charles Russell.

ALDERMASTON
9 miles SW of Reading on the A340

It was in this tranquil village, in 1840, that the William pear was first

THE OLD MANOR
Whitehouse Green, Sulhamstead, Berkshire RG7 4EA
Tel: 0118 983 2423 Fax: 0118 983 6262

Ten acres of delightful, peaceful grounds surround the **Old Manor** (circa 1600), which has been lovingly renovated and extended by owners Peter and Rosemary Sanders-Rose. Comfort, elegance and a warm, friendly atmosphere combine to make a perfect choice for a break in the country. The letting accommodation comprises two glamorous beamed suites, the East with a dressing room and en suite bathroom with bath and shower, the West with a four-poster bed and whirlpool bath. A splendid breakfast is served in the intimate dining room, and guests can join the hosts, both excellent cooks, for a family supper. No smoking. No children under 10.

The Bull Country Inn

Stanford Dingley, Nr Reading,
Berkshire RG7 6LS
Tel: 0118 974 4409

Country lanes north of the A4 lead to the village of Stanford Dingley and the 15th century **Bull Country Inn**, which since October 2000 has been owned and run by Robert and Kate Archard and Robin and Carol Walker. The pub, set in grounds of 1½ acres, has always had a loyal following, but now that it is in the hands of locals who 'liked it so much they bought it', the Bull is set to become a centre of the community once again. Traditional country inn values are maintained, and the menus offer variety and value for money.

In March 2002 a new dining room and six well-equipped Bed & Breakfast rooms were opened, adding to the amenities without detracting from the original 'inn' characteristics. The Bull is of special interest to classic car enthusiasts (Jaguars in particular) and motor sport: one of the bars is themed in this vein, while the other remains a very popular tap room with old beams, a section of wattle and daub and an ancient pub game called ring-the-bull. Throughout the year the Bull hosts folk music evenings and is visited at least twice a year by the Kennet Morris Men. A local bloodhound hunt leaves from the pub every Boxing Day. There are also monthly 'classic Saturdays', when owners of classic cars and bikes gather in the grounds.

White Tower Nursery

Aldermaston Village, Berkshire RG7 4LD
Tel: 0118 9712123 Fax: 0118 971 4101
e-mail: chrissy@whitetowernursery.freeserve.co.uk

The White Tower Nursery and Garden Centre is owned and run by the hardworking team of Chrissy and Peter Clemson, who over the past ten years have built up an excellent reputation for quality, value for money and friendly personal service. Chrissy is a real expert in the plant world, with qualifications that include City & Guilds Phase 1 and 2 in Amenity Horticulture (top in the country in Phase 2) and HNC in Plant Physiology, Pathology and Crop Protection. Peter, an electrician by profession, can, in Chrissy's words, turn his hand to anything, and between them they have made a great success of White Tower Nursery.

Herbaceous perennials are Chrissy's first love, and in the six acres of open areas and polythene tunnels a fine variety of perennials is grown, along with bedding plants, including some unusual and obscure varieties, lovingly grown from seed and ready to enhance any garden. Besides the home-grown plants the nursery stocks composts, pots and other garden accessories, and Chrissy and her staff are always on hand to offer advice on such topics as planting, identifying customers' plants, plant diseases and garden design. The nursery, which stands on the main A340, is open from 9 to 6 Monday to Saturday and from 10 to 4 on Sunday. There is ample free parking on the site.

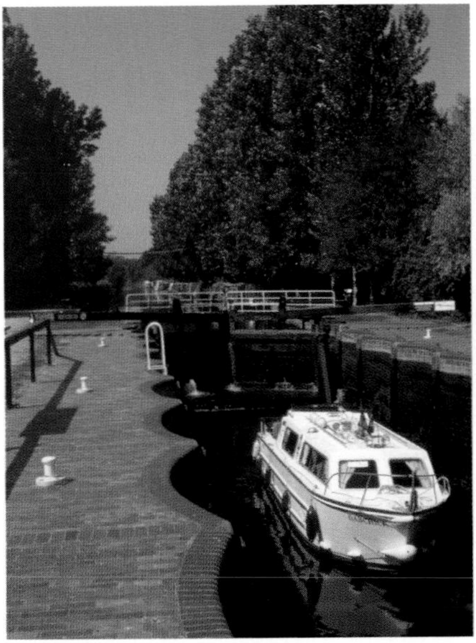

Aldermaston Wharf

propagated by John Staid, the then village schoolmaster. First known as the Aldermaston pear, a cutting of the plant is believed to have been taken to Australia where is it now called the Bartlett pear. Still retaining much of its original 12th century structure and with a splendid Norman door, the lovely **St Mary's Church** provides the setting for the York Mystery Cycle, nativity plays dating from the 14th century, which are performed here each year. Using beautiful period costumes and contemporary music, including a piece written by William Byrd, the cycle lasts a week and the plays attract visitors from far and wide. Another old custom still continued in the village is the auctioning of the grazing rights of Church Acres every three years. Using the ancient method of a candle auction, a pin, in this case a horseshoe nail, is inserted into the tallow of a candle one inch from the wick. The candle is lit while bidding takes place and the grazing rights go to the highest bidder as the pin drops out of the candle. Outside under a yew tree in the churchyard lies the grave of Maria Hale, formerly known as the Aldermaston witch. She was said to turn herself into a large brown hare and although the hare was never caught or killed, at one time a local keeper wounded it in the leg and from then on it was noticed that Maria Hale was lame!

Close to the village is a delightful walk along the Kennet & Avon Canal to **Aldermaston Wharf**. A Grade II-listed structure of beautifully restored 18th century scalloped brickwork, the wharf houses the **Kennet and Avon Canal Visitor Centre**, where the canalman's cottage contains an exhibition on the canal and information on its leisure facilities.

Woolhampton

10 miles SW of Reading on the A4

This tranquil village on the banks of the Kennet and Avon Canal had a watermill at the time of the Domesday Survey of 1086 and was mentioned again in 1351, when the manor and mill were owned by the Knights Hospitallers. The present mill, built in 1820 and extended in 1875, was powered by a brook which runs into the Kennet and was last used in 1930; it has since been turned into offices.

Aldworth

11 miles NW of Reading on the B4009

The parish Church of St Mary is famous for housing the **Aldworth Giants** - the larger than life effigies of the de la Beche family which date back to the 14th century. The head of the family, Sir Philip, who lies here with eight other members of his family, was the Sheriff of Berkshire and valet to Edward II. Though now somewhat defaced the effigies were so legendary that the church was visited by Elizabeth I. Outside, in the churchyard, are the remains of a once magnificent 1,000-year-old yew tree that was sadly damaged in a storm.

Nearby, at **Little Aldworth**, the grave of the poet Laurence Binyon, who wrote the famous lines 'At the going down of the sun and in the morning, we shall remember them' can be seen in the churchyard and, opposite the Bell Inn, is one of the deepest wells in the country. Topped by great beams, heavy cogs, and wheels, it is some 327 feet deep.

Basildon Park

Basildon

8 miles NW of Reading on the A417

This small village is the last resting place of the inventor and agricultural engineer, Jethro Tull, and his grave can be seen in the churchyard. Outside the churchyard is a classic pavilion built in memory of his parents by the late Mr Childe-Beale which is, today, the focal point of **Beale Park**. Covering some 300 acres of ancient water meadow, the park is home to a wide range of birds and animals. There are small herds of unusual farm animals, including rare breeds of sheep and goats, Highland cattle, deer, and South American llama, over 120 species of birds living in their natural habitat, and a pets' corner for smaller children. However, the park's work is not confined to the keeping of animals and, as well as planting a **Community Woodland**, an ancient reed bed has been restored. The park's other main attraction housed in the pavilion is the **Model Boat Collection**, which is one of the finest of its kind.

However, the village's main feature is the National Trust owned **Basildon Park**, an elegant, classical house designed in the 18th century by Carr of York and undoubtedly Berkshire's foremost mansion. Built between 1776 and 1783 for Francis Sykes, an official of the East India Company, the house has the unusual addition of an Anglo-Indian room. The interior, finished by JB Papworth and restored to its original splendour after World War II, is rich in fine plaster work, pictures, and furniture and the rooms open to the public include the Octagon Room and a decorative Shell Room. If the name Basildon seems familiar it is probably as a result of the notepaper: the head of the papermaking firm of Dickinson visited the house and decided to use the name for the high quality paper.

Pangbourne

5½ miles NW of Reading on the A417

Situated at the confluence of the River Pang and the River Thames, the town grew up in the late 19th and early 20th centuries as a fashionable place to live. As a result there are several attractive Victorian and Edwardian villas to be seen including a row of ornate Victorian houses known as the Seven Deadly Sins. It was here that the author Kenneth Grahame retired, living at **Church Cottage** beside the church. Graham married late in life and it was whilst

THE MODERN ARTISTS GALLERY

High Street, Whitchurch-on-Thames,
Nr Pangbourne, Berkshire RG8 7ER
Tel: 0118 984 5893 e-mail: pg@mod-art.demon.co.uk

Peggy Gibson owns and runs the **Modern Artists Gallery**, which showcases some of the finest contemporary artists from the UK and abroad. The gallery has two floors with excellent lighting, wall and floor space for paintings, sculptures and ceramics. The Gallery is situated at the foot of Whitchurch Hill and is open from 10.00am to 5.00pm Wednesday to Saturday, or by appointment.

living here that he wrote for his son *The Wind in the Willows*, the original bedtime stories based along the banks of the river between Pangbourne and Marlow.

Visitors to the town who cross the elegant iron bridge to neighbouring **Whitchurch** must still pay a toll, though now very small. The right to exact the toll has existed since 1792 and it is one of the very few surviving privately owned toll bridges. It was at **Whitchurch Lock** that the characters in Jerome K Jerome's *Three Men in a Boat* abandoned their craft, after a series of mishaps, and returned to London.

Church Cottage, Pangbourne

WINDSOR

This old town grew up beneath the walls of the castle in a compact group of streets leading from the main entrance. Charming and full of character, this is a place of delightful timber-framed and Georgian houses and shop fronts, with riverside walks beside the Thames, and a wonderful racecourse. The elegant **Guildhall**, partly built by Wren in the 17th century, has an open ground floor

for market stalls, while the council chambers are on the first floor. Concerned that they might fall through the floor onto the stalls below the council members requested that Wren put in supporting pillars in the middle of the market hall. As his reassurances that the building was sound fell on deaf ears, Wren complied with their wishes but the pillars he built did not quite meet the ceiling - thereby proving his point! The grand central station, in the heart of the town, was built in 1897 to commemorate Queen Victoria's Diamond Jubilee and it is now home to a fascinating exhibition, **Royalty and Empire**, which charts the life and times of the country's longest reigning monarch. Close by, in the High

Street, is another exhibition well worth visiting, **The Town and Crown Exhibition.** Here the development of the town and the influences of the Crown are explained in an imaginative and visual manner.

Meanwhile a trip to **The Dungeons of Windsor** provides a step back in time and an investigation of the town's history with a special regard for stories of crime and punishment from the early days of 13th century lawlessness through to the harsh Victorian era. The Household Cavalry also have their home in Windsor, at Combermere Barracks, and here is the superb **Household Cavalry Museum**, which displays collections of their uniforms, weapons, and armour from 1600 through to the present day.

In a pleasant setting close to the River Thames, **Royal Windsor Racecourse** is one of the most attractive in the country. Though less grand than neighbouring Ascot, its Monday evening meetings always bring a good crowd, but many regret the decision to give up the jumping fixtures.

The greatest attraction hereabouts is of course **Windsor Castle**, one of three official residences of the Queen (the others are Buckingham Palace and Holyrood House, in Edinburgh). The largest castle in the country and a royal residence for over 900 years, it was begun in the late 11th century by William the Conqueror as one in a chain of such defences which stood on the approaches to London. Over the years its role changed from a fortification to a royal palace; various monarchs added to the original typical Norman castle, the most notable additions being made by Henry VIII, Charles II and George IV. Various parts of the castle are open to the public, in particular the state apartments with their remarkable collection of furniture, porcelain and armour. Carvings by Grinling Gibbons are to be seen everywhere and the walls are adorned with a plethora of masterpieces, including paintings by Van Dyck and Rembrandt. The Gallery shows changing displays from the Royal Library, including works by Leonardo, Michelangelo and Holbein. On a somewhat smaller scale, but nonetheless impressive, is **Queen Mary's Dolls' House.** Designed by Sir Edwin Lutyens for Queen Mary, this is a perfect miniature palace, complete with working lifts and lights and running water. Built on a 1 to 12 scale, it took three years to complete, and 1,500 craftsmen were employed to ensure that every last detail was correct; the house was presented to the queen in 1924. In November 1992, a massive fire swept through the northeast corner of the castle and no-one in the country at the time will forget the incredible pictures of the great tower alight. Following five years of restoration, the damaged areas were re-opened to the

Windsor Castle

St George's Chapel, Windsor

public. Within the castle walls is the magnificent **St George's Chapel**. Started by Edward IV in 1478, and taking some 50 years to finish, the chapel is not only one of the country's greatest religious buildings but also a wonderful example of the Perpendicular Gothic style. It is the last resting place of ten monarchs, from Edward IV himself to Henry VIII with his favourite wife Jane Seymour, Charles I, George V with Queen Mary, and George VI, beside whom the ashes of his beloved daughter Princess Margaret were laid in February 2002. It is also the Chapel of the Most Noble Order of the Garter, Britain's highest order of chivalry. Many events will take place at Windsor and throughout the land in the course of 2002 to mark the 50th anniversary of the Queen's accession to the throne, including 'All the Queen's Horses', an equestrian spectacular due to be staged at the Royal Windsor Horse Show in May.

Frogmore House, a modest early-18th century manor house in Home Park, has over the years acted as a second, more relaxed royal residence than the nearby castle. It was bought in 1792 for Queen Charlotte, consort of George III, and was later a favourite retreat of Queen Victoria, who remarked that 'all is peace and quiet and you only hear the hum of the bees, the singing of the birds'. She and Prince Albert built a mausoleum in the grounds to house the remains of the Queen's mother, the Duchess of Kent, and their own - both Victoria and Albert are at rest here. The former library now contains furniture and paintings from the Royal Yacht *Britannia*. The house is surrounded by 30 acres of picturesque gardens containing masses of spring bulbs and some fine specimen trees.

To the south of the town lies the 4,800-acre **Windsor Great Park**, a remnant of the once extensive Royal Hunting Forest, and a unique area of open parkland, woodland, and impressive views. Within the park, at Englefield Green, is the **Savill Garden**, created by Sir Eric Savill when he was Deputy Ranger and one of the finest woodland gardens to be seen anywhere. A garden for all seasons, its attractions include colourful flower beds, secret glades, alpine meadows and a unique temperate house. The **Long Walk** stretches from the Castle to Snow Hill, some three miles away, on top of which

(Continued page 104)

Savill Garden, Windsor

WALK 3

Windsor and Eton

Start	Windsor
Distance	5½ miles (8.9km). Shorter version 3 miles (4.8km)
Approximate time	2½ hours (1½ hours for shorter version)
Parking	Windsor
Refreshments	Pubs, cafés and restaurants at Windsor and Eton, pubs at Eton Wick
Ordnance Survey maps	Landranger 175 (Reading & Windsor), Explorer 160 (Windsor, Weybridge & Bracknell)

Riverside meadows, the playing-fields of Eton and views of Windsor Castle and Eton College are the main ingredients of this flat and easy walk. Towards the end there is a particularly memorable view of Windsor Castle rising majestically above the opposite bank of the Thames. Leave plenty of time to explore the many historic attractions of Windsor.

From the banks of the Thames, Castle Hill winds up to Windsor Castle, the largest castle in Britain and a royal residence for over 900 years. It was begun by William the Conqueror in the late 11th century as one of a chain of castles defending the approaches to London, but over the centuries successive monarchs have remodelled and added to it – notably Henry II (who rebuilt the original circular keep), Henry III, Henry VIII, Charles II and George IV. Much of its present appearance dates from a particularly extensive programme of restoration and rebuilding carried out by George IV in the early 19th century. St George's Chapel, begun by Edward IV in 1478, is a masterpiece of Perpendicular Gothic architecture and contains many royal tombs. Despite all the additions and modernisation, Windsor still retains the basic plan of a Norman castle, with its varied buildings grouped around the massive 12th century (though much restored) shell keep that dominates all the views of the fortress.

Although the castle is inevitably the major draw, Windsor has other attractions, including an elegant 17th century guildhall (partly built by Wren) and the Royalty and Empire Exhibition in the Central Station. The station was built in 1897 to commemorate Queen Victoria's Diamond Jubilee and nowadays houses a display which imaginatively brings to life the celebrations of that year and the events and people of Victoria's long reign.

Across the river is Eton, whose attractive High Street leads to the red brick buildings of Eton College, founded by Henry VI in 1440 but, like Windsor Castle, added to over the centuries. Many Prime Ministers, from the Elder Pitt to Harold Macmillan, have been educated there.

Start at the pedestrianised bridge over the Thames that links Windsor and Eton, and with your back to the river and facing Windsor Castle, turn left down steps on to Thames Side to walk alongside the river. After passing the Donkey House pub go through a metal gate. Continue along a tarmac path between railings – Romney Walk – passing to the left of the station, and on meeting a tarmac track turn left along it to enter Crown Estate land. The track keeps alongside the railway line to reach a boatyard by Romney Lock.

WALK 3

Climb a stile immediately in front and walk along the riverside path to follow the Thames around a right-hand bend, passing under a railway bridge and continuing towards a road bridge. To the right are fine views across Home Park to the castle. Just before the road bridge turn sharp right across the grass to reach the road at the end of white railings, turn sharp left to cross the bridge, continue along the road for about 100 yds (91m) and turn left A on to a track that keeps along the left edge of Datchet golf-course, by trees and undergrowth bordering the river on the left.

In the far corner of the golf-course continue, by a wire fence on the right, to a public footpath sign just in front of a railway bridge. Turn left to pass under the bridge, go through a kissing-gate and then bear slightly left to continue across rough meadowland. Cross a footbridge, climb two stiles in quick succession, and walk along a narrow path to climb a third stile and emerge on to the riverbank, just to the left of a boathouse. Keep ahead along the tarmac track to a road, bear left along it and then continue along the path parallel to it. Opposite a public footpath sign turn left over a footbridge B to follow a clear, well-surfaced track across part of the playing-fields of Eton College. Just in front of a brick bridge, turn sharp right to continue along the track which curves to the left and passes through a kissing-gate by a lodge on to a road C.

For the shorter version of the walk, turn left along the road, passing Eton College and continue along Eton High Street to the starting point.

For the full walk, cross the road and go through a gate in the fence opposite, at a public footpath sign. Keep ahead across more playing-fields to cross a wide flat bridge, then join a wide track along the left margin of the sports fields (ignore the footbridge) to reach two brick cottages. Bear left along the driveway to a T-junction, turn right and keep left along the fenced lane to pass beneath the railway. Immediately beyond, keep ahead along the narrow stony path beside a ditch. Dog-leg beneath the bypass bridge and then follow the rough lane away from the embankment on a low causeway across fields to reach a four-way, waymarked footpath junction.

Turn left, cross a footbridge over Common Ditch and turn right across the meadow, keeping roughly parallel to the ditch on your right to reach a gate into a lane. Turn left and follow this around to The Greyhound pub about 200 yds (183m) away. Turn left and walk to the main road D. Turn right, cross the road and in a few paces take the signposted path on the left, the tarred route of National Cycle Route 4. Follow this straight across the lush meadows to reach the bank of the Thames E.

Turn left and follow the winding river for about 1½ miles (2.4km) back to the start, passing under both road and railway bridges again. The grand finale to the walk is the majestic view of Windsor Castle, its walls and towers rising above the opposite bank. On reaching the end of the meadows keep ahead, first along a tarmac drive and then along a road, to the bottom end of Eton High Street. Turn right to cross the bridge back into Windsor.

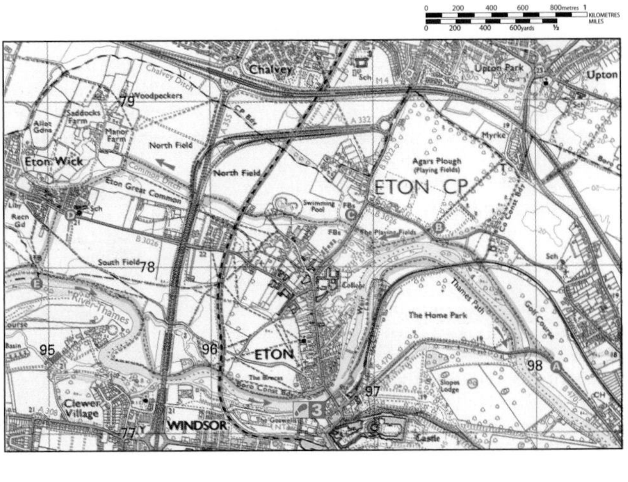

Legoland Windsor

stands a huge bronze of George III on horseback erected there in 1831. Queen Anne added the three mile ride to nearby Ascot racecourse. On the park's southern side lies **Smith's Lawn**, where polo matches are played most summer weekends. Windsor Great Park is also the setting for the Cartier International competition, polo's highlight event held every July, and the National Carriage Driving Championships.

To the southwest, set in 150 acres of parkland, is **Legoland Windsor**, where there a whole range of amazing Lego models is on display, made from over 20 million bricks.

AROUND WINDSOR

Eton

1 mile N of Windsor on the A355

Just across the River Thames from Windsor, this town has grown up around **Eton College**, the famous public school that was founded in 1440 by Henry VI. Originally intended for 70 poor and worthy scholars and to educate students

Turks Head Antiques

28 High Street, Eton, Berkshire SL4 6AF
Tel: 01753 863939

The town of Eton, just across the River Thames from Windsor, has grown up around the famous public school founded in 1440 by Henry VI. The building that houses **Turks Head Antiques** is only a little less venerable, and the legacy of its days a coaching inn can be seen in the traditional black and white frontage, the ancient beams within and the adjacent mews where coaches would enter and horses rest. Anthea Baillie has been trading in Eton since 1973, mainly in silver, and Andrew Reeve has been here since the mid-1990s, having previously been with Christies.

The small-paned bow window and the charming little shop behind it are filled with an amazing variety of interesting antique pieces, including silver, porcelain, glass, framed paintings and prints and small items of furniture, most of it dating from the Georgian period to the 1930s. The shop has a heavily beamed ceiling and a door whose stained glass window depicts the Eton College crest. The College is only five minutes away, as is Windsor Castle, and the Turks Head's neighbours include many interesting shops as well as pubs and restaurants.

Eton College

for the newly created King's College, at Cambridge University, the college has been added to greatly over the years. Of the original school buildings, only the College Hall and the kitchen have survived; the great gatehouse and Lupton's Tower were added in the 16th century and the Upper School dates from around 1690. However, the school has kept many ancient traditions over the years including the black tail mourning coats that were originally worn on the death of George III in 1820 and which are still worn today. For centuries the college has educated the great and the good, among them William Pitt the Elder, Harold Macmillan, Thomas Gray (author of *Elegy Written in a Country Churchyard*), Henry Fielding, Shelley, George Orwell and Ian Fleming. Eton has also been famous in the past for its strict discipline, personified in 1832 by a master who told the pupils when they rebelled: 'Boys, you must be pure of heart, for if not, I will thrash you until you are'.

Windsor Bridge, Eton

Slough

3 miles N of Windsor on the A355

A small settlement until the creation of a trading estate in 1920, Slough then grew rapidly from around 7,000 to 100,000. The area does have a long history, however, and a visit to **Slough Museum** makes for an interesting hour or two delving into the past. Slough has a lovely surprise in the shape of one of the most splendid churches in the county. The **Church of St Mary** at Langley Marish is a real gem, notable particularly for the private family pew of the Kedermisters, totally screened from the main part of the church, and a library filled with painted panels.

Ascot

6 miles SW of Windsor on the A329

A small village until 1711 when Queen Anne moved the Windsor race meeting to here and founded the world famous **Ascot Racecourse**. Its future was secured when the Duke of Cumberland established a stud at Windsor in the 1750s, and by the end of the century the meetings were being attended by Royalty on a regular basis. Today, Royal Ascot, held every June, is an international occasion of fashion and style with pageantry and tradition and the very best flat racing spread over four days (with an extra day in 2002 to mark the 50th anniversary of the Queen's accession to the throne).

Ascot Races

To the west of the town lies **Englemere Pond**, a Site of Special Scientific Interest and also a local nature reserve. Once part of the royal hunting ground which surrounded Windsor Castle and still owned by the Crown Estate, the main feature is the shallow acidic lake which offers a wide range of habitats from open water to marsh, for the many species of plants, birds, and animals, and insects found here.

SANDHURST

11 miles SW of Windsor on the A3095

The town is famous as being the home of the **Royal Military Academy**, the training place for army officers since it was established in 1907. The academy's **Staff College Museum** tells the history of officer training from its inception to the present day. Close by is **Trilakes**, a picturesque country park set in 18 acres with, of course, some lakes. This is a wonderful place to visit with children as there are a wide assortment of pets and farm animals which they can get

to know, including miniature horses, pygmy goats, donkeys, aviary birds, pot-bellied pigs and Soay sheep.

BRACKNELL

7 miles SW of Windsor on the A329

Designated a new town in 1948, Bracknell has developed quickly from a small place in poor sandy heathland into a large modern town with one of the first purpose built shopping centres in the country - opened in the 1960s. As well as being home to a number of high tech companies, Bracknell is also the home of the Meteorological Office.

Seen from many parts of the town and a very prominent landmark is the centrally located **Bill Hill**. At the top of the hill can be seen a circular mound of earth, hollowed out at the centre, which is all that remains of a Bronze Age round barrow. Used throughout that period, these burial mounds, which may cover either individuals or groups, are the most common prehistoric monuments in the country.

What remains of the great royal

Bracknell

Look Out Discovery Centre

Nine Mile Ride, Bracknell, Berkshire RG12 7QW
Tel: 01344 354400 Fax 01344 354422
e-mail: mark.croll@bracknell forest.govuk
website: www.bracknell forest.gov.uk/lookout

The Look Out Discovery Centre in Bracknell is a great day out for all ages. The main attraction is an exciting hands on, interactive science and nature exhibition. Budding scientists will spend many hours exploring and discovering over 70 bright, fun filled exhibits within five themes zones.

In the exhibition there is The Look Out tower. Climb the eighty eight steps and see over the Centre towards Bracknell and beyond. In the surrounding 2,600 acres of Crown Estate woodland, visitors can enjoy nature walks, a picnic area, child's play area. In the Coffee Shop you can relax over a cup of tea or take a break and have a hot lunch. The Gift Shop offers a wonderful range of gifts for every occasion or weird and wacky presents, ideal for birthday party bags at the right price. The Look Out is open daily from 10.00am - 5.00pm.

hunting ground, **Windsor Forest** (also called Bracknell Forest) lies to the south of the town and has over 30 parks and nature reserves and some 45 miles of footpaths and bridleways. Of particular interest in the area is The **Look Out Discovery Park**, an interactive science centre that brings to life the mysteries of both science and nature (see panel above). Throughout the woodland surrounding the centre there are nature trails and walks to points of interest as well as the inappropriately named **Caesar's Camp**. Not a Roman fort, this camp is an Iron Age hill fort built over 2,000 years ago but, close by, lies the Roman link road between London and Silchester. Known locally as the **Devil's Highway**, it is said to have acquired the name because the local inhabitants thought that only the Devil could have undertaken such a prodigious feat of engineering.

Binfield

8 miles SW of Windsor on the B3034

Binfield is famous as the boyhood home of the poet Alexander Pope. The family moved here after his father had amassed a fortune as a linen draper, and the boy Pope sang in the local choir and gained a local following for his poems about the Windsor Forest and the River Loddon. To the south of the village lies **Pope's Wood**, where the poet is said to have sought inspiration. Other connections include the artist John Constable, who sketched the parish church while here on his honeymoon, and Norah Wilmot, who was one of the first lady racehorse trainers to be allowed to hold a licence in her own name, having been forced to train for years in the name of her head lad. The Jockey Club abandoned this archaic ruling as recently as 1966, when a contemporary of Miss Wilmot, the 70-year-old Florence Nagle, guaranteed her place in the annals of racing history when she secured a verdict in the Court of Appeal by which the Jockey Club was obliged to grant licences to train to women. Lord Denning himself summed up the matter: 'If she is to carry on her trade without stooping to subterfuge she has to have a training licence'. Miss Wilmot saddled a winner in her own name less than 24 hours after receiving her licence; she was then aged 77 and had either run or assisted in the running of a stable for more than 50 years. Since that historic day the likes of Jenny

Holme Grange Craft Barn & Art Gallery

Holme Grange Craft Village, Heathlands Road,
Wokingham, Berkshire RG40 3AW
Tel: 0118 977 6753
website: www.holme-grange.co.uk

Holme Grange Craft Village, a varied complex of 19th and 20th Century farm buildings, is set in the heart of a rural farming area within easy reach of the M3/M4 motorways. The main buildings enclose a delightful courtyard, where snacks and light meals are served by the Tea Shoppe.

The spacious Craft Barn - once a milking barn - has retained its original wooden beams and cast-iron milking bays. It is an ideal setting in which to browse and admire the wide variety of work from around 90 local craftworkers.

The centrepiece of the village is its Art Gallery, designed to reflect the wide range of artistic talent in the area. The work of over 60 local artists - painters, sculptors, workers in wood, decorative glass and other media - is on display for viewing and purchase. The Gallery also boasts an extensive range of hand-crafted greetings cards and a wide selection of high quality silk flowers. It holds special artists' exhibitions throughout the year, and supplies a range of quality artists' materials.

The Craft Barn and Art Gallery are open seven days a week, throughout the year (closing only between Christmas and New Year). Their comprehensive web site carries all the information needed to get the most out of a visit to this artistic haven in the heart of Berkshire.

Pitman, Venetia Williams, Henrietta Knight and Mary Reveley have reached the top echelons of their profession in their own names.

Wargrave

10 miles W of Windsor on the A321

This charming village developed as a settlement in the 10th century at the confluence of the Rivers Thames and Loddon on an area of flat land in a wooded valley. The peace that generally prevails here was disturbed in 1914 when suffragettes burnt down the church in protest at the vicar's refusal to remove the word 'obey' from the marriage service. In the churchyard, undisturbed by the riot or anything since, stands the **Hannen Mausoleum**, a splendid monument that was designed for the Hannen family by Sir Edwin Lutyens in 1906.

Roy Temple Polishing

Unit 14, Sheeplands Farm, Twyford Road, Wargrave,
Nr Reading, Berkshire RG10 8DL Tel/Fax: 0118 940 2211

Roy Temple has been in the business of furniture restoration and polishing for a quarter of a century, and since the early 1990s he has based his workshop in the riverside village of Wargrave. The core work of **Roy Temple Polishing** is the restoration, repair and polishing of furniture, both antique and modern, but he also undertakes repairs at customer's premises to floors and doors, staircases and handrails, along with detailed work such as desks with leather inserts. His client base includes both private and commercial concerns and extends as far afield as Oxford and London.

Another interesting sight can be found on the outskirts of the village, at Park Place. In 1788, the estate was owned by General Henry Conway, Governor of Jersey and, in recognition of his services, the people of the island gave the general a complete **Druids' Temple**. The massive stones were transported from St Helier to the estate and erected in a 25 foot circle in the gardens of his mansion. In 1870, Park Place was destroyed by fire and the estate broken up but today the temple stands in the garden of **Temple Combe**, close to a house designed by the famed American architect, Frank Lloyd Wright. The only house of his in this country, it was built, in 1958, to an elaborate U-shaped design; its many unusual features include suede-panelled interior walls.

River Thames, Maidenhead

Maidenhead

6 miles NW of Windsor on the A4130

Transport has played a major role down the years in the history of Maidenhead, first with Thames traffic, then as a stop on the London-Bath coaching route, and finally with the coming of the railway, which helped to turn the town into a fashionable Victorian resort. The **Maidenhead Rail Bridge** was built by Isambard Kingdom Brunel in 1839 to carry his Great Western Railway over the Thames. The bridge, which comprises the widest, flattest brick arches in the world, was hailed at the time as the pinnacle of engineering achievement and has been immortalised in Turner's incredibly exciting and atmospheric painting *Rain, Steam and Speed*. **Boulter's Lock**, one of the biggest on the Thames, takes its name from an old word for a miller; a flour mill has stood on Boulter's Island since Roman times, and the island was also the home of Richard Dimbleby, the eminent broadcaster and father of the famous broadcasters David and Jonathan. To the north and west of the town, **Maidenhead Commons** and **Cock Marsh** contain a variety of habitats, including woodland, scrub thickets, grassland, ponds and riverside. Both are popular with walkers and nature-lovers: Cock Marsh is an important site for breeding waders, and both sites are rich in flora and invertebrate fauna.

Cookham

6 miles NW of Windsor on the A4094

This pretty, small town, on the banks of the River Thames, was made famous by the artist Sir Stanley Spencer, who used

Stanley Spencer Gallery, Cookham

Cookham as the setting for many of his paintings. He was born here in 1891 and was buried here on his death in 1959. The town's tribute to its most renowned resident is the **Stanley Spencer Gallery**, a permanent exhibition of his work which is housed in the converted Victorian chapel Stanley visited as a child.

DORNEY

2 miles NW of Windsor off the A308

One of the finest Tudor manor houses in England, **Dorney Court**, just a short walk from the River Thames, has been the home of the Palmer family since 1530. Built in about 1440, it is an enchanting building which also houses some real treasures, including early 15th and 16th century oak furniture, beautiful 17th century lacquer furniture, and 400 years of family portraits. It is here that

the first pineapple in England was grown in 1665.

On **Dorney Common** is the village of **Boveney**, which served as a wharf in the 13th century as timber was being transported from Windsor Forest. The flint and clapboard church of St Mary Magdalene, down by the riverside, was the setting for several scenes from Kevin Costner's film *Robin Hood Prince of Thieves*.

OXFORDSHIRE

Oxfordshire is a county covering about 1,000 square miles, contained for the most part within the Thames Basin. Between Henley and Wallingford lie the beginnings of the Chiltern Hills, while in the north are the most easterly hills of the Cotswolds as well as rich farm land based on the clay soil that stretches up from Oxford to the Midlands. In the east,

THE RESTORATION COMPANY

The Coach House, Dorney Court, Dorney, Berkshire SL4 6QL
Tel: 01628 660708

The Restoration Company enjoys the most atmospheric of settings in the old coach house of Dorney Court, one of the finest Tudor manor houses in the country. The workshop is set within a cobbled yard where horses from the riding school and livery horses are kept in ten stables. The company is owned and run by Kate Hood, who worked here for three years before taking possession in December 2001. The Restoration Company specialises in the restoration of period furniture, and the fully equipped workshop allows Kate and her assistants to work on fine furniture in a rustic setting, using the traditional methods that have been employed by craftsmen through the ages.

They keep a large stock of old, reclaimed wood, which enables the skilled staff to repair antique furniture with materials of the right age. All woodwork and finishing is undertaken by the company, whether the customer's piece of furniture needs just a little tender loving care or a complete overhaul. Dorney Court itself is well worth a visit, and the sense of history that pervades the place will not be lost on Kate, who has a degree in ancient and medieval history as well as a diploma in furniture restoration. There are some excellent walks in the locality and the village has a good pub.

Henley Regatta

Henley is one of many attractive Thamesside settlements, towards the west are Faringdon and Witney, and in the north Bicester, Chipping Norton and Banbury. The county is of course dominated by its capital, Oxford, which from the 12th century grew from a small and little known market town into one of the major seats of learning in the world. It also prospered as a central point of communication, first as a stopping point on coaching routes and later with the coming of the canals and the railways. Industry grew, too, and in the suburb of Cowley Lord Nuffield's Morris car works were a major employer. Many palaeolithic, mesolithic and neolithic finds have been made in the county, but the most eyecatching early archaeological feature is the Uffington White Horse from the Iron Age. Dorchester and Alchester were the most important sites in Roman Oxfordshire, the Saxons built many settlements along the Thames, and the Danes overran the area in the 10th and 11th centuries. The county was heavily involved in the Civil War (1642-1651) and the towns of Oxford (for 3 years the Royalist headquarters), Danbury and Wallingford were all besieged by Parliamentary forces during the conflict. The northwest region of the county lies almost wholly in the Cotswolds and is included in Chapter 7.

HENLEY-ON-THAMES

Reputed to be the oldest settlement in Oxfordshire, this attractive riverside market town has over 300 listed buildings covering several periods. The Thames has always played an important role in its life; in 1829 the first varsity boat race, between Oxford and Cambridge, took place here on the river and, within a decade, the event was enjoying royal patronage. The **Henley Regatta**, held every year in the first week of July, is a marvellous and colourful event with teams competing on the mile long course from all over the world. Opened in 1998, the **River and Rowing Museum** is a fascinating place that traces the rowing heritage of Henley, the river's changing role in the town's history, and even provides the opportunity to 'walk' the length of the River Thames, from source to sea, taking in all the locks. Housed in spacious, purpose-built premises designed by the award-winning architect, David Chipperfield, its exhibits include the boat in which the British duo, Redgrave and Pinsent, won their gold medals at the 1996 Olympics. Henley was the site of Rupert's Elm, where Prince Rupert is said to have hanged a Roundhead spy. A portion of the tree is preserved in this museum. Also situated on the riverbank, beside the town's famous 18th century bridge decorated with the faces of Father Thames and the goddess Isis, is the Leander Club, the headquarters of the famous rowing club.

Apart from the boating, which is available throughout the summer, and the pleasant walks along the riverbanks, there are lots of interesting shops, inns, and teashops in the town.

Just down river from the town centre lies **Fawley Court**, a wonderful private house that was designed by Christopher Wren and built in 1684 for a Colonel Freeman. Now owned by the Marian Fathers, the **Museum** it contains includes a library, documents relating to the Polish Kings, and memorabilia of the Polish army. The house, gardens, and museum are open to the public from March to October.

Mapledurham Estate

Mapledurham, near Reading,
Oxfordshire RG4 7TR
Tel: 01189 723350
Fax: 01189 794016
e-mail: maple@mapledurham.co.uk

Mapledurham House and Watermill nestle on the banks of the River Thames in the beautiful south Oxfordshire countryside. Visitors can watch the last working watermill in action – still producing flour – and tour the Elizabethan mansion. Cream teas are a speciality here and can be eaten in the Old Manor tearooms or on the lawns sloping down to the Thames. Arrival can also be by boat from nearby Caversham – a delightful way to start the afternoon. Open in the afternoons at weekends and Bank Holidays from Easter to the end of September.

To the northwest of Henley, at Rotherfield Greys, is another interesting house, **Greys Court**, dating originally from the 14th century but much altered down the centuries; a beautiful courtyard and a tower survive from the earliest building. A Tudor wheelhouse is among the interesting outbuildings, and the gardens offer many delights, notably old-fashioned roses and wisterias, an ornamental vegetable garden, a haha, an ice-house and the **Archbishop's Maze**, which was inspired, in 1980, by Archbishop Runcie's enthronement speech.

AROUND HENLEY-ON-THAMES

Sonning Common

3½ miles SW of Henley on the B481

An interesting feature here is the **Saxon Maze**, which was inspired by an illustration of an 8th century mythical sea creature. The grass pathways, lined by 5ft hedges, were laid to the design of Adrian Fisher, and the maze was opened in 1991.

Mapledurham

6½ miles SW of Henley off the A4074

Found down a small lane which leads to the River Thames, this tiny village is home to Mapledurham House, a Watermill, and a church. The late 16th-century home of the Blount family, **Mapledurham House** was built on the site of an older manor house and it has remained in the same family ever since. As well as viewing the great oak staircase

Mapledurham House

Mapledurham House

and the fine collection of paintings housed here, visitors will find the house's literary connections are equally interesting: Alexander Pope was a frequent visitor in the 18th century; the final chapters of John Galsworthy's *The Forsyte Saga* were set here; and it was the fictional Toad Hall in *The Wind in the Willows*. The house also featured in films, such as *The Eagle has Landed*, and the television series *Inspector Morse*.

Another attraction on the estate is the old riverside **Watermill** (see panel opposite), a handsome late-15th century construction, which stands on the site of an earlier building that was mentioned in the Domesday Book. The mill remained in operation until 1947 and it was then the longest surviving working mill on the river. Now fully restored, the traditional machinery can be seen in action grinding wholemeal flour, which is then sold through the mill shop.

The **Village Church** is also worth a visit as, during restoration work in 1863, the architect, William Butterfield, made great use of coloured brickwork and he also refaced the tower with a bold chequered pattern using flint and brick.

Goring-on-Thames

9½ miles W of Henley on the B4009

This ancient small town lies across the River Thames from its equally ancient neighbour, Streatley, and, while today they are in different counties, they were once in different kingdoms. This is a particularly peaceful stretch of the river, with the bustle of Pangbourne and Henley-on-Thames lying downstream, and it is some distance to the towns of Abingdon and Oxford further upstream.

In the 19th century, after Isambard Kingdom Brunel had laid the tracks for the Great Western Railway through Goring Gap, the village began to grow as it was now accessible to the Thames-loving Victorians. Though there are many Victorian and Edwardian villas and houses here, the original older buildings have survived, adding an air of antiquity to this attractive place.

Ewelme

9 miles NW of Henley off the B4009

At the centre of this pretty village is a magnificent group of medieval buildings, including the church, almshouses and school, which were all founded in the 1430s by Alice Chaucer, grand-daughter of the poet Geoffrey, and her husband, the Duke of Suffolk. There is a wonderfully elegant alabaster carving of Alice inside the church and under this effigy is another rather macabre carving of a shrivelled cadaver. In the churchyard is the grave of Jerome K Jerome, author of *Three Men in a Boat*, who moved to the village following the success of his book.

Watlington

8 miles NW of Henley off the B480

There are superb views over the surrounding countryside from **Watlington Hill**, which rises 700 feet above Watlington Park with its woods of

The Granary Antique And Country Furniture

31 High Street, Watlington, Oxfordshire OX9 5PZ
Tel: 01491 612530 Fax: 01491 612880

In his workshop behind a handsome old granary, Peter Hutchins produces country furniture using the finest timber and traditional craft techniques. Among the items made by Peter at **The Granary** are four-poster panelled beds in Russian redwood, oak refectory tables and elegant English dressers using mixed local hardwoods. Peter's own work is complemented by a collection of beautiful and practical antique furniture on sale in two showrooms. Each piece is personally chosen by Peter, and the range is extensive. The Granary is open from 9.00am to 5.00pm Monday to Saturday.

beech and yew. Watlington Hill and its neighbour Pyrton Hill are designated a Site of Special Scientific Interest and are home to over 30 species of butterflies and a wide variety of chalk-loving plants.

Chalgrove

10 miles NW of Henley on the B480

Chalgrove is the site of an English Heritage registered battlefield, where in 1643 Prince Rupert defeated John Hampden. An information board at the site gives details of the battle, and there is also a monument to John Hampden, a local squire and sometime MP for Buckinghamshire who refused to pay Ship Money to the King. He was taken to court in 1638 and incarcerated in the Tower of London. He was a cousin of Oliver Cromwell and in the Civil War became a leading opponent of the King.

Stonor House

Stonor

4 miles N of Henley on the B480

The village is the home of Lord and Lady Camoys and their house, **Stonor**, has been in the family for over 800 years. Set in the a wooded valley in the Chilterns and surrounded by a deer park, this attractive house dates from the 12th century though the beautiful, uniform facade is Tudor and hides much of the earlier work. The interior of the house contains many rare items, including a mass of family portraits, and there is also a medieval Catholic Chapel here that was in continuous use right through the Reformation. In 1581, Edmund Campion sought refuge at the house and an exhibition features his life and work. The gardens too are well worth a visit with their lawns, orchard and lovely lavender hedges, and they offer splendid views over the rolling parkland.

JULIAN CHRISTIAN DESIGNS LTD

Dairy Lane, Hambleden, Henley-on-Thames,
Oxfordshire RG9 3AS
Tel: 01491 413292 Fax: 01491 413232
website: julianchristian.co.uk

Julian Christian Designs is sited in an old converted
dairy building on the historic Hambleden Estate, at the
foot of the beautiful Chiltern Hills. It is approximaely 2
miles east of Henley-on-Thames, on the north side of the
River Thames and just a short distance from Hambleden
Lock.

Julian Christian Designs has quickly become synonymous with garden furniture of outstanding
design and quality. A large range of both traditional and
contemporary designs is offered, manufactured in Iroko
hardwood, a timber carefully selected for its outstanding
durabiity. Designs include the stunning 'Chelsea' triangular
table with its natural slate insert and the 'Winchester' large
round table offered with either a selection of traditional
chairs or, new for this season, specially designed curved
benches. The friendly and helpful staff will be only too
happy to discuss your requirements and demonstrate the
extensive range of outdoor furniture which is permanently
displayed in the showroom. A warm welcome is always
assured.

River Thames, Abingdon

HAMBLEDEN
3 miles NE of Henley off the A4155

Set among some of the most picturesque
Chilterns countryside, the Chiltern
Valley Winery and Brewery produces
some 120,000 bottles of wine a year and
some superb real ales. Lord Cardigan,
immortalised in the Charge of the Light
Brigade, was born in the manor house at
Hambleden; his sea chest is preserved in
the village church.

ABINGDON

This is an attractive town and one of the
country's oldest, as it grew up around a
Benedictine **Abbey** that was founded in
675. Sacked twice by the Danes for its
gold and silver, the abbey was practically
derelict by the 10th century but, under the
guidance of Abbot Ethwold, the architect
of the great Benedictine reform, it once

Frugal Food

17 West St Helen Street, Abingdon, Oxfordshire OX14 5BL
Tel: 01235 522239

Owner Valerie Stoner and her staff pride themselves on the friendly, personal and well-informed service they offer at **Frugal Food**, which occupies premises that were originally the home of a medieval merchant. Former teacher Valerie has always had a keen interest in food and health matters, and combines the two in the shop that she took over in 1991 after working there part-time. The shop itself opened in the 1970s, and over the years has built up a loyal clientele, some of whom remember it in its previous incarnation as greengrocer and dairy.

The shop window gives little clue to what lies within - an Aladdin's cave of goods and goodies in bottles and boxes and tins and packets; many products are sold loose, giving customers the maximum flexibility in terms of both choice and quantity. The range includes wholefood and organic food products, food that caters for special diets (eg gluten-free), supplements, herbal and homeopathic remedies, top-quality cheeses, hand-made chocolates, oils and vinegars and spices and preserves. They also stock a selection of baskets and hampers, which can be filled to order with customers' individual requirements. Frugal Food is open from 9.00am to 5.30pm Monday to Friday and from 9.00am to 5.00pm on Saturday.

Kingfisher Barn Holiday Cottages & Accommodation

Rye Farm, Abingdon, Oxfordshire OX14 3NN
Tel/Fax: 01235 537538 e-mail: info@kingfisherbarn.com
website: www.kingfisherbarn.com

For a short break or a relaxing holiday in quiet, scenic surroundings, **Kingfisher Barn Holiday Cottages** are the perfect choice. The cottages, Granary, Middle and Stable, were created by the conversion of old Shire horse stable buildings, and two of the three have been specifically designed for wheelchair users. Stable and Middle Cottages, sleeping four and six respectively, have all the accommodation on the ground floor, with an access ramp and wider doors.

There are ceiling hoists in the bedrooms, a wheel-in shower with seat, grab rails and sideways transfer to the toilet basin; the kitchen areas have adjustable hobs and sink height. All the rooms are efficiently heated, and accessories include tv, radio cassette player and barbecue. A heated indoor swimming pool is available by arrangement, with a hoist system if needed. The cottages are an ideal base for exploring the many places of interest in the region, and there's easy access to golf courses and beautiful riverside walks. And the town of Abingdon, only ten minutes away, has plenty to see, including several museums, a fine County Hall designed by Wren, and a wide range of shops.

again prospered and was, in its heyday, larger than Westminster Abbey. Unfortunately little remains today of this great religious house, but the **Gatehouse**, built in the late 15th century, is a splendid reminder. The largest town in the Vale of the White Horse, Abingdon was also the county town of Berkshire between 1556 and 1869, and indeed at one time the Abbot here was the largest landowner in Berkshire after the Crown.

Thames Street, Abingdon

This prosperity and importance has given the town an interesting history which can be discovered at the **Abingdon Museum** in the old County Hall. Another of the town's pleasing buildings is the **Church of St Helen**, whose steeple dominates the view southwards along the street. Originally built in the 14th century, the church was remodelled in the 15th and 16th centuries, when the town prospered from a thriving wool trade, to provide an altogether larger and more elaborate building. However, the main glory of the church, the painted

HYDE FARM NURSERIES

Marcham, Oxfordshire OX13 6NX
Tel/Fax: 01865 391054

Two very distinct enterprises are based at **Hyde Farm Nurseries**, located a short drive west of Abingdon on the A415. The telephone number above is for MARCHAM PLANTS, a series of well-stocked glasshouses on a large open site with plenty of off-road parking. Proprietor Perry Birchall's nursery, which originally specialised in fuchsias and geraniums, has expanded considerably to include special varieties of pelargonium, rare conservatory plants, rock plants, climbers, shrubs and topiary; it has built up a considerable reputation for its seasonal hanging baskets, and also stocks a full range of accessories, from pots and planters to garden ornaments, compost, fencing and sheds.

APPLAUSE

Tel/Fax: 01865 391247
e-mail: dorothea@applause-2000.demon.co.uk
website: www.applause-2000.demon.co.uk

Also located at Hyde Farm Nurseries is **Applause**, run by cat lover and cat breeder Dorothea Uebele. Her speciality breeds are Birmans, Ragdolls and Mainecoons, and viewings can be arranged by appointment. A stud service is available to approved queens. The name Applause, which is the prefix of many of the cats, was taken from a particularly beautiful fuchsia, which was one of the early specialities of the nurseries.

R&M Turnpike Forge

Clifton Hampden, Abingdon, Oxfordshire OX14 3DE
Tel: 01865 407755 Fax: 01865 407757
website: www.turnpikeforge.co.uk

Turnpike Forge, a working smithy since the early 18th century, is still in use producing a vast range of metal products for both industrial and ornamental use. The forge is located on the A415 Abingdon-Dorchester road at the site of a turnpike gate to a former tollbridge over the River Thames. The R and the M (R for Roy Hanson, M for his wife Marilyn) were added when Roy took over the forge, which he still owns and manages. Roy learnt his trade in the Armed Forces and now imparts his traditional skills to apprentices. He is a member of the British Artist Blacksmiths Association and is one of a disappearing band of true craftsmen producing hand-made goods that no machine can rival.

The current active blacksmith at the forge is Matthew Haines, who gained first place in the National Westminster Bank and the Rural Development Commissions New Entrant Training Scheme projects when he 'graduated' in 1991. In his element beside the fire and anvil, with a piece of red-hot metal to work and a 4lb hammer in his hand, he produces a wide range of goods, including made-to-measure curtain rails, gates and railings, light steel fabrications, canopies and fire baskets, garden furniture, name plates and pokers - all made to individual requirements. A fascinating display of the forge's output can be seen in the showroom, which is open Monday to Friday and most Saturdays.

Brook Farm Cottages

Milton Road, Drayton, Abingdon, Oxfordshire OX14 4EZ
Tel: 01235 820717 Fax: 01235 820262

Pam and Kevin Humphrey offer a warm welcome and genuine hospitality at **Brook Farm Cottages**, which are set peacefully within the farmyard of Brook Farm. The three cottages - the Shippen, the Old Dairy and the Old Parlour - have been stylishly converted from an old milking parlour to provide all the modern conveniences for a self-catering holiday while retaining attractive features like the original beams. Each cottage has underfloor central heating, two bedrooms, a spacious sitting room with tv, dining area and fully equipped kitchen with plenty of cupboard space. Individual courtyard gardens lead to a communal courtyard with a safe play area for children.

There is also a communal laundry room with washing machine, tumble dryer and ironing facilities. Each cottage has its own parking space. The Old Dairy and the Old Parlour can connect to sleep a maximum of nine. The cottages - no smoking and no pets - are within easy reach of the A34 (Milton Heights interchange) between three picturesque villages with a choice of nearby pubs and restaurants. Abingdon is only 3 miles away, and for lovers of walking and the countryside the Ridgeway Path is close by. Also within easy reach is Milton Manor House, a beautiful 18th century gentleman's residence designed by Inigo Jones.

St Helens Church, Abingdon

ceiling of the Lady Chapel, has been retained from the 14th century. Beside the churchyard, which contains a curious small building that was the blowing chamber for the church organ, are three sets of almshouses. The oldest, Christ's Hospital, was founded in 1446 while the other two, Twitty's Almshouses and Brick Alley Almshouses, date from the early 18th century.

AROUND ABINGDON

Dorchester

5 miles SE of Abingdon off the A4074

This small town, situated on the River Thames and just a short walk from the River Thames, was once an important Roman station called Dorocina. It was here that Christianity was established in the southwest of England by St Birinus. Known as the Apostle of the West Saxons, Birinus was consecrated in Genoa, landed in Wessex in 634, and converted the King of Wessex in the following year. In gratitude, the King gave Dorchester to Birinus and it became a centre of missionary activity.

The **Abbey Church of St Peter and St Paul** is all that remains of the Augustinian Abbey which was built on the site of the original Saxon Church in 1170. Its chief glory is the 14th century choir and the huge Jesse window, showing the family tree of Jesus, which has retained its original glass. The story of the abbey, along with the history of settlement in the area going back to neolithic times, is told in the **Abbey Museum**, which is housed in a former Grammar Schoolroom, built in 1652.

Little Wittenham

4½ miles SE of Abingdon off the A4130

This village, which has a number of pretty cottages, lies beneath the **Wittenham Clumps**, which for centuries formed an important defensive position overlooking the Thames. In the village church of St Peter are effigies of Sir William Dunch, a former MP for Wallingford, and his wife, who was the aunt of Oliver Cromwell. A little way northwest, towards the village of Long Wittenham, is the unique **Pendon Museum**, whose main attraction is a model village built in tiny scale to resemble a typical 1930s village in the Vale of the White Horse. The model is the incredibly skilled and detailed work of Roye England, an Australian who came to this country in 1925 to study. The model incorporates a model railway (Roye England's first passion) and, as a tribute to the master, who died in 1995, a tiny model of himself in the 1:76 scale of the whole model.

Wallingford

Wallingford

8 miles SE of Abingdon on the A4130

A strategic crossing point of the Thames since ancient times. Alfred the Great first fortified the town, against the Danes, and the Saxon earth defences can still be seen. It was here that William the Conqueror crossed the river on his six-day march to London. Wallingford was also an important trading town; it received its charter in 1155 and for several centuries had its own mint. During the Civil War the town was a Royalist stronghold defending the southern approaches to Oxford, the site of the Royalist headquarters. It was besieged in 1646 by the Parliamentary forces under Sir Thomas Fairfax and its walls were breached after a 12-week siege; it was the last place to surrender to Parliament. The Castle, built by William the Conqueror, was destroyed by Cromwell in 1652 but substantial earthworks can still be seen and the museum tells the story of the town from earliest days.

Blewbury

7 miles S of Abingdon on the A417

In the foothills of the Berkshire Downs, this pretty village was and remains a favoured spot for artists and writers. Among these was Kenneth Grahame, the author of *The Wind in the Willows*, who lived in a Tudor brick house in the village from 1910 to 1924. He wrote the book for his son, who tragically died while an undergraduate at Oxford. They are buried together in the churchyard of St Cross in Oxford. Mr Toad compares himself favourably with Oxford students in the book:

'The clever men at Oxford
Know all that there is to be knowed
But they none know one half as much
As intelligent Mr Toad.'

Didcot

4½ miles S of Abingdon on the A4130

The giant cooling towers of Didcot's power station dominate the skyline for miles around and there is little left to be found of the old town. But the saving grace is the **Didcot Railway Centre**, a shrine to the days of the steam engine

Didcot Railway Centre

and the Great Western Railway. Isambard Kingdom Brunel designed the Great Western Railway and its route through Didcot, from London to Bristol, was completed in 1841. Until 1892 its trains ran on their unique broad gauge tracks and the GWR retained its independence until the nationalisation of the railways in 1948. Based around the engine shed, where visitors can inspect the collection of steam locomotives, members of the Great Western Society have recreated the golden age of the railway at the centre which also includes a beautiful recreation of a country station, complete with level crossing. The locomotives on display include 4079 *Pendennis Castle*, repatriated from Australia in 2000, King class 6023 *King Edward II* and one of the streamlined and very distinctive Great Western diesel railcars, this one dating from 1940. The Firefly Trust has recently completed the building of a reproduction of the broad-gauge Firefly locomotive of 1839. Steam days are held through out the year when locomotives once again take to the broad gauge track and visitors can also take in the Victorian signalling system and the centre's Relics Display.

SUTTON COURTENAY
2 miles S of Abingdon on the B4016

A pretty village that was mentioned in the Domesday Book with an abbey that was founded in 1350. The village **Church of All Saints**, which dates back to Norman times, contains some fine stone carvings and woodwork but the real interest lies in the churchyard. Here can be found the chest tomb of Herbert Asquith, the last Liberal Prime Minister (from 1908 to 1916) and his wife; they lived by the Thames not far from the church. Also here is the grave of Eric

COUNTRY MARKETS ANTIQUES & COLLECTABLES CENTRE

Chilton Garden Centre, Newbury Road, Chilton, Oxfordshire OX11 0QN
Tel: 01235 835125 Fax: 01235 833068 website: www.countrymarkets.co.uk
e-mail: country.markets.antiques@breathemail.net

Country Markets Antiques & Collectables Centre is based within Chilton Garden Centre, the largest garden centre in South Oxfordshire. The antiques centre has been in business for over ten years, with 3,000 square feet of display area stocked with affordable antiques and collectables comprising Victorian-Edwardian and 1930s-1940s furniture, period pine furniture, country artefacts, porcelain, ceramics, silver, jewellery, pictures and prints, books, metal ware and old tools, cased fish, clocks and a veritable cornucopia of collectables. The centre also offers specialised services including restoration, re-upholstery and repairs.

WYEVALE GARDEN CENTRES

Chilton Garden Centre, Newbury Road, Chilton, Oxfordshire OX11 0QN
Tel: 01235 833900 Fax: 01235 831266

The **Wyevale Garden Centre** at Chilton is part of the largest garden centre chain in the UK, with 120 branches nationwide. Situated just off the A34 near Chilton village and the Ridgeway National Trail, it consists of two main buildings. The first houses the trees, shrubs, bedding plants and house plants, along with fencing, paving, compost, chemicals, bulbs, seeds and water garden products. The second building contains a restaurant and the antiques franchise (see entry above) and an area set aside seasonally for garden furniture or Christmas trees and decorations. There's also a well-stocked gift section.

The Fish

4 Appleford Road, Sutton Courtenay, Abingdon,
Oxfordshire OX14 4NQ
Tel: 01235 848242 Fax: 01235 848014
e-mail: mike@thefish.uk.com

In an attractive and historic Thames village a couple of miles southeast of Abingdon, **The Fish** is a comfortable and stylish pub restaurant which can seat 60, with a pleasant garden, patio and conservatory. Since 1995 it has been leased from the owning brewery by Mike and Jenny Gaffney, who have built up a strong local customer base by offering high-quality meals at competitive prices. Their chefs prepare à la carte and fixed-price menus every lunchtime and evening using top-class fresh ingredients including local meat and seafood from Devon and Cornwall. Seafood dishes are very much to the fore, ranging typically from pan-seared Cornish dived scallops flambéed in pastis to chargrilled tuna steak with a mango and crispy noodle salad, or whole plaice grilled with rock salt and black peppercorns. Meat-eaters will also find a tempting choice, and no one should miss out on the delights of the pudding menu. A simpler bistro-style menu is available Monday to Saturday lunchtimes.

Mike and Jenny are delighted to cater for special occasions and can cope with most individual dietary requirements. They are also pleased to receive overnight guests, for whom they offer two Bed & Breakfast rooms with private facilities. A short walk from The Fish is a very welcoming 16th century pub, the George & Dragon, where the Gaffneys' youngest son, Neville, is the landlord.

Blair, better known as George Orwell, author of *1984* and *Animal Farm*; several yew trees are planted here in his memory.

WANTAGE

This thriving market town in the Vale of the White Horse was, in 849, the birthplace of Alfred the Great and remained a Royal Manor until end of the 12th century. In the central market place, around which there are some fine Georgian and Victorian buildings, is a huge statue of the King of the West Saxons, who spent much of his life (he died in 899) defending his kingdom from the Danes in the north before becoming the overlord of England. An educated man for his time (as a boy Alfred had visited Rome), he not only codified the laws of his kingdom but also revived the tradition of learning.

Sutton Courtney Village

Unfortunately, only the **Church of St Peter and St Paul** has survived from medieval times and, though it was heavily restored in 1857 by GE Street,

Down Barn Farm

Sparsholt Down, Wantage, Oxfordshire, OX12 9XD
Tel: 01367 820272
e-mail: pendomeffect@aol.com www.nationaltrails.gov.uk

Penny Reid's **Down Barn Farm,** has fully organic status and enjoys a glorious setting in open countryside just off the ancient Ridgeway National Trail. The farm entrance is via a track off the minor road between Lambourn and Kingston Lisle. Penny offers comfortable accommodation in three pleasantly furnished bedrooms. Breakfast is included in the room rate, with other meals provided by arrangement. A sitting room is available for guests. Penny is an experienced endurance rider and also provides livery and escorted rides on the downs.

various features have survived from the original 13th century structure and there's also a brass commemorating the life of Sir Ivo Fitzwarren, the father of Dick Whittington's wife, Alice.

Opposite the church is the **Vale and Downland Museum Centre**, which is located in another of the town's old buildings - a house dating from the 16th century - and a reconstructed barn. Dedicated to the geology, history, and archaeology of Wantage and the Vale of the White Horse, the displays cover the centuries from prehistoric times to the present day.

Built as the home of the Wantage Sisterhood, an Anglican Order, in the 19th century, three architects were involved in the construction of **St Mary's Convent**: GE Street; William Butterfield, architect of Keble College, Oxford; and John Pearson, architect of Truro Cathedral. It was in Wantage that the first steam tramway operated, starting in 1873 and surviving until 1948.

Just to the east of the town lies **Ardington House**, a beautifully symmetrical, early-18th century building that is the home of the Baring family. Occasionally open to the public, the best feature here is the Imperial Staircase - where two flights come into one - of which this is a particularly fine example.

AROUND WANTAGE

Kingston Bagpuize

6 miles N of Wantage off the A420

The intriguing name of this straggling village goes back to Norman times when Ralf de Bachepuise, a contemporary of William the Conqueror, was given land in the area. The village grew to serve the needs of **Kingston Bagpuize House** (see panel on page 124), a fine mansion with superb gardens.

Kingston Bagpuize House

KINGSTON BAGPUIZE HOUSE & GARDEN

Kingston Bagpuize, Nr Abingdon,
Oxfordshire OX13 5AX
Tel: 01865 820259 Fax: 01865 821659
website: www.kingstonbagpuizehouse.org.uk

The Bachepuis family leased the land of the local manor during the 11th and 12th centuries, during which time the name of the village was anglicised from Bachepuis to Kingston Bagpuize. The present **Kingston Bagpuize House**, the home of Francis and Virginia Grant and their children, was built in 1660 and numbers among its many treasures a superb cantilevered staircase and gallery dominating the entrance hall. Thought to date from 1720, the main flight of stairs and gallery have no supporting columns, the great weight being borne by the walls, which are three feet thick. Striking features here include hand-painted Chinese wallpaper and Chinese porcelain vases.

The elegant proportions and symmetry of the house are shown in the marvellous drawing room, with its twin fireplaces, fine French furniture from the 18th and 19th centuries, a pair of Queen Anne cabinets in laburnum and two Hepplewhite armchairs with tapestry seats in gros point and petit point worked by sometime owner Marlie Raphael. The pine-panelled library is balanced by the oak-panelled dining room, where the paintings include a portrait of Marlie aged 3 in 1907, and a Flemish painting showing scenes from the life of St Bernard. The house is truly magnificent, but it is the gardens which bring many visitors to Kingston Bagpuize. Showing traces of much earlier gardens, the grounds contain a large collection of trees, shrubs and perennials; some of the yews are over 300 years old, while the handsome Wellingtonias were planted in the 19th century.

The influence of Francis Grant's great aunt Marlie Raphael, who owned the house from 1939 to 1976, is particularly strong in the garden: in the 1950s and 1960s she planted extensively and created the lovely woodland garden to provide year-round colour and interest. She was advised in this work by Sir Harold Hillier, whose nurseries supplied most of her plants. The present owners are restoring the gardens and have planted many trees and shrubs to complement those already growing. One of their great achievements is a minutely detailed map of the garden showing the names and exact locations of almost 300 plants. On open days a selection of home-baking is served in the tearoom in the basement of the original kitchen; there's also a small gift shop and plants for sale.

Open afternoons for 2002 are as follows: February 17 & 24; March 3, 17 & 31; April 1, 7, 20 & 21; May 5, 6 & 19; June 3, 4, 9, 16 & 30; July 7, 20, 21 & 28; August 4, 25, 26 & 28; September 7, 8, 11, 21 & 22; October 13, November 10.

House and garden are available for special events and group visits throughout the year by written appointment. Children under 5 are allowed in the garden but not in the house; no dogs.

FALLOWFIELDS COUNTRY HOUSE HOTEL

Faringdon Road, Southmoor, Oxfordshire OX13 5BH
Tel: 01865 820416 Fax: 01865 821275
e-mail: stay@fallowfields.com
website: www.fallowfields.com

Standing in ten acres of immaculate landscaped gardens, **Fallowfields Country House Hotel** dates back 300 years, but with modifications and extensions down the years the look is early Victorian Gothic. Owner Anthony Lloyd and his staff offer the warmest of welcomes, and friendly, personal service is a keynote throughout. The house has ten magnificent letting bedrooms, each with its own individual style and appeal. Tasteful colour schemes, elegant furnishings and top-quality bed linen create a relaxing ambience, and many of the rooms enjoy lovely views over the grounds and paddocks towards The Ridgeway, the oldest road in Europe. Some rooms have four-poster beds, and all have tv, radio, telephone, hairdryer and tea-making facilities.

The bathrooms combine attractive Victorian fittings with the modern luxury of power showers and spa baths. In the beautifully appointed conservatory restaurant Head Chef Alan Jefferson-Mackney uses local or home-grown organic produce in his imaginative British menus, which offer the option of light lunches and suppers or a three-course menu. A terrace set with tables and chairs under parasols is a lovely spot for enjoying an alfresco pre-dinner drink. The conservatory can be extended with a delightful marquee, creating a perfect venue for a celebration or wedding reception, and Fallowfields is licensed to conduct civil wedding ceremonies.

GARFORD

5 miles NE of Wantage off the A338

Though there is little to see now, excavations have revealed that the village was inhabited during the Iron Age; the earliest structures unearthed are timber-built round huts with pits for storing grain. At some later point a shrine was built here and with the coming of the Romans the site seems to have kept its religious significance. To the south of the village, on a tributary of the Thames, stands **Venn Watermill**, built in the late 18th century and with its machinery and wheel still intact.

STEVENTON

5 miles NE of Wantage on the A4185

In Mill Street stand the National Trust's **Priory Cottages**, former monastic buildings now converted into two houses. South Cottage contains the priory's original Great Hall, which can be visited in the summer by written appointment.

LETCOMBE BASSETT

2 miles S of Wantage off the B4001

This tiny village has a notable place in literary history: it is called Cresscombe in *Jude the Obscure*, which Thomas Hardy wrote while staying here. Earlier, Jonathan Swift spent the summer of 1714 at the village's rectory where he was visited by the poet Alexander Pope.

Just to the east of the village lies **Segsbury Camp**, which is sometimes also referred to as **Letcombe Castle**. Set on the edge of the Berkshire Downs, this massive Iron Age hill fort encloses some 26 acres of land.

KINGSTON LISLE

4½ miles W of Wantage off the B4507

Just to the southwest of the attractive

Q Gardens

Milton Hill, Steventon, Nr Abingdon,
Oxfordshire OX14 4DP
Tel: 01235 820988 Fax: 01235 820990
e-mail: enquiries@qgardens.net
website: www.qgardens.net

Steve and Sher Elphick are co-owners and managers of **Q Gardens**, which is a combination of 90-acre fruit and vegetable farm, farm shop, tea room, garden centre and pick-your-own centre. Their own produce comprises a wide variety of fruit and vegetables, honey and honey-based products such as beeswax, candles, preserves and skin creams. They also sell bread freshly baked on the premises, cider and apple juice, dairy products, ham, cakes, biscuits and flowers. The pick-your-own season runs from June to October and features, in seasonal order, cherries, strawberries, black-, red- and white- currants, tayberries, blackberries, raspberries, runner beans, plums, apples and pears - all of which can also be bought at the shop.

The garden centre, open from April to June, sells a wide range of bedding and trailing plants, pots, hanging baskets and compost, and fully trained staff are on hand to give help and advice. The latest addition to the business is the Q Tea Room, where a wide selection of freshly made rolls, baguettes, sausage rolls, cakes and pastries can be enjoyed with tea, coffee or a cold drink. The speciality cream tea is a temptation that's hard to resist, and in season strawberries with clotted cream are a very special treat.

The Asti Stud & Saddlery

Millaway Farm, Goosey, Nr Faringdon, Oxfordshire SN7 8PA
Tel: 01367 710288 Fax: 01367 710218
e-mail: info@asti-stud.co.uk website: www.asti-stud.co.uk
on-line store: http://shop.asti-stud.co.uk/trolleyed

Situated in the picturesque Vale of the White Horse off the Faringdon-Wantage road (A417), the **Asti Stud** is an ABRS and BHS approved centre offering riding activities for all ages and levels of experience with an on-site saddlery shop. The range of instructors offer tuition in general horse riding as well as dressage, show jumping, side saddle and carriage driving on well mannered horses and ponies, or clients can bring their own horse or pony. Escorted hacks around the lanes and bridleways or along the beautiful Ridgeway are also offered.

For the real horse enthusiast, the yard offers tailor made horse days and non-residential courses combining riding with education on aspects of horse care and stable management. As a Pony Club centre, the yard also offers training towards pony club tests and achievement badges. During school holiday periods, the yard organises a range of events including training days, share-a-pony mornings, mini shows, fun activities and Hot Air Balloon rides. The yard also offers a range of livery options from grass to full on a long or short term basis with excellent facilities and hay, straw, shavings and feed available on site.

The on-site saddlery shop stocks a wide range of items for horse, rider and groom as well as a range of horse gifts, books and country clothing with many items available for purchase through their website. Home produced lamb and beef is available in freezer packs and a resident saddler is available for leather, rug and saddlery repairs. The yard and shop are open 7 days a week throughout the year.

Uffington

somewhere on these downs in 871, but modern thinking now considers that it dates from about 100 BC.

Above the White Horse is the Iron Age camp known as **Uffington Castle**, and to one side is a knoll known as **Dragon's Hill** where legend has it that St George killed the dragon.

Norman Church of St John lies the **Blowing Stone** (or **Sarsen Stone**), a piece of glacial debris that is perforated with holes. When blown, the stone emits a fog-horn like sound and tradition has it that the stone was blown by King Alfred.

Uffington

5½ miles W of Wantage off the B4507

This large village was, in 1822, the birthplace of Thomas Hughes, the son of the vicar. The author of *Tom Brown's Schooldays*, Hughes incorporates many local landmarks, including the White Horse and Uffington Castle, in his well-known work. The **Tom Brown's School Museum** tells the story of Hughes' life and works.

However, the village is perhaps best known for the **Uffington White Horse**, where on the hillside a mysteriously abstract and very beautiful figure of a horse, some 400 feet long, has been created by removing the turf to expose the gleaming white chalk beneath. It is a startling sight which can be seen from far and wide, and many a tantalising glimpse of it has been caught through the window of a train travelling through the valley below. Popular tradition links it with the victory of King Alfred over the Danes at the battle of Ashdown, which was fought

Great Coxwell

8 miles NW of Wantage off the A420

This village is well known for its magnificent 13th century **Tithe Barn** and its **Church of St Giles**, which also dates from that time. A simple and elegant building, the church is often overlooked in favour of the barn, which was originally built to serve the needs of the Cistercian Abbey at Beaulieu in Hampshire who were granted the land here by King John. An impressive building that is some 152 feet long, with Cotswold stone walls of over four feet thick, this huge barn was used to store the tithe - or taxes - received from the tenants of the church land. At the Dissolution it passed into private ownership and is now owned by the National Trust.

Buscot

11 miles NW of Wantage on the A417

This small village, in the valley of the upper Thames, is home to two National Trust properties: **Buscot Old Parsonage** and **Buscot Park**. The parsonage is a lovely house, with a small garden on the banks of the River Thames, that was built of Cotswold stone in 1703. However, Buscot Park is a much grander affair, as its name might suggest, and this classic example of a late Georgian house was built in 1780. It houses the magnificent Faringdon Art Collection, which includes

TEDDY BEARS AT WITNEY

99 High Street, Witney, Oxfordshire OX28 6HY
Tel: 01993 702616'706616 Fax: 01993 702334

When Ian Pout came to Witney in 1977 as a dealer in antiques and old books and toys, teddy bears were a very small part of his business. But the bear element gradually grew, and in 1984, with the help of Gina Clayton, he opened **Teddy Bears of Witney** in his 17th century premises with low beamed ceilings and perfect homely ambience. Visitors come from all parts of the globe to this wonderful shop, where every inch of available space is taken up by bears old and new, small and large, wistful and cheerful. The stock of new bears runs to more than 1,000, each carefully selected from the world's best manufacturers and artists and beautifully displayed amidst the antique furniture.

From the traditional Steiff and Merrythought bears to contemporary designs, there is such a variety that at least one of them will capture the heart of a prospective buyer. But this is no ordinary teddy bear shop, as Ian, a keen collector, has assembled for display some of the most famous teddy bears in the world. Aloysius is the actual bear who starred in *Brideshead Revisited* as the much-loved companion of Sebastian Flyte. This renowned bear, who had spent 60 years sitting in a delicatessen in Maine before finding stardom, was bought by Ian, who commissioned from Merrythought a limited edition of 5,000 exclusively for his shop. In a sale at Christie's in 1989 Ian acquired Alfonzo, the red mohair bear who was given to Princess Xenia by her father the Grand Duke George of Russia in 1908.

Steiff produced a limited edition Baby Alfonzo, which like the original is made of red mohair and wears a cotton sateen Cossack tunic and trousers. Steiff also produced Xenia, in memory of the Princess. Theodore, the tiny pocket bear who was the favourite of the actor Peter Bull, sits in front of his own little teddy bear shop. Peter Bull, a noted teddy bear lover, was largely responsible for the resurgence of interest in teddy bears with his books and promotional television appearances in the 1960s and 1970s. Other distinguished bears on display include Boots, so called because of his wooden boots, and Othello, a black mohair Steiff bear of 1912 who was made in memory of those who lost their lives on the *Titanic*.

For all teddy bear lovers young and old Teddy Bears of Witney is a must - and it's open seven days a week.

paintings by Rembrandt, Murillo and Reynolds; one room is decorated with a series of pictures painted by Edward Burne-Jones, the pre-Raphaelite artist who was a close friend of William Morris. Painted in 1890, they reflect Burne-Jones' interest in myths and legends and tell the story of the Sleeping Beauty. The grounds of Buscot Park were largely developed in the 20th century and include a canal garden by Harold Peto, a large kitchen garden and an Egyptian avenue created by Lord Faringdon in 1969 featuring sphinxes and statues based on originals in Hadrian's Villa outside Rome. Anyone particularly interested in the work of Burne-Jones should also visit the village church, where a stained glass window showing the Good Shepherd was designed by him in 1891, when he was working with William Morris's firm, Morris and Co. The church itself is very pleasantly situated by the river just outside the village.

WITNEY

Situated in rich sheep-farming land in the valley of the River Windrush, this old town's name is derived from Witta's Island and it was once of importance as the meeting place of the Wittan, the Council of the Saxon Kings. Developed as a planned town in the early Middle Ages, under the guidance of the Bishop of Winchester, the site of the Bishop's Palace lies alongside **St Mary's Church**. With an attractive exterior, though the interior does not live up to the promise, the church provides a dramatic focus to the town's market place. By 1278, Witney had a weekly market and two annual fairs and in the centre of the market place still stands the Buttercross. Originally a shrine, the cross has a steep roof with rustic-looking stone columns; it dates from about 1600. Wool was the economic base of life here and Witney

Merchant Adventurer

1 Wesley Walk, Witney, Oxfordshire OX28 6ZJ
Tel: 01993 776022 Fax: 01993 708001

Sarah Grant came to work at **Merchant Adventurer**, liked it, and now both owns and runs it. The venture, which imports furniture and accessories from all points of the compass, occupies a handsome modern stone building in an upmarket shopping precinct not far from the main street of the former wool town of Witney. The stock in trade ranges from table decorations to dining room suites, taking in almost everything in between!

Wiggly paper snakes hang from the ceiling, sea horses and dolphins and exotic African masks cling to the walls, and display racks are are filled with all kinds of gifts and ornaments in glass, china, porcelain or ivory. Table lamps, wall and ceiling lights, mirrors, silks, rugs and carpets come in all shapes and colours and sizes, and the stand-alone larger items include tv and hi-fi units, chairs, dressers, sideboards, bookcases and tables - coffee, occasional and dining. Merchant Venturer is a perfect place to spend an hour or two exploring, whether it's looking for a gift with a difference or re-furnishing a house; opening hours are 9.00am to 5.00pm Monday to Friday and 9.00am to 5.30pm on Saturday.

developed weaving and, in particular, the making of blankets. The Witney Blanket Company was incorporated in 1710 but before that there were over 150 looms here working in the blanket trade employing over 3000 people. The **Blanket Hall**, in the High Street, has on it the arms of the Witney Company of Weavers; it was built for the weighing and measuring of blankets in an age before rigid standardisation. The trade began in the 16th century and, even though there has been a great decline in the industry since World War I, there are still a couple of blanket factories here.

Just outside the town is the **Cogges Manor Farm Museum**, which stands on the site of a now deserted medieval village of which only the church, priory, and manor house remain. The displays tell the story of the lives of those who worked the surrounding land down the centuries.

Cogges Manor Farm Museum

Witney Buttercross

AROUND WITNEY

Stanton Harcourt

4 miles SE of Witney off the B4449

This beautiful village is noted for its historic manor house **Stanton Harcourt Manor**, which dates back to the 14th century. Famed for its well preserved medieval kitchen, one of the most complete to survive in this country, the house is also renowned for its fine collection of antiques and the tranquil gardens. It was while staying here, from 1717 to 1718, that Alexander Pope translated Homer's great work, the *Iliad*. He worked in the tower, part of the original manor house and now referred to as **Pope's Tower**.

While the manor house draws many people to the village, the splendid Norman **Church of St Michael** is also

The Old Kitchen, Stanton Harcourt Manor

worthy of a visit. Naturally the Harcourt chapel dominates but there are other features of interest, including an intricate 14th century shrine to St Edburg.

Standlake

5 miles SE of Witney on the A415

A little way south of the village is the 13th century Newbridge, the second oldest bridge across the Thames. Newbridge saw conflict during the Civil War and the Rose Revived pub was used by Cromwell as a refreshment stop.

Radcot

7 miles SW of Witney on the A4095

This tiny hamlet boasts the oldest bridge across the River Thames. Built in 1154, **Radcot Bridge** represents an important crossing place and, as such, the hamlet has seen much conflict over the centuries. To the north of the bridge are the remains of a castle where, in 1141,

Kasbah

Manor Farm Antiques, Standlake,
Oxfordshire OX29 7RL
Tel: 01865 300971

Five miles southeast of Witney on the A415, **Kasbah** brings a wonderful touch of exoticism to the very English surroundings of the Oxfordshire countryside. Owner Charles Gower has spent most of his life in the world of antiques and several years ago diversified into a different sphere. Kasbah is a superb collection of beds, traditional and contemporary mosaic tables and chairs, decorative ceramics and terracotta and distinctive lighting and ornamentation; all the items have the feel of Morocco and the Middle East and all are displayed to stunning effect in various layouts in spacious, barn-style showrooms with exposed stone or colour-washed walls and raftered ceilings.

The collection represents an eclectic and elegant fusion of different cultural styles, and everything on display shows a very high standard of workmanship, being made by hand using natural materials and long-established traditional methods of manufacture. This unique range of furnishings and ornaments is designed to bring an individual and atmospheric quality to any house or garden, and can also provide eye-catching decor in a restaurant, bar or hotel.

Aston Pottery

Kingsway Farm, Aston, Nr Bampton, Oxfordshire OX18 2BT
Tel: 01993 852031 Fax: 01993 851877
website: www.astonpottery.co.uk

On the edge of the Cotswolds, on the B4449 between Standlake and Bampton, lies **Aston Pottery**, which was set up 12 years ago by Jane and Stephen Baughan to develop a range of household ceramics that offer the combination of quality, style and durability. Today they employ 25 staff and supply over 200 shops. All the pottery is hand-decorated on to a range of 45 different shapes from teapots to jugs and bowls to huge oval platters.

The working pottery itself is a complex of period Cotswold farm buildings which have been extensively renovated to provide an efficient and modern working environment for staff and visitors. The pottery includes a large shop where any one of the 125 designs can be bought, all exquisitely decorated by hand in themes featuring British animals and birds; wild and garden flowers; farmyard animals; English gardens and children's nursery sets. Through the summer months the Pottery provides a very practical and 'hands on' demonstration of how teapots are made and decorated. This lasts for approximately one hour and is geared to entertain and inform both children and adults. The pottery shop and tea room are open 7 days a week. A mail-order catalogue is available. Please log on to the website for further information.

King Stephen battled with the disenthroned Queen Matilda, while in the following century King John fought his Barons before finally conceding and signing the Magna Carta.

Kelmscott

9 miles SW of Witney off the A4095

Located near the River Thames and dating from about 1570, **Kelmscott Manor** was famously the country home of the artist and designer-manufacturer William Morris from 1871 until his death in 1896. Morris loved the house dearly and it is the scene of the end of his utopian novel *News from Nowhere*, in which he writes of a world where work has become a sought after pleasure. The house, which along with the beautiful garden is open to visitors during the summer, has examples of Morris's work and memorabilia of Dante Gabriel Rosetti, who also stayed there. Rosetti is reputed to have found the village boring, so presumably the fact that he was in love with Morris' wife, Jane, drew him here. Morris is buried in the churchyard, under a tombstone designed by his associate Philip Webb on the lines of a Viking tomb house. The church itself is interesting, the oldest parts dating from the late 12th century, and the village includes some fine farmhouses from around the end of the 17th and beginning of the 18th centuries.

Filkins

8 miles SW of Witney off the A361

This tiny Cotswold village is now the home of a flourishing community of craft workers and artists, many of whom work in restored 18th century barns. Wool has played a great part in the wealth of this area and, also sited in a converted barn, is the **Cotswold Woollen Weavers**, a working weaving museum with an exhibition gallery and a mill shop. In the same attractive village is the **Swinford Museum**, which concentrates on 19th century domestic and rural trade and craft tools.

Cotswold Wild Life Park

BRADWELL GROVE

7 miles W of Witney off the A361

The 120 acres of park and garden which make up **The Cotswold Wild Life Park** are home to a whole host of animals, many of whom roam free in the wooded estate. Rhinos, zebras, ostriches and tigers are just some of the animals in the spacious enclosures while tropical birds, monkeys, reptiles, and butterflies are all given the chance to enjoy the warmth of their natural habitat by staying indoors. With an adventure playground and a narrow-gauge railway, the park has something to offer every member of the family.

OXFORD

The skyline of this wonderful city can be seen from many of the hilltops which surround it and the view is best described by the 19th century poet, Matthew Arnold: 'that sweet City with her dreaming spires'. George Bernard Shaw was rather less effusive when he wrote: 'Very nice sort of place, Oxford, I should think, for people who like that sort of place'. However, Oxford is not all beautiful, ancient buildings but a town of commerce and industry and around the academic centre there are suburbs and factories. A city which has been the centre of the country's intellectual, political, religious and architectural life for over 800 years, it is still an academic stronghold, housing some of the finest minds in some of the finest buildings in the country.

A walled town in Saxon times, Oxford grew on a ford where the River Thames meets the River Cherwell. The first students came here in the 12th century when they were forced out of Paris, at the time Europe's leading academic centre. Intellectual pursuits were at that time chiefly religious, and as the town already had an Augustinian Abbey it soon

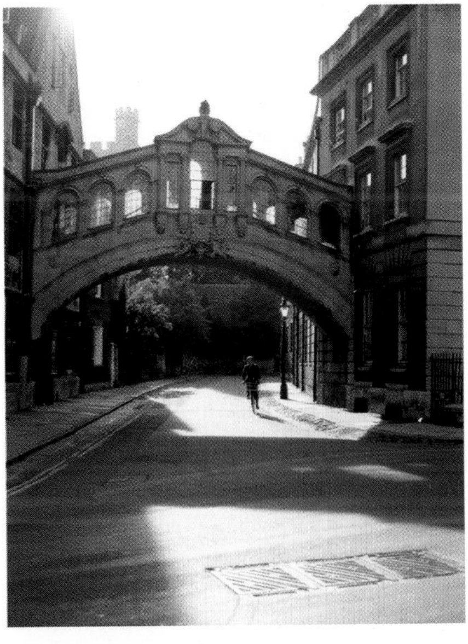

Hertford College Bridge

The Old Bank Hotel

92-94 High Street, Oxford, Oxfordshire OX1 4BN
Tel: 01865 799599 Fax: 01865 799598
e-mail: info@oldbank-hotel.co.uk website: www.oxford-hotels-restaurants.co.uk

When it first opened towards the end of 1999, the **Old Bank** was the first hotel to be created in the centre of the city for 135 years. And it is certainly very much in the centre, situated on the city's most famous thoroughfare, the High, and surrounded by historic University buildings.

The fabric of the Old Bank, at the junction of the High, Magpie Lane and Catte Street, dates from Elizabethan times, and was, as the name suggests, once used as a bank. Behind the period frontage the hotel's interior is stylishly contemporary, and the theme throughout the public rooms and the 44 guest bedrooms on four floors is one of understated elegance.

The bedrooms, which were designed by Gladys Wagner of Wagner Designs, Paris, feature clever, original combinations such as linen bed covers with velvet trimmings. All the rooms have luxurious en suite marble bathrooms with power showers, and their up-to-the-minute specification includes efficient air-conditioning, two telephone lines (one for fax or data), tv, radio and digital CD player. Room service is available day and night.

The hotel and its restaurant Quod (see panel opposite) house an impressive collection of 20th century British art personally selected by the hotel's owner Jeremy Mogford. There are original Stanley Spencer prints in each bedroom, photographic collections of the well-known local photographer Paddy Summerfield in the reception area and vast, imposing oils in the restaurant.

Besides the restaurant, the hotel has a residents' bar and lounge and a room for private dining. And it has a ghost. This is Prudence, a Puritan who fell in love with a Royalist and because they could never marry died of a broken heart. Hotel guests may or may not detect the presence of Prudence but, surrounded as they are by so many academic buildings, they will certainly feel part of University life.

became the country's leading seat of theological thinking. However, there was considerable tension between the townsfolk and the intellectuals and in the 13th century, in a bid to protect their students, the university began to build colleges - enclosed quadrangles with large, sturdy front doors. The first colleges, University (1249), Balliol (1263) and Merton (1264) were soon joined by others which to this day maintain their own individual style while all coming under the administration of the university.

Merton College was founded by Walter de Merton, Lord Chancellor of England, as a small community of scholars from the income of his Surrey estates. Though the present buildings mostly date from the 15th to 17th centuries, Mob Quad is the university's oldest. The key feature of the college is its splendid medieval library where the ancient books are still chained to the desks. Once considered the poor relation to other, wealthier colleges, **Balliol College** was founded as an act of penance by John Balliol and for many years it was reserved for only the poor students. Most of the college buildings now date from the 19th century when the college was instrumental in spearheading a move towards higher academic standards. Thought by some to have been founded by Alfred the Great, **University College** was endowed in 1249 but the present college buildings are mostly 17th century. The poet Shelley was the college's most famous scholar though he was expelled in 1811 for writing a pamphlet on atheism. Shelley drowned at the age of 30 while in Italy, and his memorial can be seen in the Front Quad.

One of the most beautiful colleges in the city, **Christ Church**, was founded in 1525 as Cardinal College by Thomas

QUOD RESTAURANT & BAR

Old Bank Hotel, 92-94 High Street, Oxford,
Oxfordshire OX1 4BN
Tel: 01865 202505 Fax: 01865 799587
e-mail: quod@oldbank-hotel.co.uk
website: www.oxford-hotels-restaurants.co.uk

All ages and tastes are catered for at **Quod Restaurant & Bar**, which opened in 1999 as part of the Old Bank Hotel. The imposing former Georgian banking hall is now a splendidly bright, welcoming room that has an up-to-the-minute feel while retaining some of the original features. The interior styling draws its inspiration from the Tuscan landscape, using earthy colours and a range of natural materials. The most eye-catching feature of the decor is the original artwork on the walls, notably some huge oil paintings by some of the country's up and coming young artists. A zinc-topped bar stands at the centre of things, and the south side of the room opens on to a terrace with elegantly simple tables and chairs set out under parasols.

The menu is also inspired by Italy, offering a good variety of pasta, pizza, salads, fish dishes and grills. Specials could run from castelluccio lentil soup with parmesan croutons and white truffle oil to monkfish and speck salad, chicken with peppers and mushrooms, and slow-roasted lamb shank served with roasted pumpkin and mint pesto. Home-made ice creams and sorbets, tiramisu and apple strudel are popular endings, and the wine list offers plenty of choice by bottle or glass. The full menu is available every day from noon to 11pm, and Quod is also open early for breakfast. A private dining room has seats for up to 24. Other Quods are in London, Birmingham and Brighton.

Christchurch College, Oxford

Wolsey and refounded as Christ Church in 1546 by Henry VIII after Wolsey had fallen from royal favour. The main gateway into the college leads through the bottom of Tom Tower (designed by Christopher Wren and home of the Great Tom bell) and into Tom Quad, the largest of the city's quadrangles. From here there is access to the rest of the college and also to the college's chapel. The only college chapel in the world to be designated a cathedral, Christ Church Cathedral is also England's smallest; it was founded in 1546 on the remains of a 12th century building.

Another splendid college well worth a visit is **Magdalen College**, which has extensive grounds that include a riverside walk, a deer park, three quadrangles and a series of glorious well manicured lawns. It was founded in 1458

The Oxford Cheese Company

17 Covered Market, Oxford, Oxfordshire OX1 3DU
Tel: 01865 721420
website: www.oxfordcheese.co.uk

Customers flock from far afield to visit and buy from this amazing shop located in the covered market. An incredible variety of English and French farmhouse cheeses are displayed in abundance, including one of the largest selections of goats' and ewes' milk cheese to be found anywhere in the UK. Naturally, Oxford Blue takes pride of place - the cheese created by the irrepressible founder and owner of the company, Baron Robert Pouget. Amongst the Barons' other creations are the washed rind ISIS cheese, the pungent Cotswold Crottin and the tangy extra matured Marksbury Farmhouse Cheddar.

The Alpha Bar

89 Covered Market, Oxford, OX1 3DU
Tel: 01865 250499

If you are a vegetarian, vegan or just after a healthy lunch, then the Alpha Bar could be the place for you. Owned by William Pouget, son of the Baron, this enterprise caters for many diets including macrobiotics and those on gluten or wheat free diets. There is not only a wide variety of sandwich and salad fillings but also home-made cakes, soups and refreshing smoothies on sale, as well as a diverse range of herbal teas and coffee.

The Hat Box

Avenue Three, The Covered Market, Oxford, Oxfordshire OX1 3DY
Tel: 01865 200844
website: www.oxfordhats.com

The aptly named **Hat Box** occupies tiny premises among a kaleidoscope of shops and stalls in Avenue 3 of Oxford's historic covered market. The shop is owned and run with a great sense of fun by Martha Lovell, who took over the business in 2001 and who knows everything there is to know about hats and millinery. Ladies' hats of all kinds fill the display space, with prices ranging from less than £10 to upwards of £300. The best of British hat-makers are featured, and the shop's top-of-the-range offering is hats made to measure in one week.

by William Waynflete, Bishop of Winchester, and its bell tower is one of the city's most famous landmarks. Oxford was closely involved in the Civil War and was for three years the King's headquarters. Several of the Colleges were pressed into service as part of the headquarters by the Royalists: Wadham and New College were both used as stores for arms and gunpowder; Magdalen was Prince Rupert's headquarters and the tower was used as Charles' lookout when the Earl of Essex laid siege to the city. The damage caused by Cromwell's men is dramatically illustrated by bullet holes in the statue of the Virgin in the wonderful **Church of St Mary**. It was in this church that the trial of the Protestant martyrs Hugh Latimer, Nicholas Ridley and Thomas Cranmer was held; they were found guilty of heresy and burned to death in a ditch outside the city walls; the three are commemorated by the Martyrs Memorial, erected in 1841 in St Giles. If Oxford was the temporary home of countless luminaries (from Wolsey, Wesley and Wilde to 12 British Prime Ministers) it is also the permanent resting place of many others. In the churchyard of St Cross are buried Kenneth Grahame (*The Wind in the Willows*), Kenneth Tynan and the composer Sir John Stainer; William Laud, 17th century Archbishop of Canterbury is buried in the chapel of St John's College; JRR Tolkien, Oxford professor and author of *The Lord of the Rings*, and the philosopher Sir Isiah Berlin lie in Wolvercote cemetery; and CS Lewis, critic and writer of the Nania series of books, is at rest in the churchyard of Holy Trinity, Headington. Many of the colleges have lovely peaceful gardens, some of them open to the public at various times, and the **University Parks** are a perfect place for a stroll at any time. As well as the college buildings, Oxford has many interesting and magnificent places to explore. At the city's central crossroads, unusually named **Carfax** and probably derived from the Latin for four-forked, is a tower, **Carfax Tower**, which is all that

Magdelen College, Oxford

Annabel Harrison

36 Little Clarendon Street, Oxford,
Oxfordshire OX1 2HU
Tel: 01865 512936

If Oxford University offered a degree in Highly Desirable Fashion, **Annabel Harrison** is where most of the practical study would take place. Located a short walk from the centre of the city, this shop offers an exciting, well-displayed range of clothes and accessories for the fashion-conscious woman about town, and luxury is the keynote of the latest collections. Featuring among the Winter 2001 stocks are Voyage Passion ('Pure Rock Chick Glamour'); See by Chloë, very special knitwear from Ischiko; more knitwear, fantastic suits and oh so soft leather jackets from Donna Karan; stylish belts and bags from Avion; the famous ranges of Armani and Nicole Farhi; and glamorous faux-fur hats from Gilly Forge - think Audrey Hepburn in *Charade*.

The leading lights in this paradise for smart dressers are Fiona Walker, who visits the fashion shows and fashion houses looking for the next exciting collections, and manageress Gill Wright, who brought extensive experience in the fashion business when she arrived from Ralph Lauren. Annabel Harrison is open from 10 to 5.30 Monday to Saturday. There's a sister shop in Cheltenham, called Alison Harrison.

Ducker & Son

6 Turl Street, Oxford, Oxfordshire)X1 3DQ
Tel: 01865 242461
e-mail: ducker.oxford@virgin.net

In traditional shop premises in the very heart of the city, the name of Ducker & Son has for more than a century been synonymous with the pinnacle of the art of bespoke shoemaking. The business has been run for more than 40 years by brothers George and Stephen Purves; they learned their trade from their father, who worked for Edward Ducker, the founder of the business, and later took over his shop. When Mr Ducker arrived in Oxford with his boot making tools in 1898 he joined at least 20 other shoemakers in the city; now there's just one, and Ducker & Son is one of the very few traditional hand-sewn shoemakers outside the West End of London.

The shop window is filled with pairs of their highly desirable shoes, whose prices range from around £200 for a machine- made pair from stock to £1000 for a made-to-order hand sewn pair and £2500 for a pair of hand made riding boots. George and Stephen make weekly trips to Northampton - the country's traditional shoemaking centre - to buy leather for the uppers, while the leather for the soles comes from America, where some of the animals are bred purely for their hides. Among the celebrities shod by Ducker & Son are Evelyn Waugh, Chris Patten, Sir Robin Day and Jeremy Paxman.

Radcliffe Camera

remains of the 14th century Church of St Martin. A climb to the top of the tower offers magnificent views across the city. One of the most interesting buildings, the **Radcliffe Camera**, was built between 1737 and 1749 to a design by James Gibb. England's earliest example of a round reading room (camera means chamber, or room), this splendid domed building still serves this purpose for the **Bodleian Library**. Named after Sir Thomas Bodley, a diplomat and a fellow of Merton College, it contains over 5½ million books and is one of the world's greatest libraries. The collection of early printed books and manuscripts is second only to the British Library in London and, though members of the University can request to see any book here, this is not a lending library and the books must be read and studied on the premises. Close by is the **Clarendon Building**, the former home of the Oxford University Press and now part of the Bodleian, and also in this part of the city is the **Bridge of Sighs**, part of Hertford College and a 19th century copy of the original bridge in Venice. In Oxford the bridge crosses a street rather than a canal. The magnificent **Sheldonian Theatre** was designed and built in the style of a Roman theatre by Christopher Wren between 1664 and 1668 while he was Professor of Astronomy at the University. It is still used today for its intended purpose, as a place for University occasions including matriculation, degree ceremonies, and the annual Encaenia, when honorary degrees are conferred on distinguished people. As well as the superb wooden interior, the ceiling has 32 canvas panels, depicting Truth descending on the Arts, which are the work of Robert Streeter, court painter to Charles II. Naturally, the city has a wealth of museums and the best place to start is at the innovative **Oxford Story**, which presents a lively review of the last 800 years of university life, from the

The Old Parsonage Hotel

1 Banbury Road, Oxford, Oxfordshire OX2 6NN
Tel: 01865 310210 Fax: 01865 311262
e-mail: info@oldparsonage-hotel.co.uk
website: www.oxford-hotels-restaurants.co.uk

Once a haven to persecuted clergy and a Royalist stronghold, the **Old Parsonage** now acts as a refuge to visitors in more peaceful times. The 17th century building, in beautiful honey-coloured stone, is located at the beginning of Banbury Road an east walk from the city centre, colleges, theatres and art galleries.

Accommodation comprises 30 individually furnished bedrooms with luxurious marble bathrooms, satellite tv, private safe, telephone and 24-hour room service.

Many of the rooms enjoy views over either the secluded walled garden or the unique roof garden. In the Parsonage Restaurant and Bar award-winning modern British cuisine is served from early morning till late at night. Residents and non-residents can enjoy anything from a morning coffee or a cream tea to a glass of champagne, a cocktail, a snack or a three-course meal with wine, served on the terrace when the weather permits.

The restaurant, whose quality is confirmed by the large number of local diners, offers a nicely varied menu that will please both traditionalists and those with a taste for more adventurous cooking.

Starters might include asparagus with hollandaise sauce, baked comice pear with stilton and walnuts, or stir-fried prawns with chilli, pesto, coriander and couscous salad. Main courses are equally diverse and tempting, from sea bass with spicy tomato sauce to calves' liver and bacon with sage and onion mash, chicken with 20 cloves of garlic and rack of lamb with crushed potatoes. Desserts round off a meal in fine style, and the excellent food is accompanied by a thoughtfully compiled wine list.

Middle Ages to the present day. The **Museum of Oxford**, with a different style, also covers the story of Oxford through a series of permanent displays showing various archaeological finds. First opened in 1683 and the oldest museum in the country, the **Ashmolean Museum** was originally established to house the collection of the John Tradescants, father and son. On display in this internationally renowned museum are archaeological collections from Britain, Europe, Egypt, and the Middle East; Italian, Dutch, Flemish, French, and English old masters; Far Eastern art, ceramics, and lacquer work and Chinese bronzes. The Ashmolean, named after the 17th century antiquary Elias Ashmole, also features many items from the Civil War, including Cromwell's death mask, his watch, King Charles' spurs and a collection of coins, among them the famous Oxford crown and a £3

coin minted by Charles. Here, too, is the **Museum of the History of Science**, a remarkable collection of early scientific instruments including Einstein's blackboard and a large silver microscope made for George III. In a splendid high-Victorian building, near the University Science Area, is the **University Museum** where the remains of a dodo, extinct since around 1680, and a mass of fossilised dinosaur remains are on display. Also here is the **Pitt Rivers Museum**, with its interesting collection taken from all over the world. Musicians will enjoy the **Bate Collection of Historical Instruments**, while those captivated by old masters should take time to visit the **Christ Church Picture Gallery**, with its collection of works by Tintoretto, Van Dyck, Leonardo da Vinci and Michelangelo. Another place worthy of a visit and a particularly peaceful haven in the city is **Oxford Botanic**

GEE'S RESTAURANT

61a Banbury Road, Oxford, Oxfordshire OX2 6PE
Tel: 01865 553540 Fax: 01865 310308
e-mail: info@gees-restaurant.co.uk
website: www.oxford-hotels-restaurants.co.uk

An ornate late-Victorian conservatory in civilised North Oxford ten minutes from the city centre is the delightful setting for **Gee's Restaurant**. Built in 1898 for the Gee family, it was converted into a restaurant in 1984, since when it has had several distinguished owner-chefs. Today, it is a popular spot with local residents, visitors to the city and business people. Sitting in the company of potted palms on cane-backed chairs at immaculately set tables, diners can choose from a menu that is modern British with Mediterranean and Asian influences.

Starters such as seared sea trout with cucumber, celery and tomato risotto with steamed cockles and home-grown sorrel, and spaghettini with broad beans, garlic and pecorino show a skilled and imaginative hand at work in the kitchen, and equally eclectic main courses might include chargrilled

veal cutlet with home-made chips and red wine mustard, rib-eye steak with a watercress and garlic butter, pan-fried smoked haddock with tagliatelle, grain mustard butter and sage, and, for vegetarians, slow-roasted peppers with couscous, harissa and smoked aubergine. A good-value two-course Express Lunch is an additional option Monday to Saturday. Gee's is open lunchtime and evening Monday to Saturday and all day Sunday; it's an ideal venue for wedding receptions, birthday parties, business functions and other special occasions.

Bridget Wheatley Contemporary Jewellery

38 Cowley Road, Oxford, Oxfordshire OX4 1HZ
Tel: 01865 722184 Fax: 01865 790858
website: www.bridgetwheatley.com

Bridget Wheatley Contemporary Jewellery is a haven of creativity and innovation. Bridget opened her shop in October 2000 with a degree from Birmingham School of Jewellery and many years' experience designing and making a wide range of jewellery. The essence of her work is simplicity allied to great attention to detail, and she takes her main inspiration from medieval and Celtic art. Bridget uses irregularly shaped freshwater pearls and richly coloured gemstones combined with gold and silver, and her work ranges from small items costing a few pounds to larger pieces such as necklaces.

The shop is bright, airy and chatty, and Bridget is happy to discuss customers' requirements, trying to find exactly the right piece for the right occasion, either from stock or as a specially made item. Alongside Bridget's own work, the shop is a showcase for an eclectic group of artists using diverse designs, materials and techniques to produce a stunning array of beautiful, totally individual pieces. The shop, which is located a leisurely ten-minute walk from the city centre, is open from 10 to 5.30 Tuesday to Saturday.

Frog Orange

4 The Parade, Windmill Road, Headington, Oxford, Oxfordshire OX3 7BL
Tel: 01865 766777 Fax: 01865 751072
e-mail: frog_orange@hotmail.com

Lucy Allen and Beck Lee moved from London in the summer of 2001 to open **Frog Orange** and bring an extra splash of colour and helping of fun to Oxford. Located in a long-established parade of shops in Headington, a mile or so from the centre of Oxford, the double-fronted shop with orange-painted walls is a veritable Aladdin's Cave of gifts and novelties, an ideal place to visit to find gifts with a difference, and a reminder that shopping can actually be fun. The range is very diverse, from greetings cards and wrapping paper to toys and jewellery. Soft toys sit waiting patiently to be hugged on the shelves of a dresser, and a whole bookcase is stocked with aromatic oils and aromatherapy products.

Mood lighting, moving image globes and decorative or scented candles are among other items on display. Frog Orange offers a free gift wrapping service and balloons for children. Opening times are 9.30 to 5.30 Monday to Friday, 10 to 5.30 on Saturday, and the shop also opens on Sundays during the run-up to Christmas.

Museum of Oxford

Garden, down by the river opposite Magdalen College. Founded in 1621, when plants were practically the only source of medicines, this was a teaching garden where the plants grown here were studied for their medicinal and scientific use. Today the garden manages to hold 8,000 species of plants in its 4½ acres, including the National collection of euphorbias. Outside the entrance is a rose garden commemorating the work of Oxford's scientists in the discovery and use of penicillin. In the same ownership as the Botanic Garden is the **Harcourt Arboretum** at Nuneham Courtenay, six miles south of Oxford off the A4074. As well as a magnificent collection of trees, the site includes a bluebell wood and a 22-acre meadow.

Oxford is also the place where the River Thames changes its name to the poetic Isis and, at **Folly Bridge**, not only are there punts for hire but river trips can be taken, both up and down stream, throughout the day and evening.

AROUND OXFORD

Garsington

4 miles SE of Oxford off the B480

The most distinguished building hereabouts is **Garsington Manor**, built on a hilltop of mellow Cotswold stone in the 16th century. Between 1915 and 1927, this was the home of the socialite Lady Ottoline Morrell who, along with her husband Philip, were unflaggingly hospitable to a whole generation of writers, artists, and intellectuals including Katherine Mansfield, Lytton Strachey, Clive Bell, Siegfried Sassoon, DH Lawrence, TS Eliot, Rupert Brooke, Bertrand Russell and Aldous Huxley. Huxley based an account of a country house party in his novel *Crome Yellow* on his experiences at Garsington, thereby causing a rift with his hostess. She found his description all too apt, and felt betrayed. Huxley insisted that he had not meant any harm, but she remained hurt and they were estranged for some time. It seems that Lady Ottoline was not very lucky in the artists on whom she lavished her attention and hospitality. DH Lawrence also quarrelled with her after drawing a less than flattering, but clearly recognisable, portrait of life at her house in *Women in Love*.

Garsington's other claim to literary fame is that Rider Haggard was sent to the school run by the Rev HJ Graham at the rectory in 1866. The present house is later, built in 1872, but across the road from the Church is a 16th century gateway from the rectory he would have

(Continued page 146)

WALK 4

Old Boars Hill

Start	Wootton, by church ¼ mile (400m) north of B4017
Distance	5 miles (8km)
Approximate time	2½ hours
Parking	Car park opposite Wootton church
Refreshments	Pub at Wootton, ¼ mile (400m) south of start
Ordnance Survey maps	Landranger 164 (Oxford), Explorer 180 (Oxford)

The gentle wooded slopes of Old Boars Hill rise to 540ft (165m) to the south-west of Oxford, and from several vantage points on this undemanding walk there are grand views over the city's 'dreaming spires'. In addition there are some equally fine views over the Thames Valley, Chilterns and Berkshire Downs. Part of the route is across land owned by the Oxford Preservation Trust, set up in 1926 to preserve the city's attractive rural setting.

Turn right out of the car park opposite Wootton church and take the first turning on the right, signposted to Old Boars Hill. Follow the lane around first a right-hand and then a left-hand bend, and opposite a house turn left **A**, at a public footpath sign to Cumnor, along a track towards stables. Pass to the right of the stables, climbing several stiles in quick succession, and continue along the right-hand edge of a field, by a hedge on the right, to turn right over a stile in the field corner. Immediately climb another stile and continue along the left-hand edge of a field, by a wire fence and hedge on the right, gradually bearing right away from the field-edge to a stile.

Climb this, keep ahead over the next field, climb another stile and continue along the left-hand edge of a field, by a wire fence on the left, following the field-edge as it bends to the right. Turn left over a stile and follow a narrow path between gardens to rejoin the lane. Turn left uphill to reach a T-junction at the top **B**.

Bear right here through a gate to enter Jarn Mound and Wild Garden, owned by the Oxford Preservation Trust and constructed under the orders of Sir Arthur Evans, the famous archaeologist, in the early 1930s. The route continues to the right, but keep ahead and climb steps to the top of Jarn Mound for the view over Oxford, the Chilterns and the Berkshire Downs, which is now unfortunately partially obscured by trees. Retrace your steps to the gate and in front of it turn left along the stony path that passes to the right of a stone commemorating Sir Arthur Evans, and follow this path through the well-wooded garden as it bears left passing through a fence on to a lane. Turn right along the lane, Ridgeway, and at a junction keep ahead along Berkeley Road. At a kissing-gate by an Oxford Preservation Trust notice and collection

WALK 4

box, turn left **C** and then turn right to follow a path across delightful, unimproved meadowland, at first keeping parallel to the lane on the right.

Later the path bears left and passes to the left of a copse, fenced tree and bench. From here there is a fine view of Oxford. Head slightly downhill, making for the left edge of the belt of trees in front where there is a stile by a metal gate. Climb the stile and then turn left along the left-hand edge of a field, by a hedge on the left. Go through a metal gate, keep ahead across the next field and go through another metal gate. Trace the right-hand edge of the next three fields to reach a metal gate into a farm lane. Turn left and in 70 yds (64m) fork left along the rough track. In a further 100 yds (91m) turn left along the waymarked bridleway, pass to the left of a cottage and, at the corner as the track turns right, go ahead over the waymarked stile and along the field edge beside a brook.

In the field corner turn right to continue along the edge of the field, by a fence on the left, and near the top of a slight rise turn left over a stile and take the narrow, enclosed path beside cupressus, continuing beyond along the path skirting scrubby pasture to meet a field road. Bear right along it – there are more fine views over Oxford to the right – heading across fields, later continuing between hedges to a T-junction of tracks **D**. Turn left along a tarmac track, which keeps along the left edge of Youlbury Wood, passing to the right of a reservoir. Take the first turning on the left, signposted to Oxford, but almost immediately turn right **E** through a gate into the Elizabeth Daryush Memorial Gardens, another piece of land owned by the Oxford Preservation Trust.

Follow a grassy path between trees and soon you reach a pond and benches, where there is a superb view ahead over the Berkshire Downs. Keep along a broad and obvious grassy path, and at a crossroads of paths about 100 yds (91m) in front of a house, bear right and continue down to a stile and public footpath sign at the bottom right-hand corner of the garden. Climb the stile to rejoin the tarmac track and turn left along it downhill. Later the track becomes a broader lane which continues through Wootton village to return to the starting point of the walk. ●

0 200 400 600 800metres 1 KILOMETRES
0 200 400 600yards ½ MILES

known. While there Haggard became friendly with a local farmer named Quartermain whom he must have remembered with affection as he used the name for his hero, many years later, in his novel *King Solomon's Mines*.

The village **Church of St Mary** is a pleasant and cosy building with fine views to the south over the Chilterns from its hill top position, but it also looks over the industrial belt to the south of Oxford. Though the interior is chiefly Victorian, the church has retained its Norman tower and inside there is an elegant memorial to Lady Ottoline.

WHEATLEY
4 miles E of Oxford on the A40

This former quarry village retains many old buildings, of which the most interesting is a curious conical lock-up. To the west, close to the M40 (junction 8), are the famous **Waterperry Gardens**

of Waterperry House (the house is not open to the public). Established as a residential gardening school for women in the 1930s, Waterperry is now part pleasure garden and part commercial garden centre. The gardens are host each year to Art in Action, which brings together many of the world's finest craftspeople.

THAME
11 miles E of Oxford on the A418

Founded in 635 as an administrative centre for the Bishop of Dorchester, Thame first became a market town in the 13th century and its importance as a commercial centre is evident by the wide main street it still has today. Lined with old inns and houses, some of which go back to the 15th century, this is a delightful place to visit.

The imposing **Church of St Mary**, tucked away at one end of the High Street,

COBWEBS DELICATESSEN & THE SUN

40 Church Road, Wheatley, Oxfordshire OX33 1NB
Tel: 01865 876543 (Cobwebs) 872264 (The Sun)

Cobwebs Delicatessen and The Sun are two places well worth visiting in the pleasant former quarry town of Wheatley. Both are owned by Helen Webb, who is personally involved in their running, along with friendly, helpful staff. Cobwebs, at the junction of Church Road and Holloway Road, is a small brick building with an 'old curiosity shop' frontage; cosy and comfortable, it combines the roles of

delicatessen, with a cornucopia of local and organic produce, crafts and gifts, and coffee shop serving light lunches. Opening times are 8.30 to 5.30 Monday to Saturday.

The Sun Inn, at No. 5 Church Road, was built in the 18th century with stones from the local quarry, which also supplied the building material for Windsor Castle. The front is bedecked with flowers in summer, earning prizes in various In Bloom competitions, and there's a large garden at the back. Inside, exposed stone, wooden floors, old beams and open fires create an inviting ambience for enjoying a drink or something from the menu of excellent home-cooked old-fashioned pub dishes. The inn has four warm, characterful en suite bedrooms, making it an ideal holiday or touring base. This part of Oxfordshire is excellent walking country, and local places of interest include the famous Waterperry Gardens; in Wheatley itself one of the more unusual buildings is a curious conical lock-up.

ANNA STEPHENS

56 North Street, Thame, Oxfordshire OX9 3BH
Tel: 01844 217999 Fax: 01844 260535
e-mail: momentum@waitrose.com

The husband and wife team of Anna Ivanovska and Stephen Hendry opened their furniture and accessories shop on January 1, 2001 after looking for premises for almost two years. A little shop that is big on quality, service and value, **Anna Stephens** stocks English pine furniture in a variety of painted, waxed or lacquered finishes. Also on display is an expanding range of contemporary oak and ethnic furniture, mattresses, divans and sofa beds, along with accessories such as silk cushions, throws and prints. Products are carefully selected with consideration of environmental impact and working conditions to the fore.

was built in the 13th century though the aisles were widened in the 14th century and the tower was heightened in the 15th century. In the centre of the chancel is a monument to Lord John Williams, and his wife, who was notorious for having helped burn Archbishop Thomas Cranmer in the 16th century. To the west of the church lies the **Prebendal House** which, in its oldest parts, dates from the 13th century. A prebend was an income granted to a priest by a Cathedral or Collegiate Church and, at Thame, the prebend was established in around 1140 by Lincoln Cathedral. A special residence for the holders of the office was first mentioned in 1234.

The town also has a famous **Grammar School**, housed in a Tudor building in Church Lane. The schoolmaster's house faces the road and over the doorway are the arms of Lord Williams, who founded the school in 1558. John Hampden, one of the Parliamentary leaders during the Civil War, was at school here and he also died at Thame. When the Civil War broke out he raised a regiment of infantry for the Parliamentary Army and fought with great bravery at Edgehill and Reading. However, he was wounded at the battle of Chalgrove Field in June 1643 and was carried back to Thame, where he died some days later in an inn which stood on the High Street. A plaque on a wall denotes the site.

ELSFIELD

2 miles N of Oxford off the A40

Elsfield was the home of the author and administrator John Buchan, 1st Baron Tweedsmuir, from 1919 to 1935, when he left to take up his appointment as Governor-General of Canada. During his time at Elsfield Manor House he wrote a number of books, including *Midwinter*, written in 1923 and partly set in the vicinity. His ashes are buried by the east wall of the churchyard of St Thomas of Canterbury. RD Blackmore, author of *Lorna Doone*, lived in Elsfield as a child while his father was the vicar.

BICESTER

Though the name (which is pronounced Bister) suggests that this was a Roman settlement, the town was not, in fact, established until Saxon times and the Roman name comes as a result of the nearby and long since vanished Roman town of **Alchester**. By the time of the 12th century, the town was the home of both an Augustinian priory and also a Benedictine nunnery. Growing up around these religious houses and its market, the town suffered a disastrous fire in the early 18th century and most of the buildings seen here today date from that time onwards. Hunting and horse-racing played as much a part in the prosperity of Bicester as agriculture though industrialisation has been sporadic. The founding here of the Army's ordnance depot in 1941 brought much new development, which continued until the 1960s.

AROUND BICESTER

Ardley

3 miles N of Bicester off the B4100

In Ardley Quarry, close to Junction 10 of the M40, scientists from Cambridge University and the Oxford University Museum of Natural History have recently discovered dinosaur tracks suggesting that large two-legged beasts from the Middle Jurassic period, about 163 million years ago, could attain speeds much faster than had previously been thought. The species is believed to be *Megalosaurus Bucklandii*, the first dinosaur ever identified. It's an interesting theory, but will it run?

Lower Heyford

6 miles W of Bicester on the B4030

Situated at a ford across the River Cherwell, which was replaced in the late 13th century by a stone bridge, the village lies on the opposite bank from its other half - Upper Heyford. To the south of the village lies **Rousham House**, a fine mansion built in the mid-17th century for Sir Robert Dormer that is set in magnificent gardens on the banks of the River Cherwell. The gardens as seen today were laid out by William Kent in 1738 and include lots of water features, sculpture and follies. Next to the house are very attractive pre-Kent walled gardens with a parterre, herbaceous borders, a rose garden and a vegetable garden. The garden is open to the public all year round while the house has limited opening.

Deddington

8½ miles NW of Bicester off the A423

Visitors to this old market town might recognise it as the place that was demolished by a runaway crane in the television adaptation of Tom Sharpe's *Blott on the Landscape*. The damage was, of course, cleverly faked and Deddington, which hovers between a small town and a large village, still retains all its medieval character. Surveyed in the Domesday Book as twice the value of Banbury, the town never developed in the same way as Banbury and Bicester, but it remains a prosperous agricultural centre with a still bustling market place. Little can now be seen of the 12th century **Deddington Castle**. This was destroyed in the 14th century and most of the building materials were put to good use in other areas of the town. However, excavations have revealed the remains of a curtain wall, a hall, and a small rectangular keep. Meanwhile, the **Church of St Peter and St Paul** is still very visible and can be found on the edge of the Market Place. In the 1630s, the church's steeple collapsed, taking part of the main building with it and, though rebuilding work begun soon afterwards, the intervention of the Civil War made this a long project. During this time, Charles I had the church bells melted down to provide his army with another cannon. Another steeple was not built and the tower was heavily buttressed to ensure that it would never collapse.

Close by is **Castle House**, where Pier Gaveston, Edward II's favourite, was held before his execution in 1312. The house's two towers were added later, in the 1650s, when the house was in the ownership of Thomas Appletree. A supporter of Cromwell, Appletree was ordered to destroy the property of Royalists and it was material from two local houses that he used in his building work.

BANBURY

Famous for its cross, cakes, and the nursery rhyme, this historic and thriving market town has managed to hang on to many of its old buildings as well as become home to Europe's largest livestock market. The famous **Banbury Cross** can be found in Horsefair where it was erected, in 1859, replacing the previous one demolished by the Parliamentarians during the Civil War. It was built to commemorate the marriage of Queen Victoria's oldest daughter to the Prussian Crown Prince, and the figures around the bottom of the cross, of Queen Victoria, Edward VII, and George V, were added in 1914.

The town's other legendary claim to fame is its cakes, made of spicy fruit pastry, which can still be bought. Banbury was also, at one time, famous for its cheeses, which were only about an inch thick. This gave rise to the expression 'thin as a Banbury cheese'.

On the east side of the Horsefair stands **St Mary's Church**, a classical building of warm-coloured stone and hefty pillars which are pleasantly eccentric touches. The original architect was SP Cockerell, though the tower and portico were completed between 1818 and 1822 by his son, CR Cockerell. The style reflects the strong influence on English architecture of Piranesi's Views of Rome, using massive shapes and giving stone the deliberately roughened appearance which comes from the technique known as rustication.

In **Banbury Museum** can be found the story of the town's development, from the days when it came under the influence of the bishops of Lincoln, through the woollen trade of the 16th century, to the present day. The effects of the Civil War on the town were also great; the Royalists held Banbury Castle and there were two sieges here. The completion of the Coventry to Oxford Canal in 1778, the coming of the railway in 1850, and the opening of the M40 in 1991 have all played their part in making Banbury a large and successful commercial town.

AROUND BANBURY

Broughton

2½ miles SW of Banbury on the B4035

The moated mansion, **Broughton Castle**, was built in 1300 by Sir John de Broughton as his manor on the site of the existing house. Extended and altered in the 16th century to turn it into a fine Tudor home, the house has been owned by the same family since 1451. Over the years, there have been several Royal visitors including Queen Anne of Denmark, wife of James I. Both James I and Edward VII used the aptly named King's Chamber, with its handpainted Chinese wall paper. The house also played a part in the Civil War as it has a secret room where leaders of the Parliamentary forces laid their plans.

Bloxham

3½ miles SW of Banbury on the A361

Dominated by the 14th century St Mary's Church, whose spire is a highly visible local landmark and its Victorian public school, this large village is one of narrow lanes and fine gentlemen's houses. The old court house, to the south of the church, contains the **Bloxham Village Museum**, where there is a permanent collection of items on display which tell the life of the inhabitants of the village and surrounding area.

South Newington

6 miles SW of Banbury on the A361

This small village of ironstone dwellings is home to the **Church of St Peter and**

Turpins Lodge Riding Centre

Lodge Farm, Hook Norton, Banbury, Oxfordshire OX15 5DQ
Tel: 01608 737033 Fax: 01608 737080
e-mail: caroline@tlrs.fsnet.co.uk
website: www.turpinslodge.co.uk

Set in delightful countryside on the eastern fringes of Hook Norton, **Turpins Lodge Riding Centre** has been based at Lodge Farm for the past 14 years. Owned and run by Caroline, John and Victoria, the riding centre has been designed to give maximum enjoyment to visitors of all ages, both for riders and for families and friends who have come to watch the riders responding to the expert tuition on offer. At the heart of the centre is an area where horses are stabled, groomed and prepared for riding.

There is a purpose-built indoor arena, with plenty of spectator seating and there is an outdoor menage and jumping arena, to test both the novice riders and those with more experience and expertise in the saddle. There's plenty of space for the horses to graze and relax when not being ridden, and the centre can cater for all livery requirements. All abilities are welcome from four years upwards, and the centre is Council licensed and ABRS approved. School holiday specials include Own a Pony days and non-residential short courses. If you can ride and wish to see the countryside, what better way than on horseback. It is essential to book in advance as groups are small and very popular.

Turpin Cottage

Lodge Farm, Hook Norton, Banbury, Oxfordshire OX15 5DQ
Tel: 01608 737033 Fax: 01608 737080
e-mail: john@turpinslodge.freeserve.co.uk
website: www.turpinlodge.co.uk

Turpin Cottage is the creation of John Romer, who has masterminded the amazing conversion of a small stone barn into a luxury cottage. The emphasis throughout is on style and quality, and the standard of workmanship is second to none. The feeling inside is reminiscent of a period country house in France, with heavy beams contributing to the atmospheric setting. The kitchen is equipped with a handsome red Aga cooker, and other accessories are concealed in beautifully crafted purpose-built units.

A wrought-iron spiral staircase leads to the upper floor, and metal ladders ascend to various areas in the work space. A spa bath is just one of many touches of luxury, and pipes under the polished wood floors provide warmth in abundance when the summer's over. Turpin Cottage, of which John is immensely and justly proud, is place to dream of, a superb holiday home for a family exploring the lovely local countryside or enjoying the delights of horse riding at the adjacent riding centre.

Vincula, which contains the best medieval wall paintings in the county. Detail and colouring are both superb in the depictions, which include the murders of Thomas à Becket and Thomas of Lancaster (a rebel against Edward II), St Margaret slaying a dragon and a wonderful Virgin and Child.

Great Tew

7 miles SW of Banbury off the B4022

One of the most picturesque villages in the county, Great Tew, a planned estate village, had fallen into such disrepair by the 1970s that it was declared a conservation area in order to save it from complete dereliction. Today, the thatched cottages and houses from the 16th, 17th and 18th centuries nestle in a fold in the landscape of rolling countryside. The big house hereabouts is Great Tew Park, dating mainly from the 19th century. Only the garden walls remain of its 17th century predecessor, owned by Lucius Carey, Lord Falkland, and a gathering place for some of the great writers and intellectuals of the day, including Edmund Waller and Ben Jonson. In the 17th century the 5th Viscount Falkland was Secretary to the Navy and gave his name to the Falkland Islands.

Swerford

7 miles SW of Banbury off the A361

Lying deep in the valley of the River Swire, Swerford once had a castle. Mounds and earthworks are all that remain, seen behind the Church of St Mary, which has architectural features from as far back as the 13th century and some fascinating gargoyles.

Hook Norton

7 miles SW of Banbury off the A361

This large village is best known for its brewery, which was set up by John Harris from his farmhouse in 1849. He started there as a maltster and after years of gaining expertise and learning from experiments he constructed a purpose-built brewery in 1872. The Brewery, which moved to its present premises in 1900, remains in the Harris family.

Swalcliffe

5 miles W of Banbury on the B4035

The village is dominated by the large **Church of St Peter and St Paul** which towers over all the other buildings here. Founded in Saxon times, the bulk of the building dates from the 12th, 13th and 14th centuries and it is the tracery in the east window which makes the church noteworthy. However, by far the most impressive building in Swalcliffe is the **Barn**, which has been acknowledged as one of the finest 15th century half-cruck barns in the country. Built as the manorial barn by New College, Oxford, in 1400-1409, it was used to store produce from the manor and never to store tithes.

Today, it is home to a collection of agricultural and trade vehicles.

To the northeast of the village, on **Madmarston Hill**, are the remains of an Iron Age hill fort which was occupied from the 2nd century BC to the 1st century AD.

Wroxton

3 miles NW of Banbury on the A422

A charming village of brown stone cottages clustered round the village pond, from which a road leads to **Wroxton Abbey**. This impressive Jacobean mansion was built by Sir William Pope, Earl of Downe, and was the home of the North family for 300 years. The gardens and grounds of the Abbey, now restored as an 18th century park, are open to the public, but the house is not. All Saints Church contains several imposing monuments including those to Sir William and his wife, Lord North, who was Prime Minister from 1770 to 1782, and the banker Thomas Coutts.

Cropredy

4 miles N of Banbury off the A423

Cropredy Bridge was the site of a Civil War battle in 1644, where the Royalists defeated Cromwell's men. The church contains some relics of the battle, including a lectern thrown into the river for safe keeping and rescued later.

Claydon

5 miles N of Banbury off the A423

Claydon is the most northerly village in Oxfordshire, a somewhat remote rural community with farms reaching almost into the village itself. Here, appropriately, is the **Granary Museum of Bygones**, a fascinating place that re-creates life on a farm about a century ago. In the farm loft are hundreds of everyday items long since replaced by their modern equivalents as well as complete re-creations of a cottage kitchen, a blacksmith's and a wheelwright's workshop.

The Green Scene

The Green, Cropredy, Oxfordshire OX17 1NH
Tel: 01295 758203 Fax: 01865 758085

Located on the green in a village just north of Banbury, the **Green Scene** comprises three separate ventures under the same roof of a 17th century stone-built cottage. Gina Cumming owns and runs the ground-floor gallery and coffee shop. The former displays the best of contemporary work by British craft designers and local artists, including watercolours, ceramics, glass, wood turning and silver jewellery. In the coffee shop, visitors can enjoy light lunches, delicious home-made pastries and fine coffee served throughout the day (the gallery and coffee shop are open from 10.30 to 5 except on Monday).

On the first floor, Sue Jeffries is the owner and manager of Chattles, which deals in antique furniture, china, silver, pictures, books and jewellery and also has a small section selling good-quality secondhand clothes. On the first floor, too, Sue's daughter Polly, a highly qualified chiropractor, runs a well-equipped chiropractic clinic whose services include aromatherapy and remedial massage and animal physical therapy (Tel: 01295 271011, e-mail: polly.jeffries@hemscott.net). The nearby Oxford Canal, the delightful local countryside and the annual Fairport music festival bring visitors from near and far, and for a growing number of them a visit to the Green Scene is an essential part of the itinerary.

3 HAMPSHIRE AND THE NEW FOREST

A county of strong contrasts, from densely populated urban areas to peaceful villages and stretches of open countryside and woodland. In the northwest are the North Downs, which are actually uplands, gently rolling, wooded hills whose folds shelter many picturesque little villages. But other parts are quite heavily populated, with prosperous towns such as Basingstoke, Aldershot and Farnborough sprawling across the map. Northeast Hampshire has one major city, Winchester, one major town, Andover, and scores of scattered villages in a part of the county with some really grand scenery, particularly as the North Downs roll westwards to meet Salisbury Plain. In the northern part are the peaceful open chalklands, while towards the south the rivers and streams and water meadows are the focus, bringing anglers from near and far for the finest trout fishing in the land. Winchester, which was already an important community in the Roman period, became the capital of the Kingdom of Wessex under the Anglo-Saxons and the capital of the whole country in the reign of Alfred the Great.

Fishing on the River Test

Winchester is best known for its wonderful Cathedral and its renowned public school, but its other attractions could easily fill a whole book, and this area of Hampshire has a great deal to offer outside its major city, from historic and pre-historic sites to Victorian extravaganza at Highclere, the largest house in the county, and nostalgia on the Watercress Line steam railway. Evidence of Iron Age occupation is particularly strong around the old wool town of Andover, most importantly at the hill fort of Danebury, which was a stronghold of the Atrebates tribe. The whole region is criss-crossed by marked trails and paths and cycle routes and some of the scenery and views are spectacular. The highest point in the region is Farley Mount, a country park with an abundant variety of flora and fauna. In the

Thatched Cottage, Wherwell

The New Forest

south of the county are further contrasts: the coastal crescent that stretches from Southampton through Fareham to Portsmouth and Havant is busy, bustling and built up, while inland there are parts of the South Downs that are as scenic and peaceful as anywhere in the county. Southampton boasts one of the finest natural harbours in the world and will be forever associated with the glamour of the transatlantic liners, which had their heyday in the 1920s and 1930s. The associations of nearby Portsmouth are not with the liners but with fighting ships such as the *Mary Rose*, *HMS Victory* and *HMS Warrior*. Portsmouth is also a popular seaside resort providing, with its neighbour Hayling Island, seven miles of sandy beaches. Sailing for pleasure is a major interest all along this part of the coast, and the fleet of yachts and powered craft berthed in and around the Solent, with Hamble as its 'capital', is one of the largest and most concentrated in the world.

One of the country's greatest natural treasures, the New Forest is a very special part of rural England. It acquired its name after William the Conqueror proclaimed it as his hunting ground and began a programme of planting thousands of trees. The largest wild area in lowland Britain, the Forest is famous for its deer and its ponies; it is ideal walking country and also has a network of waymarked cycle routes.

ADVERTISERS AND PLACES OF INTEREST

LOCATOR MAP

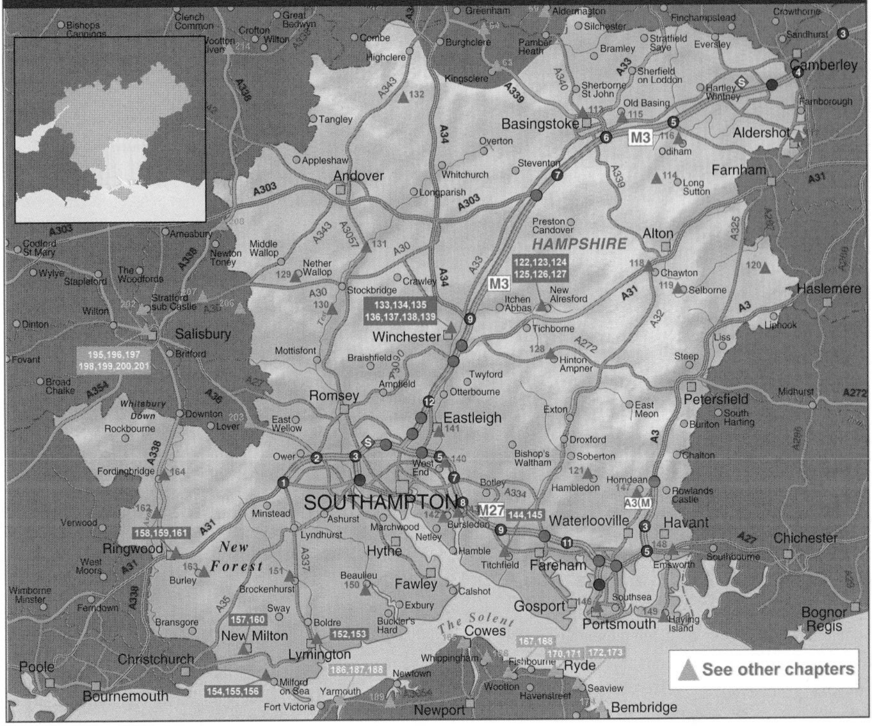

ADVERTISERS AND PLACES OF INTEREST

BASINGSTOKE

A thriving industrial and commercial town wi a long history that is not always apparent from its predominantly modern look, largely the result of London overspill. But something of old Basingstoke can still be seen, including the peaceful and evocative ruins of the 13th century Chapel of the Holy Ghost and the 14th century Church of St Michael the Archangel. The old Town Hall, dating from 1832, is now home to the **Willis Museum** with its exhibits of Basingstoke over the last 200 years and a collection of maps and clocks. The museum is named after George Willis, a clockmaker and sometime Mayor of Basingstoke, who established the museum in 1931. A more recent attraction - The **Milestones Museum** (see panel above) - was opened in November 2000, bringing Hampshire's heritage to life in an award-winning modern building.

MILESTONES MUSEUM

Leisure Park, Churchill Way West,
Basingstoke, Hampshire RG21 6YR
Tel: 01256 477766 Fax: 01256 477784
website: milestones-museum.com

Opened in November 2000, this is Hampshire's living history museum, where the county's heritage comes to life in cobbled streets with shops, factories, interactive areas, staff in period costume and superb exhibits relating to industrial and everyday life.

Among the many highlights are the Tasker and Thorneycroft collections of agricultural and commercial vehicles, and the renowned AA collection.

AROUND BASINGSTOKE

OLD BASING

2 miles NE of Basingstoke off the A30

The modern town of Basingstoke offers its residents a wide choice of up-to-date amenities, but two miles to the east, Old Basing, with its narrow streets, old cottages and the much-visited ruins of **Basing House**, could be on another planet (see panel opposite). A bridge on the site crosses the old **Basingstoke Canal**, which was opened in 1794 linking the town with London. The canal

STREET FARMHOUSE

Alton Road, South Warnborough, Nr Hook,
Hampshire RG29 1RS
Tel/Fax: 01256 862225

In an attractive Jacobean farmhouse, Colin and Wendy Turner offer quiet, comfortable Bed & Breakfast accommodation in four well-appointed bedrooms. All the rooms have washbasins, tv, and tea-makers and guests start the day with an excellent breakfast served in the elegant dining room. The farmhouse retains many original details such as beamed walls, a handsome inglenook fireplace and a vaulted kitchen ceiling. There's a large garden, and in season an outdoor heated swimming pool is available for guests' use. **Street Farmhouse** is an ideal base for country lovers, and the nearby M3 gives quick access to both London and the Southwest. Children are welcome, but not pets.

Basing House

Redbridge Lane,
Old Basing, Basingstoke,
Hampshire RG24 7HB
Tel: 01256 467294

Built on a massive scale inside the walls of a medieval castle, the house was once the largest private residence in the country. The ruins of the old and new houses, the riverside walk, the dovecotes and the spectacular 16th century grange barn add up to an attraction of great appeal, and the beauty of the place is enhanced by the recently re-created 17th century garden inside the Tudor walls. The house was sacked by Cromwell's men, with Cromwell himself present, after a long and arduous siege. The ruins include the historic Garrison gateway and the foundations and cellars of the old house, and the remains of the north wing of the new. Open Wed-Sun and Bank Holiday afternoons in summer.

was never as widely used as had been hoped and gradually fell into disuse, but large sections have now been restored and boat trips can be taken in summer from the smart Canal Visitor Centre at Mytchett, near Camberley in Surrey. On the theme of the transport of yesteryear, a passenger railway once operated between Basingstoke and Alton, and one of its stations, Cliddesden, was used for the filming of the 1937 Will Hay classic *Oh! Mr Porter*.

Preston Candover

7 miles S of Basingstoke on the B3046

This is the largest of the local Candovers (the others, to the south, are Candover Brown and Candover Chilton), with a Victorian church and the ruins of a much older church.

Steventon

8 miles W of Basingstoke off the A303/B3400

This is the village where Jane Austen was born in 1775 and where she spent the first 25 years of her life. During this time she wrote *Pride and Prejudice*, *Sense and Sensibility* and *Northanger Abbey*, though they were not published while she was here (her father offered *Pride and Prejudice* to a publisher in 1797, but he turned it down without even reading it!). The village church, where her father was rector, contains some memorials to the Austen family and also some fragments of medieval wall painting. Some of the Austens are buried in the churchyard, where a 900-year-old yew stands proudly.

Overton

8 miles W of Basingstoke on the B3400

A sizeable village near the source of the River Test, its broad main street lined with handsome Georgian houses. It was once an important staging post on the London-Winchester coach route, and the annual sheep fair was one of the largest in the county; it was held each year for centuries until coming to an end in the 1930s. The area north of Overton towards Kingsclere includes **Watership Down**, high up on a ridge, with wonderful views. This is the setting of the eponymous book by Richard Adams; it is now a nature reserve and, yes, there are lots of rabbits. The Down is on the long-distance footpath the **Wayfarer's Walk**, which runs from Inkpen Beacon just over the border in Berkshire with Emsworth on the Hampshire coast.

Sherborne St John

3 miles N of Basingstoke off the A340

One of the best known buildings in the county, **The Vyne** was built in the 16th century for Lord Sandys, Lord Chamberlain at the Court of Henry Vlll. Of particular note are the classical portico (the first in Britain when added in the 17th century), some marvellous linenfold panelling in the Oak Gallery and a Tudor chapel with Renaissance stained glass, Flemish Majolica tiles and Gothic painted vaultings. It stands in a classic parkland setting on the A340 between Sherborne St John and Bramley.

Bramley

5 miles N of Basingstoke off the A340

The **Church of St James** has immense appeal with its combination of the homely and the grand. Its main treasure is its wall paintings, notably of St Christopher and of Thomas à Becket. The south transept is the work of the renowned architect Sir John Soane - for him a rare sortie into ecclesiastical fields.

Stratfield Saye

7 miles NE of Basingstoke off the A33

The estate and **Stratfield Saye House** were presented to the Duke of Wellington as a reward for his defeat of Napoleon at Waterloo. The long two-storey house is full of Wellington relics, including books, flags and his splendidly ornate funeral carriage, made from cannon captured at Waterloo. A whole room is devoted to Wellington's beloved charger Copenhagen, who is buried in the grounds. Wellington Country Park, with fine walks and numerous attractions, is three miles away.

The Drawing Room, Stratfield Saye House

Pamber Heath

8 miles N of Basingstoke off the A340

Between the villages of Pamber Green and Pamber Heath lies **Pamber Forest**, a nature reserve where a variety of habitats, from dry open heathland to wood pasture and stream valleys, each supports its own distinctive range of wildlife. The third Pamber is Pamber End, where the ruins of a 12th century priory church can be seen.

Silchester

9 miles N of Basingstoke off the A340

Excavation continues to unearth treasures at the famous Roman site of Silchester, where earlier work gave us the most complete plan of any Roman town in Britain. The Romans called it **Calleva Atrebatum** - the Atrebates were a local British tribe who founded the settlement just before the Romans arrived. The perimeter wall can still be traced, and one of the many impressive remains is that of the 1st century amphitheatre beyond the walls. Most of the treasures discovered at the site are now in Reading Museum. Also of note in Silchester is the whitewashed 12th century **Church of St Mary**, which boasts some superb woodwork, 13th century wall paintings and a 14th century stone effigy of an early restorer. It lies within the walls of the Roman town.

ART LEGACY GALLERY

95 High Street, Odiham, Hampshire RG29 1LA
Tel: 01256 703370
e-mail: gallery@artlegacyuk.com website: www.artlegacyuk.com

Located in the main street of the Tudor village of Odiham, **Art Legacy** specialises in contemporary art for sale to discerning collectors. The Gallery exhibits a range of oil paintings, ceramics, optical glass and sculptures in cast iron, bronze and cast aluminium, all by new and renowned artists, many of whom have pieces in major museums and galleries. They include Eduardo Paolozzi, Richard Ennis, Catrin Howell, Bernard Meadows, Chris Gollon and Dennis Mitchell. International artworks can be sourced and commissions undertaken.

SHERFIELD ON LODDON

4 miles NE of Basingstoke off the A33

Follow the brown signs at Sherfield on Loddon roundabout to find **Longbridge Mill**, a restored water mill housed in a timber-framed 16th century building. Flour-milling demonstrations are given each month.

ODIHAM

7 miles E of Basingstoke on the A287

Several buildings of note in this fascinating old market town. The 15th century church is the largest in the county and has a rarity in the shape of a hudd, a portable cloth-covered wooden frame which would provide some shelter for the rector while conducting burial services in the rain. In a corner of the churchyard stands the **Pest House**, built around 1625 as an isolation ward for patients with infectious diseases, including the plague. Later an almshouse, it is now a little museum. All that remains of once grand **Odiham Castle** is an octagonal keep; the castle was only a few years old when it played host to King John on the eve of his journey to Runnymede to put his signature on Magna Carta.

LONG SUTTON

8 miles SE of Basingstoke off the A32

Set in very attractive walking, cycling and horse-riding country, Long Sutton is a classic Hampshire village complete with duckpond. The village is also home to **Lord Wandsworth School** which has a sporting pedigree and has produced many well-known sportsmen including Jonny Wilkinson, England's top-scoring fly half and a star in the Newcastle team.

HARTLEY WINTNEY

9 miles NE of Basingstoke on the A30

Riding through Hartley Wintney in 1821, William Cobbett, the author of *Rural Rides*, was delighted to see young oaks planted on the village green. These oaks, known as the Mildmay Oaks, were a gift from the Lady of the Manor, Lady Mildmay, and were planted after Trafalgar as a source of timber for ships. They were never needed for that purpose and have continued to provide the village centre with a lovely sylvan setting. South of the village, the old **Church of St Mary**, largely untouched since a renovation in 1834, features high-sided box pews along the main aisle, elegant galleries spanning the nave and transepts, and colourful funeral hatchments. A mile west of Hartley, **West Green House Garden**, in the care of the National Trust, is a series of charming gardens set around an equally appealing 18th century house. Among the highlights are stunning herbaceous beds, an ornamental kitchen garden and a grand water garden or nymphaeum.

Eversley

12 miles NE of Basingstoke on the A327

The best-known resident of this village in the far north of the county was Charles Kingsley, author of *The Water Babies* and *Westward Ho!*. Sometime chaplain to Queen Victoria, he is buried in his own churchyard, and his life is commemorated in a hall in the village. And the school gates, put up in 1951 for the Festival of Britain, include the figure of a boy chimney sweep.

Aldershot Military Museum

Queens Avenue, Aldershot,
Hampshire GU11 2LG
Tel: 01252 314598

The Museum covers the histories of Aldershot military town and the adjoining civil towns of Aldershot and Farnborough. The complex contains a rich mixture of buildings, objects, displays, vehicles and archives, and each of the several galleries has a different theme and character.

The John Reed Gallery covers the history of the Army in Aldershot from its arrival in 1854, and includes a rare example of a Victorian barrack room displayed in its original setting. Rushmoor Local History Gallery, which with the John Reed Gallery occupies a pair of unique barrack bungalows built in 1894, deals with the history of the civil towns of Aldershot and Farnborough. The Cody Gallery is named after an American, Samuel Franklin Cody, who made Britain's first powered flight at Farnborough in 1908. The Montgomery Gallery, which stood originally in the grounds of Monty's home at Isington near Alton, houses a collection of larger exhibits, including field guns and other vehicles. The museum's collection of vehicles, some here, some kept outside, ranges from the mass-produced Willys jeep of 1943 to the formidable 60-ton Chieftain tank; most are in full working order.

Aldershot

15 miles E of Basingstoke on the A331

Aldershot was a little-known village of some 800 souls until the Army decided to settle here in considerable numbers, since when the population has grown to around 55,000 and the town has become the most famous military centre in the country. The story of how Aldershot became the home of the British Army is told in the **Aldershot Military Museum**, (see panel above) which occupies the last two surviving Victorian barracks blocks in the middle of the camp. Special events are held throughout the year, and there's always a special thrill when a Chieftain battle tank is part of the show.

The airborne side of the towns is covered in the **Airborne Forces Museum** in Browning Barracks, about half a mile from the Military Museum. The Heroes Shrine in Manor Park, Aldershot commemorates the dead of the First World War, while a nearby sunken garden remembers those who fell in the Second World War. The Duke of Wellington is singled out for honour by an imposing bronze statue on Round Hill. The statue originally stood on top of the Triumphal Arch at Hyde Park Corner in London but was moved to Aldershot in 1885. The men of Aldershot became the first aviators in the country, using Farnborough Common for their flying and building their aircraft sheds where the Royal Aircraft Establishment stands today. The first occupant of the site was the Ballooning Factory, which became the Royal Aircraft Factory and then the RAE.

Farnborough

15 miles E of Basingstoke on the A331

Visitors arrive in Farnborough in their thousands for the Farnborough Air Show, held every two years, but a less well-

Harrier Hawk Jump Jet, Farnborough Air Show

known site just outside Farnborough is **St Michael's Abbey**, built in flamboyant French style by the Empress Eugenie in honour of her husband the Emperor Napoleon lll. She came to live in England with her son and was joined later in exile by her husband, who died at Chislehurst after an operation to remove bladder stones. The Emperor, the Empress and their son, who was killed in the service of the British Army in Zululand, are buried in three five-ton tombs in an ornate mausoleum next to the abbey. Also buried here is the family's devoted Corsican secretary Franchescini Pietri.

ALTON

Surrounded by hop fields and some of Hampshire's loveliest countryside, Alton has a history that can be traced to pre-Roman times. Long known for its brewing industry, it was also an important centre for cloth-making, and its position on the route from London to Winchester accounts for the large number of coaching inns in the town. One of the most important landmarks is the impressive double-nave, partly-Norman **St Lawrence's Church**, which was the scene of a dramatic episode during the Civil War. A large force of Roundheads drove some 80 Royalists into the church, killing 60 of them. The Royalist commander, Colonel Boles, made a heroic last stand from the splendid Jacobean pulpit but was eventually shot and killed. The church door and several of the Norman pillars are still scarred with the bullet marks left in that conflict. A more peaceful legacy of the past is the series of comical 11th century carvings of animals and birds, including a wolf gnawing a bone and two donkeys kicking their heels in the air. Nearby, in the old cemetery, is the grave of Fanny Adams, who, aged 8, was killed and hacked to pieces by one Frederick Baker. The story of the horrid murder was widely reported, and sailors with a macabre sense of humour began to use the phrase 'Sweet Fanny Adams' for the somewhat dubious tinned mutton which had recently been issued among their rations. In time, the saying became used for anything contemptuously

Flood Meadows, Alton

considered worthless (and eventually for nothing at all). The **Allen Gallery** in Church Street contains a fine collection of porcelain, pottery and tiles, including the famous Elizabethan Tichborne spoons. There is a delightful walled garden behind the gallery and a smart new lounge where coffee and cakes are served. In the High Street, the **Curtis Museum**, named after its founder Dr William Curtis, features exhibits of natural history, geology and archaeology, as well as the story of the local hop-picking and brewing industry. Among the highlights are the Roman Selborne Cup and the imposing Anglo-Saxon Alton Buckle, while children will make straight for the Gallery of Childhood, a colourful little gallery packed with toys, dolls and books. Alton, whose High Street was once part of the old Pilgrims Way, is the point at which the Watercress Line (see under New Alresford page 167) joins the national railway system.

On the northern edge of Alton, **Holybourne** is an ancient village constructed on the Roman town of Vindomis. The church is built on the source of the River Bourne. Mrs Gaskell, author and friend of the Brontës, lived here.

A little way east of Alton on the B3004, **St Mary's Church** in **East Worldham** contains an effigy thought to be that of Phillipa, wife of Geoffrey Chaucer. It could very well be that good lady, as their son Thomas was Lord of the Manor here from 1418 to 1434.

AROUND ALTON

CHAWTON

2 miles S of Alton off the A31

The **Jane Austen Museum** is located in Chawton House (see panel below), a redbrick property where the author lived from 1809 until shortly before her death in 1817.

Jane's mother and sister Cassandra, who lived at the house with her, are buried in the graveyard of the nearby Church of St Nicholas (Jane spent the last few weeks of her life in Winchester and is buried in Winchester Cathedral).

SELBORNE

3 miles S of Alton on the B3066

Selborne is an attractive village in a little valley in beautiful countryside, famous

JANE AUSTEN'S HOUSE

Chawton, Nr Alton, Hampshire GU34 1SD
Tel/Fax: 01420 83262
website: www.janeaustemuseum.org.uk

Jane Austen's House is a 17th century redbrick building where the author lived from 1809 until shortly before her death in 1817. Now administered as a museum, the house contains an extensive collection of family momentoes and documentary material, including first editions, copies of letters written by Jane, and needlework and patchwork made by Jane and her mother and sister. The Admiral's Room houses memorabilia of Jane's two brothers, both distinguished sailors, while another room contains a period costume exhibition. The house is open daily from 1 March to 31 December and at weekends in January and February.

for its association with the 18th century naturalist Gilbert White.

Gilbert White was buried in the graveyard of the village church, where he is commemorated by two fine stained glass windows. Also to be seen in the churchyard is the stump of a yew tree, believed to have been up to 1,400 years old when it succumbed to a storm in 1990. Parts of the top were used to make a font cover and an altar.

PETERSFIELD

A pleasant market town in a wide valley in the shadow of Butser Hill, the highest point of the South Downs. Its fine old square is looked over by an equestrian statue of King William lll in Roman dress, erected in 1753 with a bequest of £500 from the local MP Sir William Jolliffe. Some of the town's oldest houses are set around The Spain, an attractive green

(Continued page 166)

GILBERT WHITE'S HOUSE AND THE OATES MUSEUM

The Wakes, High Street, Selborne, Hampshire GU34 3JH
Tel: 01420 511275 Fax: 01420 511040

Gilbert White's House is a charmingly modest 18th century country house with a glorious garden, home of the renowned naturalist and author of *The Natural History of Selborne*, the Reverend Gilbert White (1720-1793). The rooms are furnished in period style, with many of his possessions on display, and the garden, too, has been restored to its 18th century form. Also here is the Oates Museum commemorating the life and exploits of Captain Lawrence Oates, who died on Captain Scott's ill-fated Antarctic Expedition. Books, gifts and plants are on sale in the shop, and in the Tea Parlour delicious fare based on 18th century recipes is served. Various courses, events and exhibitions are held throughout the year.

VICTORIAN DREAMS

The Old Holme School, Village Green, Crabtree Lane, Headley, Hampshire GU35 8QH
Tel: 01428 717000 e-mail: sales@victorian-dreams.co.uk
Fax: 01428 717111 website: www.victorian-dreams.co.uk

In the world of antique bedsteads **Victorian Dreams** is one of the very best names to know. The company, which is owned by Debbie Hack, was established in 1990 and is situated in a former Victorian primary school. There are hundreds of bedsteads on display, some already restored, others awaiting restoration, and at least 20 are always set up with mattresses and linen. Many of the beds are over 100 years old, and the skilled and enthusiastic workshop team produce a level of workmanship that is second to none.

Many customers enjoy choosing an unrestored bedstead, confident of the finished appearance having seen the completed examples. Every type of antique bedstead imaginable finds a place in the showrooms - brass and iron, all brass, wooden, caned and upholstered, both ornate and simple in style, and they keep in stock a comprehensive range of mattresses and linen. Victorian Dreams also stocks an extensive range of reproduction metal beds, all produced by an English family-run foundry. These beds are faithful copies of original Victorian designs, but with the benefit of being available in sizes difficult or impossible to find among the originals. Victorian Dreams, which stands on the B3002 by the village green, is open from 9.00am to 5.30pm Monday to Saturday and from 10.00am to 4.00pm on Sunday.

WALK 5

Selborne and Noar Hill

Start	Selborne village
Distance	5¼ miles (8.4km)
Approximate time	3–3½ hours
Parking	Selborne village car park
Refreshments	Pubs, tearooms and hotel in Selborne
Ordnance Survey maps	Landranger 186 (Aldershot & Guildford), Explorer 133 (Haslemere & Petersfield)

After leaving this renowned Hampshire village, the route of the walk soon leads away from the busy through-road and up into woodland to the nature reserve on Noar Hill. Continuing around the hillside, the path provides panoramic views of the surrounding farmland. It then descends through fields and along an ancient track before rising again to Selborne Hill. The final descent is made along a narrow zigzag path back into Selborne. It is well worth allowing time at the beginning or end of the walk to wander through the village and visit the museums and church.

Selborne was made famous by the eminent naturalist Gilbert White who was born here in his grandfather's vicarage in 1720. He spent most of his life in the village studying and writing about natural history and wrote the book which has made him internationally well-known, The Natural History and Antiquities of Selborne. His old home is now a museum and stands opposite the church of St Mary, built around 1180. A yew in the churchyard made news when it was blown down in the gales of 1990. By then it was around 1,400 years old and 26ft (7.9m) in girth. Unwilling to loose this important part of their history the villagers had the tree replanted. It is too early yet to tell whether it is regrowing successfully.

It is appropriate that this walk runs first through Noar Hill's ancient chalk quarries, now a nature reserve renowned for its wild flowers and attendant butterflies in summer. Thirty-five species of butterfly have been recorded here. It is also a good site for cowslips, and eleven species of orchid grow here.

Much of the local countryside is now in the hands of the National Trust, including Selborne Common, and the zigzag path cut out of the hillside by which the walk returns to Selborne was made by Gilbert White and his brother in 1753.

Leave the car park by the entrance, down the side of the Selborne Arms pub, onto the main road that runs through the village. Turn right along the road. A monkey-puzzle tree on the far side of the road is made more noticeable because of the bat boxes that surround the trunk. You soon pass the Romany Folklore Museum. Continue down the hill until reaching the Gilbert White drinking trough on the right-hand side of the road. Just after this, turn right and go over a stile and onto a footpath across a field **A**.

The path goes through a gap in the hedge, then turns left down the side of the hedge. Cross the stile at the end, then continue to follow the path slightly to the right and uphill. Cross a further stile and follow the footpath sign straight ahead. As you climb the hill you start to get some

WALK 5

good views over the surrounding countryside. Climb a further stile, turn right onto the bridleway **B**, then keep to the footpath that runs parallel with the field-edge fence.

On reaching a wider gravel track, turn left uphill, then bear right to go through a gate onto the nature reserve. This reserve, considered one of the best examples of a chalk grassland and scrub mosaic, is in the care of Hampshire Wildlife Trust. The gravel track becomes a grass ride. When the track divides, take the left-hand fork into the wood alongside a fence. Go over a stile beside a metal gate and then take the left-hand narrow grass path downhill. On reaching a wider track turn right uphill. The path continues along the side of the hill with wonderful views across the Hampshire countryside. When the path meets a bridleway turn right onto this.

Ignore the Hangers Way sign off to the left and continue along the path straight ahead. At a meeting of paths, take the one most straight ahead which bears slightly to the right and uphill. **C** Continue through the wood until the path divides, bear right here and, on reaching a field, cross the stile into it and walk along the right-hand side of the field until reaching a tarmac road. Cross the road and continue along the bridleway straight ahead. After passing alongside the field, the path enters woodland and then reaches another tarmac road. Turn left onto this road and walk down the hill for 20 yds (18m) before turning left to follow a footpath sign into the field **D**.

The path crosses the middle of the field. At the far side, go through a small gate and straight across a tarmac road to follow the bridleway up Green Lane. This, probably ancient, track takes you up Selborne Hill to reach Selborne Common, owned by the National Trust. Ignore the path signposted Selborne Church and instead go straight on, then bear right soon after onto the 'Selborne via pipeline' footpath **E**.

On coming out of the trees, a path joins from the left; continue ahead. Ignore paths from the right and left until reaching a seat on the left. It is well worth taking a short rest here to enjoy the view over Selborne village. Finally turn left in front of the seat, then right to take Gilbert White's narrow gravel track and steps down the hillside. On reaching the bottom of the hill, go through the kissing-gate and follow the path down into Selborne.

The car park is on the left at the bottom of the path. ●

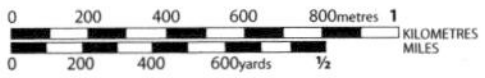

whose name commemorates the markets held here by dealers in Spanish wool. Plenty of time should be allowed for a stroll round the town and its major places of interest. The oldest building is the **Church of St Peter** with its 12th century chancel arch and splendid north nave. in the churchyard a headstone remembers the cricketer and maker of cricket balls John Small (1737-1826). **Petersfield Museum** in the old courthouse uses a good deal of local archive material in telling the history of the town from the 12th century to the present day. The **Bear Museum** was the first of its kind in Britain and is home to a varied collection of Teddy Bears, some close to celebrating their 100th birthdays. Visitors are invited to bring along their own bears so that the resident experts can shed some light on their family trees. The **Physic Garden**, set in an ancient walled burgage plot behind 16 High Street, is a charming little garden laid out in the style of the 17th century, a style that would have been familiar to the distinguished botanist John Goodyer, who lived in Petersfield. The **Flora Twort Gallery** contains the delightful drawings and paintings of local scenes produced over a period of 40 years by the accomplished eponymous artist, who bequeathed her cottage studio to Hampshire County Council on her death at the age of 91 in 1985. The restaurant on the premises has a fine reputation.

AROUND PETERSFIELD

Steep

2 miles NW of Petersfield off the A325

In **All Saints Church** are two engraved lancet windows installed in 1978 to mark the centenary of the birth of the writer and poet Edward Thomas, who moved with his family from London to Steep in 1907. He was killed in action in the First World War. On Shoulder of Mutton Hill, above the village, is a memorial stone to the poet, erected in 1937 when the hillside was dedicated to his memory.

Buriton

3 miles S of Petersfield off the A3

Buriton is a very pleasant village with a wonderful tree-lined duckpond sited in ideal walking country. The **Church of St Mary** has a notable treasure in its Norman font made of Purbeck marble. The church has for a neighbour an early 18th century manor house (in private hands) where the historian Edward Gibbon wrote much of his magnum opus, *The Decline and Fall of the Roman Empire*.

South Harting

3 miles SE of Petersfield on the B2146

The most notable building hereabouts is the National Trust's **Uppark**, a fine Wren-style country mansion built in 1690 high on the South Downs. It was extensively damaged by fire in 1989 and the restoration plans are the subject of an award-winning exhibition. The interior houses rescued paintings, fine furnishings and famous dolls houses, and the garden has been restored to the original Repton design. The servants' rooms are as they were in 1874, when the mother of HG Wells was housekeeper (he mentions Uppark fondly in his autobiography).

Chalton

5 miles S of Petersfield off the A3

Chalton is the site of **Butser Ancient Farm**, a reconstruction of an Iron Age Farm at the foot of Butser Hill. The site is in effect an open-air archaeological laboratory, where experts are undertaking studies into the lives, homes and farming methods of the ancient people who once lived here.

Thatched Cottage, East Meon

East Meon

5 miles W of Petersfield off the A3 or A272

The Meon Valley is an area of great beauty and East Meon can claim to be the loveliest village in the whole valley. It also boasts one of the finest churches in the county. The central tower of the Church of All Saints, with walls four feet thick, dates from the 12th century, while inside, the greatest treasure is the remarkable 12th century **Tournai font** in black marble, exquisitely carved with scenes that include the Creation and the Expulsion of Adam and Eve from the Garden of Eden. Only seven such fonts are known to exist in England, the work of Flemish master carvers, and East Meon's is certainly among the most magnificent of them all. Thomas Lord, founder of the cricket ground in London, and the spy Guy Burgess are buried in the churchyard in neighbouring West Meon.

Exton

8 miles W of Petersfield on the A32

A beautiful Meon Valley village with a wide expanse of grass bordering the river and close to the Old Winchester Hill archaeology trail.

Droxford

10 miles SW of Petersfield on the A32

In Droxford church there is a plaque to Izaak Walton, a great lover of the area, whose son-in-law was rector. In a siding outside Droxford station Churchill and Eisenhower set in train the D-Day invasion.

Soberton

12 miles SW of Petersfield off the A32

A wide-flung village at the point where the Meon Valley broadens and the chalk gives way to clay.

Hambledon

8 miles SW of Petersfield off the A3

A village of redbrick Georgian houses, known for its wine and even better

Painted Wood

Candover Gallery

22 West Street, Alresford, Hampshire SO24 9AE
Tel: 01962 733200
e-mail: candovergallery1@aol.com

Owned and run by potter and former pottery teacher Barbara Ling, **Candover Gallery** occupies a 200-year-old listed building in a main road location, with parking available outside or in adjacent car parks. Established by Barbara in 1984, the gallery has built up a far-reaching reputation for the quality of the work sold, for its presentation, and for the warm welcome and in-depth knowledge of contemporary work of Barbara and her staff. In bright, beautifully laid-out display areas, contemporary ceramics and glass pieces by more than 30 of the best craftsmen in Britain are on show.

Their work, as befits valued antiques of the future, is represented in many collections, both private and public, including the Victoria and Albert Museum, the Ulster Museum, and the Museum of Wales. Among the prominent artists with work on show are Walter Keller, one of today's most influential potters, whose metallic salt-glazed work is highly distinctive and instantly recognisable; Siddy Langley, who studied ceramics before becoming a glass blower, and whose work is exhibited in the UK, Europe, the USA, South America and Japan; and Anthony Stern, who at the Royal College of Art developed his own individual style of decoration, using lead crystals 'paint in glass'.

The Tapestry Centre

42 West Street, Alresford, Hampshire SO21 9AU
Tel: 01962 734944
e-mail: tapcent@ukonline.co.uk
website: www.tapestrycentre.co.uk

Watercress and wool may have been what put the lovely old town of Alresford on the map and wool is still a factor for those with an interest in needlework. Over the past 20 years, Caroline Perry has developed the **Tapestry Centre** into one of the most delightful shop of its kind. Behind the attractive frontage on West Street, there are two floors for the enthusiast or beginner. The Tapestry Centre website will tell you how to get there and you will find an unique collection of canvaswork, cross stitch and crewel embroidery.

Names include Designers Forum, Coleshill, Stitchery, Jolly Red, Russell House, Lanarte, The Crewelwork Company and the accomplished designer Hervé Lelong. Also there are trammé canvases by Stitchery, Ivo and Beverley. Many wools and threads are stocked including Appleton, Paterna, Anchor, DMC and Medici. Services are professionally carried out for stretching, mounting, framing, cushion-making, upholstery and, exceptionally, tailor-made cording in up to four wools. Apart from a good in-house choice, furniture can be custom made to fit any finished needlework. Helpful, knowledgeable staff are always on hand between 9am and 1pm and 2.15pm and 5pm Monday to Saturday.

known for its cricketing connections. It was in the Hambledon Club that the rules of the game were laid down in 1774. A granite monument stands on **Broadhalfpenny Down**, where the early games were played, and a number of cricketers are buried in the churchyard at the village church of St Peter and St Paul. Vineyards had been cultivated in England as far back as Roman times but all but disappeared in the Middle Ages. The revival started here, and the Hambledon bottles carry an appropriate cricketing logo.

NEW ALRESFORD

In the valley of the River Alre, New Alresford (pronounced Allsford) was new in about 1200, created by Geoffrey de Lucy, Bishop of Winchester, as part of a grand plan to build a waterway from Winchester to Southampton. The huge reservoir he built is smaller now, and home to otters and varied birdlife. Once among the country's leading wool markets, Alresford has long been at the centre of the watercress industry, and one of its many attractions is the **Watercress Line**. This is the nickname of the Mid-Hants Railway, which once carried wagonloads of watercress to join the lines to London and beyond. Ten miles of the line are now run by enthusiasts as a steam railway. The line runs from Alresford to Alton by way of Ropley, the engineering centre of the railway and a station with a notable display of topiary. The next stop is Medstead & Four Marks, which at 630 feet above sea level is the highest in the south of England. The gradients of up to 1 in 60 caused crews using this route to say that they were going 'over the Alps'. The steepness of the line calls for

BARN YARD FOODS 49/51A West Street Alresford, Hants. SO24 9AU Tel: 01962 733187

Barnyard Foods

49-51A West Street, Alresford, Hampshire SO24 9AB
Tel: 01962 733187 Fax: 01730 529231
e-mail: rosemarymorrish@aol,com

Healthy living is the watchword at **Barnyard Foods**, which is located up a little lane running off the main street in Alresford. Rosemary Morrish, who has owned the business for ten years, has filled the converted barn with a tremendous range of natural and organic foods, health supplements and natural remedies.

The shelves are always well stocked and even the rafters are put to good use for hanging dried flowers and herbs. In a cold cabinet is an impressive selection of sandwiches, in locally baked bread, bagettes and baps. The choice runs to about 30, from egg mayonnaise through tuna, cheese, ham, prawn and BLT, to Brie with avocado and mango chutney, and Greek with feta cheese, olives and salad. This is Alresford, so there must be some watercress – there is, garnishing either egg mayonnaise or mature cheddar with Marmite. Rosemary has put a lifetime's experience into play in serving the needs of a discerning , increasingly health conscious public, and her shop, one of the most interesting of the many specialist outlets in Alresford, is a wonderful place for anyone interested in maintaining a healthy, balanced diet.

The Handcrafted Furniture Workshop

19 Broad Street, Alresford, Hampshire SO24 9AR
Tel: 01962 733288

An alleyway off the main street leads to the **Handcrafted Furniture Workshop**, where visitors will find not only furniture but a bewildering array of other offerings. Owner Mark Davey, whose background is in arts and crafts, has built up the business over the last few years to encompass a range of products and services that is surely unequalled in the region. A gift shop, patisserie and speciality food shop give on to a beautiful garden, which in turn leads into the furniture workshop and showroom.

Superbly crafted pieces of furniture, from traditional rocking chairs to marvellous ornately framed mirrors, stand on impressive display along with stools and tables and sofas, and the services include general furniture repairs and re-upholstery. A café over the shop serves hot and cold drinks and snacks. The workshop and its offshoots really do form a unique collection of outlets and anyone visiting Mark Davey's premises will spend a very happy hour or two browsing, admiring and perhaps purchasing anything from a gift wrapped pot of jam to a dining room table.

The Eastern Art Gallery

9 Broad Street, Alresford, Hampshire SO24 9AR
Tel: 01962 736777
e-mail: info@orientalcarpets.uk.com website: www.orientalcarpets.uk.com

After a successful career in the world of corporate carpets Gary Sheppard decided to branch out on his own and took a magic carpet ride to Alresford, where he opened **The Eastern Art Gallery** in 1998. Two floors of display rooms in a building on one of the town's main streets, with parking nearby, are filled with a wide selection of beautiful hand-knotted rugs, carpets, kelims, hall runners and many other unique and desirable treasures at affordable prices, hung on the walls, spread on the floor, or rolled ready for display.

As well as selling these superb examples of the carpetmaker's craft, the gallery will buy or part exchange old rugs and carpets, undertake cleaning and repairs, provide valuations and offer a home approval service. The chief craftsman is a power packed little Iranian just four feet tall, who won a silver medal for weightlifting at the Olympic Games in 1976. In the summer months he sits outside the gallery repairing carpets and never fails to attract interested passers by.

powerful locomotives, and ferrequinologists (railway buffs) will thrill at the sight of an ex-Southern region S15 4-6-0, a Standard Class 5 4-6-0 number 73096 and most of all at the mighty 34016 *Bodmin*, a Bulleid Pacific of the West Country class. The final station is Alton, where the line joins the main railway network.

The Watercress Line

Though 800 years old, Alresford has a mainly Georgian look, the result of the major fires which ravaged the town down the years. The fulling mill and the ancient parish church are both worth a visit, and the town has many interesting specialist shops. Alresford's most famous son was Admiral Lord Rodney, a contemporary of Lord Nelson who built the grand manor house near the church. Mary Sumner, wife of a rector of the church, founded the Mothers Union here in 1876. Alresford was also the home of the author and poet Mary Russell Mitford, best known for her portraits of country life, and in particular *Our Village*. Alresford has very strong links with the early years of cricket, and

Tudor Antiques & Fine Arts

The Old Exchange, Station Road, Alresford, Hampshire SO24 9JG
Tel: 01962 735345 Fax: 01962 736345
e-mail: e&ptudor@tudor-antiques.co.uk
website: www.tudor-antiques.co.uk

World travellers Eric and Penelope Tudor bring style, personality and a wealth of experience to **Tudor Antiques & Fine Arts**, their excellent enterprise located in the former telephone exchange. Over the years they have built up a significant reputation as specialists in dining room furniture, and in a 2,000 square feet showroom they keep a considerable stock of tables, chairs, sideboards and cabinets to suit all tastes.

The diverse stock is English, Continental and Oriental from the 17th to the 19th centuries, and this is *the* place to come to furnish a classic Georgian dining room or lounge, to find a French Provincial refectory table, or chairs. If an Oriental conversation piece is what's required, the showrooms can provide that too, as the displays also include pieces from China, Tibet and Mongolia, providing one of the most extensive selections of Oriental furniture in the South of England. Smaller items such as mirrors, clocks and fireside accessories are on show, ready to complete the transformation of a room. The Tudors offer in addition an interior design service and can provide valuations for insurance and probate.

Mitford wrote: *'Hampshire is the Greece of cricketers, and Alresford the Athens.'*

A short way north of Alresford on the B3046 stands the imposing shell of **Northington Grange**, a grand neo-classical country mansion built around 1815 by William Wilkins and inspired by a tour of Greece. The most notable feature of the Grecian facade is the row of vast Doric columns, said to be based on the Temple of Theseus in Athens.

AROUND NEW ALRESFORD

Hinton Ampner

4 miles S of New Alresford on the A272

The River Itchen, renowned for trout and watercress beds, rises a little way west of Hinton Ampner to begin its 25-mile journey to the sea at Southampton; the Itchen Way follows the river throughout its course. **Hinton Ampner House and Gardens** (see panel opposite), now in the care of the National Trust, was largely the creation of Ralph Dutton, the 8th and last Lord Sherborne.

Tichborne

2 miles W of New Alresford off the A31

Two famous stories will be forever associated with this lovely village of thatched and half-timbered cottages. The legend of the **Tichborne Dole** dates from the time of Henry I, when the owner of Tichborne Park, the dastardly Sir Roger Tichborne, told his crippled wife Mabella that she could have her dying wish to provide food for the poor, but only from an area she could crawl round. The brave woman managed to encircle an area of more than 20 acres of arable land, while holding a flaming torch. Ever since then the Park's owners have provided bags of flour every year to the villagers of Tichborne and Cheriton, and the field is still known as 'The Crawls'. Equally notorious is the episode of the **Tichborne Claimant**, a sensational trial of 1871 involving a certain Arthur Orton, son of a Wapping butcher, who appeared from his home in Wagga Wagga, Australia, claiming to be the heir to the estate. Although he bore no resemblance to the rightful heir, Roger Charles Doughty Tichborne, who had disappeared while sailing round the world, he was 'recognised' and supported in his claim by Roger's mother, who disliked her husband's family and was determined to believe the impostor. Orton's claim was rejected in a trial that lasted 100 days, and he was put on trial for perjury; after a further 188 days he was found guilty and sentenced to 14 years in prison.

A mile or so south of Tichborne, on the B3046, is the village of **Cheriton**, whose church is thought to stand over a prehistoric burial ground. In 1644, the Battle of Cheriton, fought near Cheriton Wood, resulted in the deaths of 2,000 men as the Roundheads defeated the Royalists.

ANDOVER

A picturesque market town with a history going back to Saxon times. One outstanding landmark is the hilltop **Church of St Mary**, which was completely rebuilt in the 1840s with a generous gift from Dr William Goddard, a retired headmaster of Winchester College. The interior is said to have been modelled on Salisbury Cathedral; it falls a little short of that marvellous building but is nonetheless worth a visit. Dominating the market place in the town centre is the handsome Guildhall, built in 1825, and many of the old coaching inns that once filled the town

Hinton Ampner Gardens (National Trust)

Bramdean, Alresford, Hampshire SO24 0LA
Tel: 01962 771305

The **Hinton Ampner** of today is largely the creation of Ralph Dutton, the 8th and last Lord Sherborne. Born here in 1898, he inherited the house in 1936 and set about remodelling the house and garden in a carefully considered marriage of modern gardening, neo-Georgian building and neo-Classical furnishings. His plan for the garden was to lead visitors gently from mood to mood; the design is formal but the planting informal, and he created delightful walks with unexpected vistas by the thoughtful siting of trees and statues. What he wanted above all from a garden was tranquillity, and any visitor to Hinton Ampner would agree that he achieved it triumphantly. There are, just as Ralph Dutton planned, delights and surprises at every turn.

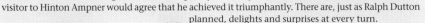

The lily pond, which he laid out on his father's croquet lawn, is home to nine different varieties of water lily and a good number of golden orfe and goldfish. The Sunken Garden, the first area planned by Dutton, boasts some of the wonderful topiary that is such an identifying feature of Hinton Ampner.

The Long Walk is a perfectly straight path linking the east and west extremities of the garden and featuring an avenue of 30 clipped Irish yews. The Dell, the Philadelphus Walk, the Yew Garden and the Temple - built as a folly, gazebo and resting place - are other highlights of this quite superb garden.

Ralph Dutton also greatly altered the house, more or less demolishing his grandfather's gloomy Victorian mansion and restoring the Georgian style that he much preferred. In 1960 a fire badly damaged the house and its contents, and in its subsequent rebuilding Dutton made further changes and set about collecting Regency furniture and Italian paintings to replace those lost in the fire.

On his death in 1985, there being no heir, Ralph Dutton bequeathed the house, the gardens and the hamlet of Hinton Ampner to the National Trust. The house is privately tenanted but the ground-floor rooms can be visited at certain times.

still stand. Andover was an important stopping place on the major routes to and from London, Oxford and Southampton, and as many as 50 coaches a day would stop at the inns to change horses and to allow the passengers to stretch their legs and take refreshment. The story of the town from pre-Roman times is told in the **Andover Museum & the Museum of the Iron Age** in Church Close.

Another way of getting to know the town is to join a guided walk on the heritage trail starting at the Tourist Information Centre; also starting from the TIC are two trails which lead to collections of poems in praise of the lovely Test Valley. The poems, set in granite or bronze, are scattered through the town and lead the walker past public works of art by the River Anton. **The Test Vale Tapestry** is a fascinating piece of community embroidery which is kept in the Council Offices and can be seen by appointment. Four miles west of Andover at **Weyhill**, signposted from the main A303, a great day out for the family can be enjoyed at the **Hawk Conservancy and Country Park**, home to more than 200 birds from all over the world. Thrilling flying displays take place three times a day and include owls, eagles, falcons, kites and hawks. Seven of the 22 acres have been developed into a wild flower meadow and conservation area dedicated to the Conservancy's founder Reg Smith. The October Weyhill Fair was an event of great importance in its day and appears as the Weydon Priors Market in Thomas Hardy's *Mayor of Casterbridge*, where the future mayor sells his wife and child.

A little further along the A303 thrills of a different kind are guaranteed at **Thruxton Motor Racing Circuit**, whose annual calendar of events takes in many aspects of the sport, including Formula Three, Touring Cars, Superbikes, Trucks and Karts.

AROUND ANDOVER

MIDDLE WALLOP
7 miles SW of Andover off the A343

The middle of three villages strung out along the valley of the Wallop Brook, a tributary of the Test, Middle Wallop became famous during the Battle of Britain, when the nearby airfield was the base for squadrons of Spitfires and Hurricanes. Many of the old buildings have been incorporated into the **Museum of Army Flying**, which is home to an important collection of military kites, balloons, aircraft and helicopters. Dioramas trace the development of Army flying from the days before the First World War with a display of 35 aircraft

DANEBURY VINEYARDS

Nether Wallop, Nr Stockbridge, Hampshire SO20 6JX
Tel: 01264 781851 Fax: 01264 782212
e-mail: patrick.westropp@danebury.com

Seven acres of vineyards on gently sloping, south-facing fields make up **Danebury Vineyards**, whose white and sparkling wines are characterised by their clean, crisp, fruity flavour. The vineyards are surrounded by a windbreak of beech trees and the chalk and flint stone in the region means the grapes develop a balanced level of acidity. In addition our long summer days allow for maximum ripening. The first plantings were in 1988, since when the owners have applied expertise and experience to improve the methods of pruning and training. The

raising of the growing wires is an example, not only making tending the vines less backbreaking but improving the airflow and reducing the risk of damage through ground frost.

Cossack is a refined sparkling wine made from a blend of Auxerrois and Rulander grape varieties. The grapes are hand-picked, with only fruit in its prime selected, and after malolactic fermentation and bottling the wine goes through a second fermentation to produce the distinctive taste of a high-quality sparkling wine. Pyrrhus is made from Schonburger grapes and is produced by cold fermentation which accentuates the fresh, fruity character of the wine. This is horseracing country, and the wines are named after Danebury trained Derby winners - Pyrrhus the First in 1846 and Cossack in 1847. Visitors are welcome, though there are no set visiting times, and lunches and dinners can be arranged by appointment for wine-tasting parties.

and the finest collection of military gliders in Europe. Explorers' World is the Museum's interactive science and education centre, with a number of hands-on activities and a fine camera obscura giving an amazing view of the surrounding countryside.

Middle Wallop

Nether Wallop

7 miles SW of Andover off the A30

Nether Wallop is the prettiest of the Wallops, its stream lined with willows, many of its houses thatched or timbered. The most notable building in the village is the **Church of St Andrew** with its striking medieval wall paintings. Almost 1,000 years old, they lay hidden beneath plaster for centuries until being rediscovered in the 1950s. The most impressive and unusual of the paintings depicts St George fighting the Dragon. Outside the church is a curiosity in the shape of a dark grey stone pyramid, 15ft high, with red stone flames rising from its tip. This imposing piece was erected at his own expense and in his own memory by Francis Couce, a local doctor who died in 1760.

Nether Wallop

Stockbridge

7 miles S of Andover on the A30

The trout-rich River Test flows through, under and alongside the broad main street of Stockbridge, which attracts visitors from near and far with its antique shops, art galleries and charming tea rooms. Fishing on the Test is strictly controlled at this point by two exclusive clubs, both with long waiting lists.

South of the A30, on a minor road from Stockbridge to Houghton lie **Houghton Lodge Gardens & Hydroponicum**. An 18th century 'Cottage Ornée' surrounded by lawns and trees stands by the Test, with lovely views over the valley - understandably this is a favourite location for films and television. Chalkcob walls shelter a kitchen garden with ancient espaliered fruit trees, glasshouses and herb garden. The hydroponic greenhouse tour includes a lecture on 'How to grow plants easily at home with soil and toil and without pesticides'.

Dairy Barn Farm Shop

North Houghton, Stockbridge, Hampshire SO20 6LF
Tel/Fax: 01264 811405
e-mail: DairyBarnShop@aol.com website: www.dairybarn.co.uk

Top-quality meat with real flavour is the speciality of **Dairy Barn Farm Shop**, which hardworking Sue Gotting and her husband Christoph opened in August 1999 in response to requests from friends and relations who had already enjoyed the unique flavour of meat from their traditional British breeds. All their animals are truly free-range and are raised non-intensively, without feed additives, on unfertilised, herb-rich pasture. Beef comes only from British minority and rare cattle breeds kept on the farm or sourced from local breeders. Delicious, full-flavoured lamb is also produced from native British breeds, including the Manx Loghtan, Wensleydale and Ryeland. Pork with exceptional taste and texture is produced from happy free-range Tamworth, Gloucester Old Spot and British Saddleback pigs, and the dry-cured bacon makes an unforgettable breakfast.

The superb eating qualities of these breeds have been known for centuries, and increased demand will ensure a steady rise in their population, safeguarding breeds which are part of our national heritage. Also available through the shop are many varieties of burgers and sausages, all with a minimum of 95% meat. Other local produce for sale includes seasonal organic vegetables, speciality breads, luxury ice cream, the finest dairy goods, smoked fish and poultry, free-range eggs and woollen goods. The shop is open from 10 to 6 Wednesday to Saturday, and they also have a mail order service with goods delivered by refrigerated courier service. Dairy Barn was a prize-winner in Henrietta Green's Food Lovers Fair 2000 with their Dexter beef and are members of Hampshire Fare. Christoph has another string to his bow: he is talented violin maker, with his own workshop close to the farm.

The Mayfly

Testcombe, Nr Stockbridge, Hampshire SO20 6AX
Tel: 01264 860283

The Test is probably the best-known trout fishing river in the world, and the **Mayfly**, originally an early 19th century farmhouse, has strong claims to be the most famous of the pubs along its banks. Barry and Julie Lane's 'Inn by the River' enjoys an idyllic setting right on the bank, by the A3057 3 miles from Stockbridge and 4 miles from Andover. Attractive and inviting from the outside, with its gables and steeply raked roof, the pub is even more appealing within, where old beams and a wealth of fishing pictures, prints and equipment set a splendidly traditional tone. When the sun is shining, tables and chairs outside by the river make a truly wonderful setting for enjoying a drink and a snack and leaving the rest of the world far behind.

Food and drink play important roles at the Mayfly, with real ales and excellent ciders to accompany anything from a light snack to a full-scale meal. From the all-day buffet come soup, quiche, smoked trout, a vast selection of cheeses and a variety of cold meats and salads, while the hot choice typically runs from lasagne with salmon to Lancashire hot pot, from vegetarian harvester pie to chicken tandoori. Barry, who has been here as licensee for 16 years, describes his beloved Mayfly not as a pub, nor as a restaurant, but as a venue. And venue it certainly is, a place to be sought out not as a 'staging post' on a tour but as a destination with its own unique appeal. Between trips to this delightful spot there's plenty to see and do in the vicinity, including working up a thirst on the Test Way, exploring the charming market town of Andover or browsing for antiques in Stockbridge.

Two miles northwest of Stockbridge off the A30 is the impressive **Danebury Iron Age Hill Fort**, whose earthworks, ditches and banks were excavated over a period of years to give us a detailed view of life more than 2,000 years ago. Many of the finds from the site are now in Andover Museum.

Longparish

5 miles E of Andover on the B3048

A straggling village on a stretch of the River Test famed for its excellent trout fishing. A Longparish resident, Colonel Peter Hawker, notes in his diary for 1818 that he landed a ton of the fish in that year! **Longparish Upper Mill**, in a lovely location on the river, is a large flour mill with a working waterwheel. Visitors can see the restoration work in progress.

Whitchurch

6 miles E of Andover on the B3400

A little town on the River Test that was once the first important coach stop on the London-Exeter run. Its coaching inns have gone but it has a unique attraction in the **Whitchurch Silk Mill**, the last working silk mill in the South of England. The waterwheel has been fully restored but the power is now provided by electricity, and the mill functions as a museum making silks for interiors and costume dramas, with a costume exhibition and a shop. The mill, which stands on Frog Island on the Test, provided some of the silk for the costumes in the BBC's acclaimed production of *Pride and Prejudice*. Bere Mill, on the eastern edge of Whitchurch, is a weatherboarded mill on the Test where a Frenchman, Henri Portal, set up a paper-making business in the 18th century.

Appleshaw

4 miles NW of Andover off the A342

Many of the houses that stand on either side of the village's broad single street are thatched, and the old-world atmosphere is enhanced by the clock installed in the middle of the street to celebrate Queen Victoria's Diamond Jubilee. The village's most notable buildings are the neo-Gothic parish church and the Georgian former vicarage.

Tangley

6 miles NW of Andover off the A342/A343

Tangley sits among woods on a hilltop high above Tangley Bottom, the low-lying ground which forms the county boundary with Wiltshire. Its mostly Victorian church is notable for its rare lead font, the only one of its kind in Hampshire and one of only a handful in the country. Dating back to the 1600s, it is decorated with Tudor roses, crowned thistles and fleurs-de-lys. The old Roman road from Winchester to Cirencester, the Icknield Way, runs through the parish of Tangley, which includes the parishes of Vernham Dean and Hatherden. Most of this

Freefolk, nr Whitchurch

part of the county is designated an Area of Outstanding Natural Beauty, and the views are stupendous.

Highclere Gardens

Highclere

14 miles N of Andover on the A343

Sir Charles Barry, architect of the Houses of Parliament, was in similarly exuberant mood when engaged on the rebuilding of **Highclere Castle** for the 3rd Earl of Carnarvon. The largest mansion in the whole county is a really splendid, grandiose affair, with turrets at the angles and a huge pinnacled tower in the centre. It occupies the site of a former Palace of the Bishops of Winchester, and the lovely park and gardens in which it stands is one of the finest of all the works of Lancelot 'Capability' Brown. The interior of the castle is no less ornate than the outside, with a mixture of Gothic, Moorish and rococo styles and a wealth of old masters and other treasures. In the basement is an exhibition of ancient artefacts collected by the 5th Earl, who was with Howard Carter on the 1922 expedition

that discovered the tomb of Tutankhamun. This fascinating hoard had lain undiscovered in the basement for almost 70 years before being found in a hidden chamber by a butler. Highclere Castle has been used as a location for many films and television productions, including *Inspector Morse*.

BURGHCLERE
15 miles N of Andover off the A34

A couple of miles from Highclere, the **Sandham Memorial Chapel** hides a unique and very moving treasure behind a fairly unprepossessing redbrick facade. The interior walls are entirely covered with murals by Stanley Spencer and reflect his own experiences as an orderly in the First World War. Most of the scenes depict soldiers in the day-to-day business of war, but one wall shows the resurrection of soldiers killed in combat. In the foreground is a pile of white crosses cast aside by the soldiers. This marvellous expressionist work, which took five years to complete and is considered to be among Spencer's finest, was commissioned in the 1920s by Mr and Mrs Behrend in memory of a relation, Lieutenant Sandham, who died in 1919 of an illness contracted during the Macedonian campaign. There is no lighting in the chapel, so the murals are best viewed on a bright day.

WINCHESTER

Winchester is one of the country's most historic cities, with settlements dating back to the Iron Age. It was an important military base from Roman times (they called it Venta Belgarum), and King Alfred chose it as the capital of his kingdom of Wessex, which at the time included most of southern England. The

CORNFLOWERS

17 College Street, Winchester, Hampshire SO23 9LX
Tel: 01962 621234

The coat of arms above a window is the clue that **Cornflowers** belongs to the ancient Winchester College. Until opening as a gift shop 10 years ago, the building served as the College tuck shop. Two large windows invitingly display the delightful range of gifts inside. Visitors, who are welcome to browse, will find a huge choice to suit very pocket and every occasion. Naturally, the shop also sells a range of items pertaining to the college, including College 'crest' and Trusty Servant engraved glassware, cassettes and CD's of music by Winchester College Quiristers, cufflinks, tea-towels, guide books and much more.

Among other goods are the very popular Burgess Dorling & Leigh range of china, and in addition, jewellery and silk scarves, soft toys, greetings cards and a beautiful range of silk flowers. Also available

are items connected with Jane Austen, who spent the last months of her life in Winchester. She died in a house in College Street and is buried in nearby Winchester Cathedral. Cornflowers is open from 10 to 5 Monday to Saturday and 11 to 4 on Sundays and Bank Holidays. It is a fascinating spot to end a visit to Winchester College, the oldest public school in England. The College was founded in 1382 by Bishop William of Wykeham to provide education for 70 poor and needy scholars. Guided tours of the College take place daily through the year, except on Tuesday and Thursday afternoons and Sunday mornings.

Woodruffs Of Winchester

32 The Square, Winchester, Hampshire SO23 9EX
Tel: 01962 877738 Fax: 01962 877875
e-mail: sales@woodruffs.co.uk
website: www.woodruffs.co.uk

Harry and Sandie Whorwood left careers in the Civil Service and opened **Woodruffs of Winchester**, turning an empty shell into a shop with a fine reputation for quality, diversity and attention to detail.

The four floors of this handsome city-centre building are filled with an enormous range of goods both traditional and innovative. One floor houses stationery, with a wide range of unusual greetings cards, luxury gift wrap and georgeous ribbons. The toiletry floor assails the customer with enticing aromas of luxurious and modern offerings from Molton Brown, I'Coloniali, Bloom and Gant for Men. The more established selections from Crabtree & Evelyn and Floris have an enormous presence, and the French ranges from L'Occitane, Lothantique and Roger & Gallet introduce the Gallic expertise in perfumery products. There are also exciting and ground breaking ranges of new and different soaps, bath lotions and shampoos to try and enjoy.

The top two floors are equally interesting and tempt the customer with exciting products. The mezzanine floor is well known for its ranges of room fragrances and candles. The stock is continually changing but staples include Kenneth Turner, Diptyque from France, Crabtree & Evelyn and Floris. Lothantique from France is proving popular and is set to join the big boys of the fragrance world. Jewellery also features well on this floor with fashion selections from Elle, YSL and Coeur du Lion. Around this framework other exciting hand made and fun crystal adornments prove popular with young and old. Watches are represented by Mondaine who make the renowned Swiss Railway Clock and Wenger who are notable for supplying their Army. The Swiss company of Swatch provides an extremely reliable fashion accessory which is well known to all. Scandinavian watches from Skagen and Jacob Jensen have proved extremely popular with their undeniable expertise in clean and crisp design. Pen aficionados will not be disappointed in the ranges from Tombow, Lamy and Rotring.

The top floor is well known for its ranges of gadgets for men and for its stunning home ranges. The Danes are represented by the design houses of Rosendahl, Tommy Larson and PO Select. These bring to the shop a contemporary clean feel which is becoming increasingly popular. CD holders, vases, key rings, oil and wine carafes, and wine accessory ranges are well represented. Oregon Scientific and Jacob Jensen, who are well known for weather centres and home accessories, bring an extra dimension for men's gift buying which adds to other well known ranges such as Toollogic and Leatherman. The rest of the floor is alive with small and original hand made dog and cat figurines, Josie Firmin chinaware, photo frames and other home accessories.

The visitor to Winchester will be well advised to seek out The Square, known locally as the Bond Street of Winchester. They would be disappointed if they did not visit this shop because, as the sign above the door reads: "... things are different at Woodruffs".

decline that set in after the Imperial Legions returned to Rome was halted by Alfred in the late 800s, and two centuries later, on the site of a 7th century Saxon cathedral, work began on the magnificent **Winchester Cathedral**, which has ever since brought worshippers and sightseers from all over the world. The work was started by Bishop Wakelin on a swampy site that necessitated foundations of vast logs. Bishop William of Wykeham added ribs and mouldings and fan vaulting in the 14th century, essentially creating the building we see today. The Cathedral, which has the longest nave of any in Europe, is filled with priceless treasures, including sumptuous medieval monuments and copies of the Winchester Bible and Bede's *Ecclesiastical History*. The tombs of King Canute, Ethelwulf, William ll (Rufus), Jane Austen and Izaak Walton are among the many in the Cathedral, along with that of St Swithin, to whom the Cathedral is dedicated. St Swithin was a 9th century bishop who, at his own humble request, was buried in the Cathedral grounds, not inside the building itself. When, on 15th July 971, his remains were brought inside on the orders of Bishop Aethelwold and honoured with a fine shrine, it rained heavily for 40 days, a phenomenon that was said to show the Saint's displeasure. Ever since that day it has been said that if it rains on July 15th it will rain for 40 days. One of the statues in the Cathedral is that of a less well known figure, a diver named William Walker. This man spent seven years from 1906 laboriously removing the logs that had supported the Cathedral for 800 years and replacing those rotting foundations with cement. The area around the Cathedral provides a wealth of interest for the visitor: the Deanery,

CREATIVE CRAFTS

11 The Square, Winchester, Hampshire SO23 9ES
Tel: 01962 856266 e-mail: sales@creativecrafts.co.uk
website: www.creativecrafts.co.uk

Thirty years ago Anthony Wilson bade farewell to the engineering trade and opened **Creative Crafts** in Chandlers Ford, moving to Winchester in 1983. The aim of the shop, probably the most comprehensive craft shop in the country, is to supply all the materials for a very extensive range of arts and crafts. The artist, whether beginner or professional, is catered for by an impressive array of colours, papers and brushes by leading suppliers. The needleworker will find materials and kits for various techniques, and in the basement is an amazing range of other crafts, including basketry and seating, candlemaking, modelling in clay and other materials, glass painting, flower making, lapidary, metal work and jewellery, paper crafts and pergamano, patchwork and quilting, rug making, soft toys, quilling, upholstery, printing and dyeing, spinning and weaving.

The shop also stocks a large range of books and videos (some for hire) which will give instruction and insight into a new or existing hobby. Children are encouraged to learn a craft or extend their school knowledge with basic kits and accessories. Helpful staff, experts themselves in one or more crafts, are always on hand with help and advice, and they will try to find anything that's not in stock. The shop, which stands in The Square almost opposite the Cathedral, is open from 9.00am to 5.30pm Monday to Saturday.

Cadogan And Company

30-31 The Square, Winchester, Hampshire SO23 9EZ
Tel: 01962 877399
website: www.cadoganandcompany.co.uk

In a superb city-centre location, with parking adjacent, **Cadogan and Company** has built up an enviable reputation for style and quality in ladies' and gentlemen's fashion and accessories. Owner Alexander Edwards, who has spent all his working life in the retail trade, came to this address ten years ago and turned what was effectively an empty shell into one of the city's leading private retailers.

Housed in a prestigious modern development, the shop is on three levels of open -plan display areas, all subtly lit and professionally laid out on stands and consoles, racks and shelves. Alexander travels the world seeking out what he knows will appeal to his discerning clientele, including elegant leather fashion garments and accessories from Italy.

Quality is the keynote throughout the range of goods on display, from indoor and outdoor fashion wear to boots and shoes, hats, nightwear, woollens, scarves and ties. Among the accessories are top-of-the-range suitcases, travel bags and accessories for the journey, umbrellas, the best leather briefcases and desk supplies, haberdashery, gold and silverware and a selection of lovely gifts, from glass and china ornaments to diaries, barometers and hip flasks.

Highly professional management and staff are on hand to attend to every need of customers at this superb shop, which is open from 9.30 to 5.30 Monday to Saturday. Within walking distance of the shop are most of the major places of interest in the city, including the wonderful Cathedral, the City Museum and the College, the oldest public school in England. Tradition and modern amenities stand side by side in Winchester, and Cadogan and Company fully deserves its place right in the heart of the city.

occupied continuously since the 13th century; the **Pilgrims' Hall** with its marvellous hammerbeam roof; **Cheyney Court**, once the Bishops' courthouse; Dean Garnier's Victorian garden; Kingsgate, one of two surviving ancient city gates, and beyond it the simple, evocative Church of St Swithin; Jane Austen's House, where the novelist spent the last six weeks of her life until her death in 1817; the renowned College with its beautiful chapel, founded in 1382 by Bishop William of Wykeham to provide education for 70 'poor and needy scholars': motto 'Manners Maketh Man'; and **Wolvesey Castle**, the chief residence of the medieval Bishops of Winchester. Here it was in 1554 that Queen Mary first met Philip of Spain: the wedding banquet was held in the Castle the very next day.

Westgate Museum, Winchester

Other parts of this wonderful city are no less fascinating. In and around the historic High Street are the 15th century Buttercross and the nearby little Church

THOMPSON ANTIQUES

13-15 Stockbridge Road, Winchester, Hampshire SO22 6RN
Tel: 01962 853152 / 866633 Fax: 01962 864173

On the western side of Winchester, in a road where parking is not only possible but easy, **Thompson Antiques** is well worth a long and leisurely visit by anyone with an interest in antiques or in the general spectrum of arts and crafts. Anne Thompson, a lady with years of experience in the antiques business, runs the shop while her husband travels at home and overseas in search of interesting hand-crafted pieces both antique and modern. And interesting is certainly the word for the stock on display in the large, well-laid out showroom, where small gift items share the space with large pieces of antique furniture and everything in between.

Among the smaller goods could be anything from brass letters and numbers to china figurines, model boats, decorative candles, lampshades and photo frames, while the bulkier items could include sideboards, dressers, chaises longues and complete dining room suites, some in rustic pine with matching wooden chairs or pew-style seating. The owners offer a traditional upholstery service and bespoke furniture can be made to order. Winchester is a city of diverse historic and cultural interest, but when it comes to antiques and the crafts Thompson Antiques really is in a class of its own for interest and variety.

of St Lawrence in the Square; the City Museum; the 16th century God Begot House, where a curfew bell tolls every evening at 8 o'clock; and a fine bronze of Horse and Rider by Elizabeth Frink. King Alfred's statue dominates the Broadway, and in nearby Bridge Street the **Winchester City Mill** is a fine example of the industrial past preserved for posterity. In the care of the National Trust, this is an 18th century water-powered corn mill with a working water-wheel, mill races and island garden. The only surviving part of the old **Winchester Castle** is the Great Hall, once the centre of court and government life, where hangs the renowned Round Table, long associated with King Arthur but perhaps dating only from Tudor times. Behind the Hall, Queen Eleanor's Garden is a faithful representation of a medieval garden. The castle grounds are the site of the historic **Peninsula**

Barracks, now occupied by several military museums, among them the Gurkha Museum; the King's Royal Hussars Museum, whose displays include the Charge of the Light Brigade; the Light Infantry Museum, telling the story of a modern regiment and featuring the Fall of the Berlin Wall and the Gulf War; and the **Royal Green Jackets Museum**, whose nine battle models include one of Waterloo with 22,000 model soldiers and horses, plus a sound and light commentary. The regiments combining to make the Royal Green Jackets have won no fewer than 55 Victoria Crosses, many of which are displayed here in their campaign cases. **The Balfour Museum** on Stockbridge Road tells the story of the Red Cross in Hampshire, and the **Historic Resources Centre** in Hyde Street offers access to collections of historic records for the area; it is located near the site of **Hyde Abbey**, which

THE CLOCK-WORK-SHOP

6a Parchment Street, Winchester, Hampshire SO23 8AT
Tel: 01962 842331 Mobile: 07885 954302
website: www.clock-work-shop.co.uk

Everyone visiting the historic city of Winchester should take time to look in at the **Clock-Work-Shop**, which occupies two floors of an old building in a side street just off the main street. Owned by Peter Ponsford-Jones and run by him and his partners Kevin Hurd and Richard Scorey, the shop specialises in the sale, purchase, repair, restoration, after care and valuation of antique clocks, mostly English and mostly from the period from the 17th century to the First World War. Around 100 clocks are usually on display, including carriage clocks, wall clocks, mantel clocks and long case clocks, and the shop also deals in fine antique barometers and has a small stock of pocket watches.

The shop hours are 9 to 5 Monday to Saturday, when all the clocks are available to view, but

customers can 'visit' the shop at any time of the day or night by accessing the splendid website, which includes comprehensive details, including photographs and prices, of the full stock. A typical entry from the long case clock catalogue: 'A very handsome 8 day longcase of super quality. The silvered dial is particularly beautiful - a real work of the engraver's art! The oak case has excellent colour, finish and proportions. A most original clock. Circa 1780. Local delivery and set-up'. With notes as interesting and tempting as these, a browse through the website could easily result in a real-life visit to the shop! All sales and repairs carry a 3-year guarantee.

recent excavation has revealed as the probable site of King Arthur's final burial place. Visitors can study new information panels in the old abbey gateway.

Two years after Jane Austen was buried in the Cathedral, the poet John Keats stayed in Winchester and wrote his ode *To Autumn*. The inspiration for the 'Season of Mist and Mellow Fruitfulness' was a daily walk past the Cathedral and College and through the water meadows beside the River Itchen. A detailed guide allows visitors to follow this walk, one of many marked walks in and around the city. A mile south of the Cathedral across the meadows is the oldest and one of the loveliest almshouses in Britain. The **Hospital of St Cross** was founded in 1132 by Henri du Blois, grandson of William the Conqueror, and extended in 1446 by Cardinal Beaufort, son of John of Gaunt, Chancellor of England and successor to William of Wykeham. Many original features survive in the Hospital, where pilgrims would meet and crusaders gather on the eve of sailing from Southampton. The tradition of hospitality lives on in the restored Hundred Men's Hall, and the Wayfarer's Dole is still given at the porter's gate to all travellers who request it.

AROUND WINCHESTER

Crawley

7 miles NW of Winchester off the B3049

A pretty village with a duck pond and an interesting social history: it is possibly a unique example of an early-20th century model village. The estate was bought in 1900 by the Philippi family, who set about adding faithful fakes to the village's store of traditional cottages. They also thought modern by providing the villagers with a state-of-the-art bath house and a rollerskating rink, but had the sensitivity not to touch the Church of St Mary, whose roof was, and still is, supported by mighty wooden columns.

Itchen Abbas

4 miles NE of Winchester on the B3047

On the north bank of the River Itchen, this is the village where Charles Kingsley is believed to have written *The Water Babies*. One of the gravestones in the churchyard is in memory of John Hughes, who died in 1825 aged 26, thought to be the last person to be hanged for horse-stealing. In the nearby hamlet of **Avington**, John, the brother of the poet Shelley, is remembered in a monument in the 18th century Church of St Mary in the grounds of Avington Park. **Avington Park** is one of the finest stately homes in England and William Cobbett's assessment in his *Rural Rides*, when he described it as one of the prettiest places in the county, is as true today as when he wrote the words in 1830. The State rooms on view include the Ballroom, the Red Drawing Room and the Library; each has its own unique attractions, and in the grounds the iron bridge over the River Itchen is a rare feature that dates from the 18th century.

Twyford

5 miles S of Winchester on the B3335

Hampshire churchyards are well known for their splendid old yew trees, and the tree that shelters Twyford's church is a particularly fine specimen. The Victorian church of striped brick and flint was designed by Alfred Waterhouse, architect of the Natural History Museum in London. There are pleasant walks on Shawford Down and along the Itchen Navigation, an early 18th century canal that runs from Winchester to Southampton. An interesting piece of industrial heritage is **Twyford Pumping Station**, a late-19th century waterworks with a working steam engine and boiler, water softening plant and lime kilns, and a regular programme of special steam open days.

Otterbourne

7 miles S of Winchester off the A33

Otterbourne was the home of the prolific Victorian novelist Charlotte Young, whose best known work is *The Heir of Redcliffe*. She was a friend and publicist of the churchman and poet John Keble, sometime vicar of nearby Hursley. The two are buried in the churchyard of St Matthew, Otterbourne. Charlotte Young is commemorated by a beautiful ornamental screen in the Lady Chapel of Winchester Cathedral.

ROMSEY

A prosperous market town on the River Test, with many historic buildings. **Romsey Abbey** was founded as a nunnery in 907 by Edward the Elder, son of Alfred the Great, and later in the same century King Edgar established the Benedictine Order here. The present building dates from between 1120 and 1230 and contains some of the very finest architecture of the period. The most spectacular feature is the nave, which soars to over 70 feet and extends for 76 feet. The Abbey's many treasures include the Romsey Rood, which shows Christ with arms spread and the hand of God descending from the clouds. At the time of the Dissolution of the Monasteries, when so many ecclesiastical buildings were destroyed, the people of Romsey, who had always used part of the Abbey as their parish church, managed to make an agreement with Henry VIII to purchase the Abbey. The price was £100 and the bill of sale, signed and sealed by Henry, is displayed in the south choir aisle. Close by the Abbey, in Church Court, stands the oldest secular building in Romsey, **King John's House**. Built probably around 1240 and therefore not for King John, it nonetheless served royalty in its time, including Edward I and his retinue, who scratched their coats of arms on to the plaster walls. The house is open for guided tours during the summer.

Romsey Abbey

A surprise for railway fans stands behind the infants' school in Winchester Road. This is **Romsey Signal Box**, a preserved vintage signal box in working order, with signals, track and other artefacts.

Romsey's most famous son is undoubtedly Lord Palmerston, three times Prime Minister during the 1850s and 1860s. A bronze statue in the Market Place honours this flamboyant statesman,

Walking and Cycling in Hampshire

Hampshire County Council Information Centre
Mottisfont Court, High Street, Winchester, Hampshire SO23 8ZB
Tel: 01962 870500 Textline: 0808 100 2454
website: www.hants.gov.uk/leisure/paths.html or www.hants.gov.uk/leisure/walks/guided/

With over 3,000 miles of rights of way, Hampshire has an enviable network of footpaths, bridleways and byways that criss-cross the county's rolling hills and heaths, downland and forest. To encourage people to explore these wonderful assets **Hampshire County Council** co-ordinates twice yearly a programme of guided walks offering more than 450 walks, cycle rides, and events. All walks and cycle rides are led by experienced people. They have also created a series of eleven long distance routes, which includes the South Downs Way National Trail. Each route has its own distinctive waymark.

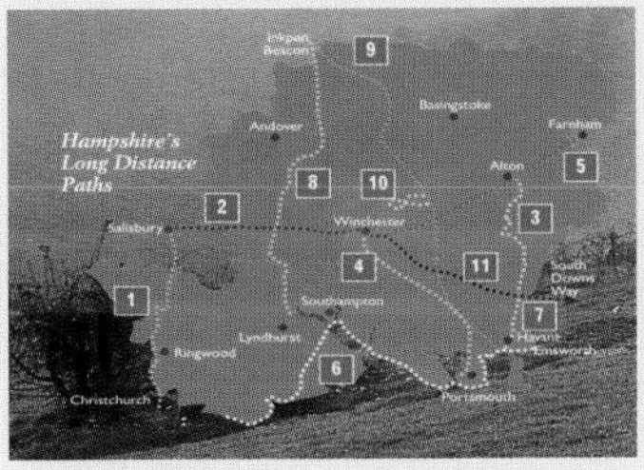

Two Off Road Cycle Packs are also published by the County Council, each containing details of 12 self guided routes that range from three to 26 miles in length. The trails are designed to suit a variety of tastes and come in a handy water resistant pocket sized pack. Some of the routes link with each other and offer short cuts, making them ideal for families with children as well as casual cyclists.

Information packs or leaflets on each long distance path, copies of the Off Road Cycle Packs and a Guided Walks Programme are available from Hampshire County Council Information Centres

who lived just south of town at the family home, **Broadlands**. One of the finest stately homes in the country, this gracious Palladian mansion by the River Test was built for an earlier member of the Palmerston family by Henry Holland and is set in lovely grounds landscaped by the industrious Lancelot 'Capability' Brown. The elegant interior houses important collections of furniture, porcelain, sculpture and paintings, including several Van Dycks) acquired by the Palmerstons. The house passed to the Mountbatten family and it was first opened to the public in 1979 by Lord Louis Mountbatten. The present owner, Lord Romsey, the grandson of Lord Louis, established the Mountbatten Exhibition, which follows Lord Louis' remarkable career as sailor, commander,

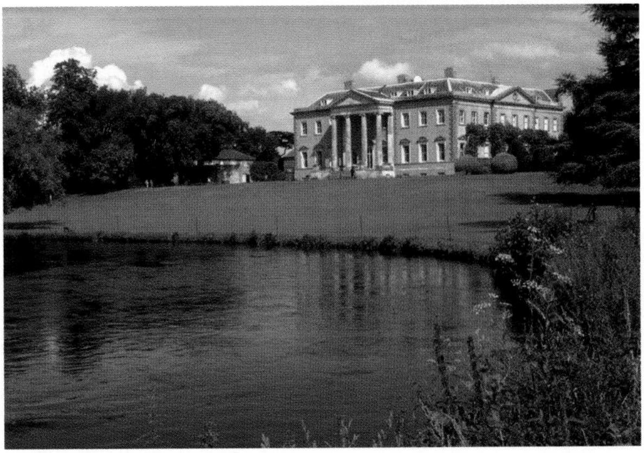

Broadlands

statesman, diplomat and sportsman. Lord Mountbatten is buried at Romsey Abbey.

AROUND ROMSEY

Ampfield

3 miles NE of Romsey on the A3090

Ampfield was once a centre of the pottery industry, and bricks made from local clay were used to build the Church of St Mark in the 1830s. One of the vicars was the father of Thomas the Tank Engine's creator the Rev W Awdry, who spent his childhood here. The chief attraction in the vicinity is the **Sir Harold Hillier Gardens & Arboretum**, begun by the renowned eponymous gardener. He started the unique collection in 1953 and the 180-acre site is now home to the greatest assembly of hardy trees and shrubs in the world. Justly billed as 'a garden for all seasons', it features among its 40,000 plants champion trees, the largest winter garden in the country and 11 National Plant Collections, including *quercus* and *hamamelis*.

Mottisfont

4 miles N of Romsey off the A3057

Mottisfont's little Church of St Andrew boasts a wealth of 15th century stained glass, including a superb Crucifixion, and should not be overlooked on a visit to **Mottisfont Abbey**. Built as an Augustinian priory in the 12th century, the building was adapted to a country mansion after the Dissolution and further much modified in the 18th century. Some parts of the priory survive, including the monks' cellarium, an undercroft with vast pillars, but the main attraction inside is the drawing room decorated as a Gothic trompe l'oeil fantasy by Rex Whistler. He was also to have designed the furniture, but World War ll intervened and he was killed in action. The superb grounds contain the National Collection of old-fashioned roses, established in 1972, a candidate for England's largest London plane tree and a lovely pollarded lime walk designed by Sir Geoffrey Jellicoe. Sir Geoffrey trained as an architect and brought an architectural quality to many of his garden and outdoor designs, which include a water garden in Hemel Hempstead, the Kennedy Memorial at Runnymede and a theme park in Texas.

Braishfield

4 miles NE of Romsey off the A3090

A scattered village in open country, almost in the shadow of Farley Mount. This country park covers 1,000 acres and from its top, just under 600 feet, the views are superb. The park abounds in wildlife and supports a wide variety of trees. Braishfield's **All Saints Church** (1885) is notable for the coloured bricks that are a signature of the architect and restorer Butterfield.

East Wellow

3 miles W of Romsey off the A27

The **Church of St Margaret** is the burial place of Florence Nightingale, who lies beneath the family monument. The simple inscription is FN 1820-1910. The church has many interesting features, including 13th century wall paintings and Jacobean panelling. Florence's family home was the nearby country mansion Embley Park.

Ower

5 miles SW of Romsey off the A31

Paultons Park is a leisure park with over 40 attractions ranging from thrilling rides and a Rio Grande railway to bird gardens, museums and dinosaurs.

SOUTHAMPTON

From this historic port Henry V set sail for Agincourt in 1415, the Pilgrim Fathers embarked on their voyage to the New World in 1620, and in 1912 the great liner *Titanic* steamed majestically into the Solent on her first and last journey. The crusaders set out from here, as did troops by the million in the Napoleonic and World Wars. As a major sea port, Southampton was an obvious target for enemy bombing, and indeed suffered greatly, but a surprising number of ancient buildings survived the bombardment, including about half of the one-mile circuit of the medieval town walls; visitors can follow the 'Walk the Walls' signposts to guide them round the walls. Perhaps the most impressive feature of the walls is **Bargate**, one of the finest medieval city gates in the country and now a museum of local history and folklore. The **Museum of Archaeology** is housed in God's House Tower, a massive stone building that was also part of the medieval town defences. It contains one of the most important archaeological collections in the country, with fascinating displays of Roman, Saxon and medieval objects excavated from local sites. The story of Southampton as seen through the eyes of residents is told in the **Tudor House Museum**, a 500-year-old building which has been a family home, artist's studio, dye house and bookbinder's premises. The garden is an authentic reconstruction of a 16th century knot garden with herbs and flowers of the period, a fountain and bee skeps. The lifestyle of the wealthy is the theme of the **Medieval Merchant's House**, which has been restored inside and out to appear just as when it was built in about 1290. The days of the luxury liner have not quite passed, and watching big ships like the *Aurora, Oriana* or *Queen Elizabeth II* from Western Esplanade and Town Quay is still a thrilling experience. The story of the liners and the port is told in the **Maritime Museum**, which is located on the corner of historic Bugle Street and Town Quay in a medieval wool house that once saw service as a prison for Napoleonic soldiers. Southampton was also at the centre of the developing aircraft industry, and in the **Southampton Hall of Aviation** visitors learn about the numerous local aircraft companies, including the Supermarine works where the chief engineer and aircraft designer RJ Mitchell created the legendary Spitfire and the S6B Seaplane that won the 1931 Schneider Trophy with a speed of 340mph. A Spitfire is among the aircraft on show, the largest of which is the four-engined Sandringham flying boat, whose flight deck is accessible to visitors on a guided tour.

Ocean Village Marina

At Totton, in a neck off Southampton Water, **Eling Tide Mill** is probably the only surviving tide mill in the world still producing flour on a daily basis. A mill has stood on the site since Domesday, but the present building dates from the 18th century. Abandoned in the 1940s and opened again after restoration in the 1980s, it takes advantage of the renowned double tide to stage milling demonstrations - and the flour it produces is for sale. It also serves as a museum, combining history, science and technology under one roof. Notable natives of Southampton include Izaak Watts (the hymnologist who wrote '*O God our Help in Ages Past*'), the composer Charles Dibdin and the painter Sir John Millais.

AROUND SOUTHAMPTON

West End

3 miles NE of Southampton off the A27

On the northern outskirts of Southampton, **Itchen Valley Country Park** is a great place for a family outing, with miles of waymarked trails, picnic and barbecue areas, children's play areas and an adventure playground. High Wood Barn Visitor Centre contains all the information about the 440-acre park, plus hands-on exhibitions and an aquarium. In the old fire station on the main street is a local history museum whose exhibits include the story of Arthur Henry Rostron, captain of the Cunard liner *Carpathia*, which rescued over 700 passengers from the *Titanic*. Captain Rostron became Commodore of the line, was knighted and retired to the village. His grave is in the old burial ground near the museum.

Eastleigh

4 miles NE of Southampton on the A335

A Saxon settlement mentioned in a charter of 932, Eastleigh waited 900 years before expanding rapidly with the arrival of the railway from London. In the heart of town, in an old Salvation Army building, **Eastleigh Museum** (see panel opposite) looks at the town in the 1930s. Visitors can meet local engine driver Mr Brown and his wife in their home and see a faithful re-creation of part of the Southern Railway locomotive works. The railway connection (Eastleigh Works were among the largest in the country) is commemorated by Jill Tweed's sculpture *The Railwayman* in the town centre. Just outside town, **Lakeside Country Park** is home to a variety of wildlife and a great place for sailing and fishing; its miniature steam railway is a popular family attraction.

Bishops Waltham

10 miles NE of Southampton on the B3335/B2177

A charming and historic small town that from 900 to 1869 was the country residence of the Bishops of Winchester.

Itchen Valley Country Park

High Wood Barn, Allington Lane, West End, Southampton, Hampshire SO30 3HQ
Tel/Fax: 023 8046 6091 e-mail: ivcp@eastleigh.gov.uk

A superb family day out is guaranteed at **Itchen Valley Country Park**, whose 440 acres of water meadows, ancient woodland, conifer plantations and grazing pasture span the River Itchen between Eastleigh and Southampton. The various areas support a great variety of bird life, insect and plant life and there are trails, cycle routes, picnic sites and a host of children's activities. The High Wood Barn Visitor Centre, built in 17th century style from timber recovered from the great storm of 1987, contains information, interactive exhibits, a café and a shop.

Eastleigh Museum

25 High Street, Eastleigh, Hampshire SO50 5LF
Tel: 023 8064 3026 Fax: 023 8065 3582
e-mail: musmst@hants.gov.uk
website: www.hants.gov.uk/museum/eastlmus/index

Right in the heart of town, **Eastleigh Museum** is the ideal place to take a break from shopping and discover what life was like in the town in the past. Visitors can meet Mr and Mrs Brown, a local engine driver and his wife, and see the re-creation of their home including the living room, scullery, back yard and outhouse. Also re-created is part of the Southern Railway locomotive works and a steam engine footplate. The museum always offers something new to see with special exhibitions, including art, crafts, photography, local history and natural history, as well as the work of local artists and societies. In the local studies area visitors can dig deeper into the area's past and even do some family history research. Tea, coffee and snacks are served in the Whistle Stop Café.

The sumptuous palace entertained many monarchs, among them Richard the Lionheart returning from the Crusades, Henry V mustering his army before sailing for Agincourt and Henry Vlll entertaining Charles V of Spain to a feast fit for a king (or even two kings). The palace, which was erected by the serial builder Henry (Henri) de Blois in 1136, was enlarged by William of Wykeham, who died at the palace in 1404. The palace was largely destroyed in the Civil War, but the ruins are impressive, especially the Great Hall with its three-storey tower. A mile or so out of town, on the B2177, **Waltham Chase Mill** is a 19th century watermill being restored to full working order. Between the town and the mill is the Moors Nature Reserve, where a source of the River Hamble rises through bubbling sand.

Netley

4 miles SE of Southampton off the A3025

A Victorian town on the shores of the Solent, Netley was brought into prominence by the vast military hospital built here after the Crimean War. The designer of **Netley Hospital** was EO Mennie and the foundation stone was laid by Queen Victoria in 1856. The chapel, with its distinctive 100ft tower, now houses an exhibition about the hospital, but the rest of the buildings were demolished after a fire in the 1960s. The hospital, which became known throughout the world, also found fame in fiction as the place where Conan Doyle's Dr Watson trained as an army doctor. Netley Cemetery is the final resting place of many nationalities, both of servicemen and of the civilian staff who worked at the hospital. The site of the hospital has been developed as the **Royal Victoria Country Park**, with 100 acres of woods and coastline offering pleasant walks and splendid views over Southampton Water. A miniature steam railway runs for a mile round the park.

Netley Abbey, founded in the 13th century, is an extensive and imposing ruin in a quiet setting among lawns and trees. Jane Austen was a frequent visitor to this romantic spot, and Horace Walpole, writing in the mid-18th century, declared that *'these are not the ruins of Netley but of Paradise'.*

Bursledon

4 miles SE of Southampton on the A3025

A village that, like its neighbours, is linked inextricably with ships and shipbuilding. Twenty Viking longships were sunk by King Alfred's men in a battle on the river here, and many of the sailors who were killed are buried beneath the Church of St Leonard. Nelson's flagship at the Battle of Copenhagen, the *Elephant*, was built in a yard that is still in the business.

Just off Junction 8 of the M27, Manor Farm Country Park is a working farm of a bygone age on the banks of the Hamble river. Among its many attractions are a Victorian schoolroom, vintage machinery, traditional farm animals and demonstrations of Victorian farm activities.

In a magnificent hilltop setting, **Bursledon Windmill** is the only one surviving in Hampshire; it was built by a Mrs Phoebe Langtry in 1814 at a cost of £800. Inactive from the time of depression in the 1880s, the tower mill was restored to full working order between 1976 and 1991. Its sails - a fine sight on a hilltop setting - revolve whenever a good northerly or southerly wind blows, producing stoneground

flour for sale. Next to the mill is the Windmill Wood Nature Trail, a woodland habitat supporting a wide variety of wildlife including woodpeckers.

The village has another relic of the county's industrial heritage in the shape of **Bursledon Brickworks**, the last surviving example in the country of a steam-driven brickworks. Built in 1897, the works closed in 1974 but have been lovingly restored and are open to the public. Among the special features are displays on the history and technique of brickmaking, and visitors can buy traditional building products in the shop.

BOTLEY
4 miles SE of Southampton on the A334

This attractive village of redbrick houses on the Hamble is as pleasant now as when William Cobbett, the 19th century writer and political commentator,

PICKWELL FARM SHOP

Pickwell Farm, Grange Road, Bursledon, Nr Southampton, Hampshire SO31 8GD
Tel: 02380 404616 Fax: 02380 406421

The mother and son team of May and Andrew Draper run the splendidly named **Pickwell Farm Shop** & Nursery, whose 56 acres of land include ten acres of Pick Your Own produce. At least 32 varieties of fruit and vegetables are for picking or for sale at various times of the year, and the goods in the attractive modern redbrick shop also includes milk from local suppliers, free-range eggs and home-baked cakes. Behind the shop is the nursery, where trees and shrubs, roses, bedding plants, peat and compost can be bought. Pickwell is open 7 days a week.

MAGIC FLUTE ARTWORKS

231 Swanwick Lane, Lower Swanwick, Southampton, Hampshire SO31 7GT Tel: 01489 570283
e-mail: art@magicfluteartworks.co.uk

A charming redbrick building in a village close to the River Hamble is home to **Magic Flute Artworks**, owned and run since 1997 by artist Bryan Dunleavy. In the gallery Bryan sells his own work and the work of other Hampshire artists, as well as picture frames, framing materials and artists' materials. Bryan organises occasional exhibitions and supervises painting holidays in the area, and for visitors staying awhile his wife offers Bed & Breakfast accommodation in three cosy bedrooms.

described it as *'the most delightful village in the world....it has everything in a village I love, and none of the things I hate'*. The author of *Rural Rides* lived a very comfortable, well-to-do life in Botley between 1804 and 1817 and is honoured by a memorial in the Market Square. **Botley Mills**, on a site mentioned in the Domesday Book, consist of an 18th century water mill and an early-20th century roller mill; the mills are being restored as a museum of flour milling.

Halfway between Botley and the pretty village of **Wickham**, on the A334, **Wickham Vineyard** was established in 1984, and its original six-acre planting had expanded to 18 acres of vines. The vineyard and the modern winery are open for visits, as is the adjacent nature reserve, where the sparrowhawk and the great spotted woodpecker can be seen, along with a wealth of meadow flowers. Wickham was the home of William of Wykeham, Chancellor of England, Bishop of Winchester and founder of Winchester College and New College, Oxford. The mill by the bridge over the River Meon is of particular interest to American visitors as it contains beams from the American frigate *Chesapeake*, captured in 1813 off Boston by the British frigate *Shannon*.

Hamble

6 miles SE of Southampton on the B3397

Hamble was a major trading post in the 14th century and an important centre of the shipbuilding industry. Famous now as a yachting centre, the village takes its name from the river, just ten miles in length, that flows past on its way to Southampton Water. Some 3,000 craft have berths in the Hamble Estuary, and in the high season there's an amazing variety to be seen, from vintage barges to the sleekest modern vessels. The area south of the village is **Hamble Common**,

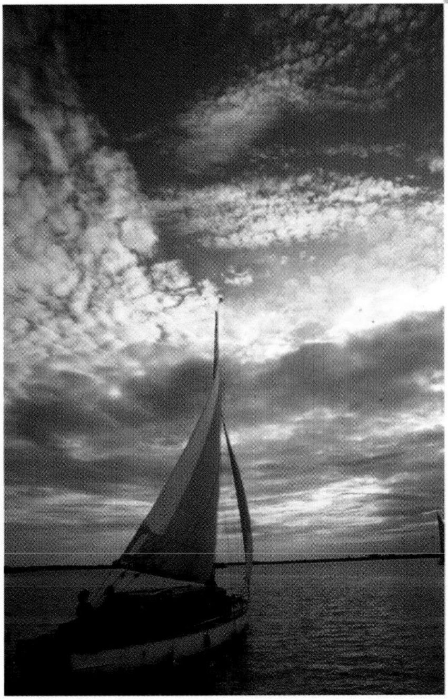

Sailing, Hamble Estuary

55 acres of coastal heath with a wide range of habitats and a correspondingly extensive variety of flora and fauna. Along the shore are the remains of Iron Age settlements, a Tudor castle and a Napoleonic gun battery. The castle was built on the orders of Henry Vlll in 1543 as part of a defence against a feared French invasion; it has disappeared apart from a few foundation stones which can be seen at low tide. At the eastern tip of the Common is a Bofors anti-aircraft gun, installed in 1989 to replace the gun that helped to protect the docks and oil terminals during World War ll.

Fareham

10 miles SE of Southampton on the A27

Much expanded since Thackeray described it as a 'dear little old Hampshire town', Fareham still has considerable charm, and the handsome

Tussie Mussie Spode

35 The Square, Titchfield, Hampshire PO14 4AQ
Tel/Fax: 01329 842174
e-mail: pam@onlyspode.com website: www.onlyspode.com

Several rooms in a handsome Georgian house in the centre of Titchfield are devoted to elegant displays of new Spode tableware and giftware. Owner Pam Hodgkinson created **Tussie Mussie Spode** Show House Shop in 1997 as a completely new way to sell china from the world-famous Spode company of Stoke-on-Trent. Tussie Mussie sells ONLY SPODE china and provides a unique service for discerning Spode buyers based on years of experience and close personal contacts at Spode. As Pam says, no one knows more about Spode....except Spode! The shop is based in Pam's home, and Tussie Mussie displays new Spode as it might be seen in the home, not behind glass in a store that offers many other ranges. Using Spode is part its joy, and in the 200 years since Josiah Spode perfected bone china the Stoke factory has consistently produced beautiful products.

The latest are displayed in Pam's six Show House Shop rooms (blue room, kitchen, bathroom, dining room, schoolroom and attic bedroom) which visitors can browse at leisure, experiencing Spode in real home surroundings and perhaps making choice easier. At least 60 dinner services are on display, plus literally dozens of giftware items, many of them priced at under £10. The main ranges include the classic Willow pattern - developed by Josiah Spode in about 1790, Blue Italian, Woodland, Signatures and Penny Lane.

For 2002 comes the Golden Jubilee Collection celebrating the 50th year of the Queen's reign, a superb collection in bone china and Blue Room Imperial ware. The highlight of this collection is the limited edition Lions Head Vase. The shop is open from 10 to 6 Wednesday to Saturday, but special appointments are possible, and of course the very comprehensive website is available 24 hours a day. The gift wrap service is free and telephone orders can be accepted for same day collection.

Chamomile Cottage

35 The Square, Titchfield, Hampshire PO14 4AQ
Tel: 01329 842174 e-mail: pam@onlyspode.com
Fax: 01329 842174 website: www.onlyspode.com/cottage.htm

Tucked away in a private courtyard at the rear of Tussie Mussie Spode is a delightful B&B with a difference. It's a four-room former cobblers cottage which is available for long or short lets. The cottage has full central heating and includes all the things you expect today. After a completely relaxing night's sleep guests make their own breakfast, for which everything is provided: there's the choice of a full breakfast cooked on the AGA/Rayburn (we'll show you how) or more simply fruit juice, cereals and often cold meats and cheeses. The separate bathroom with bath and shower is just along the corridor, and at the end is the living room and a staircase to the attic bedroom set amongst the old rafters. The attic bedroom has a double bed, though the cottage can easily sleep two more. Two Z-beds can be set up downstairs (or upstairs) and children are always welcome. For little ones, there is a cot.

Outside there is a small, walled garden for the private use of guests, where the Camellia and Wisteria are delightful features in Spring and a variety of flowers and herbs grow throughout the summer. Chamomile Cottage has its own entrance so guests can come and go without disturbing the main house. Titchfield Village Square is right outside, so there's lots of handy eating places, pubs and shops nearby.

houses on the High Street reflect the prosperous days as a shipbuilding centre. Many aspects of the town's history are exhibited in **Westbury Manor Museum**, located in a large 17th century farmhouse on the outskirts of town. Also nearby are the Royal Armouries at **Fort Nelson**, whose displays of artillery dating from the Middle Ages form one of the finest collections of its kind in the world. Among the 300 guns on display are a wrought-iron monster of 1450 that could fire a 60kg granite ball almost a mile, Flemish guns captured at Waterloo and bits of the notorious Iraqi supergun. Daily gun firings take place at noon and 3pm, and the dramatic interpretations include accounts of the defence of Rorke's Drift, experiences under shellfire in the World War l trenches and a Royalist eyewitness account of the execution of Charles l. The fort was built on the orders of Lord Palmerston as part of the defences of the Royal Dockyards against a possible French invasion. The French attack never materialised, but the fort saw service in World War ll as part of Britain's anti-aircraft defences as an enormous ammunition depot. Abandoned in the 1960s, it has subsequently been restored by Hampshire County Council. Most of it is now open to the public, and visitors can take a guided tour round the ramparts, the tunnels and underground ammunition stores, the barracks and the Victorian kitchen.

Titchfield

8 miles SE of Southampton on the A27

Two miles west of Fareham stands the village of Titchfield, where the ruins of a 13th century abbey can be seen. The abbey reflects the former prominence of Titchfield, which was an important market centre and thriving port on the River Meon. The parish church contains a notable treasure in the shape of the **Wriothesley Monument**, carved by a Flemish craftsman in 1594. This remarkable and massive piece is a triple tomb chest depicting Thomas Wriothesley, the 1st Earl of Southampton, with his wife and son. The Earl it was who converted part of the abbey into a house, in which the 3rd Earl, Henry Wriothesley, entertained William Shakespeare.

Gosport

12 miles SE of Southampton on the A32

Gosport is the site of another of Palmerston's forts - the circular **Fort Brockhurst**, in virtually original condition, is open for visits - and of the **Royal Naval Submarine Museum**. Located at *HMS Dolphin*, the museum has many exhibits relating to the development of submarines and submarine warfare, and visitors can look over *HMS Alliance*, a submarine built towards the end of World War ll. Another, much earlier submarine, known as *Holland 1*, is also on display. Gosport's splendid **Holy Trinity Church** contains an organ that was once played by Handel when he was music master to the Duke of Chandos at Little Stanmore in Middlesex. The town of Gosport bought the organ when the Duke died. Gosport's original railway station still stands, a fine colonnaded building of 1842.

PORTSMOUTH

Located at Portsmouth is the country's leading naval base, which Richard the Lionheart ordered to be built in 1194. Down the centuries the docks have been extended and the defences improved to maintain the strategic importance in times of war. In 1495 the first dry docks were built and in the next century Henry

VIII built Southsea Castle and also built many fighting ships including the ill-fated ***Mary Rose***. At **Flagship Portsmouth** (see panel below), people come from all over the world to see the historic ships in the naval dockyard.

Other museums (there are at least a dozen in the city) that should not be missed are the **City Museum & Record Office**, with period room settings from the 17th century to the 1950s; the **Industrial Heritage Museum** of WM Treadgold & Co; and the **City of Portsmouth Preserved Transport Depot** with 21 vintage and veteran passenger vehicles on show. Portsmouth's literary connections include Jane Austen, who mentions the city in her novel *Mansfield Park*, and while living in Southampton she visited Portsmouth to see her brothers Francis and Charles, both of whom reached very high rank in the Navy. Other distinguished sons of Portsmouth include Isambard Kingdom Brunel and the yachtsman Alec Rose. Like Southampton, Portsmouth suffered badly during World War ll, losing the majority of its fine 17th and 18th century buildings. **St George's Church**, a handsome Georgian building of 1754, was damaged by a bomb but has been splendidly restored, and the barn-like Beneficial Boys School, built in 1784, is another survivor. In the **Royal Garrison**

Flagship Portsmouth

Porters Lodge, Building 1/7, College Road,
HM Naval Base, Portsmouth, Hampshire PO1 3LJ
Tel: 023 9286 1533 e-mail: enquiries@flagship.org.uk
Fax: 023 9229 5252 website: www.flagship.org.uk

Flagship Portsmouth, in the historic dockyard, is home port to three of the greatest ships ever built, but has many other attractions. The latest of these is the blockbusting Action Stations, where visitors can test their skills and abilities through a series of high-tech interactive displays and simulators.

The most famous of the ships is undoubtedly *HMS Victory*. From the outside it's a majestic three-master, but inside it's creepily claustrophobic except for the Admiral's and Captain's spacious, mahogany-panelled quarters. The *Mary Rose*, the second largest ship in Henry VIII's fleet, was putting out to sea, watched proudly by the King from Southsea Common, when she suddenly heeled over and sank. All 700 men on board lost their lives. The impressively preserved remains of the ship are now housed in the timber-clad Mary Rose Museum. *HMS Warrior* was the Navy's first iron-clad warship and the most formidable fighting ship the world had seen in 1860: bigger, faster and more heavily armed than any warship afloat, built of iron and powered by both sail and steam. Her size and might proved to be a deterrent to potential enemies and she never actually had to go to war.

Boat trips round the harbour give a feel of the soul of the city that has been home to the Royal Navy for more than 800 years, and the most attractive part, picturesque Old Portsmouth, can be seen to advantage from the little ferry that plies the short route to Gosport.

The Royal Naval Museum is the most fascinating of its kind, with a marvellous exhibition of the life and deeds of Nelson, and the interactive Dockyard Apprentice Exhibition explains the skills and crafts of 1911 that went into the building of the world's finest fighting ships, the Dreadnoughts.

Church, Catherine of Braganza married Charles ll in 1662. The major art gallery in Portsmouth is the **Aspex Gallery**, whose role is to provide the people of Portsmouth and visitors with opportunities to experience some of the most innovative, contemporary visual arts produced locally, nationally and internationally.

Southsea Beach

Southsea, the southern section of the city, also offers much to interest the visitor. Charles Dickens was born in Southsea in 1812, the second of seven children, and the house of his birth in Old Commercial Road is now a museum. Some of his personal belongings, from a paperweight to the couch on which he died at his last home, in Kent, are on display in the museum. A large collection of Dickens memorabilia is kept in the City Library, and the Tourist Information Centre will supply details of **Dickens Celebrity Guide Walks**. Two of Dickens' mistresses - Maria Sarah Winter (née Beadnell) and the actress Ellen Walton-Robinson (née Ternan) are buried in Highland Road cemetery in Southsea; Dickens himself is buried in Westminster Abbey. The **D-Day Museum** commemorates the Allied invasion of Europe in 1944; pride of place among the many evocative exhibits must go to the remarkable 83-metre Overlord Embroidery. The **Royal Marines Museum** highlights some of the Marines' outstanding achievements throughout the world and is home to a world-famous collection of medals, including the ten Victoria Crosses awarded to Royal Marines. The Museum is housed in Eastney Barracks, and also at Eastney is a splendid old engine house with a pair of magnificent James Watt beam engines. One of the engines is in steam when the house is open, on the last complete weekend of every month. **Portsmouth Sea Life Centre**, on Clarence Esplanade at Southsea, reflects the city's rich maritime history with a themed interior that includes lifeboats, a ship's bridge, a tropical reef observatory and close encounters with all sorts of sea creatures, from shrimps to sharks.

Southsea Castle was built in 1545 by Henry Vlll to protect Portsmouth against the French; in the early 19th century it was altered to accommodate extra guns and men, and a walk through the tunnels that surround the moat is one of the highlights of a tour of the castle. A little way out to sea from the Hovercraft Terminal on Clarence Esplanade stands **Spitbank Fort**, a monumental Victorian fort with 50 rooms and a maze of passages. Four of these forts were built offshore, part of a later defence against the French threat. This one can be reached by ferry from Southsea Pier.

At the head of Portsmouth Harbour, **Portchester Castle** is not only the grandest medieval castle in the county but also stands within the best-preserved site of a Roman fort in northern Europe. Sometime around 280AD the Romans

Porchester Castle

enclosed eight acres of this strategic headland and used it as a base for ships clearing the Channel of pirates. The original walls of the fort were 20ft high and 10ft thick, though their depth was much reduced down the years by local people pillaging the stone for their own buildings. The castle dates back to 1120, though the most substantial remains are those of the royal palace built for Richard ll at the very end of the 14th century. Also within the walls of the Roman enclosure is Portchester Church, a superb Norman building that was part of an Augustinian Priory. The priors for some reason moved inland, leaving the church in disuse; it remained thus for more than 550 years until Queen Anne personally donated £400 for its restoration. One of the glories of the church is a 12th century font of carved Caen stone.

AROUND PORTSMOUTH

Rowlands Castle

5 miles N of Portsmouth off the A3

A small village with a long green and the remains - largely obscured by the railway - of a medieval castle. Roland was a local hero who slew a foreign giant.

One of the south of England's most elegant stately homes is nearby **Stansted Park**, a fine example of Caroline Revival architecture. The first house on the site was an 11th century hunting lodge, and Stansted House was built on the present site in 1688. Much altered and extended over the next two centuries, the house was burnt down in 1900 and rebuilt to the same blueprint. Set in 1,750 acres of lovely park and woodland, the house is full of treasures, among them 18th century Brussels tapestries, fine English furniture and a collection of bird paintings by Dutch Old Masters. The servants' quarters, kitchen and wine cellars provide a fascinating insight into life below stairs. The grounds include a beech avenue, an arboretum, Ivan Hicks' 'Garden in Mind', a garden centre and an exquisitely decorated secluded chapel.

Horndean

5 miles N of Portsmouth off the A3

A busy village that has a long association with the brewing industry. The company of **George Gale**, founded at Horndean in 1847, opens its doors to visitors for a guided tour that includes the techniques of brewing and the opportunity to taste prize-winning ales and country wines.

Queen Elizabeth Country Park, at Gravel Hill, Horndean, is part of the landscape of the South Downs and is located in an Area of Outstanding Natural Beauty. Open throughout the year, its 1,400 acres include walking and cycle trails, adventure play trails, horse riding, and picnic and barbecue areas. It's

Horndean Antiques

69 London Road, Horndean, Hampshire PO8 0BW
Tel/Fax: 02392 592989
e-mail: info@horndean-antiques.co.uk
website: www.horndean-antiques.co.uk

Established in Horndean for over 30 years, **Horndean Antiques** is run by David A Roebuck, a local cabinet-maker who maintains the founder's ideals of quality and tradition. Fronting the premises is the antique shop selling pieces from the 1600s into the 1900s as well as traditional handmade furniture. In the workshops cabinet-making and French polishing remain the backbone of the business. The craftsmen working here have all served a full apprenticeship to acquire the skills needed for the careful carrying out of restoration work on furniture and long case clocks.

Conservation is important and at Horndean Antiques the craftsmen's knowledge covers gentle cleaning and wax polishing through to full French polishing. Over the years they have been called upon to restore and make many unusual wooden pieces, from miniature items to large architectural features. The 'Carlton House' desk was made by a young cabinet-maker, James Tallack, in the final year of his apprenticeship, and typifies the quality of workmanship here - James is the fourth Horndean Antiques apprentice to win an award for excellent work. Leathering and tooling is also carried out on the premises to writing boxes, Davenports, desks and tables in a variety of colours. Although they take pieces of any age, the mainstays have always been the restoration of antique furniture and clocks and commissions for handmade furniture. Open Monday to Friday and Saturday morning.

a naturalist's paradise, with many species of butterflies and wild orchids, and a large area is designated as a National Nature Reserve. The many Roman and Iron Age sites in the Park are preserved as Scheduled Ancient Monuments. The Park is dominated by the three hills of **Butser**, **War Down** and **Holt Down**, which provide a contrast between the dramatic downland and beautiful woodland.

Emsworth

6 miles NE of Portsmouth on the A27

A picturesque village located in the upper reaches of Chichester Harbour, Emsworth is a popular spot with sailors, walkers, birdwatchers and artists. In the 18th century it was the main port in the harbour, and was later important for the production of oysters, but the main maritime activity now is yachting.

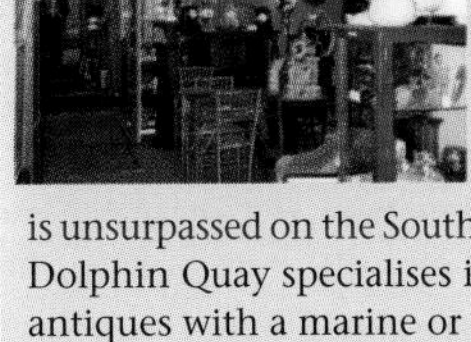

Dolphin Quay Antiques

Queen Street, Emsworth, Hampshire PO10 7BU
Tel: 01243 379994 e-mail: enquiries@dolphin-quay-antiques.co.uk
website: www.dolphin-quay-antiques.co.uk

Nancy and Malcolm Farmer own and run **Dolphin Quay Antiques**, where three showrooms offer the visitor a range of highly desirable antiques that is unsurpassed on the South Coast in terms of quality and variety. As well as the finest antique furniture, Dolphin Quay specialises in antique clocks and watches, vintage sporting apparel and luggage, and antiques with a marine or naval theme, including pond yachts, models, paintings, books and Royal Navy and shipping line memorabilia. Also on display are the decorative arts represented by art nouveau and art deco pieces, jewellery, silver, Doulton ware, china and ceramics. Open seven days a week.

Emsworth Museum is filled with exhibits reflecting the history of the village, particularly from the great fishing days. One of the many model ships on display is the *Echo*, which was the largest sailing fishing vessel to work out of any British port. The author PG Wodehouse lived in Record Road, where a blue plaque marks his house.

A short distance to the west is the Saxon village of **Warblington**, of which little survives but the ruins of a 16th century castle and the **Church of St Thomas à Becket**, with its little tower and timbered spire, which has some Roman bricks, Saxon archways, medieval floor tiles and, in the churchyard, a pair of stone grave-watchers' huts. From these huts men could guard the graves from body-snatchers - a group of criminals who stole corpses until it was officially outlawed by the Anatomy Act of 1832. There are some interesting gravestones in the cemetery, some to drowned sailors, one to Augustus Short, the first Bishop of Adelaide. The cemetery is on the path of the long-distance Solent Way, one of many marked walks in the county.

Havant

6 miles NE of Portsmouth off the A27

The town of Havant developed from a network of springs and a Roman crossroads into a leading centre for the manufacture of leather goods, gloves and parchment. Its modern leisure and recreation facilities are extensive, but for a feel of the history of the place a visit to **Havant Museum** is rewarding. Special exhibitions cover arts, crafts, local and social history, and natural history, and three rooms are given over to an important collection of firearms.

Hayling Island

4 miles S of Havant on the A3023

With its five-mile sandy beach, Hayling Island has been a traditional family seaside holiday resort for 150 years, but one that manages to retain much of its rural character, particularly in the northern part. The island lies between **Langstone** and **Chichester Harbours**; much of the former is given over to an RSPB reserve which in winter is home to up to 20,000 migrant wading birds as well as year-round residents. The **Hayling Billy Trail**, once the old Hayling Billy railway line, provides access for walkers, cyclists and horse-riders, and there are excellent views over the harbour for birdwatching. At South Hayling stands the parish church of St Mary, which combines formal Early English and the freer Decorated styles. The southern part of the island is more developed as a resort, with arcades, beach huts and houses from the 1930s, which is

The Terracotta Pot Shop

Eastoke Corner, Hayling Island, Hampshire PO11 9LU
Tel/Fax: 023 9263 7590
e-mail: sales@theterracottapotshop.co.uk
website: www.theterracottapotshop.co.uk

Handmade, frost resistant, terracotta from Greece is the speciality of the **Terracotta Pot Shop**, which Rosemary Satchwell started in 1997 and now occupies light, airy and spacious corner premises. The pots are in three main styles: sandy-coloured pots from Crete in designs similar to those used thousands of years ago; silky smooth pots with patterns and pots with an unusual rough finish, both in a darker terracotta. The shop opens every day in summer and Wednesday to Sunday in winter and also stocks antique pots, hand-painted Greek ceramics, Mexican patio heaters, Spanish cookware and Greek olive oil products. At junction of Rails Lane and Seafront.

when the island really began to boom as a holiday destination. Hayling is something of a mecca for board sailors. Not only does it provide some of the best sailboarding in the country for beginners and experts alike, it is also the place where the sport was invented. Many places claim that honour but Peter Chilvers has a High Court ruling to prove it. In 1982 a judge decided that Mr Chilvers had indeed invented the sailboard at Hayling in 1958. As a boy of ten, he used a sheet of plywood, a tent fly sheet, a pole and some curtain rings to make his conveyance and sail up one of the island's creeks.

Autumn in the Forest

THE NEW FOREST

The New Forest has been a very special part of rural England ever since William the Conqueror set it aside as his private hunting ground 900 years ago. Seizing some 15,000 acres that the Saxons had laboriously reclaimed from the heathland, he began a programme of planting thousands of trees. To preserve the Forest against any threat to the wildlife he would be hunting (especially deer) he adopted all the rigorous hunting laws of the Saxons and introduced many of his own. Anyone who killed a deer would himself be killed. If he shot at a deer and missed, his hands were cut off; and anyone who disturbed a deer during the breeding season had his eyes put out. Certain rights, some of them still in force, were granted to the Forest dwellers: pasturage, the right to graze livestock; turbage, the right to cut turf; estover, the right to cut wood for fires; pannage, the right to let pigs forage for food. An Act of Parliament of 1851 sanctioned the permanent removal of the deer on the grounds that they were causing great damage to the trees, but it proved impossible to kill them all and today there are still plenty of deer roaming in the 145 square miles of the Forest. They number about 2,000; fallow deer, mainly descended from the original herds, make up the majority, but there are also small numbers of red and roe deer, along with some sika deer, which were first introduced at the end of the 19th century. Visitors are more likely to see the famous wild New Forest ponies, and the signs that warn against feeding or even approaching them should be taken very seriously: they can be very dangerous and do not need feeding - the Forest provides everything they need. The keen-eyed bird-watcher might be rewarded with the sight of a tiny Dartford warbler or the spectacular hobby, a small type of predatory falcon. The Forest, less than half of which is actually wooded, is of great importance in terms not only of recreation and conservation but also of commerce: the Forestry Commission maintains an annual production of 36,000 tonnes of timber from the mainly conifer plantations. The Forest is ideal walking country, with vast tracts virtually unpopulated but criss-crossed by hundreds of footpaths and bridleways. The Commission has also established a network of waymarked cycle routes which make the most of the scenic attractions and are also designed to help protect the special nature of the Forest.

LYNDHURST

The only town of any size in the New Forest, Lyndhurst was the administrative centre of William's Forest. The most striking building in this compact little town is the **Church of St Michael and All Angels**, rebuilt in the mid-19th century in what Sir John Betjeman described as 'the most fanciful, fantastic Gothic style that I have ever seen'. The rebuilding, the work of George Gilbert Scott's pupil William White, coincided with the heyday of the Pre-Raphaelite movement, and the church contains some fine stained glass by Burne-Jones from the firm of William Morris. The most famous work of all is the huge mural by Lord Leighton depicting the parable of the wise and foolish virgins. In the churchyard is the grave of Alice Liddell, who, as a young girl, was the inspiration for Alice in Lewis Carroll's *Alice in Wonderland*. As Mrs Reginald Hargreaves, Alice lived all her married life in Lyndhurst and lost two sons in the First World War. Next to the church is the Queen's House. Originally built as a hunting lodge, and still showing medieval and Tudor elements, it has been host to many sovereigns (and changes its name to King's House when the monarch is male). The last monarch to stay was George lll, who graciously allowed loyal villagers to watch through the window as he ate dinner. The house is now the Headquarters of the Forestry Commission and is also home to the **Verderers' Court**, an institution dating back to Norman times which still deals with matters concerning the Forest's ancient commoning rights. The verderers sit in public ten times a year, working in close partnership with the Forestry Commissioners in managing the Forest and reconciling the needs of the commoning system (the right to rent land and graze livestock) with the demands concomitant with the Forest being a major recreational and tourist attraction. Another duty of the verderers is to appoint five agisters, stockmen who are responsible for the day-to-day supervision of the 5,000 ponies and cattle roaming in the Forest. The main car park in the High Street is the location of the **New Forest Museum & Visitor Centre**, where many aspects of the Forest - the development of the trees, the ponies, the deer, the human inhabitants - are covered in detail by audio-visual shows, exhibits and interactive displays. Animals of a more reclusive kind are the theme of the **New Forest Reptile Centre** situated two miles west of town and open every day from Easter to October. Here visitors can be sure to see the reptilian inhabitants of the Forest that might otherwise elude even the

New Forest Ponies

most observant traveller in the Forest itself, including the sand lizard and the rare smooth snake. Lyndhurst's High Street, an attractive thoroughfare of mainly Edwardian buildings, slopes down to Bolton's Bench, a tree-crowned knoll where ponies can often be seen grazing. At the other end of town Swan Green, surrounded by picturesque cottages, is a much-photographed setting for summer cricket matches.

AROUND LYNDHURST

Minstead

3 miles NW of Lyndhurst off the A337

A village of picture-postcard appeal, looked over from a hill by the 13th century **Church of All Saints**, which has almost a cottagey appearance. It features an unusual triangular nave, a triple-decked pulpit and an open fireplace. During the 18th century, the gentry of Minstead regarded attending church as a duty that should be made as agreeable as possible. Three of the most affluent residents paid to have the church fabric altered so that they could each have their own entrance door leading to a private parlour complete with the fire and comfortable chairs. The squire of Minstead even installed a sofa on which he could doze during a sermon, which at the time would normally last a minimum of an hour. Sir Arthur Conan Doyle, the creator of Sherlock Holmes, and his wife are buried in the churchyard. Though the detective, with his pipe and deerstalker, is the best-known of the author's creations, he actually preferred to write historical novels, some of which were set in Hampshire. His own favourite among these novels was *The White Company*, which is set in part in the New Forest.

Conan Doyle loved the New Forest and had a home near Cadnam, a short distance northwest of Minstead. Minstead's other main attraction is **Furzey Gardens**, eight acres of delightful woodland gardens laid out by Hew Dalrymple in the 1920s. The informal landscape enjoys views over the New Forest towards the Isle of Wight. Beautiful banks of azaleas and rhododendrons, heathers and ferns surround a picturesque water garden, and among the notable species to be found are spectacular Chilean fire trees and the strange Bottle Brush tree.

Just north of Minstead, across the A3 at Canterton Glen, stands the **Rufus Stone**, said to mark the spot where William Rufus (William ll, son of William the Conqueror) was killed while hunting by an arrow shot by Sir Walter Tyrell. His entourage sped off in all directions to report the event and William's body was carried on the cart of Purkis the charcoal-burner to Winchester, where William's brother Henry had already arrived to proclaim himself King. Rufus, the most unpopular of monarchs, was buried in

The Rufus Stone

the Cathedral without ceremony and almost without mourning. The story goes that Tyrell fled to France, reversing his horse's shoes in a bid to thwart pursuers......but there were none.

Ashurst

3 miles NE of Lyndhurst on the A35

There are several family attractions here. The **New Forest Butterfly Farm** in Langley Wood houses butterflies, birds and insects in a garden and jungle setting. **Longdown Dairy Farm** shows the workings of a modern dairy farm and is home to the **National Dairy Council Museum Collection**. The **Otter, Owl and Wildlife Conservation Park**, set in 25 acres of ancient woodland, contains Europe's largest gathering of multi-specied otters, owls and other indigenous wildlife including deer, wild boar, lynx, foxes, polecats, pine martens, badgers, Scottish wild cats and hedgehogs, all in their natural surroundings. Ashurst Lodge, now a private house, contains the remains of an Elizabethan industrial site where saltpetre was mined. The Forestry Commission offers visitors the opportunity of camping in the heart of the Forest, and the site at Ashurst is one of three offering full facilities.

Marchwood

6 miles E of Lyndhurst on the A326

A community with strong links with both woodland and water. Ships of the Royal Fleet Auxiliary are based at the military port, which was built in 1943 for the construction of the Mulberry Harbours. On the western edge of the village, the woodland of Crookedhays Copse is a haven of wildlife.

Hythe

8 miles SE of Lyndhurst off the A35

This is one of the very best places to watch the comings and goings of the big ships on Southampton Water, and no visit here is complete without taking a ride up the pier on the quaint little electric train, the oldest electric pier train in the world; from the end of the pier a ferry plies the short route across to Southampton. Hythe is the birthplace of the Hovercraft - its inventor Sir Christopher Cockerell lived in the village. In the 1930s Hythe was the home of the British Powerboat Company and of TE Lawrence (Lawrence of Arabia) while he was testing the RAF 200 series powerboats.

Beaulieu

7 miles SE of Lyndhurst on the B3056

This historic settlement on the banks of the Beaulieu river has been a popular place to visit for many centuries - it was here in 1202 that King John gave an area

Beaulieu Abbey

then known as Bellus Locus (Beautiful Place in Latin, Beaulieu in French) to the Cistercian monks. The **Abbey** passed into the ownership of the Earl of Southampton in 1538; he pulled most of it down, and used some of the stones in the construction of Calshot and Hurst Castles. But many parts survive, and a stately home grew up around the Abbey's imposing gatehouse. In the grounds of Lord Montagu's estate is the **National Motor Museum** (see panel below), one of the country's premier attractions, with over 300 vehicles covering all aspects of motoring and glorious gardens which are worth a visit in their own right. Among the exhibits are the landspeed record holders *Bluebird* and *Golden Arrow*, Grand Prix cars, an Outspan Orange car, vintage motorcycles and commercial vehicles and thousands of models. Many of the exhibits and activities, both inside and outside, are geared towards children, making a visit to Beaulieu an outstanding treat for all ages. Montagu family treasures are on display in **Palace House**, formerly the gatehouse of the Abbey, and visitors can meet characters from Victorian days who will talk about their lives in service.

Fawley

12 miles SE of Lyndhurst on the A326

Oil is king here, and the terminals and

Beaulieu National Motor Museum

Beaulieu, Brockenhurst, Hampshire SO42 7ZN
Tel: 01590 612345 Fax: 01590 612624
e-mail: info@beaulieu.co.uk
website: www.beaulieu.co.uk

The **National Motor Museum**, in the grounds of Lord Montagu's estate, houses over 300 vehicles covering all aspects of motoring. Among the exhibits - the oldest dates from 1896 - are world landspeed record-breakers *Bluebird* and *Golden Arrow*, Damon Hill's championship winning Formula 1 Williams Grand Prix car, an Outspan Orange car, Ariel and Vincent motorcycles and a large number of commercial vehicles.

One of the many permanent displays is an accurate reconstruction of a 1938 garage complete with forecourt, servicing bay, machine shop and office.

Many Montagu family treasures are now on display in **Palace House**, formerly the Great Gatehouse of Beaulieu Abbey, where visitors can meet characters from Victorian days, among them the butler, housemaid and cook, who will talk about their lives. The old monks' refectory houses an exhibition of monastic life, and embroidered wall hangings designed and created by Belinda, Lady Montagu, depict the story of the Abbey from its earliest days. The glorious gardens are an attraction in their own right, and there are plenty of rides and drives for young and old alike - including a monorail that runs through the roof of the Museum in the course of its tour of the estate.

refineries of what is probably the largest oil plant in Europe create a science fiction landscape; standing bravely apart is the village church, a link with earlier days, looking out over Southampton Water. Fawley is where some islanders from Tristan da Cunha settled after fleeing a volcano that threatened their island in 1961; a model of one of the boats they used for their escape can be seen in the chapel. Also of note in Fawley is **Cadland House**, whose 8-acre garden overlooking the Solent was designed for the banker Robert Drummond by Capability Brown. It houses the national collection of leptospermums and also features a splendid kitchen garden and a modern walled garden. Beyond the refineries a road leads off the B3053 Calshot road to **Ashlett Creek** and another world, the natural, unrefined world of creeks, mud flats and bird-haunted marshland.

Calshot

14 miles SE of Lyndhurst on the B3053

The RAF were based in both World Wars at Calshot, where seaplanes were prepared and tested for the Schneider Trophy races. The hangars once used by the RAF are now the Calshot Activity Centre, whose many activities include an artificial ski slope. At the very end of a shingle spit stands one of Henry VIII's coastal defence castles. This is **Calshot Castle**, which is now restored as a pre-World War 1 garrison. Visitors can admire the view from the roof of the keep, walk round the barrack room looking like it did before World War 1 and see the exhibition of the Schneider air races. A little way to the west is **Lepe**, one of the major embarkation points for the 1944 D-Day invasion. The area at the top of the cliffs at Lepe is now a country park, and there's safe swimming off the beach.

Exbury

10 miles SE of Lyndhurst off the B3054

Created by Lionel de Rothschild in the 1920s and still run by members of the family, **Exbury Gardens** fully justify the reaction of one visitor, who described them as 'Heaven with the gates open'. On hundred and fifty gardeners and workmen took 10 years to create the gardens, and Rothschild sent expeditions to the Himalayas to find the seeds he wanted. He himself bred hundreds of varieties of plants and the displays of rhododendrons, camellias and azaleas which he planted are renowned the world over. The 200-acre grounds are a delight to visit in spring, summer or autumn, with May perhaps the best time of all. Many varieties of the Exbury specialities are on sale in the plant centre, where there's also a gift shop, tea room and restaurant.

Exbury's **Church of St Catherine** is best known for its moving, lifelike bronze memorial to two brothers who were killed in action in World War 1. The work was commissioned by the brothers' parents and executed by Cecil Thomas, a gifted young sculptor who was a friend of the brothers. The area around Exbury and Lepe is featured in Nevil Shute's sad story *Requiem for a Wren*, which describes the preparations made in the New Forest for the D-Day landings. Shute himself was an aero-engineer as well as a writer, and for a time worked here on a top-secret pilotless plane.

Buckler's Hard

10 miles SE of Lyndhurst off the B3056

Across the river from Exbury, Buckler's Hard is a popular spot for berthing yachts and cruisers and has a long and distinguished history of shipbuilding. Many fighting ships were built here, including one of London's favourites,

HMS Agamemnon, which saw service at both Copenhagen and Trafalgar. It was a ship Nelson loved in spite of the fact that it was while he was in command, in a battle off Corsica, that he lost an eye. The village was created by the 2nd Duke of Montagu in the early 1700s for the main purpose of receiving and refining sugar from his estates in the West Indies. His grand plans involved the building of a number of broad streets but in fact only one was ever constructed, grass-verged and running down to the water's edge.

One of its buildings is now a Maritime Museum which tells the story of Buckler's Hard from the earliest sugar cane days. Displays include models of ships, among them *Victory*, *Agamemnon* and the yacht *Bluebottle*, which Prince Philip raced with success. A special display recounts the exploits of Sir Francis Chichester, who sailed round the world in *Gypsy Moth* from his home port of Bucklers Hard.

A lovely riverside walk passes through **Bailey's Hard**, a former brickworks where the first naval vessel built on the river was completed in 1698. Henry Adams, the most distinguished of a family of shipbuilders, lived in the village in what is now the Master Builders Hotel. In the summer, half-hour cruises on *Swiftsure* depart from the pier at Buckler's Hard.

Brockenhurst

3 miles S of Lyndhurst on the A35

A large village in a lovely setting in the heart of the New Forest. Forest ponies are frequent visitors to the main street and the village green (they naturally have right of way!). The **Church of St Nicholas** has a vast graveyard with a yew tree that is probably the oldest tree in the whole region. In the graveyard lie many soldiers, many of them from New Zealand, who had died of their injuries in a nearby military hospital. But the best

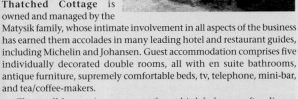

known grave is that of Harry Mills, known as Brusher Mills, who brushed the New Forest cricket pitch and followed the occupation of snake-catcher.

LYMINGTON

An ancient seaport and market town, Lymington was once a major manufacturer of salt, with hundreds of salt pans between the quay and the tip of the promontory at Hurst Castle. **St Barbe Museum**, in New Street, tells the story of the area between the New Forest and the Solent, with special reference to the salt industry (salt was made here beside the sea for hundreds of years), boatbuilding, smuggling and the area at war. There is also a changing exhibition of the work of artists both local and world-renowned - the gallery has in the past hosted works by artists as diverse as David Hockney

LYMINGTON LARDER

13 High Street, Lymington, Hampshire SO41 9AA
Tel: 01590 676740
e-mail: eatlocal@uk2.net website: www.lymington.larder.co.uk

In a bay-windowed Georgian shop, **Lymington Larder** was taken over in 2000 by Charles du Parc who has a lifelong love of cheeses and a commitment to locally produced food. The delicatessen stocks farmhouse cheeses from the South of England and a select range of Continental cheeses; dry-cured bacon, sausages, butter, jams and chutneys from local sources, as well as fresh-baked pies and pasties. Hampers, business lunches and mail order are other services offered, and there is a cosy café area providing sandwiches, baguettes and light lunches using food from the delicatessen. The shop is a member of the Guild of Fine Food Retailers.

STANWELL HOUSE HOTEL

High Street, Lymington, Hampshire SO41 9AA
Tel: 01590 677123 Fax: 01590 677756
e-mail: sales@stanwellhousehotel.co.uk
website: www.stanwellhousehotel.co.uk

Jane McIntyre's **Stanwell House Hotel** is a Georgian building in the heart of Lymington, carefully updated to provide all the expected modern comforts while maintaining a civilised period atmosphere. The emphasis throughout is on comfort and service, and there are 29 bedrooms include Elgars Cottage (two bedrooms) and five luxury suites . All the rooms are dramatic and different and the suites have old silks and velvets, touches of Ralph Lauren and Mulberry, four-poster beds and some with roll-top baths, complemented by modern conveniences such as power showers, tv, trouser press and kettles

discreetly hidden within pieces of Georgian furniture.

Excellent food is

served by candlelight in the award winning Bistro. The 3 star hotel also has a smart cocktail bar, light, bright conservatory with York stone flags, an eclectic collection of furnishings and old prints on the walls. Other amenities include a patio and walled garden, a conference room and an in-house clothing store.

and Goya. The broad High Street leading up from the quay is a hive of activity on Saturday, when the market established in the 13th century is held.

The Isle of Wight ferry runs from Walhampton, just outside Lymington, where a notable building is the Neale Obelisk, a memorial to Admiral Neale erected in 1840. At **Hordle**, just north of the A337 between Lymington and New Milton, **Apple Court** is a delightful garden with an important collection of hostas.

AROUND LYMINGTON

Boldre

2 miles N of Lymington off the A337

Boldre is a pretty little village on the River Lymington, with a charming square-towered 13th century church. 'The village is here, there and everywhere', wrote Arthur Mee in the 1930s, describing the agglomeration of hamlets - Pilley, Portmore and Sandy Dow - that make up the parish of Boldre. Mee approved of the church and also praised an 18th century rector, the Rev William Gilpin, who found fame with his books describing his travels round Britain. After the Second World War, the church at Boldre became a shrine to *HMS Hood*, sunk by the *Bismarck* in 1941 with the loss of 1,400 lives. A service in memory of the victims is held every year. Figures remembered by memorials in the church include the Rev Gilpin, John Kempe, a 17th century MP for Lymington and Richard Johnson, a vicar who was on the first sailing of convicts to Botany Bay in 1788 and who built the first church in Australia. The interior of the church has been changed very little down the centuries, one exception being some modern windows designed by Alan Younger. In School Lane, **Spinners** is a charming, informal woodland garden with a national collection of trilliums.

Sway

3 miles N of Lymington off the A337

This rural village and the surrounding countryside were the setting for much of Captain Marryatt's *Children of the New Forest*, an exciting tale set in the time of the Civil War and written a year before Marryatt died in 1848. In Station Road, **Artsway** is a visual arts centre that was originally a coach house; the site contains a garden and a gallery. South of the village is a famous 220ft folly called **Peterson's Tower**. This curiosity was built by a retired judge, Andrew Peterson, in honour of his late wife and as proof of the efficacy of concrete. The tower was originally topped by a light that could be seen for many miles, but it was removed on the orders of Trinity House as a potential source of confusion to shipping. The judge's ashes were buried at the base of his folly but were later moved to be next to his wife in the churchyard at Sway.

Milford-on-Sea

5 miles SW of Lymington on the B3058

An unspoilt resort village with a parish church dating from the 13th century. A shingle spit extends a mile and a half from Milford, and at the end, less than a mile from the Isle of Wight, stands **Hurst Castle**, another in the chain of coastal fortresses built by Henry VIII. Charles I was imprisoned here before being taken to London for his trial and execution. The castle was modernised during the Napoleonic Wars and again in the 1860s, when the massive armoured wings were added. Two of the huge guns installed in

(Continued page 212)

WALK 6

Pennington Marshes

Start	Harbour, Keyhaven
Distance	6 miles (9.7km)
Approximate time	3 hours
Parking	Small free parking area by the harbour wall. Alternatively use the official car park (free in winter)
Refreshments	Pubs in Keyhaven and Pennington
Ordnance Survey maps	Landranger 196 (Solent & the Isle of Wight) and Outdoor Leisure 22 (New Forest)

The route of this mainly waterside walk runs through Pennington Marshes with the Solent to one side and both salt and freshwater marshes to the other. Paths are flat and in the main well surfaced and dry, but along short lengths waterproof footwear is advisable.

Pennington marshes are a nature reserve run by Hampshire County Council and are part of a Site of Special Scientific Interest. The marshes are important as a stopping-off point for migrating birds in spring and autumn. They are also important as feeding grounds for winter visitors escaping the extreme cold of their far-northern breeding grounds. One regular visitor from the Arctic is the brent goose which all but died out in the 1930s but whose numbers have now recovered well. Rarer, avocet, arctic skua, snow bunting and osprey have been seen. The marsh is also, with the Beaulieu River estuary, one of the major breeding sites on the south coast of England for common, sandwich and little terns.

Follow the tarmac lane that runs beside the inner wall of the harbour away from Keyhaven. Ignore a track to the right and carry straight on to a five-bar gate, going around it. Ignore a tall green metal gate on your left with a footpath sign beside it and continue ahead. Soon the tarmac road becomes a gravel track. On the right the sails of boats can be seen apparently moving across a dry landscape. In fact they are passing along a stretch of the Solent in front of the Isle of Wight.

Walk around a five-bar gate tarmac road, continuing straight on down the lane ahead. When the road bends left, turn right down a narrow gravel footpath between fences **A**.

Go around a further five-bar gate at the end of the path and onto a tarmac lane that bears right. Pass a row of old fishermen's cottages on the left and continue down the lane which bears left. Just before a public footpath sign, turn right onto a narrow gravel track and follow the blue marker signifying the Solent Way **B**.

WALK 6

Bear right at a T-junction on the path to follow a narrow track that leads down the right-hand side of an inlet. On the left the masts of the boats at Lymington Marina are evident, and a chimney in the distance points to the position of Fawley Power Station near Southampton. On reaching the lock that feeds or cuts off water to this inlet, go up the steps beside it and turn right to follow the sea wall. **C**

The shapes of earlier dykes and salt pans can be seen on the right. More information on this salt industry, which thrived for around 600 years, is given under Walk 19.

Continue to follow the sea wall back to Keyhaven. This new wall, started in 1991, is already providing a base for hardy salt surviving plants. It has been designed to include sluices and flaps to allow salt water to pass through to the marshes inside the wall so that plant life and feeding birds will not be affected. The path then follows the shoreline.

From here the lighthouse at Hurst Spit and Hurst Castle can be seen. Like Calshot Castle, Hurst was one of a series of forts built by Henry VIII to defend the coast. Since then it has been used, among other things, as a prison. Its most famous prisoner was Charles I who was held here for a short time before being returned to London for his trial and execution. Follow the path back alongside the harbour.

You can visit Hurst Castle by boat or by walking along the pebble beach. It is about 6 miles (9.5km) there and back. A boat leaves the harbour regularly for Hurst Castle in summer. ●

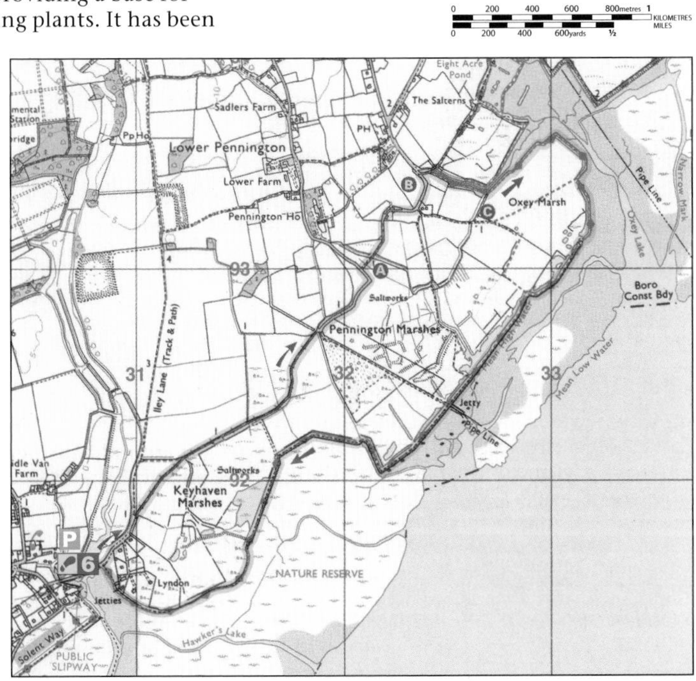

the 1870s can still be seen. The castle was used as a garrison during World War II and is now in the care of English Heritage. Access is either along the beach or by ferry from Keyhaven. Between Milford and Everton are **Braxton Gardens** and Everton Grange Lake, where visitors can tour the walled garden with its beautiful roses, see the knot garden planted with germander and cotton lavender, fish in the lake or buy something in the plant centre or farm shop.

New Milton

4 miles W of Lymington on the A337

A lively little town with a superb stretch of coastline minutes away at Barton-on-Sea. The best-known landmark in the town is the splendid **Water Tower** of 1900. Late-Victorian providers of water services seem to have enjoyed pretending that their water towers and sewage treatment plants were in fact castles, and the specimen at New Milton is

Landfall

96 High Street, Milford-on-Sea, Hampshire SO41 0QE
Tel: 01590 643951 website: www.newforest-online.co.uk

There's no better place for seeking out the perfect gift for any occasion than **Landfall**, a delightful little high street shop which Ethne Moody has owned and run for 30 years. Antiques, jewellery and books are her main specialities, but browsers will also find a merry jumble of bric-a-brac, brassware, crockery, mirrors, pictures and small items of furniture. Many of Ethne's customers are loyal locals, but the shop also attracts holidaymakers in the know who consider Landfall as essential a part of their itinerary as Hurst Castle or the New Forest. The welcome is unfailingly warm and friendly, and the shop is open from 9.00am to 5.30pm Monday to Saturday and from 2.00pm to 5.00pm on Sunday.

Carringtons Antiques

100 High Street, Milford-on-Sea, Hampshire SO41 0QE
Tel: 01590 644665

Peter and Kerry Lee originally from London and, with a background in the trade, moved to Milford in the mid-1980s and opened **Carringtons Antiques** towards the end of 1999. Behind and attractive white-painted shopfront on Milford's main street, the Lees keep a constantly changing stock of antiques, concentrating mainly on porcelain and china, linen, pictures and items of furniture, and attending trade fairs throughout the South of England. Spares and repairs for oil lamps are a speciality, and Carrington Antiques will undertake house clearances and valuations. The shop is open from 10.00am to 5.00pm Tuesday to Saturday.

Braxton Rose And Herb Garden

Lymore Lane, Milford-on-Sea, Hampshire SO41 0TX
Tel: 01590 642008 Fax: 01590 645259

Braxton Gardens are comprised of three individual gardens - the courtyard garden with pool and fountain, the walled herb garden featuring a germander and cotton lavender knot garden, and the wonderful rose garden, one of the best in Hampshire, planted with over 450 David Austin roses of almost 100 varieties. The gardens are one of the largest stockists of these superb roses, and are also well known for their extensive range of herbs and alpines. Other attractions on site are a gift shop selling jams, chutneys, cards, stationery and cosmetics, and a café with a good selection of teas, coffees, scones and cakes. Braxton Gardens are generally open from 10.00am to 5.00pm, with admission and parking free.

Chewton Glen

New Milton, Hampshire BH25 6QS
Tel: 01425 275341 Fax: 01425 272310
e-mail: reservations@chewtonglen.com
website: www.chewtonglen.com

Set in 130 acres of immaculate lawns, parkland and woodland on the edge of the New Forest, Martin and Brigitte Skan's magnificent 'hotel, health and country club' has no equal in its class in Britain and few anywhere in the world. **Chewton Glen** dates from the early 1700s and was remodelled in the Palladian style in the 1890s. When Martin bought it in 1966, the hotel had just eight bedrooms but expansion and acclaim followed quickly. Martin and his Swiss-born wife have seen the hotel grow to 59 rooms and suites, the grounds from 30 to 130 acres, and the staff from 6 to 175.

The bedrooms are spread between the Old House, the Garden Wing, the Coach House Wing and the Croquet Lawn Wing. All are individually designed and decorated, using the finest fabrics and wallpapers. They all have king-size or twin beds, a trouser press, personal safe, hairdryer, 10-channel satellite tv and cosseting bath robe and slippers for each guest. Complimentary sherry, mineral water and shortbread are provided in each room, many of which have air conditioning and CD systems. The interior design is overseen with faultless taste by Brigitte, both in the bedrooms and in the lounges and cosy bar. Captain Frederick Marryat wrote his classic *Children of the New Forest* while staying here in 1846 (the house was owned at the time by his brother) and the rooms are all named after characters, ships or places in the much loved stories.

Pierre Chevillard's cooking has garnered an impressive array of awards including a Michelin star and The Times' Hotel Restaurant of the Year. Pierre and his team of 24 chefs offer a range of menus and dishes conceived and executed with well-honed skills, from the familiar (tournedos with gratin dauphinois; bread and butter pudding) to sublime specialities such as his signature dish of braised fillet of sea bass with shiitake mushrooms, beansprouts, ginger and coriander. And it's not just the food that wins the awards: in 2000, readers of the American magazine, Gourmet, voted Chewton Glen 'Best Country House Hotel in the World' and of course Chewton Glen is the only privately owned Five Red Star Hotel in Britain. Pol Roger conferred the Best European Wine List Award. The room rate includes the use of the 9-hole par-3 golf course, the indoor swimming pool (also an outdoor pool in summer), the indoor and outdoor tennis courts, the croquet lawn and the amazing Health Club. Inspired by a Roman spa, the club offers state of the art aerobic machines in the air conditioned gym, the pool, whirlpool, saunas, steam room scented with eucalyptus and an extensive range of massage, beauty, body and hair treatments. Looking after the guests as always been the number one priority at Chewton Glen, and under managing director Peter Crome service moves with the smoothness of a Rolls Royce at this most exceptional and civilised of hotels.

Millers Antiques Limited

Netherbrook House, Christchurch Road,
Ringwood, Hampshire BH24 1DR
Tel: 01425 472062 Fax: 01425 472727
e-mail: mail@millers-antiques.co.uk
website: www.millers-antiques.co.uk

Millers Antiques Limited was established in Chelsea in 1897 and has been based in Netherbrook House, Ringwood, since the 1960s. The listed Queen Anne house and extensive Georgian outbuildings set round a courtyard make ideal showrooms. Millers carry a wide range of interesting and unusual antique furniture and accessories. English and Continental furniture, majolica, treen, copper and brass, Quimper and decorative pieces feature in the stock.

Alan, the grandson of the founder, and his wife Carole travel many miles each year to find the antiques which fill their showrooms. Millers Antiques also offer the highest quality restoration services in addition to packing and shipping both to the UK and worldwide. Opening hours at Millers Antiques Limited are Monday to Friday 9.30 to 5 (with early closing on Monday afternoon) and Saturday 10 to 3. Any other time to visit can be arranged by appointment.

Bettles Gallery

80 Christchurch Road, Ringwood, Hampshire BH24 1DR
Tel: 01425 470410

Bettles Gallery is situated on the southern edge of the old market town of Ringwood bordering the New Forest at a crossing point of the River Avon. Bournemouth and the coast are only a short distance away, and the area is rich in scenic and historic attractions. The Gallery was opened in 1989 in a 300-year-old building with low ceilings, oak beams and an inglenook fireplace, all of which contribute to a friendly, intimate atmosphere. The Gallery specialises in British Studio Ceramics and Contemporary Paintings and over the years has built up a first-class reputation for the quality of work on display. The eight or nine solo or group exhibitions held each year attract collectors from far afield. Recent exhibitions have featured ceramics by John Maltby, Mike Dodd and David Leach and paintings by Brian Graham and Peter Joyce.

Work from leading potters and promising newcomers is always on show and as an added dimension interesting ceramic jewellery and carefully selected paintings, mostly by artists from the South of England with leanings towards impressionistic and the abstract, are also on display. The Gallery is a member of the Independent Craft Galleries Association, of which Gill and Roger Bettle are committee members. It works closely with local businesses and organisations to promote an awareness of contemporary arts and crafts by means of talks and displays, and welcomes visits from student groups. The Gallery is open from 10 to 5 Tuesday to Friday and from 10 to 1 on Saturday. There is free parking at the rear of the Gallery.

THE POTTERY

Danestream Farm, Sway Road, New Milton, Hampshire BH25 5QU
Tel: 01425 627066

Valerie Sparkes, who took an honours degree in ceramics at Bristol University, is the owner of **The Pottery**, which she established at Danestream Farm in 1993. She produces a unique range of colourful contemporary pottery on the premises, and visitors can watch the process in the workshop behind the display area. Valerie's speciality is blue and white pottery, all hand-thrown and hand-painted. All the pieces - mugs, jugs, plates, bowls, teapots - are both attractive and practical, and the full range of her wares is available for sale in the shop. There's ample off-road parking next to the shop, which is open Wednesday to Saturday (9.30-1.15 & 2.15-5.30) and Sunday morning.

particularly striking. Three storeys high, with a castellated parapet, the octagonal building has tall, narrow windows - ideal for water authority archers to see off attackers disputing their water bills! At Bashley Crossroads, west of New Milton, the **Sammy Miller Museum & Farm Trust** is a mecca for motorcycle enthusiasts, with the finest collection of fully restored machines in Europe. The two galleries house over 200 rare and classic models, and the Rocket Gold Star, the 1958 Velocette LE200, the AJS V4, the 1936 Indian Four, the 1951 497cc McCandless prototype Norton Twin and the streamlined Mondial racer are just a few of the machines on display for the bikers to drool over. Special events are held on selected Sundays in the summer months.

The village of **Wootton** lies a couple of miles north of New Milton, with forest to the north and west.

RINGWOOD

Situated on the western edge of the New Forest at a crossing point of the River Avon, Ringwood has been modernised and greatly extended in recent years, but its centre still boasts a number of elegant Georgian houses, both large and small. **Ringwood Meeting House**, built in 1727 and now a museum, is an outstanding example of an early Non-Conformist chapel, complete with the original, rather austere fittings. **Monmouth House** is of much the same period and stands on the site of an earlier building in which the Duke of Monmouth was confined after his unsuccessful attempt to oust James ll. The Duke, the illegitimate son of Charles II, had been discovered hiding in a ditch just outside the town and despite his pleas for mercy to his uncle the King he was beheaded at Tower Hill a few days later. The records at Ringwood's parish church tell of a gardener called Bower who used to drink 16 pints of ale a day! Ringwood was granted its market charter in 1226, and a lively market is still held every Wednesday.

A few miles west of town and into Dorset stretches the mighty Ringwood Forest, which contains the **Moors Valley Country Park** and its delightful narrow-gauge steam railway.

In Crow Lane, at **Crow**, just north of Ringwood, is the **New Forest Owl Sanctuary**, with a vast collection of owls (400 birds in 100 aviaries), three flying displays every day, lectures and films. The sanctuary is also home to three pairs of breeding red squirrels. Bruce Berry, the founder of the sanctuary, and his dedicated staff have put hundreds of birds back into the wild, often after treatment in the Hospital Unit, which is

Timber!

5 Star Lane, Ringwood, Hampshire BH24 1AL
Tel: 01425 483505
e-mail: sanastephens@yahoo.co.uk
website: www.loveorganic.com

Whether you live in the Ringwood area, or are just passing by, **Timber!**, is a fascinating organic shop not to be missed, with something for everyone. This unique shop sells stationary and unusual gifts, cosmetics, jewellery, adult's and children's clothing, toys, paints and home-decorating products including flooring! This might seem a vast range of products to have, but one common feature pulls them all together - they are all natural/ organic/ fair trade. Proprietor, Mrs Stephens, was determined to provide products to consumers that do not destroy the planet or exploit the people who made them.

"We have truly beautiful products and are proud of our ethics. We're a happy and friendly shop with lots of regularly satisfied customers."

Timber! is certainly progressive - many of their goodies are made by the creative local community and they also provide a locally grown organic vegetable box scheme. Timber! also sell all the organic seeds, fertilizers, composts and baby plants for your organic garden.

St Martin's Gallery

Old Church, Mockbeggar Lane, Ibsley, Ringwood, Hampshire BH24 3PR
Tel: 01425 489090 Fax: 01202 885282

St Martin's Church, built in 1654 and restored in 1832 after a fire, found a new role in 1998 when Pamela Denton opened it as an art gallery. The original altar, font and organ have been incorporated in the design, making a really beautiful and atmospheric setting for showing both local and international art. Apart from pictures and prints, the stock includes ceramics, glassware, jewellery and small items of furniture, along with what is probably the finest selection of artificial flowers in the South of England. Tea, coffee and cakes are available, served either in the gallery or out in the garden.

New Forest Cider

Littlemead, Pound Lane, Burley, Nr Ringwood, Hampshire BH24 4ED
Tel/Fax: 01425 403589

Cider-making was a way of life 100 years ago, and at **New Forest Cider** they still make it the old-fashioned way from local orchard apples and cider fruit. Visitors can watch the process and buy draught cider drawn from barrels in the cowshed, and there are usually some farm animals to see. Bed & Breakfast and self-catering accommodation is available at the farm, which is easy to find just 300 yards from the Post Office in Pound Lane. The farm is open most times throughout the year.

totally funded by donations and sponsorship.

AROUND RINGWOOD

BURLEY

3 miles SE of Ringwood off the A31

Great walking, cycling and horse riding around an attractive village high above the Avon that was once a noted centre for smuggling. It also has, down the years, a strong association with witches, and though the last paid-up witch got on her broomstick and high-tailed it to America nearly 50 years ago, the town still has some witchcraft shops. Burley is home to New Forest Cider, where cider is still made the old-fashioned way. A mile northwest of Burley is Castle Hill, where traces of an Iron Age fortress can be seen.

FORDINGBRIDGE

7 miles N of Ringwood on the A338

Mentioned in the Domesday Book, the town unsurprisingly takes its name from ford and bridge, and the medieval Great Bridge, upstream from the ford, is a major feature of the town with its seven elegant arches. The bohemian painter Augustus John (1878-1961) loved Fordingbridge and spent much of the last 30 years of his life at Fryern Court, an austere Georgian house just north of the town. Much of the painter's colourful life was the subject of scandal, often on a national scale, but the townspeople were proud of their most famous resident and erected a robust, rugged bronze statue of the painter by a recreation ground near the bridge. The Early English parish church has many fine features and should not be missed on a visit to Fordingbridge. Also well worth a visit is **Branksome China Works**, where visitors can see how the firm, established in 1945, makes its fine porcelain tableware and famous animal studies. They're a sociable crowd here, with an annual carnival and the Fordingbridge Show in July and a grand civic fireworks display on the Saturday nearest Guy Fawkes Day.

Two miles west of Fordingbridge off the B3078 - follow the signposts - is **Alderholt Mill**, a restored working water-powered corn mill standing on Ashford Water, a tributary of the Hampshire Avon. The site includes an arts and crafts shop and a place for the sale of refreshments and baking from the mill's own flour.

North of Fordingbridge on the A338 is the lovely and largely unspoilt 17th century village of **Breamore**, which has a very interesting little church with Saxon windows and other artefacts. Most notable, in the south porch, is a Saxon rood, or crucifixion scene. **Breamore House**, set above the village overlooking the Avon Valley, was built in 1583 and contains some fine paintings, including works of the 17th and 18th century Dutch

Breamore House

Rockbourne Roman Villa

Rockbourne, Fordingbridge, Hampshire SP6 3PG
Tel: 01725 518541

Rockbourne Roman Villa, the largest of its kind in the region, was discovered in 1942 when oyster shells and tiles were found by a farmer in the course of digging out a ferret. A local chartered surveyor and noted antiquarian, the late AT Morley Hewitt, recognised the significance of the finds and devoted 30 years of his life to the villa. Excavations of the site, which is set in idyllic countryside, have revealed superb mosaics, part of the amazing underfloor heating system and the outline of the great villa's 40 rooms. Many of the hundreds of objects unearthed are on display in the site's museum, and souvenirs are for sale in the well-stocked museum shop.

School and a unique set of 14 Mexican ethnological paintings; superb period furniture in oak, walnut and mahogany; a very rare James l carpet and many other items of historical and family interest. The house has been the home of the Hulse family for well over 250 years, having been purchased in the early 18th century by Sir Edward Hulse, Physician in Ordinary at the Courts of Queen Anne, George l and George ll. In the grounds of the house, the **Countryside Museum** is a reconstructed Tudor village: a wealth of rural implements and machinery, replicas of a farm worker's cottage, smithy, dairy, brewery, saddler's shop, cobbler's shop, general store, laundry and school. Amenities for visitors include a tea shop and a children's adventure play area. The Museum's Millennium project was the restoration of an extremely rare Bavarian four-train turret clock of the 16th century. On **Breamore Down** is one of those oddities whose origins and purpose remain something of a mystery: this is a mizmaze, a circular maze cut in the turf down as far as the chalk. Further north can be seen part of Grim's Ditch, built in late-Roman times as a defence against the Saxons.

A short distance east of Breamore, on the B3080, is the village of **Woodfalls**, situated on the border with Wiltshire.

Rockbourne

3 miles NW of Fordingbridge off the B3078

One of the prettiest villages in the region, Rockbourne lies by a gentle stream at the bottom of a valley. An attraction that brings in visitors by the thousand is **Rockbourne Roman Villa** (see panel above).

A mile or so beyond the Roman Villa, looking out on to the downs, is the little village of **Whitsbury**, a major centre for the breeding and training of racehorses.

The New Forest is a place of unique beauty, a place where man and nature have always been in harmony. This is the way it will continue if visitors adhere to the few simple rules issued by the authorities. These are based on common sense principles designed to protect the environment; to protect the animals from the humans and the humans from the animals; and to ensure that this remarkable corner of the English countryside remains the special place it was when singled out by William the Conqueror more than nine centuries ago.

4 ISLE OF WIGHT

Compton Bay

The largest island off the English coast is a delightful self-contained community covering an area of 147 square miles, half of which is designated an Area of Outstanding Natural Beauty. The 67 miles of coastline include chalk and sandstone, sandy beaches, marshes and estuaries and deep coastal ravines, while inland are ancient forests, farmland, downs and river valleys. The National Trust cares for 17 miles of the coastline, including the Needles Headland, the best known and most photographed spot on the island. Excavation sites have revealed more than 120 million years of history, with visible evidence of occupation by Stone Age, Bronze Age and Iron Age communities. The Romans arrived under Vespasian - they called the island Vectis - and for many centuries after them the islanders lived isolated lives, disturbed occasionally by French raiders but largely cut off from the mainland. That state of isolation changed dramatically in the 1840s, when Queen Victoria and Prince Albert bought an estate near East Cowes and built Osborne House. Poets, authors and artists followed, and before long the world at large came to enjoy the peace, the scenery and the wide-ranging appeal of the Garden Island, an appeal that has endured to this day. The Isle of Wight is a paradise for walkers, with hundreds of miles of footpaths and trails, and in 1999 the Walking Festival was launched to commemorate the island becoming the first county to achieve the Countryside Commission's National Target for Rights of Way. It's also a popular place for cyclists, while for those who want to do little but laze and bathe and comb there are no fewer than 23 major beaches. The coastal communities provide all the needs of holidaymakers, and keen anglers and yachtsmen are in their element. Cowes Week is the annual highlight in many yachtsmen's lives and the most fashionable event in the yachting calendar.

Sailing at Cowes

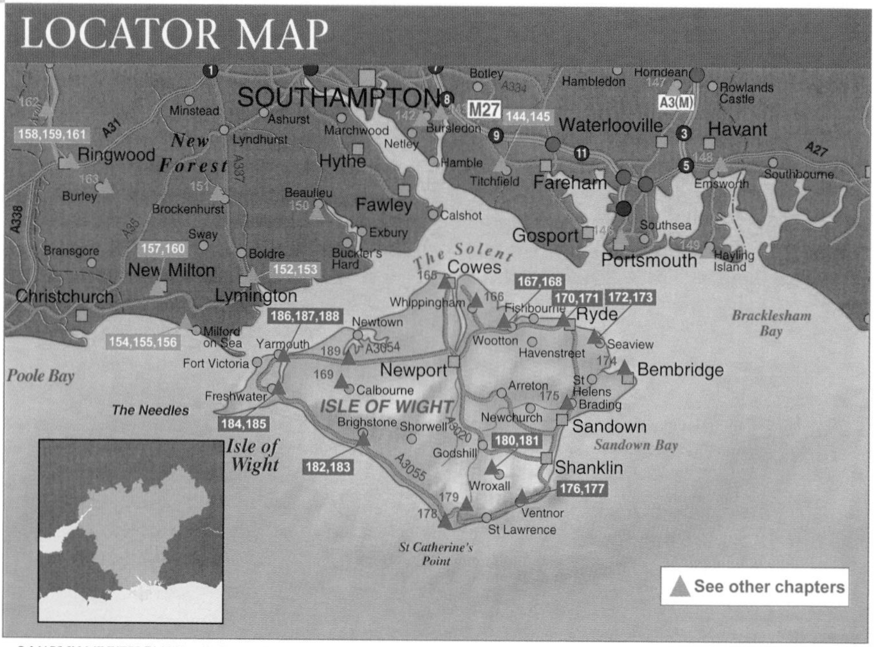

ADVERTISERS AND PLACES OF INTEREST

COWES

Sunset at Cowes

A chain ferry links the two parts of Cowes across the River Medina. West Cowes is renowned as the home of the Royal Yacht Squadron, and **Cowes Week** is a rendezvous for sailors from all over the world and a firm fixture in the social calendar. The Prince Regent, later George IV, was the senior flag officer of what was originally the Yacht Club for 20 years, and the 'Royal' was added when he became King in 1820. His brother William IV renamed it the Royal Yacht Squadron in 1833. On a platform at the Squadron's headquarters, previously one of Henry VIII's castles, stand 22 brass cannon from William's yacht the *Royal Adelaide*. Shipbuilding was for centuries the main industry of East Cowes, spanning ships for the Royal Navy, lifeboats, flying boats and seaplanes. Many of the seaplanes took part in the Schneider Trophy races, which brought great excitement to the Solent in the inter-war years. Sir Donald Campbell's *Bluebird* was built here, and the hovercraft had its origins in what is

Cowes Pottery & Crafts

12-13 Shooters Hill, Cowes, Isle of Wight PO31 7BG
Tel/Fax: 01983 293357
e-mail: cowpotwight@aol.com

Gifts and fancy goods from 50p to £500 are the stock in trade of **Cowes Pottery & Crafts**, a double-fronted shop in a pedestrian precinct that's perfect for a leisurely browse. Jill Dyvig-Smith, a skilled potter, has owned and run the shop for many years, establishing an enviable reputation for the variety, quality and value for money to be found in the shop. Once inside, customers come face to face with a merry jumble of gifts that fill every shelf and every rack - and most of the wall space and floor space as well! From trinkets to treasures, there really is a gift to suit all ages and all occasions, and something pretty to wrap it in.

There's pottery, naturally, and there are toys and clocks and cards and lamps, glassware and linen, aquatic designer mobiles and souvenirs of the Island. The shop, which is open 9.30 to 5.30 Monday to Saturday and 10.30 to 4.30 on Sunday, has a strong local following and is also a popular place with yachtsmen and with many of the thousands of tourists who visit the Island each year. Cowes is a town of many attractions, from the excitement of the annual Regatta to the fascinating museums, the marvellous model railway exhibition and the grandeur of nearby Osborne House, built as 'a modest country home' for Queen Victoria and Prince Albert.

Sailing off Cowes

now the home of Westland Aerospace. Westland's factory doors were painted with a giant Union Jack to mark the Queen's Jubilee in 1977 - a piece of patriotic paintwork that has been retained by popular demand. Two museums in Cowes have a nautical theme. The **Sir Max Aitken Museum** in an old sailmaker's loft in West Cowes High Street houses Sir Max's remarkable collection of nautical paintings, instruments and artefacts, while the **Cowes Maritime Museum** charts the island's maritime history and has a collection of racing yachts that includes the Uffa Fox pair *Avenger* and *Coweslip*. (Uffa Fox, perhaps the best known yachtsman of his day, is buried in the Church of St Mildred at Whippingham.) On the Parade, near the Royal Yacht Squadron, the **Isle of Wight Model Railways Exhibition** has for almost 20 years been one of the most admired attractions of its kind in the country. The displays include models spanning the whole history of railways, from the *Rocket* to *Eurostar*. Some are set in a British landscape, others against a stunning Rocky Mountains backdrop, and there is even a low-level layout which small children can operate and see without being lifted.

A romantic landmark on the east bank of the Medina is Norris Castle, built in the 18th century for Lord Henry Seymour. The 12-year-old Princess Victoria stayed here and was so charmed that when she returned as Queen with Albert to look for a retreat she tried to buy it. She failed, and instead made plans for the construction of **Osborne House**, a mile south of East Cowes. Designed in the style of an Italian villa by Thomas Cubitt with a little help from Albert, the new Osborne House was built as 'a modest country home' between 1845 and 1850. If it was modest, it was modest only by royal standards. The scale and grandeur of what became Victoria's favourite country house are impressive, and the interior decor has recently been restored in the original colours. Visitors can admire the Indian Room, the marbled pillars and the magnificent paintings, look in on the Queen's private study and bedroom, or take a peek below stairs at the Table Deckers rooms where the staff prepared the royal meals. The landscaped gardens are no less majestic than the house, and there are dazzling views from the terrace. A short stroll or a carriage ride away is the delightful Swiss Cottage, originally the royal children's playhouse, where refreshments and souvenirs are on sale. On view in the Swiss Cottage chalet are the royal children's gardening tools and Queen Victoria's bathing machine. Osborne House and its grounds were, not surprisingly, the setting for some of the scenes in the film *Mrs Brown* with Judi Dench and Billy Connolly.

AROUND COWES

Whippingham

3 miles S of Cowes on the A3021

Queen Victoria also acquired **Barton Manor** (see panel below) at nearby Whippingham, a peaceful retreat whose grounds are occasionally open to the public. Prince Albert had a hand in the design of the gardens and of the ornate Church of St Mildred, where the contractor and co-designer was AJ Humbert, who was also responsible for Sandringham. The royal family regularly worshipped at St Mildred's, which is predictably full of royal memorials, including a monument to Victoria's son-in-law Prince Henry of Battenberg, who succumbed to malaria in Africa at the age of 38. Alfred Gilbert's wonderful art nouveau screen in the chancel arcade is a unique work of art, and other notable pieces are a bronze angel and the font, both of them designed by Princess Louise, a daughter of the Queen, a memorial to Albert and a chair used by the Queen.

Wootton

3 miles SE of Cowes on the A3054

Wootton is the western terminus of the Isle of Wight Steam Railway, with an old wooden booking office and signal box moved from elsewhere on the island. It is also the home of **Butterfly World & Fountain World.** This complex comprises a sub-tropical indoor garden

Barton Manor

Whippingham, East Cowes,
Isle of Wight PO32 6LB
Tel: 01983 292835 Fax: 01983 293923

The estate of Barton is first mentioned in the Doomsday Book of 1086, and later an Augustinian oratory was founded. That fell into gradual decline, and from the 15th to the 19th centuries the estate was run as a farm. When Queen Victoria and Prince Albert bought Osborne House, **Barton Manor** and its estate became their home farm and the Prince had a new set of farm buildings erected. In 1902, after the Queen's death, King Edward VII made a gift of Osborne to the nation and kept Barton Manor for himself. It was eventually sold by the Crown in 1922 and has been in private hands ever since. Today the property is owned by the film and stage entrepreneur Robert Stigwood, who is also a keen conservationist. The gardens are a real delight with many treasures and surprises including the rhododendron walk, the splendid rose maze, a water garden, a secret garden and the national collections of Watsonia and red hot pokers. The estate is open on four special days in the year in aid of the local Earl Mountbatten Hospice.

Minghella

Minghella (IW) Ltd, The Minghella Centre, High Street, Wootton, Isle of Wight PO33 4PL
Tel: 01983 883545 Fax: 01983 883242
e-mail: info@minghella.co.uk
website: www.minghella.co.uk

The **Minghella** family are the best known manufacturers of ice cream in the region, and their melt-in-the-mouth masterpieces are supplied not only throughout the island but to a large part of the mainland through outlets such as Tesco and Safeway. Edward and Gloria Minghella are intimately involved in the business, but the day-to-day management is in the hands of their daughter Gioia, who was formerly a head teacher. Quality and purity are keynotes of their luxury ice cream, and their repertoire runs to some 66 flavours - details of the range on offer can be seen at their showroom and factory in the High Street.

Among the most popular are oriental ginger and honey and a range of 'spirited' creations such as whisky and marmalade, Grand Marnier and orange and the recent award-winning rum and raisin. The milk and the double cream used in making the ice cream all comes from an island herd of Jersey cows, and the sugar used is unrefined brown. They even make an ice cream without sugar and with very little fat, thus bringing a generous helping of non-calorific joy to those for whom ice cream had become a forbidden fruit: this one is charmingly called La Dolce Vita. Minghella also produce a mouthwatering range of sorbets and will undertake commissions for gateaux and set pieces for parties and special occasions.

The Minghella family may have conquered this cool corner of the market, but they are well known on the Isle of Wight and now throughout the world for other exploits. Edward and Gloria have held or still hold prominent positions in the administrative and commercial life of the Island (she has been Mayor of Medina and is a Deputy Lieutenant and magistrate; he has been President of the local Chamber of Commerce), but the name of Minghella is best known nowadays through the achievements of their son Anthony, the screenwriter and director responsible for such outstanding films as *Truly, Madly, Deeply*, *The English Patient* and *The Talented Mr Ripley*. Dominic is also making a name for himself as a writer, Loretta is a distinguished lawyer and Edana, who was recently awarded a doctorate in Professional Studies, having devoted her life to reasearch into mental health services, is now a senior research manager in the public sector. So ice cream isn't the only market where this talented family has the opposition licked!

Lushington Garden Buildings

Lushington Hill, Wootton, Isle of Wight PO33 4NR
Tel: 01983 882216 Fax: 01983 884442
e-mail: lushingtongardenbuildings@hotmail.com

Paul, Jonathan and Matthew Young are the proprietors of **Lushington Garden Buildings**, a successful and well-known Island business which the brothers started in 1986. Along with a faithful team of skilled craftsmen, they manufacture high quality, made-to-measure timber sheds, workshops, garages, summerhouses and internally lined and insulated cabins. The results of their handiwork are displayed on a one-acre site where there are over 70 show buildings on display. Customers can create and design their own garden building to suit their personal requirements by choosing from a selection of different roof designs, roof pitches, roof overhangs, verandas, doors, windows, roof coverings, external claddings and decorative finishes.

All buildings have the option of being internally insulated and lined to provide a comfortable, usable garden room for summer and winter use which is suited to almost any purpose. All buildings are made from pressure treated Scandinavian joinery grade redwood and are base coat prime treated as standard. Each building is individually made to a high specification at an affordable price. Lushington Garden Buildings offer a delivery service and installation service throughout Southern England. Site surveys, written quotations and cad drawings are also available.

with hundreds of exotic butterflies flying free; a colourful Italian garden with computer-controlled fountains; a Japanese garden with Oriental buildings and a koi carp lake; and a five-acre garden centre.

Havenstreet

4 miles SE of Cowes off the A3054

Headquarters and nerve centre of the **Isle of Wight Steam Railway**. Havenstreet has a small workshop and museum, gift shop and refreshment room. The locomotives working the line date back as far as 1876 and include a tiny A1 class engine acquired from the London, Brighton & South Coast Railway in 1913, and a W14, named *Calbourne*, which was built in 1891 and came to the island in 1925. The carriages and goods wagons are of a similar vintage.

The road south from Cowes to Newport (A3020) passes by the edge of **Parkwood Forest**, 1,000 acres of ancient royal hunting forest now managed by the Forestry Commission. From the car

Isle of Wight Steam Railway

park and picnic area a waymarked trail leads through the forest, which is one of the few remaining 'safe houses' for the red squirrel.

NEWPORT

The island's capital, Newport was once a busy shipping centre on the Medina, and many of the old riverside warehouses are still standing. One of them houses the important Quay Arts Centre and another the **Classic Boat Museum**. Beautifully restored sailing and power boats, along with engines, equipment and memorabilia, are all under cover, and there's also a café, shop and chandlery on the premises. Among the highlights are a 1910 river launch and *Lady Penelope*, a fabulous speedboat once owned by the fabulous Lady Docker. Alongside this museum is another, equally fascinating, the **Isle of Wight Bus Museum**, which houses an impressive line-up of island buses and coaches and a former Ryde Pier tram. The buses include a 1920s Daimler and a Bristol Lodekka that completed a successful trip to Nepal. There are several fine old buildings in the High Street, the most renowned and distinctive being the porticoed **Guildhall**, designed by John Nash in 1813. It stands on the site of an earlier building where Charles I met the Parliamentary Commissioners in 1648 in an attempt to keep the throne. The Guildhall now houses a museum where classic displays combine with the latest in computer technology to bring alive the history of the island.

In **St Thomas' Church** is the tomb of the tragic Princess Elizabeth, daughter of Charles, who died of a fever at the age of 14 while a prisoner at Carisbrooke Castle. Her brother Henry was also imprisoned at Carisbrooke but he lived and was allowed to go into exile. Elizabeth's grave was discovered during building work on a new church, whose foundation stone was laid by Prince Albert in 1854. Queen Victoria ordered that a memorial be erected in her honour, and another fine memorial honours Sir Edward Horsey, who governed the island from 1565 to 1582.

A monument to Queen Victoria stands in St James' Square, and opposite it a bronze bust of Lord Mountbatten, who was Governor of the island until his death in 1979. In 1926 a **Roman Villa** was discovered in Avondale Road, and subsequent excavations and reconstructions have produced an exhibition that gives an accurate insight into how the occupants of a late Romano-British villa lived and how

Carisbrooke Castle

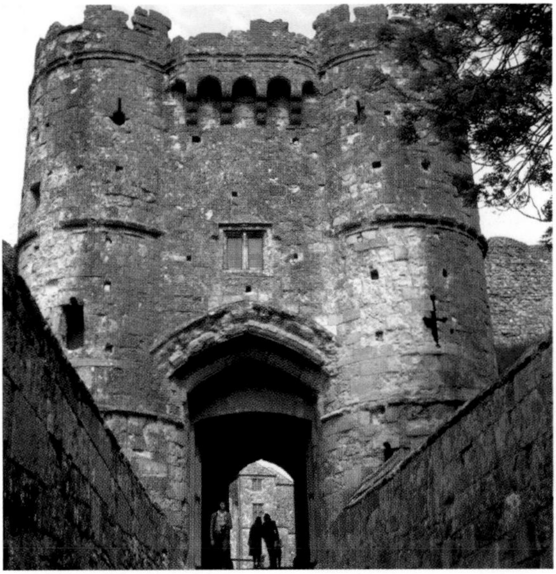

Castle Entrance

sophisticated and ingenious were the villa's designers and builders. The narrow streets and passageways of old Newport were the scene of many hauntings and dastardly deeds down the years and visitors can see the sights and hear the tales on the **Newport Ghost Walk**, organised every Wednesday night.

A mile or so southwest of Newport, **Carisbrooke Castle** is one of the most impressive in England. Standing high on a ridge overlooking **Carisbrooke**, once the island's capital, the castle is a beautifully preserved Norman fortress on the site of a Roman fort. It is best known as the place where, in 1647, Charles 1 sought refuge and a passage to France from the castle's governor, Colonel Hammond. The Colonel imprisoned the King before sending him back to the mainland and the scaffold. Visitors with a head for heights can walk the ramparts and admire the view; see traces of the bowling green constructed for the King's amusement; look around the 800-year-old Great Hall and the museum and see the window which Charles tried to squeeze through in a bid to escape. A well at the end of the courtyard is worked by donkeys, who are splendidly looked after at a centre in the castle grounds. Concerts and plays are performed in the castle during the summer months.

Well worth a visit in Carisbrooke itself is **St Mary's Church**, which contains the elaborate canopied tomb of Lady Wadham, an aunt of Jane Seymour. The Perpendicular tower is covered with carvings, including a clearly discernable group of singers.

AROUND NEWPORT

Calbourne

5 miles SW of Newport on the B3401

In the picturesque village of Calbourne, All Saints Church is a remarkably original 13th century building whose treasures include a handsome 16th century brass of William Montacute, son of the Earl of Salisbury. The most enchanting part of the village is Barrington Row, usually known as Winkle Street, a row of charming old cottages opposite the village stream (Caul Burn) and an ancient sheepwash.

The grandest building in the neighbourhood is historic Swainston Manor, now a luxurious hotel. Earlier buildings on the site were owned by royalty and by Bishops of Winchester; the 12th century Bishops Chapel still stands next to the hotel.

The Water Mill & Museum of Rural Life

Calbourne, Isle of Wight PO40 3JN
Tel: 01983 531227

On the B3401 between Newport and Freshwater, the **Water Mill** is just one of many attractions on an 11-acre landscaped valley site which no visitor to the island should miss. A mill on this site was mentioned in the Domesday Book and a fine example of a 17th century Water Mill is still working today. In 1963 it was opened as a tourist attraction by the family who had owned the mill since 1878. The present owners, Sally and Tony Chaucer have continued to develop the site's historic importance.

The Domesday Book records 34 water-powered mills on the island, and the Calbourne Mill is the last survivor. For centuries it used the traditional stone grinding process, but modern technology caught up with it in the late 19th century, when an additional roller plant was constructed in 1894 by Henry Simon. The plant was driven by a portable steam engine which was replaced in 1970 by a suction gas engine that gave reliable service for the remainder of the mill's working life. Milling takes place every day at 3pm except Saturday, producing flour for the bread and cakes which are on sale in the café and shop.

The mill is only one of many fascinating features on the site, which also incorporates the Museum of Rural life. Here the visitor can see a fine collection of agricultural implements and machinery and other vintage exhibits - there's even a classic fire engine. Some of the items on display are impressive in their size, none more than the enormous gun that guards the entrance to the mill. Originally intended to protect the Needles approach to Portsmouth, the gun, one of four built in the 1870s, weighs 38 tons and is almost 20 feet in length. Grandma's Kitchen contains an expanding collection of domestic bygones, and there's a fascinating assembly of washing machines down the years. Traditional skills are practised in the wheelwright's shop and in the smithy. The grounds around the mill stream and pond provide picturesque walks, and a picnic area has been set aside in a quiet spot.

On the B3401 between Newport and Freshwater, the **Water Mill** (see panel above) is just one of many attractions on an 11-acre landscaped valley site, which no visitor to the island should miss.

Arreton

3 miles SE of Newport on the A3056

Probably the most beautiful historic house on the island is **Arreton Manor**. There was a house on this site long before Alfred the Great mentioned Arreton in his will of 885, and the manor was owned by successive monarchs from Henry VIII to Charles I. The Norman church at Arreton was rebuilt in the 13th century; one of its most prized possessions is a 15th century brass - headless, alas - of Harry Hawles, who was killed fighting with Henry V at the Battle of Agincourt. A more modern treasure is the Burma Star window. In a coach house next to the church is the **Island Brass Rubbing Centre**, where visitors can learn the simple craft of brass rubbing and create their own rubbing of a knight, or buy something ready rubbed from the stock. One of the knights is friend Harry Hawles, whose head has been restored for rubbing purposes. Oliver Cromwell's grandson William is buried in the churchyard.

A mile southeast of Arreton stands the oldest grand house on the island,

Haseley Manor, with a history that traces back to around 1300. **Robin Hill** is an adventure park at Downend with a head-spinning variety of rides and slides and runs and trails.

NEWCHURCH

7 miles SE of Newport on the A3056

Amazon World is a popular family attraction that tells the story of the rain forest with the help of a large number of exotic animals and birds - conservation is the name of the game here. One of the highlights in Newchurch is the annual Garlic Festival, held on a weekend in August. The village church and its steeple are clad in wood.

RYDE

For many visitors to the island, Ryde is the arrival point. Foot passengers on the ferry from Portsmouth disembark at the end of Ryde Pier, which was one of the first to be built; the coast shelves very gently at this point, and before the construction of the pier passengers had an inconvenient cart ride from ferry to shore. The half-mile long pier is served by an electric railway that runs to Sandown and Shanklin. Steam locomotives gave way in 1967 to a small fleet of electric trains (1938 stock) which had recently been retired from duty on London Transport's Northern Line. The line connects with the Isle of Wight Steam Railway at Smallbrook Junction. Ryde is blessed with a five-mile sandy beach, which, along with all the usual seaside attractions and a marina, makes it a popular holiday spot. Reminders of its Georgian and Victorian heyday are still there in abundance, among them a fine arcade in Union Street opened in 1837, the year of Queen Victoria's accession. The town has some important churches: **All Saints**, designed by Sir George Gilbert Scott, the Roman Catholic **St Mary's**

FIFTY-ONE

51 Union Street, Ryde, Isle of Wight PO33 2LF
Tel: 01983 563666

Wednesday, 11th July 2001 saw the opening of **Fifty-One** and the fulfilment of a lifelong ambition of Barbara Hooper to become the proprietor of her very own *Country Living*-style shop. In the centre of town, with the beach and other attractions within easy reach, Fifty-One has a traditional frontage with a large and impressive expanse of window space to attract shoppers.

Inside, every inch of display space is taken up with a vast range of things to enhance the home, from china, glassware and small decorative objects to fabrics and soft furnishings, bed linen, furniture and antiques.

Gifts to suit all occasions and pockets can be bought and prettily wrapped, and the shop also offers a service for designing and making curtains and blinds. In the short time since it opened, Fifty-One, on one of the town's main shopping streets, has proved a magnet for discerning, house-proud shoppers, both local residents and visitors, and an inspiration for anyone looking to fit the right present to the right occasion. Opening hours are 9.30 to 5.30 Monday to Saturday.

Elizabeth Pack

29-30 Cross Street, Ryde,
Isle of Wight PO33 2AA
Tel: 01983 812252 Fax: 01983 613900

A family concern with a history going back to Victorian times, **Elizabeth Pack** is known throughout the Island and indeed way beyond it as the leading ladies fashion house of the Isle of Wight. Occupying a handsome three-storey building in a prime town-centre site, the business has been run for the past 30 years by a remarkable lady, Elizabeth Barrow, who has spent practically all her life in the worlds of drapery and fashion.

Elizabeth numbers local celebrities among her loyal clientele, who stay loyal in the certain knowledge that the lady and the shop will never let them down; nothing is too much trouble, no notice too short, and on more than one occasion her dresses have been sent across the world by special express courier. She knows all the leading manufacturers and has access to many of the major collections, enabling her to produce just the right garment or garments for any occasion, from a dinner dress to a complete wardrobe. The bridal service is something of a speciality, supplying everything from the bridal gown to top-to-toe outfitting for the bridesmaids and ushers. The shop has plenty of space to show off the clothes to the best advantage, and the stock includes a complete range of clothes, all accessories, jewellery and shoes.

Shoppers hesitating before making a final decision can relax with a cup of coffee and a snack in the Coffee Bean café on the first floor. Down the years the Elizabeth Pack trademarks of quality, style and professionalism have won both local and national recognition, and the business has rightly gained international standing. Ryde is a town of wide and varied appeal, with attractions as diverse as ex-London Underground trains and a George Gilbert Scott church, but there's only one Elizabeth Barrow and there's only one Elizabeth Pack!

with a Pugin chapel, and **St Thomas**, which is now a heritage centre featuring an exhibition of memorabilia associated with the transportation of convicts to Australia - many of the convicts left these shores in ships moored off Ryde. In the theatre standing on the site of the present Ryde Theatre, Mrs Jordan gave her last British performance and Ellen Terry her first. Dorothea (Dorothy) Jordan was noted for her comic and tomboy roles and for the fact that she bore 10 children by the Duke of Clarence, later King William IV. A popular society figure, her portrait was painted by Reynolds and Gainsborough. Ellen Terry, the favourite leading lady of Sir Henry Irving, had a long and intimate correspondence with George Bernard Shaw. To continue the theatrical theme, the theatre troupe of Vincent Crummles spent a week in Ryde performing *Nicholas Nickleby*.

In the middle of **Appley Park** stands **Appley Tower**, built as a station for troops guarding Spithead and now open to the public as a centre for fossils, crystals, natural gems, oracles and rune readings. Another public space is **Puckpool Park**, a leisure area behind the sea wall between Ryde and Seaview. It surrounds what was once a battery, built in the 19th century; its last gun was removed in 1927. At the Westridge Centre, just off the A3055 road to Brading, **Waltzing Waters** is an indoor water, light and music spectacular performed several times daily in a comfortable modern theatre.

AROUND RYDE

FISHBOURNE

2 miles W of Ryde on the A3054

Fishbourne is the port where the car ferry from the mainland docks. Nearby **Quarr Abbey** is a handsome redbrick Benedictine monastery built around 1910 near the ruins of a 12th century Cistercian Abbey. The old abbey, founded by a certain Baldwin de Redvers, enjoyed 400 years of prestige and influence, owning much of the land and many of the grand houses, before its destruction in 1536.

The stone for the original Quarr Abbey at Fishbourne came from the quarries at nearby **Binstead**, where a major family draw is **Brickfields Horse Country**, a centre that is home to more than 100 animals, from magnificent shire horses to miniature ponies, farm animals and pets. Open daily throughout the year, the numerous attractions include racing pigs (the Lester Piglet Derby!), wagon rides, a parade of Cowboys and Indians, a blacksmith's forge and museums focusing on carriages, tractors and many aspects of farm life. The shire horses are the particular pride and joy of the centre's owner Phil Legge, whose Montgomery and Prince won him top honours in an All-England ploughing match.

SEAVIEW

2 miles SE of Ryde off the B3330

A pleasant village, and one that is aptly named, as it commands fine views of Spithead, the open sea and the Napoleonic forts that were built to defend the Solent and Portsmouth from the marauding French. Once a haunt of smugglers and a centre of the island's important salt industry, it is now a favourite holiday base, with a gently sloping sandy beach and a calmer air than the bustling major resorts.

A short distance west of Seaview on the B3330 lies **Flamingo Park Waterfowl & Water Gardens**, whose colonies of flamingos, penguins, macaws and waterfowl are among the largest in the country. Visitors are encouraged to join

Holiday Home Services (Seaview)

Madeira Road, Seaview, Isle of Wight PO34 5BA
Tel: 01983 811418 Fax: 01983 616900
e-mail: brochure@seaview-holiday-homes.co.uk
website: www.seaview-holiday-homes.co.uk

Seaview is a village of unspoilt charm, a seaside location with safe, sandy beaches, a place for swimming, sailing or windsurfing - or relaxing totally and enjoying the escape from the mainland bustle. The narrow streets are a picturesque mixture of little whitewashed cottages and grand Victorian and Edwardian houses, and many of the properties - more than 60, in fact - are available for hire throughout the year on a self-catering basis through **Holiday Home Services (Seaview)**. The service is run by Diana Stansfield, who brings warmth, charm and great professionalism to the business of managing her clients' properties.

The range of the properties is impressive, the smallest offering a cosy little nest for two, the largest catering for families or groups of up to a dozen. At the smaller end of the scale are a number of compact one-bedroom flats, while typifying the largest and grandest is a six-bedroom Edwardian house with gardens and off-road parking. Some of the properties have a ban on pets and/or smoking, so be sure to ask when you book. All are fully equipped with all the necessities for an independent, go-as-you-please holiday. Most are very close to the amenities of the village and some enjoy sea views. Cleaning and babysitting services can be provided on request, and cots and high chairs are either available for hire or already supplied.

The delights of Seaview are on the doorstep, and many other attractions and places of interest can be reached easily and quickly by car or public transport. Notable among these are two unmissable family treats. Flamingo Park, on the B3330 between Seaview and Ryde, is home to flamingos, penguins, swans, cranes and many other birds. Visitors can join in the fun by helping to feed the penguins, macaws and parrots as well as the koi carp and giant carp. Waltzing Waters, just off the main Ryde-Sandown road, is billed as the world's most elaborate water, light and music production. Holiday Home Service have linked up with Red Funnel and Wight Link Ferries so all accommodation and travel arrangements to the Isle of Wight can be made with just one telephone call, fax or e-mail to Holiday Home Services (Seaview).

The Priory Bay Hotel

Priory Drive, Seaview, Isle of Wight PO34 5BU
Tel: 01983 613146 Fax: 01983 616539
e-mail: enquiries@priorybay.co.uk
website: www.priorybay.co.uk

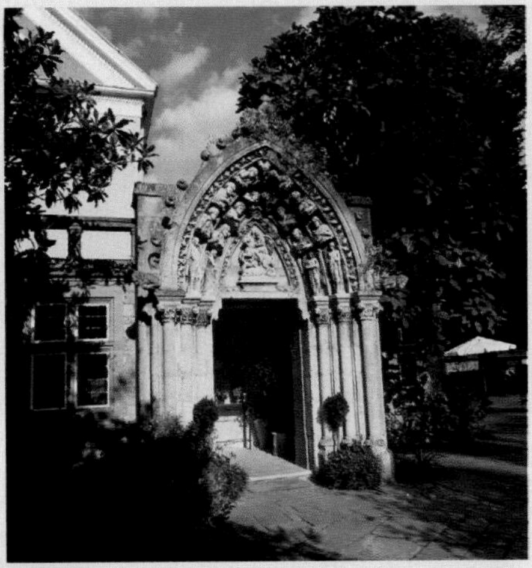

A thousand years of history have created a unique atmosphere and architectural legacy at the **Priory Bay Hotel**, which enjoys a wonderful secluded setting only a couple of miles from Ryde. Long before the Domesday Book was written there was a Cluniac monastery here, occupying a site that commands breathtaking views over the Solent and Spithead. The oldest surviving building is an attractive thatched barn dating from about 1100 that is believed to have been part of the original priory farm.

A 15th century portal provides an imposing entrance to the hotel, and Tudor farmers and Georgian gentry have made their contributions to a charming medley of beautiful buildings. As a result, each of the bedrooms has its own very distinctive character, but all are superbly furnished and appointed. As an alternative to the hotel's rooms, self-catering accommodation of a very high standard is available in either the historic Tithe Cottages or in splendid modern cottages in the grounds. The grounds are no less appealing than the hotel itself. Seventy acres of peaceful woodland, lawns and terraced gardens were reputedly designed by Gertrude Jekyll, and it is recorded that Queen Victoria sat beneath the magnificent magnolias.

The hotel has its own private beach, a par 3 9-hole golf course, an outdoor swimming pool and tennis courts, and sailing, riding and many other outdoor activities can be arranged locally. The gardens produce many of the vegetables and herbs for the kitchen, where the chefs make excellent use of fresh local ingredients for the menus in the main restaurant and, in summer, the Beach Restaurant or out on the terraces - all open to non-residents. The style is Modern European, and typical dishes on the table d'hote menu could be prawn and basil ravioli in a lobster consommé, roasted pigeon with a champagne sauce, sea bass with a fennel confit or a trio of fish cooked in beer batter.

The superb bedrooms, the elegant, civilised day rooms, the fine food, the solicitous service and the lovely grounds guarantee a wonderful holiday without ever leaving the premises, but there's plenty to see and do in the vicinity, including Flamingo Park Waterfowl and Water Gardens and the manifold attractions of Ryde.

Flamingo Park Waterfowl & Water Gardens

in feeding the birds and also the giant carp and koi carp.

St Helens

4 miles S of Ryde on the B3330

A small village with a very large green that was once dotted with open wells and is now used as a cricket and football ground. There are some excellent walks in the area, both on the common and on the Duver (it rhymes with lover), an expanse of grass and dunes reaching down to the harbour at Bembridge. The stretch of water off the coast, known as St Helen's Roads, has seen some significant moments in history, notably as the point from which, in 1346, Edward lll launched his invasion of Normandy, and as an assembly point for part of the D-Day landing force in the Second World War.

Bembridge

5 miles SE of Ryde on the B3395

Once a thriving fishing village, Bembridge is now a popular sailing centre and a holiday base. The maritime connection remains strong, and visitors can take a guided tour round the lifeboat station or spend a fascinating few hours in the **Maritime Museum and Shipwreck Centre** (see panel below).

Art lovers should find time to visit the **Ruskin Gallery**, where an impressive collection of paintings and manuscripts of the 19th century artist are

The Shipwreck Centre & Maritime Museum

Sherborne Street, Bembridge, Isle of Wight PO35 5SB
Tel: 01983 872223 Fax: 01983 873125

Open every day from March to October, the centre is overflowing with relics and objects recovered from the sea and shipwrecks, including pirate gold and silver. The setting is Providence House, a mid-18th century building which was a bakery until 1973 and opened as a museum in 1978.

Special exhibits include Diver's Corner, charting the history and development of diving equipment from the 1840s; a fine collection of model ships; Bembridge Lifeboat Past & Present, detailing the background of the local lifeboat from 1867 to the present day; photographs of Bembridge village as it used to be; and the sad story of the disappearance of the submarine *HMS Swordfish* in 1940.

The most macabre and unusual exhibit is the 'merman', a gruesome-looking creature that is actually a Victorian trick by sailors in the Far East by grafting the mummified head of a monkey on to the body and tail of a dead fish. These 'mermen' were popular attractions at Victorian fairs, and this one never fails to intrigue visitors to this fascinating place.

The Museum, which has a shop selling gifts and souvenirs, was founded and is still owned by Martin Woodward, a renowned diver who started salvage diving on shipwrecks in 1968. He is the present coxswain of the Bembridge lifeboat.

housed, and Bembridge Gallery in the High Street, featuring the work of island artists. Half a mile south of Bembridge on the B3395 stands one of the island's best known landmarks, **Bembridge Windmill**. In the care of the National Trust, it is the last surviving windmill on the island, dating from about 1700 and last used in 1913. Much of the original wooden machinery is still in place, as are the sails, and there are spectacular views from the top floor. In common with many parts of the island, this is excellent walking land, and the coastal path from Bembridge to Sandown has the bonus of fine sea views. On top of Bembridge Down stands the Victorian Fort Bembridge.

BRADING

5 miles S of Ryde on the A3055

One of the oldest towns on the island, Brading was granted its first Royal Charter by Edward l in 1285. But its history goes back a good deal further, certainly to the Bronze Age. The Romans were here, too, and the **Roman Villa** discovered here in 1880 is one of the most complete in Britain. Among the many other interesting buildings in the town is the 12th century **Church of St Mary**, whose features include a processional passage under the west tower and wooden monuments to the Oglander family, who for 800 years were the most important family on the island. There is a particularly poignant monument, sculpted in great detail, to Elizabeth Rollo, who died in 1875 at the age of one. The church is said to stand on the spot where St Wilfrid converted the islanders to Christianity in 680 (another source has it that Christianity came to the island by way of King Caedwalla of Wessex, who put to death the majority of the islanders when they

W STAY & SON

Quay Lane Farm, Quay Lane, Brading, Isle of Wight PO36 0AT
Tel/Fax: 01983 407077

The premises of **W Stay & Son**, ornamental blacksmiths since 1790, are located off Quay Lane not far from the High Street, the railway station and the estuary of the River Yar. The family skills have been handed down through the generations, and the business is now in the safe hands of Tim Stay and his son William (Will). Decorative metalwork is their speciality, and customers who go along with a sketch of what they have in mind can be sure that their idea will take physical shape just the way they wanted.

The excellent Stay catalogue illustrates the range of their handiwork, starting with a variety of gates ('first impressions are everything') and

progressing to garden furniture that is both functional and very attractive, light fittings to put the finishing touches to gardens, paths and barbecue areas, and miscellaneous pieces that could include anything from fireguards and candelabras to weather vanes and bespoke pub signs. Brading is one of the oldest settlements on the Island, dating back to the Bronze Age, and the family firm of W Stay & Son fully deserves its distinguished place in the annals of this delightful little town. The premises are open from 9 to 4 Monday to Friday and from 8 to 12 on Saturday. Quay Lane starts at the High Street by the Wax Museum and ends in a footpath that runs to St Helens further up the coast.

refused to take up the faith he sought to impose). Next to the church is the diminutive town hall, where stocks and a whipping post are reminders of how justice was summarily dispensed.

The **Isle of Wight Wax Works** presents 2,000 years of local history with sound, light and animation, along with animal exhibits from around the world, a chamber of horrors, a haunted mansion, an exhibition of oddities and a display of candle carving. The **Lilliput Museum of Antique Dolls & Toys**, in the High Street, is home to an impressive collection of exhibits dating from around 2,000BC to 1945. The 2,000 items include tin toys, model trains, teddy bears, dolls houses and dolls, among them some very rare German and French bisque dolls.

Lilliput Museum of Antique Dolls & Toys

Two notable houses with long and distinguished histories are close to the town. **Nunwell House**, set in five acres of lovely gardens, is the former home of the Oglander family. Guided tours take in an old kitchen exhibition and a military collection assembled by the family. The six acres of grounds include a rose garden (originally a bowling green) and an arboretum. It was in Nunwell House that Charles I passed his last night of freedom. **Morton Manor** dates back as far as 1249, with major rebuilding carried out in 1680. It stands in the most exquisite gardens, frequent winner of the Isle of Wight in Bloom awards. Features include an Elizabethan sunken garden surrounded by a 400-year-old box hedge, dazzling herbaceous borders, ponds and waterfalls and 90 varieties of Japanese maples. In 1981 the Trzebski family added a vineyard, which visitors are welcome to include in a tour of the house and gardens.

Just outside Brading is another vineyard: Adgestone Vineyard is the oldest on the island, having been established in 1968. Guided tours take place daily, and pony and trap rides are an added attraction.

SANDOWN

'A village by a sandy shore' was how a guide book described Sandown in 1870. Since then it has grown into the island's leading holiday resort, with miles of flat, safe sands, a traditional pier, abundant sports and leisure facilities and a number of attractions for all the family.

John Wilkes, sometime Member of Parliament and Lord Mayor of London, was one of the first celebrities to be taken with the village, and as a town Sandown was host to many other distinguished visitors, including Lewis Carroll, Charles Darwin, George Eliot and Henry Wadsworth Longfellow. Above the library, the **Museum of Isle of Wight Geology** offers an insight into millions of years of fossil history, with special displays relating to ammonites and dinosaurs. A new attraction, a Dinosaur Museum, was added to the tourist trail in 2001.

Two miles west of Sandown, near Apse Heath, is a National Trust area known as **Borthwood Copse**. The trees there range from coppiced chestnut and hazel to ancient oaks, and in spring the bluebells blossom into a colourful carpet.

AROUND SANDOWN

SHANKLIN

1 mile S of Sandown on the A3055

Shanklin is Sandown's more sedate neighbour, sharing the same sweeping bay but differing in many respects from its brasher brother. The old village stands on a 150ft cliff from which the ground slopes gently down to the safe, sheltered beach with its long seafront esplanade. With its scenic setting, numerous public gardens and healthy climate, Shanklin has had wide appeal down the years. Charles Darwin and Longfellow were great fans, and John Keats wrote some of his best-known poems while staying here. The grassy open space known as Keats Green commemorates his sojourn. The village has survived largely intact at the head of one of the island's most renowned landmarks, **Shanklin Chine**.

Shanklin Chine

First opened in 1817 and a former refuge of smugglers, this 300 feet deep wooded ravine, mysterious and romantic, has long fascinated visitors with its waterfalls and rare flora. In the Heritage Centre at the top of the chine a special millennium exhibition **A Century of Solent Sea & Sail 1900-2000** has joined the PLUTO display: during the Second World War a vast tank, part of the PLUTO (**Pipe Line Under the Ocean**) project for pumping fuel across the Channel to supply the troops involved in D-Day, was hidden in Shanklin. The Chine also has a memorial to the Royal Marines of 40 Commando who used the Chine as an assault course before the disastrous assault on Dieppe in 1942.

GODSHILL

4 miles W of Shanklin on the A3020

A short drive inland from Shanklin leads to the charming village of Godshill, which with its stone-built thatched cottages and its medieval **Church of All Saints** is one of the most popular stops on the tourist trail. The double-naved church, whose 15th century pinnacled tower dominates the village, contains some notable treasures, including a 15th century wall painting of Christ crucified on a triple-branched lily, a painting of Daniel in the Lions' Den and many monuments to the Worsleys and the Leighs, two of the leading island families.

Godshill has much to entertain visitors, including the magical **Model Village** with its 1/10th scale stone houses, trains and boats, even a football match taking place on the green, and the **Natural History Centre** with its famed shell collection, minerals and aquarium. The miniature village was built with the help of model-makers from Elstree film studio and after two years' preparation was opened to the public in 1952. The models are made of coloured cement and the detail is quite incredible. Real straw was prepared in the traditional way for thatching; the church on the hill took 600 hours of work before being assembled in its position; each house has its own tiny garden with miniature trees and shrubs. The airfield is in the style of small landing strips of the 1920s and 1930s, and the little railway is modelled on the older Island systems. Things get even smaller in the model garden of the model Old Vicarage, where there is another (1/100 scale) model village with yet another Old Vicarage, and within its garden another (1/1,000 scale) model village - a model of a model of a model! Also in Godshill is the **Nostalgia Toy Museum**, where 2,000 Dinky, Corgi and Matchbox toys and 1960s dolls bring back childhood memories.

VENTNOR

With its south-facing aspect and the protection of St Boniface Down, Ventnor enjoys a particularly mild climate. A series of terraces rises from the sandy beach, and most of the houses were built with balconies and large windows to make the most of the generous rations of sunshine.

Before the 1830s Ventnor had been a small, remote fishing village with something of a reputation for smuggling, but after a famous doctor, Sir James Clarke, reported the virtues of its climate, the visitors started to arrive. The railway, which came in 1866, assisted the boom, and soon the village of 300 became a town of 5,000. Much of its Victorian charm remains intact (partly because of the limited geographical scope for expansion) and the meteorological advantages allowed the development of one of its chief attractions, **Ventnor Botanic Garden**, which stands a mile west of town on the site of the former Royal National Chest Hospital. Many hundreds of rare and exotic plants flourish in the temperate surroundings, and the centre received a huge boost in the spring of 2000 with the opening of an exciting new **Visitor Centre** whose exhibits include an interactive display called The Green Planet - the Incredible Life of Plants. Many unusual varieties are for sale in the shop. Snuggling in the Garden is the **Smuggling Museum**, whose 300 exhibits illustrate 700 years of smuggling lore.

Back in town, the **Coastal Visitor Centre** provides a fascinating and educational insight into the island's coastal and marine environment, with special features on animal and plant life,

Pie In The Sky

3 Church Street, Ventnor, Isle of Wight PO38 1SW
Tel: 01983 854199

A visit to **Pie in the Sky** is like taking a trip back in time. The owner, Bridget Boudewijn, gave up a career in Art & Design to open this delightful Victorian-era shop in the lovely, peaceful little town of Ventnor. Pie in the Sky started life as the Candy Shop, which has left the legacy of sweets in jars on the shelves, and many of the older regulars remember from their childhood. The stock has now greatly expanded and includes health foods, honey from near and far (including Andrew Reid's prize-winning local honey), vegetarian ready meals, free-range eggs, herbs and spices and a range of photographic gift and greetings cards that show the beauty and diversity of the Island.

coastal defences and living with landslides - a problem very familiar to the island as well as to many parts of England's south coast. Two museums that tell of local life are the **Longshoreman's Museum** and the **Ventnor Heritage Museum**. One of the highlights of the year is the Crab Fair, held annually just outside Ventnor.

Outside town, **St Boniface Down**, the first National Trust acquisition on the Island, is a must for the serious walker, and a climb to the top of the highest point on the island (almost 800 feet) is rewarded with stupendous views. These are the most southerly chalk downs in the country and are designated both Area of Outstanding Natural Beauty and Site of Special Scientific Interest. On nearby Bonchurch Down wild goats were introduced to control the holm oaks, while New Forest ponies live on Luccombe Down, the site of several Bronze Age burial mounds.

A little way east of Ventnor, the quiet village of **Bonchurch** stands at the start of the six-mile strip of land called the Undercliff. This remarkable feature, which runs along the coast to Blackgang, is marked by towering cliffs that offer protection from the elements and have also inspired poets and artists with their rugged, romantic beauty. The poet Algernon Swinburne spent some of his childhood in Bonchurch, and is buried in the churchyard of St Boniface. Charles Dickens wrote part of *David Copperfield* while staying in Bonchurch. His first impressions of the place were very favourable (' I think it is the prettiest place I ever saw') and he seemed likely to make it his permanent home, but he soon grew to dislike the weather and the place and returned to his familiar Broadstairs.

AROUND VENTNOR

St Lawrence

1 mile W of Ventnor on the A3055

Nestling in the heart of the Undercliff, the ancient village of St Lawrence has a 13th century church that once laid claim to being the smallest in Britain. It was extended in 1842 but remains diminutive, measuring just 20 feet by 12 feet. Close to the village is the **Rare Breeds Waterfowl Park** set in 30 acres by the coast. The park includes one of the largest collections in Britain of rare farm animals, plus animals and birds from all over the world. The meerkats who arrived in 1999 have been so successful at breeding that their quarters have had to be extended. Other arrivals for the millennium were the first litter of Kune Kune pigs from New Zealand. Not far away, old farm buildings were converted into **Isle of Wight Studio Glass**, where

The Hermitage Country House

St Catherine's Down, Isle of Wight PO38 2PD
Tel: 01983 730010 e-mail: hermitage@melvillehall.co.uk
website: www.hermitage-iow.co.uk

The **Hermitage Country House**, a late Victorian building bought by the Wells family in 1990, enjoys a quiet, remote setting at the top of St Catherine's Down. The four beautifully appointed bedrooms, all have bathrooms en suite, central heating, tv, radio and tea-makers, feature antique furniture and fully restored antique beds that give their unique style to each of the rooms.Guests have the use of a drawing room overlooking the patio, and the gardens and surrounding area offer quiet seclusion and delightful country walks. No children or pets.

The Buddle Inn

St Catherine's Road, Niton, Isle of Wight PO38 2NE
Tel: 01983 730243 e-mail: buddleinn@aol.com

Good food, good ale and genuine hospitality are a way of life at the **Buddle Inn**, where John and Pat Bourne have been the welcoming hosts since the 1980s. Originally built as a farmhouse in Elizabethan times, the inn is rich in old-world charm, with original flagstones and beams, exposed stone walls and an inglenook fireplace. Abandoned tunnels are a legacy of smuggling days, and a sign in the bar reads 'This grand old inn was used by smugglers and customs men - but never on the same night'. Six traditional ales, including a local brew, local cider and even local wine are served in the bar, and a full range of food is also available, from a simple sandwich to a lobster feast.

skills old and new produce glass of the highest quality. Lord Jellicoe, hero of Jutland, lived for some years in St Lawrence and often swam in Orchard's Bay, a small cove where Turner sketched.

The coast road continues through the village of Niton to **St Catherine's Point**, the most southerly and the wildest part of the island, in an area of Special Scientific Interest. Steps lead down to St Catherine's lighthouse and a path leads up to the summit of St Catherine's Hill, where the remains of a much older lighthouse, known as the Pepperpot, can be seen. Close by is the Hoy Monument erected in honour of a visit by Tsar Nicholas I.

Blackgang Chine, at the most southerly tip of the island, has been developed from an early Victorian scenic park into a modern fantasy park with dozens of attractions for children. Also inside the park are two heritage exhibitions centred on a water-powered sawmill and a quayside, with displays ranging from cooper's and wheelwright's workshops to a shipwreck collection, a huge whale skeleton and a 19th century beach scene complete with a bathing machine. The coastline here is somewhat fragile, and a large slice of cliff has been lost to storms and gales in recent years.

Wroxall

2 miles W of Ventnor on the B3327

Owls, falcons, vultures and donkeys all call Wroxall their home! **Appuldurcombe House** (see panel opposite), once the grandest mansion on the whole island with gardens laid out by Capability Brown, was badly bombed in 1943 and has never been lived in since. The **Owl & Falconry Centre**, in what used to be the laundry and brewhouse, stages daily flying displays with birds of prey from around the world and holds courses in the centuries-old art of falconry.

Heaven for 200 donkeys and many other animals is the **Isle of Wight Donkey Sanctuary** at Lower Winstone Farm. The rescue centre is a registered charity relying entirely on donations, and visitors have several ways of helping, including the Adopt a Donkey scheme.

Appuldurcombe House

Wroxall, Nr. Ventnor, Isle of Wight PO38 3EW
Tel: 01983 852484 Fax: 01983 840188
website: www.appuldurcombe.co.uk

Appuldurcombe House was once the grandest and most striking house on the Island, and its 18th century baroque elegance is notable still in the partly restored building (it suffered bomb damage in 1943 and has not been lived in since). Visitors can stroll in the 11 acres of grounds designed by Capability Brown and maybe enjoy a picnic. The Owl & Falconry Centre is set up in the imaginatively restored servants' quarters and brewhouse. It puts on daily flying displays, featuring owls and other birds of prey from around the world. There is an excellent shop, a café for light refreshments, a photographic exhibition of the history of the house and a newly restored barn for indoor flying displays in poor weather. Open daily.

Shorwell

7 miles S of Newport on the B3399

An attractive village of thatched stone cottages. South of the village, just off the Newport-Brighstone road, is **Yafford Mill**, an 18th century water mill restored to working order. Also on the site are a farm park with rare farm animals, owls, monkeys and Sophie the seal; nature walks; a narrow gauge railway; a tea room and a gift shop. The **Church of St Peter** is notable for its ornate decor, its 500-year-old stone

Little Span Farm

Rew Lane, Wroxall, Nr Ventnor, Isle of Wight PO38 3AU
Tel/Fax: 01983 852419
e-mail: info@spanfarm.co.uk website: www.spanfarm.co.uk

Little Span Farm is a working arable and stock farm set in an area of outstanding natural beauty on the southwest side of Wroxall. Owner Felicity Corry offers a choice of guest accommodation - Bed & Breakfast or Self-Catering. In the 17th century stone farmhouse, for non-smoking B&B, are two double bedrooms with en suite bathrooms and a twin-bedded room with private bathroom; each has tv and tea-making facilities. Alternatively, guests could opt for a self-catering holiday in Stable Cottage, a 18th century stone barn that was once the home of the farm's carthorses and now offers spacious 'upside-down' accommodation. The open-plan beamed living/dining room has views across farmland towards Stenbury Down, with French doors opening on to a sun terrace with a barbecue.

Adjoining this area is a roomy farmhouse kitchen, while below, reached by a spiral staircase, are a double bedroom with en suite shower room and a twin room and a children's room that share a bathroom. This cottage has a small, sloping rear garden. Further accommodation is available in the old Brew House and Harvester's Cottage, both newly converted to provide every comfort while retaining the character of the buildings. These can be let as one unit, or the Brew House as self-catering for up to six guests and Harvester's for B&B for up to four. Children are welcome throughout, and dogs can be accommodated by arrangement. The location is ideal for walking and family holidays, and Ventnor Golf Course is no more than a long putt away. The farm itself has a nature trail featuring an ancient woodland with badger setts and nesting buzzards, and children can help with bottle-feeding the lambs.

pulpit, the many monuments to the Leigh family and a carefully restored 15th century wall painting of St Christopher with all his usual travelling paraphernalia. The church also has a real oddity in a painting on wood of the Last Supper, brought from Iceland in 1898.

Brighstone

8 miles S of Newport on the B3399

One of the prettiest villages on the island, Brighstone was once notorious as the home of smugglers and wreckers. But in the late 19th century the villagers assembled a lifeboat crew; its first skipper was one James Buckett, a former smuggler who was forced to serve five years in the Navy as punishment for his crimes. The National Trust runs a shop in a picturesque row of thatched cottages, and a little museum depicting village life down the years - including some relics of the lifeboat.

The island has long been known for its fossil finds, especially relating to dinosaurs and on a clifftop near the village the bones of a completely new species of predatory dinosaur were unearthed. The 15ft carnivore, which lived in the cretaceous period about 120 million to 150 million years ago, has been named *cotyrannus lengi* after Gavin Leng, a local collector who found the first bone. On Military Road (A3055) near Brighstone, the **Dinosaur Farm Museum** (see panel below) came into being following the unearthing in 1992 of the skeleton of a brachiosaurus, at the time the Island's largest and most spectacular dinosaur discovery. This unique attraction follows the tale of this and other finds. Visitors are invited to bring their own fossils for identification, and the Farm also organises guided fossil tours at various locations on the Island.

A mile or so west of Brighstone, the National Trust is also responsible for **Mottistone Manor Garden**, a charming hillside garden alongside an Elizabethan manor house. The garden is particularly known for its herbaceous borders and terraces planted with fruit trees. The Mottistone Estate extends from Mottistone Down in the north to the coast at Sudmoor. On **Mottistone Common**, where New Forest ponies graze, are the remains of a neolithic long barrow known as the Longstone. There are two stones, one standing upright, the other, smaller, on its side. A local story has it that the first stone was thrown there by St Catherine in a contest with the Devil for control of the island. The second stone, thrown by the Devil, fell just short of the first, so the upright stone thrown by St Catherine represents the triumph of good over evil. Back on the coast road, Compton Bay (excellent

Dinosaur Farm Museum

Military Road, Nr Brighstone, Isle of Wight PO30 4PG
Tel/Fax: 01983 740844

Following the discovery of a fossilised dinosaur skeleton on the farm in 1992, the **Dinosaur Farm Museum** was founded to continue work on this skeleton and others unearthed on this dinosaur-rich island. Visitors can see the bones being identified, preserved and catalogued and can also bring their own fossils for identification. The museum shop is stocked with dinosaur-themed souvenirs and fossils, and there's an attractive tea room in the 17th century farmhouse. Opening times are Sunday, Tuesday and Thursday from Easter to the end of September (10.00-17.00), every day in July and August, and Sundays and various other dates in October. The owners of the site, Barbara and Geoff Phillips, offer accommodation in a number of six-berth caravans in the grounds.

Rose Cottage

Thorncross Farm, Thorncross, Brighstone, Nr Newport,
Isle of Wight PO30 4PN
Tel: 01983 740291 Fax: 01983 741408

Rose Cottage is a thatched 17th century cottage situated in the hamlet of Thorncross in an area of outstanding natural beauty close to the downs and the sea. Recently modernised without in any way detracting from its original character and charm, the cottage offers quiet, comfortable self-catering accommodation for up to four people, with radiator heaters providing a warm, cosy ambience at any time of year. On the ground floor are the beamed living room with inglenook fireplace and cottage-style furniture, and the comprehensively equipped kitchen with a door leading out into the garden. The bathroom is also located on the ground floor, while upstairs is a large beamed bedroom with a double bed, two single beds, a dressing table, wardrobe and three bedside cabinets.

The large, well-tended garden, with lawn, patio and garden furniture, is a perfect spot to relax and unwind, and the whole area around the cottage is a delight to explore, whether on foot, on a bicycle or in a car. The Isle of Wight Cycle Route passes by the front door and walkers can take the Coastal Footpath, which runs round the whole Island, or branch out on the many scenic inland forest and downland trails. This locality is also famous for its fossils, and a dinosaur discovered a mile away is now the star of the show at the Dinosaur Farm Museum in nearby Brighstone. Mr and Mrs Russell, the owners of Rose Cottage, have a no smoking, no pets policy.

surfing) and Compton Down (National Trust) is a wild area rich in wildlife and affording superb views. On top of nearby Brook Down is a group of Bronze Age barrows known as the Five Barrows.

Freshwater

8 miles W of Newport on the A3055

A bustling town with good shopping and a village atmosphere. It was put on the map by Alfred, Lord Tennyson, who lived at Farringford House (now a hotel) and later bought the house with the money he made from his poem *Maud*. A dedicated walker, Tennyson was often to be seen on the dramatic High Down in his cloak and wide-brimmed hat. After his death the area was renamed **Tennyson Down** and a cross erected high on the cliffs in his memory. The cliffs are a favoured nesting place of many birds, including cormorant, shag, fulmar and razorbill. There are more remembrances of Tennyson in the **Church of All Saints** on a hill high above the River Yar. Lady

Freshwater Bay

Ye Old Village Clock Shop

3 Moa Place, School Green Road, Freshwater, Isle of Wight PO40 9DS
Tel: 01983 754193

Ron and Sandra Tayler, antiquarian horologists with more than 30 years experience, run **Ye Old Village Clock Shop**, whose showrooms are the finest of their kind on the Island. Dealers and restorers in fine antique clocks, dating from 1600 to 1900. There is a wide, varied range stocked and on display are carriage, mantle, long case and wall clocks. Also mechanical music and automata when available. A clock restoration service is undertaken for customers. Normal opening hours are 9.30 to 1 o'clock Monday, Wednesday, Friday and Saturday.

Seahorses

Victoria Road, Freshwater, Isle of Wight PO40 9PP
Tel/Fax: 01983 752574 e-mail: seahorsesiow@lineone.net

In a peaceful and secluded setting near to Freshwater Bay, **Seahorses** is a substantial period house offering a friendly, homely atmosphere in which to enjoy a relaxing break. Run by Boris and Brenda Moscoff, the house has four spacious double and family rooms with en suite facilities, tv and tea-makers; large dining and leisure areas include 2½ acres of lovely grounds. The proprietors welcome children and adults with learning difficulties with their carers or families. Pets are also welcome. Art and craft courses can be arranged by Boris, himself a talented artist, and guests can use the studio on the premises.

Emily Tennyson is buried in the churchyard and there is a touching memorial to their son Lionel, 'an affectionate boy' who died at the age of 32 while returning from India. Freshwater's most distinguished son is Robert Hooke (1635-1703), known for his Law of Elasticity and for his wide-ranging researches into subjects as far apart as the crystal structure of snowflakes and the position of the stars.

The town has gradually spread southwards towards **Freshwater Bay**, where Julia Margaret Cameron, the pioneer photographer, was persuaded by her friend Lord Tennyson to settle. Her home was **Dimbola Lodge**, which now attracts thousands of visitors with its permanent exhibition of her work and changing exhibitions of the work of other distinguished photographers. The gift of a camera as a Christmas present from her daughter and son-in-law in 1863 sparked an immediate enthusiasm in Julia for this new art form and soon she was welcoming and photographing the cream of Victorian society. Tennyson, Thackeray, Darwin and GF Watts and his wife the actress Ellen Terry all at some time lived locally, and frequent guests included Lewis Carroll, Robert Browning and Edward Lear. The poet Henry Taylor wrote of the Lodge: *'....a house indeed to which everyone resorted for pleasure and in which no man, woman or child was ever known to be unwelcome.'*

Freshwater Bay is the start point of the 15-mile Tennyson Trail, which ends at Carisbrooke.

Totland, on the coast west of Freshwater, is a popular holiday spot with safe bathing in **Totland Bay**. Just outside Totland is Headon Warren, from where the coastal path runs to Alum Bay. On a hill a little way inland is the Victorian Gothic Christ Church with a massive lych gate made from timbers from *HMS Thunderer*, which saw action at the Battle of Trafalgar.

Two miles west of Freshwater, **Alum Bay** is a popular tourist spot famous for its multi-coloured sand and its spectacular chair lift. The Bay is the site of the **Needles Park**, with children's entertainment, a sand shop, sweet factory and glass blowing studio. Here, too, are **The Needles**, the island's best-known landmark. A continuation of the cliffs at the western tip of the island, they comprise three jagged slabs of rock, with a striped red-and-white lighthouse at the end of the most westerly. There was a fourth, known as Lot's Wife, which collapsed into the sea in 1764. The sea has gouged deep caves out of the stacks, which are a particularly spectacular sight when viewed close up from a pleasure boat. Two of them are known as Lord Holmes' Parlour and Kitchen, named after a 17th century Governor of the Island who once entertained his guests in the Parlour and kept his wine cool in the Kitchen. In the car park at Alum Bay is a monument to Marconi, who sent messages to a tug in Alum Bay and set up the first wireless station here in 1897. The first paid Marconigram was sent in the following year by Lord Kelvin. A clifftop walk leads to the **Needles Old Battery**, one of many forts built under the direction of Lord Palmerston against the threat of a French invasion. Two original gun barrels are mounted in the parade ground, and there are various displays explaining the battery's function, including a children's guide, exhibition and quiz sheets. A 200ft tunnel with a spiral staircase leads down to a searchlight position with dramatic views of the Hampshire and Dorset coastline.

Alum Bay

The Needles

YARMOUTH

A fascinating, picturesque little place with old stone quays, narrow streets and attractive old houses. It has had its ups and downs - up in the heady days when it returned two Members of Parliament to Westminster, down when it lost both and was declared a rotten borough. In the mortuary chapel of the 13th century

The Alchemist Gallery

Foresters Hall, High Street, Yarmouth,
Isle of Wight PO41 0PL Tel/Fax: 01983 760226
e-mail: annetoms@alchemistgallery.co.uk
website: www.alchemistgallery.co.uk

In the picturesque little harbour town of Yarmouth, the **Alchemist Gallery** occupies the spacious first floor of the old meeting hall of the Ancient Order of Foresters. The generous floor and wall space, pine-lined roof and tall windows provide an ideal setting for exhibiting contemporary applied art.

Paintings, ceramics, glass, textiles, jewellery, turned and carved wood, photographs, artist's cards and hand made prints are all on display. Work is drawn from around the South, with leading artists from the Island well represented. Mini exhibitions within the larger space change periodically, constantly creating new interest. Also to be seen are contributions from small designer led companies from Britain, France and Scandinavia.

The Alchemist Gallery is open every day from Easter to Christmas. Closed mid-week after the Christmas break until Easter (except the Spring Half Term week). Admission is free. Regrettably, there is currently no wheel chair access.

Angela's Delicatessen

The Square, Yarmouth, Isle of Wight PO41 0NS
Tel/Fax: 01983 761196

Next to the Town Hall in Yarmouth's main square, **Angela's Delicatessen** is owned and run by 100% foodies Angela and Don Hollist, who enjoy searching on their travels for new products, particularly from small producers. Two large windows crammed with goodies tempt visitors inside, where they can browse to their heart's content among the stock assembled by people with a genuine passion for good food. Traditional cheeses, many unpasteurised and with some excellent blues; home-cooked hams, other meats and speciality sausages; savoury pies and pastries cooked fresh throughout the day; oak-smoked kippers from Craster; Morecambe Bay potted shrimps; excellent pâté maison and smoked salmon pâté; interesting wines; ingredients from all over the world, especially China and Thailand - all this and much more makes Angela's Delicatessen a must for people who love their food. Trying to find new and interesting foods keeps Angela and Don very busy, but as they love their food so much they regard it as a labour of love. They also offer an outside catering service, and, with so many yachtsmen dropping anchor in town, they sell a lot of frozen meals 'to go'. Usual opening hours are 8 to 5 every day.

Church of St James is an intriguing statue on the tomb of Governor Holmes. During one of the many conflicts with the French, he captured a ship on board which was a sculptor with an unfinished statue of Louis XIV. He was travelling to Versailles to model the King's head from life. The Governor thought that the statue of the King, even though it was in full French armour, would be just right for his own tomb, and he ordered the sculptor to model his head instead of the King's. One of the most interesting buildings, but one that is easy to miss down by the ferry, is **Yarmouth Castle**, built by Henry Vlll in 1547 after the town had been sacked by the French. This was the final fortress in his coastal defence system, and a climb to the battlements provides the best views of the comings and goings of ships in the Solent. The estuary of the River Yar is rich in wild life, especially bird life.

AROUND YARMOUTH

FORT VICTORIA

1 mile W of Yarmouth off the A3054

Another of the forts built by Lord Palmerston as a defence against a feared French invasion. They were never used in active service and became known as Palmerston's Follies. The area around the fort has been converted into one of the island's major leisure complexes, with unspoilt beaches, walks and tours and a wide range of attractions including a sunken history exhibition, an aquarium, a planetarium and the largest model railway layout in Britain. The trains, points, signals, sound effects and level crossings are controlled by computers, using two PCs and over 40 microprocessors. The scale is HO and the setting is Germany.

SALTY'S

Quay Street, Yarmouth, Isle of Wight PO41 0PE
Tel: 01983 761550
e-mail: nmgreen@virgin.net

The name smacks of the sea, and indeed the sea is in the blood of the Green family who own **Salty's**. The quayside restaurant is run by Jo Green and her daughter Nicky, and her son Jamie is the skipper of his own fishing boat. Several years ago the building was part of the pub that stands next door; the Greens acquired the premises and created the atmospheric downstairs bar and the upstairs restaurant that was once a sail loft. An excellent range of beers, wines and spirits is served in the bar, along with classic pub dishes such as chilli, Cumberland sausages and steak & kidney pudding, and tapas and fruits de mer in the summer, while in the nautically themed restaurant the emphasis is firmly on fresh fish and shellfish, the great majority of it caught locally.

Starters like oysters, gravad lax and sardines with tapenade en croûte are preludes to some really superb main courses that could be plain and simple - grilled plaice, crab or lobster salad, traditional fish & chips - or a little more elaborate, such as seared tuna steak served with wok-fried Chinese greens, sun-dried chilli and sesame seeds, or local Dover sole with a sabayon of Baileys and Dijon mustard. Meat-eaters are not forgotten, and a meal at Salty's ends with some mouthwatering desserts. In summer the bar and restaurant are open Tuesday to Sunday lunch, in winter the bar Thursday to Sunday lunch and the restaurant Friday evening to Sunday lunch.

The New Inn

Main Road, Shalfleet, Isle of Wight PO30 4NS
Tel/Fax: 01983 531314
e-mail: martinbullock@virgin.net
website: www.thenew-inn.co.uk

Easy to find on the main Newport-Yarmouth road, the **New Inn** has been at the heart of village life since the 17th century. The present building dates from around 1750 and has retained all the best traditional features, including beamed ceilings, flagstones, panelling and open fires. With owner Martin Bullock and head chef Mark McDonald at the helm, the pub has gone from strength to strength, and has recently added The Good Pub Guide's award of Isle of Wight Dining Pub of the Year 2002 to its many other accolades.

Mark's food is absolutely outstanding, with local produce used as much as possible, and a great variety offered on menus that run from sandwiches and baguettes to superb fish dishes and Sunday roasts. The seafood platter, with crab, lobster and tiger prawns, is justly renowned, and other choices range from herby grilled sardines or country vegetable soup for starters to whole grilled plaice, hake fillets with a lemon and tarragon sauce, chicken breast with honey and cream and gammon steak topped with Stilton. The top-notch food is complemented by four real ales and a wine list that tours the world. The bars have smoking and non-smoking areas, and the pub has a spacious beer garden.

Newtown

5 miles E of Yarmouth off the A3054

Founded in the 13th century by a Bishop of Winchester, Newtown once had a large, busy harbour, but silting led to its decline as a maritime centre and the harbour is now a nature reserve. At its height, the town was the most important on the Island and regularly sent two MPs to Westminster; among them were John Churchill, later the 1st Duke of Marlborough, and Prime Minister George Canning. The town's most notable building is the **Old Town Hall**, erected in 1699 and now owned by the National Trust. A small, unassuming building of brick and stone, it contains many interesting documents and memorabilia. The records include the exploits of Ferguson's Gang, an anonymous group of benefactors who gave donations to save selected properties. It is not recorded why this building was chosen, but in 1934 one of the gang went into the National Trust offices and discreetly dropped £500 on the secretary's desk to save the town hall.

At Porchfield, 2 miles east of Newtown, fun in the country for the whole family is promised at **Colemans Animal Farm**, where visitors are encouraged to stroke and feed the animals. Children will also love the huge wooden play area, the sandpit, the straw maze and the mini-farm with pedal tractors.

5 WILTSHIRE AND SALISBURY PLAIN

Wiltshire is a county that is rich in the monuments of prehistoric man; it also boasts one of the highest concentrations of historic houses and gardens in the country. This makes it a great place for the tourist, and it's also a perfect choice for walkers, cyclists and lovers of nature, with wide open spaces, woodland and downland and a number of chalk streams that are home to a huge variety of wetland wildlife. The industrial heritage, too, is strong, taking in Brunel's Great Western Railway and the railway town of Swindon, brewing at Devizes and carpet-making at Wilton. And the county has many surprises, from the white horses carved in hillsides and the mysterious crop circles to the ancient hill forts and the greatest mystery of them all, the stone circles of Stonehenge - how *did* those stones get from the Marlborough Downs and the mountains of Pembrokeshire and what *was* their use? Pepys didn't have the answer when writing in his Diary in June 1668:

Stourhead Gardens

'.....to Stonage, over the plain and some great hills, even to fright us. Come thither, and find them as prodigious as any tales I ever heard of them, and worth going this journey to see. God knows what their use was! They are hard to tell, but yet may be told.'

.......and we don't have the full answer now.

The jewel in the crown of Wiltshire is the city of Salisbury, at the confluence of the rivers Avon, Wylye, Bourne and Nadder, with its glorious cathedral, a masterpiece of the Early English style, and many other fine buildings. The cathedral for the episcopal see stood originally at nearby Old Sarum, a flourishing town in medieval days that lost its status when a 12th century

Avebury Stone Circles

Stonehenge, nr Amesbury

bishop moved flock, stock and barrel down the hill to the more amenable surroundings of Salisbury and began to build a new cathedral. Atmospheric ruins are all that remains of Old Sarum. Westbury, at the western edge of the chalk downlands of Salisbury Plain, was an important centre of the medieval cloth and wool trades and still boasts some handsome buildings from the days of great prosperity. Like Old Sarum, Westbury was formerly a 'rotten borough', returning two MPs until the 1832 Reform Act stopped the cheating (Old Sarum was the more notorious, having two MPs at a time when it had no voters!). Stourhead, a beautiful Palladian mansion full of treasures, stands in magnificent grounds laid out by Henry Hoare, and another house filled with wonderful things is Longleat, whose grounds contain the famous safari park. The National Trust village of Lacock, the market town of Devizes with its extraordinary flight of locks on the Kennet and Avon Canal, the historic abbey town of Malmesbury, the lovely Vale of Pewsey and the ancient 4,500-acre Savernake Forest, designated a Site of Special Scientific Interest, are other attractions that no visitor to this wonderful county should miss.

ADVERTISERS AND PLACES OF INTEREST

LOCATOR MAP

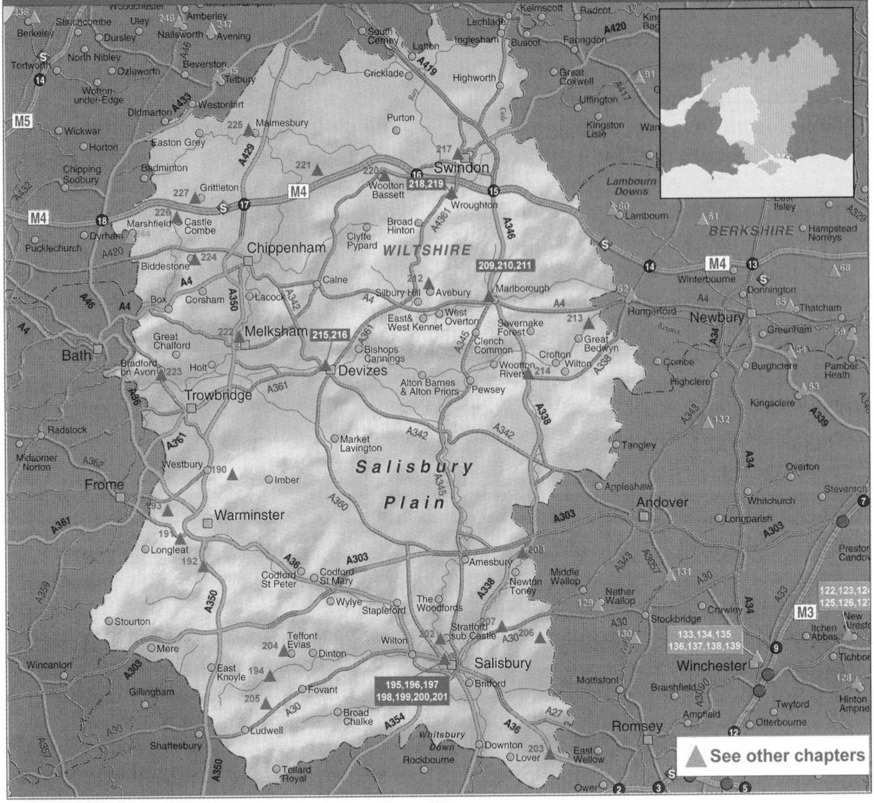

ADVERTISERS AND PLACES OF INTEREST

WESTBURY

Westbury, at the western edge of the chalk downlands of **Salisbury Plain**, was a major player in the medieval cloth and wool trades, and still retains many fine buildings from the days of great prosperity, including some cloth works and mills, Westbury was formerly a 'rotten borough' and returned two MPs until 1832, when a Reform Bill put an end to the cheating. Scandal and corruption were rife, and the **Old Town Hall** in the market place is evidence of such goings-on, a gift from a grateful victorious candidate in 1815. This was Sir Manasseh Massey Lopes, a Portuguese financier and slave-trader who 'bought' the borough to advance his political career.

All Saints Church, a 14th century building on much earlier foundations, has many unusual and interesting features, including a stone reredos, a copy of the Erasmus Bible and a clock with no face made by a local blacksmith in 1604. It also boasts the third heaviest peal of bells in the world.

On the southern edge of town is another church well worth a visit. Behind the simple, rustic exterior of St Mary's, Old Dilton, are a three-decker pulpit and panelled pew boxes with original fittings and individual fireplaces. Just west of Westbury, at **Brokerswood**, is **Woodland Park and Heritage Centre**, 80 acres of ancient broadleaf woodland with a wide range of trees, plants and animals, nature trails, a lake with fishing, a picnic and barbecue area, a tea room and gift shop, a museum, a play area and a narrow-gauge railway.

By far the best-known Westbury feature is the famous **Westbury White Horse**, a chalk carving measuring 182 feet in length and 108 feet in height. The present

WHITE HORSE POTTERY

Newtown, Nr Westbury, Wiltshire BA13 3EE
Tel: 01373 864772 Fax: 01373 300389

The White Horse Pottery is located on the B3098 at the junction of the road that leads to the famous White Horse carved in chalk in the hillside. The pottery premises were built 150 years ago by the Church of England as a school (it looks like a small church), a role it retained until the 1960s. Many fine features survive, including the slate roof, bell tower and church-style mullion windows, and the old playground at the back is now the car park. The pottery is both home and workplace to Trevor and Susanne Pictor, who work with clay to produce a wide variety of terracotta and glazed pots and bowls and jugs, with everything hand-thrown on the wheel.

They accept commissions - 'if it's round, we make it' - and Susanne also makes a range of wall and kitchen tiles. Visitors can see the whole pot-making process, from preparing the clay to throwing, shaping and finishing. Once the pots are dried they are fired in the gas kiln and sold as terracotta or glazed and fired again Several different glazes are used, including a stunning bright blue. Normal opening hours are 10 to 5 Tuesday to Saturday, but Trevor and Susanne hold regular special events at the pottery, including group evening visits, a hands-on day at Christmas time and Pizza Pot evenings, when visitors can enjoy home-cooked pizzas and make pots at the same time.

steed dates from 1778, replacing an earlier one carved to celebrate King Alfred's victory over the Danes at nearby Ethandun (Edington) in 878. The white horse is well looked after, the last major grooming being in 1996. Above the horse's head are the ruins of Bratton Castle, an Iron Age hill fort covering 25 acres.

Westbury White Horse

AROUND WESTBURY

WARMINSTER

4 miles S of Westbury on the A350

Warminster is a historic wool, corn-trading and coaching town with many distinguished buildings, including a famous school with a door designed by Wren. In addition to the 18th and 19th century buildings, Warminster has a number of interesting monuments: the Obelisk with its feeding troughs and pineapple top erected in 1783 to mark the enclosure of the parish; the Morgan Memorial Fountain in the Lake Pleasure Grounds; and *Beyond Harvest*, a statue in bronze by Colin Lambert of a girl sitting on sacks of corn. Warminster's finest building is the Church of St Denys, mainly 14th century but almost completely rebuilt in the 1880s to the design of Arthur Blomfield. The **Dewey Museum**, in the public library, displays a wide range of local history from Iron Age times to the present day, including the Victor Manley collection of geology. To the west of town is the 800ft **Cley Hill**, an Iron Age hill fort with two Bronze Age barrows. Formerly owned by the Marquess of Bath, the Hill was given to the National Trust in the 1950s and is a renowned sighting place for UFOs. (The region is also noted for the appearance of crop circles and some have linked the two phenomena.)

Purely Organic

Deverills Trout Farm, Longbridge Deverill, Warminster, Wiltshire BA12 7DZ
Tel: 01985 841093
website: www.purelyorganic.co.uk

Purely Organic, located in the village of Longbridge Deverill on the A350 Warminster-Blandford road, attracts health-conscious and environmentally aware visitors from near and far with its range of organic fair trade products. The best known of these are the trout, which are among the best and most natural in the country. The spring water used is drawn at a constant temperature from 35 metres down, and flows first through organic watercress beds which enrich it with natural freshwater shrimps, minnows, sticklebacks and the like which provide an excellent, nourishing base for the diet of the trout. The fish grow from natural exercise rather than additives in their food, making them firm and fibrous and totally unlike river or lake trout, which can often be both earthy and mushy.

Purely Organic sells the trout fresh, smoked, in paté or fish cakes, and other produce on sale in the well-stocked shop include soups (watercress is wonderful), local honey, dairy products, meat, general groceries, eggs from hens and ducks, flour for bread, ice creams, soft drinks and sandwiches, organic plant seeds and the Green Things range of body products. Purely Organic, which is owned and run by Tony and Eleanor Free, won the Gold Prize in the 1999 Green Apple Awards for services to the environment. The shop is open from 9 to 6 seven days a week.

Longhorn Western Riding Ltd

Longhedge Farm, Corsley, Nr Warminster, Wiltshire BA12 7QZ
Tel/Fax: 01373 832495
e-mail: clare@cejbayman.freeserve.co.uk
website: www.webcom.com/tli/longhorn

On a dairy farm in the heart of the countryside by the Longleat Estate, **Longhorn Western Riding** is owned and run by Clare Bayman, who has been with horses all her life and has many years' experience of teaching riding, jumping and dressage. Longhorn's horses are a mixture of American Quarter horses, Appaloosas and native British horses such as Exmoors, Cobs and Connemaras. All are trained Western and ridden in authentic American saddles and bridles.

There are between 16 and 20 horses to choose from, and all levels of ability are catered for, from those who have never ridden to those who were born in the saddle. The Longhorn trails meander through the 6,000-acre Estate of the Marquess of Bath, and out of the saddle the Estate's attractions include the famous Safari Park, the world's largest maze and a children's playground. Stabling is provided for visitors who bring their own horses, and a range of accommodation is available in the vicinity. There are several B&Bs on the edge of the Longleat Estate; one has a barn that can accommodate a party of eight. Lord Bath's 'local', the Bath Arms, has bedroom accommodation for up to 12. Jeans and Western wear are standard attire at Longhorn.

On the northern edge of Warminster **Arn Hill Nature Reserve** forms a circular walk of two miles along public footpaths through woodland and open downland.

Imber

5 miles E of Westbury off the B3098

The part of Salisbury Plain containing the village of Imber was closed to the public in 1943 and has been used by the Army ever since for live firing. The evicted villagers were told that they could return to Imber after the War, but the promise was not kept and the village remains basically inaccessible. A well-marked 30-mile perimeter walk skirting the danger area takes in Warminster, Westbury, Tilshead in the east and Chitterne in the south.

Codford St Peter & Codford St Mary

8 miles SE of Westbury on the A36

Sister villages beneath the prehistoric remains of Codford Circle, an ancient hilltop meeting place which stands 617 feet up on Salisbury Plain. The church in Codford St Peter has one of Wiltshire's finest treasures in an exceptional 9th century Saxon stone carving of a man holding a branch and dancing. East of Malmpit Hill and visible from the A36 is a rising sun emblem carved by Australian soldiers during World War l. In the military cemetery at Codford St Mary are the graves of Anzac troops who were in camp here. Anzac graves may also be seen at nearby Baverstock.

Wylye

10 miles SE of Westbury off the A36

Peace arrived in Wylye in 1977, when a bypass diverted traffic from the busy main roads. It had long been an important junction and staging post on the London-Exeter coaching route. A statue near the bridge over the River Wylye (from which the village, Wilton and indeed Wiltshire get their names) commemorates a brave postboy who drowned here after rescuing several passengers from a stagecoach which had overturned during a flood.

Above the village is the little-known **Yarnbury Castle**, an Iron Age hill fort surrounded by two banks and an outer bank. To the west is a triangular enclosure from Roman times which could have held cattle or sheep. From the 18th century to World War l Yarnbury was the venue of an annual sheep fair.

Longleat

6 miles SW of Westbury off the A362

1999 saw the 50th anniversary of the opening of **Longleat House** to the public. The magnificent home of the Marquess of Bath was built by an ancestor, Sir John Thynne, in a largely symmetrical style, in the 1570s. The inside is a treasure house of old masters, Flemish tapestries, beautiful furniture, rare books.....and Lord Bath's murals. The superb grounds of Longleat House were landscaped by Capability Brown and now contain one of the country's best known

Longleat House

venues for a marvellous day out. In the famous **safari park** the Lions of Longleat, first introduced in 1966, have been followed by a veritable Noah's Ark of exotic creatures, including elephants, rhinos, zebras and white tigers. The park also features safari boat rides, a narrow-gauge railway, children's amusement area, garden centre and the largest hedge maze in the world.

Stourhead Gardens

Stourton

9 miles SW of Westbury off the B3092

The beautiful National Trust village of Stourton lies at the bottom of a steep wooded valley and is a particularly glorious sight in the daffodil season. The main attraction is, of course, **Stourhead**, one of the most famous examples of the early 18th century English landscape movement. The lakes, the trees, the temples, a grotto and a classical bridge make the grounds, laid out by Henry Hoare, a paradise in the finest 18th century tradition, and the gardens are renowned for their striking vistas and woodland walks as well as a stunning selection of rare trees and specimen shrubs, including tulip trees, azaleas and rhododendrons. The house itself, a classical masterpiece built in the 1720s in Palladian style for a Bristol banker, contains a wealth of Grand Tour paintings and works of art, including furniture by Chippendale the Younger and wood carvings by Grinling Gibbons. On the very edge of the estate, some three miles by road from the house, the imposing King Alfred's Tower stands at the top of the 790ft Kingsettle Hill. This 160ft triangular redbrick folly was built in 1772 to commemorate the king, who reputedly raised his standard here against the Danes in 878. Also part of the estate, Whitesheet Down is grazed by cattle in the summer and sheep in the winter to maintain the wide variety of wildlife. The estate has several acres of open water, and the most interesting area for nature conservation is Six Wells Bottom with ponds that pre-date the 18th century landscaping.

Stourhead Gardens

MERE

12 miles SW of Westbury off the A303

A small town nestling below the downs near the borders with Dorset and Somerset. The town is dominated by **Castle Hill**, on which Richard, Earl of Cornwall, son of King John, built a castle in 1253. Nothing of the castle remains, though many of the stones were used in building Mere's houses. The Church of St Michael the Archangel in High Gothic style features some fine medieval and Victorian stained glass, carved Jacobean pews, an unusual octagonal font and a 12th century statue of St Michael slaying a dragon. **Mere Museum**, in the public library in Barton Lane, is principally a local history collection with a good photographic archive. Displays are changed regularly but a permanent feature is a large, detailed map of Mere drawn in colour by a local artist. This is a great area for rambling, one of the best spots being the Whitesheet Hill Nature Trail with wonderful views and a wealth of plants and insects, including some rare chalk-loving butterflies.

EAST KNOYLE

14 miles S of Westbury on the A350

Two items of interest here. A simple stone monument marks the birthplace, in 1632, of Sir Christopher Wren, son of the village rector of the time. East Knoyle Windmill is a tower mill on a circular base, without sails and unused for over a century. It offers good views over Blackmoor Vale and has a large grassy area for picnics.

TOLLARD ROYAL

6 miles SE of Shaftesbury on the B3081

Tollard Royal is a historic village atop **Zigzag Hill** in the heart of Cranborne Chase. King John had a small estate here which he used on his hunting trips. **King**

NOBLES DELICATESSEN

The Square, Tisbury, Salisbury, Wiltshire SP3 6JP
Tel: 01747 870452 Fax: 01747 871981
e-mail: shop@nobles.co.uk

Antony and Fiona Dodd-Noble are the dynamic and enthusiastic couple who run **Nobles Delicatessen**, which occupies a traditional double-fronted shop in the centre of Tisbury. The look is of a typical old-fashioned grocery, but the briefest of inspections within will reveal that this is far from a run-of-the-mill grocery business. The shelves and display tables are stacked high with top-quality groceries and provisions, in bottles, in tins, in packets or set out on delicatessen counters and a salad bar. Nobles also operates as a coffee shop, with a few tables and chairs laid out for shoppers wanting to relax with a cup of the finest, freshest coffee.

Customers can serve themselves from the herb and spice boxes, and draught liquor, including sherry, whisky and brandy, is sold 'by anything from a tablespoon to a bucket'. The owners offer an outside catering service for dinner parties and all sorts of special occasions, including weddings and christenings. Nobles is open all day Monday to Saturday and is well worth a diversion. The historic town of Tisbury can be reached by minor roads from all directions: east of the A350, north of the A30, south of the B3089.

Lacewing Framing & Restoration

Douglas McLeod and Lacewing Framing, 44 Trinity Street,
Salisbury, Wiltshire SP1 2BD
Tel: 01722 337565

In a residential area of the city, but at no great distance from the major places of interest, **Douglas McLeod & Lacewing Framing** is a double-fronted shop with a gallery to the rear. In the shop are many fine examples of period and contemporary frames and mirrors along with samples of the vast range of different frames made to order. The gallery is full of beautiful old frames, overmantles, mirrors and pictures including oil paintings, watercolours and prints.

This thriving business of framing and restoration is run by Douglas and Susie McLeod. All traditional skills of carving, gilding and paint effects are used, restoration, repairs and cleaning of frames, oil paintings and works of art on paper are undertaken within fixed quotations. Their fully staffed large workshop is equipped with all traditional hand and machine tools and is capable of carrying out the most demanding and intricate tasks. Anyone who appreciates art and superb craftsmanship will enjoy a visit to this outstanding enterprise.

lynnelucas

26 Catherine Street, Salisbury, Wiltshire SP1 2DA
Tel/Fax: 01722 339960

"lynne**lucas**" the shop and Lynne Lucas the shop's owner have built up an excellent local reputation as stockists of high-quality ladies fashion clothes and accessories. In the well-lit interior, racks of suits and dresses feature the designs of, among others, Max Mara, Max Mara Weekend, Gerard Darel, Ghost, Renato Nucci, Annette Gortz, Sand, Sonja Marohn and Claudia Strater. The shop is located right in the heart of the city, close to many places of interest, making it easy for the well-dressed lady to acquire not only a new wardrobe but also an insight into the fascinating history of one of the country's most glorious medieval cities.

The Silver Gift Gallery

2a Bridge Street, Salisbury, Wiltshire SP1 2LX
Tel: 01722 410595

Gifts for all occasions at all prices make up the varied stock at the **Silver Gift Gallery**, which occupies a prominent corner site in a busy and attractive shopping complex in the heart of Salisbury. Owner Sandra Barnes is a real enthusiast, and her shop attracts a constant stream of visitors drawn by the irresistible window display into the pleasant, well-lit Aladdin's Cave within. Silver is the name of the game, with items ranging from small, inexpensive gifts to serious ornamental and ceremonial jewellery.

John's House is a part-stone, part-timber residence whose fine condition is largely due to the efforts of General Pitt Rivers, an eminent Victorian archaeologist who inherited the estate and spent the last 20 years of his life unearthing Bronze Age remains. His collection is housed in the Salisbury and South Wiltshire Museum, where a gallery is named in his honour.

Ludwell

2 miles E of Shaftesbury on the A30

Near the village is the National Trust-owned **Win Green Hill**, the highest point in Wiltshire, crowned by a copse of beech trees set around an ancient bowl barrow. From the summit there are wonderful views as far as the Quantock Hills to the northwest and the Isle of Wight to the southeast.

SALISBURY

The glorious medieval city of Salisbury stands at the confluence of four rivers, the Avon, Wylye, Bourne and Nadder. Originally called New Sarum, it grew around the present Cathedral, which was built between 1220 and 1258 in a sheltered position two miles south of the site of its windswept Norman predecessor at Old Sarum. Over the years the townspeople followed the clergy into the new settlement, creating a flourishing religious and market centre whose two main aspects flourish to this day.

One of the most beautiful buildings in the world, **Salisbury Cathedral** is the only medieval cathedral in England to be built in the same Early English style - apart from the spire, the tallest in England, which was added some years later and rises to an awesome 404 feet. The Chapter House opens out of the cloisters and contains, among other treasures, one of the four surviving originals of Magna Carta. Six hundred thousand visitors a year come to marvel at this and other priceless treasures, including a number of magnificent tombs. The oldest working clock in Britain and possibly in the world is situated in the fan-vaulted north transept; it was built in 1386 to strike the hour and has no clock face. The Cathedral is said to contain a door for each month, a window for each day and a column for each hour of the year. A small statue inside the west door is of Salisbury's 17th century **Boy Bishop**. It was a custom for choristers to elect one of their number to be bishop for a period lasting from St Nicholas Day to Holy Innocents Day (6-28 December). One year the boy bishop was apparently literally tickled to death by the other choristers; since he died in office, his statue shows him in full bishop's regalia.

Salisbury High Street and Gate

Milford Hall Hotel & Restaurant

206 Castle Street, Salisbury, Wiltshire SP1 3TE
Tel: 01722 417411 Fax: 01722 419444
e-mail: milfordhallhotel@cs.com
website: www.milfordhallhotel.com

The core of **Milford Hall Hotel** is a handsome Georgian manor house which was expanded to create a comfortable and convenient hotel offering period charm and up-to-date amenity. This thoughtful mix of old and new - the modern extension is set in the grounds of the old house - extend beyond bricks and mortar to encompass the warmth and comfort of traditional English hospitality while catering for today's guests, including business people and families with children. Milford Hall has 31 bedrooms, all offering en suite bathroom, tv, radio, trouser press, hairdryer and hospitality tray; all these are in the newer part and 20 are on the ground floor.

Within the Georgian house are four additional rooms of character, each a luxuriously furnished, traditional double bedroom. The Clarendon Room has a four-poster bed and the Longford Room a superb half-tester bed. The Brasserie @ 206 is a new addition to the hotel and offers a superb range of fresh fish, meat and vegetarian dishes to suit all tastes. Open 7 days a week to residents and non-residents alike, the restaurant is proud to display its AA Rosette for high standards of cuisine. The lounge is a great place to relax, and in the bar guests can meet friends for a drink and a chat. The Fonthill Room is an ideal venue for ballroom-style meetings or for private business entertaining. The Lounge Room, with French windows opening out on to the gardens, is also available for meetings. The Alderman Room, in a quiet part of the hotel with ground-floor access from the car park or hotel reception, is a much larger which will accommodate up to 80 in a theatre-style layout.

With two dedicated conference and function rooms, the hotel has the flexibility to handle all kinds of events - from meetings and seminars to wedding receptions and parties.The hotel is also a licensed venue for civil marriages. Milford Hall has no leisure facilities of its own but is able to offer residents complimentary use of the local leisure centre and swimming pool which are within easy walking distance. Also close at hand are the manifold attractions of the city of Salisbury, including shops, museums and the glorious Cathedral, which ranks among the most beautiful buildings in the world. Sue Wilson is the Marketing Manager for this hotel and also for the sister hotel the Old Bell in Malmesbury.

The Close, the precinct of the ecclesiastical community serving the cathedral, is the largest in England and contains a number of museums and houses open to the public. **Salisbury and South Wiltshire Museum**, in the 17th century King's House, is the home of the Stonehenge Gallery and a designated archaeological collection of national importance. Displays include early South Wiltshire, the Giant and Hob Nob, Romans and Saxons, the Pitt Rivers collection (see under Tollard Royal), Old Sarum, ceramics, costume, lace, embroidery and Turner watercolours. A few doors away is **The Royal Gloucestershire, Berkshire and Wiltshire Museum** housed in a 13th century building called the Wardrobe, which was originally used to store the bishop's clothes and documents. The museum tells the story of the county regiments since 1743 and the exhibits include Bobbie the Dog, the hero of Maiwand, and many artefacts from foreign campaigns. The house has tea room and a riverside garden with views of the famous water meadows. The historic **Medieval Hall** is the atmospheric setting for a 30-minute history of Salisbury in sound and pictures. **Mompesson House**, a National Trust property, is a perfect example of Queen Anne architecture notable for its plasterwork, an elegant carved oak staircase, fine period furniture and the important Turnbull collection of 18th century drinking glasses. In the Market Place is the **John Creasey Museum** and the **Creasey Collection of Contemporary Art**, a permanent collection of books, manuscripts, objects and art. Also in the Market Place, in the library, is the **Edwin Young Collection**

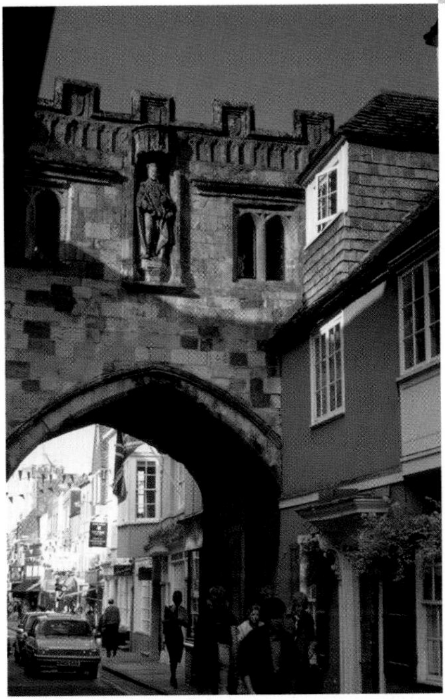

Cathedral Close, Salisbury

of 19th and early 20th century water-colours, drawings and oil paintings of Salisbury and its surrounding landscape.

Salisbury racecourse, a short drive west of the city, stages flat racing during the summer months.

There are many other areas of Salisbury to explore on foot and a short drive takes visitors to the ruins of **Old Sarum** (see panel opposite), abandoned when the bishopric moved into the city. Traces of the original cathedral and palace are visible on the huge uninhabited mound, which dates back to the Iron Age. Old Sarum became the most notorious of the 'rotten boroughs', returning two Members of Parliament, despite having no voters, until the 1832 Reform Act stopped the cheating. A plaque on the site commemorates Old Sarum's most illustrious MP, William Pitt the Elder.

Fisherton Mill

108 Fisherton Street, Salisbury, Wiltshire SP2 7QY
Tel: 01722 415121

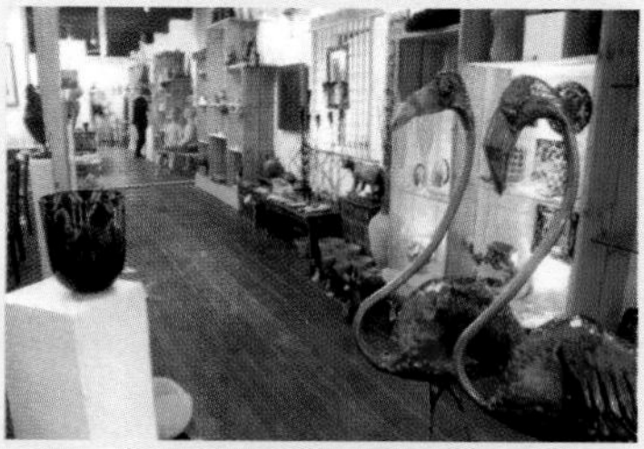

Built in 1880 as a grain mill, **Fisherton Mill** is now the venue for the South of England's largest independent art gallery. Spread over three floors, a hay loft and a courtyard, the gallery, which is owned by George Baylis, retains many of the mill's original features, notable wooden floors polished by years of grain sacks being dragged, staircases, beamed ceilings, cast-iron pillars and fine old pieces of machinery. On the ground floor is a lifestyle shop selling an array of accessories both functional and decorative, including ceramics, textiles, glass, jewellery, sculpture and painting. The first floor houses a collection of fine contemporary British furniture standing amid paintings and sculptures, while the Beams Gallery is an exhibition space that's an ideal setting for both themed and mixed media exhibitions.

The White Gallery on the second floor is the mill's largest exhibition space, which with over 60 metres of wall space and 3,000 square feet of floor space can accommodate and show to great effect large-scale paintings and sculptural pieces. The courtyard is used as a seasonal space for exhibiting large sculptures and garden pieces and also provides a fairweather space for sampling the delights created by Michael Fox, owner-chef of the café and restaurant. Inside or out, visitors can enjoy anything from a simple snack or pastry to a full-scale meal.

Hollyhock

25-27 New Street, Salisbury, Wiltshire SP1 2PH
Tel: 01722 411051

Hollyhock, which Annie Brocklebank has owned for 10 years, is a large, well-designed shop with an impressive stock of ladies designer clothes and accessories. Annie and her staff assure shoppers of friendly, attentive service as they work their way through the racks and shelves. Designer lines include Caroline Charles, Christian Lacroix, Beppi Bondi, Paddy Campbell, Ischiko, Paul Costelloe, Oui, Lamberto Losani, Mirina Rinaldi and many more, with sizes ranging from 8 to 24. Hollyhock has a lovely surprise in the shape of a beautiful rear garden with views of the Cathedral.

OLD SARUM

Tel: 01722 335398 website: www.english-heritage.org.uk

Situated high above Salisbury Plain, **Old Sarum**, the site of the ancient city of Salisbury, was first settled in the Iron Age when a massive hill fort was created here. Later occupied by the Romans (several Roman roads converge here), the town grew in Saxon times within its prehistoric ramparts until, by the time of the Norman Conquest, there were two palaces here along with Salisbury's first great cathedral. People continued to live at Sarum until the 16th century, although a new town grew up around the 13th century cathedral, and in the 19th century Old Sarum was one of the country's most notorious 'rotten boroughs'. Today, the massive earth ditches and ramparts remain intact and there are spectacular views across the Salisbury and the surrounding countryside.

AROUND SALISBURY

BRITFORD

1 mile S of Salisbury on the A338

Lying within branches of the Wiltshire Avon, Britford has a moated country house and a fine Saxon church with some early stone carvings. An ornate tomb is thought to be that of the Duke of Buckingham, who was beheaded in Salisbury in 1483. Nearby **Longford Castle**, mainly 16th century, houses an interesting collection of paintings.

DOWNTON

5 miles S of Salisbury off the A338

The Saxons established a meeting place, or moot, on an earlier earthwork fortification, and it was in commemoration of that ancient parliament that the present **Moot House** was built on the foundations of the old castle. The building and its garden stand opposite a small 18th century amphitheatre built to resemble the Saxon moot. In 1955, a Roman villa comprising seven rooms and a bath house was discovered nearby.

LOVER

6 miles SE of Salisbury off the A338

In the vicinity of this charmingly-named village is the National Trust's **Pepperbox Hill** topped by an early 17th century octagonal tower known as **Eyre's Folly**. Great walking, great views, and a great place for nature-lovers, with a variety of plant and bird life.

WILTON

3 miles W of Salisbury on the A30

The third oldest borough in England, once the capital of Saxon Wessex. It is best known for its carpets, and the **Wilton Carpet Factory** on the River Wylye continues to produce top-quality carpets, maintaining a worldwide reputation for quality that goes back 300 years. Wilton carpets as we know them today were created by a French carpet weaver who was brought to England by the Earl of Pembroke in the early part of the 18th century to teach the local weavers his skills. In 1835 redundant handlooms were brought from the Axminster factory in Devon and set up in Wilton. Luxurious hand-knotted Axminsters, with each tuft individually tied by hand, were made alongside traditional Wiltons up to 1958. Visitors can tour the carpet-making exhibition in the historic courtyard then go into the

New Forest Lodge

Southampton Road, Landford, Salisbury,
Wiltshire SP5 2ED
Tel: 01794 390999 Fax: 01794 390066
e-mail: reservations@newforestlodge.co.uk
website: www.newforestlodge.co.uk

Easily found on the A36 Salisbury-Southampton road, **New Forest Lodge** offers, well-appointed accommodation in 14 bedrooms comprising doubles, twins and family rooms. All have luxury en suite bathrooms with power showers. Short or long stays are equally welcome, and for golfers an attractive package is available in conjunction with the nearby Hamptworth Golf Club. Bedrooms and public rooms have all been refurbished, and a very smart boardroom for up to 14 delegates has everything needed for a business meeting.

On the same site and under the same management is the Keepers Restaurant, open seven days a week for breakfast, lunch and dinner. A snack menu is available for lighter lunches, and in the evening guests can dine by candle-light from a regularly changing à la carte menu. The cooking combines the best of traditional and contemporary British styles with dishes that range from seared breast of pigeon with rocket salad to a trio salmon with creamed leeks, chargrilled steaks and chump of Welsh lamb with gratin potatoes and pancetta. Sunday lunch is served until 4 o'clock, and the restaurant has a patio and garden area that comes into its own in the summer.

Howard's House Hotel

Teffont Evias, Nr Salisbury, Wiltshire SP3 5RJ
Tel: 01722 716392 e-mail: enq@howardshotel.com
Fax: 01722 716820 website: www.howardshousehotel.com

Built as a farmhouse in 1623 and restored in 1989, **Howard's House** stands in a quintessential English garden of rolling lawns, ancient box hedges, a pond with a fountain and secret corners for daydreaming and quiet contemplation. In this most civilised of settings nine luxurious bedrooms were created, each with its own bathroom, bathrobes, telephone, tv and hairdryer. Floral prints and pastel shades combine to enhance the feeling of informality and relaxation, and the sitting room offers abundant comfort and calm, with French windows open to the garden in summer and a log fire glowing warmly in winter.

In the beautifully appointed dining room (no smoking) tip-top produce is handled with skill and flair on outstanding table d'hote and à la carte dinner and Sunday lunch menus. Typical choices might include pan-seared king scallops with oven-baked tomatoes and a saffron vinaigrette, Gressingham duck breast with wild mushroom risotto, roast root vegetables and a beetroot jus, and char-sealed fillet of Scotch beef with a rosemary galette, garlic confit, green beans and Madeira. Howard's House is a real gem of a hotel and an ideal place for a relaxing break, for country walks or for visiting the many places of historic interest in the area.

modern factory to see the carpets made on up-to-date machinery using traditional skills and techniques. Alongside the factory is the Wilton Shopping Village offering high-quality factory shopping in a traditional rural setting.

Wilton House is the stately home of the Earls of Pembroke. When the original house was destroyed by fire in 1647, Inigo Jones was commissioned to build its replacement. He designed both the exterior and the interior, including the amazing Double Cube Room, and the house was further remodelled by James Wyatt. The art collection is one of the very finest, with works by Rembrandt, Van Dyke, Rubens and Tintoretto; the furniture includes pieces by Chippendale and Kent. There's plenty to keep children busy and happy, notably the Wareham Bears (a collection of 200 miniature costumed teddy bears), a treasure hunt quiz and a huge adventure playground. There's a Tudor kitchen, a Victorian laundry and 21 acres of landscaped grounds with parkland, cedar trees, water and rose gardens and an elegant Palladian bridge. During World War ll the house was used as an operations centre for Southern Command and it is believed that the Normandy landings were planned here. Open daily late March-end October.

The Church of St Mary and St Nicholas is a unique Italianate church built in the style of Lombardy by the Russian Countess of Pembroke in 1845. The interior is resplendent with marble, mosaics, richly carved woodwork and early French stained glass.

Broad Chalke

7 miles W of Salisbury off the A354

A Saxon village where the 17th century diarist John Aubrey had a small estate. A warden of the parish church, he was also a keen angler and wrote of his beloved River Ebble: *'There are not better trouts in the Kingdom of England than here'*. The designer and photographer Cecil Beaton spent his final years in Broad Chalke and is buried in the churchyard of All Saints.

Fovant

8 miles W of Salisbury on the A30

The **Fovant Badges** are badges carved in the chalk hillside by troops during the First World War. They include the Australian Imperial Force, the Devonshire Regiment, 6th City of London Regiment, the London Rifle Brigade, the Post Office Rifles, the Royal Corps of Signals, the Royal Wiltshire Yeomanry,

(Continued page 268)

Old Wardour Castle

Tel: 01747 870487
website: www.english-heritage.org.uk

One of the most romantic ruins in England (15 miles west of Salisbury), **Old Wardour Castle** was built in the late 14th century for John, 5th Lord Lovel and its six-sided design, with many suits of rooms for guests, is unique in this country. Lord Lovel had been inspired by the castles then being built in France and he was determined to copy the style for his new home. As well as providing security, the castle was a place for luxurious living and was also designed to impress. Besieged twice during the Civil War, the castle was badly damaged in the second siege, in 1644, and was never restored. When Wardour New Castle was built in the 1770s, the old castle was left as an ornamental featured deliberately integrated into the landscaped gardens to be admired as a romantic ruin. It has featured in the film, *Robin Hood, Prince of Thieves* and is a venue for regular special events during the summer.

WALK 7

Fovant Down

Start	Fovant, by the church at the north end of the village
Distance	4½ miles (7.2km)
Approximate time	2 hours
Parking	By Fovant church
Refreshments	Pubs at Fovant
Ordnance Survey maps	Landranger 184 (Salisbury & The Plain), Pathfinders 1261, ST82/92 (Shaftesbury) and 1262, SU02/12 (Salisbury (South) & Broad Chalke)

There are poignant memories of World War I both at the start of the walk in Fovant churchyard and on Fovant Down, famed for its carvings of regimental badges. After an initial ascent and descent to the west of the village, a steady climb leads on to the crest of the down followed by a walk along the wooded ridge. The views from here are superb. The descent takes you across the face of the down past some of the badges, though these are best viewed from the bottom. The final part of the walk is through the attractive village of Fovant.

At the start of the walk you might like to enter the peaceful and attractive churchyard of Fovant's medieval church. Here are the graves of soldiers from all over the British Empire who died from injuries received during World War I.

Begin by walking back along the lane to a crossroads, turn left and at a public bridleway sign to the A30, turn right on to a tarmac track **A**. After a few yards this becomes a grassy path, enclosed between hedges and trees, which heads gently uphill through a steep-sided valley to a fork.

Continue along the right-hand enclosed path – this is narrow and likely to be overgrown – which descends gently to reach the A30 to the right of a farm **B**. Cross over and take the lane ahead, signposted to Broad Chalke and Bowerchalke. Where the lane bends right in front of a chalk pit, bear left over a stile **C**, at a public footpath sign to Fovant Down. Continue along the sunken path ahead, climbing steadily up to the ridge of the down, head up through bushes near the top and turn right over a stile to a crossroads **D**. Turn left and walk along a broad, ridge top track through a narrow strip of woodland. After emerging into open country, extensive views open up across the sweeping downs on both sides.

WALK 7

Where the track curves right, turn left over a stile **E** and keep ahead along the right edge of the earthworks of Chiselbury Fort, an Iron Age hill fort which, at a height of 662ft (201m), enjoys a commanding position and magnificent views. Shortly after following the curve of the fort gradually to the left, look out for a stile in a fence on the right and head across to climb it.

Bear left and follow a faint, grassy path steeply and diagonally downhill, passing between some of the regimental badges, to the bottom corner of the down. Continue through bushes, keep ahead to climb a stile and walk along the left edge of a field to a metal gate in the corner. At this point look back for a good view of the Fovant Badges, a series of regimental badges carved on the side of the down by troops stationed here in World War I.

Go through the gate and turn left along a straight, enclosed track, passing to the left of a large farmhouse. Later the track bears left, then turns right and continues between houses to emerge on to a lane on the edge of Fovant. Keep ahead through the village to the main road **F**, cross over and continue along the lane opposite through this long and strung out village. At a fork in front of the village hall take the left-hand lane, signposted to Tisbury, and at a crossroads turn right along Church Lane to return to the start. ●

0 200 400 600 800metres 1 KILOMETRES
0 200 400 600yards ½ MILES

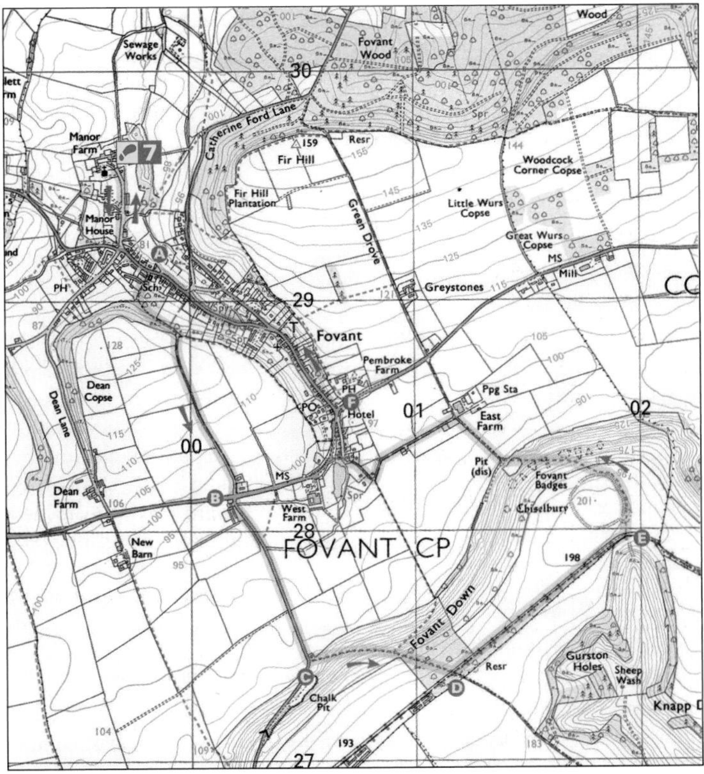

the Wiltshire Regiment and the YMCA. The badges can be seen from the A30.

Dinton

9 miles W of Salisbury off the A30

There are two National Trust properties to visit near this lovely hillside village. **Little Clarendon** is a small but perfectly formed Tudor manor house with three oak-furnished rooms open to visitors; **Philipps House** is a handsome white-fronted neo-Grecian house with a great Ionic portico. Built by the early 19th century architect Jeffrey Wyattville for William Wyndham, it stands in the beautiful landscaped grounds of Dinton Park.

Teffont Evias

9 miles W of Salisbury off the B3089

Teffont Evias is a quiet little village with some handsome houses built with stone from the local Chilmark quarries. Close by, on the road that connects with the A303, is **Farmer Giles Farmstead**, a 175-acre working farm where a wide variety of farm animals can be seen at close quarters.

Stapleford

6 miles NW of Salisbury

One of a number of delightful unspoilt villages including the three Langfords and **Berwick St James**, where the grid of the medieval board game Nine Men's Morris can be seen on a stone bench in the church porch. At Stapleford there was once a castle belonging to Waleran, chief huntsman of William the Conqueror.

Woodford Valley

6 miles N of Salisbury off the A345

A seven-mile stretch between Salisbury and Amesbury contains some of the prettiest and most peaceful villages in the county, among them **Great Durnford** with its Norman church and restored mill, **Lake**, with an imposing Tudor mansion, and **Middle Woodford**, where the internationally renowned **Heale Garden and Plant Centre** lies within the grounds of 16th century Heale House in an idyllic setting by a tributary of the Avon. Much of the garden was designed by Harold Peto (1854-1933), whose own garden at Iford Manor (see under Bradford-on-Avon) is in the Italianate style that he so favoured. Highlights at Heale include a superb collection of plants, shrubs and roses, a water garden and a Japanese bridge and teahouse made in 1910 with the help of four Japanese gardeners.

Amesbury

8 miles N of Salisbury on the A345

Queen Elfrida founded an abbey here in 979 in atonement for her part in the murder of her son-in-law, Edward the Martyr, at Corfe Castle. Henry ll rebuilt the abbey's great Church of St Mary and St Melor, whose tall central tower is the only structure to survive from the pre-Norman monastery. A mile to the north of Amesbury, the A345 passes along the eastern side of **Woodhenge**, a ceremonial monument even older than Stonehenge. It was the first major prehistoric site to be discovered by aerial photography, its six concentric rings of post holes having been spotted as cropmarks by Squadron Leader Insall in 1925. Like Stonehenge, it seems to have been used as an astronomical calendar. When major excavation was carried out in the 1920s, a number of neolithic tools and other artefacts were found, along with the skeleton of a three-year-old child whose fractured skull suggested some kind of ritual sacrifice.

Two miles west of Amesbury at the

Stonehenge

remains of ceremonial and domestic structures, many of them accessible by road or public footpath. The great stone blocks of the main ring are truly massive, and it seems certain that the stones in the outer rings - rare bluestones from the Preseli Hills of west Wales - had to be transported over 200 miles. Stonehenge's orientation on the rising and setting sun has always been one of its most remarkable features, leading to theories that the builders were from a sun-worshipping culture or that the whole structure is part of a huge astronomical calendar ...or both. The mystery remains, and will probably remain for ever.

junction of the A303 and A344/A360 stands **Stonehenge** itself, perhaps the greatest mystery of the prehistoric world, one of the wonders of the world, and a monument of unique importance. The World Heritage Site is surrounded by the

Nigel Northeast Cabinet Maker

Back Drove, Furniture Workshop, West Winterslow, Wiltshire SP5 1RY
Tel: 01980 862051 e-mail: nigel@nigelnortheast.co.uk
Fax: 01980 863986 website: www.nigelnortheast.co.uk

Handmade, high-quality bespoke furniture is the speciality of **Nigel Northeast, Cabinet Maker**, now in his 20th year since starting the business and whose workshops are located in an area renowned for centuries for its craftsmen. Nigel and his team, all highly trained in traditional skills, pass those skills on to apprentices, who are trained in all aspects of cabinet making, from the choice of wood to handcut dovetailing and the final hand polishing. Only solid timbers are used, with veneers for decoration only; the workshops keep an extensive stock of traditionally dried timber, indigenous to the area and some of which was recovered from the great storm of January 1990.

The choice of English hardwood covers oak, ash, walnut, yew, acacia, sycamore, sweet chestnut and cherry, while the imported timber is mainly mahogany. Items in an exquisite catalogue range from magazine racks and small occasional tables to dining room suites, and Nigel and the team are happy to be briefed on one-off commissions to customers' design and finish, or they will make pieces according to customers' specifications. The firm offers a wide range of other services including antique restoration, French polishing, insurance work, flood and fire damage restoration, gallery and exhibition design and modern spray finishes. They will collect and deliver any piece for restoration directly to the customer's home.

The Beadles

Middleton, Middle Winterslow, Nr Salisbury,
Wiltshire SP5 1QS
Tel: 01980 862922 Fax: 01980 863565
e-mail: winterbead@aol.com
website: www.guestaccom.co.uk/754.htm

The Beadles is a delightful modern Georgian-style house in a lovely quiet garden setting off the A30 seven miles east of Salisbury. Owners Anne-Marie and David Yuille-Baddeley offer warm, comfortable accommodation in tastefully appointed double and twin-bedded rooms with en suite bathrooms, telephone, tv and tea/coffee making facilities. Breakfast (also evening meals by arrangement) is served in the elegant dining room, and picnic meals are available on request.

The house is a tranquil and very civilised base for exploring the Wessex region, and the owners are happy to advise on what to see and how to get there: Salisbury with its magnificent Cathedral, Stonehenge, Wilton House, renowned for its fabulous art collection, the beautiful New Forest and Thomas Hardy country are all within easy reach, and for walkers the historic Clarendon Way runs nearby. The Beadles, which is a non-smoking establishment, is open all year, with special seasonal breaks and discounts for stays of longer than three days. Children over 12 are welcome, and the house has ample car parking space and facilities for meetings.

Cholderton Rare Breed Farm Park

Amesbury Road, Cholderton, Salisbury, Wiltshire SP4 0EW
Tel: 01980 629438
website: www.rabbitworld.co.uk

Cholderton Farm Park, set in beautiful countryside just off the A303, first opened its gates in 1987, since when it has developed into one of the most popular family attractions in the county, and the winner of several awards from the tourist industry. Owned and run by Pamela and Jeremy McConnell and their family, the park is home to a large number of rare breeds. Rabbit World is just one small part, with over 50 breeds on show in spacious pens, often in family units. The under-cover unit also displays information on rabbit life and history and has a pen where children can sit and stroke some of the younger rabbits.

Also under cover are a poultry unit with 18 breeds and a sheep unit (see the seaweed-eating sheep!), while outdoor attractions include a waterfowl pond, water gardens, a nature trail, a woodland adventure playground and a separate area for very young visitors. There are picnic areas both in and out of doors, and a cafeteria in the farmhouse serves lunches, snacks and speciality cream teas. During peak times of year additional attractions are added, including tractor and trailer rides and the famous Cholderton 'Pork Stakes' pig races. The farm also has a formal educational side, with lectures, videos and a comprehensive teachers pack for visiting school groups. The farm is open every day from the end of March to the end of October; also open out of season at weekends (10.30-16.00) for parties and educational visits by arrangement.The majority of the park is accessible by wheelchair.

STRATFORD-SUB-CASTLE

2 miles NE of Salisbury off the A343

Old Sarum is not the only impressive mound hereabouts, as three miles to the east is the Iron Age hill fort of **Figbury Rings**. Above it, the bleak expanse of Porton Down is a largely undisturbed conservation area where the great bustard has been making a comeback. This large, long-legged bird was once a common sight on Salisbury Plain and is incorporated in Wiltshire's coat of arms.

NEWTON TONEY

8 miles NE of Salisbury on the A338

Close to this pleasant village is **Cholderton Rare Breeds Farm Park** set in beautiful countryside and a major family attraction since opening to the public in 1987 (see panel opposite). Highlights include Rabbit World, tractor and trailer rides, pig racing, a woodland adventure playground, nature trail and a cafeteria serving excellent clotted cream teas. The park is also home to many endangered farm animals.

MARLBOROUGH

Famous for its public school and its wide high street, Marlborough is situated in the rural eastern part of Wiltshire in the upland valley of the Kennet, which flows through the town. It was once an important staging post on the coaching run from London to Bath and Bristol, and the presence of the A4 means that it still has easy links both east and west. Its main street, one of the finest in the country, is dignified by many Tudor houses and handsome Georgian colonnaded shops, behind which are back alleys waiting to be explored. St Mary's Church, austere behind a 15th

THE BOWMOORE GALLERY

4 London Road, Marlborough, Wiltshire SN8 1PH
Tel: 01672 513593 or 0781 8054448
e-mail: bowmoore@supanet.com

Geri Denning owned and ran the **Bowmoore Gallery** for over 30 years in Gloucestershire and London. She recently moved the Gallery to Marlborough, a delightful town which she regards as ideal for exhibiting paintings and sculptures. The Gallery promotes a number of talented artists, whose works cover a wide range that includes naive, impressionist, abstract and contemporary British. Among the artists featured are Lucy Rawlinson, who specialises in village and country landscapes; Bryan Hanlon, who uses oil, watercolour, pastel, tempera and bronze in traditional landscapes and wildlife works; Tony

Myer, local Avebury scenes; and Ann Stevens, a sculptor specialising in small figures.

The Gallery always has in stock a large selection of oil paintings, watercolours and sculptures from 1880 onwards. Prices range upwards from as little as £50, and the Gallery also sells a wide variety of beautiful and original gifts, including ceramics, pots, cushions, wooden platters and photo frames. Bowmoore Gallery holds regular exhibitions and private viewings, and in the summer the courtyard is the perfect setting.

century frontage, stands in **Patten Alley**, so named because pedestrians had to wear pattens (an overshoe with a metal sole) to negotiate the mud on rainy days. The porch of the church has a ledge where churchgoers would leave their pattens before entering. Other buildings of interest include those clustered round The Green (originally a Saxon village and the working-class quarter in the 18th and 19th centuries); the turn-of-the-century Town Hall looking down the broad High Street; and the ornate 17th century Merchant's House, now restored as a museum.

Marlborough College was founded in 1843 primarily for sons of the clergy. The Seymour family built a mansion near the site of the Norman castle. This mansion was replaced in the early 18th century by a building which became the Castle Inn and is now C House, the oldest part of

The Table Gallery Company

4 Kingsbury Street, Marlborough, Wiltshire SN8 1HU
Tel/Fax: 01672 5111188
e-mail: tablegallery@btinternet.com website: www.tablegallery.com

A Grade II-listed building dating back almost 300 years is the atmospheric setting for Paul Martin's **Table Gallery**, a double-fronted shop specialising in antique and country furniture from the 17th, 18th and early 19th centuries. Most of the pieces are English or French, the materials oak, elm or fruit woods, and the vast majority of the stock comes from farms in North Wales and Snowdonia, or from farmhouses all over France.

The coolly contemporary interior has plenty of space and excellent lighting that focuses on each piece, enabling it to be viewed from all angles like a sculpture in an art gallery. An excellent reference library is at the disposal of customers to browse through while enjoying a cup of coffee. The Gallery undertakes polishing and restoration work and offers a service of finding exactly what the customer is looking for, along with authenticating and valuing. Items in stock range from decorative treen to spice cupboards, chairs and stools, settles and dressers.

Harper's

44a Kingsbury Street, Marlborough, Wiltshire SN8 1JE
Tel: 01672 514395 Fax: 01672 514829
e-mail: harperslifestyle@aol.com website: www.harpers-lifestyle.com

Owner Jayne Jensen offers 'contemporary style for you and your home' in her delightful shop, **Harper's.** Her stock is an eclectic mix of tempting items, from Jasper Conran crystal, Alessi goods, side tables and superb leather sofas to beautiful fashion, including Fenn Wright & Manson, Nougat and L.K.Bennett footwear. Also on display for sale are jewellery, accessories, pretty gifts and a small range of carefully chosen antiques. Jayne recently opened the Crown Hotel in Marlborough in true Harper's style: elegant decor, beautiful antiques and traditional English cooking.

the College. A mound in the private grounds of the school is linked with King Arthur's personal magician Merlin. It was said that he was buried under this mound and gave the town its name 'Merle Barrow' or Merlin's Tomb. Among the many notable pupils of the college were William Morris and John Betjeman.

Savernake Forest

AROUND MARLBOROUGH

Savernake Forest

2 miles E of Marlborough off the A346

The ancient woodland of **Savernake Forest** is a magnificent 4,500-acre expanse of unbroken woodland, open glades and bridle paths. King Henry VIII hunted wild deer here and married Jane Seymour, whose family home was nearby. Designated an SSSI (Site of Special Scientific Interest), the forest is home to abundant wildlife, including a small herd of deer and 25 species of butterfly. One day each winter the Forest is closed to prevent rights of way being established.

West Overton

3 miles W of Marlborough off the A4

The area between Marlborough and Avebury sees the biggest concentration of prehistoric remains in the country. The scattered community of West Overton stands at the foot of **Overton Hill**, the site of an early Bronze Age monument called **The Sanctuary**. These giant standing stones are at the southeastern end of West Kennet Avenue, an ancient pathway which once connected them to the main megalithic circles at Avebury (see panel page 272). Overton Hill is also the start point of the Ridgeway long-distance path, which runs for 80 miles to the Chilterns. Just off this path is **Fyfield Down**, now a nature reserve, where quarries once provided many of the great stones that are such a feature of the area. **Devil's Den** long barrow lies within the reserve. The local legend that Satan sometimes appears here at midnight attempting to pull down the stones with a team of white oxen has not in recent times been corroborated.

East and West Kennet

4 miles W of Marlborough on the A4

West Kennet Long Barrow, one of Britain's largest neolithic burial tombs, is situated a gentle stroll away from the twin villages. The tomb is of impressive proportions - 330' long, 80' wide and 10' high - and is reached by squeezing past some massive stones in the semicircular forecourt.

Silbury Hill

5 miles W of Marlborough on the A4

The largest man-made prehistoric mound in Europe, built around 2800BC, standing 130' high and covering five acres. Excavation in the late 1960s revealed some details of how it was

(Continued page 276)

WALK 8

Avebury, West Kennett and Silbury Hill

Start	Avebury
Distance	6½ miles (10.5km)
Approximate time	3 hours
Parking	National Trust car park at Avebury
Refreshments	Pub and café at Avebury
Ordnance Survey maps	Landranger 173 (Swindon & Devizes), Pathfinders 1169, SU07/17 (Marlborough Downs) and 1185, SU06/16 (Devizes & Marlborough)

This fascinating walk links the most outstanding collection of prehistoric remains in the country. From the stone circle at Avebury, the route heads up on to the downs and follows a section of the Ridgeway into the village of East Kennett. It then continues to the impressive West Kennett Long Barrow, and the final stretch, mainly by the infant River Kennet, takes you past the intriguing Silbury Hill, the largest artificial mound in Europe. Allow plenty of time in order to appreciate these unique monuments to the full.

A 17th century antiquarian wrote of the great stone circle at Avebury that 'it did as much excel Stonehenge, as a cathedral does a parish church'. Constructed sometime between 2700 and 1700 BC and the focal point of the most important group of prehistoric monuments in the country, it is undeniably impressive, even in an incomplete state. It is also more complex than it seems, with two smaller circles within the main outer ring of stones, and protected by a ditch and embankment. The size of the circle and the proximity of the other monuments suggest that it must have been a major political and/or religious centre of Neolithic Britain.

Partially enclosed by the stone circle, the village of Avebury is a most attractive place in its own right, with an Elizabethan manor house and fine medieval church.

Begin by taking the tarmac path, signposted Avebury Village and Stone Circle, that leads from the far corner of the car park. Follow it to a road and turn right (A) through the village, passing through the outer circle. Where the road turns left by the Red Lion, keep straight ahead along a lane (Green Street). Pass through the stone circle again and after passing a farm, the lane becomes a rough track which heads steadily uphill on to a ridge.

At a crossroads of tracks turn right on to the Ridgeway (B) and follow a track across the downs. The views from here are extensive and wide ranging. Eventually the track descends gently to emerge on to the busy A4 (C). To the left is a group of tumuli and on the other side of the road is the Sanctuary, formerly a double circle of stones linked to Avebury by a stone avenue.

WALK 8

Some of the stones that formed this processional avenue survive beside the lane between West Kennett and Avebury.

Walk along the enclosed track opposite, continue downhill along the right edge of a field and in the bottom corner follow the field edge round to the left to a footpath sign. Turn right through a gap, cross a bridge over the River Kennet and continue along a tarmac drive to a lane. Keep ahead but after a few yards turn right **D** at a wall corner along an enclosed path, which leads to a lane. Here turn right through the village of East Kennett and just before the lane crosses the river, turn left along a track.

At a junction of tracks and paths, keep straight ahead along a tree-lined track for a few yards , then turn right **E** on to a path enclosed by trees, with a wire fence on the right. Climb a stile and walk along the left edge of a field, following the field edge as it bears to the left. Climb a stile at the far end, cross a tarmac track and continue along the track ahead. Where it ends, keep along the right edge of a field and, in the field corner, go through a gap on to a well-surfaced path **F**.

The route continues ahead but turn left and head gently uphill in order to visit West Kennett Long Barrow. This stone-chambered tomb, dating from around 3700 BC, is the largest burial chamber in England, nearly 350ft (107m) long. The three huge stones at the entrance were probably placed there when the tomb was sealed up.

As you retrace your steps downhill, the view is dominated by the imposing bulk of Silbury Hill. Follow the path to the left, turn right through a metal kissing gate and cross a bridge over the river. Keep ahead and go through another metal kissing gate on to the A4. Turn left and soon after crossing the River Kennet again you arrive at Silbury Hill, the largest man-made mound in Europe, 130ft (40m) high and covering an area of over 5 acres. So well built was it that there has hardly been any erosion over a period of nearly 5000 years. However, investigations and excavations have failed to find out the exact purpose of this incredible feat of construction, which remains one of the great mysteries of prehistory.

Walk back along the road and just after re-crossing the river, turn left over a stile to continue along the left edge of a field, by a wire fence and later the river on the left. Follow the Kennet back to Avebury, negotiating a number of stiles and gates. On reaching a road, turn right and almost immediately left into the car park.

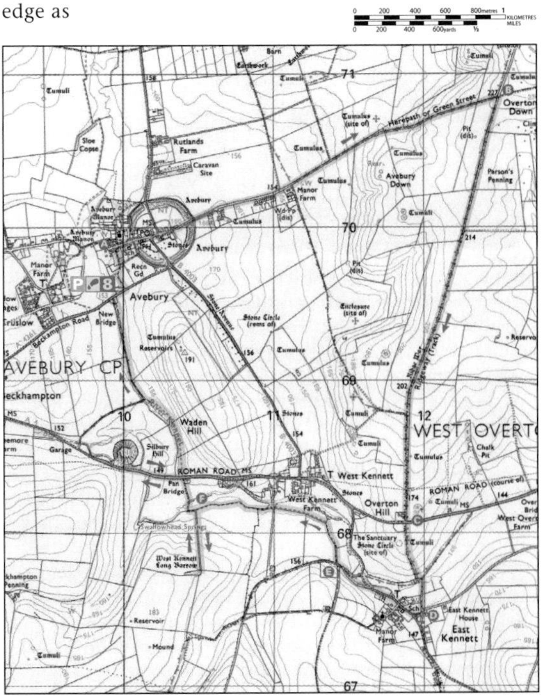

constructed but shed little light on its purpose. Theories include a burial place for King Sil and his horse and a hiding place for a large gold statue built by the Devil on his way to Devizes. Scholarship generally favours the first.

Silbury Hill

Avebury

6 miles W of Marlborough on the A4361

A 28-acre World Heritage Site is the centre of the **Avebury Stone Circles**, the most remarkable ritual megalithic monuments in Europe (see panel below). Many of the archaeological finds from the site are displayed in Avebury's **Alexander Keiller Museum**, which also describes the restoration of the site by Keiller in the 1930s.

Avebury has a gem from Elizabethan times in **Avebury Manor**, which stands on the site of a 12th century priory. The house and its four-acre walled garden, which features a wishing well, topiary, a rose garden and an Italian walk, are owned by the National Trust. Open daily except Monday and Thursday.

Avebury Stone Circles

Avebury, Wiltshire

A 28-acre World Heritage Site is the centre of the **Avebury Stone Circles**, the most remarkable ritual megalithic monuments in Europe. A massive bank and ditch enclose an outer circle and two inner circles of stones. The outer circle of almost 100 sarsen stones (sand and silica) enclose two rings with about 40 stones still standing. Archaeologists working on the site found the remains of a long-vanished avenue of stones leading south towards Beckhampton.

This discovery seems to vindicate the theory of the 18th century antiquary William Stukeley, who made drawings of the stone circles with this avenue marked. The stones in the avenue had disappeared so completely (perhaps destroyed out of some superstition in the Middle Ages) that few believed Stukeley. The research team from Southampton, Leicester and Newport Universities uncovered a series of subterranean features which appear to be buried stones and the sockets in which they were set. Two large stones, known as Adam and Eve, had always been known about on this route, but there were no further traces until the team's discoveries in 1999.

The **Avebury Stones** bear testimony to the enormous human effort that went into their construction: some of the individual stones weigh 40 tons and all had to dragged from Marlborough Downs. The Avebury stones are in two basic shapes, which have been equated with male and female and have led to the theory that the site was used for the observance of fertility rites.

Great Bedwyn

6 miles SE of Marlborough off the A4

In the chancel of the 11th century Church of St Mary the Virgin is the tomb of Sir John Seymour, the father of Henry VIII's

The Harrow Inn

Little Bedwyn, Nr Marlborough, Wiltshire SN8 3JP
Tel/Fax: 01672 870871 e-mail: dining@harrowinn.co.uk
website:www.harrowinn.co.uk

Roger Jones and his wife Sue took over the **Harrow Inn** in 1998 and turned it from a quiet country local alehouse-cum-post office into a mecca for lovers of good food and good wine. Roger made his name in London and now attracts a clientele from near and far to enjoy fine dining in a charming setting in the Wiltshire countryside off the A4 or A338 southwest of Hungerford. On a corner site on the outskirts of the village, the Michelin-recommended inn is an angular building with a chequered brick facade, and inside are several separate dining areas with wine-coloured walls, gentle lighting, well-chosen prints and immaculate table settings.

Roger's daily changing menu is a tour de force, a tempting succession of dishes distinguished by fine fresh flavours and novel combinations. Everything on the menu is sure to get the gastric juices flowing, and seafood dishes always feature prominently: grilled squid with spiced prawn stuffing and chilli jam; medallions of monkfish Madras with a pea and mint purée, fillet of turbot with seared scallops and a ragout of wild mushrooms. Game comes to the fore in its season with such dishes as warm salad of snipe with black pudding, or roast woodcock with a Pedro Ximenez reduction and parsnip wafers. The outstanding food is complemented by a magnificent wine list that contains real treasures at realistic prices. The Harrow has exclusive deals with many top growers, and the value is obtained by dealing not through wine merchants but directly with importers or vineyards. Closed Sunday evening, Monday and Tuesday.

third wife Jane. Nearby is **Lloyds Stone Museum**, a monument to the skills of the English stonemason. Among the items on display are an assortment of tombstones and a stone aeroplane with an 11ft wingspan. A mile or so north of Great Bedwyn lies the tiny village of Little Bedwyn.

Crofton

6 miles SE of Marlborough off the A338

The eastern end of the Vale of Pewsey carries the London-Penzance railway and the Kennet and Avon Canal, which reaches its highest point near Crofton. The site is marked by a handsome Georgian pumping station which houses the renowned **Crofton Beam Engines**. These engines - the 1812 Boulton & Watt and the 1845 Harvey of Hayle - have been superbly restored under the guidance of the Canal trust. The 1812 engine is the oldest working beam engine in the world, still in its original building and still doing its original job of pumping water to the summit level of the Canal. Both engines are steamed from a hand-stoked, coal-fired Lancashire boiler. The brick chimney has also been restored, to its original height of 82 feet.

Wilton

8 miles SE of Marlborough off the A338

A footpath of about a mile links the Crofton Beam Engines with Wilton. This is the smaller of the two Wiltshire Wiltons and is the site of the **Wilton Windmill**. This traditional working mill, the only one operating in the county, was built in 1821 after the Canal Company has taken the water out of the River Bedwyn for their canal, thereby depriving the water mills of the power to drive their mills. The mill worked until 1920, when the availability of steam power and electricity literally took the wind out its sails. After standing derelict for 50 years the mill was restored at a cost of £25,000 and is now looked after by the Wilton Windmill Society. This superb old mill is floodlit from dusk until 10pm, making a wonderful sight on a chalk ridge 550 feet above sea level.

CLENCH COMMON
2 miles S of Marlborough on the A345

This is a lovely part of the world for walking or cycling. The Forestry Commission's West Woods, particularly notable for bluebells in May, has a picnic site, and nearby is Martinsell Hill topped by an ancient fort.

WOOTTON RIVERS
4 miles S of Marlborough off the A345

An attractive village with a real curiosity in its highly unusual church clock. The **Jack Sprat Clock** was built by a local

man from an assortment of scrap metal, including old bicycles, prams and farm tools, to mark the coronation of King George V in 1911. It has 24 different chimes and its face has letters instead of numbers.

ALTON BARNES AND ALTON PRIORS
6 miles SW of Marlborough off the A345

The largest **White Horse** in Wiltshire can be seen on the hillside above Alton Barnes; cut in 1812, it is 54 metres high and 51 metres long and is visible from Old Sarum, 20 miles away. According to the local story the original contractor ran off with the £20 advance payment and the work was carried out by one Robert Pile, who owned the land. The runaway contractor was later arrested and hanged for a string of offences. Other notable Wiltshire White Horses in the locality are at Hackpen, just north of Marlborough (cut to commemorate

WESTCOURT BOTTOM

Burbage, Marlborough, Wiltshire SN8 3BW Tel: 01672 810924
e-mail: westcourt.b-and-b@virgin.net website: www.westcourtbottom.co.uk

Bill and Felicity Mather offer Bed & Breakfast accommodation of exceptional style and quality at **Westcourt Bottom**, their large 17th century thatched cottage on the edge of Burbage, five miles south of Marlborough. The three bedrooms are spacious, very comfortable and full of character, with half-timbers among the many eyecatching original features and hairdryers, coffee, tea and biscuits. The log fire sitting room, with tv for guests, is equally appealing, and guests also have the use of a large, beautiful garden with a swimming pool.

The atmosphere throughout is relaxed and informal, and the cottage is an ideal place to unwind and a perfect base from which to explore the surrounding area on foot, by cycle or by car. Savernake Forest is very close by, on the other side of the Kennet & Avon Canal, and also just a leisurely walk away are two legacies of past industrial times, the Wilton Windmill and the Crofton Beam Engines. Stonehenge, the Avebury Circles and the West Kennet Long Barrow are all within an easy drive. A full English breakfast with free-range produce and home-made bread, jam and juices starts the day at Westcourt Bottom, and local pubs offer a good selection of both lunch and evening meals.

Queen Victoria's coronation) and at Pewsey (see below). To the north of Alton Barnes, high up on a chalk ridge, are the remains of three prehistoric hill forts, Knap Hill, Adam's Grave and Rybury.

Pewsey

7 miles S of Marlborough on the A345

In the heart of the beautiful valley that bears its name, this is a charming village of half-timbered houses and thatched cottages. It was once the personal property of Alfred the Great, and a statue of the king stands at the crossroads in the centre. The parish church, built on a foundation of sarsen stones, has an unusual altar rail made from timbers taken from the *San Josef*, a ship captured by Nelson in 1797.

Attractions for the visitor include the old wharf area and the **Heritage Centre**. In an 1870 foundry building it contains an interesting collection of old and unusual machine tools and farm machinery. The original **Pewsey White Horse**, south of the village on Pewsey Down, was cut in 1785, apparently including a rider, but was redesigned by a Mr George Marples and cut by the Pewsey Fire Brigade to celebrate the coronation of King George VI. **Pewsey Carnival** takes place each September, and the annual Devizes to Westminster canoe race passes through **Pewsey Wharf**.

A minor road runs past the White Horse across Pewsey Down to the isolated village of **Everleigh**, where the Church of St Peter is of unusual iron-framed construction. Rebuilt on a new site in 1813, it has a short chancel and narrow nave, an elegant west gallery and a neo-medieval hammerbeam roof.

DEVIZES

At the western edge of the Vale of Pewsey, Devizes is the central market town of Wiltshire. The town was founded in 1080 by Bishop Osmund, nephew of William the Conqueror. The bishop was responsible for building a timber castle between the lands of two powerful manors, and this act brought about the town's name, which is derived from the Latin ad divisas, or 'at the boundaries'. After the wooden structure burnt down, Roger, Bishop of Sarum, built a stone castle in 1138 that survived until the end of the Civil War, when it was demolished. Bishop Roger also built two fine churches in Devizes. Long Street is

Devizes Castle

The Healthy Life

4 Little Brittox, Devizes, Wiltshire SN10 1AR
Tel: 01380 725558 Fax: 01380 727772
e-mail: health@thehealthylife.co.uk
website: www.thehealthylife.co.uk

The denizens of Devizes are lucky to have a quite outstanding natural food shop and café owned and run by two experts in their fields, and located in a pedestrianised area in the centre of town. Peter Vaughan, graduate of the Academy of Culinary Arts and qualified in nutrition and herbalism, specialises in 'body-friendly' food and has made frequent broadcasts on radio and television. In 1999 he opened **The Healthy Life** with Judith Dain, whose expertise includes the link between diet and behaviour. In the food shop, a good selection of products are available, many of which are ethically sourced, organic or biodynamic, along with a fresh takeaway section, and a range of supplements, herbal remedies and skin-friendly toiletries.

Healthy light lunches are served in the upstairs café, which in the evening becomes a private dining room where groups of between 8 and 25 can enjoy a fine dining experience with three balanced courses prepared by Peter and complemented by The Healthy Life wines and a selection of organic beers. For parties of fewer than eight a number of evenings each month are set aside for public bookings, and regular cookery demonstrations give parties of 12 or more the chance to learn the secrets of Peter's recipes and to have all their culinary questions answered.

Urban Rustics

No.1 Old Swan Yard, Devizes, Wiltshire SN10 1AT
Tel/Fax: 01380 725593
e-mail: chrispoyser@genie.co.uk
website: www.urbanrustics.co.uk

Take a brother and sister team, place in a small period shop in the centre of a delightful Wiltshire market town, add an eclectic choice of home accessories - and you have **Urban Rustics**. In Old Swan Yard, a small complex of niche retailers, Kate Filby and Christopher Poyser have combined an individual and closely edited collection of furniture, lighting and lifestyle accessories from Scandinavia, France and the Far East with the best of home-grown collections from the likes of Cath Kidston, Wallace Saks, Ella Doran and Ever Trading.

The result is a dynamic mix of goodies with a focus on clean, contemporary design and integrity of materials, a look that is both influenced by fashion and beyond it. Whether the item sought is a linen tablecloth, a Mongolian lamb love rug, the latest uber-hip CD from the likes of Claude Challe of Buddha Bar fame, ironically kitsch clasp purse or the severest of glass vases, the siblings have most bases covered. Staffed by just the two of them, and on two floors, the shop has a relaxed, welcoming and completely informal ambience where locals often swing by to swap gossip, pick up pressies and catch up with the latest deliveries. Service is friendly, personal and downright cheeky, with free gift wrapping offered as a matter of course. In short, Urban Rustics is the perfect attitude-free zone in which to indulge in a little hardcore retail therapy - proof, if proof were needed, that civilisation does indeed extend beyond the M25.

lined with elegant Georgian houses and also contains the **Wiltshire Heritage Museum**, which has a splendid collection of artefacts from the area, and an art gallery with a John Piper window and regularly changing exhibitions.

Devizes Visitor Centre offers a unique insight into the town. The Centre is based on a 12th century castle and takes visitors back to medieval times, when Devizes was home to the finest castle in Europe and the scene of anarchy and unrest during the struggles between Empress Matilda and King Stephen. An interactive exhibition shows how the town came to be at the centre of the 12th century Civil War and thrived as a medieval town, many traces of which remain today, and on into the present.

Many more of the town's finest buildings are situated in and around the old market place, including the Town Hall and the Corn Exchange. Also here is an unusual **market cross** inscribed with the story of Ruth Pierce, a market stall-holder who stood accused, in 1753, of swindling her customers. When an ugly crowd gathered round her, she stood and pleaded her innocence, adding "May I be struck dead if I am lying". A rash move, as she fell to the ground and died forthwith.

Devizes stands at a key point on the Kennet & Avon Canal, and the **Kennet and Avon Canal Museum** tells the complete story of the canal in fascinating detail. Many visitors combine a trip to the museum with a walk along the towpath, which is a public footpath. The route of the canal involved overcoming the rise of 237 feet from the Avon Valley to Devizes. The engineer John Rennie devised the solution, which was to build one vast flight of locks, 29 in all of which 16 were set very close together down Caen Hill. The **Devizes Locks** Discovery Trail descends from Devizes Wharf, through the town and to the bottom of the flight at Lower Foxhangers, returning by way of open countryside and the village of Rowde. Each July the Canalfest, a weekend of family fun designed to raise funds for the upkeep of the canal, is held at the Wharf, which is also the start point of the annual Devizes-Westminster canoe race held every year on Good Friday.

AROUND DEVIZES

Bishops Cannings

4 miles NE of Devizes on the A361

The bishops of Salisbury once owned a manor here and built the very grand parish church before they started work on the Cathedral. This church, dedicated to St Mary, has often been likened to the Cathedral and does indeed bear some resemblance, notably in its tall, tapering spire. This is Moonraker country, and according to legend a group of 17th century smugglers from Bishops Canning fooled excisemen when caught recovering dumped brandy kegs from a pond known as the Crammer. The smugglers pretended to be mad and claimed that the moon's reflection on the pond was actually a cheese, which they were trying to rake in. The ruse worked, so who were the real fools? A hollow in the downs west of the village was the scene of a bloody Civil War battle in 1643, when the Royalist forces under Prince Rupert's brother Maurice defeated the Parliamentarian forces at Roundway Down. According to a local legend the cries of the dead can be heard coming from a burial ditch on the anniversary of the battle (July 13).

Market Lavington

5 miles S of Devizes on the B3098

The 'Village under the Plain' is home to a little museum in the former

STEAM - Museum Of The Great Western Railway

Kemble Drive, Swindon, Wiltshire SN2 2TA
Tel: 01793 466646 Fax: 01793 466615
website: www.steam-museum.org.uk

The award-winning **STEAM, the Museum of the Great Western Railway**, is located in a beautifully restored building at the heart of Swindon Railway Works, where for nearly 150 years thousands of men and women worked for the Great Western Railway. The main activity was the building of great steam locomotives, the last being 92220 *Evening Star*, one of a fleet of powerful 2-10-0 freight engines which were destined to have all too short a working life. The star of the show in the Museum is 6000 *King George V*, which stands in a platform at the head of the 'Bristolian' express. Visitors can climb aboard the footplate of this marvellous thoroughbred and relive the glory days of 'God's Wonderful Railway'. Another of the great GWR locomotives was the Castle class, and here visitors can actually walk underneath *Caerphilly Castle* as it stands in its inspection pit.

The sounds, sights and smells of the railway works live on in the workshops, where locomotives and carriages are restored, and one section of this fascinating place contains GWR accessories and road vehicles, including the famous Scammell 'mechanical horse', which could turn on a sixpence but sometimes had a mind of its own. The great figure of early railway days was the engineer Isambard Kingdom Brunel, whose story is told together with that of the thousands of less famous workers, from the navvies to drivers, signalmen and station masters, who built and operated the railway. There are many hands-on opportunities to relive the action, from building bridges to working the signals, shunting the wagons and driving the steam trains, and special events and family activities are held regularly throughout the year.

All areas of the Museum are accessible to wheelchairs, and visitors who run out of steam can relax awhile in the stylish balcony café, open daily for drinks, cakes, pastries and light lunches. In the Steam Shop, an impressive range of GWR and railway gifts, books and souvenirs is for sale. A short walk from STEAM Museum is the Railway Village Museum, whose exhibits include a restored Victorian railway worker's cottage. STEAM Museum is open every day, the Railway Village Museum from Easter to the end of October. STEAM was funded by a partnership that brought together the Heritage Lottery Fund, Swindon Borough Council, Carillion Development Management and BAA McArthurGlen.

schoolmaster's cottage behind the old village school. Displays at **Market Lavington Museum** include a Victorian kitchen and archive photographs.

SWINDON

Think Swindon, think the Great Western Railway. Think GWR, think Isambard Kingdom Brunel. The largest town in Wiltshire, lying in the northeast corner between the Cotswolds and the Marlborough Downs, was an insignificant agricultural community before the railway line between London and Bristol was completed in 1835. Swindon Station opened in that year, but it was some time later, in 1843, that Brunel, the GWR's principal engineer, decided that Swindon was the place to build his locomotive works. Within a few years it had grown to be one of the largest in the world, with as many as 12,000 on a 320-acre site that incorporated the Railway Village; this was a model development of 300 workmen's houses built of limestone extracted from the construction of Box Tunnel. This unique example of early-Victorian town planning is open to the public as the **Railway Village Museum**, with a restored Victorian railway worker's cottage. Lit by gas, the cottage contains many original fittings such as the range and copper in the kitchen.

The Great Western Railway Museum (see panel opposite) moved from the same site in Faringdon Road in the autumn of 1999 to a new home in the former GWR works in Kemble Drive, with a new name, a great deal more space and a host of new interactive exhibits. **STEAM** has the collection of locomotives (the stars are 6000 *King George V*, heading The Bristolian in the station platform, and the Castle class *Caerphilly Castle*), nameplates, signalling equipment and an exhibition of the life and achievements of Brunel; it also focuses on the human aspect of a hard industry, telling the story of the men and women who built and repaired the locomotives and carriages of the GWR (God's Wonderful Railway) for seven generations. The last locomotive to be built at the works was 92220 *Evening Star*, a powerful 2-10-0 freight engine of a type that proved surprisingly versatile but were destined to have all too short a working life. Engineering work continued on the site until 1986, when the works finally closed. STEAM has a Café and a shop with an impressive range of GWR and other railway gifts, books, souvenirs and pocket-money toys. It's family-friendly, and all areas are fully accessible to wheelchairs. The site now also contains the **National Monuments Record Centre** - the public archive of the Royal Commission on the Historical Monuments of England, with 7 million photographs, documents and texts.

There's lots more to Swindon than the legacy of the GWR: it's a bustling and successful commercial town with excellent shopping and leisure facilities and plenty of open spaces. One such is **Coate Water Country Park** on the Marlborough road. In an elegant early-19th century house on the Bath Road, **Swindon Museum & Art Gallery** contains a variety of displays on the history, archaeology and geology of the town and the surrounding area and also houses a fine collection of 20th century British art

AROUND SWINDON

LATTON

7 miles NW of Swindon on the A419

A lovely old village with some delightful 17th century Cotswold-stone cottages and

Robert Mullis Rocking Horse Maker

55 Berkeley Road, Wroughton, Swindon, Wiltshire SN4 9BN
Tel: 01793 813583 Fax: 01793 813577
e-mail: robert@rockinghorses.freeserve.co.uk
website: www.rockinghorsemaker.com

Robert Mullis, Rocking Horse Maker, is a man dedicated to the craft of making wooden rocking horses which are both wonderful reminders of a bygone age and unique testimonies to up-to-the-minute craftsmanship. Robert was apprenticed to a long-established form of Wiltshire agricultural contractors in the village of his birth, where he acquired a love of timbers and the knowledge of woodworking techniques which he has put to excellent use in his craft ever since. That craft developed from a single rocking horse which he made simply 'for something to do' into a thriving business that produces rocking horses to individual requirements for a worldwide market. The first stage in the creation of these splendid creatures is the careful selection of timber - ash, beech, walnut, oak, American tulipwood, utile or whatever the customer specifies. The hand of the master craftsman transforms the blocks into the horse. Each horse is unique, characterised by a painstaking attention to detail, from the choice of the finest horse hair to specialist glass eyes and genuine leather for the tack. There are two styles - the Georgian-style bow rocker and the later Victorian style with safety stand - and three finishes: modern dapple grey, antiqued dapple grey or polished. A choice of sizes, hair colour, stirrups, saddle and tack means that every horse is truly the customer's own. And it doesn't stop at horses, as special commissions are undertaken for all sorts of whimsical and fantasy creatures.

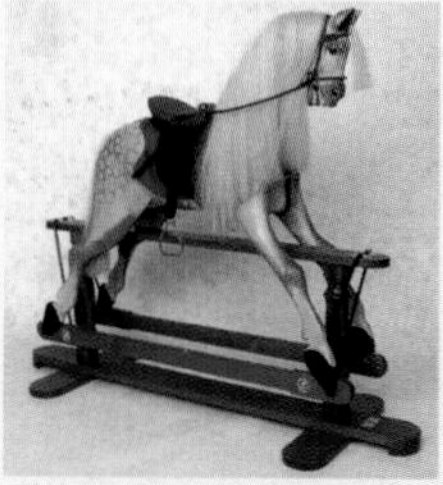

Robert Mullis Restoration Services Ltd

55 Berkeley Road, Wroughton, Swindon, Wiltshire SN4 9BN
Tel: 01793 813583 Fax: 01793 813577
e-mail: robert@rockinghorses.freeserve.co.uk
website: www.rockinghorsemaker.com

Robert Mullis is a master craftsman who has turned his skills to the manufacture of beautiful wooden rocking horses, but in his workshop in Wroughton he also runs a thriving business restoring these splendid creatures, many of them cherished family treasures. A fair percentage of the horses arrive looking forlorn and neglected but they leave looking fresh, bright-eyed and ready to bring joy to generations ahead. Few, if any, horses are completely beyond repair, and for Robert no commission is too small nor any challenge too great. And the same skill and pride that go into the making of his own horses are applied to the rebuilding or refurbishment of horses who have seen better days; the same time-honoured techniques and materials - gesso and glue, horse hair, polish and paint, carefully mixed and applied, transform his charges and give them a new lease of life.

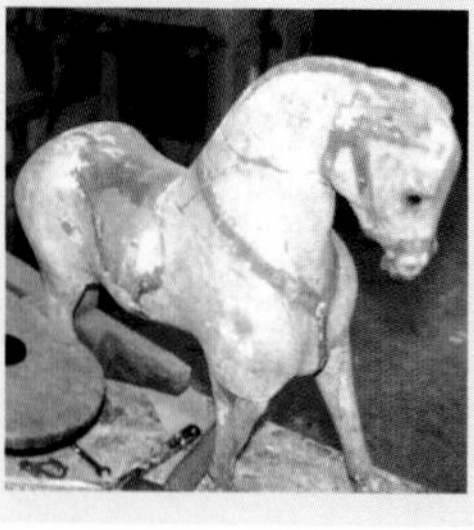

If the time comes when a restored horse needs a companion Robert Mullis will always be happy to discuss a new commission, perhaps in the style of the restored horse. The workshop is located in the village of Wroughton, which lies three miles south of Swindon on the A4361. Other local attractions include country parks, a nature reserve and the National Museum of Science and Industry at Wroughton Airfield, but for anyone who appreciates the highest standards of craftsmanship there's only one Robert Mullis.

larger Victorian houses. It was once an important junction of the **Wiltshire & Berkshire** and **Thames & Severn Canals**.

Cricklade

6 miles N of Swindon off the A419

The only Wiltshire town on the Thames was an important post on the Roman Ermin Street and had its own mint in Saxon times. There are many buildings of interest, notably the Church of St Sampson, with its cathedral-like four-spired tower, where a festival of music takes place each September; the famous school founded by the London goldsmith Robert Jenner in 1651; and the fancy Victorian clock tower. **Cricklade Museum** contains displays on social history, Roman occupation, Rotten Borough elections and an archive of 2,000 photographs. **Rotten Borough** was the name given to depopulated electoral districts, which retained their original representation, maintained either by the Crown or by local aristocratic patrons to control seats. Just before they were largely abolished by the far-reaching Reform Act of 1832, 140 of the 658 seats in Parliament were Rotten, of which 50 had fewer than 50 voters. The Reform Act also extended the franchise, but even after it was passed the total electorate in the country was less than a million. Nearby **North Meadow** is a National Nature Reserve where the rare snakeshead fritillary grows. Cricklade is the centre of the Cricklade Corridor Trust set up to secure the maximum economic, heritage, leisure and environmental benefits from a number of projects between Swindon and Cricklade and beyond. These include railway and canal restoration, nature conservation and the development of a branch of the National Cycle Network.

Highworth

5 miles NE of Swindon on the A361

The name is appropriate, as the village stands at the top of a 400ft incline, and the view from **Highworth Hill** takes in the counties of Wiltshire, Gloucestershire and Oxfordshire. There are some very fine 17th and 18th century buildings round the old square, and the parish church is of interest: built in the 15th century, it was fortified during the Civil War and was attacked soon after by Parliamentarian forces under Fairfax. One of the cannonballs which struck it, is on display outside. The church contains a memorial to Lieutenant Warneford, who was awarded the VC for destroying the first enemy Zeppelin in 1915.

Wroughton

3 miles S of Swindon on the A4361

Wroughton Airfield, with its historic Second World War hangars, is home to the **National Museum of Science and Industry's** superb collections, including Air Transport and Aviation, Land Transport and Agriculture, Radar and Firefighting Equipment.

Nearby **Clouts Wood Nature Reserve** is a lovely place for a ramble, and a short drive south, by the Ridgeway, is the site of **Barbury Castle**, one of the most spectacular Iron Age forts in southern England. The open hillside was the scene of a bloody battle between the Britons and the Saxons in the 6th century; the Britons lost and the Saxon kingdom of Wessex was established under King Cealwin. The area around the castle is a country park.

Broad Hinton

5 miles S of Swindon off the A4361

In the church at Broad Hinton is a memorial to local bigwig Sir Thomas Wroughton, who returned home from hunting to find his wife reading the Bible instead of making his tea. He seized the Bible and flung it into the fire; his wife retrieved it but in doing so severely burnt her hands. As punishment for his blasphemy Sir Thomas's hands and those of his four children withered away (very hard on the children, surely). The monument shows the whole handless family and a Bible with a corner burnt off.

Clyffe Pypard

6 miles W of Swindon off the A4361

Only traces remain of this medieval village remain. Sir Nikolaus Pevsner, the renowned architectural historian, lived nearby and is buried in the churchyard.

Lydiard Tregoze

2 miles W of Swindon off the A3102

On the western outskirts of Swindon, **Lydiard Park** is the ancestral home of the Viscounts Bolingbroke. The park is a delightful place to explore, and the house, one of Wiltshire's smaller stately homes, is a real gem, described by Sir Hugh Casson as "a gentle Georgian house, sunning itself as serenely as an old grey cat". Chief attractions inside include the little blue Dressing Room devoted to the 18th century society artist Lady Diana Spencer, who became the 2nd Viscountess Bolingbroke. St Mary's Church, next to the house, contains many monuments to the St John family, who lived here from Elizabethan times. The most striking is the **Golden Cavalier**, a life-size gilded effigy of Edward St John in full battledress (he was killed at the 2nd Battle of Newbury in 1645).

Wootton Bassett

3 miles W of Swindon off the A3102

A small town with a big history. Records go back to the 7th century, and in 1219 King Henry lll granted a market charter

(the market is still held every Wednesday). The first known mayor of Wootton Bassett was John Woolmonger, appointed in 1408. A later mayor was acting as town magistrate when a drunk was brought before him after an overnight drinking spree. When asked by the mayor whether he pleaded guilty to drunkenness, the man said "You knows your worship was just as drunk as I was" (he was on the same spree). "Ah well", said the mayor. "That was different. Now I am the mayor and I am going to fine you five shillings."

The most remarkable building in Wootton is the **Old Town Hall**, which stands on a series of stone pillars, leaving an open-sided ground-floor area that once served as a covered market. The museum above, open on Saturday mornings, contains a rare ducking stool, silver maces and a mayoral sword of office.

A section of the **Wilts & Berks Canal** has been restored at **Templars Fir**. In May 1998 about 50 boats of all kinds were launched on the canal and a day of festivities was enjoyed by all. The railway station, alas, has not been revived after falling under the Beeching axe in 1966.

CHIPPENHAM

This historic settlement on the banks of the Avon was founded around 600 by the Saxon king Cyppa. It became an important administrative centre in King Alfred's time and later gained further prominence from the wool trade. It was a major stop on the London-Bristol coaching run and is served by the railway between the same two cities. Buildings of note include the Church of St Andrew (mainly 15th century) and the half-timbered Hall, once used by the burgesses and bailiffs of the Chippenham Hundred. The new **Chippenham Museum and Heritage Centre** in the Market Place tells the story of the town from the Jurassic onwards, and the displays focus on Saxon Chippenham, Alfred the Great, Brunel's railway, the celebrated cheese market, Victorian living conditions and Chippenham curiosities. At Hardenhuish Hall on the edge of town, John Wood the Younger of Bath fame built the Church of St Nicholas; completed in 1779, it is notable for its domed steeple and elegant Venetian windows.

In the flood plain to the east of Chippenham stands the 4½ mile footpath known as **Maud Heath's Causeway**. This remarkable and ingenious walkway consisting of 64 brick and stone arches was built at the end of the 15th century at the bequest of Maud Heath, who spent most of her life as a market trader trudging her often muddy way between her village of Bremhill and Chippenham. She died a relatively wealthy woman, and the land and property she left in her will provided sufficient funds for the upkeep of the causeway, which is best seen near the hamlet of Kellaways. A statue of Maud, basket in hand, stands overlooking the flood plain at Wick Hill.

AROUND CHIPPENHAM

Calne

5 miles E of Chippenham on the A4

A former weaving centre in the valley of the River Marden; the prominent wool church reflects the prosperity of earlier times. One of the memorials in the church is to Dr Ingenhousz, who is widely credited with creating a smallpox vaccination before Jenner, and another remembers the King of the Gypsies, who died of smallpox in 1774. Dr Joseph

Bowood House

Priestley, who discovered oxygen, lived on The Green.

A short distance from Calne, to the west, stands **Bowood House**, built in 1625 and now a treasury of Shelborne family heirlooms, paintings, books and furniture. In the Bowood Laboratory Dr Joseph Priestley, tutor to the 1st Marquess of Lansdowne's son, conducted experiments that resulted in the identification of oxygen. The house is set in lovely Capability Brown grounds with a lake and terraced garden. The mausoleum was commissioned in 1761 by the Dowager Countess of Shelborne as a memorial to her husband and was Robert Adam's first work for them. A separate woodland garden of 60 acres, with azaleas and rhododendrons, is open from late April to early June.

The **Atwell Motor Museum**, on the A4 east of Calne, has a collection of over 70 vintage and classic cars and motorcycles from the years 1924 to 1983.

Lacock

4 miles S of Chippenham on the A350

The National Trust village of Lacock is one of the country's real treasures. The quadrangle of streets - East, High, West and Church - holds a delightful assortment of mellow stone buildings, and the period look (no intrusive power cables or other modern-day eyesores) keeps it in great demand as a film location. Every building is a well-restored, well-preserved gem, and overlooking everything is **Lacock Abbey**, founded in 1232 by Ela, Countess of Salisbury in memory of her husband William Longsword, stepbrother to Richard the Lionheart. In common with all monastic houses Lacock was dissolved by Henry Vlll, but the original cloisters, chapter houses, sacristy and kitchens survive.

Much of the remainder of what we see today dates from the mid 16th century, when the abbey was acquired by Sir William Sharington. He added an impressive country house and the elegant octagonal tower that overlooks the Avon. The estate next passed into the hands of the Talbot family, who held it for 370 years before ceding it to the National Trust in 1944.

The most distinguished member of the Talbot family was the pioneering photographer William Henry Fox Talbot, who carried out his experiments in the 1830s, mainly at the Abbey. The **Fox Talbot Museum** commemorates the life and achievements of a man who was not just a photographer but a mathematician, physicist, classicist, philologist and transcriber of Syrian and Chaldean cuneiform. In 1839 William Henry Fox Talbot presented to the Royal Society 'an account of the art of photogenic drawing or the process by which natural objects may be made to delineate themselves without the aid of the artist's pencil' - photography, in short. Louis Daguerre was at the same

Lacock Abbey

time demonstrating a similar technique in France, and it is not certain which of the two pioneers should be called the father of photography. But it was indisputably true that Fox Talbot invented the positive/negative process that permitted multiple copies. The Museum is located in an old barn at the entrance to the Abbey and contains Fox Talbot memorabilia and a collection of early cameras. Fox Talbot also remodelled the south elevation of the abbey and added three new oriel windows. One of the world's earliest photographs shows a detail of a latticed oriel window of the abbey; the size of a postage stamp, it is the earliest known example of a photographic negative.

Trowbridge

13 miles S of Chippenham on the A350

The county of town of Wiltshire, and another major weaving centre in its day. A large number of industrial buildings still stand, and the Town Council and Civic Society have devised an interesting walk that takes in many of them. The Trowbridge Museum, located in the town's last working woollen mill, has a variety of interesting displays, including a reconstructed medieval castle and tableaux of a weaver's cottage and Taylor's drapery shop. It also features some working textile looms. The chancel of the parish church of St James, crowned by one of the finest spires in the county, contains the tomb of the poet and former rector George Crabbe, who wrote the work on which Benjamin Britten based his opera *Peter Grimes*. Trowbridge's most famous son was Isaac Pitman, the shorthand man, who was born in Nash Yard in 1813.

Corsham

3 miles SW of Chippenham off the A4

Pevsner was very much taken with Corsham, asserting that it had no match in Wiltshire for the wealth of good houses. The town's prosperity was based on the two main industries of cloth-weaving and stone-quarrying. **Corsham Court**, based on an Elizabethan house of 1582, was bought by Paul Methuen in 1745 and later housed his inherited collection of paintings. The present house and grounds are chiefly the work of John Nash, Capability Brown, Thomas Bellamy and Humphry Repton, a top-pedigree setting for the treasures within, which include paintings by Caravaggio, Fra Filippo Lippi, Reynolds, Rubens and Van Dyck and furniture by Chippendale. The house has been used as the location for several films, including *Northanger Abbey* and *Remains of the Day*. Among other important buildings in Corsham are Almshouses erected in 1668 by Dame Margaret Hungerford, the old market house (town hall) and a row of 17th century Flemish weavers' cottages. Mansion House, now a youth centre, was the home of Robert Neale, a leading clothier and sometime MP for Wootton Bassett. His firm produced the red coats worn by the Duke of Wellington's troops. The parish church, St Bartholomew's, contains tombs and memorials to some of Corsham's eminent clothiers, and also the famous flat-stone grave of Sarah Jarvis, who died in 1753 at the age of 107 having grown a third set of teeth! A unique attraction is the **Underground Quarry Centre**, the only shaft stone mine in the world open to the public. Opened in 1810, it is reached by 159 steps, and helmets, lamps and a guide are provided for a fascinating tour that tells the story of Bath stone from rock face to architectural heritage.

Box

6 miles SW of Chippenham on the A4

Bath stone is still quarried at this delightful spot, which is best known for one of the most remarkable engineering feats of its time, **Box Tunnel**. The 1.8 mile railway tunnel took five years to excavate and when completed in 1841 was the longest such tunnel in the world. According to local legend the sun shines through its entire length on only one occasion each year - sunrise on April 9, the birthday of its genius creator Isambard Kingdom Brunel.

Melksham

7 miles S of Chippenham on the A350

Once an important weaving centre, Melksham was also very briefly in vogue as a spa town. It didn't make much of a splash, being overshadowed by its near neighbour Bath, so it turned to manufacturing and was given a boost when the Wiltshire & Berkshire Canal was opened. The canal, built between 1795 and 1810, linked the Kennet and Avon Canal with Abingdon, on the Thames. The Wilts & Berks was abandoned in 1914, but much of its path still exists in the form of lock and bridge remains, towpaths and embankments.

Holt

9 miles SW of Chippenham on the B3107

The village was once a small spa, and the old mineral well can still be seen in a factory in the village. Right at the heart of the village is **The Courts**, a National Trust English country garden of mystery with unusual topiary, ponds, water gardens and an arboretum; the garden is mainly the work of Sir George Hastings and was created in the reign of Edward VII. The house, where local weavers came to settle disputes until the end of the 18th century, is not open to the public.

Moorlands

The Coach House, Station Approach, Melksham, Wiltshire SN12 8BN
Tel/Fax: 01225 702155
e-mail: moorlandsnet@aol.com website: www.moorlandsuk.co.uk

Owner Jacky Moore offers self-catering holiday accommodation at **Moorlands**, in four single storey cottages built to the highest traditional standards. Sleeping either two or four, they are beautifully furnished and equipped, with fitted carpets, double glazing and heating; each has either one or two bedrooms, a bathroom, a comprehensively equipped kitchen, and a lounge/dining area with patio doors looking out on to a secluded garden. A coin-operated laundry and a payphone are on site. The cottages are suitable for guests with walking difficulties, and one has been planned specifically with disabled guests in mind. No pets, no smoking.

Kennet and Avon Canal, Bradford-on-Avon

Great Chalfield

9 miles SW of Chippenham off the B3107/3109

Great Chalfield Manor, completed in 1480, is a delightful moated manor house with an impressive great hall and a tiny parish church.

Bradford-on-Avon

13 miles SW of Chippenham on the A363

An historic market town at a bridging point on the Avon, which it spans with a superb nine-arched bridge with a lock-up at one end. The town's oldest building is the **Church of St Lawrence**, believed to have been founded by St Aldhelm around 700. It 'disappeared' for over 1,000 years, when it was used variously as a school, a charnel house for storing the bones of the dead, and a residential dwelling. It was re-discovered by a keen-eyed clergyman who looked down from a hill and noticed the cruciform shape of a church. The

surrounding buildings were gradually removed to reveal the little masterpiece we see today. Bradford's Norman church, restored in the 19th century, has an interesting memorial to Lieutenant-General Henry Shrapnel, the army officer who, in 1785, invented and gave his name to the shrapnel shell. Another of the town's outstanding buildings is the mighty **Tithe Barn**, once used to store the grain from local farms for Shaftesbury Abbey, now housing a collection of antique farm implements and agricultural machinery. The centrepiece of the museum in Bridge Street is a pharmacy which has stood in the town for 120 years before being removed lock, stock and medicine bottles to its new site.

Off the A363, **Barton Farm Country Park** offers delightful walks in lovely countryside by the River Avon and the Kennet and Avon Canal. It was once a medieval farm serving Shaftesbury Abbey. Barton Bridge is the original packhorse bridge built to assist the transportation of grain from the farm to the tithe barn.

Half a mile south of town by the River Frome is the Italian-style **Peto Garden** at **Iford Manor**. Famous for its romantic, tranquil beauty, its steps and terraces, statues, colonnades and ponds, the garden was laid out by the architect and landscape gardener Harold Ainsworth Peto between 1899 and 1933. He was inspired by the works of Lutyens and Jekyll to turn a difficult hillside site into 'a haunt of ancient peace'.

Outside Bradford, off the A366, the charming 15th century Westwood Manor has many interesting features, including Jacobean and Gothic windows and ornate plasterwork.

Home Farm

Harts Lane, Biddestone, Chippenham, Wiltshire SN14 7DQ
Tel: 01249 714475 Fax: 01249 701488
e-mail: audrey.smith@homefarmbandb.co.uk
website: www.homefarmbandb.co.uk

Ian and Audrey Smith welcome guests to **Home Farm**, their creeper-clad 17th century farmhouse, which stands in a large garden on a 200-acre working farm close to the centre of Biddestone. Flagstone floors and oak staircases preserve the period character, and the owners offer delightful Bed & Breakfast accommodation in a large family room sleeping four and another sleeping three, both with en suite shower rooms, and a double room with a private shower room. Each room has its own individual style and colour scheme, and all have tv, radio, hairdryer and a particularly well-stocked hospitality tray.

A hearty breakfast is served in the cosy oak-beamed dining room, and the farm has a spacious, comfortable drawing room where guests can relax round the fire. Peace and tranquillity are guaranteed at this civilised spot, and the village in which it stands is in a designated Area of Outstanding Natural Beauty. The village, which has a beautiful 12th century church, is surrounded by lanes and footpaths where visitors can enjoy a leisurely stroll or step out on a more serious walk on the Macmillan Way or the Ridgeway. Two pubs serving excellent meals are within strolling distance, and local amenities include the Wiltshire Cycle Way and several golf courses.

Biddestone

3 miles W of Chippenham off the A420

A lovely village where Cotswold stone cottages, old farmhouses and a 17th century manor cluster round the green.

MALMESBURY

England's oldest borough and one of its most attractive. The hilltop town is dominated by the impressive remains of the **Benedictine Malmesbury Abbey**, founded in the 7th century by St Aldhelm. In the 10th century, King Athelstan, Alfred's grandson and the first Saxon king to unite England, granted 500 acres of land to the townspeople in gratitude for their help in resisting a Norse invasion. Those acres are still known as King's Heath and are owned by 200 residents who are descended from those far-off heroes. Athelstan made Malmesbury his capital and is buried in the abbey, where several centuries later a monument was put up in his honour.

The abbey tower was the scene of an early attempt at human-powered flight when in the early part of the 11th century Brother Elmer strapped a pair of wings to his arms, flew for about 200 yards and crashed to earth, breaking both legs and becoming a cripple for the rest of his long life. The flight of this intrepid cleric, who reputedly forecast the Norman invasion following a sighting of Halley's Comet, is commemorated in a stained glass window. Another window, by Burne-Jones, portrays Faith, courage and Devotion. The octagonal **Market Cross** in the town square is one of many interesting buildings that also include the Old Stone House with its colonnade and gargoyles, and the arched Tolsey Gate, whose two cells once served as the town jail.

In the **Malmesbury Athelstan Museum** in the Town Hall are displays of lace-making, costume, rural life, coins, early bicycles and tricycles, a manually-operated fire engine, photographs and maps.

A more recent piece of history concerns the **Tamworth Two**, the pigs who made the headlines with their dash for freedom. Their trail is one of many that can be followed in and around the town.

AROUND MALMESBURY

Castle Combe

8 miles SW of Malmesbury on the B4039

The loveliest village in the region, and for some the loveliest in the country, Castle Combe was once a centre of the

Castle Combe

The Old Bell Hotel & Restaurant

Abbey Row, Malmesbury,
Wiltshire SN16 0AG
Tel: 01666 822344 Fax: 01666 825145
e-mail: info@oldbellhotel.com
website: www.oldbellhotel.com

Luxurious accommodation, comfortable public rooms, fine food and top-notch service have long been keynotes at the **Old Bell Hotel**, which was founded by Walter Loring, sometime Abbot of Malmesbury, in 1220. The building was constructed alongside the cloisters of the Abbey to house the many visitors who came to study in the Abbey library, and traces of that original hostelry can still be seen in stone arches and window surrounds and in the canopied fireplace below what was the Great Hall. Major additional building took place in Edwardian times, and the hotel of today has 31 splendidly appointed bedrooms, all with private bathrooms and most with bath and integral shower. Telephone, tv, clock radio, hairdryer and modem points are standard accessories, and many rooms contain period double beds. The rooms are named after people associated down the centuries with the Old Bell, among them Abbot Loring, Harry Brakspear, who designed the Edwardian extension, and Sir John Rushout, whose family owned the manor in the 19th century.

Families with children are not just welcome, they are really well catered for, with cots or zed beds provided in the bedrooms at no extra cost, a supervised den where little ones can be left to romp in safety, and a special selection of children's meals. Log fires, friendly old furniture and paintings are features in the public rooms, and in fine weather the lovely gardens and lawns come into their own. The hotel has established a proud tradition of serving the best of proper British cooking, accompanied by a carefully chosen list of wines from around the world. The Old Bell's Sunday lunches in particular have become something of an institution, with roasts carved in time-honoured style from the trolley, plates of fresh vegetables, fish and seafood - some smoked in the hotel's own smokehouse, English cheeses, home-baked bread and fruit pies with clotted cream. Booking is advisable for this splendid feast. A stroll round Malmesbury, with its wealth of historic buildings, will generate an appetite which the Old Bell is well able to satisfy, whatever the day or time. Sue Wilson is the Marketing Manager here and also at the sister establishment the Milford Hall Hotel in Salisbury.

Situated between Cirencester and Bath and very close to Westonbirt Arboretum (Junction 17 off the M4, 5 minutes).

The Gallery On The Bridge

The Street, Castle Combe, Wiltshire SN14 7HU
Tel/Fax: 01249 782201

Alison Holland spent many years as a professional hairdresser before changing direction and opening her **Gallery on the Bridge** in the picturesque village of Castle Combe. Selling fine art, local crafts and interesting hand-made collectibles, the premises are as attractive as any in this lovely spot, with small-paned windows, exposed stone walls and old beams and doors. Alison has put every inch of space to the best possible use: on dressers, on the bare stone walls, on glass shelves and in cleverly-lit recesses a truly wonderful collection of items is on display for purchase, including original water colours, Caroline Smith pottery, Spode and Royal Worcester china and some outstanding glass pieces.

All the studio glass is produced by individual glass blowers and each piece is signed by its maker. Eight miles southwest of Malmesbury on the B4039, Castle Combe is the loveliest village in the region, and for many the loveliest in the whole country; it is an entirely appropriate setting for this splendid little gallery, which visitors should definitely find time to look round when exploring all the other attractions.

Neeld Arms

Grittleton, Wiltshire SN14 6AP
Tel: 01249 782470
e-mail: neeldarms@zeronet.co.uk

After many years of selling to the licensed trade Charles West moved to the other side of the bar when he became the owner of the **Neeld Arms**. This long-established country inn has for many years been the focal point for hospitality and good food and drink in the village of Grittleton, which is located off the A350 or B3049 a few miles northwest of Chippenham. In the cosy, old-fashioned bar, with beams, open fires and lots of inviting nooks and snugs, real ales and a selection of wines accompany tasty, appetising home-cooked fare on menus that change on a daily basis to make the best use of mainly local produce.

Home-made pork, apricot terrine served with warm piccalilli makes a splendid starter or snack meal, and hearty main courses listed on the blackboard might include spicy lamb sausages with mash, peas and gravy, roast partridge on pearl barley and juniper risotto, or the ever-popular steak & kidney pie. The Neeld Arms has another string to its bow in the shape of six comfortable bedrooms for Bed & Breakfast accommodation; all have en suite facilities, tv, tea/coffee-making kit and lots of thoughtful little extras.

prosperous wool trade, famed for its red and white cloth, and many of the present-day buildings date from the 15th and 16th centuries, including the Perpendicular Church of St Andrew, the covered market cross and the manor house, which was built with stones from the Norman castle that gave the village its name. One of the Lords of the Manor in the 14th century was Sir John Fastolf, who was reputedly the inspiration for Shakespeare's Falstaff. A small museum dealing with the village's history is open on summer Sunday afternoons.

Easton Grey

3 miles W of Malmesbury on the B4040

Here the southern branch of the River Avon is spanned by a handsome 16th century bridge with five stone arches. A manor house has overlooked the village since the 13th century, and the present house, with a classical facade and an elegant covered portico, dates from the 18th century. It was used as a summer retreat by Herbert Asquith, British Prime Minister from 1908 to 1916, and in 1923 the Prince of Wales was in residence during the Duke of Beaufort's hunting season at Badminton.

Grittleton

7 miles S of Malmesbury off the A429

The big house here is Grittleton House, designed in the 1840s by James Thomson for Joseph Neeld, sometime MP for Chippenham. Thomson also designed St Margaret's Church at nearby Leigh Delamere; the church features a splendid bellcote and some beautiful stained glass.

6 ROYAL FOREST OF DEAN AND WEST GLOUCESTERSHIRE

Wild wood, royal hunting ground, naval timber reserve, important mining and industrial area. The **Royal Forest of Dean**, one of England's few remaining ancient forests, has been all these, and today its rich and varied landscape provides endless interest for walkers, historians and nature-lovers. It covers an area of some 30,000 acres and lies in an area bordered by the Severn Estuary to the south and the Wye Valley to the west, effectively isolated from the rest of England and from Wales. As a result, 'this heart-shaped land' (Dennis Potter's description) has developed a character all its own. Following the last Ice Age an area of some 120,000 acres between the Rivers Severn, Wye and Leadon became covered with deciduous forest and remained so until about 4000BC, when the farmers of the New Stone Age began clearing the land with their state-of-the-art flint axes, felling vast numbers of trees; coppicing was started about this time, and the new shoots growing from the bases of the trees provided the timber of the future. The Forest has long been home to a variety of wildlife, and it was the presence of deer that led Edmund Ironside to designate it a royal hunting ground in the 11th century. Iron ore deposits were first discovered in the Forest 2,500 years ago and were exploited by the Romans, but it was not until the 1600s that mineral began to be extracted on a large scale. The most ruinous development in the Forest was the demand for timber for the process of iron smelting; at one time 72 furnaces were operating in the area, depleting the timber supplies to such an extent that a major replanting programme was initiated in the 1660. The Victorians exploited another of the Forest's natural resources, coal, removing up to a million tons a year at the height of demand. This industry more or less came to an end in the 1930s, and the Forest has gradually reclaimed most of the workings. In 1938 the Forest was made into a Forest Park, the first to be created in England, balancing the needs of conservation and recreational use with commercial timber production. The Forest of today has many attractions for visitors: walking and cycling, arts and crafts, caves and mines, birds and natural habitat, railways and museums, beautiful and distinctive churches - in short, something for everyone.

In the northwest of the county the Leadon Valley, a peaceful and picturesque part of the world, has strong literary connections, including the influential Dymock poets, while in the Severn Vale lush meadows lie along the river, famous for its tidal bore and haven for thousands of wildfowl and wading birds. The Wildfowl and Wetlands Trust at Slimbridge, founded in 1946 by Peter Scott, and historic Berkeley Castle are among the diverse attractions here.

LOCATOR MAP

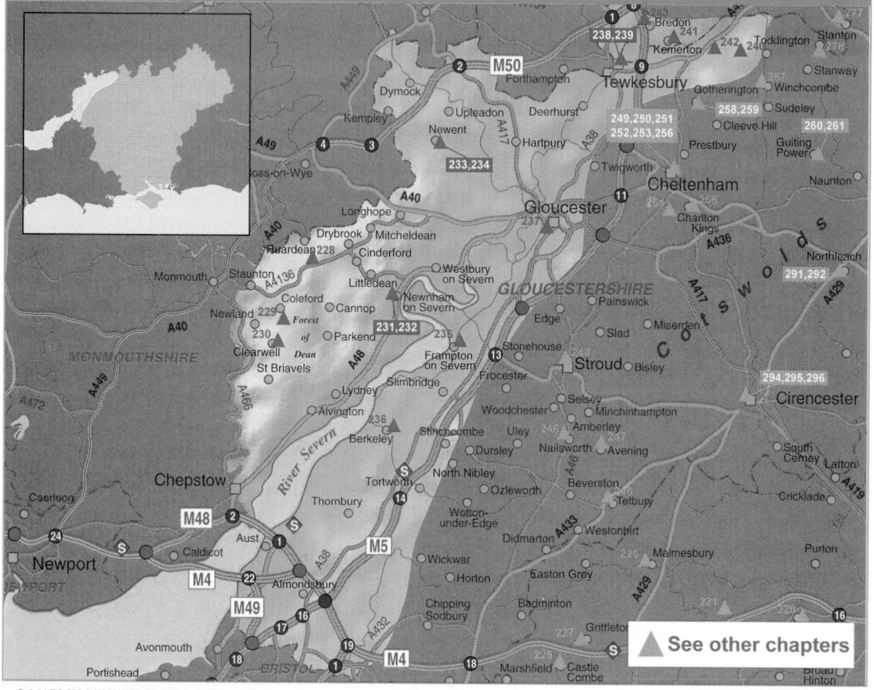

ADVERTISERS AND PLACES OF INTEREST

228 The Pine Centre At Forest Joinery, Lydbrook, Gloucestershire Page 300

229 Coleford Garden Centre, Coleford, Gloucestershire Page 301

230 Clearwell Caves, Coleford, Gloucestershire Page 302

231 Forest Guild, Newnham-on-Severn, Gloucestershire Page 304

232 Swan House Country Guest House, Newnham-on-Severn, Gloucestershire Page 305

233 Roses Country Fayre, Newent, Gloucestershire Page 306

234 Three Choirs Vineyards, Newent, Gloucestershire Page 307

235 Tanhouse Farm Cottages, Frampton-on-Severn, Gloucestershire Page 308

236 The Jenner Museum, Berkeley, Gloucestershire Page 312

237 The National Waterways Museum, Gloucester, Gloucestershire Page 316

238 Pickwicks Of Tewkesbury, Tewkesbury, Gloucestershire Page 318

239 Woodend Farm, Tewkesbury, Gloucestershire Page 318

240 The Gardeners Arms, Alderton, Gloucestershire Page 319

241 Upper Court & Courtyard Cottages, Kemerton, nr Tewkesbury, Gloucestershire Page 320

242 Ye Olde Hobnails Inn, Little Washbourne, nr Tewkesbury, Gloucestershire Page 321

243 Bredon Pottery, Bredon, nr Tewkesbury, Gloucestershire Page 324

LONGHOPE

A good start point for a tour in and around the Forest of Dean is Longhope, a pleasant settlement south of the A40 Gloucester to Ross-on-Wye road.

Longhope is the location of the **Harts Barn Crafts Centre**, situated in a hunting lodge built by William Duke of Normandy and housing an array of working crafts including jewellery, pine furniture, art gallery, hand-made gifts, glassware, dried flowers and picture framing. Open Tuesday to Sunday, the Centre has a tea shop and restaurant.

AROUND LONGHOPE

MITCHELDEAN

2 miles W of Longhope on the A4136

A peaceful community on the northern fringe of the forest. A mile or so south of the village is **St Anthony's Well**, one of many throughout the land said to have magical curative powers. The water at this well is invariably icy cold and bathing in it is said to provide a cure for skin disease (St Anthony's Fire was the medieval name for a rampant itching disease). The monks at nearby Flaxley Abbey swore by it.

DRYBROOK

4 miles W of Longhope off the A4136

Hidden away at Hawthorns Cross on the edge of the Forest is the **Mechanical Organ Museum** with a vast collection of mechanical music spanning 150 years. The museum is open at Easter and on Tuesday and Thursday afternoons in April, May, July and August.

RUARDEAN

2 miles W of Drybrook on the A4136

A lovely old village whose **Church of St John the Baptist**, one of many on the fringe of the forest, has many interesting features. A tympanum depicting St George and the Dragon is a great rarity, and on a stone plaque in the nave is a curious carving of two fishes. These are thought to have been carved by craftsmen from the Herefordshire School of Norman Architecture during the Romanesque period around 1150. It is part of a frieze removed with rubble when the south porch was being built in the 13th century. The frieze was considered lost until 1985, when an inspection of a bread oven in a cottage at nearby Turner's Tump revealed the two fish set into its lining. They were rescued and returned to their rightful place in the church. Ruardean was the birthplace in the 1840s of James and William Horlick, later to be become famous with their Horlicks formula. Their patent for 'malted milk' was registered in 1883 and the granary where the original experiments were carried out still remains in the village. Ruardean Hill is 951 feet above sea level and on a clear day Herefordshire, the Black Mountains and the Brecon Beacons can all be seen.

From Ruardean, country roads lead westward to the sister villages of **Upper** and **Lower Lydbrook**. These tranquil villages were once major producers of pig iron, rivals even for Sheffield, and when the extraction of iron ore and coal was at its height their position on the northwest edge of the forest made then ideally suited for the processing of the ore. The first commercially viable blast furnace in the area was sited here at the beginning of the 17th century. For several centuries flat-bottomed barges were loaded at Lower Lydbrook with coal bound for Hereford, 25 miles upstream; this river trade continued until the 1840s, when it was superseded, first by the Gloucester-Hereford Canal and then by the Severn and Wye Railway. The

THE PINE CENTRE AT FOREST JOINERY

Unit 4, Waterloo Business Park, Lydbrook,
Gloucestershire GL17 9LR
Tel/Fax: 01594 860116
e-mail: pineinlydbrook@aol.com
website: www.pineinlydbrook.co.uk

David and Bridget Staines have been making fine
furniture for 20 years and set up in Waterloo Business
Park in 1999. **The Pine Centre** has showrooms which
are now the largest in the area, and their clientele has
expanded from mainly local to nationwide. Fitted and
free-standing furniture, handmade kitchens are their specialities, and they also undertake general
carpentry commissions.

The furniture is available in a number of ranges,
including Mexican, Farmhouse, Barley Twist, Budget,
Peruvian, Malvern, Cottage and Shaker, and bespoke
pieces can also be made to order in the wood of the
customer's choice or hand-painted to the customer's
design. Bespoke pieces account for 50 per cent of the
business. The Pine Centre is open Monday, Tuesday,
Thursday, Friday and Saturday from 9 to 5.30 and
Sunday from 10 to 4 (Closed Wednesday). Coming from
the direction of Gloucester, turn right off the A4136 on
to the B4234 - first right after Brierley Esso garage.

actress Sarah Siddons lived in Lydbrook
as a child, in the Old House dating from
the 15th century.

COLEFORD

A former mining centre which received
its royal charter from Charles 1 in the
17th century in recognition of its loyalty
to the Crown. It was by then already an
important iron processing centre, partly
because of the availability of local ore
deposits and partly because of the ready
local supply of timber for converting
into charcoal for use in the smelting
process. It was in Coleford that the
Mushet family helped to revolutionise
the iron and steel industry. Robert
Forester Mushet, a freeminer, discovered
how spiegeleisen, an alloy of iron,
manganese, silicon and carbon, could be
used in the reprocessing of 'burnt iron'

and went on to develop a system for
turning molten pig iron directly into
steel, a process which predated the more
familiar one developed later by Bessemer.

Coleford, still regarded as the capital of
the Royal Forest of Dean, is a busy
commercial centre with an interesting
church and a number of notable
industrial relics. The Forestry
Commission is housed at Bank House
and has information on all aspects of the
Forest. There are miles of waymarked
walks and cycle trails in the Forest, and
the famous Sculpture Trail starts at
Beechenhurst Lodge. Coleford is home to
the **Great Western Railway Museum**,
housed in an 1883 GWR goods station
next to the central car park and another
treat for railway fans is the **Perrygrove
Railway**, where a narrow gauge steam
train takes a 1½ mile trip through
farmland and woods. Nearby is another

Coleford Garden Centre

Lambsquay Road, Milkwall, Coleford, Gloucestershire GL16 8QA
Tel: 01594 832700

Coleford Garden Centre occupies a 3-acre site a mile outside Coleford in pleasant rural surroundings close to the historic Clearwell Caves. A quarry and brickworks once stood on the site, where for the past four years Malcolm Butler has been developing the Centre into a source of all things to do with the garden. There's an extensive range of trees, shrubs, plants, seeds and seed potatoes, and accessories on display in the spacious glass-framed shop area range from compost, fertilisers and pesticides to hedge trimmers, fish ponds, pumps, greenhouses, garden furniture, pots and tubs, garden ornaments and bird feeders.

visitor attraction, also on the B4228 just south of town. This is **Puzzle Wood**, where 14 acres of open-cast ore mines have been redesigned as a family attraction, with paths forming an unusual maze, breathtaking scenery, wooden bridges, passageways through moss-covered rocks and lots of dead ends and circles.

Forest of Dean

AROUND COLEFORD

NEWLAND
1 mile SW of Coleford off the A466

Newland's Church of All Saints is often known as the **Cathedral of the Forest** because of its impressive size. Its aisle is almost as wide as its nave and its huge pinnacled tower is supported by flying buttresses. Like many churches in the county, it was built during the 13th and 14th centuries and remodelled by the Victorians. Inside, it has a number of interesting effigies, including an unusual brass relief of a medieval miner with a pick and hod in his hand and a candlestick in his mouth. Other effigies depict a forester in 15th century hunting gear with a hunting horn, a sword and knife; and, from the 17th century, an archer with wide-brimmed hat, bow, horn and dagger.

CLEARWELL
2 miles S of Coleford off the A466

Clearwell Caves (see panel on page 302) are set in an area of special landscape value, just on the outskirts of the historic village of Clearwell, which boasts a castle, pretty church, chapel and several good pubs. This is the only remaining working iron mine in the Forest of Dean out of the very many that once worked here.

Clearwell Caves

Near Coleford, Royal Forest of Dean,
Gloucestershire GL16 8JR
Tel: 01594 832535 Fax: 01594 833362
e-mail: rw@clearwellcaves.com
website: www.clearwellcaves.com

Clearwell Caves are set in an area of special landscape value, on the outskirts of the historic village of Clearwell, which boasts good walks, a castle, a handsome church, as well as several good pubs and hotels. The Caves are part of the last remaining working iron mine in the Forest of Dean and the last ochre mine in the UK.The Caves are part of a natural cave system that became filled with iron ore around 180 million years ago. Working for ochre began by at least the Bronze Age, over 4000 years ago and as a result the Caves complex now consists of many miles of passageways and hundreds of caverns.

Visitors are offered a wide range of activities, from a leisurely and fascinating self guided underground walk, descending over 100 feet, to a more strenuous adventure caving trip or even a Natural Paint workshop. The Cave shop is a treat in itself with unusual gift ideas, books, souvenirs and a wide range of spectacular minerals and crystals from around the world. And of course you can buy ochre mined here.

Don't miss the Tearoom, which provides a good range of freshly prepared lunches and refreshments, and some very interesting mining artefacts displayed around the ceiling and walls. An unusual day out for all ages and a great underground experience.

A memorable visit can be completed by wandering down to see Clearwell village, the lovely French Gothic-style church and the pretty surrounding countryside; there are several walks from the Caves that explore surface mining remains, some with spectacular views over the Welsh mountains and the Wye Valley.

Cannop

4 miles E of Coleford on the B4226

Cannop Valley has many forest trails and picnic sites; one of the sites is at Cannop Ponds, picturesque ponds created in the 1820s to provide a regular supply of water for the local iron-smelting works. Nearby is **Hopewell Colliery**, a true Forest of Dean free mine where summer visitors can see old mine workings and some of the old tools of the trade, then relax with a snack from the café.

Staunton

3 miles NW of Coleford on the A4136

Lots to see here, including a Norman church with two stone fonts and an unusual corkscrew staircase leading up past the pulpit to the belfry door. Not far from the village are several enormous mystical stones, notably the **Buckstone** and the **Suck Stone**. The former, looking like some great monster, used to buck, or rock, on its base but is now firmly fixed in place. The Suck Stone is a real giant, weighing in at many thousands of tons. There are several other stones in the vicinity, including the **Near Harkening** and **Far Harkening** down among the trees, and the Long Stone by the A4136 at Marion's Cross.

Parkend

3 miles SE of Coleford off the B4234

A community once based, like so many others in the area, on the extraction of minerals. In the early years of the 19th century, before steam engines arrived and horses did all the donkey work, Parkend became a tramroad centre and laden trams ran from coalpits, iron mines, quarries, furnaces and forges to river-borne outlets at Lydbrook and Lydney. New Fancy Colliery is now a delightful picnic area, with a nearby hill affording breathtaking views over the forestscape. Off the B4431, just west of Parkend, is the RSPB's **Nagshead Nature Reserve**, with hundreds of nest boxes in a woodland site with footpaths, waymarked trails and a summer information centre.

St Briavels

5 miles S of Coleford on minor roads

On the edge of a limestone plateau high above the Wye Valley, this historic village is named after a 5th century Welsh bishop whose name appears in various forms throughout Celtic Wales, Cornwall and Brittany, but nowhere else in England. In the Middle Ages St Briavels was an important administrative centre for the royal hunting forest and also a leading manufacturer of armaments, supplying weapons and ammunition to the Crown. In 1223 it is believed that Henry lll ordered 6,000 crossbow bolts (called quarrels) from here. The ample Church of St Mary the Virgin, Norman in origin, enlarged in the 12th and 13th centuries and remodelled by the Victorians, is the scene of a curious and very English annual custom, the St Briavels **Bread and Cheese Ceremony**. After evensong a local forester stands on the Pound Wall and throws small pieces of bread and cheese to the villagers, accompanied by the chant 'St Briavels water and Whyrl's wheat are the best bread and water King John can ever eat'. This ceremony is thought to have originated more than 700 years ago when the villagers successfully defended their rights of estover (collecting wood from common land) in nearby Hudnalls Wood. In gratitude each villager paid one penny to the churchwarden to help feed the poor, and that act led to the founding of the ceremony. Small pieces of bread and cheese were considered to bring good luck, and the Dean Forest miners would keep the pieces in order to ward off harm.

St Briavels Castle, which stands in an almost impregnable position on a high promontory, was founded by Henry l and enlarged by King John, who used it as a hunting lodge. Two sturdy gatehouses are among the parts that survive and they, like some of the actual castle buildings, are now in use as a youth hostel.

LYDNEY

The harbour and the canal at Lydney, once an important centre of the iron and coal industries and the largest settlement between Chepstow and Gloucester, are well worth exploring, and no visit to the town should end without a trip on the **Dean Forest Railway**. A regular service of steam and diesel trains operates between Lydney Junction, St Mary's Halt and Norchard. At **Norchard Railway Centre**, headquarters of the line, are a railway museum, souvenir shop and details of restoration projects, including the extension of the line to Parkend. Air-conditioned classic coaches in the platform serve light snacks on steam days. The backbone of the locomotive fleet (this is for real railway buffs) are 5541, a Churchwood-designed Prairie tank engine, and 9681, an 0-6-0 pannier tank built in 1948, when GWR was becoming BR. Popular events throughout the year include Days Out with Thomas, Santa Specials and Steam Footplate Experience Courses.

One of the chief attractions in the vicinity is **Lydney Park Spring Gardens and Roman Temple Site**. The gardens, which lie beside the A48 on the western outskirts, are a riot of colour, particularly in May and June, and the grounds also contain the site of an Iron Age hill fort and the remains of a late-Roman temple excavated by Sir Mortimer Wheeler in the 1920s. The builders of this unusual temple were probably wealthy Romanised Celts; the mosaic floor, now lost, depicted fish and sea monsters and was dedicated to Nodens, the Roman-Celtic god of healing whose emblem was a reclining dog with curative powers. The nearby museum houses a number of Roman artefacts from the site, including the famous 'Lydney Dog', and a number of interesting items brought back from New Zealand in the 1930s by the first Viscount Bledisloe after his term there as Governor General. Also in the park are traces of Roman iron-mine workings and Roman earth workings.

AROUND LYDNEY

Alvington

2 miles SW of Lydney on the A48

In the churchyard at Alvington are the graves of the illustrious Wintour family, protagonists in the defeat of the Spanish Armada. Half a century after that event came Sir John Wintour's remarkable escape from Cromwell's men at what is now known as **Wintour's Leap**. Captain Wintour, adventurer, Keeper of the Forest of Dean and sometime secretary to Queen Maria Henrietta of the Netherlands, was at the head of a Royalist force defeated at Blockley, near Chepstow, by Parliamentary troops. Wintour is said to have escaped the battle, which took place in 1644, by riding up by the Wye and hurling himself and his horse into the river from the cliffs.

NEWNHAM-ON-SEVERN

One of the gateways to the Forest, and formerly a port, Newnham lies on a great bend in the river. Its heyday was at the beginning of the 19th century, when a quay was built and an old tramway tunnel converted into what was perhaps the world's first railway tunnel. The village has many interesting buildings which can be visited by following the Millennium Heritage Walk plaques installed by the parish council with funds provided by an open-air jazz concert.

AROUND NEWNHAM-ON-SEVERN

Westbury-on-Severn

3 miles NW of Newnham on the A48

The village, bounded on three sides by the river, is best known for the National Trust's **Westbury Court Garden**, a formal Dutch water garden laid out between 1696 and 1705. Historic varieties of apple, pear and plum, along with many other species introduced to England before 1700, make this a must for any enthusiastic gardener. The house was long ago demolished, and the only building to survive is an elegant two-storey redbrick pavilion with a tower and weather vane. Also worth a visit in Westbury is the Church of Saints Peter, Paul and Mary with its detached tower and wooden spire. Walmore Common is winter home to thousands of swans as well as many wading birds and unusual flora. Westbury is an excellent spot to watch the famous **Severn Bore**. This is a tidal wave that several times a month makes its way along the river; the bore travels at an average speed of about 16 kilometres an hour and has been known to reach a height of 2 metres. The Severn Estuary experiences the second highest tide anywhere in the world, and the difference between the lowest and highest tide in any one day can be more than 14.5 metres. These high, or spring tides, occur on several days in each lunar cycle throughout the year.

Littledean

2 miles NW of Newnham on the road to Cinderford

Places of interest here include the 13th century church, the 18th century prison and, just south of the village, **Littledean Hall**, reputedly the oldest inhabited house in England. The house has Saxon and Celtic remains in the cellars and is thought to have originated in the 6th century; it became a Royalist garrison during the Civil War. Highlights in the grounds, from which balloon flights launch, include a Roman temple site, a Victorian walled garden and a number of ancient chestnut trees. Open 11-5 every day in summer.

CINDERFORD

3 miles NW of Newnham on the A4151

A former coal-mining community with evidence of the mines visible among the trees.

At Camp Hill in the nearby hamlet of Soudley is **Dean Heritage Centre**, where four galleries tell the story of the Forest and its people. It is a perfect setting for a family day out with woodland walks, café, adventure playground and children's activity room, museum and crafts shops, farm animals and woodland crafts, including charcoal burning and woodturning. A level trail runs round Soudley Ponds, a designated Site of Special Scientific Interest.

At nearby **Awre**, an ancient crossing place of the Severn, the Church of St Andrew has changed little in its 700 years. Its most notable possession is a massive mortuary chest carved from a single piece of wood and used as a laying out place for bodies recovered from the Severn. In the churchyard are examples of headstones featuring the local speciality - cherubs.

NEWENT

Capital of the area of northwest Gloucestershire known as the Ryelands, and the most important town in the Vale of Leadon, Newent stands in the broad triangle of land called Daffodil Crescent. The rich Leadon Valley soil was traditionally used for growing rye and raising the renowned Ryelands sheep, an ancient breed famed for the quality of its wool. The town was one of the county's principal wool-trading centres, and the wealth produced from that trade accounts for the large number of grand merchants' houses to be seen here. The most distinctive house in Newent is the splendid timber-framed **Market House**, built as a butter market in the middle of the 16th century, its upper floors supported on 16 oak pillars that form an open colonnade. The medieval **Church of St Mary** has many outstanding features, including the shaft of a 9th century Saxon cross, the 11th century 'Newent Stone' and the 17th century nave. Royalist troops had removed the lead from the roof to make bullets, an act which caused the roof to collapse during a snowstorm in 1674. A new nave was started after Charles ll agreed to donate 60 tons of timber from the Forest of Dean. The 150ft spire is a landmark for miles around.

The Shambles Museum of Victorian Life is virtually a little Victorian town, a cleverly laid out jumble of cobbled streets, alleyways and squares, with shops and trades tucked away in all corners, and even a mission chapel and a Victorian conservatory.

Three Choirs Vineyards

Newent, Gloucestershire GL18 1LS
Tel: 01531 890223 Fax: 01531 890877
e-mail: ts@threechoirs.com
website: www.threechoirs.com
(Rooms: www.rooms@threechoirs.com)

Three Choirs Vineyards is one of the great success stories of English wines, which are now exported and enjoyed all over the world. Three Choirs is England's leading producer of single estate wines, and Thomas Shaw and his staff invite visitors to stroll among 70 acres of carefully cultivated vines, where experts nurture well-chosen modern varieties alongside world-renowned grapes such as Pinot Noir. A choice of three tours is available to suit all visitor needs: the Self-Guided Tour including the vineyards walk video, exhibition, viewing gallery and wine tasting; the Guided Tour with a member of staff as guide to explain the processes involved; and the Vineyard Game, a treasure hunt with clues related to the vineyard and wines to be tasted and identified.

All the wines - white, red, rosé and sparkling - are available in the vineyard shop, along with a range of gifts for wine and food lovers. The main activities of the vineyard are complemented by the major attractions of the Vineyard Restaurant and the overnight accommodation. The restaurant (all non-smoking) serves modern English cuisine on a menu that changes with the seasons; it is open every lunchtime except Monday and in the evening from Tuesday to Saturday. Eight spacious twin or double letting bedrooms came on stream in May 2000, providing an ideal base for getting to know the vineyard and its products or for exploring the Cotswolds and the Welsh Borders. All the rooms are en suite, with private terraces overlooking the lovely vineyards.

There aren't too many windmills in Gloucestershire, but at **Castle Hill Farm** just outside town is a working wooden mill with great views from a balcony at the top.

AROUND NEWENT

A mile south of Newent is the **National Bird of Prey Centre** housing one of the largest and best collections of birds of prey in the world. Over 110 aviaries are home to eagles, falcons, owls, vultures, kites, hawks and buzzards. Between 20 and 40 birds are flown daily at the Centre, which is open every day from February to November.

On the road north towards Dymock, set in 65 acres of rolling countryside, the **Three Choirs Vineyard** is the country's largest wine producer (see panel above).

Dymock

3 miles N of Newent on the B4216

At the heart of the village is the early Norman Church of St Mary, whose unusual features include a tympanum depicting the Tree of Life, a 13th century stone coffin lid, stained glass by Kempe and the last ticket issued at Dymock station, in 1959. A corner of the church is dedicated to the memory of the **Dymock Poets**, a group who based themselves in Dymock from before the First World War. The group, which comprised Lascelles Abercrombie (the first to arrive), Rupert Brooke, John Drinkwater, Wilfred Gibson, Edward Thomas and Robert Frost, sent out its New Numbers poetry magazine from Dymock's tiny post office; it was also from here that Brooke published his *War Sonnets*, including *The Soldier* (*'If I should*

TANHOUSE FARM COTTAGES

Frampton-on-Severn, Gloucestershire GL2 7EH
Tel/Fax: 01452 741072
e-mail: tanhouse-farm@lineone.net
website: www.tanhouse-farm.co.uk

Mike and Caroline Williams offer outstanding self-catering accommodation in two beautifully restored and converted old farm buildings that comprise **Tanhouse Farm Cottages**. The Old Stables, sleeping four, is set in a private courtyard behind a magnificent medieval tithe barn. Furnishings are mainly in traditional oak and the cottage has a wealth of exposed beams. On the ground floor are a dining area with a table and chairs for 6; a well-designed and comprehensively equipped kitchen with plenty of cupboard and worktop

space; a utility room with washing machine, tumble dryer and freezer; a bedroom with twin beds; a bathroom with bath, separate shower, WC, basin and shaver point; and a lounge with a comfortable suite, grandfather clock, tv, video and hi-fi. Stairs lead from the lounge up to the master bedroom, which has a mass of exposed elm beams and a romantic oak-panelled four-poster bed with matching furniture. The back garden has barbecue facilities and there's undercover parking space.

Adjacent to the Old Stables, also with a garden, BBQ and undercover parking, is the Old Priests Cottage dating from the mid-17th century. This is similar in style and specification, except that both bedrooms are upstairs; the bathroom is accessed from the twin room. Hot water and central heating are oil-fired in both the Old Stables and the Old Priests Cottage. The cottages are only a five-minute walk from the banks of the Severn Estuary and the Gloucester Sharpness Canal, both of which are ideal for leisurely strolls and watching superb sunsets. The Severn, boasting the

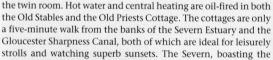
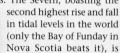

second highest rise and fall in tidal levels in the world (only the Bay of Funday in Nova Scotia beats it), is famous for its Bore, a tidal wave that travels 20 miles upstream reaching heights of up to 8 feet at its peak.

The village of Frampton-on-Severn is a great place to watch this phenomenon and is also renowned for having the longest village green in England. The beautiful Cotswolds are a short drive to the east, while to the west, via Gloucester or the Severn Bridge, lies the Royal Forest of Dean. Closer to hand is the Wildfowl and Wetland Trust at Slimbridge, six miles by road or a mile-and-a-half walk along the canal towpath. Fishing, cycle hire, snooker and clay pigeon shooting can all be arranged by Mike and Caroline.

die, think only this of me: That there's some corner of a foreign field that is forever England...'). Brooke and Thomas died in the War, which led to the dissolution of the group. Two circular walks from Dymock take in places associated with the poets. Dymock boasts some fine old brick buildings, including the White House and the Old Rectory near the church, and outside the village, the Old Grange, which incorporates the remains of the Cistercian Flaxley Abbey. Many other literary figures are associated with the Forest. Dennis Potter, born at Coleford in 1935 the eldest son of a Forest coal-miner, is renowned for writing the screenplays for some of television's most memorable programmes, including *Pennies From Heaven* and *The Singing Detective*. But he also wrote with passion about the Forest in *The Glittering Coffin* and *The Changing Forest: Life in the Forest of Dean Today*. Mary Howitt, born in Coleford in 1799, is known as a translator, poet and author of children's books. It was as a translator that she met a Danish story-teller called Hans Christian Andersen, who asked Mary to translate his stories into English.

UPLEADON

2 miles N of Newent off the B4215

The **Church of St Mary the Virgin** features some fine Norman and Tudor work but is best known for its unique tower, half-timbered from bottom to top; even the mullion windows are of wood. The church has a great treasure in its Bible, an early example of the Authorised Version printed by the King's printer Robert Barker. This was the unfortunate who later issued an edition with a small but rather important word missing. The so-called Wicked Bible of 1631 renders Exodus 20.14 as "Thou shalt commit adultery".

KEMPLEY

3 miles NW of Newent on a minor road

A village famous for its cider and also for having two churches, of very different age and significance. The Church of St Mary, easily the most popular church in the area, dates from the end of the 11th century and would be a gem even without its greatest treasure. That treasure, in the chancel, is an almost complete set of 12th century frescoes, the most renowned in the region and among the finest in the land, protected by Reformation whitewash and Victorian varnish. Their subjects include St Peter and the Apostles, Christ with his feet resting on a globe, and the de Lacy family, local lords of the manor. The red sandstone Church of St Edward the Confessor was built in 1903 by the 7th Earl Beauchamp in the style of the Arts and Crafts Movement using exclusively local materials.

This is the area of **Dymock Woods**, an area of Forestry Commission woodland famous for its daffodils.

Three miles south of Newent, on National Trust land, stands **May Hill**. It rises to nearly 1,000 feet and its domed summit is planted with trees commemorating Queen Victoria's Golden Jubilee (1887), Queen Elizabeth ll's Silver Jubilee (1977) and the Queen Mother's 80th birthday (1980). The reward for climbing to the top is a quite magnificent view that stretches over Gloucestershire, and, on a clear day, as far as Bristol.

SOUTH GLOUCESTERSHIRE AND THE VALE OF BERKELEY

FRAMPTON-ON-SEVERN

8 miles SW of Gloucester off the A38

The 22-acre Rosamund Green,

incorporating a cricket ground and three ponds, is one of the largest village greens in England, formed when the marshy ground outside the gates of **Frampton Court** was drained in the 18th century. The court is an outstanding example of a Georgian country house, built in the Palladian style in the 1730s and the seat of the Clifford family ever since. Fine porcelain, furniture and paintings grace the interior, and in the peacock-strutted grounds an ornamental canal reflects a superb Orangery in Dutch-influenced strawberry gothic. A unique octagonal tower was built in the 17th century as a dovecote.

On the other side of the green is **Frampton Manor**, the Clifford family's former home, built between the 12th and 16th centuries. This handsome timber-framed house is thought to be the birthplace of Jane Clifford, who was the mistress of Henry II and bore him two children. The manor, which has a lovely old walled garden with some rare plants, is open by written appointment. At the southern edge of the village stands the restored 14th century Church of St Mary with its rare Norman lead font. The church stands beside the **Sharpness Canal**, which was built to allow ships to travel up the Severn Valley as far as Gloucester without being at the mercy of the estuary tides. The canal has several swing bridges and at some of these, as at Splatt Bridge and Saul Bridge at Frampton, there are splendid little bridge-keeper's cottages with Doric columns.

To the west of Frampton, on a great bend in the river, is the Arlingham Peninsula, part of the **Severn Way Shepperdine-Tewkesbury long-distance walk**. The trail passes close to Wick Court, a 13th century moated manor house. The land on which the village of **Arlingham** stands once belonged to the monks of St Augustine's Abbey in Bristol who believed it to be the point where St Augustine crossed the Severn on his way to converting the heathen Welsh tribes.

The Severn naturally dominated life hereabouts and at **Saul**, a small village on the peninsula, the inhabitants decorated their houses with carvings of sailors, some of which, in bright, cheerful colours, can be seen today. The village lies at the point where two canals cross. Two separate waterways, the Stroudwater Navigation and the Thames & Severn Canal, once linked the Severn and the Thames, a route of 37 miles. The canals, known collectively as the **Cotswold Canals**, were abandoned in respectively 1933 and 1954 but most of the route is intact and since 1972 the **Cotswold Canals Trust** has worked in partnership with local authorities on restoration work; the aims of the Trust are: to promote for the benefit of the community the re-opening of the canals; to promote the restoration of the two waterways to give a balance between the needs of navigation, development, recreation, heritage, landscape conservation, wildlife and natural habitats; to promote the use of all the towpath as the Thames & Severn Way long distance footpath; and to achieve restoration of the Cotswold Canals as a navigable route from Saul Junction to the Thames. Continuing round the bend in the river, **Epney** is the point from which thousands of baby eels are exported each year to the Netherlands and elsewhere to replenish their own stocks. A mile or so inland from Epney is the historic hamlet of **Moreton Valence**, whose 15th century church has an impressive Norman doorway with a depiction of the Archangel Michael thrusting a spear into a dragon's mouth. Also to be seen here are the ramparts of a 14th century castle, once the property of the De Valence family.

Slimbridge

4 miles S of Frampton on the A38

The **Wildfowl and Wetlands Centre** was founded as a trust on the banks of the Severn in 1946 by the distinguished naturalist, artist, sailor and broadcaster Peter (later Sir Peter) Scott. He believed in bringing wildlife and people together for the benefit of both, and the Trust's work continues with the same aims. Slimbridge has the world's largest collection of ducks, geese and swans, and spectacular flamingoes among the exotic wildfowl. Also at the centre are a tropical house, pond zone, children's play area, wildlife art gallery, restaurant and gift shop, and there are magnificent views from the observation tower. Sir Peter died in 1989 and his ashes were scattered at Slimbridge, where he had lived for many years. A memorial to him stands at the entrance to the Centre.

Berkeley Castle

Berkeley

6 miles S of Frampton off the A38

The fertile strip that is the Vale of Berkeley, bounded on the north by the Severn and on the south by the M5, takes its name from the small town of Berkeley, whose largely Georgian centre is dominated by the Norman **Berkeley Castle**. Said to be the oldest inhabited castle in Britain, and home to 24 generations of the Berkeley family, this wonderful gem in pink sandstone was built between 1117 and 1153 on the site of a Saxon fort. It was from here that the barons of the West met before making the journey to Runnymede to witness the signing of Magna Carta by King John in 1215. Edward ll was imprisoned here for several months after being usurped from the throne by his wife and her lover, and eventually met a gruesome death in the dungeons in the year 1327. Three centuries later the castle was besieged by Cromwell's troops and played an important part in the history of the Civil War. It stands very close to the Severn and once incorporated the waters of the river in its defences so that it could, in an emergency, flood its lands. Visitors passing into the castle by way of a bridge over a moat will find a wealth of treasures in the **Great Hall**, the circular keep, the state apartments with their fine tapestries and period furniture, the medieval kitchens and the dungeons. The Berkeley family have filled the place with objects from around the world, including painted glassware from Damascus, ebony chairs from India and a cypress chest that reputedly belonged to Sir Francis Drake. Security was always extremely important, and two remarkable signs of this are a four-poster bed with a solid wooden top (no nasty surprises from above in the night) and a set of bells once worn by the castle's dray horses and now hanging in the dairy. Each horse wore bells with a distinctive chime so that if an outsider attempted to gain entrance as a carter his strange bells would betray him. The castle is

The Jenner Museum

Berkeley, Gloucestershire BL13 9BH
Tel: 01453 810631 Fax: 01453 811690
e-mail: manager@jennermuseum.com
website: www.jennermuseum.com

Born in Berkeley in 1749, Edward Jenner returned here after completing his medical training and his house, The Chantry, is now home the **Jenner Museum** where this pioneering doctor and immunologist's life and work is explored. Intrigued by the country lore that said that milkmaids who caught the mild cowpox could not catch smallpox, one of the most feared diseases of all time, Jenner set about developing a means of vaccinating against smallpox, which he successful did in 1798. In 1967, the World Health Organisation masterminded a final global plant to eradicate the disease and, in 1980, smallpox was declared dead. Not only did Jenner develop the first vaccination but his discovery has now been developed into one of the most important parts of modern medicine – immunology. Along with his work on smallpox, Jenner also made several other important contributions to medicine: he was probably the first to link angina with hardening of the arteries, he described rheumatic heart disease and he purified important medicines. Both Jenner's medical work and also his work as a naturalist and geologist are described here through numerous displays and exhibits.

surrounded by sweeping lawns and Elizabethan terraced gardens. Special features include a deer park, a medieval bowling alley, a beautiful lily pond and a butterfly farm with hundreds of exotic butterflies in free flight.

The parish church of St Mary, which contains several memorials to the Berkeley family, has a fine Norman doorway, a detached tower and a striking east window depicting Christ healing the sick. A curious piece of carving in the nave shows two old gossips with a giant toad sitting on their heads. Next to the castle and church is the **Jenner Museum**, (see panel above) once the home of Edward Jenner, the doctor and immunologist who is best known as the man who discovered a vaccine against smallpox. The son of a local parson, Jenner was apprenticed to a surgeon in Chipping Sodbury in 1763 at the tender age of 14. His work over several decades led to the first vaccination against smallpox, a disease which had killed many thousands every year. His beautiful Georgian house in Church Lane has a state-of-the-art display showing the importance of the science of immunology, and in the grounds of the house is a rustic thatched hut where Jenner used to vaccinate the poor free of charge and which he called the Temple of Vaccinia. The east window of the church is a memorial to Jenner, while in the churchyard is the grave of Dicky Pearce, one of the last court jesters, who died in 1728.

At **Sharpness**, a mile or so west of Berkeley, the world's first nuclear power station operated between 1962 and 1989. It marks the entrance to the **Gloucester & Sharpness Canal**, opened in 1827 to bypass the tricky waters of the lower Severn. Sixteen miles in length, it has a lock from the tidal River Severn at Sharpness and a lock back into the River Severn at the head of Gloucester Docks, from which the River Severn Navigation runs 43 miles north to Stourport. There are several interesting villages in the vicinity, including Breadstone, which has a church built entirely of tin.

THORNBURY

The woollen industry was important here in late medieval times, and the church, set away from the centre near the site of the old manor house, reflects the prosperity of those days. The side chapel is dedicated to the Stafford family, the local lords of the manor, whose emblem, the Staffordshire knot, is much in evidence. Edward Stafford, 3rd Duke of Buckingham, was responsible for starting work on **Thornbury Castle** in 1511 but did not live to see its completion. Charged with high treason by Henry VIII, he was beheaded on Tower Hill in London in 1522. The building was competed by Anthony Salvin in the 1850s.

AROUND THORNBURY

Aust

3 miles W of Thornbury on the B4461

The English end of the original Severn Suspension Bridge is located here. Completed in 1966, it replaced the ferry service which had plied this unpredictable stretch of water since Roman times. The bridge carries the M4 across the wide river mouth into South Wales.

Almondsbury

6 miles S of Thornbury on the A38

The Church of St Mary has some fine windows, including a memorial to Charles Richardson, the 19th century engineer who designed the original Severn Tunnel. A curious event took place in 1817 at nearby Knole Park when a young woman arrived at the door of the local squire saying that she was an Oriental princess who had been kidnapped and taken on board a ship, from which she had escaped by jumping overboard. The squire believed the story and 'adopted' Princess Caraboo, who soon became the toast of Bath. Her fame spread far enough to come to the attention of her former Bristol landlady, who identified the fake princess as a certain Mary Baker, a penniless woman from Devon. The embarrassed squire raised the money to send the impostor to Philadelphia. She returned some years later to Bristol, where she died in 1865.

CHIPPING SODBURY

This pleasant market town was one of the earliest examples of post-Roman town planning, its settlement being arranged in strips on either side of the main street in the 12th century. The town once enjoyed prosperity as a market and weaving centre, and it was during that period that the large parish church was built.

A mile or so to the east, on a loop off the A432, is **Old Sodbury**, whose part-Norman church contains some exceptional tombs and monuments. One of these is a carved stone effigy of a 13th century knight whose shield is a very rare wooden carving of a knight. Also in the church is the tomb of David Harley, the Georgian diplomat who negotiated the treaty which ended the American War of Independence. A tower just to the east of the church marks a vertical shaft, one of a series sunk to ventilate the long tunnel that carried the London-South Wales railway through the Cotswold escarpment. Opened in 1903, the 2½ mile tunnel required its own brickworks and took five years to complete.

A lane leads south from Old Sodbury to **Dodington House**, built between 1796 and 1816 where previously an Elizabethan house stood. It was designed in lavish neo-Roman style by the classical architect James Wyatt, who was killed in a carriage accident before seeing his work completed. The house, whose interior is even more ornate than the facade, is open daily in the summer. Connected to the house by an elegant conservatory is the private Church of St Mary, also designed by Wyatt, in the shape of a Greek cross.

AROUND CHIPPING SODBURY

Badminton

4 miles E of Chipping Sodbury off the B4040

The **Badminton Park** estate was founded by Edward Somerset, the son of the Marquis of Worcester, whose 25-foot monument stands in the little church next to the main house. The central section of the house dates from the 1680s and contains some marvellous carvings in lime wood by Grinling Gibbons. The rest of the house, along with the grounds and the many follies and gateways, is the work of the mid-18th century architect William Kent. The house contains an important collection of Italian, English and Dutch paintings. The game of badminton is said to have started here during a weekend party in the 1860s. The Duke of Beaufort and his guests wanted to play tennis in the entrance hall but were worried about damaging the paintings; someone came up with the bright idea of using a cork studded with feathers instead of a ball. In such a moment of inspiration was the game born, and it was one of the guests at that weekend bash who later took the game to Pakistan, where the first rules were formalised.

Many of the buildings on the estate, including the parish church and the estate villages of Great and Little Badminton, were designed in an ornate castellated style by Thomas Wright. The park is perhaps best known as the venue of the Badminton Horse Trials, which annually attract the best of the international riders, and spectators in their thousands.

Didmarton

7 miles NE of Chipping Sodbury on the A433

Plenty of interest here, notably the medieval Church of St Lawrence, left alone by the serial remodellers of Victorian times and retaining its original three-storey pulpit and antique box pews. Across the road a semicircle of stones marks the site of **St Lawrence's Well**, which the saint himself, after a personal visit, promised would never run dry. In the centre of the village, **Kingsmead House** has two oddities in its garden: an octagonal gazebo from which the owner could get the first view of the stagecoaches arriving from Bath and a Gothic hermit's house made of yew.

Horton

3 miles N of Chipping Sodbury off the A46

On high ground northeast of the long, narrow village stands the National Trust's **Horton Court**, a part-Norman manor house rebuilt for William Knight, the man given the task of presenting Henry VIII's case to the Pope when the King was trying to divorce Catherine of Aragon. Among the many interesting features is a covered walkway resembling a Roman cloister. The 12th century Great Hall survives from the earlier building.

Wickwar

5 miles N of Chipping Sodbury on the B4060

A market town of some importance in days gone by, Wickwar had its own mayor and corporation and two breweries; in the 1890s it became the first town in the west to install electric street lighting. Wickwar boasts a number of handsome Georgian buildings, notably the town hall with its distinctive bell tower and arches. A round tower close to the church marks a vertical shaft sunk in 1841 to ventilate the railway tunnel that runs below. To the east, across South

Moon Ridings and up on to the ridge, stands the **Hawkesbury Monument**, designed in Chinese style and erected in 1846 as a memorial to Lord Robert Somerset of Badminton, a general at the Battle of Waterloo. It has 145 steps, and the reward for climbing to the top is great views along the Cotswold escarpment and across the Severn to the Welsh mountains.

GLOUCESTER

The capital city of Gloucestershire first gained prominence under the Romans, who in the 1st century AD established a fort to guard what was then the lowest crossing point on the Severn. A much larger fortress soon followed, and the settlement of Colonia Glevum became one of the most important military bases, crucial in confining the rowdy Celts to Wales. William the Conqueror held a Christmas parliament and commissioned the Domesday Book in Gloucester, and also ordered the rebuilding of the abbey, an undertaking which included the building of a magnificent church that was the forerunner of the superb Norman Cathedral. The elaborate carved tomb of Edward ll, murdered at Berkeley Castle, is just one of many historic monuments in **Gloucester Cathedral**; another, the work of the Wedgwood designer John Flaxman, remembers one Sarah Morley, who died at sea in 1784, and is shown being delivered from the waves by angels. The ashes of the educationalist Dorothea Beale, who founded St Hilda's College, Oxford, are buried in a vault in the Lady Chapel. The exquisite fan tracery in the cloisters is the earliest and among the finest in existence, and the great east window, at 72 feet by 38 feet, is the largest surviving stained-glass window in the country. It was built to celebrate the English victory at the Battle of Crécy in 1346 and depicts the coronation of the Virgin surrounded by assorted kings, popes and saints. The young King Henry lll was crowned here, with a bracelet on his little head rather than a crown.

Gloucester Cathedral

The old area of the city around Gloucester Cross boasts some very fine early buildings, including St John's Church and the Church of St Mary de Crypt. Just behind the latter, near the house where Robert Raikes of Sunday School fame lived, stands an odd-looking tower built in the 1860s to honour Hannah, the wife of Thomas Fenn Addison, a successful solicitor. The tower was also a memorial to Raikes.

Three great inns were built in the 14th and 15th centuries to accommodate the scores of pilgrims who came to visit Edward ll's tomb, and two of them survive. The galleried New Inn, founded by a monk around 1450, doubled as a theatre and still retains the cobbled courtyard. It was from this inn that Lady Jane Grey was proclaimed Queen. Equally old is The Fleece Hotel in Westgate Street, which has a 12th century stone-vaulted undercroft. In the same street is **Maverdine**

House, a four-storey mansion reached by a very narrow passage. This was the residence and headquarters of Colonel Massey, Cromwell's commander, during the Civil War siege of 1643. Most of the region was in Royalist hands, but Massey survived a month-long assault by a force led by the King himself and thus turned the tide of war.

Gloucester Docks were once the gateway for waterborne traffic heading into the Midlands, and the handsome Victorian warehouses are always in demand as location sites for period films. The docks are now home to several award-winning museums. The **National Waterways Museum** (see panel below), on three floors of a beautiful warehouse, is entered by a lock chamber with running water and tells the fascinating story of Britain's canals with films, hands-on displays and floating historic boats.

The **Robert Opie Collection** at the **Museum of Advertising and Packaging** takes a nostalgic look at the 40s, 50s, 60s and 70s with the aid of toys and food, fashions, packaging and a continuous screening of vintage TV commercials. Soldiers of Gloucestershire uses archive film, photographs and life-size reconstructions to tell the history of the county's regiments.

Elsewhere in the city **Gloucester City Museum and Art Gallery** houses treasures from all over the county to reveal its history, from dinosaur bones and Roman remains to antique furniture and the decorative arts. Among the highlights are the amazing **Birdlip Mirror**, made in bronze for a Celtic chief just before the Roman conquest, two Roman tombstones and a section of the Roman city wall revealed under the cut-away gallery floor. English landscape painting is represented by Turner,

The National Waterways Museum

Llanthony Warehouse, Gloucester Docks, Gloucester,
Gloucestershire GL1 2EH
Tel: 01452 318056 Fax: 01452 318066
e-mail: marketing@nwm.demon.co.uk website: www.nwm.org.uk

There's so much to see and do for all ages at the award-winning **National Waterways Museum** located in a splendid Victorian warehouse in historic Gloucester Docks. The Museum charts the fascinating 300-year story of Britain's inland waterways through interactive displays, touch-screen computers, working models and historic boats. Visitors can find out what made the waterways possible, from the business brains and design genius to the hard work and sweat of the navvies, and try their hand at designing and painting a narrow boat, building a canal and navigating a boat through a lock.

The Museum has a working blacksmith's forge, a floor of displays dedicated to waterway trade and cargoes, a marvellous interactive gallery and family room where weights and pulleys, water playareas, period costume, large jigsaw puzzles and brass rubbings bring history to life in a way that is both instructive and entertaining. The museum shop sells unusual gifts and souvenirs and refreshment is provided in the café. There are computerised information points throughout the Museum and visitors can even take to the water themselves on a 45-minute boat trip running along the adjacent Gloucester & Sharpness Canal between Easter and October. The National Waterways Museum is owned by the Waterways Trust, which preserves, protects and promotes our waterway heritage while giving new life to their future.

Gainsborough and Richard Wilson. Timber-framed Tudor buildings house **Gloucester Folk Museum**, where the exhibits include farming, fishing on the Severn, the port of Gloucester, the Civil War, a Victorian schoolroom, a dairy, an ironmongery and a wheelwright's workshop. **Gloucester Transport Museum** has a small collection of well-preserved vehicles and baby carriages housed in a 1913 former fire station. The **House of the Tailor of Gloucester**, in College Court, is the house sketched by Beatrix Potter in 1897 and used in her tale *The Tailor of Gloucester*. It now brings that story to life, complete with Simpkin the Cat and an army of helpful mice.

In the southwestern suburbs of Gloucester are the ruins of **Llanthony Abbey**. The explanation of its Welsh name is an interesting one. The priory of Llanthony was originally founded in the Black Mountains of Wales at the beginning of the 12th century, but the inmates were so frightened of the local Welsh that they begged the Bishop of Hereford to find them a safer place. The Bishop passed their plea to Milo, Earl of Hereford, who granted this plot of land for a second priory bearing the same name as the first. Llanthony Secunda was consecrated in 1136. On a nearby hill the monks built St Ann's Well, whose water was - is - believed to cure eye problems.

In a hangar at Gloucestershire Airport is the **Jet Age Museum**, whose exhibits include a Meteor and a Javelin.

AROUND GLOUCESTER

Hartpury

5 miles NW of Gloucester on the A417

There are two very interesting listed buildings here: a rare medieval set of bee hives in a building known as a bee bole, and, in the churchyard, a Soper stone tomb with a shrouded body on top. At nearby **Ashleworth** is a magnificent 14th century tithe barn with a stone-tiled roof, projecting porches and elaborate interlocking roof timbers.

Twigworth

2 miles N of Gloucester off the A38

Twigworth is the home of **Nature in Art**, a renowned museum of wildlife art housed in 18th century Wallsworth Hall.

Pauntley

8 miles N of Gloucester on the A417

The penniless orphan boy who in the pantomime fable was attracted by the gold-paved streets of London and who became its Lord Mayor was born at **Pauntley Court**. Richard Whittington, neither penniless nor an orphan, was born here about 1350, one of three sons of landowner Sir William de Whittington and Dame Joan. He became a mercer in London, then an important financier and was three times Mayor (not Lord Mayor - that title had not been invented). He married Alice Fitzwarren, the daughter of a wealthy landowner from Dorset. The origin of the cat connection is unclear, but an event which could have contributed to the myth was the discovery in 1862 of the carved figure of a boy holding a cat in the foundations of a house in Gloucester. The carving can be seen in Gloucester Museum.

Redmarley d'Abitot

9 miles NW of Gloucester on the A417

This hilltop village, built on the red marle (clay) from which it takes its name and once the property of the French d'Abitot family, was for a time the home of the actress Lily Langtry, mistress of the Prince of Wales, later King Edward VII. The link with the actress is remembered in two streets in the village - Drury Lane and Hyde Park Corner.

Pickwicks Of Tewkesbury

Church Street, Tewkesbury, Gloucestershire GL20 5RX
Tel/Fax: 01684 290397
website: www.tmgcon.com/pickwicks

Built as merchant's house in the 14th century, near the magnificent 12th century Abbey, **Pickwicks of Tewkesbury** has since 1990 been the base of operations for John and Mary Green, leading merchants in tea and coffee. A narrow doorway in the black-and-white timbered frontage leads into a display area filled with everything to do with tea and coffee, and at the back there are seated areas serving teas, coffees and light refreshments. The stock includes over 200 teapots, and tea and coffee equipment from Bodum and other leading manufacturers. And of course there's the tea and the coffee.

Tea is available in over 40 varieties, and the top of the range in terms of price and exclusivity is the Jasmine Chung Hao from China; besides the 40 there are black teas flavoured with anything from almonds to wild cherry. The choice of coffees is equally impressive, divided on the price list between high, strong and medium roast and including the wonderful and highly prized Jamaican Blue Mountain. The mail order service is an expanding part of the business, with teas and coffees sent anywhere in the UK. Coffee can be sent as whole beans or ground for any of the following: percolator, cafetière, permanent filter, espresso, paper filter or Turkish.

Woodend Farm

Tewkesbury, Gloucestershire GL20 6EE
Tel: 01684 299749 Fax: 01684 291554
e-mail: cotswoldcharm@woodendfarm.co.uk
website: www.woodendfarm.info

On the A38 two miles north of Tewkesbury, with sweeping views across the Cotswolds, **Woodend Farm** makes an ideal touring base and is also a perfect venue for a country house party. Owner Philip Workman, has converted a number of buildings on the estate into stylish, comfortable self-catering accommodation for small or large groups. The 7-bedroomed, creeper-clad redbrick farmhouse with its bakehouse annexe offers generous living space for up to 18 guests, with a huge farmhouse kitchen complete with oil-fired Aga, large leafy gardens, a children's playground and a heated outdoor swimming pool.

Also available to guests is a unique complex of four individually styled cottages providing equally splendid accommodation for parties of 2 to 22 people. The Banquet Barn has its own kitchen, cloakrooms and blazing log fire, and after meeting and eating together in style, guests can retire to the peace and privacy of their individual cottages, which also have all the facilities needed for self-catering. The third possibility is the Coach House, a very characterful detached, centrally heated cottage with four bedrooms sleeping up to 10 guests. It has a large beamed lounge, a farmhouse-style kitchen and a lawned leisure area with access from a spiral staircase leading off the balcony.

TEWKESBURY

A town of historic and strategic importance close to the confluence of the Severn and Avon rivers. Those rivers also served to restrict the lateral expansion of the town, which accounts for the unusual number of tall buildings. Its early prosperity was based on the wool and mustard trades, and the movement of corn by river also contributed to its wealth. Tewkesbury's main thoroughfares, High Street, Church Street and Barton Street, form a Y shape, and the area between is a marvellous maze of narrow alleyways and small courtyards hiding many grand old pubs and medieval cottages. At the centre of it all is **Tewkesbury Abbey**, the cathedral-

Tewkesbury Abbey

sized parish church of St Mary. One of the largest and grandest parish churches in the country, it was founded in the 8th century and completely rebuilt in the

THE GARDENERS ARMS

Beckford Road, Alderton, Gloucestershire GL20 8NL
Tel: 01242 620257

In a village just off the B4077 between Teddington and Toddington, the **Gardeners Arms** is a beautiful old black and white thatched building dating from the late 15th century. Major refurbishment has not lessened the terrific period appeal of the place, which boasts massive stone walls, ancient beams and an original well that is a talking point in the bar, where it functions as a table for resting drinks.

Proprietors Mike Wakeman and Wendy Fear have built up a strong following at the Gardeners with the well-kept real ales (the annual beer festival is a popular summer occasion) and the excellent food served lunchtime and evening and all day on Sunday.

In the restaurant, the main à la carte and fixed price menus provide an impressive choice to suit all

tastes and appetites, and the fish specials are always in great demand. A lighter bar snack menu is available at lunchtime, with a choice that runs from doorstep sandwiches, jacket potatoes, fajita wraps and salad bowls to beef or chicken burgers, fishcakes with a lime butter sauce (an all-time favourite dish), battered cod and rump steaks. Regular theme nights, music nights and quiz nights mean that there's nearly always something entertaining going on at this most congenial of pubs, which has ample car parking space and a large garden with two petanque pitches.

Upper Court & Courtyard Cottages

Kemerton, Nr Tewkesbury, Gloucestershire
GL20 7HY
Tel: 01386 725351 Fax: 01386 725472
e-mail: diana@uppercourt.co.uk
website: www.uppercourt.co.uk

Upper Court is a magnificent Georgian manor with 15 acres of grounds that include a two-acre lake, a dovecote and a watermill on a site recorded in the Domesday Book. The Manor is the home of Bill and Diana Herford, and their house is a perfect place for a private party or special celebration; a marquee by the lake is an idyllic setting for a wedding party, and the main reception rooms in the house are available for small conferences and seminars.

The guest bedrooms, all with en suite facilities, tv and tea-makers, have either twin beds or four-posters and are appointed with great style and taste, with English chintz, antique porcelain, pictures and needlework; one of the rooms is on the ground floor. There are plenty of magazines to read by the fire in the drawing room, and meals can be served in the dining room or on the lawn (breakfast can also be taken in the bedrooms). Adjoining the main house are the Courtyard Cottages, offering self-catering accommodation of the highest standard in five beautifully appointed cottage sleeping from 2 to 10. Excellent home-cooked meals can be brought to the cottages, and private dinner parties can be arranged in the manor house for cottage guests.

Children are welcome in the cottages, but pets are not permitted in the cottages or in the manor house. The gardens and grounds (National Garden Scheme) are superb and the lake is home to a variety of wildfowl, swans, ducks, geese and herons. Fly-fishing is available, and other amenities on site include a heated swimming pool (July and August), an all-weather tennis court and a croquet lawn. Diana and Bill are the most friendly and helpful hosts and their son Oliver is a rising young potter with his own studio on the premises. Kemerton is one of the prettiest villages on Bredon Hill, a beauty spot immortalised in the poem by AE Housman. The clay pigeon shooting on the hill is highly recommended, and a walk to the summit is rewarded with wonderful views covering parts of at least five counties.

11th. It was once the church of the Benedictine Abbey and was among the last to be dissolved by Henry Vlll. In 1540, it was saved from destruction by the townspeople, who raised £453 to buy it from the Crown. Many of its features are on a grand scale - the colossal double row of Norman pillars; the six-fold arch in the west front; and the vast main tower, 132 feet in height and 46' square, the tallest surviving Norman main tower in the world. The choir windows have stained glass dating from the 14th century, and the abbey has more medieval monuments than any besides Westminster. A chantry chapel was endowed by the Beauchamps, an influential family that married into another, that of Richard Neville, Warwick the Kingmaker.

Three museums tell the story of the town and its environs: the Little Museum, laid out like a typical old merchant's house; Tewkesbury Museum, with displays on the social history and archaeology of the area; and the **John Moore Countryside Museum**, a natural history collection displayed in a 15th century timber-framed house. The museum commemorates the work of John Moore, a well-known writer, broadcaster and naturalist, who was born in Tewkesbury in 1907.

The **Battle of Tewkesbury** was one of the fiercest in the Wars of the Roses. It took place in 1471 in a field south of the town which has ever since been known as Bloody Meadow. Following the Lancastrian defeat, those who had not been slaughtered in the battle fled to the Abbey, where the killing began again. Abbot Strensham intervened to stop the massacre, but the survivors, who included the Duke of Somerset, were handed over to King Edward IV and executed at Market Cross. The 17-year-old son of Henry VI, Edward Prince of Wales, was killed in the conflict and a plaque marking his final resting place can be seen in the Abbey. One of the victors of the battle was Gloucester, later Richard III. Tewkesbury was again the scene of military action almost two centuries later during the Civil War. The town changed hands several times during this period and on one occasion Charles I began his siege of Gloucester by requisitioning every pick, mattock, spade and shovel in Tewkesbury.

AROUND TEWKESBURY

KEMERTON
3 miles NE of Tewkesbury off the B4079

The village of Kemerton, below Bredon Hill and only a mile from the Vale of Evesham, is the scene of an annual tug of war between teams from local villages.

(Continued page 324)

Ye Olde Hobnails Inn

Little Washbourne, Nr Tewkesbury, Gloucestershire GL20 8MQ
Tel: 01242 620237

East of Tewkesbury on the B4077, **Ye Olde Hobnails Inn** is a country hostelry of great age and immense character. The focal point of one of the smallest communities in the county, Susan Ashton's splendid inn stands in extensive gardens with play areas for children. Inside, all is old-fashioned charm, and with its excellent food, real ales and good wines, it's a perfect spot to stop for a relaxing drink and a meal. Lunchtime brings classic pub fare, including the very popular Hobnail baps, while in the evening an à la carte menu offers a first-class choice of home-cooked dishes, with some extra special puddings to round things off in style.

WALK 9

Deerhurst, Apperley and the River Severn

Start	Deerhurst, by Odda's Chapel, signposted from B4213
Distance	7 miles (11.3km)
Approximate time	3½ hours
Parking	Deerhurst
Refreshments	Pub near Mumford's Farm, pub at Haw Bridge, pub on riverside path
Ordnance Survey maps	Landrangers 150 (Worcester & The Malverns, Evesham & Tewkesbury) and 162 (Gloucester & Forest of Dean), Explorer 179 (Gloucester, Cheltenham & Stroud)

From Deerhurst, noted for its Saxon church and chapel, the route crosses fields to Apperley and continues by the banks of a disused canal to reach the River Severn. The final 3 miles (4.8km) is a pleasant and relaxing walk beside the river, following the Severn Way. As this is an almost entirely flat walk, there are wide and extensive views in all directions, eastwards to the line of the Cotswolds and westwards – across the river – to the impressive profile of the Malverns.

Saxon churches are something of a rarity but in the small village of Deerhurst there are two. The walk starts by Odda's Chapel, a small late-Saxon chapel built by Odda, a kinsman of Edward the Confessor, in 1056. Nearby is the church which, although mainly medieval, retains some of its original Saxon stonework, arches and doorways. It was founded as a monastery, probably during the 8th century, and was a place of some importance in Saxon England but declined after the Norman Conquest with the rise of the great abbeys of Evesham, Tewkesbury and Gloucester in the locality. After its suppression in the 15th century, it became a parish church.

Where the lane ends at the car park, turn left over a stile, at a public footpath sign, and walk diagonally across a field in the direction indicated by a yellow arrow. Look out for a stile on the right at the end of a line of trees and head across to climb it. Continue across the next field and climb a stile in the far corner onto a narrow lane.

Turn right, follow the lane around a left-hand bend and at a right-hand bend, keep ahead **A**, passing to the left of a gate, to a stile. Climb it, walk along an enclosed path, by a young plantation on the right, climb another stile and keep straight ahead across a field to climb a stile on the far side. Keep in the same direction across a playing-field to a road, turn right and, at a public footpath sign, turn left over a stile. Continue by a fence on the left, climb a stile in the field corner, keep ahead to climb another, walk across the end of a garden and climb another stile. Bear slightly left across a field, climb a stile in the far corner, continue in the same

WALK 9

direction across the next field and climb a stile onto a road in front of the Farmers Arms B.

Turn right and, at a public footpath sign, turn right over a stile and head gently uphill in a straight line between widely spaced trees. In the top, right-hand corner, climb two stiles in quick succession and continue over the brow of a hill to another stile. Climb it, walk across the next field, climb a stile in the right-hand corner and continue along a fence-lined path to emerge onto a lane in Apperley C. The main part of the village – with its green, pond and brick-built church – is to the right.

Turn left and at a public bridleway sign – where the lane bears right in front of a new housing estate – turn left onto an enclosed path. This attractive, tree-lined path descends gently to a road. Cross over and continue along the enclosed track opposite. The track later bends right, turns left in front of a gate and finally crosses a footbridge to a T-junction D. Turn right along a path that keeps beside the disused Coome Hill Canal on the left for just over ¾ mile (1.2km), eventually going through a gate onto a lane. The canal was built in 1796 to link the coalfields of the Forest of Dean with Cheltenham. It closed in 1876, and the area is now a nature reserve.

Turn left along the lane to cross a bridge over the disused canal and after ¼ mile (400km) turn right over a stile to join the Severn Way E. Walk across a meadow, bearing right to keep parallel with the riverbank, and at its far edge turn first right and then left to climb a stile. Bear left across the next meadow and climb two stiles in quick succession. Now continue along the riverbank to a road, climbing several stiles. In the last field before the road, look out for a stile on the left about half-way along it. Climb the stile, turn right and head across to climb another one and walk along a track, passing to the left of a house. At a fork, take the left-hand path, which heads up to the road to the right of Haw Bridge F.

Cross over, climb the stile opposite and continue by the River Severn back to Deerhurst. At one point the route keeps along the edge of a caravan site and passes the Coalhouse Inn but otherwise it is mainly across meadows beside the river, crossing several stiles. Soon after passing the Yew Tree Inn on the opposite side of the river, you see Odda's Chapel over to the right. At a public footpath sign in front of a large, solitary oak tree, turn right along a track and go through a gate to return to the start. ●

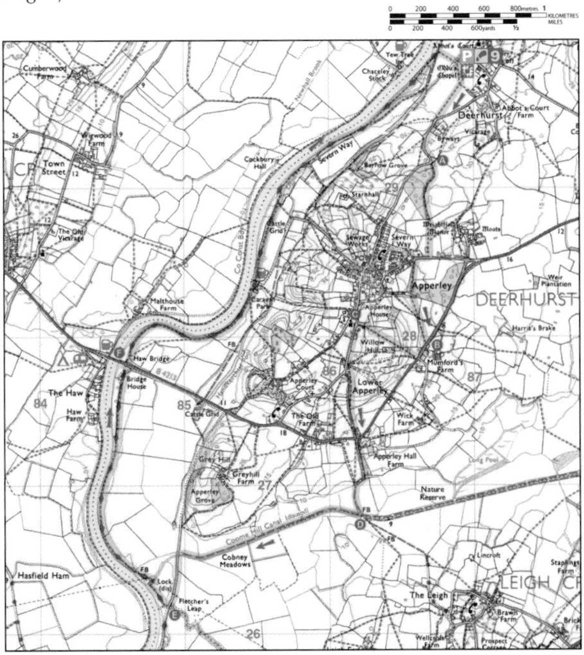

Bredon Pottery

High Street, Bredon, Nr Tewkesbury, Gloucestershire GL20 7 LW
Tel: 01684 773417
e-mail: bredonpottery@aol.com

In a village four miles east of Tewkesbury on the Gloucestershire-Worcestershire border, **Bredon Pottery** is run by Tony and Sue Davies, who make a range of decorated earthenware pottery for use in the house, kitchen, conservatory and garden. The kitchenware is in two different styles: blue and white, with a fresh, bright, lively look, and a traditional slipware range in the earthier colours of browns, yellows and black. They also produce a range of garden pots and planters in a variety of shades of grey, brown and terracotta. All the pottery is ovenproof and dishwasher-proof, and every piece is both practical and attractive. Everything is made and fired at the Pottery and visitors can sometimes see the wares taking shape in the workshop that adjoins the shop, where a large range of the pottery is on display.

Tony and Sue belong to both the Gloucestershire Guild of Craftsmen and the Worcestershire Guild of Designer Craftsmen, and they exhibit regularly with both these groups. Customers can see the wares on display at such prestigious venues as the Three Counties Show at Malvern or the Gloucestershire Guild Exhibition at Painswick. The owners are happy to undertake commissions for special occasions such as births and weddings, encouraging customers to visit in person to discuss the details of an individual piece; the Pottery, which is located on the main street of the village, is open from 10 to 6 Tuesday to Saturday. If you are making a special journey, please phone to confirm they are open.

Bredon

4 miles NE of Tewkesbury on the B4080

Bredon Barn is a 14th century barn built of Cotswold stone, with a splendid aisled interior and unusual stone chimney cowling.

Deerhurst

3 miles S of Tewkesbury off the A38

On the eastern bank of the Severn, a village whose current size and status belies a distinguished past. The church, with a distinct Celtic feel, is one of the oldest in England, with parts dating back to the 7th century, and its treasures include a unique double east window, a 9th century carved font, a Saxon carving of the Virgin and Child and some fine brasses dating from the 14th and 15th centuries. One depicts the Cassey family, local landowners, and their dog Terri.

Another Saxon treasure, 200 yards from the church, is **Odda's Chapel**, dedicated in 1056 and lost for many centuries before being gradually rediscovered after 1885 under an unsuspecting half-timbered house. The connection was then made with a stone inscribed with the date of consecration discovered in 1675 and now on view in the Ashmolean in Oxford.

Forthampton

3 miles W of Tewkesbury off the A438

This unspoilt Severn Vale village is dominated by the ancient Church of St Mary and by **Forthampton Court**, sometime home to the abbots of Tewkesbury and still retaining its fine 14th century banqueting hall, chapel and a medieval wood-based picture of Edward the Confessor. Near the churchyard can be seen relics of harsher times - a set of stocks and a whipping post complete with manacles.

7 THE COTSWOLDS

Cheltenham

'The most English and the least spoiled of all our countrysides.' So wrote JB Priestley in 1933 in his *English Journey*, and 70 years on his verdict would surely have been the same. Part of the Jurassic uplands that cross the country from the southwest to the northeast, the Cotswold escarpment runs for 50 miles from Dyrham to Chipping Campden, mainly in Gloucestershire but also taking in part of north Oxfordshire. The general height is about 650 feet, but Cleeve Hill, the highest point, rises to over 900 feet. The county has a wealth of Neolithic remains, particularly long barrows, while the Bronze Age is represented by large numbers of round barrows, mainly in the Cotswolds. This area also contains many Iron Age hill forts, the majority in secure sites on the escarpment. The Romans, too, left their mark in roads and the remains of villas and camps, the best of the former being at Chedworth near Cheltenham. The oolitic limestone that makes up the Cotswolds produces fine building material, and the mellow stone buildings are one of the most characteristic features of the region. These range from pretty little cottages nestling in the valleys to sturdy barns and handsome churches, some modest, others built on the grand scale with wealth derived from the wool trade. The best of these are at Cirencester, Fairford, Chipping Campden and Northleach. In the Middle Ages Gloucestershire was renowned throughout Europe as the source of prime wool: 'In Europe the best wool is English. In England the best wool is the Cotswold.' The Cotswolds were ideal grazing grounds and the abbeys and monasteries raised huge flocks. The Church and the merchants became rich, and reminders of those days are present in abundance in the churches, in the houses and in the mills, which

River Thames, Lechlade

at one time were numbered in their hundreds; many still survive, often restored to working order.

Walkers of all energy levels are very well catered for in the Cotswolds, from pottering round parish paths to long-distance hiking on the Cotswold Way, and the number of published cycling trails grows each year.

Blenheim Palace

LOCATOR MAP

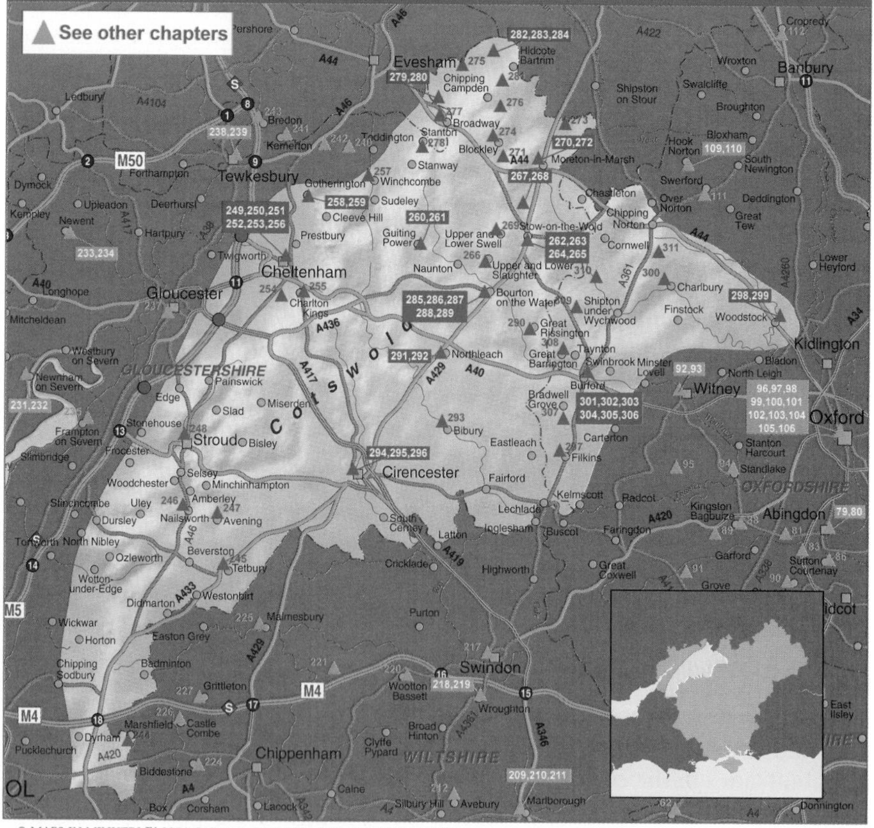

ADVERTISERS AND PLACES OF INTEREST

SOUTH GLOUCESTERSHIRE AND THE SOUTHERN COTSWOLDS

DYRHAM
5 miles E of Bristol on the A46

The National Trust-owned **Dyrham Park** stands on the slope of the Cotswold ridge, a little way south of the site of a famous 6th century battle between Britons and Saxons. This striking baroque mansion, used as a location for the filming of *Remains of the Day*, houses a wonderful collection of artefacts accumulated by the original owner William Blathwayt during diplomatic tours of duty in Holland and North America (he later became Secretary of State to William lll). Among the most notable are several Dutch paintings and some magnificent Delft porcelain. The west front of the house looks out across a terrace to lawns laid out in formal Dutch style; much of the estate is a deer park, which perhaps it was originally, as the word Dyrham means 'deer enclosure' in Saxon. A charming little church in the grounds has a Norman font, a fine 15th century memorial brass and several memorials to the Winter and Blathwayt families.

MARSHFIELD
10 miles E of Bristol on the A420

This old market town was once the fourth wealthiest town in Gloucestershire, after Bristol, Gloucester and Cirencester, its prosperity based on the malt and wool industries. Its long main street has many handsome buildings dating from the good old days of the 17th and 18th centuries, but not many of the coaching inns remain that were here in abundance when the town was an important stop on the London-Bristol run. Among the many notable buildings

LANNOWE ORIENTAL TEXTILES

Tel: 01225 891487 Fax: 01225 891182
e-mail: joanna@lannowe.co.uk

Joanna Titchell has worked with textiles and carpets for 25 years and runs her business from two workshops in South Gloucestershire. The services offered by her business cover restoration, conservation, washing, dyeing, and plate photography. Oriental rugs, antique carpets, kilims, Indian dhurris, European tapestries, embroidery and needlework are all handled with great care and skill, and Joanna's customers range from individuals with cherished items to museums and stately homes. Her business began in London in 1976 and moved to South Gloucestershire soon after.

Now operating from two workshops, the business gives training and employment to many local people and has built up a large pool of expertise. The main workshop is located in a converted malting house behind a Georgian frontage in a row of Cotswold stone houses. On entering, the visitor is overwhelmed by hundreds of hanks of brightly coloured fabrics used in the conservation and restoration processes; by the huge carpets under restoration; and by the feast of colours in the dyeing and colour matching areas. Visits are strictly by appointment, and a telephone call will reveal the exact location of the workshop!

are the **Tolzey market hall** and the imposing Church of St Mary, which boasts a fine Jacobean pulpit and several impressive monuments from the 17th and 18th centuries. Each Boxing Day brings out the **Marshfield Mummers**, who take to the streets to perform a number of time-honoured set pieces wearing costumes made from newspapers and accompanied by a town crier. On the northern edge of town is a folk museum at Castle Farm.

Westonbirt Arboretum

A lane leads south through a pretty valley to the delightful hamlet of **St Catherine's**, whose church contains a splendid 15th century stained-glass window with four lights depicting the Virgin Mary, the Crucifixion, St John and St Peter. The great manor house, St Catherine's Court, now privately owned, once belonged to the Benedictine priory at Bath.

Westonbirt

9 miles NE of Chipping Sodbury on the A433

Westonbirt Arboretum, three miles south of Tetbury, contains one of the finest collections of temperate and shrubs in the world - 18,000 of them spread over 600 acres of glorious Cotswold countryside. Wealthy landowner Robert Stayner Holford founded this tree wonderland by planting trees for his own interest and pleasure. His son, Sir George Holford, was equally enthusiastic about trees and continued his father's work until his death in 1926, when he was succeeded by his nephew, the 4th Earl of Morley. Opened to the public in 1956 and now managed by the Forestry Commission, the arboretum has something to offer all year round: a crisp white wonderland after winter snows, flowering shrubs and rhododendrons in spring, tranquil glades in summer, glorious reds and oranges and golds in the autumn. The grounds provide endless delightful walks, including 17 miles of footpaths, and there's a visitor centre, plant centre, café and picnic areas.

Tetbury

11 miles NE of Chipping Sodbury on the A433

A really charming Elizabethan market town, another to have prospered from the wool trade. Its most famous building is the stone-pillared 17th century **Market House** in the heart of town, but a visit should also take in the ancient **Chipping Steps** connecting the market house to the old trading centre, and the Church of St Mary, an 18th century period piece with high-backed pews, huge windows made from recovered medieval glass and slender timber columns hiding sturdy iron uprights. **Tetbury Police Museum**, housed in the original cells of the old police station, has a fascinating collection of artefacts, memorabilia and uniforms from the Gloucestershire Constabulary.

Tetbury Church

Two miles northwest of Tetbury, west of the B4104, stands **Chavenage House**, a beautiful Elizabethan mansion built of grey Cotswold stone on earlier monastic foundations in the characteristic E shape of the period. The elegant front aspect has remained virtually unchanged down the years, and the present owners, the Lowsley-Williams family, can trace their lineage back to the original owners. Two rooms are covered with rare 17th century tapestries, and the house contains many relics from the Cromwellian period. Cromwell is known to have stayed at the house, and during the Civil War he persuaded the owner, Colonel Nathaniel Stephens, a relative by marriage, to vote for the King's impeachment. According to the Legend of Chavenage the owner died after being cursed by his daughter and was taken away in a black coach driven by a headless horseman. The present owner, who conducts tours round the property, welcomes visitors to 'Gloucestershire's second most haunted house' (Berkeley Castle is the most haunted!). In 1970 an astonishing find was made in the attic - a portfolio of watercolours by George IV of plans for the restoration of Windsor Castle.

Beverston

2 miles W of Tetbury on the A4135

The same Robert Stayner Holford who started the Westonbirt Arboretum built the model village of Beverston in conjunction with the architect Lewis Vulliamy. Their aim was to combine rural practicality with improved standards of accommodation, and the limestone terraces and model farms can be seen from the main road. The village also had a castle, once occupied by Earl Godwin, father of King Harold, and the earthworks are still visible.

Wotton-under-Edge

10 miles W of Tetbury on the B4508

A hillside former wool town with a number of interesting buildings: Berkeley House with its stone Jacobean front; the terraced house that was the family home of Isaac Pitman and where he devised his renowned method of shorthand; the Perry and Dawes almshouses; and the Church of St Mary with memorials to Lord Berkeley and his wife Margaret.

Tortworth

8 miles N of Chipping Sodbury off the B4509

Overlooking the village green stands the Church of St Leonard, which contains some fine 15th century stained glass and a pair of canopied tombs of the Throckmorton family, former owners of the Tortworth Park estate. In a field over the church wall are several interesting trees, including an American hickory, a huge silver-leafed linden and two Locust trees. Nearby, and the most famous of all, is the famous **Tortworth Chestnut**, a massive Spanish chestnut which the diarist John Evelyn called 'the great chestnut of King Stephen's time'. Certainly it was well established by Stephen's time (1130s), and a fence was put up to protect it in 1800. At that time a brass plaque was put up with this inscription:

'May man still guard thy
venerable form
From the rude blasts and
tempestuous storms.
Still mayest thou flourish
through succeeding time
And last long last the
wonder of the clime.'

And last it has; its lower branches have bent to the ground and rooted in the soil, giving the impression of a small copse rather than a single tree.

Ozleworth

8 miles NE of Chipping Sodbury on minor roads

A secluded hamlet with a very unusual circular churchyard, one of only two in England. The church itself has a rare feature in a six-sided Norman tower. Also at Ozleworth is the National Trust's **Newark Park**, built as a hunting lodge by the Poyntz family in Elizabethan times. James Wyatt later converted it into a castellated country house. Open by appointment only.

This is great walking country, and one of the finest walks takes in the **Midger Wood Nature Reserve** on its way up to **Nan Tow's Tump**, a huge round barrow whose tomb is said to contain the remains of Nan Tow, a local witch.

DURSLEY

One of the most notable buildings in this former centre of the cloth-making trade is the 18th century market hall standing on 12 pillars at a busy town-centre junction. It has a bell turret on its roof and a statue of Queen Anne facing the fine parish church. William Shakespeare reputedly spent some time in Dursley after being spotted poaching, and there is a reference to a bailiff from the town in *Henry IV*. Cloth is still produced in the mill at Cam on the northern edge of Dursley, continuing a tradition started in the 16th century. Local legend is rich in stories about **Cam Long Down**, a small, isolated peak that is sometimes claimed as the scene of King Arthur's last battle. One story concerns the Devil, who decided one day to cart away the Cotswolds and dam the Severn. On setting out with his first cartload he met a cobbler and asked him how far it was to the river. The cobbler showed him one of the shoes he was taking home to mend and replied, 'Do you see this sole? Well,

I've worn it out walking from the Severn.' This persuaded the Devil, who was obviously a lazy devil, to abandon his task; he tipped out his load, creating the hill that can be seen today.

STINCHCOMBE
3 miles W of Dursley off the A4135

Stancombe Park, on the southern edge of Stinchcombe, is a handsome country house built in 1880 on the site of a Roman villa, whose mosaic floor can be seen in Gloucester Museum. The gardens at Stancombe are occasionally open to the public.

NORTH NIBLEY
2 miles SW of Dursley on the B4060

This village was the birthplace, around 1494, of William Tynedale, the first man to translate and print the Old and New Testaments. He used the original sources instead of the approved Latin, for which heresy he was burnt at the stake in Belgium in 1536. 350 years later the imposing **Tynedale Monument**, paid for by public subscription, was erected on the ridge above the village to commemorate his life and work. Standing 111 feet high on the escarpment, it is one of the most prominent landmarks on the Cotswold Way and offers superb views. North Nibley is also the site of the last 'private' battle in England, which took place in 1471 between rival barons William Lord Berkeley and Viscount de Lisle.

ULEY
11 miles NE of Chipping Sodbury on the B4066

Calm and quiet now, Uley was once a busy centre of commerce, mainly in the cloth-making industry. The most distinguished house in the area is **Owlpen Manor**, a handsome Tudor country house set in formal Queen Anne terraced yew gardens. Inside, contrasting with the ancient polished flagstones and the putty-coloured plaster, are fine pieces of William Morris-inspired Arts and Crafts furniture; there's also a rare beadwork collection and some unique 17th century wall hangings.

The village lies in the shadow of **Uley Bury**, a massive Iron Age hill fort which has thrown up evidence of habitation by a prosperous community of warrior farmers during the 1st century BC. Another prehistoric site, a mile along the ridge, is Uley Long Barrow, known locally as **Hetty Pegler's Tump**. This chambered long barrow, 180 feet in length, takes its name from Hester Pegler, who came from a family of local landowners. Adventurous spirits can crawl into this Neolithic tomb on all fours, braving the dark and the dank smell to reach the burial chambers, where they will no longer be scared by the skeletons that terrified earlier visitors. The walls and ceilings of the chamber are made of huge stone slabs infilled with drystone material.

A little further north, at the popular picnic site of **Coaley Peak** with its adjoining National Trust nature reserve, is another spectacular chambered tomb, **Nympsfield Long Barrow**.

NAILSWORTH

This small residential and commercial town was once, like so many of its neighbours, a centre of the wool trade. Several of the old mills have been modernised, some playing new roles, others plying their original trades. **Ruskin Mill** is a thriving arts and crafts centre. **Stokescroft** is an unusual 17th century building on Cossack Square. During restoration work in 1972 scribblings found on an attic wall

GREEN SPIRIT

Market Street, Nailsworth, Gloucestershire GL6 0BZ
Tel: 01453 835735 Fax: 835538

Owner Michael Chivers has put his experience in the field of organic and wholefoods, to excellent use in Green Spirit. Serving Nailsworth as both shop and café, Green Spirit stocks and serves only the best quality food and produce, much of it sourced locally. Honey comes from the bees at Ruskin Mill; milk and yoghurt and cheese from farms in the area; bread and cakes from local bakers; bacon, ham and sausages from the Royal Estate at Highgrove; essential oils from Hambledon. Also on sale are herbal remedies, wheat-free and dairy-free produce and organic wines, and the café is open for tea, coffee, soups and light snacks such as houmus with toast.

suggested that soldiers had been billeted there in 1812 and 1815. Perhaps this is why it is known locally as 'the Barracks'. It is thought to have housed Russian prisoners during the Crimean War, which accounts for the name of the square.

AVENING

2 miles SE of Nailsworth on the B4014

History aplenty in this ancient village. Each September it celebrates 'Pig Face Sunday', a festival harking back to the days when wild boar roamed the Cotswolds causing damage to crops, livestock and even human beings. One rogue animal caused such havoc that when it was caught it was hanged from an oak tree before being roasted and eaten.

In Hampton Fields to the northeast of the village is the extraordinary **Avening Long Stone**, standing eight feet high and

pierced with holes. This prehistoric standing stone is said in local legend to move on Midsummer's Eve.

STROUD

The capital of the Cotswold woollen industry, Stroud stands on the River Frome at a point where five valleys converge. The surrounding hill farms provided a constant supply of wool, and the Cotswold streams supplied the water-power. By the 1820s there were over 150 textile mills in the vicinity; six survive, one of them specialising in green baize for snooker tables. A stroll round the centre of town reveals some interesting buildings, notably the **Old Town Hall** dating from 1594 and the **Subscription Rooms** in neo-classical style. An easy walk from the centre is **Stratford Park**, a large park containing dozens of trees

THE BELL AT AVENING

29 High Street, Avening, Gloucestershire GL8 8NF
Tel/Fax: 01453 836422 website: www.thebellatavening.co.uk

Two cottages and a bakery were converted into a public house in the 19th century, and today the **Bell at Avening** retains its period charm intact. Cotswold stone walls, original beams, darkwood furnishings, upholstered bench seats and log fires create a lovely welcoming ambience in the two bars, and landlord Graham Hackney has the services of a top-class resident chef to provide an excellent range of dishes to enjoy with a glass or two of one of the many real ales on tap. This splendid free house on a corner site in the main street is also a good choice for an overnight stay, with three letting bedrooms in a renovated granary at the back of the pub.

FOUR CLOCKS ANTIQUES

14 George Street, Stroud, Gloucestershire GL5 3DY
Tel: 01453 767681 Fax: 01453 812719

In the antiques business for 20 years, David Partridge moved to George Street from premises elsewhere in Stroud in Millennium Year. **Four Clocks Antiques** is located in the town centre near the Tourist Information centre and takes its name from the Four Clocks Monument, a well-known Stroud landmark. The goods that David has for sale change constantly, both in the attractive window display and in the 650 square feet of shop space, which is filled with an interesting collection of general antiques, arms and armour, porcelain and jewellery - a wide-ranging choice that provides plenty of opportunity for browsing and buying a very special gift.

both ordinary and exotic. Lots of ducks on the pond.

FROCESTER
4 miles W of Stroud off the A419

In the grounds of the village-centre chapel stands the wonderful **Frocester Tithe Barn**, a massive 186 feet in length and looking much as it did when built on the instructions of Abbot John de Gamages between 1284 and 1306.

SELSLEY
2 miles S of Stroud off the A46

All Saints Church, built in the 1860s by wealthy mill-owner Sir Samuel Marling, is notable chiefly for its exceptional stained glass. This was commissioned from William Morris and Company and features designs by many of the Morris partnership, including Philip Webb, Burne-Jones, Ford Madox Brown, Dante Gabriel Rossetti and Morris himself.

WOODCHESTER
2 miles S of Stroud off the A46

Woodchester Park Mansion is one of Britain's most intriguing Victorian country houses. Building started in 1854 and was halted abruptly in 1868, three-quarters finished, with the scaffolding in place and the workmen's tools abandoned. What stands now, as in 1868, is a vast shell with gargoyles and

flying buttresses on the Gothic facade, and all the props and stays and tools inside. The mansion is now used as a training ground for stonemasons.

AMBERLEY
3 miles S of Stroud off the A46

In the churchyard at Amberley lie the remains of PC (Percival Christopher) Wren, whose best known work is *Beau Geste*, a romantic tale of the French Foreign Legion.

MINCHINHAMPTON
4 miles SE of Stroud off the A419

A scattered community on a ridge between two picturesque valleys, Minchinhampton acquired its market charter as far back as 1213. The area is good for walking and exploring, with the old stone quarries at Ball's Green and the National Trust woodland and grassland at **Minchinhampton and Rodborough Commons**. The majority of the commons are open to walkers and riders, and nature-lovers might spot rare butterflies such as the Chalkhill Blue, the tiny Green Hairstreak and the Duke of Burgundy Fritillary. The Commons are also famous for their grassland species, including the lovely Pasque flower, whose resurgence has been assisted by the introduction of a small herd of Belted Galloways to help manage the rich grassland areas of the lower slopes.

Bisley

4 miles E of Stroud on minor roads

Country roads lead across from Stroud or up from Oakridge Lynch to the delightful village of Bisley, which stands 780 feet above sea level and is known as 'Bisley-God-Help-Us' because of the winter winds which sweep across the hillside. Bisley's impressive All Saints Church dates from the 13th century and was restored in the early 19th by Thomas Keble, after whose poet and theologian brother John Keble College, Oxford was named. The font has two carved fish inside the bowl and a shepherd and sheep on the base. In the churchyard is the Poor Souls' Light, a stone wellhead beneath a spire dating from the 13th century. It was used to hold candles lit for souls in purgatory. Below the church are the **Seven Wells of Bisley** (also restored by Thomas Keble), which are blessed and decorated with flowers each year on Ascension Day. At the top of the village is a double lock-up built in 1824, with two cells beneath an ogee gable.

The village's main claim to fame is the story of the Bisley Boy. When Bisley was a rich wool town it had a royal manor, Over Court, where the young Princess Elizabeth (later Queen Elizabeth l) often stayed. The story goes that during one of those visits the princess, then aged 10, caught a fever and died. Fearing the wrath of her father Henry Vlll, her hosts looked for a substitute and found a local child with red hair and remarkably similar physical characteristics except for the rather important fact that the child was a boy called John Neville. Could this explain the Virgin Queen's reluctance to marry, her problem with hair loss and her 'heart that beats like a man's, or was the story made up to fit those facts? Alas, we will never know.

VALE OF GLOUCESTER AND THE CENTRAL COTSWOLDS

Slad

2 miles N of Stroud on the B4070

Immortalised by Laurie Lee in his autobiographical *Cider With Rosie*, the sprawling village of Slad in the valley of the same name was for centuries a centre for milling and the production of fruit. Cider gave way to champagne on March 13, 2002 after a Polish-bred horse called Galileo, trained by Tom George at Slad, was successful in one of the big novice hurdles at the Cheltenham Festival. A Roman villa was found in the Valley, and the votive tablets found on the site are now in Gloucester Museum.

Miserden

5 miles NE of Stroud off the B40470 or A417

Miserden Park Gardens, with views over the lovely Golden Valley, were created in the 17th century and are known for their spectacular spring bulbs, perennial borders, roses, topiary and an avenue of Turkish hazels.

Painswick

4 miles N of Stroud on the A46

This beautiful little town, known as the 'Queen of the Cotswolds', prospered with the wool trade, which had its peak in the second half of the 18th century. At that time 30 mills provided power within the parish, and the number of fine houses and farms in and around the town are witness to those days. Many of them are built of the pale grey limestone that was quarried at Painswick Hill.

St Mary's Church, which dates from around 1380, was the site of one of many local skirmishes in the Civil War when a party of Parliamentary soldiers came

Sue's Crafts

38 High Street, Cheltenham, Gloucestershire GL50 1EE
Tel/Fax: 01242 254477
e-mail: sue@suescrafts.com
website: www.suescrafts.com

On a corner site at the eastern end of the High Street is **Sue's Crafts**, which stocks an amazing variety of products connected with all aspects of needlecraft. Run by Sue and Dave Walker and their daughter Georgina, the shop has built up a customer base that extends over a wide area. Needles and pins, haberdashery items of all kinds, wools and fabrics, threads and ribbons and silk flowers, braids and beads, tools to make up quilts and cushions, paints, printed canvases, tapestry, rug and cross stitch kits by the hundred, frames in finished or kit form, rubber stamping, quilling, parchment craft requirements, greetings cards - all this and much more fills the little shop, which really is an Aladdin's Cave for anyone interested in or adept at needlework.

They started in 1994 selling at craft shows, exhibitions, hospitals and steam rallies and moved into the shop in 1999; over the past three years thay have greatly extended the range of craft items. What started as a hobby for Sue has developed into a full-time career: the mail order side of the business is expanding rapidly, and in the basement qualified teachers conduct courses on all kinds of crafts.

Catherine Shinn Decorative Textiles

7 Suffolk Parade, Cheltenham, Gloucestershire GL50 2AB
Tel: 01242 574546 e-mail: sales@catherineshinn.com
Fax: 01242 578495 website: www.catherineshinn.com

When Catherine Shinn opened her shop in the 1980s, she continued a family interest reaching back five generations. At **Catherine Shinn Decorative Textiles** she and her staff have gathered the skills and stock to produce a range of furnishing accessories, using traditional methods and fabrics from the 17th century to the present day. There is an extensive collection of antique textiles, as well as trimmings, cushions, pin cushions, bell pulls, needlework pictures, hangings and much more. Another speciality is a range of unique hand-blown glass decorations, many made from moulds in use since late Victorian times. Open from10 to 5 Monday to Saturday.

Venezia

6 Montpellier Avenue, Cheltenham, Gloucestershire GL50 1SA
Tel: 01242 521953 Fax: 01242 522343
e-mail: linda@veneziagifts.co.uk website: www.veneziagifts.co.uk

The magic and opulence of Venice are captured in Cheltenham in **Venezia**. Some years ago owner Linda Burridge opened the nearby Montpellier Gallery, featuring some of Venice's leading artists, and her love of all things Venetian inspired her to open the Venezia gift shop. Here, she has assembled a delightful collection including masks, pictures, glass, marbled papers, glamorous dresses, jackets and scarves, ranging from the eminently affordable to the extravagantly luxurious. Venezia also provides a chance to assist in the saving of Venice from the sea, as with each purchase a percentage is donated to the Venice in Peril fund.

under cannon fire, which did considerable damage to the building. In 1643 King Charles l spent the night at Court House before the siege of Gloucester. In the grounds of early-18th century **Painswick House**, on the B4073 at the northern edge of town, **Painswick Rococo Garden**, hidden away in magnificent Cotswold countryside, is a unique restored 18th century garden with plants from around the world and a maze planted in 1999 with a path structure in the shape of '250' to commemorate the garden's 250th anniversary. Other attractions are carpets of snowdrops in early spring, a kitchen garden, a specialist nursery, a children's nature trail, a gift shop and a restaurant.

A little further north, at Cranham, **Prinknash Abbey Park** (call it Prinnage) comprises an active monastery, chapel, working pottery, gift shop and tearoom. The Benedictine monks of Caldey Island moved here in 1928 when the old house was made over to them by the 20th Earl of Rothes in accordance with the wishes of his grandfather. They no longer occupy the old house, having moved into the impressive new monastery in 1972. The abbey chapel is open daily for solitude and contemplation. Visitors can have a guided tour round the pottery and buy a hand-made Prinknash pot. Part of the abbey gardens are given over to the **Prinknash Bird & Deer Park**, where visitors can feed and stroke the fallow deer and see the waterfowl, the peacocks and the African pygmy goats. By the lake is a charming two-storey Wendy House.

Edge

4 miles N of Stroud on the A473

Straddling a hilltop across the Spoonbed Valley, Edge has two delightful village greens and the mid 19th century Church of St John the Baptist with an ornate spire. To the west of the village lies **Scottsquarr Common**, an area of Special Scientific Interest with an abundance of wild flowers and butterflies and spectacular views.

CHELTENHAM

Smart, fashionable Cheltenham: a small, insignificant village until a mineral spring was accidentally discovered in 1715. According to tradition, the first medicinal waters were discovered when locals saw pigeons pecking at salty deposits which had formed around a spring. A local man, William Mason, built a pump room and began Cheltenham's transformation into one of Europe's leading Regency spa towns. Mason's son-in-law was the astute Captain Henry Skillicorne, who added a meeting room, a ballroom and a network of walks and carriageways, and called it a spa. A number of other springs were soon discovered, including one in the High Street around which the first Assembly Rooms were built. In 1788 the Royal seal of approval came in the shape of King George lll, who spent five weeks taking the

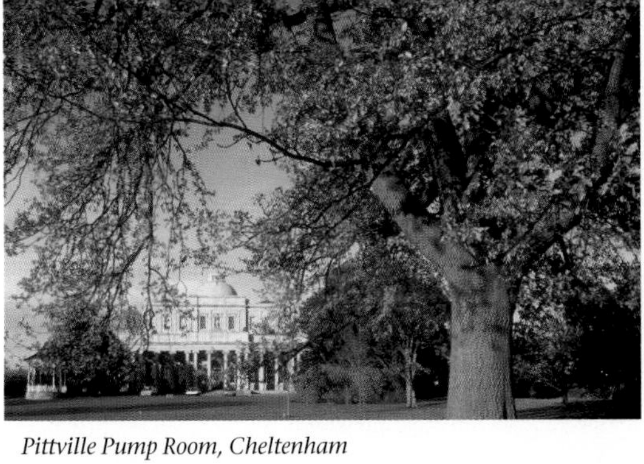

Pittville Pump Room, Cheltenham

Syreford Gallery

41 Great Norwood Street, Cheltenham, Gloucestershire GL50 2BQ
Tel: 01242 702272 Fax: 01242 255235
e-mail: caroline@syrefordgallery.co.uk

'A lot of quality in a small space' is one of the many complimentary remarks made by visitors to **Syreford Gallery**. Here since April 1998 after occupying a private house on the outskirts of town, Caroline Davis's gallery was set up to support recent graduates and now showcases new contemporary work by both young and more established artists. The pieces on display, every one of them unique, include paintings, sculptures, ceramics, metalwork, textiles and photography, and the gallery is open to visitors from 10 to 5 Tuesday to Saturday.

The Courtyard

22 Montpellier Spa Road, Cheltenham, Gloucestershire GL50 1UL
Tel: 01242 517412 e-mail: jane@22montpellier.co.uk
website: www.22montpellier.com

World travellers Jane and Bruce Reynolds settled in Cheltenham in the late 1980s and for the past two years have offered two luxurious apartments for self-catering guests. The **Courtyard** is part of a Regency building, close to some of the best shops and restaurants in town and comprises two bedrooms, a beautifully appointed bathroom, a kitchen/diner, utility room and large sitting room with tv, video and music centre. It also has a small courtyard garden with cast-iron furniture. In the same road, the Regency Maisonette offers equally outstanding accommodation; both apartments have the ETC Four Star rating. Minimum stay is 3 nights and a parking permit is available if required.

Cheltenham Pot & Plant Centre

Kidnappers Lane, Leckhampton, Nr Cheltenham,
Gloucestershire GL53 0NP Tel/Fax: 01242 513401

Cheltenham Pot & Plant Centre, run by partners Matt and Carl, is located just off the A46 five minutes drive south of Cheltenham. The bright, spacious display areas stock an enormous variety of pots in all shapes and sizes and styles, including the Clough Mill range, as well as ornaments and statues in stone and marble, and garden furniture made in Evesham. Locally grown annuals, perennials, alpines and shrubs are the basis of the plant side of the business, along with accessories such as peat, compost and bark chippings. The partners and their staff offer personal service and expert advice at the Centre, which is open from 9 to 5 seven days a week.

Six Ways Antiques

199 London Road, Charlton Kings, Cheltenham,
Gloucestershire GL52 6HU Tel: 01242 510672
e-mail: bob.sommer@lineon.net

Two miles outside Cheltenham on the A40 London road, **Six Ways Antiques** is owned and run by Bob and Jill Sommer, whose joint expertise covers many aspects of the antiques and allied trades. Their centre comprises 14 units filled with a vast array of antiques and collectables including furniture, china, glass, prints, silver, plate, flatware, linen, toys, painted furniture and much more. Six Ways also undertakes furniture restoration, upholstery and house clearances. Visitors are welcome call in to buy, sell or browse; the centre is open seven days a week, admission is free and there's ample free parking directly opposite.

Cheltenham Art Gallery & Museum

Clarence Street, Cheltenham, Gloucestershire GL50 3JT
Tel: 01242 237431 Fax: 01242 262334
e-mail: artgallery@cheltenham.gov.uk website:
www.cheltenhammuseum.org.uk

Cheltenham Art Gallery & Museum is one of only 52 museums in the country officially designated as a museum with an outstanding collection. In this case it comprises furniture, silver, jewellery, ceramics, carvings and textiles, produced by the Arts & Crafts Movement, whose members were inspired by the ideology of William Morris. The Museum also has a fine collection of paintings from the 17th century onwards, and 20th century gems. Among other highlights are displays on the history and archaeology of the area and special events, talks and exhibitions take place throughout the year. There is also a café and gift shop.

waters with his family and made Cheltenham a highly fashionable resort. An entirely new town was planned based on the best features of neoclassical Regency architecture, and as a result very few buildings of any antiquity still stand. One of these is the Church of St Mary, with parts going back to the 12th century and some very fine stained glass.

Skillicorne's walks and rides are now the tree-lined Promenade, one of the most beautiful boulevards in the country, its crowning glory the wonderful Neptune's Fountain, modelled on the Fontana di Trevi in Rome and erected in 1893. Housed in Pittville Park in the magnificent Pump Room overlooking gardens and lakes north of the town centre is the **Pittville Pump Room Museum**, which uses original period costumes to bring alive the story of Cheltenham from its Regency heyday to the 1960s. Special exhibitions are held throughout the year. **Cheltenham Art Gallery and Museum** (see panel above) has an acclaimed collection of furniture and silver, much of it made by Cotswold craftsmen and inspired by William Morris's Arts and Crafts Movements. Also Oriental porcelain, English ceramics, fine paintings and changing special exhibitions. Gustav Holst was born in 1874 in a terraced Regency house in Clarence Road, which is now the **Holst Birthplace Museum and Period House**. The original piano of the composer of *The Planets* is the centrepiece of the story of the man and his works, and there's a working kitchen, a Regency drawing room and a nursery.

Cheltenham Ladies College, where the pioneering Miss Dorothea Beale was principal, was founded in 1854. Two remarkable modern pieces of public art take the eye in the centre of town. The **Wishing Fish Clock** in the Regent Arcade is a work in metal by the famous artist and craftsman Kit Williams: below the clock, from which a mouse pops out when disturbed by the arrival of an egg laid by a duck on high, is suspended a 12 feet fish, which celebrates the hour by swishing its tail and blowing bubbles, to the delight and fascination of shoppers below. The mechanical parts of the clock are the work of the renowned local clockmaker Michael Harding. Off the High Street are the **Elephant Murals**, which portray an event that occurred in 1934 when three elephants from a travelling circus escaped and raided a provision shop stocked with corn - an incident which older locals with long memories still recall. **Cheltenham Racecourse**, two miles north of town, is the home of National Hunt Racing, staging numerous top-quality races highlighted by the March Festival when the Gold Cup and the Champion Hurdle find the year's best steeplechaser and best hurdler. Several other festivals have their home in Cheltenham, including the International Jazz Festival (April), the International Festival of Music (July) and the International Festival of Literature (October).

Prestbury

1 mile NE of Cheltenham on the A46

Racing at Cheltenham started at Cleeve Hill but moved to land belonging to **Prestbury Park** in 1819, since when all the great names in steeplechasing and hurdling have graced the Prestbury turf. But Prestbury's greatest son was not a jump jockey but the amazing Fred Archer, undisputed champion of flat race jockeys, born in the village in 1857. In the King's Arms hangs a plaque with this inscription:

'At this Prestbury inn lived
FRED ARCHER the jockey

Who trained upon toast,
Cheltenham water & coffee.

The shoe of his pony
hangs in the bar

Where they drink to his prowess
from near and from far

But the man in the street
passes by without knowledge

That twas here Archer
swallowed his earliest porridge.'

Cleeve Hill

3 miles NE of Cheltenham on the B4632

The Cotswolds rise to their highest point, over 1,000 feet above sea level, at **Cleeve Cloud** above Prestbury and a mile from the village of Cleeve Hill. The views from here are magnificent, and also worth the climb is a massive Neolithic long barrow known as **Belas Knap**, where excavations have revealed the bones of more than 30 people. It is very unusual in having a false entrance at the north end, apparently leading to no chambers.

Winchcombe

6 miles NE of Cheltenham on the B4632

The Saxon capital of Mercia, where in medieval times the shrine of St Kenelm, martyred here by his jealous sister in the 8th century, was second only to that of Thomas à Becket as a destination for pilgrims. Winchcombe grew in importance into a walled town with an abbot who presided over a Saxon parliament. The abbey was destroyed in 1539 after the Dissolution of the Monasteries and all that remains today is a section of a gallery that is part of the George Inn. As well as pilgrims, the abbey gave rise to a flourishing trade in wool and sheep.

One of the most famous townsmen of the time was Jack Smallwood, the Jack o' Newbury who sponsored 300 men to fight at Flodden Field in 1513 and was a leading producer of woollen goods. Silk and paper were also produced, and for a few decades tobacco was grown locally - a fact remembered in place names such as Tobacco Close and Tobacco Field. This activity ceased in 1670 when a law was passed banning home-produced tobacco in favour of imports from the struggling colony of Virginia.

ISBOURNE MANOR HOUSE

Castle Street, Winchcombe, Gloucestershire GL54 5JA
Tel: 01242 602281 e-mail: felicity@isbourne-manor.co.uk
website: www.isbourne-manor.co.uk

Felicity and David King open the beautiful part-Georgian, part-Elizabethan
Isbourne Manor House to guests looking for a warm, personal welcome, a
peaceful, civilised ambience and the highest standards of comfort. Set in lovely gardens by the River
Isbourne, the house has three superbly appointed letting bedrooms with en suite or private facilities,
and a host of cosseting little extras including fresh fruit and flowers. Guests have the use of two
elegant day rooms, and the day starts with a generous breakfast featuring the best local ingredients
and Felicity's home-made preserves. No pets and no smoking in the Manor House.

The decline that followed had the effect of stopping the town's development, so many of the old buildings have survived largely unaltered. These include St Peter's Church, built in the 1460s and known particularly for its 40 grotesques and gargoyles, the so-called Winchcombe Worthies. **Winchcombe Folk and Police Museum**, in the Tudor-style Town Hall by the Tourist Information Centre, tells the history of the town from neolithic times to the present day and also keeps a collection of British and international police uniforms and equipment.

A narrow passageway by an ordinary-looking house leads to **Winchcombe Railway Museum and Garden**, a wonderland full of things to do: the railway museum contains one of the largest collections of railway equipment in the country, and visitors can work signals and clip tickets and generally get misty-eyed about the age of steam. The Cotswold garden is full of old and rare plants.

A mile or so north of Winchcombe stand the ruins of **Hailes Abbey**, founded in 1246 by Richard, Earl of Cornwall. Richard, caught in a storm at sea, vowed that he would found a religious house if he survived and in 1245 his brother Henry III gave him the manor at Hailes to do it. It was built on such an ambitious scale that the Cistercian monks were hard pressed to maintain it, but after a wealthy patron donated a phial said to contain the blood of Christ the abbey soon became an important place of pilgrimage and a lucrative source of funds; it was even mentioned in Chaucer's Canterbury Tales. The authenticity of the phial, which had been confirmed by the future Pope Urban IV, was questioned at the time of

Hailes Abbey

The Bugatti Trust

Prescott Hill, Gotherington, Nr Cheltenham,
Gloucestershire GL52 9RD
Tel: 01242 677201 e-mail: trust@bugatti.co.uk
Fax: 01242 674191 website: www.bugatti.co.uk/trust

Recommended to visitors with an interest in design, art in engineering as well as the history of the motor car.

Ettore Bugatti designed and built beautiful and world leading racing and sports cars in the 1920's and 1930's. There were numerous other sensational Bugatti products from the 'Royale' to world speed record trains and aricraft. The whole story of the Bugatti family from Carlo, Ettore's artist father, to the sad demise of the family control of the Molsheim factory in the 1950's, can be seen at the **Bugatti Trust**. The Trust is a Bugatti research centre and small museum, containing an amazing collection of drawings, documents, photographs, artefacts and a few cars. This history is an inspirational combination of art and engineering. Open Monday-Friday 10.00am-4.30pm. Free entry.

The Bugatti Owners' Club

Prescott Hill, Gotherington, Nr Cheltenham,
Gloucestershire GL52 9RD
Tel: 01242 673136 Fax: 01242 677001
e-mail: club@bugatti.co.uk
website: www.bugatti.co.uk/club

The Bugatti Owners' Club was founded in 1929 for enthusiasts of the Bugatti car. Its home is the world-famous Prescott Hill, which provides drivers and spectators with motor sport at its exhilarating best, set in glorious Cotswold country. The Club Secretary will happily provide callers with an application form for membership, details of Club Days and special events, which can include non-competitive runs up the famous hill and use of the Prescott Lodge Restaurant. You don't have to own a Bugatti to join the Club, but for members who are Bugatti owners the Club has a very comprehensive spare parts scheme.

The Club also has a wide range of Bugatti regalia items and memorabilia for sale, many of them highly collectable. The Prescott course is very demanding, and there are competitive events on six weekends a year. Spectators are very welcome and Prescott has good facilities. In the paddock the cars and drivers are accessible and there's a friendly atmosphere that has to be experienced to be fully appreciated. Prescott is an ideal location for business or social entertaining, and Prescott Lodge can cater in style for up to 150. One of the most memorable days out is provided by driving the hill climb in your own road car, at the Drivers School. A fully qualified, championship winning team of instructors impart encouragement and instruction to develop and improve driving techniques. The course includes blackboard teaching, walking the course, and individual and convoy observed runs. Climbs are video-recorded and played back at the end of the session.

the Dissolution and it was destroyed, and with it the abbey's main source of income. The abbey fell into disrepair and the only significant parts to survive are the cloister arches. Some of the many artefacts found at the site, including medieval sculptures and decorated floor tiles, are on display in the abbey's museum. Some of the medieval glass from the abbey is now in the church at Stanton.

Sudeley

1 mile S of Winchcombe off the B4632

Set against the beautiful backdrop of the Cotswold Hills, the site of **Sudeley Castle** has royal connections going back a thousand years. The restored medieval stately mansion was the last home, and burial place, of Catherine Parr, sixth and last wife of Henry VIII. King Charles I stayed at the castle, and his nephew, Prince Rupert, established his garrison headquarters here during the Civil War. The interior of the castle, restored by the owning Dent family in sumptuous Victorian style, is a treasure house of old masters (Turner, Rubens, Van Dyck), tapestries, period furniture, costumes and toys, and the beautiful grounds include a lake, formal gardens and a 15ft double yew hedge. Among the many other attractions are an exhibition on the evolution of the gardens, 'The Lace and Times of Emma Dent', a gift shop, plant centre, restaurant and adventure playground.

Sudeley Castle

Gotherington

5 miles NE of Cheltenham on the A435

This is the location of the famous **Prestbury Hillclimb**, scene of hillclimb championships and classic car meetings as well as the location of the **Bugatti Trust** (see panels opposite).

Toddington

8 miles NE of Cheltenham on the B4632/B4077

Toddington Station is the northern terminus of the restored **Gloucestershire Warwickshire Railway**, from where steam or diesel trains run on a round trip of 13 miles through delightful countryside by way of Winchcombe and Gotherington. The line is open all year and there is a programme of special events and gala days.

Stanway

9 miles NE of Cheltenham on the B4077

A charming village clustered round Jacobean **Stanway House**, whose contents include fine paintings, two superb Broadwood pianos, a shuffleboard table and a Chippendale exercising chair on which keep-fit enthusiasts of the time would bounce for half an hour a day. The grounds are equally interesting, with a tithe barn, water mill, ice house, brewery, dogs' cemetery and a pyramid erected in honour of John Tracy from the owning family. Another resident was Thomas Dover, the sea captain who rescued

(Continued page 346)

WALK 10

The Guitings and Guiting Wood

Start	Car park at the western end of Critchford Lane, about ¾ mile (1.25km) south-west of Kineton
Distance	6½ miles (10.5km)
Approximate time	3 hours
Parking	After passing into the gated section of the road to the west of Critchford Ford, turn left at the crossroads to find a small gated car park half-hidden amongst chestnut trees and sheep-pens
Refreshments	Pubs at Kineton and Guiting Power
Ordnance Survey maps	Landranger 163 (Cheltenham & Cirencester) and Outdoor Leisure 45 (The Cotswolds)

This is a walk well worth doing, both for the section through Guiting Wood, a large expanse of woodland mainly covering the slopes of the valley of the little Castlett stream, and the enjoyable interludes along quiet lanes and through fields. In addition, three small attractive villages are passed through.

Turn to the right from the car park and head back to Critchford Lane; turn left along the lane so that the lovely manor house is on the right. Excavations in the meadow here have uncovered the remains of an Iron Age farmstead dating from the 3rd to 1st centuries BC. The site has produced valuable finds, including a wide variety of pottery. It seems that animals were herded here, and grain harvested, the latter being stored in a series of pits.

After the field gate at the end of this meadow turn right to pass behind the manor house. Before the next gate turn to the left off the made-up drive and follow the line of a wooden fence. This leads up to the edge of Guiting Wood.

Keep the wood on the right for the length of two long fields and just before the end of the second of these look for a clearly waymarked path into the woods **A**. You will pass by an ancient right-of-way stone on the left. Timber operations make the following short stretch very muddy in wet weather and brambles add to the difficulties. In autumn, however, the colours of the wide variety of trees are an adequate compensation.

At a footpath crossroads keep straight on; the way now starts to descend, and soon becomes steeper. The trees here are young and scrubby, and the path slippery. Turn right at the footpath junction at the bottom. The path now is very narrow and overgrown in places and ends where a stile gives on to a lane **B**. Turn right here for an easier passage through the remainder of Guiting Wood.

The lane leads mainly downhill until it crosses a tiny stream, with a pumping station on the left. Hazel trees abound here. Past the stream the lane climbs quite steeply; keep along it, ignoring various inviting alternatives. The view back from the summit of the hill at Louisehill Plantation towards Guiting Wood illustrates the wide variety of trees it contains.

Now the lane descends gently to Temple Guiting where it meets a busier road which we follow by turning right to Kineton. At this point a detour can be made to visit the church at Temple Guiting **C**, which is reached in three minutes by turning left at the junction to find almost immediately a footpath on the right leading to it. The small village lies ahead on the other side of the River Windrush.

The church dates from the 12th century, the heyday of the Knights Templar who gave the village its name. The most notable features of this lovely, tranquil building for visitors to see are the remains of medieval glass in the middle window on the south side (the Metropolitan Museum in New York is said to own the other figures which came from this set) and the remarkably ornate arms of George II worked in plaster by John Switzer in 1742 which are mounted above the entry to the bell-tower.

Returning to the junction by New Barn Farm, turn away from the church to follow the lane to Kineton, with lovely views of hills and woodland to the east. Here the Half Way House is noted for its food and drink.

Continue along the lane and after ½ mile (800m) look for a waymarked footpath on the right **D**, opposite a pair of semi-detached cottages. This leads across a field to follow a hedge on the left. A lane is crossed and the footpath continues on the other side. Cross a stream by a footbridge and then keep the stream on the left, finally crossing a stile to reach a lane which leads to the village green of Guiting Power. There are two pubs to be found in this village: the Farmers' Arms downhill from the war memorial, about 200 yds (184m) away, and Ye Olde Inne (or Th' Ollow Bottom) which is passed on the way out of the village by turning to the right at the war memorial. The village church, though heavily restored by the Victorians, still retains two Norman doorways.

Just after the village sign, walking north-westwards out of the village, turn to the right down a lane marked with an 'Unsuitable for Motors' sign. Leave the lane by the sandy track on the left, which follows the contours of the hill for a pleasant ten minutes of walking until the starting point comes into view on the right. ●

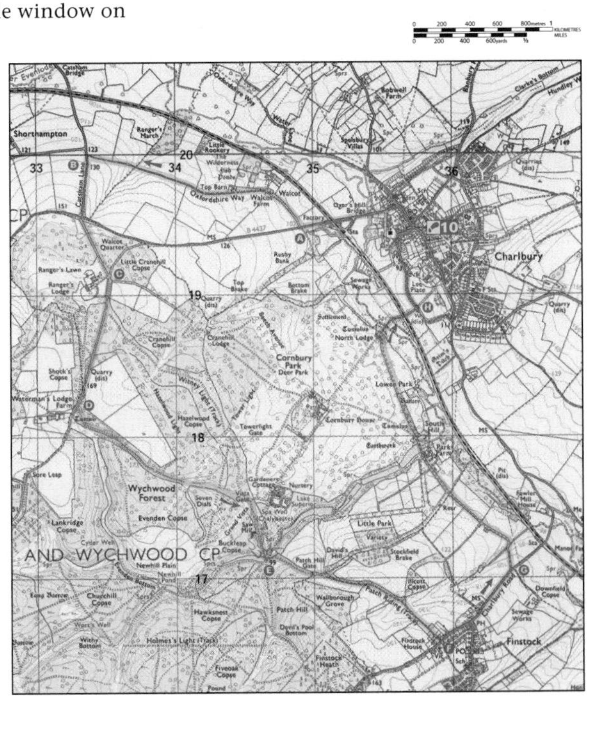

Alexander Selkirk from a desert island, an event which gave Daniel Defoe the inspiration for *Robinson Crusoe*. Also of note in Stanway is a thatched cricket pavilion resting on mushroom-shaped stones. The pavilion was a gift from JM Barrie, the author of *Peter Pan*, who was a regular visitor to the village.

Stanton

10 miles NE of Cheltenham on the B4632

One of the prettiest spots in the Cotswolds, an attractive village of steeply-gabled limestone cottages dating mainly from the 16th and 17th centuries. The whole village was restored by the architect Sir Philip Scott in the years before World War I; his home between 1906 and 1937 was **Stanton Court**, an elegant Jacobean residence built by Queen Elizabeth I's Chamberlain. The village church, dedicated to St Michael and All Angels, has many interesting features, including some stained glass from Hailes Abbey and a number of medieval pews with scarred ends caused perhaps by the leashes of dogs belonging to local shepherds. Most of the glass is the much more modern work of Sir Ninian Comper (1864-1960), the Aberdeen-born architect and prolific designer of church fittings and furnishings; stained glass was one of his specialities. John Wesley is said to have preached in the church. Beyond Stanton, on the road to Broadway, the National Trust-owned **Snowshill Manor** is an elegant manor house dating from Tudor times; once the home of Catherine Parr, it contains a fascinating collection of crafts and artefacts assembled by the last private owner, Charles Paget Wade.

Guiting Power

8 miles E of Cheltenham off the A436

A neat collection of Cotswold stone cottages round a triangular green. Noteworthy features include the part-Norman St Michael's Church and a World War I memorial cross. Close by is

Cotswold Farm Park

Guiting Power, Nr Stow-on-the-Wold, Gloucestershire GL54 5UG
Tel: 01451 850307 Fax: 01451 850423
e-mail: info@cotswoldfarmpark.co.uk website: www.cotswoldfarmpark.co.uk

Established in 1971, the **Cotswold Farm Park** was the first Rare Breeds Farm to open to the public. With over 50 flocks and herds of British breeds of farm animals on site, visitors can listen to their tales of survival using the hand-held audio tour. Attractions include pets corner, adventure playground, farm safari ride, indoor tractor school, soft play area, woodland walk, farm nature trail, gift shop and restaurant, and seasonal demonstrations of lambing, shearing, milking and animals at work. Open Easter to the end of September.

Cotswold Farm Park (see panel above), which celebrated its 30th birthday in 2001. This typical Cotswold hill farm is home to over 50 breeding flocks and herds of British breeds of sheep, cattle, pigs, goats, horses, poultry and waterfowl. Among the many other attractions are shearing and spinning demonstrations, fleece sales, safari rides and a host of activities guaranteed to keep children happy for hours.

Naunton

9 miles E of Cheltenham off the B4068

There's plenty to see in this unspoilt village founded in Saxon times, including two churches and a magnificent 15th dovecote. For the more energetic, the Black Horse Walk is a full day's walk across hillsides and through woods and water meadows, taking in Upper and Lower Slaughter and including lunch at the Black Horse Inn.

STOW-ON-THE-WOLD

At 800 feet above sea level, this is the highest town in the Cotswolds, and the winds sometimes prove it. The town's main source of wealth in earlier times was wool; twice-yearly sheep fairs were held on the Market Square, and at one such fair Daniel Defoe records that over 20,000 sheep were sold. Those days are remembered today in **Sheep Street** and **Shepherds Way**. The square holds another reminder of the past in the town stocks, used to punish minor offenders. The sheep fairs continued until they were replaced by an annual horse fair, which was held until 1985. The Battle of Stow, in 1646, was the final conflict of the Civil War, and after it some of the defeated Royalist forces made their way to St Edward's Church, while others were cut down in the market square. The church, which suffered considerable

The Roman Court Hotel

Fosseway, Stow-on-the-Wold, Gloucestershire GL54 1JX
Tel: 01451 870539 Fax: 01451 870639
e-mail: info@theromancourthotel.co.uk
website: www.theromancourthotel.co.uk

Vito Logozzi and his family offer a warm Italian welcome at the **Roman Court Hotel**, a converted coaching inn south of Stow. The hotel incorporates the 50-cover La Villa Romana Restaurant where the cooking combines the best of British and Italian influences. Guests can meet for a drink in the convivial bar, or enjoy an alfresco drink or meal in the charming palazzo courtyard. The Roman Court has 17 well-appointed bedrooms, all with private bathrooms, telephone, tv and tea-makers. Some of the rooms are ideal for families and all have a baby listening service.

Hamptons Delicatessen

1 Digbeth Street, Stow-on-the-Wold,
Gloucestershire GL54 1BN
Tel: 01451 831733 Fax: 01451 831975
e-mail: sales@hamptons-hampers.co.uk
website: www.hamptons-hampers.co.uk

For the past 15 years **Hamptons Delicatessen** has been providing a wide range of top-quality foods to discerning customers living in or visiting the Cotswolds. Richard Bufton's marvellous shop is packed with shelf upon shelf of mouthwatering goodies, including bespoke teas and coffees, local honey and preserves, chutneys and pickles and mustards, patés, Glenfiddich whisky cake, Duchy original organic biscuits and Charbonnel & Walker chocolates.

Occupying a prominent display space is the extensive Cottage Delight range of speciality foods, among them such treats as pickled walnuts in port, venison paté, plum pudding and tropical fruits in rum. But the real speciality here is the superb range of cheeses, including the local Stow Truckle and Stow Blue among the 60 or so varieties usually on display. A growing part of the business is the range of Food Hampers, which can be bought at the shop or by mail order, ready made or made up to the customer's individual choice. Hampers can be provided throughout the year, presented in either open or traditional lidded baskets. Shop hours are 9 to 5 Monday to Saturday and 11 to 4.30 Sunday.

Susan Megson Gallery

Digbeth Street and The Square, Stow-on-the-Wold,
Gloucestershire GL54 1BR
Tel: 01451 870484 (Glass Gallery) 01451 870712 (Home & Garden)
Fax: 01451 831051 e-mail: suemegsongallery@aol.com
website: www.susanmegsongallery.com

In the centre of the beautiful hilltop town of Stow-on-the-Wold, Susan Megson Gallery is in fact two galleries in one, just a few steps apart. Behind the small bay-windowed frontage there's plenty of well-lit display space for the galleries, one devoted to glass art and one with other mixed media art. In the Glass Gallery (Susan is herself an expert in the field of hand-blown glass) are the works of over 50 artists, including renowned British artists Bob Crooks, Stewart Hearn, Catherine Hough, Amanda Brisbane, Richard Golding (Okra Glass) and Sue Shaw (Jewellery). The gallery also has a wonderful representation of artists from abroad which includes Italian glass-makers such as Formia, Zanetti, Antichi Angeli and Punto Arte. The United States are represented by Fox Fire, Eikholt Glass, Black Beans & Rice, Vandermark Merritt, Cohn-Stone and Ableman, to name just a few. Other countries represented in the gallery are Australia, Canada, France, Romania and Iceland.

The Home and Garden Gallery, on The Square, which focuses on ceramics, bronzes, metal sculptures and paintings, includes a wide variety of artists in each field. Ceramists such as Melanie Adkins, John Hines, Brian Andrew, John Culver, Peter Ilsley, Stephen Kingsford and David Hart are well represented. Bronzes and metal sculptures by John Mellows, Yves Lohe, Inver Art, Farthing Foundry and Suzie Marsh, paintings by Jill Healing, Nicky Belton, Ian Fennelly and Italian frescoes by Roberta Ricchini are regular contributors to the work on display. The Galleries are open from 10 to 5 Tuesday to Saturday, from 11 to 4 on Sunday and from 10 to 5 on Monday during the summer.

damage at this time, has been restored many times down the centuries, not always to its advantage, but one undoubted treasure is a painting of the Crucifixion in the south aisle, thought to be the work of the 17th century Flemish artist Gaspard de Craeyer. The church is dedicated to King Edward the Martyr, who was murdered at Corfe Castle by his stepmother Elfrida. Other buildings of note in the town are the 15th century Crooked House and the 16th century Masonic Hall. On Digbeth Street stands the Royalist Hotel, said to be the oldest inn in England; an inn has certainly stood on the site since 947. In Park Street is the **Toy and Collectors Museum**, housing a charming display of toys, trains, teddy bears and dolls, games and books, along with textiles and lace, porcelain and pottery.

Stow on the Wold

John Davies Gallery

Church Street, Stow-on-the-Wold,
Gloucestershire GL54 1BB
Tel: 01451 831698 Fax: 01451 832477
e-mail: daviesart@aol.com
website: the-john-davies-gallery.co.uk

David Prentice: *Lighting up Time*
Oil on Canvas, 31in x 35in.

The **John Davies Gallery** has been attracting lovers of art and paintings for 25 years and its owner and founder, John Davies, is widely recognised as one of the leading dealers outside London in his field. The Gallery specialises in both period and contemporary work, and holds regular exhibitions. High quality British and Continental landscape and figure paintings dating from 1890-1960 are presented to the highest standards, but not at extreme prices, and originality of condition and sensitive framing are hallmarks of the establishment.

The friendly and homely premises, which houses a number of well-lit, domestic size galleries, is easy to walk around; visitors are treated warmly and courteously, and are not subjected to the 'hard sell'; Radio 3 is often heard in the background. Many interesting contemporary artists from England, Wales and Scotland feature, many of whom are achieving distinguished careers. The gallery is the main agent for the work of David Prentice, whose powerful and progressive landscapes derived from the Malverns and Snowdonia, have created a very strong interest in recent years.

The Old Mill

Mill Lane, Lower Slaughter,
Gloucestershire GL54 2HX
Tel: 01451 820052 Fax: 01451 822127
website: oldmill-lowerslaughter.com

On a site dating back at least to the time of the Domesday Book, the **Old Mill** is one of the outstanding attractions of Lower Slaughter, which in 2001 was voted the most beautiful village in the Cotswolds. Owner Gerald Harris, a former top jazz singer, has transformed the mill into an award-winning gift and craft shop with Big Band music from the 30s and 40s playing - all available on CD along with many other unusual gifts not seen elsewhere, including prints and original artwork from local artists. The mill is also home to a museum and an ice cream parlour selling wonderful hand made organic ice cream (free tastings!) and a riverside tea room where visitors can enjoy top quality ground coffee and leaf tea - both served in cafetieres.

The village of Lower Slaughter is in a well known walking area - in fact there are 6 walks dedicated to walking the Slaughters (Upper and Lower Slaughter) and the shop has its own book called "Footsteps from the Mill" - all great walks a must. Remember when you arrive in the village of Lower Slaughter, park where you can and then follow the brown footpath signs to the "Mill Museum" - approximately 200 yards with idillic riverside cottages to see on the way. A fantastic place to visit.

Longborough Farm Shop

Longborough, Nr Stow-on-the-Wold,
Gloucestershire GL56 0QZ
Tel: 01451 830469 Fax: 01451 830413
e-mail: longborough.farmshop@ukonline.co.uk

On the A424 2 miles north of Stow-on-the-Wold, Katharine Assheton's **Longborough Farm Shop** is a foodie paradise, an absolute must for anyone driving or touring in the area. Under the beams of the stone-walled shop there's an amazing, mouthwatering display of specialist foods in packets and jars and tins, along with cakes baked by local ladies, cider, mead and fruit wines, and an assortment of food-related gifts, cards, candles and table accessories.

From the fruit farm (some pick-your-own available) come a variety of apples, plums and pears, strawberries, raspberries, tayberries and blackberries, and asparagus in its short but sensational season. The cheeses, kept of course in tip-top condition, are mostly English, but perhaps the stars of the show are the superb meats, including local Dexter beef, Jacob lamb, pork from Gloucester Old Spot pigs and bacon and sausages from Dorset. There's game, too, with pheasant, partridge and venison all on sale in their seasons. This marvellous place is open seven days a week from Easter to Christmas and Monday to Saturday January to Easter.

Cottage Barn

Sunnybank, Chapel Lane, Longborough, Gloucestershire GL56 0QR
Tel/Fax: 01451 830695 e-mail: rupert.williams-ellis@talk21.com
website: www.cotswoldscottage.co.uk

Visitors come from all over the world to enjoy the peace and freedom of a self-catering holiday at **Cottage Barn**, which is a conversion of an18th century Cotswold stone farm building and stands in the garden of owners Rupert and Mandy Williams-Ellis. Accommodation comprises three bedrooms, bathroom, well-equipped kitchen, conservatory/dining area and spacious sitting room with tv and video. Exposed stone walls, oak beams, a log-burning stove help to create a really delightful ambience, and the property has its own entrance and parking, a patio terrace and a small lawned garden area. No smoking or pets in the cottage. A 17th century watermill is also available in Snowdonia.

Rectory Farmhouse

Lower Swell, Nr Stow-on-the-Wold, Gloucestershire GL54 1LH
Tel: 01451 832351

At the far end of a private drive a mile west of Stow-on-the-Wold, **Rectory Farmhouse** is a fine 17th century Cotswold stone building kept in immaculate condition by owner Sybil Gisby. She provides superior Bed & Breakfast accommodation in three superb double bedrooms, all with lofty beamed ceilings, traditional furnishings, central heating and luxurious en suite bathrooms with cast-iron baths and power showers. The rooms enjoy stunning views over open countryside towards Stow. Home-made preserves are a feature of the excellent breakfasts served in the dining room, and guests have the use of a lovely relaxing sitting room.

Cox's Architectural Salvage Yard

10 Fosse Way Business Park, Moreton-in-Marsh,
Gloucestershire GL56 9NQ
Tel: 01608 652505 Fax: 01608 652881
e-mail: coxs@fsbdial.co.uk
website: www.salvo.co.uk

An extensive range of beautiful and interesting items salvaged from the past is on show at **Cox's Architectural Salvage**, which is owned and run by Peter Watson, ably assisted by Dick Goodman. The large showroom and its enclosed yard house what is essentially a constantly changing museum, and visitors can spend many a happy hour browsing through literally thousands of items, from doorknobs and knockers to vast stone monuments. Cox's buy and sell all manner of architectural antiques, reclaimed beams, floorboards, stone flags, church interiors, pub furniture, garden ornaments and statuary, stained glass and doors, doors and more doors - up to 1,200 usually in stock.

The business is run in strict accordance with the Salvo Code, undertaking, among other things, not knowingly to buy any items removed from listed buildings or scheduled monuments without specific listed building or scheduled monument consent. Where possible, Cox's keep a record of the provenance of items, including date of manufacture, from where it was salvaged and previous owners. In addition to the reclaimed items, Cox's stocks a wide range of paints and oils, waxes and polishes for restoring wood to its original finish. The yard is open from 9 to 5 Monday to Saturday.

Batsford Park: Arboretum, Garden Centre & Falconry Centre

Batsford Park, Moreton-in-Marsh, Gloucestershire GL56 9QB
Tel: 01386 701441 Fax: 01386 701829
e-mail: batsarb@batsford.freeserve.co.uk
website: www.batsford-arboretum.co.uk

Batsford Park is a place of several unique attractions, comprising an arboretum and wild garden, a garden centre and a falconry centre. The Arboretum contains a rare and beautiful collection of over 1,500 species and varieties of trees, shrubs, bamboos and wild flowers set in 55 acres of typical Cotswold countryside. Visitors can wander along magical meandering paths and by the side of streams, discovering delights and surprises at very turn, including a Japanese Rest House, a hermit's cave and a number of magnificent bronze statues from the Far East, origin-ally collected by Lord Redesdale. Each season brings its own special magic to this jewel in the Cotswold crown: in spring the snowdrops and daffodils; in early summer the magnolias and the Japanese cherry blossom; in autumn the reds and yellows and golds of the deciduous trees; and in winter the fairyland of frost and the waterfall of icicles suspended above the frozen lake.

The Arboretum and gift shop are open daily from the beginning of February to mid-November, otherwise at weekends only. In the Apple Store Tea Room, teas, coffees and snacks can be enjoyed either inside or out on the terrace overlooking the garden. The Garden Centre at Batsford is a specialist plantsman's centre with many rare and unusual trees, shrubs, alpine plants, herbaceous and perennials, and a wide range of garden sundries, compost, mulches, terracotta and glazed pots, seeds and gifts. Advice is available on the stock of ferns, bamboos, Japanese maples and magnolias, many of which can be seen growing to maturity in the Arboretum. Cotswold Falconry Centre is home to a large collection of falcons, hawks, owls, kites and vultures, which are flown at regular intervals throughout the day, enabling all visitors to see and admire their remarkable grace, speed and agility. The site has many breeding aviaries, including the owls in Owl Wood, and at various times of the year the birds are either nest building, sitting on eggs or feeding their young. In the Cotswold School of Falconry the Centre holds introductory courses, hunting days and a 3-day hands-on falconry experience. Adoption schemes, whereby a bird can be adopted for a year, have proved very popular, especially as gifts. The Centre is open from mid-February to mid-November and has a picnic area, refreshments and gift shop.

Upper & Lower Swell

1 mile W of Stow on the B4077 & B4068

A couple of Swells, neighbouring villages on the banks of the River Dikler. Lower Swell's focal point is the triangular village green, while the large mill pond is one of Upper Swell's many delights. Nearby, in Condicote Lane, is **Donnington Trout Farm** with a hatchery, smokery, farm shop and a lake for fly fishing.

Moreton-in-Marsh

4 miles N of Stow on the A429

A bustling market town at the junction of the A44 and the A429 Fosse Way, Moreton was once an important stop on the coaching route between London and the West Midlands. Its broad main street is lined with handsome 17th and 18th century buildings, while from earlier days are the old town gaol, the White Hart, where Charles I took refuge during

Grimes House Antiques & Fine Art

High Street, Moreton-in-Marsh, Gloucestershire GL56 0AT
Tel: 01608 651029 e-mail: grimes_house@cix.co.uk
website: www.grimeshouse.co.uk

Stephen and Val Farnsworth run an antique shop with a difference. A veritable Aladdin's Cave, **Grimes House Antiques & Fine Art** combines furniture, collectable boxes, porcelain and probably the largest collection of antique cranberry glass in the world with a superb collection of paintings in traditional style by some of today's finest artists. Through a delightful courtyard gallery, at the rear of the shop, is a fine art print department with an excellent selection of limited edition prints both framed and unframed. Grimes House also keeps a comprehensive stock of artists materials and a distinctive range of greetings cards, and offers a bespoke picture framing service.

The Farriers Arms

Todenham, Nr Moreton-in-Marsh, Gloucestershire GL56 9PF
Tel: 01608 650901 Fax: 01608 650403

Situated in the heart of the Cotswolds 3 miles north of Moreton-in-Marsh, the **Farriers Arms** developed alongside the old village smithy and has for centuries been the social hub of the village. Owned by Steven and Susan Croft, it has built up a strong reputation for the quality and choice of food and drink and retains the character of a typical Cotswold pub, with exposed stone walls, flagstones, rustic furniture and ancient beams adorned with horse brasses.

A range of real ales is on tap in the bars, along with a comprehensive list of wines available by glass or bottle. Daily wine specials are announced on a blackboard, while another board lists the day's dishes, all home-prepared using fresh local produce wherever possible. British and Continental influences are evident throughout a mouthwatering choice that could include chicken liver parfait with Cumberland sauce, local pork and chive sausages in a Dijon cream, whole grilled plaice served with a lemon and caper butter and linguine with roasted artichokes, peas and shaved parmesan. The regulars at this outstanding pub include a team of serious dominoes players who figure prominently in the local league.

the Civil War, and the Curfew Tower with its clock and bell dated 1633. In Bourton Road, the **Wellington Aviation Museum** has a collection of World War II aircraft paintings, prints and models and a detailed history of the Wellington bomber. A mile east of town on the A44 stands the **Four Shires Stone** marking the original spot where the counties of Gloucestershire, Oxfordshire, Warwickshire and Worcestershire met. Moreton-in-the-Marsh is the scene, every Tuesday, of the biggest open-air street market in the Cotswolds.

Blockley

7 miles N of Stow off the A44/A429

Silk-spinning was the main industry here, and six mills created the main source of employment until the 1880s. As far back as the Domesday book water mills were recorded here, and the village also once boasted an iron foundry and factories making soap, collars and pianos. The mills have now been turned into private residences and Blockley is a quieter place. One of the chief attractions for visitors is **Mill Dene Garden**, set around a mill
in a steep-sided valley. The garden has hidden paths winding up from the mill pool, and at the top there are lovely views over the Cotswolds. Also featured are a grotto, a potager, a trompe l'oeil and dye plants.

Chipping Campden

10 miles N of Stow on the B4081

The 'Jewel of the Cotswolds', full of beautifully restored buildings in golden Cotswold stone. It was a regional capital of the wool trade between the 13th and 16th centuries and many of the fine buildings date from that period of prosperity. In the centre of town is the Jacobean Market Hall, built in 1627 and

one of many buildings financed by the noted wool merchant and financier Sir Baptist Hicks. He also endowed a group of almshouses and built Old Campden House, at the time the largest residence in the village; it was burnt down by Royalists to prevent it falling into the hands of the enemy, and all that survives are two gatehouses and the old stable block. The 15th century Church of St James was built on a grand scale and contains several impressive monumental brasses, the most impressive being one of William Grevel measuring a mighty eight feet by four feet.

Chipping Campden

Dover's Hill, a natural amphitheatre above the town, is the scene of the **Cotswold Olympics**, founded in the 17th century by Captain Robert Dover, whom we met at Stanway House. The Games followed the traditions of ancient Greece and added some more down-to-earth activities such as shin-kicking and bare-knuckle boxing. The lawlessness and hooliganism that accompanied the games led to their being closed down in 1852 but they were revived in a modern form in 1951 and are still a popular annual attraction on the Friday following the spring bank holiday.

Broadway

10 miles NW of Stow on the A44

Just over the border into Worcestershire, where the Cotswolds join the Vale of Evesham, Broadway is one of the glories of the Cotswolds, a showpiece village with an abundance of scenic and historic attractions. The renowned Lygon Arms entertained both King Charles and Oliver Cromwell, and **Broadway Tower** at the top of Fish hill affords spectacular views over the Severn Vale.

Hidcote Bartrim

3 miles NE of Chipping Campden off the B4632

Hidcote Manor Garden is one of the most famous in the country, a masterpiece created in the first years of

The Churchill Arms

Paxford, Nr Chipping Campden, Gloucestershire GL55 6XH
Tel: 01386 594000 Fax: 01386 594005
e-mail: info@thechurchillarms.com
website: www.thechurchillarms.com

Food, drink and accommodation are all outstanding at the **Churchill Arms**, a handsome 18th centurybuilding in Cotswold stone. In the capable hands of Leo Brook-Little and his wife Sonya Kidney, this fine old free house retains a good deal of period charm with flagstones, beams and a log-burning stove. Sonya, a highly talented chef of international renown, does the cooking and blackboards announce a mouthwatering, daily changing selection of her marvellous dishes typified by grilled herring fillet with oats and an English mustard sauce, chicken chasseur and slow-braised shoulder of lamb with celeriac mash. Sweets such as sticky toffee pudding or a trio of parfaits provide a perfect finale, with a platter of interesting cheeses as an alternative.

Another blackboard lists the wines - one half in white chalk, the other in red chalk. For guests staying overnight there are six en suite bedrooms, each with its own character and name, all with tv, refreshment tray and good-quality toiletries. The pub has ample car parking space and a beer garden with an area for playing the ancient game of Aunt Sally. The Churchill family were important local landowners in the 1920s and at the time of the depression did not impose rent increases on their tenants. The area thus escaped the worst effects of the depression and indeed remains affluent to this day. Paxford lies a couple of miles east of Chipping Campden in an area of great scenic beauty and historic interest. Among the many places to visit are Chipping Campden itself, with its abundance of fine buildings, and the arboretum and falconry centre at Batsford.

Whiteacres

Station Road, Broadway, Worcestershire WR12 7DE
Tel: 01386 852320 Fax: 01386 852674
e-mail: whiteacres@btinternet.com

Three minutes walk from the centre of Broadway, **Whiteacres** is a classic late-Victorian villa with a lovely cottage-style garden and ample off-street parking. Hosts Jenny and Stan Buchan escaped from the worlds of commerce and industry and now offer Bed & Breakfast accommodation in a relaxing, home-from-home ambience. The five letting bedrooms are all en suite and each is individually furnished; two have four-poster beds and all are equipped with tv, tea/coffee-making facilities, hairdryers and many thoughtful little extras to add to the comfort and enjoyment of your stay.

Rooms at the back overlook the garden, while those at the front have the benefit of a view of the Cotswold escarpment. There's a pleasant lounge where guests can watch satellite tv or play one of a selection of games available, and the day at Whiteacres starts with an excellent breakfast. Jenny and Stan guarantee a warm welcome and are pleased to offer advice on what to see and do in the neighbourhood. Broadway, just over the Worcestershire border in the heart of the Cotswolds, is one of the most beautiful villages in Britain, and many other towns and villages, gardens and historic buildings are within an easy drive. Accredited by the AA and the English Tourism Board with 4 diamonds, plus a Silver Award from the ETC.

the 20th by the eminent horticulturist Major Lawrence Johnston. A series of small gardens, each with a different character and appeal, Hidcote is renowned for its rare shrubs and trees, herbaceous borders and unusual plant species from all parts of the globe. Visitors can refresh themselves in the tea bar or licensed restaurant.

UPPER AND LOWER SLAUGHTER

2 miles SW of Stow off the A429/B4068

Broadway Tower

The Slaughters (the name means nothing more sinister than 'muddy place') are archetypal Cotswold villages set a mile apart on the little River Eye. Both are much visited by tourists, much explored and much photographed; they are also much as they have always been, since virtually no building work has been carried out since 1904. Francis Edward Witts, author of the *Diary of a Cotswold Parson*, was the rector here between 1808 and 1854.

At Lower Slaughter, the **Old Mill**, with its tall chimney and giant waterwheel, is a prominent feature by the river. This

THE MOUNT INN

Old Snowshill Road, Stanton, Nr Broadway,
Worcestershire WR12 7NE
Tel/Fax: 01386 584316
e-mail: pub@the mountinn.co.uk
website: www.the mountinn.co.uk

The Mount Inn is a traditional Cotswold inn that started life as a farmhouse in the early 17th century. Sometime later it became a cobblers, then a tea room and an off-licence, and now, as the village pub, it offers a warm welcome from long-standing tenants Lynda and Colin Johns to familiar faces and occasional visitors, who include many walkers - this is great walking country and the pub stands on a hilltop above Stanton on the main Cotswold Way. A large inglenook fire keeps things cosy in the winter, and horse harnesses, brasses, cartoons of regulars and a display of foreign currency contribute to a varied and interesting decor in the bars.

The local Donnington Ales are excellent thirst-quenchers, and excellent home-cooked food is served every session except Sunday evening. At lunchtime there's an extensive snack menu, while in the evening a full dinner menu is served. The no-smoking dining room, which contains a fascinating selection of cricket memorabilia, has seats for 25, and the rest of the pub can seat up to 60 inside; the garden area can accommodate another 60 around picnic-style tables, and there are seats for 30 on the patio, which offers outstanding views over the rooftops of the village to the Cotswold Hills and the Welsh mountains beyond. In the garden is a large aviary with cockatiels, budgies, finches and quail, along with non-flying rabbits and guinea pigs. The pub has ample off-road parking.

Lowerfield Farm

Willersey, Nr Broadway, Worcestershire WR11 5HF
Tel: 01386 858273 e-mail: info@lowerfield-farm.co.uk
Fax: 01386 854608 website: www.lowerfield-farm.co.uk

Lowerfield Farm offers genuine farmhouse comfort and hospitality in a 17th century Cotswold farmhouse. Owner Jane Hill and her family, provide luxurious accommodation in three cosy, comfortable bedrooms, elegantly furnished, with panoramic views, en suite bathrooms, tv, clock radio, hairdryer and tea/coffee-making facilities. One room is located on the ground floor. A full traditional English breakfast is served in the dining room or farmhouse, and a three-course evening meal can be taken by arrangement. The family also run Cowslip Self-Catering Cottages (see under Chipping Campden).

Cowslip Cottages

Lowerfield Farm, Willersey, Broadway, Worcestershire WR11 5HF
Tel: 01386 858273
e-mail: info@cowslip-cottages.co.uk website: www.cowslip-cottages.co.uk

Cowslip Cottages, is a small, locally based enterprise specialising in looking after privately owned self-catering holiday cottages. Two of the cottages are in Chipping Campden: Molly's Cottage with two double bedrooms, a flagstone-floored bathroom, cosy sitting room and a good-sized fitted kitchen with French windows opening on to a garden terrace. and Benfield Cottage, equally well appointed and has an en suite double bedroom. In Toddington, on the peaceful 18th century square, are two superb, characterful cottages fitted and furnished to a very high standard, both with two bedrooms and everything needed for a delightful self-catering holiday.

The Ebrington Arms

Ebrington, Nr Chipping Campden, Gloucestershire
Tel: 01386 593223

In a pretty village two miles east of Chipping Campden, the **Ebrington Arms** is a lovely old Cotswold inn long celebrated for its excellent hospitality. That tradition is being maintained in fine style by Graham and Sara Springett, who have carried major refurbishment without losing any of the inn's period charm. Imaginative food, accompanied by a good selection of wines and real ales, is served lunchtime and evening, and the owners have expanded the role of the inn by creating two en suite bedrooms for guests staying overnight.

Nineveh Farm

Campden Road, Mickleton, Gloucestershire GL55 6PS
Tel: 01386 438923
e-mail: stay@ninevehfarm.co.uk website: www.ninevehfarm.co.uk

A fine Georgian farmhouse with flagstones, beams and antique furnishings, **Nineveh Farm** nestles at the foot of Bakers Hill in feature gardens surrounded by open farmland. Owners Alison and Michael Yardley offer Bed & Breakfast accommodation in 5 well-appointed bedrooms in the main house or in the Garden House, a cedar cottage with French windows. All rooms have en suite or private facilities, tea-makers, hairdryers and radio-alarms, and guests have the use of a sitting room with tv and local maps and guides. The day starts with a hearty traditional English breakfast, before you enjoy the delights of the countryside and Stratford-upon-Avon.

restored 19th century flour mill is open for visits and has a tearoom and ice cream parlour.

BOURTON-ON-THE-WATER
4 miles S of Stow on the A429

Probably the most popular of all the Cotswold villages. The willow-fringed River Windrush flows through the centre, crossed by several delightful low-arched pedestrian bridges, two of which date from the late 18th century. The golden stone cottages are pretty as a picture, and among the notable larger buildings are St Lawrence's Church, with its 14th century chancel and rare domed Georgian tower, and a manor house with a 16th century dovecote. In the High Street, **Miniature World - The Museum of Miniatures** is a unique exhibition of miniature scenes and models that took the country's leading master miniature makers 3½ years to complete. Bourton is a great place for miniatures, as there is also the famous **Model Village** with church music and the model of the model, and **Bourton Model Railway** with over 40 British and Continental trains running on three main displays in OO, HO and N gauge. The **Cotswold Motor Museum and Toy Collection**, in an 18th century water mill, has a fascinating collection of antique toys, a display of historic advertising signs and 30 or so (full-size!) cars and motorcycles. Bourton has Europe's only **Perfumery Exhibition**, a permanent attraction where perfumes are manufactured on the premises; the exhibition explored the origins of perfume and includes 'smelly-vision' in a specially constructed cinema, a perfume quiz and a beautiful perfume garden where all the plants have been selected for their aroma. A five-minute walk from the town centre brings visitors to **Birdland Park & Gardens** set in seven

BRYMBO

Honeybourne Lane, Mickleton,
Nr Chipping Campden,
Gloucestershire GL55 6PU
Tel: 01386 438890 Fax: 01386 438113
e-mail: enquiries@brymbo.com
website: www.brymbo.com

Gené and Barry Jeffrey's **Brymbo** is an attractively converted farm building set in the beautiful, peaceful Cotswold countryside. The Bed & Breakfast accommodation, all on the ground floor, consists of five non-smoking bedrooms - two twins, two doubles and a family room - all with central heating, tv and tea-making facilities. Sunflower and Apricot have en suite shower rooms, while Peach, Cornflower and Lilac share two bathrooms.

Guests have the use of two sitting rooms, one with a log fire, the other with splendid panoramic views; the breakfast room, where a cooked traditional or vegetarian breakfast is served, shares the views and enjoys the morning sunshine. An extensive selection of local guide books, maps and information makes it easy for guests to plan their days, and the owners also have videos about the surrounding area. Brymbo has ample car parking space and a large garden where on balmy evenings guests can relax by the pond or beneath the pergola. It is an ideal base for a walking or cycling holiday, and Chipping Campden, sometimes called 'the Jewel of the Cotswolds', is only 3 miles away.

Myrtle House

Mickleton, Nr Chipping Campden,
Gloucestershire GL55 6SA
Tel: 01386 430032
e-mail: kate@myrtlehouse.co.uk
website: www.myrtlehouse.co.uk

On the B4622 in the pleasant village of Mickleton, **Myrtle House** is an elegant Grade II-listed Georgian building. Genial owners Kate and Phil Rush offer excellent Bed & Breakfast accommodation in five spacious guest rooms, all with en suite facilities, hairdryer, tv, radio-alarm clock and tea-makers. Children are welcome, and the owners can provide a cot, high chair and extra bed. Well-behaved pets are also welcome.

The bedrooms, each with its own individual style and charm, are non-smoking, but puffing is permitted in the comfortable residents' lounge, where an open fire keeps things cosy in the winter months; local guide books and maps are provided for guests to browse through and plan their days. Guests have the use of a secluded walled garden, and off-street parking is available in the courtyard. A full English breakfast is served in the dining room, and with a little notice picnics and pre/post theatre snacks can be made up (Stratford is an easy drive away). Mickleton, one of the northern gateways to the Cotswolds, is an excellent base for walking, cycling or touring. Broadway, Chipping Campden and Stow-on-the-Wold are all within an easy drive, along with a number of historic houses and nationally important gardens.

Lansdowne Villa Guest House

Lansdowne, Bourton-on-the-Water, Gloucestershire GL54 2AR
Tel: 01451 820673 Fax: 01451 822099
website: www.smoothound.co.uk/hotels/lansdownevilla

Relaxation is the watchword at **Lansdowne Villa Guest House**, where Jenny and Bernard Harris offer guests a warm, personal welcome and a pleasant, comfortable stay. Their mid-Victorian house has 12 letting bedrooms (non-smoking), all with en suite facilities, central heating, tv, radio-alarm and tea/coffee makers. A full English breakfast is served in the dining room and dinner is available by arrangement. Lansdowne Villa stands at the quiet western end of one of the prettiest of Cotswold villages, close to the River Windrush and a short stroll from the centre and all its attractions.

The Water Gallery

Windrush Cottage Shop, Riverside, Bourton-on-the-Water,
Gloucestershire GL54 2DP
Tel: 01451 822255

In the delightful bay-windowed **Water Gallery** overlooking the River Windrush, Heather Mead has assembled an outstanding collection of paintings, prints and craftwork. Local artists and local scenes are very much to the fore and, always in demand, are framed 19th century maps of every county in England, Nigel Hemming's pictures of gun dogs and prints by the Dutch artist Willem Haenraets. Among other exclusive products are Maasai scenes of African landscapes and the 'Walk in the Country' range of animals. Open seven days a week, the Water Gallery also offers a picture framing service.

acres of woodland, water and gardens. The natural setting is home to over 500 birds, including flamingos, pelicans, cranes, storks and waterfowl; there are over 50 aviaries of parrots, falcons, pheasants, hornbills, toucans, touracos and many others, and tropical, temperate and desert houses are home to the more delicate species. Open all year, Birdland has a café and facilities for children, including a play area, pets corner and penguin feeding time.

Bourton on the Water

Two attractions outside the village are the Iron Age **Salmonsbury Camp** and **Folly Farm**, home to Europe's largest domestic waterfowl and wildlife conservation area, with over 160 rare breeds. Also at this major attraction off the A436 Cheltenham road are spectacular lavender fields, a garden centre and a coffee shop.

Great Rissington

7 miles S of Stow off the A424

Great Rissington lies halfway between Bourton and Burford, nestling on a hillside overlooking the valley of the Windrush.

Northleach

10 miles S of Stow on the A429

A traditional market town with some truly magnificent buildings. It was once a major wool-trading centre that rivalled Cirencester in importance and as a consequence possesses what now seems a disproportionately large church. The

Wold Galleries

Halford House, Station Road, Bourton-on-the-Water,
Gloucestershire GL54 2AA Tel: 01451 822092
e-mail: wold.galleries@virgin.net website: www.woldgalleries.co.uk

Wold Galleries opened in 1972, since when the priority has been to nurture up and coming artists and show the finest contemporary work available at an affordable price. Owned and run by Kit and Ella Havelock-Davies, the Galleries, located in a Grade II-listed building, feature the work of 30 to 40 artists, some local, whose talents spread across the mediums of oil, watercolour, pastel, acrylic, glass, ceramic and bronze. Included in the display are works by Russian painters, and by two highly regarded Spanish artists. The owners also offer a picture-framing service. Browsers are welcome at the Galleries, which are open from 10 to 5 every day except Tuesday.

The Cotswold Shop

High Street, Bourton-on-the-Water, Gloucestershire GL54 2AN
Tel: 01451 820547

The Cotswold Shop, on the main street of one of the most delightful villages in the Cotswolds, is a gem of a place, the perfect spot to visit when looking for a special little gift or a well-deserved personal treat. The bow window and the shop behind are full of goodies, including the huge range of old fashioned sweets, biscuits presented in boxes with village scenes, teas from Jacksons of Piccadilly, Cotswold honey and locally made preserves, and luxurious chocolates and toffees. The shop is also a stockist for the fine Moorcroft Pottery from Staffordshire, including the most recent limited edition pieces.

The Lamb Inn

Great Rissington, Nr Burford, Gloucestershire GL54 2LP
Tel: 01451 820388 Fax: 01451 820724
website: www.thelamb-inn.co.uk

Overlooking the Windrush Valley between the towns of Burford, Bourton-on-the-Water and Stow-on-the-Wold, the **Lamb Inn** is an ideal base for exploring the scenic and historic attractions of the Cotswolds. Many visitors to the area are keen walkers, and there's no better place to pause than Paul and Jacqueline Gabriel's fine old inn, whose sturdy stone walls, old beams and log fires contribute to a delightful atmosphere in keeping with its 300 years. The hosts provide the warmest of welcomes, and visitors can look forward to excellent food, traditional ales and fine wines. In the à la carte restaurant head chef Tony Harrison has brought the cuisine to new heights with his combination of time-honoured classics and innovative specials drawing their inspiration from near and far.

Among the most popular dishes on his seasonal menus are crab & prawn samosa with salad leaves and red pesto, chargrilled local pheasant with roast peppers and forest berry sauce, and, for a memorable dessert, prune and armagnac crème brûlée with almond brittle. Guests staying overnight have a choice of 14 rooms, each one individually designed to reflect its shape and character; top of the range are the splendid suites, two of them with four-poster beds. Two fascinating features in the bar area are memorabilia of a Wellington bomber that crashed in the garden in 1943 and a picture gallery of Guide Dogs for the Blind, an institution which the inn sponsors.

Keith Harding's World Of Mechanical Music

The Oak House, High Street, Northleach, Gloucestershire GL54 3ET
Tel: 01451 860181
e-mail: keith@musicbox.10.demon.co.uk
website: www.mechanicalmusic.co.uk

Keith Harding's love for mechanical music began 40 years ago in London, and since 1986 he has been based in a handsome period house in the main street of Northleach. Visitors of all ages will find plenty to amuse and delight them, as **Keith Harding's World of Mechanical Music** has the finest selection of musicals and automata, both antique and modern, to be found anywhere. The shop holds a large stock of musical boxes and clocks, puzzles, games and gifts of all kinds, videos and CDs and, for the collector, a large range of books on mechanical music, musical boxes and clocks. It is also a living museum of various kinds of self-playing musical instruments that were the proud possessions of former generations, from a tiny singing bird concealed in a snuff box to a mighty red Welte Steinway reproducing piano of 1907.

The instruments are introduced and played by the guides in the form of a live musical entertainment show, and the tours include demonstrations of restored barrel organs, barrel pianos, musical boxes, polyphons, automata, reproducing pianos, phonographs, gramophones and antique clocks, all in a period setting that enhances the enjoyment of a visit to this unique place. Keith Harding and his dedicated team are specialist craftsmen unrivalled in their field, and everything on show is maintained in perfect working order; customers' pieces can be restored and estimates are free. Opening times are 10 to 6 daily.

Church of St Peter and St Paul, known as 'the Cathedral of the Cotswolds', is a fine example of Cotswold Perpendicular, built in the 15th century with pinnacled buttresses, high windows and a massive square castellated tower. Treasures inside include an ornately carved font and some rare monumental brasses of which rubbings can be made (permits obtainable from the Post Office). An old country prison is now home to the **Cotswold Heritage Centre**, with displays telling the story of social history and rural life in the Cotswolds.

At **Yanworth**, a couple of miles west of Northleach off the A429 Fosse Way, is what must be the region's oldest stately home, the National Trust's **Chedworth Roman Villa**, a large, well-preserved Romano-British villa discovered by chance in 1864 and subsequently excavated to reveal more than 30 rooms and buildings, including

The Dolls House

Market Place, Northleach, Nr Cheltenham, Gloucestershire GL54 3EJ
Tel/Fax: 01451 860431 e-mail: dollshouse@northleach.wyenet.co.uk

1971 saw the opening of England's first specialist dolls house shop in London and in 1995, Michal Morse moved her shop to the quiet market town of Northleach. **The Dolls House** contains an enchanting collection of hand-made dolls houses and miniature furniture, all in the scale of 1:12 and all irresistible to both children and collectors. The houses are modelled on various periods, from Tudor and Georgian to Victorian and Edwardian, and the accessories include both mass-produced items and hand-made, many of the latter exclusive to the shop. The Dolls House is open from 10 to 5 Thursday to Saturday; other days vary, so it's best to phone before setting out.

a bath house and hypocaust. Some wonderful mosaics are on display, one depicting the four seasons, another showing nymphs and satyrs. The villa lies in a beautiful wooded combe overlooking the valley of the Colne; a natural spring rises at the head of the combe, and the presence of this source of fresh water was probably the main reason for choosing this site.

Arlington Row

BIBURY

15 miles S of Stow on the B4425

William Morris, founder of the Arts & Crafts Movement, described Bibury as 'the most beautiful village in England' and, apart from the tourists, not a lot has changed since he made the claim. The Church of St Mary, with Saxon, Norman

and medieval parts, is well worth a visit, but the most visited and most photographed building in Bibury is **Arlington Row**, a superb terrace of medieval stone cottages built as a woolstore in the 14th century and converted three centuries later into weavers' cottages and workshops. Fabric

DIANE BREEN GALLERY

The Street, Bibury, Nr Cirencester, Gloucestershire GL7 5NP
Tel: 01285 740736
website: www.dianebreen.com

The delightful **Diane Breen Gallery**, in a picturesque setting overlooking the River Coln, is just a brief stroll downstream from the National Trust's Arlington Row. The Gallery, which Diane Breen created in 1997, has on display a wide selection of traditional and contemporary original paintings by acclaimed Cotswold and national artists. Among the works featured are English watercolour landscapes by David Rust, Colin Tuffney and Elizabeth Chalmers; moody, atmospheric pastels by Christopher Stinchcombe; and vibrant contemporary works by Anuk Naumann and Michael Ibbotson.

The Gallery also specialises in the signed limited editions of exquisite English flower studies by Anne Cotterill. New editions of these beautiful pictures are introduced regularly throughout the year; they are limited to 100, so they sell out very quickly. In addition, the Gallery keeps a good range of unusual and fine ceramics, hand-made glassware finished in gold and silver leaf, hand-painted crystal glassware and silk embroidered miniature textiles. Opening hours are Thursday to Sunday from 11 to 5. Monday, Tuesday and Wednesday are studio days, when Diane, herself a talented and prolific artist, will be working in her studio above the Gallery. Visitors are welcome on these days, but should telephone or e-mail to arrange a time.

produced here was supplied to nearby **Arlington Mill** for fulling, a process in which the material was cleaned in water and beaten with mechanically-operated hammers. Today the mill, which stands on the site of a corn mill mentioned in the Domesday Book, is a museum with a collection of industrial artefacts, crafts and furniture, including pieces made in the William Morris workshops.

CIRENCESTER

The 'Capital of the Cotswolds', a lively market town with a long and fascinating history. As Corinium Dobonnorum it was the second largest Roman town in Britain (Londinium was the largest). Few signs remain of the Roman occupation, but the award-winning **Corinium Museum** features one of the finest collections of antiquities from Roman Britain, and reconstructions of a Roman kitchen,

Church of St John the Baptist, Cirencester

POLO CANTEEN

29 Sheep Street, Cirencester, Gloucestershire GL7 1OW
Tel: 01285 650977 Fax: 01285 642777
website: www.polocanteen.co.uk

Polo Canteen, two minutes walk from the shops and spires of Cirencester town centre, is a stylish restaurant run by owner/chef Paul Welch. One of the Cotswolds' most highly regarded and most distinctive privately-run restaurants, it offers an outstanding selection of dishes making excellent use of the finest and freshest local produce, complemented by an alluring, well-chosen wine list. Everything, from the bread to the desserts, is made on the premises, and in addition to the full à la carte menu there's a daily changing selection of chef's specials.

Typical dishes run from chicken and wild mushroom terrine or dill and lime marinated salmon (starter or main course) to chargrilled tuna with potato and olive compote, breast of duck with herb mash and a rich roast gravy, and pepper-sauced sirloin steak. There's always plenty of choice for vegetarians, and desserts such as pecan pie or baked apples in butterscotch round things off in style. The game of polo, played regularly at Cirencester Park, provides the inspiration for the colonial-style decor, and the restaurant is the perfect setting for intimate tête-à-têtes, family celebrations and - thanks to the famously large round tables - small parties and wedding receptions. The whole restaurant can be hired for private functions. Polo Canteen is open 12 to 2 and 7 to 10 Monday to Saturday.

Parlour Farm Antiques

Unit 12B, Wilkinson Road, Lovelane Industrial Estate, Cirencester, Gloucestershire GL7 1YT
Tel: 01285 885336 Fax: 01285 885338
e-mail: info@parlourfarm.com
website: www.parlourfarm.com

Nick Grunfeld's **Parlour Farm Antiques** has gained an international reputation for providing the very highest quality at the very best price, coupled with relaxed, informal and efficient service. It was initially established as a major importer of restored antique pine and offers an ever changing selection that includes unique or unusual items as well as regular stock items for sale. The Farm has now added bespoke solid wood kitchens to its repertoire, making an immediate impact on the market with a combination of top-quality workmanship, unbeatable prices and vast choice of core units - all of which can, when necessary, be adapted to suit individual requirements.

A specialist design service includes an on-site visit, design, drawings, informal discussions at the Farm, production of working drawings and liaison throughout the whole painless procedure. Garden chairs, tables, benches and accessories are another speciality of Parlour Farm, where all the wood used in their products originates from controlled durable natural resources and is subject to a strictly controlled production process. The warehouse, which has over 7,500 sq ft of stock and display space, is open from 10 to 5 seven days a week.

Rankine Taylor Antiques

34 Dollar Street, Cirencester, Gloucestershire GL7 2AN
Tel: 01285 652529
website: www.antiquesnews.co.uk/rankine-taylor

Anyone who thinks that the traditional old-style English antique shop is a thing of the past should pay a visit to **Rankine Taylor Antiques** behind the great parish church in Dollar Street, Cirencester. Behind the large double shop front are several showrooms, each filled with an eclectic collection assembled by Leslie Rankine Taylor over the 33 years since her move from her native Edinburgh. The shop specialises in 17th, 18th and early 19th century furniture, along with silver, glass and associated objects, but the owner's real passion is for any rare and interesting objects, and browsers will find delights and surprises at every turn.

The Scottish influence remains strong, with bagpipes on Burns Night and shinty sticks from the Isle of Skye in one of the regularly changing artistic and original window displays, which have become famous both locally and with visitors from all over the world. In the shop, many of the displays are on a theme, perhaps ecclesiastical or nautical, with anything from a naval officer's hat to a ship's anchor. Rankine Taylor Antiques is open six days a week (and Sundays by appointment) and there's a private car park for customers opposite the shop.

dining room and garden give a fascinating and instructive insight into life in Cirencester of almost 2,000 years ago.

The main legacy of the town's medieval wealth is the magnificent **Church of St John the Baptist**, perhaps the grandest of all the Cotswold 'wool churches', its 120ft tower dominating the town. Its greatest treasure is the Anne Boleyn Cup, a silver and gilt cup made for Henry VIII's second wife in 1535, the year before she was executed for adultery. Her personal insignia - a rose tree and a falcon holding a sceptre - is on the lid of the cup, which was given to the church by Richard Master, physician to Queen Elizabeth I. The church has a unique three-storey porch which was used as the Town Hall until 1897. Cirencester today has a thriving crafts scene, with workshops in the **Brewery Arts** House, a converted Victorian brewery. Sixteen resident craftworkers include a basket maker, jeweller, textile weaver, ceramicist and stained glass artist. A shop in the centre sells the best in British work, and there are galleries, a coffee house and arts and crafts classes and workshops. **Cirencester Open Air Swimming Pool**, next to the park, was built in 1869 and is one of the oldest in the country. Both the main pool and the paddling pool use water from a private well.

South Cerney

3 miles SE of Cirencester off the A419

Two areas of flooded gravel workings form the **Cotswold Water Park**, an increasingly important wetland area with a greater area of water than the Norfolk Broads. The area, which includes **Keynes Country Park**, is a centre for water sports, fishing, bird-watching, walking and cycling.

Fairford

9 miles E of Cirencester on the A417

A welcoming little town in the valley of the River Coln, with many fine buildings of the 17th and 18th centuries and an abundance of inns as evidence that this was an important stop on the London-Gloucester coaching run. John and Edmund Tame, wealthy wool merchants, built the superb late-Perpendicular **Church of St Mary**, whose greatest glory is a set of 28 medieval stained glass windows depicting the Christian faith in picture-book style. John Tame's memorial stone, along with those of his wife and son, are set into the floor of the church.

Lechlade

12 miles E of Cirencester on the A417

Lechlade stands at a point where the Rivers Leach and Coln meet the Thames. A statue of Old Father Thames overlooks **St John's Lock**, the highest navigable point on the river, where barges loaded with building stone bound for Oxford and London have given way to pleasure

Lechlade

Cotswold Woollen Weavers

Filkins, Nr Lechlade,
Gloucestershire GL7 3JJ
Tel: 01367 860491 Fax: 01367 860661
e-mail: wool@naturalbest.co.uk
website: www.naturalbest.co.uk

'Where Fleece Becomes Fabric' is the apt slogan of the renowned manufacturers and retailers **Cotswold Woollen Weavers**, where the traditions of fine woollen weaving continue and flourish. The Martin family and their staff welcome visitors to their working woollen mill, where the age-old crafts of spinning and weaving are practised and the traditional machinery brings the Industrial Revolution to life. In the Mill Shop the Cotswold Woollen Weavers range of Woolmark cloths, garments, knitwear, rugs and accessories, all woven at Filkins, can be purchased.

In the Exhibition Areas displays explain how fleece becomes fabrics and tell the fascinating story of wool in the Cotswolds. This is a story that weaves its way into many aspects of Cotswold life, from the very landscape to the mills, the famous 'wool churches' and the people themselves. To this day the Lord Chancellor sits in Parliament on the Woolsack to mark the great importance of the old wool trade. Visitors can pause awhile in the coffee shop or picnic area, or take the opportunity to explore the tranquil village of Filkins, which is located less than a mile off the A361 between Lechlade and Burford. Cotswold Woollen Weavers is open 10 to 6 Monday to Saturday and 2 to 6 on Sunday; admission and parking are free.

The Craftsmen's Gallery

1 Market Street, Woodstock, Oxfordshire OX20 1SU
Tel/Fax: 01993 811995
e-mail: richard.marriott@btclick.com website: www.craftsmensgallery.co.uk

In the 14 years since he started the **Craftsmen's Gallery**, owner Richard Marriott has built a strong customer base of artists and art-lovers. Art and craft materials to meet all needs are stocked on the ground floor, along with hand-crafted work by British craftsmen in ceramics, wood, pewter, bronze and other materials. Here and in the basement are original works of art in watercolours, oils and pastels, and etchings and prints by talented contemporary artists. The Craftsmen's Gallery also provides a complete bespoke picture framing service.

Cheneys

Market Street, Woodstock, Oxfordshire OX20 1UY
Tel: 01993 813534
e-mail: cheneywoodstock@netscapeonline.co.uk

Cheneys, with its original Blue and White window, is a well-established attraction in Woodstock's Market Street. The speciality is English Blue and White China, whose many patterns are attractively displayed on pine dressers and tables. This display, along with the friendly service, draws loyal customers from home and abroad - some even call in just to say hello to Gus the Westy with his smart blue collar! Cheneys are stockists for Bridgewater, Brixton, Burleigh, Luneville, Moorland, Spode and Rye pottery and provide everything from a single jug to a dinner service through to a wedding list.

craft. Halfpenny Bridge, which crosses the Thames in the town centre, has a tollhouse at its eastern end. The slender-spired Church of St Lawrence is said to have inspired Shelley to write his *Stanzas in a Summer Evening Churchyard*. The verses are inscribed on a stone at the churchyard entrance.

Kelmscott

2 miles E of Lechlade off the A417

Set in a romantic garden close to the Thames, just over the border into Oxfordshire, **Kelmscott Manor** was the country home of William Morris from 1871 to 1896 (see Chilterns chapter).

Inglesham

1 mile S of Lechlade off the A361

The splendidly unspoilt Church of St John the Baptist dates mainly from the 13th century, with some notable later additions. The chief features are important wall paintings, 15th century screens, 17th and 18th century pulpit and box pews and, perhaps its greatest treasure, a Saxon carving of the Virgin and Child blessed by the Hand of God.

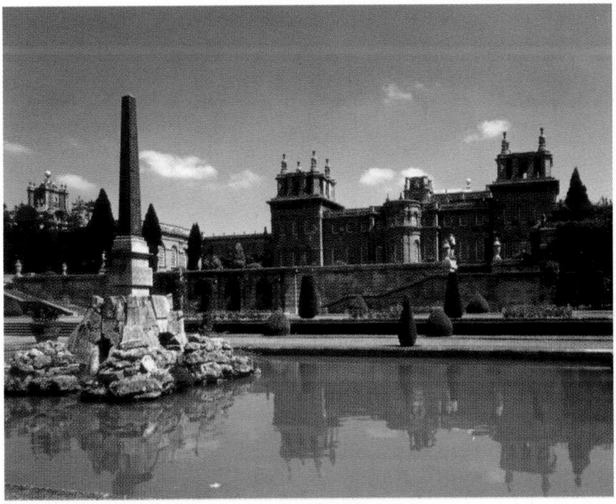

Blenheim Palace

This is one of many churches in the care of the Churches Conservation Trust, formerly known as the Redundant Churches Fund. The trust was established to preserve churches which though no longer needed for regular worship are of historic or architectural importance.

Eastleach

12 miles E of Cirencester off the A417

The twin villages of Eastleach Martin and Eastleach Turville face each other across the River Leach and are usually referred to jointly as Eastleach.

THE OXFORDSHIRE COTSWOLDS

Woodstock

8 miles NW of Oxford on the A44

Situated in the Glyme Valley, in an area of land that was originally part of the Wychwood Forest, the name of this elegant Georgian market town means a 'place in the woods'. To the north of the River Glyme is the old Saxon settlement, while on the opposite bank lies the town that was developed by Henry II in the 13th century to serve the Royal Park of Woodstock. There had been hunting lodges for the Kings of England here long before the Norman Invasion and it was Henry I who established the deer park around the manor of Woodstock. It was while at his palace here that Henry II first seduced Rosamund, whom he is said to have housed in a bower in the park. One story tells how Henry's wife, Queen Eleanor, managed to uncover the couple by following an unravelled ball of silk that had become attached to her husband's spur. Rosamund, the daughter of a local nobleman, became a nun at the Godstow Nunnery ,where she also bore him several children.

This long since disappeared medieval palace was also the birthplace of the Black Prince in 1330 and Princess Elizabeth was held prisoner here in 1558 during the reign of her sister, Queen Mary. On ascending the throne, a grateful Elizabeth I granted the town a second weekly market and two fairs for its loyalty. The palace was damaged during the Civil War, when it served as a Royalist garrison, and the last remains were demolished in 1710.

While the new town became an important coaching centre, many of the old inns survive to this day, and prospered as a result of the construction of the Oxford Canal and later the railway. The old town's trade was glovemaking and traditionally a pair of new gloves are presented to a visiting monarch. Today's visitors can look round both the factory and showroom of **Woodstock Gloves**.

The town is also home to the **Oxfordshire County Museum**, which is housed in the wonderful and imposing 16th century **Fletcher's House**. As well as the permanent displays on the life of the county through the centuries, the museum has a peaceful garden open to the public; at the entrance can be seen the old town stocks. It is the magnificent **Blenheim Palace**, one of only a handful of sites in the country to be included on the World Heritage List, which brings most people to Woodstock. The estate and the cost of building the palace was a gift from a grateful Queen Anne to the heroic John Churchill, 1st Duke of Marlborough, for his victory at the Battle of Blenheim during the Spanish War of

Blenheim Palace

Succession. However, the Queen's gratitude ran out before the building work was complete and the duke had to pay the remainder of the costs himself. As his architect, Marlborough chose Sir John Vanbrugh, whose life was even more colourful than that of his patron. He was at once both an architect (although at the time of his commission he was relatively unknown) and a playwright, and he also had the distinction of having been imprisoned in the Bastille in Paris. The result of his work was the Italianate palace (built between 1705 and 1722), which is now seen sitting in a very English park that was designed by Charles Bridgeman and Henry Wise and later landscaped by Capability Brown. Unfortunately, once completed, the new house did not meet with universal approval: it was ridiculed by Jonathan Swift and Alexander Pope, and Marlborough's wife, Sarah, who seems to have held the family purse strings, delayed paying Vanbrugh as long as possible.

A marvellous, grand place with a mass of splendid paintings, furniture, porcelain, and silver on show, visitors will also be interested in the more intimate memorabilia of Sir Winston Churchill. Born here in 1874, Churchill was a cousin of the 9th Duke and the family name remains Churchill.

First grown by George Kempster, a tailor from Old Woodstock, the Blenheim Orange apple took its name from the palace. Though the exact date of the first apple is unknown, Kempster himself died in 1773 and the original tree blew down in 1853. So famous did the spot where the tree stood become that it is said that London-bound coaches and horses used to slow down so that passengers might gaze upon it.

Bladon

1½ miles S of Woodstock on the A4095

The village lies on the southern edge of the Blenheim estate and it was in the churchyard here in 1965 that Sir Winston Churchill was laid to rest in a simple grave after a state funeral. Also interred here are his parents, his brother John, and his daughters. The ashes of his wife Clementine were buried in his grave in 1977.

North Leigh

4½ miles SW of Woodstock off the A4095

The Saxon-towered St Mary's Church is well worth a visit, and just to the north of the village lies the **Roman Villa**, one of several known to have existed in this area. Little remains apart from the foundations and some mosaic flooring, but this is enough to measure the scale of the place; it had over 60 rooms, two sets of baths and a sophisticated underfloor heating system, all built round a courtyard and clearly the home of a prosperous farming family.

Finstock

5 miles W of Woodstock on the B4022

A charming village with two notable literary associations. It was in 1927, at the 19th century Holy Trinity Church, that TS Eliot was baptised at the age of 38 following his controversial conversion to Catholicism. The novelist and churchwoman Barbara Pym lived in retirement with her sister in a cottage in the village; she died in 1980 and is buried in the churchyard. A lectern in the church is dedicated to her memory.

Charlbury

5 miles NW of Woodstock on the B4026

Now very much a dormitory town for Oxford, Charlbury was once famous for its glovemaking as well as being a centre of the Quaker Movement - the simple Friends' Meeting House dates from 1779 and there is also a Friends' cemetery. **Charlbury Museum**, close to the Meeting House, has displays on the traditional crafts and industries of the town and the town's charters given by Henry III and King Stephen can also be seen. Well known for its olde-worlde **Railway Station**, built by Isambard Kingdom Brunel, complete with its fishpond and hanging baskets, the town has two interesting great houses.

On the other bank of the River Evenlode from the main town lies **Cornbury Park**, a large estate that was given to Robert Dudley by Elizabeth I. Although most of the house now dates from the 17th century, this was originally a hunting lodge in Wychwood Forest that has been used since the days of

The Gallery At Newington House

Newington House, Sheep Street, Charlbury,
Oxfordshire OX7 3RR
Tel: 01608 811501 Fax: 01608 811586
e-mail: gallrynewingtnho@aol.com
website: www.thegalleryatnewingtonhouse.co.uk

Newington House is a bay-windowed building dating from the Georgian era, located on Charlbury's main street next to the Bull Inn. The ground floor was converted into a shop in Victorian times and is now home to The Gallery at Newington House, established in the spring of 2001. The owner is Wendy Wilson, a graduate of Chelsea School of Art and a practising abstract artist with paintings in a number of private collections.

The Gallery shows a broad range of contemporary arts and crafts, including painting, sculpture, ceramics, glass and jewellery, both figurative and abstract. The front room holds current shows, while the back room contains selections from previous shows and specialist artists. Both rooms are simple white and wood, leaving the focus firmly on the art on display. The Gallery is open from 11 to 5 Wednesday to Saturday or by appointment. Charlbury is a pleasant Cotswold town on the Oxfordshire Way, with some lovely walks on the outskirts or along the River Evenlode. One of its most distinguished buildings is its railway station, built by none other than Isambard Kingdom Brunel.

Burford House Hotel

99 High Street, Burford, Oxfordshire OX18 4QA
Tel: 01993 823151 e-mail: stay@burfordhouse.co.uk
Fax: 01993 823240 website: www.burford-house.co.uk

Burford House is a charming town house hotel with friendly, caring resident owners in Jane and Simon Henty. They make their guests feel welcome from the moment they arrive, and they and their staff put a premium on personal service. Each of the seven en suite bedrooms has its own individual appeal and all are superbly equipped, with tv, telephone, hairdryer and a number of thoughtful little extras. The sitting rooms are equally cosy and inviting, and the paved flower garden is a lovely spot for taking afternoon tea.

Salt Gallery

4 Bear Court, 38 Lower High Street, Burford,
Oxfordshire OX18 4RR Tel: 01993 822371
e-mail: saltgallery@btinternet.com website: www.saltgallery.com

Set in a Cotswold stone courtyard, the **Salt Gallery** houses a superbly presented display of British pottery and glass. It is owned and run by Chris King, who set up the gallery in premises where he had previously been a customer. Among the artists whose work is on display are Norman Stuart Clarke and Siddy Langley (glass); Steve Harrison, Rebecca Harvey, Mark Smith and Ruthanne Tudball (salt & soda glaze pottery); John Leach, Steve Taylor and Peter Swanson (ash/woodfired pottery); and work by Emily Myers, Gilda Westermann, Clare Wratten, David Garland and Paul Bye. The Salt Gallery is open from 10 to 4.30 Thursday to Monday.

Henry I. Glimpses of the house can be seen from the walk around the estate.

Lying just to the west of the town is **Ditchley Park**, a restrained and classical house built in the 1720s by James Gibbs. The interiors are splendid, having been designed by William Kent and Henry Flitcroft, and Italian craftsmen worked on the stucco decorations of the great hall and the saloon; the first treated to give an impression of rich solemnity, the second with a rather more exuberant effect.

The house has associations with Sir Winston Churchill, who used it as a weekend headquarters during World War II. Appropriately enough, given that Sir Winston had an American mother, Ditchley Park is now used as an Anglo-American conference centre.

BURFORD

Often referred to as The Gateway to the Cotswolds, Burford is an attractive old market town of honey coloured Cotswold stone found on the banks of the River Windrush. It was the site of a battle between the armies of Wessex and Mercia in 752, and after the Norman Conquest the town was given to William I's brother, Bishop Odo of Bayeux. Lying on important trade routes, both north-south and east-west, the town prospered and its first market charter was granted in 1087. In the 16th century, the town was an important centre of the woollen trade and it was used as the setting for *The Woolpack*, in which the author Celia Harknett describes the medieval wool trade in Europe. After the decline in the wool, Burford became an important coaching centre and many of the old inns can still be seen today.

Burford

The **Church of St John the Baptist** was built on the wealth of the wool trade and this grand building has the atmosphere of a small cathedral. Originally Norman, the church has been added to over the centuries and there are several interesting monuments and plaques to be found. In the south wall of the tower stair is a carved panel, dated around AD 100, which is thought to show the Celtic fertility goddess Epona, with two male supporters and a horse. In the nave north aisle a monument erected to Edmund Harman, the barber-surgeon to Henry VIII, shows North American natives - possibly the first representation of Red Indians in the country. In the south porch is a small plaque which commemorates three Leveller mutineers who were imprisoned in the church by Cromwell's men and shot in the churchyard in 1649.

The Levellers were troops from Cromwell's army who mutinied against what they saw as the drift towards the authoritarian rule they had been fighting against. While they were encamped at Burford, the Levellers were taken by surprise by

(Continued page 378)

WALK 11

Wychwood Forest

Start	Charlbury
Distance	7 miles (11.25km)
Approximate time	4 hours
Parking	Charlbury
Refreshments	Pubs at Charlbury, pub at Finstock
Ordnance Survey maps	Landranger 164 (Oxford), Explorer 180 (Oxford) and Explorer 191 (Banbury, Bicester and Chipping Norton)

For many years public access to Wychwood Forest was forbidden and its sylvan charms were hidden from view. Fortunately a waymarked 1½ mile (2.5km) route through it has now been opened up, forming the highlight of a pleasantly varied walk in the gently rolling country of the Evenlode valley. As well as the forest, the walk includes an attractive old town, deer park and extensive views across farmland to the hills beyond.

The quiet town of Charlbury has a fine situation on the slopes of the Evenlode valley, overlooking the expanses of Wychwood Forest on the western slopes. It was once noted for its glove-making industry and has a number of old houses dating back to the 16th and 17th centuries. Dominating the town is the tower of its medieval church.

Begin at the top end of Church Street by taking the road signposted to Chipping Norton and Burford. Turn left down Dyers Hill and follow the road for 1D†2 mile (800m) out of the town, over the River Evenlode and over the railway. About 200 yds (184m) past the railway bridge turn right **A**, at a bridleway and Oxfordshire Way sign, along a tarmac drive to Walcot Farm. Continue, passing cottages on the right, along the bridleway to Chilson, which is now a broad track, for nearly 1 mile (1.5km) to go through a metal gate and on to a lane **B**. Turn left along the lane for 1¼ miles (2km), keeping ahead over the B4437 to enter Wychwood Forest.

The present forest is but a remnant of the vast medieval royal hunting ground that once extended over much of western Oxfordshire and was a favourite with Norman kings. A number of deer parks were carved from the forest, including Cornbury and Blenheim, and over the years it became progressively reduced in size and was finally disafforested in 1856.

Bear right at a junction **C** and walk along the lane to a waymarked stile and 'Circular Walk' footpath sign on the left **D**. Climb the stile to follow a route

WALK 11

well waymarked with yellow-topped posts and white plastic markers through the forest for the next ½ miles (2.5km) along undulating paths and broad rides, through beautiful woodland and grassy glades. After crossing the end of a narrow lake on the right, turn sharp left E, still following the waymarked route, and head up to a stile. Climb over and keep ahead to soon emerge from the trees, continuing along a path, at first by the side of woodland on the left, later across fields and finally between cottages, to reach a road almost opposite Finstock's small 19th-century church F.

Turn left along the road – passing a road on the right that leads to the pub and Finstock village – for½ mile (800m), turning left along a tarmac drive at a 'Circular Walk' sign G. Keep along this tree-lined track for nearly 1½ miles (2.5km) as you pass through Cornbury Park, a 600-acre (268 ha) deer park originally carved from Wychwood Forest. Soon after passing the end of a lake on the left, go through a white gate with a footpath sign to the right of the drive, and keep ahead along the right-hand side of the park boundary fence, with woodland on the right and fine views across the deer park to the left. Continue over four stiles, finally going through a metal gate by a handsome lodge and keeping ahead a few yards to a door with a footpath sign on it. Go through that to turn right along the broad drive of Cornbury Park – to the left are the entrance gates and a glimpse of the 17th century mansion.

Cross the River Evenlode and the railway, continue to a road and turn left H into Charlbury, making for the church. Turn right by the church up the broad, handsome Church Street back to the starting point.

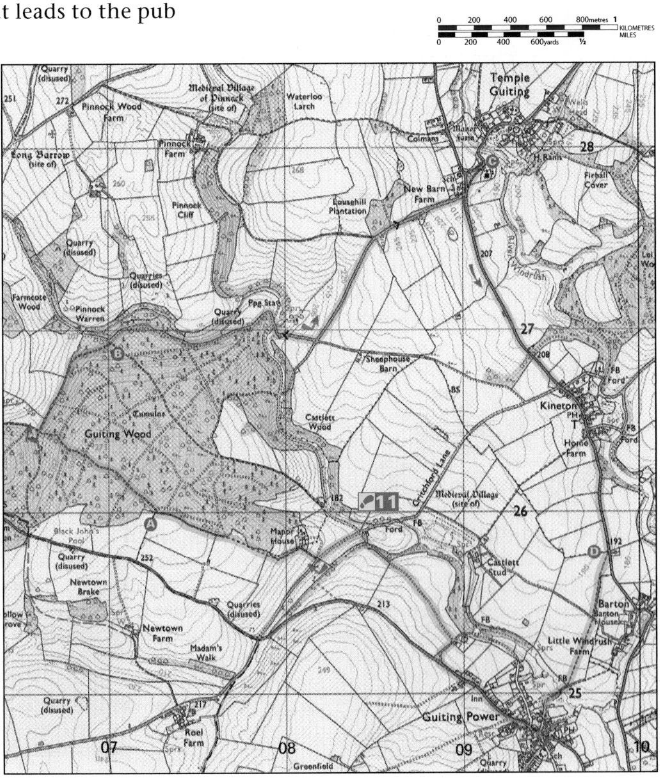

The Stone Gallery

93 High Street, Burford, Oxfordshire OX18 4QA
Tel: 01993 823302
e-mail: mail@stonegallery.co.uk
website: www.stonegallery.co.uk

The Stone Gallery is a family-run business based in the main street of the scenic Cotswold town of Burford. Established in 1918 in Newcastle, it was bought by Tilly Marshall in 1937 and has been in her family ever since, with three generations involved in the day-to-day running. Tilly herself maintains the accounts and works in the shop, and her son Simon, his wife Veral and their son Tom all design and handmake their own jewellery on the premises. The pieces they create are displayed to stunning effect in the shop, and if nothing is exactly right for a particular customer one of the family can be commissioned to make a unique piece that is guaranteed to be just right.

The family's work has won many accolades, and Tom Marshall recently had the honour of visiting the Prime Minister at Number Ten after a piece of his work was short-listed in a competition to create gifts for the leaders at the G8 Summit. Apart from stocking the Marshall family's work, the Gallery also has on display a large selection of jewellery by the internationally renowned silversmiths Georg Jensen; and works by artists of worldwide repute such as Sir Jacob Epstein, Dante Gabriel Rossetti and LS Lowry - the last was a close friend of the family. The Marshalls' collection of modern and antique glass paperweights is known far and wide and is one of the largest for sale in Europe. Another speciality of this unique business is enamel boxes, both antique and modern collector's items as well as many that make perfect gifts.

The town of Burford is an ideal base for a holiday touring the Cotswolds, with several good hotels and a number of notable inns, some dating back to the days when Burford was an important stop on the coaching routes. The grand Church of St John the Baptist, built on the wealth of the wool trade, and the 16th century courthouse, now a museum, are both well worth visiting, but no visit is complete without a look round this splendid Gallery, which is open from 9 to 6 Monday to Saturday.

BURFORD WOODCRAFT

144 High Street, Burford,
Oxfordshire OX18 4QU
Tel: 01993 823479
e-mail: enquiries@burford-woodcraft.co.uk
website: www.burford-woodcraft.co.uk

Visitors to historic Burford should take the opportunity to browse in the relaxed and friendly atmosphere in one of only a handful of galleries specialising in wood. Surrounded by the beautiful architecture of the Cotswolds, **Burford Woodcraft** is at the top of the High Street of this famous old wool town, looking down into the Windrush Valley. It is here in a listed building with oak beams that contemporary British craftsmanship in wood has been successfully promoted for more than 20 years. The ethic remains the same - work is selected carefully by Robert and Jayne Lewin from over 80 British designer makers for its good design, quality of finish and originality. The skill and talent displayed encompasses the unusual, creative and practical, with more than a hint of fun. The natural beauty and diversity of wood, the smell and the unique touch bind the extensive collection together through carving, furniture making, sculpting and turning. The one-off pieces, furniture (Robert is one of the designer makers), mirrors, sculpture, jewellery, bowls and platters co-exist with boxes, desk and kitchen ware, jewellery boxes, small accessories, games, toys and much more. Commissions are welcomed and regularly sought. An exhibition is held each autumn, making Burford Woodcraft the perfect place for seeking out Christmas presents that cannot fail to surprise and please:

'A treasure trove of goodies to tempt and delight; nativities and advent rings; birds with flapping wings; boxes for jewels and secret things; crackers with puzzles; surprises that Santa brings'. But any time's the right time to visit this unique gallery, whose reputation for its wide range of handmade British contemporary work is excellent. The commitment it has for providing pieces that are of a high quality, designed and created with inspiration and lovingly made, is very strong. The gallery is open weekdays from 9.30 to 5 and on Sunday from 11 to 4.45.

Cromwell's forces. After a brief fight, some 340 prisoners were taken and placed under guard in the church. The next day a court martial was held and three of the rebels were shot as an example to the rest, who were made to watch the executions. They were spared similar punishment when their leader recanted in a sermon.

The town's old court house, built in the 16th century with an open ground floor and a half-timbered first floor, is now home to the **Tolsey Museum**. An interesting building in its own right, the collection on display here covers the history of the town and the surrounding area. Other buildings worth seeking out include the 16th century **Falkland Hall**, the home of a local wool and cloth merchant Edmund Sylvester, and **Symon Wysdom's Cottages**, which were built in 1572 by another of the town's important merchants.

Burford also has more recent literary associations, as the writer Compton Mackenzie lived here before World War I. In his novel, *Guy and Pauline*, which was published in 1915, the town featured as 'Wychford'.

Great Barrington

2 miles NW of Burford off the A40

Connected to its smaller neighbour Little Barrington by a medieval bridge over the River Windrush, this old quarry village has an attractive church and some fine old cottages.

Taynton

1½ miles NW of Burford off the A424

Up until the end of the 19th century Taynton was a quarrying village, with the limestone taken from the quarries used in the construction of Blenheim Palace, Windsor Castle, St Paul's Cathedral as

Just Fabrics

Burford Antique Centre, Cheltenham Road, Burford, Oxfordshire OX18 4JA
Tel: 01993 823391 e-mail: fabrics@justfabrics.co.uk

Just Fabrics, on the A40 Burford roundabout, offers huge savings on an impressive selection of competitively priced own weaves and clearance fabrics from leading designers. Every design theme is covered, from sumptuous upholstery fabrics, embroidered designs, classic florals, checks and stripes through to coolly contemporary natural fabrics and colours. Just Fabrics experienced sales consultants are there to advise on fabric choice, ranges and colour matches, with convenient parking for visitors. Once fabric samples have been selected a mail-order service provides the perfect shopping solution. Shop hours are Monday to Saturday 9.30-5.30, Sunday & Bank Holidays 12-4. Answer machine out of shop hours.

Antiques @ The George

104 High Street, Burford, Oxfordshire OX18 4QJ
Tel: 01993 823319

Antiques @ The George, is a fascinating, multi-dealer antiques centre located on two floors right in the heart of the historic Cotswold town of Burford. The ancient building, once Burford's premier coaching inn, where King Charles II and Nell Gwynne often stayed, houses 18 dealers displaying a wide selection of interesting items including porcelain, glass, pictures and paintings, ceramics, oriental pieces, furniture, silver, books and postcards. Most of the objects date from the 19th century.

Cotswold Wildlife Park Ltd

Burford, Oxfordshire OX18 4JW
Tel: 01993 823006 Fax: 01993 823807 website: www.cotswoldwildlifepark.co.uk

Cotswold Wildlife Park is one of the leading family attractions in the county. The Walled Garden and the Tropical House are home to exotic plant life and animals who thrive in the environment, while the 140 acres of parkland contain fine specimen trees including the Giant Redwood, Wellingtonia, Cedar and a huge 600-year-old oak. Here, too, are many endangered species of animals, among them Asiatic lions, Amur leopards, Red Pandas and Giant Tortoises. Snacks and hot meals are served in the Oak Tree Restaurant, and amenities for children include a farmyard, adventure playground and narrow-gauge railway.

well as many Oxford colleges and local buildings.

Cornwell

9 miles N of Burford off the A436

This village had the distinction of being renovated in the 1930s by Clough Williams Ellis, best known for creating the remarkable Italianate Welsh holiday village of Portmeirion.

Chastleton

10 miles N of Burford off the A44

Chastleton is home to one of the best examples of Jacobean architecture in the country. In 1602, Robert Catesby, one of the Gunpowder Plot conspirators, sold his estate here to a prosperous wool merchant from Witney, Walter Jones. A couple of years later, Jones pulled the house down and built **Chastleton House**, a splendid Jacobean manor house

Trevor Waugh Studio

Trevor Waugh Studio, Home Buildings, Great Barrington, Burford, Oxfordshire OX18 4UR
Tel/Fax: 01451 844781
website: www.trevorwaugh.com

Trevor Waugh, born in London in 1952, studied at the Slade School of Fine Art and Croydon College of Art before embarking on a successful career as a freelance illustrator. In 1988 he moved to the Cotswolds, where the strong colours of the countryside harmonising with the local stone inspired him to paint watercolours. He has become very well known for his paintings of farm animals as well as florals and garden scenes in Cotswold settings. Many of his most popular paintings have been printed on greetings cards, and his work also appears on Primavera tapestries, bone china and kitchenware.

Travelling overseas has given him the opportunity to widen the scope of his subject matter, and he derives great pleasure from the indigenous peoples and animals wherever he goes. He has painted, taught and demonstrated his art in places as far afield as Dubai and Tennessee, and exhibits regularly at the Medici Gallery in Bond Street, London, and the Majilis Gallery in Dubai. In his studio in Great Barrington, Trevor paints, runs his watercolour courses and sells his paintings, limited edition prints, greetings cards and other interesting wares. As it is a working studio, it is open by appointment only (call Michele Waugh for more information), but visitors are welcome from March to Christmas on Fridays and Saturdays between 9.30 and 2.30.

The Merrymouth Inn

Stow Road, Fifield, Nr Burford, Oxfordshire OX7 6HR
Tel: 01993 831652 Fax: 01993 830840
e-mail: alan.flaherty@btclick.com
website: www.cotswold-inn.co.uk

Situated in the heart of the Cotswolds between Burford and Stow, the **Merrymouth Inn** can trace its history back to the 13th century, when it was a traveller's hospice associated with the nearby Bruern Abbey. Over the years it has been a hunting lodge and a brewery-owned hostelry, and it is now a splendid, inviting free house owned and run by the Flaherty family. The interior is rich in period appeal, with beams and exposed stone, and there may be features as yet unrevealed, including underground passages from the cellar to the Abbey. Stables and other outbuildings have been sympathetically converted into en suite accommodation and a restaurant.

The nine bedrooms, each with its own appeal, are stylish, comfortable and well equipped (telephone, tv, hairdryer, tea-makers), and overnight guests can look forward to a splendid breakfast with sausages from the local butcher and free-range eggs from the neighbour's hens. Fresh local produce is also a key factor in Tim Flaherty's much acclaimed cooking, and the beautiful restaurant is an equally perfect venue for a romantic dinner for two or a celebration party. Tim's specialities include braden rost (hot-smoked salmon) with sour cream, Murimuth chicken (named after the village's owners of many centuries ago) and some delectable puddings.

The Tollgate Hotel

Church Street, Kingham, Oxfordshire OX7 6YA
Tel: 01608 658389 Fax: 01608 659467
e-mail: info@the-tollgate.com
website: www.the-tollgate.com

In a peaceful Cotswold village with a lovely 12th century church, the **Tollgate** is a warm, friendly hotel created from a Georgian farmhouse. Owners Joan and Elaine ensure a real home-from-home atmosphere, and a stay in this delightful place is guaranteed to lift the spirits and recharge the batteries. Overnight accommodation comprises 10 individually decorated bedrooms, all with en suite facilities, tv and hospitality tray. One room on the ground floor is suitable for disabled guests; children and pets are welcome in the rooms in a converted barn in the garden.

A talented young chef, Tim Pearson, prepares splendid meals to enjoy in the non-smoking restaurant, and light lunches are also available; afternoon tea is served in the garden in the summer, and picnics can be provided for guests planning a day exploring the local attractions. The Tollgate has a really inviting lounge bar where a log fire burns in the feature fireplace with its ancient beam and hood. Kingham is a charming place, and the historic towns of Burford, Stow-on-the-Wold and Bourton-on-the-Water are all within very easy reach.

with a dramatic five-gabled front and a garden where the original rules of croquet were established in 1865. One of the finest and most complete Jacobean houses in England, it is filled with a remarkable collection of furniture, textiles and items both rare and everyday. The house is in the care of the National Trust and is open at certain times in the summer with advance booking.

Over Norton

11 miles N of Burford off the A3400

To the northwest of the village lies the **Rollright Stones** - one of the most fascinating Bronze Age monuments in the country. These great gnarled slabs of stone stand on a ridge which offers fine views of the surrounding countryside. They also all have nicknames: the **King's Men** form a circle; the **King Stone** is to the north of the circle; and, a quarter of a miles to the west, stand the **Whispering Knights**, which are, in fact, the remnants of a megalithic tomb. Naturally, there are many local legends connected with the stones and some say that they are the petrified figures of a forgotten king and his men that were turned to stone by a witch.

Shipton-under-Wychwood

4 miles NE of Burford on the A361

The suffix 'under-Wychwood' derives from the ancient royal hunting forest, **Wychwood Forest**, the remains of which lie to the east of the village. The name has nothing to do with witches - wych refers to the Hwicce, a Celtic tribe of whose territory the forest originally formed a part in the 7th century. Though cleared during the Middle Ages, it was still used as a royal hunting forest until the mid-17th century. By the late 18th century there was little good wood left and the clearing of the forest was rapid to provide arable land.

The forest was one of the alleged haunts of Matthew Arnold's scholar gypsy and in the poem, published in 1853, Arnold tells the legend of the brilliant but poor Oxford scholar who, despairing of ever making his way in the world, went to live with the gypsies to learn from their way of life.

The village itself is centred around its large green, which is dominated by the tall spire of 11th century **St Mary's Church**. Here, too, can be found **The Shaven Crown**, now a hotel, which was built in the 15th century as a guest house for visitors to the nearby (and now demolished) Bruern Abbey. Finally, there is the superb **Shipton Court**, built around 1603, which is one of the country's largest Jacobean houses.

Chipping Norton

10 miles NE of Burford on the A44

The highest town in Oxfordshire, at 650 feet above sea level, Chipping Norton was once an important centre of the wool trade and King John granted the town a charter to hold a fair to sell wool. Later changed to a **Mop Fair**, the tradition continues to this day when the fair is held every September.

The town's medieval prosperity can be seen in the fine and spacious **Church of St Mary** which was built in 1485 with money given by John Ashfield, a wool merchant. The splendid east window came from the Abbey of Bruern, a few miles to the southwest, which was demolished in 1535 during the Dissolution. As with many buildings in the town, there has been substantial 19th century remodelling and the present church tower dates from 1823. However, in 1549, the minister here, the Rev Henry Joyce, was charged with high treason and hanged from the then tower because he refused to use the new prayer book introduced by Edward VI.

Still very much a market town today - the market is held on Wednesdays - Chipping Norton has been little affected by the influx of visitors who come to see this charming place. The **Chipping Norton Museum** is an excellent place to start any exploration and the permanent displays here cover local history from prehistoric and Roman times through to the present day.

Found just to the west of the town centre is **Bliss Tweed Mill**, an extraordinary sight in this area as it was designed by a Lancashire architect, George Woodhouse, in 1872 in the Versailles style. With a decorated parapet and a tall chimney which acts as a local landmark, this very northern looking mill only ceased operation in the 1980s.

The Hall, Minster Lovell

MINSTER LOVELL
4½ miles E of Burford off the B4047

One of the prettiest villages along the banks of the River Windrush, Minster Lovell is home to the ruins of a once impressive 15th century manor house. **Minster Lovell Hall** was built about 1431-42 and was, in its day, one of the great aristocratic houses of Oxfordshire,

the home of the Lovell family. However, one of the family was a prominent Yorkist during the Wars of the Roses and, after the defeat of Richard III at Bosworth Field, he lost his lands to the Crown. The house was purchased by the Coke family in 1602, but around the middle of the 18th century the hall was dismantled by Thomas Coke, Earl of

LOWER COURT COTTAGES

Lower Court Farm, Chadlington, Chipping Norton, Oxfordshire OX7 3NQ Tel: 01608 676422 Mobile: 07976 883175 e-mail: jpauling@lineone.net

Picturesque cottages in beautiful rural surroundings provide delightful self-catering accommodation, ideal for touring, walking, cycling or simply relaxing. Each cottage has two or three bedrooms, bathroom, fully equipped kitchen, comfortable lounge with tv, and a lovely secluded garden. Alfie's Cottage is next to Lower Court Farm, Jasmine Cottage is in the tiny, pretty village of Fifield, Honeysuckle Cottage in Lower Oddington and Rose Cottage overlooks the green in the village of Evenlode, named after the river that runs through it. Bed linen is provided and owner Juliet Pauling can provide a grocery service. Bookings are from Saturday to Saturday. Short breaks available.

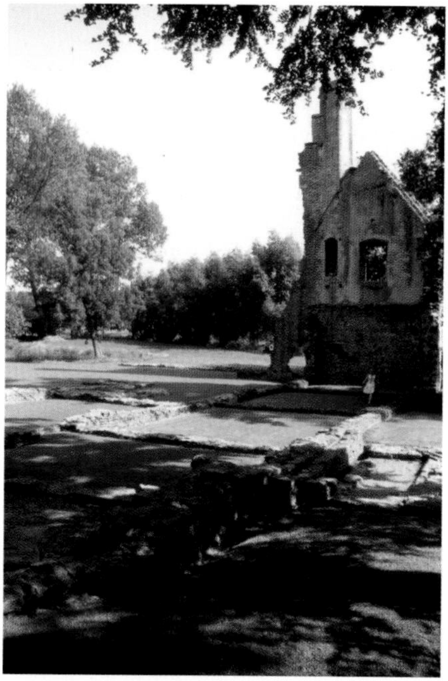

Leicester, and the ruins became lowly farm buildings. They were rescued from complete disintegration by the Ministry of Works in the 1930s and are now in the care of English Heritage. What is left of the house is extremely picturesque, and it is hard to imagine a better setting than here, beside the River Windrush. One fascinating feature of the manor house which has survived is the medieval dovecote, complete with nesting boxes, which provided pigeons for the table in a way reminiscent of modern battery hen houses.

Swinbrook

2 miles E of Burford off the A40

The Fettiplace family lived in a great manor house in this peaceful village in the valley of the Windrush. The manor has long gone, but the family is remembered in several impressive and highly distinctive monuments in the Church of St Mary. The family home of the Redesdales was also at Swinbrook, and in the churchyard are the graves of three of the six Mitford sisters, who were daughters of the 2nd Baron Redesdale. Nancy, Unity and Pamela are buried here.

TOURIST INFORMATION CENTRES

BEDFORDSHIRE

DUNSTABLE

Dunstable Library
Vernon Place
Dunstable
Bedfordshire
LU5 4HA

Tel: 01582 471012

website: www.bedfordshire.gov.uk
e-mail: dunstable-tic@bedfordshire.gov.uk

BEDFORD

10 St. Pauls Square
Bedford
Bedfordshire
MK40 1SL

Tel: 01234 215226

website: www.bedford.gov.uk

LUTON

65 -67 Bute Street
Luton
Bedfordshire
LU1 2EY

Tel: 01582 401579
Fax: 01582 487886

MILTON KEYNES

890 Midsummer Boulevard
Milton Keynes
Bedfordshire
MK9 3QA

Tel: 01908 558300

e-mail: visitor.information@miltonkeynes.gov.uk
website: www.miltonkeynes.gov.uk

SANDY

5 Shannon Court
High Street
Sandy
Bedfordshire
SG19 1AG

Tel: 01767 682728

SANDY

London Road
Sandy
Bedfordshire
SG19 1EX

Tel: 01767 682728

BERKSHIRE

BRACKNELL

The Look Out
Discovery Park
Nine Mile Ride
Bracknell
Berkshire
RG12 7QW

Tel: 01344 354409

website: www.bracknell-forest.gov.uk

MAIDENHEAD

Maidenhead Library
St Ives Road
Maidenhead
Berkshire
SL6 1QU

Tel: 01628 796502

e-mail: maidenhead.tic@rbwm.gov.uk
website www.maidenhead.gov.uk

NEWBURY

The Wharf
Newbury
Berkshire
RG14 5AS

Tel: 01635 30267

e-mail: tourism@newburydc.gov.uk
website: www.westberks.gov.uk

READING

Town Hall
Blagrave Street
Reading
Berkshire
RG1 1QH

Tel: 01189 566226

website: www.readingtourism.org.uk

WINDSOR

24 High Street
Windsor
Berkshire
SL4 1LH

Tel: 01753 743900

e-mail: windsor.tic@rbwm.gov.uk
website: www.windsor.gov.uk

BUCKINGHAMSHIRE

AMERSHAM

London Road
Amersham
Buckinghamshire
HP7 0TU

Tel: 01494 729492

AYLESBURY

8 Bourbon Street
Aylesbury
Buckinghamshire
HP20 2RR

Tel: 01296 330559

e-mail:
info@aylesburytourist.org.uk
website: www.aylesburyvale.net

BUCKINGHAM

Old Gaol Museum
Market Hill
Buckingham
Buckinghamshire
MK18 1JX

Tel: 01280 823020

e-mail: old.gaol@line1.net
website: www.mkheritage.co.uk

HIGH WYCOMBE

Pauls Row
High Wycombe
Buckinghamshire
HP11 2HQ

Tel: 01494 421892

MARLOW

31 High Street
Marlow
Buckinghamshire
SL7 1AU

Tel: 01628 483597

WENDOVER

The Clock Tower
High Street
Wendover
Buckinghamshire
HP22 6DU

Tel: 01296 696759

website: www.chilternweb.co.uk
wendover

GLOUCESTERSHIRE

BOURTON-ON-THE-WATER

Victoria Street
Bourton-on-the-Water
Gloucestershire
GL54 2BU

Tel: 01451 820211

CHELTENHAM

77 Promenade
Cheltenham
Gloucestershire
GL50 1PP

Tel: 01242 522878
Fax: 01242 255848

e-mail: tic@cheltenham.gov.uk

Fee charged for booking local accommodation

CHIPPING CAMPDEN

Rosary Court
High Street
Chipping Campden
Gloucestershire
GL55 6AL

Tel: 01386 841206

CIRENCESTER

Corn Hall
Market Place
Cirencester
Gloucestershire
GL7 2NW

Tel: 01285 654180
Fax: 01285 641182

Fee charged for booking local accommodation

COLEFORD

High Street
Coleford
Gloucestershire
GL16 8HG

Tel: 01594 812388

e-mail: tourism@fdean.gov.uk

Fee charged for booking local accommodation

GLOUCESTER

28 Southgate Street
Gloucester
Gloucestershire
GL1 1PD

Tel: 01452 421188
Fax: 01452 504273

e-mail:tourism@gloscity.gov.uk

Fee charged for booking local accommodation

GLOUCESTER DOCKS

National Waterways Museum
Llanthony Warehouse
Gloucester Docks
Gloucestershire

KEYNES COUNTRY PARK

Shorncote
Cirencester
Gloucestershire
GL7 6DF

Tel: 01285 861459

MORETON-IN-MARSH

Cotswold District Council
Offices
High Street
Moreton-in-Marsh
Gloucestershire

Tel: 01608 650881

NAILSWORTH

1 Fountain Street
Nailsworth
Stroud
Gloucestershire

Tel: 01453 832532

NEWENT

7 Church Street
Newent
Gloucestershire
GL18 1PU

Tel: 01531 822468

PAINSWICK

(Seasonal opening)
The Library
Stroud Road
Painswick
Gloucestershire

Tel: 01452 813552

STOW-ON-THE-WOLD

Hollis House
The Square
Stow-on-the-Wold
Gloucestershire
GL54 1AF

Tel: 01451 831082

STROUD

1 John Street
Stroud
Gloucestershire
GL5 1AE

Tel: 01453 765768

TETBURY

(Seasonal opening)
Shop 1
33 Church Street
Tetbury
Gloucestershire
GL8 8JG

Tel: 01666 503552

e-mail:
tetburytourism@yahoo.co.uk

Fee charged for booking local accommodation

TEWKESBURY

The Museum
64 Barton Street
Tewkesbury
Gloucestershire
GL20 5PX

Tel: 01684 295027

WINCHCOMBE

(seasonal opening)
The Town Hall
High Street
Winchcombe
Gloucestershire
GL54 5LJ

Tel: 01242 602925

WOTTON-UNDER-EDGE

The Heritage Centre
The Chipping
Wotton-under-Edge
Gloucestershire

Tel: 01453 521541

HAMPSHIRE

ALDERSHOT

Aldershot Military Museum
Queens Avenue
Aldershot
Hampshire
GU11 2LG

Tel: 01252 320968
Fax: 01252 320968

ALTON

7 Cross and Pillory Lane
Alton
Hampshire
GU34 1HL

Tel: 01420 88448
Fax: 01420 543916

ANDOVER

Town Mill House
Bridge Street
Andover
Hampshire
SP10 1BL

Tel: 01264 324320
Fax: 01264 345650

BASINGSTOKE

19-20 Westminster House
Potters Walk
Basingstoke
Hampshire
RG21 7LS

Tel: 01256 814681 (direct line)
Fax: 01256 475748

e-mail:
d.hayward@basingstoke.gov.uk

EASTLEIGH

The Point
Leigh Road
Eastleigh
Hampshire
SO50 9DE

Tel: 023 8064 1261
Fax: 023 8062 7818

e-mail: touristinformation@
eastleigh.gov.uk
website : www.eastleigh.gov.uk/

FARNBOROUGH

Farnborough Library
Pinehurst
Farnborough
GU14 7JZ

Tel: 01252 519466 (direct line)
Fax: 01252 511149

FAREHAM

Westbury Manor
West Street
Fareham
Hampshire
PO16 0JJ

Tel: 01329 221342
Fax: 01329 282959

FLEET

The Harlington Centre
236 Fleet Road Fleet
Hampshire
GU13 8BY

Tel: 01252 811151
Fax: 01252 812191

FORDINGBRIDGE

(summer only)
Salisbury Street
Fordingbridge
SP6 1AB

Tel: 01425-654560

GOSPORT

1 High Street
Gosport
Hampshire
PO12 1BX

Tel: 023 9252 2944
Fax: 023 9251 1687

HAVANT

1 Park Road
South Havant
Hampshire
PO9 1HA

Tel: 023 9248 0024
Fax: 023 9248 0024

HAYLING ISLAND

Beachlands Seafront
Hayling Island
Hampshire
PO11 OAG

Tel: 023 9246 7111
Fax: 023 9246 3297

LYMINGTON

St Barb Museum & Visitor Centre
New Street
Lymington
Hampshire SO41 9BH

Tel: 01590 689000
Fax: 01590 689000

LYNDHURST & NEW FOREST

New Forest Museum & Visitor Centre
Main Car Park
Lyndhurst
Hampshire
SO43 7NY

Tel: 023 8028 2269
Fax: 023 8028 4404

PETERSFIELD

County Library
27 The Square
Petersfield
Hampshire
GU32 3HH

Tel: 01730 268829
Fax: 01730 266679

PORTSMOUTH (SOUTHSEA)

Clarence Esplanade
Southsea
Portsmouth
Hampshire
PO5 3ST

Tel: 023 9283 2464
Fax: 023 9282 7519

e-mail: tic@portsmouthcc.gov.uk

PORTSMOUTH

Continental Ferry Port TIC
Terminal Building
Portsmouth
PO2 8QN

Tel: 023 9283 8635

e-mail: tic@portsmouthcc.gov.uk

PORTSMOUTH

The Hard
Portsmouth
PO1 3QJ

Tel: 023 9282 6722
Fax: 023 9282 2693

e-mail: tic@portsmouthcc.gov.uk

RINGWOOD

(summer only)
The Furlong
Ringwood
BH24 1AZ

Tel: 01425 470896 (& Fax)

ROMSEY

1 Latimer Street
Romsey
SO51 8DF

Tel: 01794 512987

ROWNHAMS

M27 Services (Westbound)
Southampton
SO16 8AP

Tel: 023 8073 0345

SOUTHAMPTON

9 Civic Centre Road
Southampton
SO14 7FJ

Tel: 023 8022 1106
Fax: 023 8083 2082

SOUTHAMPTON AIRPORT

Wide Lane
Southampton
SO18 2HG

no telephone enquiries

WINCHESTER

The Guildhall
Broadway
Winchester
SO23 9LJ

Tel: 01962 840500

e-mail:
tourism@winchester.gov.uk

HERTFORDSHIRE

BIRCHANGER GREEN

Welcome Break Service Area
Junction 8 of M11 Motorway
Bishop's Stortford
Hertfordshire
CM23 5QZ

Tel: 01279 508656
Fax : 01279 508625

BISHOP'S STORTFORD

The Old Monastery
Windhill
Bishop's Stortford
Hertfordshire
CM23 2ND

Tel: 01279 655831
Fax : 01279 653136

HEMEL HEMPSTEAD

Dacorum Information Centre
Marlowes
Hemel Hempstead
Hertfordshire
HP1 1DT

Tel: 01442 234222
Fax: 01442 230427

e-mail:
postmaster@dacoruminfo.co.uk

HERTFORD

10 Market Place
Hertford
Hertfordshire
SG14 1DG

Tel: 01992 584322
Fax: 01992 534724

ST ALBANS

Town Hall
Market Place
St Albans
Hertfordshire
AL3 5DJ

Tel: 01727 864511
Fax: 01727 863533

ISLE OF WIGHT

ISLE OF WIGHT TOURISM

General Information:
Tel: 01983 813818

Accommodation Booking
Service:(01983) 813813

website: www.islandbreaks.co.uk/

COWES

The Arcade
Fountain Quay
Cowes
Isle of Wight
PO31 3AR
Tel: 01983 813818
Fax: 01983 280078

NEWPORT

The Guildhall
136 High Street
Newport
Isle of Wight
PO30 1TY

Tel: 01983 813818
Fax: 01983 823811

RYDE

81-83 Union Street
Ryde
Isle of Wight
PO33 2LW

Tel: 01983 813818
Fax: 01983 567610

SANDOWN

8 High Street
PO36 8DA
Tel: 01983 813818
Fax: 01983 406482

SHANKLIN

67 High Street
Shanklin
Isle of Wight
PO37 6JJ

Tel: 01983 813818
Fax: 01983 863047

VENTNOR

34, High Street
Ventnor
Isle of Wight
PO38 1RZ

Tel: 01983 813818
Fax: 01983 856232

YARMOUTH

The Quay
Yarmouth
Isle Of Wight
PO41 4PQ

Tel: 01983 813818
Fax: 01983 761047

OXFORDSHIRE

ABINGDON

25 Bridge Street
Abingdon
Oxfordshire
OX14 3HN

Tel: 01235 522 711
Fax: 01235 535 245

BANBURY

Banbury Museum
8 Horsefair
Banbury
Oxfordshire
OX16 0AA

Tel: 01295 259855
Fax: 01295 270556

BICESTER

Unit 6A
Bicester Village
Pingle Drive
Bicester
Oxfordshire
OX6 7WD

Tel: 01869 369055
Fax: 01869 369054

BURFORD

The Brewery
Sheep Street
Burford
Oxfordshire
OX18 4LP

Tel: 01993 823 558
Fax: 01993 823 590

CHERWELL VALLEY

Motorway Service Area
J10/M40 Northampton Road
Ardley
Bicester
Oxfordshire
OX6 9RD

Tel: 01869 345888
Fax: 01869 345777

CHIPPING NORTON

The Guildhall
Chipping Norton
Oxfordshire
OX7 5NJ

Tel: 01608 644379
Fax: 01608 644379

e-mail:
chippingnortonvic@westoxon.gov.uk

DIDCOT

The Car Park
Station Road
Didcot
Oxfordshire
OX11 7NR

Tel: 01235 813243

FARINGDON

7a Market Place
Faringdon
Oxfordshire
SN7 7HL

Tel: 01367 242191
Fax: 01367 242191

HENLEY-ON-THAMES

King's Arms Barn
Kings Road
Henley on Thames
Oxfordshire
RG9 2DG

Tel: 01491 578034
Fax: 01491 411766

OXFORD

The Old School
Gloucester Green
Oxford
Oxfordshire
OX1 2DA

Tel: 01865 726871
Accom: 01865 726871
Fax: 01865 240261

e-mail: tic@oxford.gov.uk

THAME

Market House
North Street
Thame
Oxfordshire
OX9 3HH

Tel: 01844 212834
Fax: 01844 212834

WALLINGFORD

Town Hall
Market Place
Wallingford
Oxfordshire
OX10 0EG

Tel: 01491 826 972
Fax: 01491 832 925

WANTAGE

Vale and Downland Museum
19 Church Street
Wantage
Oxfordshire
OX12 8BL

Tel: 01235 760176
Fax: 01235 760176

WITNEY

51A Market Square
Witney
Oxfordshire
OX8 6AG

Tel: 01993 775802
Fax: 01993 709261

WOODSTOCK

Oxfordshire Museum
Part Street
Woodstock
Oxfordshire
OX20 1SN

Tel: 01993 813276
Fax: 01993 813632

e-mail:
tourism@westoxon.gov.uk

WILTSHIRE

AMESBURY

Redworth House
Flower Lane
Amesbury
Wiltshire
SP4 7HG

Tel: 01980 622833
Fax: 01980 625541

e-mail:
amesburytic@salisbury.gov.uk

BRADFORD-ON-AVON

34 Silver Street
Bradford-on-Avon
Wiltshire
BA15 1JX

Tel: 01225 865797
Fax: 01225 868722

CHIPPENHAM

The Citadel
Bath Road
Chippenham
Wiltshire
SN15 2AA

Tel: 01249 706333
Fax: 01249 460776

e-mail:
tourism@northwilts.gov.uk

CORSHAM

Arnold House
31 High Street
Corsham
Wiltshire
SN13 0EZ

Tel: 01249 714660
Fax: 01249 716164

e-mail:
corshamheritage@northwilts.gov.uk

DEVIZES

Cromwell House
Market Place
Devizes
Wiltshire
SN10 1JG

Tel: 01380 729408
Fax: 01380 730319

MALMESBURY

Town Hall
Market Lane
Malmesbury
Wiltshire
SN16 9BZ

Tel: 01666 823748

MARLBOROUGH

George Lane Car Park
Marlborough
Wiltshire
SN8 1EE

Tel: 01672 513989
Fax: 01672 513989

MELKSHAM

Church Street
Melksham
Wiltshire
SN12 6LS

Tel: 01225 707424
Fax: 01225 707424

e-mail:
visitmelksham@westwiltshire.gov.uk

MERE

The Square
Mere
Warminster
Wiltshire
BA12 6JJ

Tel: 01747 861211
Fax: 01747 861127

SALISBURY

Fish Row
Salisbury
Wiltshire
SP1 1EJ

Tel: 01722 334956
Fax: 01722 422059

SWINDON

37 Regent Street
Swindon
Wiltshire
SN1 1JL

Tel: 01793 530328 (01793 466454)
Fax: 01793 434031
e-mail:
infocentre@swindon.gov.uk

TROWBRIDGE

St Stephen's Place
Trowbridge
Wiltshire
BA14 8AH

Tel: 01225 777054
Fax: 01225 777054
e-mail:
visittrowbridge@westwiltshire.gov.uk

WARMINSTER

Central Car Park
Warminster
Wiltshire
BA12 9BT

Tel: 01985 218548
Fax: 01985 846154

WESTBURY

The Library
Edward Street
Westbury
Wiltshire
BA13 3BD

Tel: 01373 827158
Fax: 01373 827158

INDEX OF ADVERTISERS

A

B

C

D

E

F

G

H

I

J

K

L

M

N

O

P

Q

R

S

T

U

V

W

Y

INDEX OF WALKS

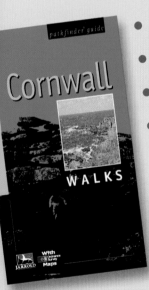

pathfinder guide

45

Norfolk

WALKS

26

pathfinder guide

Dartmoor

WALKS

JARROLD

Mapping sourced from **O/S Ordnance Survey**

n ambitious sche
-Off Channel nav
ats is currently be

st sluice was constru
John Rennie and the
923. The steady shrink
s it dried out after dra
was blown away by th

es the former salt-marshes,
ed for agriculture, and the
lood wall can soon be seen

walk along the top – this
place to watch for
s and other waders as
who wait till the last
azily taking to their
e walking along
ood wall difficult. Silence
and into mud. Silence
qualities here.
t the end of the path
e flood bank lead
s waterfront.

bridleway to a track. Cross over and
continue until you see an isolated brick
building ahead. Look for a bridleway to
the left ⒷⒹ about 100 yds (91m) before
this building – there is a signpost at the
end of a hedge.

Cross a field to the end of another

hedge and follow it to come to a footpath junction Ⓔ. Turn left here to take
the direction shown on the signpost to
leave the edge of the large field of
sandy soil. Cross a lane to continue on
the other side, heading for the small
spire of Sudbourne church, just to be
seen above trees. Note the numerous
footprints in the soil – deer and hares
are numerous here. The path turns left

42 ● WALK 14

Orford and its castle

LK 19

JARROLD

publishing

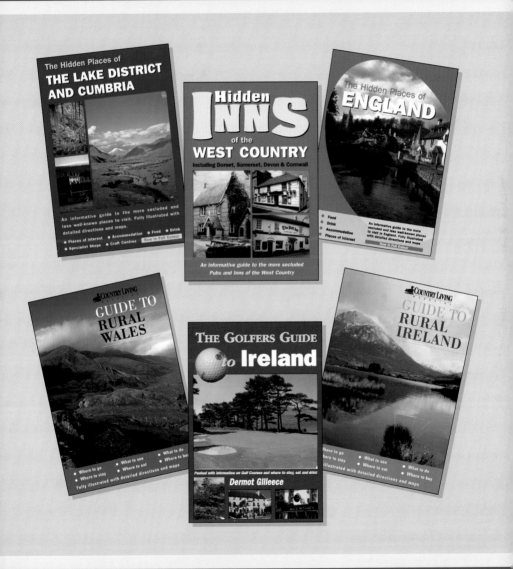

ORDER FORM

To order any of our publications just fill in the payment details below and complete the order form. For orders of less than 4 copies please add £1 per book for postage and packing. Orders over 4 copies are P & P free.

Please Complete Either:

I enclose a cheque for £ ______ made payable to Travel Publishing Ltd

Or:

Card No: ______ Expiry Date: ______

Signature: ______

NAME: ______

ADDRESS: ______

TEL NO: ______

Please either send, telephone, fax or e-mail your order to:

Travel Publishing Ltd, 7a Apollo House, Calleva Park, Aldermaston, Berkshire RG7 8TN
Tel: 0118 981 7777 Fax: 0118 982 0077 e-mail: karen@travelpublishing.co.uk

	Price	*Quantity*
Hidden Places Regional Titles		
Cambs & Lincolnshire	£7.99	....
Chilterns	£8.99	....
Cornwall	£8.99	....
Derbyshire	£7.99	....
Devon	£8.99	....
Dorset, Hants & Isle of Wight	£8.99	....
East Anglia	£8.99	....
Gloucestershire & Wiltshire	£7.99	....
Heart of England	£7.99	....
Hereford, Worcs & Shropshire	£7.99	....
Highlands & Islands	£7.99	....
Kent	£8.99	....
Lake District & Cumbria	£8.99	....
Lancashire & Cheshire	£8.99	....
Lincolnshire & Nottinghamshire	£8.99	....
Northumberland & Durham	£8.99	....
Somerset	£7.99	....
Sussex	£7.99	....
Thames Valley	£7.99	....
Yorkshire	£7.99	....

	Price	Quantity
Hidden Places National Titles		
England	£11.99	....
Ireland	£11.99	....
Scotland	£11.99	....
Wales	£11.99	....
Hidden Inns Titles		
Heart of England	£5.99	....
Lancashire & Cheshire	£5.99	....
South	£5.99	....
South East	£5.99	....
South and Central Scotland	£5.99	....
Wales	£5.99	....
Welsh Borders	£5.99	....
West Country	£5.99	....
Country Living Guides to Rural England		
East Anglia	£9.99	....
South of England	£9.99	....
South East of England	£9.99	....
West Country	£9.99	....

Total Quantity ______ Total Value ______

READER REACTION FORM

The *Travel Publishing* research team would like to receive reader's comments on any visitor attractions or places reviewed in the book and also recommendations for suitable entries to be included in the next edition. This will help ensure that the *Country Living series of Rural Guides* continues to provide its readers with useful information on the more interesting, unusual or unique features of each attraction or place ensuring that their visit to the local area is an enjoyable and stimulating experience. To provide your comments or recommendations would you please complete the forms below and overleaf as indicated and send to:

The Research Department, Travel Publishing Ltd,
7a Apollo House, Calleva Park, Aldermaston, Reading, RG7 8TN.

Your Name:

Your Address:

Your Telephone Number:

Please tick as appropriate: Comments ☐ Recommendation ☐

Name of Establishment:

Address:

Telephone Number:

Name of Contact:

READER REACTION FORM

Comment or Reason for Recommendation:

....

....

....

....

....

....

....

....

....

....

....

READER REACTION FORM

The *Travel Publishing* research team would like to receive reader's comments on any visitor attractions or places reviewed in the book and also recommendations for suitable entries to be included in the next edition. This will help ensure that the *Country Living series of Rural Guides* continues to provide its readers with useful information on the more interesting, unusual or unique features of each attraction or place ensuring that their visit to the local area is an enjoyable and stimulating experience. To provide your comments or recommendations would you please complete the forms below and overleaf as indicated and send to:

The Research Department, Travel Publishing Ltd,
7a Apollo House, Calleva Park, Aldermaston, Reading, RG7 8TN.

Your Name:

Your Address:

Your Telephone Number:

Please tick as appropriate: Comments ☐ Recommendation ☐

Name of Establishment:

Address:

Telephone Number:

Name of Contact:

READER REACTION FORM

Comment or Reason for Recommendation:

....

....

....

....

....

....

....

....

....

....

....

INDEX TO TOWNS & PLACES OF INTEREST

A

B

C

F

G

M

N

T

Y